United States Naval Observatory, Jospeh Winlock

Tables to Facilitate the Reduction of Places of the Fixed Stars

United States Naval Observatory, Jospeh Winlock

Tables to Facilitate the Reduction of Places of the Fixed Stars

ISBN/EAN: 9783337405717

Printed in Europe, USA, Canada, Australia, Japan

Cover: Foto ©Andreas Hilbeck / pixelio.de

More available books at **www.hansebooks.com**

TABLES

TO

FACILITATE THE REDUCTION OF PLACES

OF THE

FIXED STARS.

PREPARED FOR THE USE OF

THE AMERICAN EPHEMERIS AND NAUTICAL ALMANAC.

SECOND EDITION.

PUBLISHED BY AUTHORITY OF THE SECRETARY OF THE NAVY

BUREAU OF NAVIGATION,
NAVY DEPARTMENT.
1873.

PREFACE.

The following tables were prepared under the direction of Prof. JOSEPH WINLOCK, now Director of Harvard College Observatory, while Superintendent of the *American Ephemeris and Nautical Almanac*. They have been used in the preparation of the portions of that work which relate to the fixed stars, commencing with the volume for 1865; except that some modifications of the mean places and annual motions of the standard stars have been introduced in the present volume and in the Ephemeris for 1870. These changes are given in Table XXIX.

A few tables, not directly required in the construction of the Ephemeris, have been added to make the series more complete.

The essential features of these tables are those of BESSEL's *Tabulæ Regimontanae* and WOLFERS' *Tabulæ Reductionum ;* but they differ from them in form and arrangement, in using the constants of STRUVE and PETERS, and in providing for small terms in the reduction of star-places, which are usually neglected. It has not been thought necessary, however, to include in Table XXIV, which contains the reductions of places of the standard stars, any of the stars of WOLFERS' list, except a and δ Ursæ Minoris; as the corrections for differences of mean place and annual motion for the other stars are easily supplied.

The computations have been made by assistants in the Nautical Almanac office, of whom Mr. W. P. G. BARTLETT and Mr. G. W. HILL deserve special mention. To the latter I am indebted for a careful revision of the tables and proofs, and the materials for the introductory explanations. He has also prepared the articles on the *Derivation and Reduction of Star Places*, and the places of β^1 Scorpii, β and η Draconis, and 61^1 Cygni, which are given in the Introduction.

These tables are published with the hope that they will afford aid to astronomers in future work, while they exhibit the construction and character of that portion of the *American Ephemeris* to which they relate.

J. H. C. COFFIN,

Prof. Math. U. S. Navy, Superintendent of Nautical Almanac.

WASHINGTON, *February*, 1869.

CONTENTS.

SPECIAL TABLES, FOR STANDARD STARS OF THE AMERICAN EPHEMERIS.

DESCRIPTION AND USE OF THE TABLES.

These tables comprise—

1. *General tables*, which serve to form the arguments depending on time and place, or give those quantities, which are functions of the time and are independent of the place of any particular star. They extend from 1750 to 1900. A table for computing precessions in right ascension and declination, and *Supplementary Tables* of small terms in nutation have been added.

2. *Special Tables* for the standard stars of the *American Ephemeris and Nautical Almanac* for the years 1865 to 1880, giving their mean places and annual motions, and the means of reducing to their apparent places on any day within that period.

GENERAL TABLES.

TABLE I contains the longitudes of the principal Observatories from Washington, as given by Dr. GOULD in the *American Ephemeris* for 1870. West longitudes* are considered as positive.

d is the longitude in hours, minutes, and seconds.
d' in decimals of a day.
d'' in decimals of a year.

TABLE II gives for each calendar date the number of days from Jan. 0 in common years, or from Jan. 1 in bissextile years.

TABLE III contains the equivalents of hours and minutes in decimals of a day and a year.

TABLE IV gives for each midnight the part of a tropical year elapsed from noon of Jan. 0 in common years, Jan. 1 in bissextile years. For noon subtract $0^y.00137$.

Adding k'' from Table VI, d'' from Table I, and the part of a year from Table III, corresponding to the hours and minutes after mean midnight, we have for any given time the fraction of the year, τ, elapsed from the beginning of the fictitious year. In this table 1 day $= 0^y.00273791$.

TABLE V, contains for each fifth year, STRUVE and PETERS† values of the annual precession of the equinoxes, &c., viz:

Luni-solar precession, $\psi = 50''.3798 - 0''.0002168\,(t - 1800)$
General precession, $\psi' = 50''.2411 + 0''.0002268\,(t - 1800)$
$m = 46''.0623 + 0''.0002849\,(t - 1800) = 3^s.07082 + 0^s.0000190\,(t - 1800)$
$n = 20''.0607 - 0''.0000863\,(t - 1800)$, and its logarithm
$\pi = 0''.4776 - 0''.000007\;(t - 1800)$
$M = 172°\;45'\;31'' + 33''.23\,(t - 1800)$
in which t is the number of years:

The annual precession of a fixed star is—

In *Right ascension*, $\Delta a = m + n \sin a \tan \delta$
    Declination, $\Delta \delta = n \cos a$
    Longitude, $\Delta \lambda = $ Gen. Prec. $+ \pi \cos (\lambda - M) \tan \beta$
    Latitude, $\Delta \beta = - \pi \sin (\lambda - M)$

TABLE VI contains for Washington mean noon of Jan. 0 in common years, Jan. 1 in bissextile years, of each year from 1750 to 1900, the following quantities:

1. Arg. I, which is Arg. I of HANSEN and OLUFSEN's *Tables du Soleil*, augmented by $0^d.01553$ for the constants added in the tables of inequalities, reduced to the meridian of Washington, and corrected for the inequalities of long period in Tables VI, VII, and VIII of that work.

---

* Longitudes should be reckoned west, or east, to the meridian where the local reckoning of the day changes. This may be assumed as $+ 7^h$ or $- 17^h$ from Washington.
† Dr. C. A. F. PETERS, *Numerus Constans Nutationis*, pp. 66, 71, &c.

2. Arg. II, which is Arg. V of HANSEN and OLUFSEN's tables, and is used in finding the secular inequality of Arg. I from Table VII.

Arg. I + *its inequalities* + d' + *day of year*, (the day of the year including the fractional part corresponding to the local mean time,) is the argument of solar nutation and aberration in Tables VII, X, XI, XVIII, and XIX. In general it will be sufficient to add to Arg. I the secular inequality in Table VII multiplied by $(t - 1850)$. But if we wish to take into account the periodic pertubations of the sun, as is done in the preparation of the *American Ephemeris*, it will be necessary to use Arg. I + *its inequalities* of HANSEN and OLUFSEN's tables. The difference, however, cannot exceed $0^d.011$, and will seldom attain this limit.

3. Arg. III, which is the number of days after, (or when negative, before) the time when the longitude of the moon's ascending node was 0. It is derived from PEIRCE's *Tables of the Moon*. Its period, in 1850, is $6798^d.39$ nearly.

Arg. III + d' + *day of year*, or, if it exceed the limit of the table,
Arg. III + d' + *day of year*—$6798^d.39$,

is the argument of those terms of nutation which depend on the longitude of the moon's node, in Tables VIII, XII, and XIII.

4. The mean obliquity of the ecliptic, as obtained from PETERS.[*]

$$\omega = 23° 27' 54''.22 - 0''.4645 (t - 1800) - 0''.0000014 (t - 1800)^2$$

5. The mean time elapsed since the sun's mean longitude was 280°, the beginning of Bessel's *fictitious year*.

k is its value in hours, minutes, and seconds.
k'　　　　in decimals of a day,
k''　　　　in decimals of a year.

It is also the longitude of Washington from the *fictitious meridian* of Table XXIV, or the meridian on which the mean sun was at the beginning of the fictitious year.

$k + d$ will be the longitude of any place reckoned west from the fictitious meridian. The sidereal time at this meridian when the fictitious year begins is always $18^h 40^m = 280°$; and at any other meridian $18^h 40^m - (k + d.)$

TABLE VII contains for each 10 days—

1. The secular inequality of Arg. I due to the change of eccentricity and perigee of the sun's orbit, derived from Table IX of HANSEN and OLUFSEN's tables. This inequality is to be multiplied by $(t - 1850)$, t being the entire number of years, and the product added to Arg. I. The argument of this column is

Arg. II + d' + *day of year*.

2. The precession of the equinoxes in longitude, which is used in reducing longitudes from the mean equinox of one date to the mean equinox of another date. It is given for 1850. Its variation in 100 years is

$$\triangle p = + .000452 p, p \text{ being the value in the table.}$$

3. The aberration of the sun's longitude, to be applied to the sun's true longitude to obtain its apparent longitude. Its value, with STRUVE's[†] constant is

$$\triangle \odot = - 20''.4451 - 0''.3429 \cos (280°.4 - \odot).$$

The argument of this and the following column is

Arg. I + *its inequalities* + d' + *day of year*.

4. The solar nutation for the epoch 1850.[‡]

In *Longitude*, $\triangle \lambda = - 1''.2694 \sin 2 \odot + 0''.1477 \sin (\odot + 82° 34')$
Right ascension, $\triangle a = - 0^s.0776 \sin 2 \odot + 0^s.0090 \sin (\odot + 82° 34')$

and of the *obliquity*, increased by the mean motion in the fraction of the year,

$$\triangle \omega = - 0''.4645 \tau + 0''.5508 \cos 2 \odot + 0''.0092 \cos (\odot + 280° 21')$$

TABLE VIII contains, also for the epoch 1850, the lunar nutation,[‡]

* PETERS' *Numerus Constans Nutationis*, pp. 66, 71.
† STRUVE's *Constant de l'Aberration*, p. 47.
‡ PETERS' *Numerus Constans Nutationis*, pp. 46–48.

In *Longitude,* $\Delta\lambda = -17''.2491 \sin \Omega + 0''.2073 \sin 2\,\Omega$

In *Right Ascension,* $\Delta a = -1^s.0549 \sin \Omega + 0^s.0127 \sin 2\,\Omega$

Of the *Obliquity,* $\Delta\omega = +9''.2235 \cos \Omega - 0''.0896 \cos 2\,\Omega$

The equation of the equinoxes, or the reduction from the mean to the true equinox of date, is the sum of the solar and lunar nutations in longitude and right ascension, respectively, in Tables VII and VIII.

The true obliquity at date is the sum of the mean obliquity for the beginning of the year, and the two variations of the obliquity in the same tables.

The variations in 100 years of these values are—

In *Longitude,* $-0''.0172 \sin \Omega$

In *Right ascension,* $-0^s.00115 \sin \Omega$

In the *Obliquity,* $+0''.0009 \cos \Omega$

The terms omitted, which exceed $0''.007$, are—

In *Longitude,*	In *Right Ascension,*	In the *Obliquity,*
$+0''.0125 \sin (2 \odot - \Omega)$	$+0^s.00077 \sin (2 \odot - \Omega)$	$-0''.0067 \cos (2 \odot - \Omega)$
$-0.2041 \sin 2\,\mathfrak{C}$	$-0.01248 \sin 2\,\mathfrak{C}$	$+0.0886 \cos 2\,\mathfrak{C}$
$-0.0339 \sin (2\,\mathfrak{C} - \Omega)$	$-0.00208 \sin (2\,\mathfrak{C} - \Omega)$	$+0.0181 \cos (2\,\mathfrak{C} - \Omega)$
$-0.0261 \sin (3\,\mathfrak{C} - l')$	$-0.00160 \sin (3\,\mathfrak{C} - l')$	$+0.0113 \cos (3\,\mathfrak{C} - l')$
$+0.0677 \sin (\mathfrak{C} - l')$	$+0.00414 \sin (\mathfrak{C} - l')$	
$+0.0115 \sin (\mathfrak{C} + l')$	$+0.00070 \sin (\mathfrak{C} + l')$	
$+0.0150 \sin (\mathfrak{C} + l' - 2 \odot)$	$+0.00092 \sin (\mathfrak{C} + l' - 2 \odot)$	

In these and preceding formulæ,

$\odot$ = the sun's true longitude.

Ω = the mean longitude of the moon's ascending node.

$\mathfrak{C}$ = the moon's mean longitude.

l' = the longitude of the sun's perigee.

l' = the longitude of the moon's perigee.

TABLE IX contains the values for different years of the coefficients and auxiliary angles, which enter into the expressions for *A, B,* and *E,* as denoted by BESSEL, and hereafter given. They are derived from PETERS' *Numerus Constans Nutationis.*

TABLE X contains, for 1850, those terms in *A* and *B* which depend on the sun's longitude, viz:

$A_\odot = -.02519 \sin 2 \odot + .00294 \sin (\odot + 82° 34')$

$B_\odot = -0''.5508 \cos 2 \odot - 0''.0093 \cos (\odot + 280° 21')$

The argument is

Arg. I + *its inequalities* + d' + *day of year.*

TABLE XI contains, for the same argument, the variations of $A_\odot$ and $B_\odot$ in 100 years, or

$\delta A_\odot = -.000063 \cos (\odot + 83°.2) - .000020 \sin (\odot + 83°.2)$

$\delta B_\odot = +0''.0003 \cos 2 \odot + 0''.00028 \sin (\odot + 280°.4) + 0''.00001 \cos (\odot + 280°.4)$

These are to be multiplied by $\frac{1}{100}(t - 1850)$, and the products added to $A_\odot$ and $B_\odot$ taken from the preceding table.

TABLE XII contains the terms in *A* and *B,* which depend on the longitude of the moon's node, viz:

$A_\Omega = -.34236 \sin \Omega + .00410 \sin 2\,\Omega$

$B_\Omega = -9''.22355 \cos \Omega + 0''.08955 \cos 2\,\Omega$

The coefficients are for 1850. The argument is

Arg. III + d' + *day of year,* or if it exceed 3400^d,

Arg. III + d' + *day of year* — $6798^d.39$,

(the day of the year including the fractional part corresponding to the local mean time.)

When the argument is negative the sign of A_{Ω}, as given in the table, must be changed: the sign of B_{Ω} remains the same.

TABLE XIII contains, for the same argument, the variations of A_{Ω} and B_{Ω}, or

$$\delta A_{\Omega} = -.00031 \sin \Omega$$

$$\delta B_{\Omega} = -0''.0009 \cos \Omega - 0''.0001 \cos 2\ \Omega, \text{(in units of the 4th decimal place.)}$$

These are to be multiplied by $\frac{1}{100}$ $(t-1850)$ and the products added to A_{Ω} and B_{Ω} of Table XII. When the argument is negative δA_{Ω} changes sign.

By means of Tables IV, VI, VII, X, XI, XII, and XIII, we obtain

$$A = \tau + A_{\odot} + \text{\textit{its sec. var.}} + A_{\Omega} + \text{\textit{its sec. var.}}$$

$$B = \qquad B_{\odot} + \text{\textit{its sec. var.}} + B_{\Omega} + \text{\textit{its sec. var.}}$$

the logarithms of which are given in the American Ephemeris for Washington mean midnight. With the longitude and Table III we may also find their values for any other place and time.

The terms of short period, which depend on 2 $\mathbb{C}$ and $\mathbb{C} - \Gamma'$ may be supplied from Table XVII, and several other small terms from Table XXXVI.

TABLE XIV gives for 1850,

$$E_{\odot} = -0''.0035 \sin 2\ \odot, \qquad \text{and its variation in 100 years,}$$

$$\delta E_{\odot} = +0''.0005 \sin 2\ \odot, \qquad \text{in units of the 4th decimal place.}$$

The argument is

Arg. I $+$ *its inequalities* $+$ d' $+$ *day of year.*

TABLE XV gives for 1850,

$$E_{\Omega} = -0''.0483 \sin \Omega + 0''.0015 \sin 2\ \Omega, \qquad \text{and its variation in 100 years,}$$

$$\delta E_{\Omega} = +0''.0069 \sin \Omega - 0''.0001 \sin 2\ \Omega, \text{(in units of the 4th decimal place.)}$$

The argument is Arg. III $+$ d' $+$ *day of year*, or Arg. III $+$ d' $+$ *day of year* $-$ 6798^d.39. When it is negative the signs of E_{Ω} and δE_{Ω}, as given in this table, must be changed.

$\delta E_{\odot}$ and δE_{Ω} are to be multiplied by $\frac{1}{100}$ $(t-1850)$.

From Tables XIV and XV we have

$$E = E_{\odot} + \text{\textit{its sec. var.}} + E_{\Omega} + \text{\textit{its sec. var,}}$$

or, in time, $\frac{1}{15}$ of this value.

TABLE XVI gives for Washington mean noon of Jan. 0 in common years, Jan. 1 in bissextile years,

Arg. IV, the number of mean days elapsed since twice the moon's longitude was 0,

Arg. V, the number of days since the moon's mean anomaly ($\mathbb{C} - \Gamma'$) was 0, together with multiples of their periods.

TABLE XVII gives the terms in A and B, which depend on 2 $\mathbb{C}$ and $\mathbb{C} - \Gamma'$, viz:

$$A_{\mathbb{C}} = -.00405 \sin 2\ \mathbb{C}, \qquad\qquad B_{\mathbb{C}} = -0''.0886 \cos 2\ \mathbb{C}$$

$$A'_{\mathbb{C}} = +.00135 \sin (\mathbb{C} - \Gamma'),$$

in units of the fifth decimal place for A, and of the fourth for B.

Arg. for $A_{\mathbb{C}}$ and $B_{\mathbb{C}}$, Arg. IV $+$ d' $+$ *day of year;*

Arg. for $A'_{\mathbb{C}}$, Arg. V $+$ d' $+$ *day of year;*

each diminished by the largest contained multiple of its period.

Reductions of right ascensions and declinations, which depend on $\mathbb{C}$ and $\mathbb{C} - \Gamma'$, are given in Tables XXXI — XXXIV.

TABLE XVIII contains for the epoch 1850, and for each tenth of the argument,

Arg. I $+$ *its inequalities* $+$ *d'* $+$ *day of year*,

the logarithms of

$$C = -20''.4451 \cos \omega \cos \odot = -18''.7553 \cos \odot \,.$$
$$D = -20''.4451 \sin \odot$$

The variation of log. C in 100 years is $+ 0.00004,25$.

Changes of index in this table are indicated by :

TABLE XIX contains, for the same epoch and argument, H and the logarithms of h and i from the formulæ

$$h \sin H = C, \quad i = C \tan \omega = -8''.1389 \cos \odot$$
$$h \cos H = D$$

The variations in 100 years are

$$\delta H = +0'.17 \sin 2 H, \quad \delta. \log h = +0.00004,25 \sin^2 H$$
$$\delta. \log i = -0.0002,25.$$

————

The quantities A, B, C, D, E, or h, H, i, together with f, g, G from the formulæ,

$$f = m A + E, \qquad g \cos G = n A$$
$$g \sin G = B,$$

serve for reducing the mean right ascension and declination of a star at the beginning of the year to its apparent place at date.

If a_o, δ_o are the star's mean right ascension and declination at the beginning of the year;

a, δ, the star's mean right ascension and declination, and

a', δ', the star's apparent right ascension and declination, for the time, τ, reckoned from the beginning of the year and expressed in fractional parts of a tropical year;

μ and μ', the annual proper motion of the star in right ascension and declination, respectively;

ω, the obliquity of the ecliptic, in Table VI;

m, n, the coefficients for precession in Table V;

and with BESSEL's notation,

$$a = \tfrac{1}{15}(m + n \sin a \tan \delta) \qquad\qquad a' = n \cos a$$
$$b = \tfrac{1}{15} \cos a \tan \delta \qquad\qquad\qquad b' = -\sin a$$
$$c = \tfrac{1}{15} \cos a \sec \delta \qquad\qquad\qquad c' = \tan \omega \cos \delta - \sin a \sin \delta$$
$$d = \tfrac{1}{15} \sin a \sec \delta \qquad\qquad\qquad d' = \cos a \sin \delta$$

we have for the reduction to the apparent place at date, the formulæ,

$$a' - a_o = A a + B b + C c + D d + E + \tau \mu$$
$$\delta' - \delta_o = A a' + B b' + C c' + D d' + \tau \mu':$$

or the formulæ,

$$a' - a_o = f + g \sin (G + a) \tan \delta + h \sin (H + a) \sec \delta + \tau \mu$$
$$\delta' - \delta_o = g \cos (G + a) + h \cos (H + a) \sin \delta + i \cos \delta + \tau \mu'.$$

Except for stars of high declination, the mean right ascension and declination of the star, or the values of a, b, &c., for the beginning of the year, instead of their values for the date, may be used.

If greater accuracy is required the small terms in A and B from Tables XVII and XXXVI may be supplied; or instead of the former, the terms in the reductions of right ascension and declination in Tables XXXI — XXXIV: and for stars near the pole we may also add such of the following terms as may be of sufficient magnitude:

In *Right Ascension.*	In *Declination.*

$$\left.\begin{array}{l} +0\overset{s}{.}000003 \;\; \tau^2 \sin a \\ -0.000149 \;\; \tau^2 \cos a \end{array}\right\} \tan \delta$$

$$\left.\begin{array}{l} -0.0000650 \;\; \tau^2 \sin 2a \quad \cdot \\ +0.0000103 \sin 2\,\Omega \cos 2a \\ -0.0000107 \cos 2\,\Omega \sin 2a \end{array}\right\} \tan^2 \delta$$

$$\left.\begin{array}{l} +0.0000620 \sin 2 \odot \cos 2a \\ -0.0000622 \cos 2 \odot \sin 2a \end{array}\right\} \sec^2 \delta$$

$$\left.\begin{array}{l} +0.0000513 \sin(\odot+\Omega)\cos 2a \\ -0.0000507 \cos(\odot+\Omega)\sin 2a \\ +0.0000097 \sin(\odot-\Omega)\cos 2a \\ -0.0000053 \cos(\odot-\Omega)\sin 2a \end{array}\right\} \tan \delta \sec \delta$$

$$\left.\begin{array}{l} +0\overset{''}{.}000975 \;\; \tau^2 \sin^2 a \\ -0.000023 \cos 2\,\Omega \\ -0.000080 \cos 2\,\Omega \cos 2a \\ -0.000077 \sin 2\,\Omega \sin 2a \\ +0.000040 \cos 2\odot \\ -0.000467 \cos 2\odot \cos 2a \\ -0.000465 \sin 2\odot \sin 2a \end{array}\right\} \tan \delta$$

$$\left.\begin{array}{l} -0.00004 \cos(\odot+\Omega) \\ -0.00038 \cos(\odot+\Omega)\cos 2a \\ -0.00038 \sin(\odot+\Omega)\sin 2a \\ -0.00038 \cos(\odot-\Omega) \\ -0.00004 \cos(\odot-\Omega)\cos 2a \\ -0.00007 \sin(\odot-\Omega)\sin 2a \end{array}\right\} \sin \delta \tan \delta$$

TABLE XX, for the computation of the annual precession of a star in right ascension and declination, contains for the epoch 1850.0

$$\Delta_o a = 1\overset{s}{.}33709 \sin a, \text{ or its logarithm, and}$$
$$\Delta\delta = 20''.0564 \cos a,$$

the signs of which are given with the *hour* of the argument.

For any date t, expressed in years and parts of a year, the argument is the star's mean right ascension at that time;

$$\log. \Delta_o a = \text{its tab. value} - 0.00000,187 \; (t - 1850);$$

the annual precession in right ascension is

$$\Delta a = 3\overset{s}{.}07177 + \Delta_o a \tan \delta + 0\overset{s}{.}00001,9 \; (t - 1850),$$

in which δ is the star's mean declination at the time t;
and the annual precession in declination

$$\Delta\delta = \text{tab. value} - 0''.000086 \cos a \; (t - 1850.)$$

The table gives $- 0''.0086 \cos a$, the variation in 100 years of the tabular value of $\Delta\delta$. Its sign, as given in the table, must be changed when a is between 6^h and 18^h.

The variation of the annual precession in 100 years is

In *Right Ascension.*	In *Declination.*

$$\begin{array}{l} +0\overset{s}{.}00190 \\ +0.00650 \sin 2a \\ -0.000573 \sin a \tan \delta \\ +0.029868 \cos a \tan \delta \\ +0.013000 \sin 2a \tan^2 \delta \end{array}$$

$$\begin{array}{l} -0\overset{''}{.}0086 \cos a \\ -0.4480 \sin a \\ -0.1950 \sin^2 a \tan \delta \end{array}$$

by which the annual precession found for one epoch may be reduced to another.

Adding to the annual precession the proper motion of the star referred to the same equinox and equator, we have the annual variation in right ascension and declination. The whole motion between two dates, t and t', may be found by multiplying the annual motion at the middle time, $\frac{1}{2}(t' + t)$, by $(t' - t)$ the number of years in the interval.

This table and these expressions are, however, not sufficiently rigorous for stars near the pole, for which it is necessary to take into consideration second and higher differences of the motion.

SPECIAL TABLES

For the Standard Stars of the American Ephemeris.

TABLE XXI contains the mean right ascensions and declinations for 1860.0 of the 198 fixed stars, whose apparent places are given in the *American Ephemeris*, commencing with the volume for 1865. The magnitudes, annual variations, (which include precession and proper motion,) secular variations, or changes in 100 years of the annual variations, and proper motions are also given.

The differences of these places and annual variations from those employed in the *American Ephemeris* for 1865–1869 will be found in Table XXIX.

The places and proper motions of 48 northern circumpolar stars and 128 time stars have been taken from Dr. B. A. Gould's *Standard Places of Fundamental Stars, U. S. Coast Survey, Second Edition*, Washington, 1866; of α Canis Majoris, α Geminorum, (the mean of the components), α Canis Minoris, γ Draconis, and α Cephei, from Wolfers' *Tabulæ Reductionum Astronomicarum*, Berlin, 1858: of β¹ Scorpii, η and β Draconis, and 61¹ Cygni, from a discussion of nearly all available observations by Mr. G. W. Hill, hereafter given; and of 13 stars south of — 40° dec. from the *British Nautical Almanac* for 1848. The magnitudes, except of the 13 southern stars, are Argelander's. Circumpolar stars are indicated by a *

The mean right ascension, or declination, of a star for any year *t* will be its

$$R.\ A.,\ \text{or}\ Dec.,\ \text{for}\ 1860.0 + \left[An.\ var. + sec.\ var. \times \tfrac{1}{200}(t - 1860)\right](t - 1860).$$

For a star near either pole it may be necessary also to include terms of the third and higher powers of the time. The coefficients of these terms for the northern circumpolar stars will be found in Gould's *Standard Places of Fundamental Stars* already referred to.

Tables XXII and XXIII contain the mean places of the same stars for the beginning of each year from 1865–1872 and 1873–1880, respectively. The hours and minutes of right ascension are given only for the first year on each page; when the seconds exceed 60ˢ they must be diminished by the requisite number of multiples of 60ˢ, and the minutes increased by the same number. A similar remark applies to the degrees of declination.

The year is supposed to begin when the sun's mean longitude is 280°.

Tables XXIV–XXVIII contain the quantities necessary to obtain, for any date from 1865 to 1880, the apparent places of as many of these stars as are not found in Wolfers' *Tabulæ Reductionum*. Tables for α and δ Ursæ Minoris are also given; but Wolfers' tables for the remaining 42 stars require no other appreciable change than for differences of mean place and proper motion.

Table XXIV contains for each star—

$$\triangle_{\odot} a = A_{\odot} a + B_{\odot} b + C\,c + D\,d + \tau\,(a + \mu)$$
$$\triangle_{\odot} \delta = A_{\odot} a' + B_{\odot} b' + C\,c' + D\,d' + \tau\,(a + \mu')$$
$$\triangle_{\Omega} a = A_{\Omega} a + B_{\Omega} b + E_{\Omega}$$
$$\triangle_{\Omega} \delta = A_{\Omega} a' + B_{\Omega} b'$$

in which the same notation is used as in pages iii and iv.

To $\triangle_{\odot} a$ and $\triangle_{\odot} \delta$ have been added the small terms, given on page vi, which depend on τ^2 and $\odot$, and to $\triangle_{\Omega} a$ and $\triangle_{\Omega} \delta$ those which depend on Ω, whenever they are of sufficient magnitude.

The first two of this set of quantities include precession and proper motion for the fractional part of the year denoted by τ, aberration and solar nutation; the other two comprise the principal terms of lunar nutation.

The times of the star's conjunction in right ascension with the true and mean suns, and, for a circumpolar star, of its opposition to the mean sun, are also given.

The meridian on which the mean sun is at the time its longitude is 280° is called the *fictitious* meridian for the following year; and the astronomical mean time of that instant at that meridian is Jan 0 0ʰ of common years, Jan. 1 0ʰ of bissextile years. The corresponding sidereal time is Jan. 0 18ʰ 40ᵐ, or in bissextile years, Jan. 1 18ʰ 40ᵐ.

$\triangle_{\odot} a$ and $\triangle_{\odot} \delta$ are first given for the upper transit of the star at this meridian which immediately precedes, or follows, this date, according as the right ascension of the star is less, or greater, than 18ʰ 40ᵐ; and then for every tenth transit throughout the year.

viii

They are the proper values for 1870, but may be reduced to any other year by adding to each $\frac{1}{10}(t-1870) \times$ *its Var. in 10 years*, (t being the entire year, exclusive of the fractional part.)

The columns headed *Diff. for 10 days* are the first differential coefficients of $\triangle_{\odot}a$ and $\triangle_{\odot}\delta$, respectively, with regard to the time, the unit of which is 10 days. Both the *Var. in 10 years* and the *Diff. for 10 days* are expressed in units of the last decimal place of the quantities to which they belong, and are given for the same dates.

$\triangle_{\Omega}a$ and $\triangle_{\Omega}\delta$ are also given for the same first transit, and then for every hundredth transit of the same meridian in each year from 1865 to 1880.

The common argument given for both sets of quantities is the number of sidereal days from the star's first transit. But for $\triangle_{\odot}a$ and $\triangle_{\odot}\delta$ are also given the calendar dates, both sidereal and mean,[*] the repetition of which for $\triangle_{\Omega}a$ and $\triangle_{\Omega}\delta$ is unnecessary.

To the mean day is appended the fractional part expressing the astronomical mean time of the star's transit, the sidereal time being the star's right ascension. But, as the argument for a time of transit, the entire day only is to be regarded, whether sidereal or mean, and the part of a day neglected.

It is to be noted, however, that in bissextile years the dates of the months January and February, as given in the table, should be increased by one day.

The quantities in this table, being given for the time of the upper transit of the star at the fictitious meridian, may be reduced to the time of transit at any other meridian for the same date, by interpolating for its longitude from the fictitious meridian of the year; which, expressed in days, is $k' + d'$ of Tables VI and I.[†]

And for the nth transit at that meridian after any tabular date the interval for interpolation will be $n + k' + d'$. For a back interpolation n is negative.

1. If then the apparent place of a star is required for the time of its upper transit of any meridian on a specified day, the argument with which to enter the table for the star will be

The *sid. day* $+ k' + d'$, for the column *Sidereal Day;*
or, except in the case hereafter mentioned,

The *mean day* $+ k' + d'$, for the column *Mean Day,*
(neglecting, however, the fraction of a day in this column.)

On the mean day when the star is in conjunction with the mean sun there will be two transits, the first occurring near the commencement, the other near the close of the day; and it will be necessary to state which is meant.

The preceding argument applies to the first of these in a forward interpolation. For the other, and for the succeeding transits in the period of ten days in which the conjunction occurs, that is, after the conjunction and until the next tabular date, the argument should be

The *mean day* $+ k' + d' + 1^d.$

So also for a back interpolation, the argument, as first stated, applies to the second of the two transits, which occur on the day of conjunction. For the first, and for the preceding transits until the next preceding tabular date, the argument should be

The *mean day* $+ k' + d' - 1^d.$

But it may be more convenient, when the mean day is given, to reduce it to the sidereal day, by adding to it

$1^d,$	before	$\delta * $ *Mean Sun,*	$\}$ if $a < 18^h 40^m.$
$2^d,$	after	" "	
$0^d,$	before	" "	$\}$ if $a > 18^h 40^m.$
$1^d,$	after	" "	

---

[*] Jan.—0 76, at the top of col. *Mean day*, on p. 92, is Dec. 30.24, or in bissextile years, Dec. 31.24, of the preceding year. Other negative dates are to be regarded in the same way.

[†] $k' + d'$ sometimes exceeds 1^d, or the whole circumference. It should, however, be used without any reduction.

Then by adding $k' + d'$ we have the argument* to be used with the column *sidereal day*.

On the day of conjunction the first of the two transits is before, the second is after, the time of conjunction.

2 If the apparent place of a circumpolar star at the time of its lower transit on any day is wanted, the argument to be used with the column *sidereal day* will be

$$\text{The sid. day} + k' + d' + 0^d.5, \quad \text{if } a < 12^h,$$
$$\text{The sid. day} + k' + d' - 0^d.5, \quad \text{if } a > 12^h;$$

or

$$\text{The mean day} + k' + d' + 1^d.5, \quad \text{before } \vartheta * \textit{Mean Sun,} \left.\right\} \text{ if } a < 6^h 40^m.$$
$$\text{The mean day} + k' + d' + 2^d.5, \quad \text{after} \qquad ``$$
$$\text{The mean day} + k' + d' + 0^d.5, \quad \text{before} \qquad `` \left.\right\} \text{ if } a > 6^h 40^m.$$
$$\text{The mean day} + k' + d' + 1^d.5, \quad \text{after} \qquad ``$$

Two lower transits occur on the mean day of the star's opposition to the mean sun. The remarks respecting two transits on the same day apply here as in the case of upper transits.

The argument for a lower transit to be used with the column *Mean Day*, excluding as before the fractional part af a day in that column, will be

$$\text{The mean day} + k' + d' - 0^d.5,$$

from the conjunction to the succeeding opposition with the mean sun;

$$\text{The mean day} + k' + d' + 0^d.5,$$

from the opposition to the succeeding conjunction; with the same modification, however, at the date of two transits, as in the case of an upper culmination.

3. For a specified sidereal time, *sid. day* $+ s$, the argument will be

$$\text{The sid. day} + k' + d' + (s - a),$$

in which convenience requires that $s - a$ should be expressed in decimals of a day.

4. For a specified mean time, the argument, with which to enter the column *Mean Day*, will be

$$\text{The mean time} + k' + d';$$

and the fractional part of the day in this column must be taken into account.† For $\triangle_{\odot} a$ and $\triangle_{\odot} \delta$ the column of *Mean Day* is easily supplied from columns one and two of the table.

Forming the argument in either of these cases and taking the nearest, or the next preceding, tabular date, let

$$T = \tfrac{1}{10}(\textit{Arg.} - \textit{Tab. date for } \triangle_{\odot} a \text{ and } \triangle_{\odot} \delta),$$
$$T_1 = \tfrac{1}{100}(\textit{Arg.} - \textit{Tab. date for } \triangle_{\Omega} a \text{ and } \triangle_{\Omega} \delta).$$

T will be the coefficient by which to multiply the *Diff. for 10 days* of $\triangle_{\odot} a$, $\triangle_{\odot} \delta$, and their *Var. in 10 years;*

T_1, the coefficient of the *Diff. for 100 days* of $\triangle_{\Omega} a$ and $\triangle_{\Omega} \delta$; and $\tfrac{1}{2} T^2$ and $\tfrac{1}{2} T_1^2$, respectively, the coefficients of the second differences of the two sets of quantities; provided the first differences, like the *Diff. for 10 days* of $\triangle_{\odot} a$ and $\triangle_{\odot} \delta$ in the table, are reduced‡ to the tabular date employed.

If we use as 2d difference the mean of the differences of the *Diff. for 10 days*, or the *Diff. for 100 days*, which immediately precede and follow the tabular date, $\tfrac{1}{6} T^2$ and

---

* This also is the argument for the similar tables of BESSEL'S *Tabulæ Regiomontanae* and WOLFERS' *Tabulæ Reductionum.*

† The mean time interval in this case, *Arg. — Tab. date*, should be increased by $\tfrac{1}{400}$ part.

‡ This is done with sufficient exactness by subtracting from the mean of the 1st differences, which immediately precede and follow the tabular date, one-sixth of the corresponding third differences; *i. e.*
$$\triangle_0' = \tfrac{1}{2}(\triangle_i' + \triangle_i') - \tfrac{1}{12}(\triangle_i''' + \triangle_i'').$$

$\frac{1}{6} T_1{}^3$ will be, respectively, the coefficients of the 3d difference, which it is sometimes necessary to take into account. But if the nearest tabular date is used, T or T_1 will be numerically less than $\frac{1}{2}$, and the coefficient of the 3d difference will be less than $\frac{1}{48}$.

Adding the several products, indicated above, to the primary quantities to which they belong, we shall have $\triangle_\odot a$, $\triangle_\odot \delta$, the *Var. in* 10 *years* of each, $\triangle_\Omega a$ and $\triangle_\Omega \delta$ reduced to the specified time. Then, if .

a_0 and δ_0 are the mean right ascension and declination of the star at the beginning of the year, a' and δ', its apparent right ascension and declination at the stated time, the required apparent place of the star is found by the following formulæ :

$$a' = a_0 + \triangle_\odot a + its \; Var. \; in \; 10 \; y. \times \tfrac{1}{10}(t - 1870) + \triangle_\Omega a,$$
$$\delta' = \delta_0 + \triangle_\odot \delta + its \; Var. \; in \; 10 \; y. \times \tfrac{1}{10}(t - 1870) + \triangle_\Omega \delta ;$$

to which, however, should be added in the case of several circumpolar stars several small terms supplied by subsequent tables; and, for other stars also, the terms depending on $\mathbb{C}$ and $\mathbb{C} - I''$, when they are regarded as of sufficient importance.

The essential features of this table belong also to the corresponding tables of Bessel's *Tabulæ Regiomontanæ* and Wolfers' *Tabulæ Reductionum*. The peculiar arrangement with respect to the argument, employed first by Bessel, presents this great advantage, that the argument and coefficients for interpolation are the same for all stars at their respective times of transits over the same meridian on the same sidereal day; that is, from 0^h of sidereal time until the succeeding 0^h. And for each successive sidereal day the argument increases by 1 day.

In constructing an ephemeris of the stars, for each tenth transit, like that of the *American Ephemeris*, the coefficients for interpolation are the same for every date throughout the year, as well as every star, viz :

$$T = \tfrac{1}{10}(k' + d'), \qquad T_1 = \tfrac{1}{100}(k' + d');$$

or, if it is desired that the ephemeris shall commence n days later,

$$T = \tfrac{1}{10}(n + k' + d'), \qquad T_1 = \tfrac{1}{100}(n + k' + d').$$

Thus for 1868 and the meridian of Washington, to commence Jan. 1,

$$1^d + k' + d' = + 1^d.649, \qquad T = + 0.1649, \qquad T_1 = + 0.01649;$$

and for 1870, to commence Jan. 0.

$$1^d + k' + d' = + 1^d.164, \qquad T = + 0.1164, \qquad T_1 = + 0.01164.$$

To the numbers in the column *Mean Day* we may simply add n, or more rigidly $n - .00274 \, (n + k' + d')$.

Table XXV contains for 51 Cephei, σ Octantis, and λ Ursæ Minoris terms in right ascension and declination to be multiplied by $\frac{1}{100}(t - 1870)^2$; that is, a secular variation of the secular variation. The argument is the same as for $\triangle_\odot a$ and $\triangle_\odot \delta$ in Table XXIV.

Table XXVI contains, also for the same argument, the motion of $\odot + \Omega$ and $\odot - \Omega$, expressed in thousandths of the circumference.

Table XXVII contains for a Ursæ Minoris, 51 Cephei, σ Octantis, and λ Ursæ Minoris, terms in right ascension and declination, (on page vi,) which depend on $\odot + \Omega$ and $\odot - \Omega$. The argument is $\odot + \Omega$, or $\odot - \Omega$, as given on page 249 for the star at the beginning of the year, + the motion for the date in Table XXVI; rejecting 1000 when the sum exceeds that number. The sign to be used is that written on the same side as the argument.

Table XXVIII contains for a Ursæ Minoris, 51 Cephei, δ Ursæ Minoris, and λ Ursæ Minoris, terms which depend on $2 \, \mathbb{C}$, viz :

$$\triangle_{\mathbb{C}} a = - \, 0^s.0125 \sin 2 \, \mathbb{C} - [0^s.00542 \sin 2 \, \mathbb{C} \sin a + 0^s.00590 \cos 2 \, \mathbb{C} \cos a] \tan \delta$$
$$\triangle_{\mathbb{C}} \delta = - \, 0''.0813 \sin 2 \, \mathbb{C} \cos a + 0''.0886 \cos 2 \, \mathbb{C} \sin a.$$

The "argument 2 ☾" is the number of sidereal days since 2 ☾ = 0. It is given for the beginning of each fictitious year on page 253, and is formed for any date by adding to the argument for the year, the argument for $\triangle_{\odot} a$, &c., in Table XXIV, expressed in sidereal days, *i. e.*

The sid. day $+ k' + d'$,   for the upper transit,
The sid. day $+ k' + d' + (s - a)$,   for any sidereal time;

and subtracting the largest contained multiple of the period. As in Table XXIV, the argument is the same for the four stars at their transits over the same meridian on the same sidereal day..

The terms are given for every tenth of a sidereal day, an interval sufficiently small to dispense with interpolation. It will be noticed, however, that the table is arranged so that there is an interval of a sidereal day, instead of a tenth of a day, in the argument; so that, starting with the argument for the commencement of a daily ephemeris, we have only to write down the numbers from the proper column of the table, in the order in which they are given; and, when we arrive at the end of the table, to go back to the beginning, and so on until the period of the ephemeris is completed. This advantage is afforded by the fact that the period of the argument is 13.698 sidereal days, so that, assuming it as 13.7 days, will, after a whole year, make the argument in error less than $0^{d}.05$. If we add $0^{d}.025$ to the argument at the beginning of the year, the arguments obtained for the middle of the year will be correct; and at the beginning and end will be in error less than $0^{d}.03$.

Thus for the upper transit of *a* Ursæ Minoris at the meridian of Washington, 1870, Jan. 1.

Arg. 2 ☾ $+ $ *sid. day* $+ k' + d' = 5^{d}.88 + 2^{d} + 0^{d}.16 = 8^{d}.04$, and adding $0^{d}.025$, we have $8^{d}.1$ as the argument with which to commence.

TABLE XXIX contains the reductions of the places of the stars, as given in the *American Ephemeris* for the years 1865–1869, to those adopted in these tables and in the *Ephemeris* for 1870. The epoch is 1865.

TABLE XXX gives for the beginning of each year Dr. AUWERS'[*] correction of the position of *a* Canis Majoris, *Sirius*, due to orbital motion, viz:

$$q = + 0^{s}.0647 - 0^{s}.000718 \, (t - 1860) + 0^{s}.1510 \cos (u + 1^{\circ} \, 6')$$
$$r = - 0''.630 - 0''.00044 \, (t - 1860) + 1''.445 \sin (u + 23^{\circ} \, 30')$$

in which *u*, the eccentric anomaly from the inferior apsis, is found by the formulæ

$$u - e \sin u = n \, (t - T),$$

from the elements

$T = 1793.830$,   passage through the inferior apsis,
$e = \quad 0.6010$, the eccentricity,
$n = \quad 7^{\circ}.28475$, mean annual motion in orbit,
        $49^{y}.418$, period of revolution.

It is substituted for the *Tabula Subsidiaria* of WOLFERS.

SUPPLEMENTARY TABLES,
Of small terms in nutation.

TABLES XXXI and XXXIII contain terms in the reduction of mean right ascensions and declinations, which depend on 2 ☾, viz:

$$\triangle'_{\mathstrut ☾} a = - 0^{s}.0125 \sin 2 ☾.$$
$$\triangle''_{\mathstrut ☾} a \div \tan \delta = - 0^{s}.00542 \sin 2 ☾ \sin a - 0^{s}.00590 \cos 2 ☾ \cos a$$
$$\triangle'_{\mathstrut ☾} \delta = - 0''.0813 \sin 2 ☾ \cos a + 0''.0886 \cos 2 ☾ \sin a$$

The arguments are,

Side Arg. = *Arg. IV* (Table XVI) $+ d' + $ *day of year,*
Hor. Arg. = *u*,

---

subtracting from the former the largest contained multiple of the period. The signs of $\Delta''_\zeta a$ and $\Delta'_\zeta \delta$, as given in the table, are to be changed when $a > 12^h$.

TABLES XXXII and XXXIV contain terms which depend on $\mathbb{C} - \Gamma'$, viz:

$$\Delta'''_\zeta a = + 0^s.0041 \sin (\mathbb{C} - \Gamma'),$$
$$\Delta^{iv}_\zeta a \div \tan \delta = + 0^s.00180 \sin (\mathbb{C} - \Gamma') \sin a,$$
$$\Delta''_\zeta \delta = + 0''.0270 \sin (\mathbb{C} - \Gamma') \cos a,$$

The arguments are,

Side Arg. = *Arg. V* (Tab. XVI) $+ d' + $ *day of year.*
Hor. Arg. = a.

The signs of $\Delta^{iv}_\zeta a$ and $\Delta''_\zeta \delta$, as given in the table, are to be changed, when a is found at the bottom.

TABLE XXXV contains for Washington mean noon of Jan. 0 in common years, Jan. 1 in bissextile years, arguments for small terms in nutation, viz:

Arg. VI, for terms in $2 \odot - \Omega$, with its inequalities.
Arg. VII,   " $2 \odot - 2 \Omega$ "
Arg. VIII,   " $2 \odot - 2 \Gamma'$ "
Arg. IX,   " $2 \Gamma' - \Omega$
Arg. X,   " Γ'

In each case the argument is the number of mean days since the quantity was 0. The period of each is also given.

TABLE XXXVI contains the following small terms:

In A.		In B.	For *Arg.*	
$-.00011 \sin (3 \odot - \Gamma)$,*		$-0.0027 \cos (3 \odot - \Gamma)$,*		I.
$+.00025 \sin (2 \odot - \Omega)$,		$+0.0067 \cos (2 \odot - \Omega)$,	"	VI.
$-.00005 \sin 2(\odot - \Omega)$,			"	VII.
$+.00010 \sin 2(\odot - \Gamma')$,			"	VIII.
$+.00009 \sin (2\Gamma' - \Omega)$,		$+0.0024 \cos (2\Gamma' - \Omega)$,	"	IX.
$+.00005 \cos \Gamma'$ $\}$		$-0.0023 \sin \Gamma'$ $\}$	"	X.
$+.00004 \sin 2\Gamma'$ $\}$		$+0.0008 \cos 2\Gamma'$ $\}$		

They are expressed in the table in units of the *fifth* decimal place for A, and of the *fourth* for B.

The Argument in each case will be the *Argument* for the beginning of the year, from Table VI or XXXV, $+$ *its inequalities* $+ d' + $ *day of the year*, diminished by the largest contained multiple of its period.

EXAMPLES.

1. Required, for Washington mean midnight July 12, 1868, the obliquity of the ecliptic, the equation of equinoxes in longitude and right ascension, and the quantities A, B, C, D, E, f, g, G, h, H and i.

Preparation of the Arguments.

		I.	II.	III.	IV.	V.
		d	d	d	d	d
Tab. VI, XVI,	for 1868 . .	2.273	2.7	$- 2984.61$	0.054	19.01
II, III,	for July 12, 12^h.	193.500	193.5	193.50	193.500	193.50
I,	for Washington.	0.000	0.0	0.00	0.000	0.00
VII,	$.001,16 \times 18.5 =$	$+ 0.021$				
— *Multiples of Period*					$- 191.251$	-192.88
Arguments for date . . .		195.794	196.2	$- 2791.11$	2.303	19.63

* The assumed value of Γ is $279°\,56'$, which is nearly its value in 1825.

HANSEN's *Arg.* I $+$ *its inequalities* is 195^d.791, which differs only 0^d.003 from the preceding value.

	VI.	VII.	VIII.	IX.	X.
Tab. XXXV, for 1868	21.4^d	118^d	192^d	242^d	1009^d
" inequalities . . .	— .3	0	0		
I, II, III, for Wash. July 12, 12^h	193.5	193	193	193	193
—Multiples of Period . . .	— 177.8	—173	—206		
Arguments for date	36.8	138	179	435	1202

	Ob. of eclip.	*Eq. of Eq'x.*			τ
		In *Long.*	In *R.A.*		
Tab. VI, for 1868 .	23° 27′ 22″.63	″	$\cdot$	Tab. VI,	$k'' = +$ 0.00178^y
VII, for *Arg.* I.	— 0.65	$+$ 0.80	$+$ 0.049	IV, for July 12	0.52979
VIII, for *Arg.* III.	— 7.85	— 9.38	— 0.574	I, III,	0.00000
For date . .	23 27 14.13	— 8.58	— 0.525	$\tau = +$ 0.53157

		A.	*B.*	*E.*
	$\tau =$	$+$.53157		
Tab. X, XIV, for *Arg.* I . .		$+$.01618	$+$0.4010″	$+$0.0023″
XI, "		$+$.00001	0.0000	
XII, XV, for *Arg.* III .		—.18612	$+$7.8438	—0.0263
XIII, "		—.00003	$+$0.0001	

$$A = +.36161 \quad B = +8.2449 \quad E = -\ 0.024 = -0.002°$$

log. *A* = 9.55824	log. *g* sin *G* = log. *B* = 0.91618		
Tab. V, log. *n* = 1.30222	log. *g* cos *G* = log. *n A* = 0.86046		
" log. *m* = 1.66353	log. tan *G* = 0.05572	*G* = 48° 39′.9	
" log. *m A* = 1.22177	log. sin *G* = 9.87556	log. *g* = 1.04062	
m A = $+$16″.664	$f = m A + E$ = $+$ 16″.640 = $+$ 1^s.109		

	log. *C*	log. *D*	log. *h*	*H*	log. *i*
Tab. XVIII, XIX, for *Arg.* I.	0.82787	1.28068n	1.30612	160° 34′.7	0.4653

If it is desired to include in *A* and *B* the terms of short period, depending on $\mathfrak{C}$ and $\mathfrak{C} - l'$, and other small terms of nutation, we have

		A.	*B.*
Tab. XVII,	for *Arg.* IV	—.00353	—0″.0434
"	" *Arg.* V	— 131	
Tab. XXXVI	for *Arg.* I	— 8	— 17
"	" *Arg.* VI	$+$ 24	$+$ 18
"	" *Arg.* VII	$+$ 5	
"	" *Arg.* VIII	— 7	
"	" *Arg.* IX	$+$ 7	— 12
"	" *Arg.* X	— 7	— 17
	Corrected	$A = +$.35691	$B = +$8.1987

2. Required for 1848, April 7, 10^h, Greenwich mean time, the logarithms of *A*, *B*, *C*, and *D*, and *E*, omitting the terms of short period and small terms in *A* and *B*.

		I.	II.	III.	τ
Tab. VI,	for 1848	2.128^d	2.6^d	+3307.17^d	+0.00135^y
II, III, IV,	for April 7, 10^h . .	97.417	97.4	97.42	+0.26672
I,	for Greenwich . . . —	0.214	— 0.2	— 0.21	—0.00059
VII,	—.000,61 × 1.7 = — 0.001				
— *Period*				—6798.39	
Arguments at date		99.330	99.8	—3394.01	0.26748

	A	B	log C.	log. D	E
τ = .26748					
Tab. X, XIV, XVIII, for *Arg.* I.	—.01206	—0.4475	1.25083n	0.80536n	—0.0020
XI, for *Arg.* I	.00000	0.0000			
XII, XV, for *Arg.* III . .	—.00166	+9.3128			—0.0003
XIII, for *Arg.* III . . .	—.00000	0.0000			
	+.25376	+8.8653			—0.0023
Logarithms	9.40442	0.94769	1.25083n	0.80536n	

3. Required the apparent place of η Virginis for its upper transit at Berlin, March 23, 1869.

1869, March 23.

Table I, for Berlin . $d' = — 0.251$

VI, for 1869 $k' = + 0.406$

Arg. for col. *Mean day* in Tab. XXIV, March 23.155

For $a < 18^h 40^m$ and date before ☽ ✳ *Mean Sun*, + 1.

Arg. for col. *Sidereal day* in Tab. XXIV, · March 24.155 = 83.155

From either argument* we find

$T = + 0.3155;$ for interpolation of $\Delta_\odot a$ and $\Delta_\odot \delta$.

$T' = — 0.1685,$ " " $\Delta_\Omega a$ and $\Delta_\Omega \delta$.

Table XXII, η Virginis, 1869.0, $a_o = 12^h\ 13^m\ 12^s.274$ $\delta_o = + 0^\circ\ 3'\ 41''.82$

Table XXIV, $\begin{cases} \Delta_\odot a = +1.945 & \Delta_\odot \delta = —12.69 \\ \Delta_\Omega a = —0.768 & \Delta_\Omega \delta = + 5.36 \end{cases}$

Apparent place $a' = 12\ 13\ 13.451$ $\delta' = + 0\ 3\ 34.49$

The Berlin mean time of transit, from Table XXIV, is March 23.50, for which from Table XVI, Arg. IV = 10^d.2, Arg. V = 25^d.4. With these we may take from Tables XXXI — XXXIV,

$\Delta'_{☾} a = + 0.012$ $\Delta'_{☾} \delta = — 0.08$

$\Delta'''_{☾} a = — 0.002$ $\Delta''_{☾} \delta = + 0.01:$

but these terms of short period are usually neglected.

4. Required the apparent place of λ Ursæ Minoris at its lower transit at Greenwich, Nov. 1, 1877.

1877, Nov. 1.

Table I, for Greenwich $d' = — 0.214$

VI, for 1869 $k' = + 0.469$

For $a > 6^h 40^m$ and date after ☽ ✳ *Mean Sun*, + 1.5

Arg. for col. *Sidereal day* in Table XXIV, Nov. 2.755 = 306^d.755

$T' = — 0.3245,$ for interpolation of $\Delta_\odot a$ and $\Delta_\odot \delta$ from Nov. 6,

$T_1 = + 0.0675,$ " " $\Delta_\Omega a$ and $\Delta_{☾} \delta$ from 300^d.

* Neglecting decimals in the column *Mean day.*

From Table XXIV we have

For Nov. 6 $\Delta_{\odot}a = -\overset{s}{6}9.24$ $\Delta_{\odot}\delta = +\overset{''}{2}6.63$

$.7 \times (-5^s.70)$ $= -\ 3.99$ $.7 \times (-.83)$ $= -\ .58$

$T \times (-13^s.22 + 0^s.40 \times \frac{1}{2} T) = +\ 4.31$ $T \times (-.33 - .54 \times \frac{1}{2} T) = +\ .08$

$\frac{1}{6} T^3 \times 0^s.33$ $=\ 0.00$ $\frac{1}{6} T^3 \times .00$ $=\ .00$

For date $\Delta_{\odot}a = -\ 68.92$ $\Delta_{\odot}\delta = +\ 26.13$

For 1877, 300^d. $\Delta_{\Omega}a = -\overset{s}{2}3.42$ $\Delta_{\Omega}\delta = -\overset{''}{5}.38$

$T_1 \times (-.92 + .18 \times \frac{1}{2} T_1) = -\ 0.06$ $T_1 \times (+.61 + .03 \times \frac{1}{2} T_1) = +\ .04$

For date $\Delta_{\Omega}a = -\ 23.48$ $\Delta_{\Omega}\delta = -\ 5.34$

	$\odot + \Omega$	$\odot - \Omega$	$2\ \mathbb{C}_d$
Tables XXVII, XXVIII, for 1877	733	824	8.02
XXVI, XXIV, Nov. 2. 8	793	883	306.76
— Multiples of periods	−1000	−1000	−301.36
Arg's at date	526	707	13.4

Table XXIII, λ Urs. Min. 1877.0, $a_0 = 19\ \overset{m}{4}7\ \overset{s}{1}5.84$ $\delta_0 = +88\ \overset{'}{5}6\ \overset{''}{9}.15$

XXIV, $\Delta_{\odot}a = -1\ \ 8.92$ $\Delta_{\odot}\delta = +26.13$

       " $\Delta_{\Omega}a = -\ \ .23.48$ $\Delta_{\Omega}\delta = -\ 5.34$

XXV, $-0^s.11 \times .49$ $= -\ \ 0.05$ $-0''.05 \times .49 = -\ 0.02$

XXVII,   for $\odot + \Omega = 526$ $-\ \ 0.10$ $-\ 0.01$

     "   " $\odot - \Omega = 707$ $+\ \ 0.01$ 0.00

XXVIII,   " $Arg.\ 2\mathbb{C} = 13.4$ $-\ \ 0.18$ $-\ 0.07$

Apparent place $a' = 19\ \overset{m}{4}5\ \overset{s}{4}3.12$ $\delta'_0 = +88\ 56\ 29.84$

The Greenwich mean time of the lower transit is Nov. 1.73, for which we should find the sum of the small terms in Table XXXVI to be only $-0^s.008$ in R. A. and $+0''.002$ in Dec.

5. What is the mean place of ψ^1 Draconis for 1755.0, or 105 years before 1860?

Table XXI,   for 1860.0, $a = 17\ \overset{m}{4}4\ \overset{s}{2}6.134$ $\delta = +72\ \overset{'}{1}2\ \overset{''}{5}9.31$

-105 (An. Var. $-\frac{105}{800}$ Sec. Var.), $+\ 1\ 54.942$ $+\ 2\ 41.66$

$-\frac{105^3}{100} \times 0^s.000002^*$, $-\ \ 0.023$

For 1755.0 $a = 17\ 46\ 21.053$ $\delta = +72\ 15\ 40.97$

FORMULÆ USED IN THE CONSTRUCTION OF THE TABLES.

Many of the formulæ used in the construction of the tables have been given in the preceding pages. Others, however, could not be conveniently introduced.

Table VI. From Hansen and Olufsen's *Tables du Soleil*, Intr. p. 12, we have for Paris mean noon of Jan. 0 in a common year, Jan. 1 in a bissextile year,

Arg. I $= 1.905307 - \frac{1}{4}r + 0.00721714 (t' - 1850) + 0.00000003101 (t' - 1850)^2$,

Arg. V $= 2.3470 + 0.0053032 (t' - 1850)$.

t' being the entire number of the year, and r the remainder after its division by 4.

From Peirce's *Tables of the Moon*, Intr. p. 5, we have

$$\Omega = 13\ \overset{'}{5}5\ \overset{''}{5}2.6 - 190''.63366070\ i + 6''.0355\ \frac{i^2}{10^9} + 2''.3744\ \frac{i^3}{10^{16}},$$

in which i denotes the number of mean solar days from 1801, Jan. 0 0^h, mean time of Washington. From this we readily find

Arg. III $= -263^d.0838 + i\ -6798^d.37965\ n - 0^d.001463\ n^2$,

n denoting a whole number, so taken that Arg. III may be numerically less than 3399^d.2, or half the period.

According to BESSEL (*Astronomische Nachrichten*, No. 134,) the mean longitude of the sun for mean noon of Paris of Jan. 0 in common years, Jan. 1 in bissextile years, of the year 1800 + *t* is

$$279° 54' 1''.36 + 27''.605844\, t + 0''.0001221805\, t^2 - 14'\, 47''.083\, f,$$

where *f* denotes the remainder after dividing *t* by 4, and the mean daily motion of the sun is $59'\, 8''.3302$. Whence for mean noon of Washington,

$k = +\, 2^h\, 52^m\, 0^s.0 + 11^m\, 12^s.18798\, t + 0^s.002975\, t^2 - 6^h \times f.$
$k' = +\, 0^d.11944447 + 0^d.0077799535\, t + 0^d.000000034433\, t^2 - \tfrac{1}{4}f.$
$k'' = +\, 0^y.00032703 + 0^y.000021350\, t - 0^y.00068448\, f.$

Table XVI. From PEIRCE's *Tables of the Moon* we also have

$$\mathbb{C} = 107\overset{\circ}{}\, 55'\, 40''.5 + 47435''.02808897\, i + 8''.598\, \tfrac{i^2}{10^9} + 3''.6483\, \tfrac{i^3}{10^{14}}$$

$$I' = 266\quad 4\quad 51.3 + \quad 401.05783886\, i - 27.217\, \tfrac{i^2}{10^9} - 13.750\, \tfrac{i^3}{10^{12}};$$

whence

$$\mathbb{C} - I' = 201\overset{\circ}{}\, 50'\, 49''.2 + 47033''.97025011\, i + 35''.815\, \tfrac{i^2}{10^9} + 17''.398\, \tfrac{i^3}{10^{14}}$$

$$\text{Arg. IV} = \overset{d}{8}.19101 + i - 13.6607909\, n + 0.033826\, \tfrac{n^2}{10^9},$$

$$\text{Arg. V} = 15.4493 + i - 27.5545524\, n + 0.57815\, \tfrac{n^2}{10^9}.$$

in which *i* denotes the number of mean days from Washington mean noon of 1801, Jan. 0, and *n* is a whole number denoting in each case the number of entire periods of the argument.

Table XXXV. From the preceding values of $\odot$, Ω and I' are derived,

$$\text{Arg. VI} = \overset{d}{91}.800 + i - .177.84380\, n \qquad \text{for terms in } 2\,\odot - \Omega$$
$$\text{Arg. VII} = 82.753 + i - 173.31004\, n \qquad\qquad `` \quad 2\,(\odot - \Omega)$$
$$\text{Arg. VIII} = 15.783 + i - 205.89262\, n \qquad\qquad `` \quad 2\,(\odot - I')$$
$$\text{Arg. IX} = 573.790 + i - 1305.4655\, n \qquad\qquad `` \quad 2\,I' - \Omega$$
$$\text{Arg. X} = 2388.412 + i - 3231.455\, n \qquad\qquad `` \quad I'$$

in which *i* is reckoned from the same epoch as before.

Tables XXI — XXVIII.

ON THE DERIVATION AND REDUCTION OF PLACES OF THE FIXED STARS,
By Mr. G. W. HILL, *Assistant in Nautical Almanac Office.*

The co-ordinates of the stars are affected by three distinct causes; first, by the motion of the earth's axis and the equinox, which produces precession and nutation; second, by the motion of the star itself and of the solar system in space, the combined effect of which is denoted as proper motion; third, by the motion of light, the effect of which is called aberration.

1. Let us first consider the effect of precession alone. If *a* and *δ* denote the right ascension and declination of a star at any time, its rectangular co-ordinates will be, its distance being assumed as unity,

$$\left.\begin{array}{l} x = \cos \delta \cos a, \\ y = \cos \delta \sin a, \\ z = \sin \delta. \end{array}\right\} \tag{1}$$

To pass to any new system we shall have the known equations

$$\left.\begin{array}{l} x' = ax + by + cz, \\ y' = a'x + b'y + c'z, \\ z' = a''x + b''y + c''z. \end{array}\right\} \tag{2}$$

But in the case where we wish to obtain the differentials of *x*, *y*, *z* for an infinitesimal time d*t*, *a*, *b'*, and *c''* are each unity, being the cosines of angles infinitely small; and all the other constants will contain d*t* as a factor. Hence we may write

$$\frac{dx}{dt} = by + cz,$$

$$\frac{dy}{dt} = a'x + c'z, \qquad\qquad (3)$$

$$\frac{dz}{dt} = a''x + b''y.$$

The equation $x^2 + y^2 + z^2 = 1$, gives us $x\dfrac{dx}{dt} + y\dfrac{dy}{dt} + z\dfrac{dz}{dt} = 0$. Substituting in this the above values of $\dfrac{dx}{dt}$, &c., there result these three equations of condition between the six remaining constants,

$$b + a' = 0,$$
$$c + a'' = 0, \qquad\qquad (4)$$
$$c' + b'' = 0.$$

Hence

$$\frac{dx}{dt} = by + cz,$$

$$\frac{dy}{dt} = -bx + c'z, \qquad\qquad (5)$$

$$\frac{dz}{dt} = -cx - c'y.$$

It belongs to Celestial Mechanics to deduce the values of the three remaining coefficients of these equations. When precession alone is considered $c' = 0$, and $-b$ and $-c$ are the quantities m and n, whose values have been previously given. Thus we have, the unit of t being one year,

$$\frac{dx}{dt} = -my - nz,$$

$$\frac{dy}{dt} = mx, \qquad\qquad (6)$$

$$\frac{dz}{dt} = nx.$$

If the values of x, y, and z are now substituted in these equations we readily find that

$$\frac{da}{dt} = m + n \sin a \tan \delta,$$

$$\frac{d\delta}{dt} = n \cos a. \qquad\qquad (7)$$

Differentiating these and always eliminating $\dfrac{da}{dt}$ and $\dfrac{d\delta}{dt}$ by means of the primitive equations we obtain

$$\frac{d^2 a}{dt^2} = \frac{dm}{dt} + \frac{n^2}{2} \sin 2a + \left[\frac{dn}{dt} \sin a + mn \cos a\right] \tan \delta + n^2 \sin 2a \tan^2 \delta;$$

$$\frac{d^2 \delta}{dt^2} = -mn \sin a + \frac{dn}{dt} \cos a - n^2 \sin^2 a \tan \delta;$$

$$\frac{d^3 a}{dt^3} = \frac{mn^2}{2} + \tfrac{3}{2} mn^2 \cos 2a + \tfrac{3}{2} n \frac{dn}{dt} \sin 2a$$
$$+ \left\{(2n^2 - m^2 + 3n^2 \cos 2a) n \sin a + \left(2m \frac{dn}{dt} + n \frac{dm}{dt}\right) \cos a\right\} \tan \delta$$
$$+ \left\{3 mn^2 \cos 2a + 3n \frac{dn}{dt} \sin 2a\right\} \tan^2 \delta$$
$$+ 2n^3 \sin a (1 + 2 \cos 2a) \tan^3 \delta,$$

$$\frac{d^3 \delta}{dt^3} = -\left(2m \frac{dn}{dt} + n \frac{dm}{dt}\right) \sin a - (m^2 + n^2 \sin^2 a) n \cos a$$
$$- \left\{\tfrac{3}{2} mn^2 \sin 2a + 3n \frac{dn}{dt} \sin^2 a\right\} \tan \delta - 3n^3 \sin^2 a \cos a \tan^2 \delta.$$

$$\qquad\qquad (7)$$

The right ascension and declination of a star so far as regards precession are then found by the formulæ

$$
\left.
\begin{aligned}
a &= a_0 + \left(\frac{da}{dt}\right)_0 t + \tfrac{1}{2}\left(\frac{d^2 a}{dt^2}\right)_0 t^2 + \frac{1}{2..}\left(\frac{d^3 a}{dt^3}\right)_0 t^3 + \&c., \\
\delta &= \delta_0 + \left(\frac{d\delta}{dt}\right)_0 t + \tfrac{1}{2}\left(\frac{d^2\delta}{dt^2}\right)_0 t^2 + \frac{1}{2..}\left(\frac{d^3\delta}{dt^3}\right)_0 t^3 + \&c.
\end{aligned}
\right\} \quad (8)
$$

2. Let us next consider the effect of proper motion. If the values of $\frac{da}{dt}$ and $\frac{d\delta}{dt}$ for any star are obtained from observation for a certain epoch, we may compute the functions $m + n \sin a \tan \delta$, and $n \cos a$, and subtract them from these quantities; the remainders μ and μ' are the effect of proper motion in right ascension and declination at that epoch. But to deduce the values of μ and μ' for any time in general, we may adopt the assumption that the proper motion is uniform on the arc of a great circle, and on this supposition derive the rigorous values of the differential coefficients of a and δ with respect to the time.

Considering now the effect of proper motion only, let

ρ denote the velocity of the star's motion on the arc of a great circle,

χ, the angle of position of this arc,

a' and δ', the right ascension and declination of the star at the end of the time t.

The consideration of the spherical triangle formed by the pole of the equator and the two positions of star, will give these equations

$$
\left.
\begin{aligned}
\sin \delta' &= \sin \delta \cos \rho\, t + \cos \delta \sin \rho\, t \cos \chi, \\
\cos \delta' \cos (a' - a) &= \cos \delta \cos \rho\, t - \sin \delta \sin \rho\, t \cos \chi, \\
\cos \delta' \sin (a' - a) &= \sin \rho\, t \sin \chi.
\end{aligned}
\right\} \quad (9)
$$

Eliminating ρ and χ by means of the equations

$$
\rho \sin \chi = \mu \cos \delta, \qquad \rho \cos \chi = \mu',
$$

we derive from the first and third of the preceding equations the following values of a' and δ' in series arranged according to the powers of t:

$$
\left.
\begin{aligned}
a' &= a + \mu\, t + \mu\,\mu' \tan \delta.\ t^2 - \tfrac{1}{3}\left[\mu^3 \sin^2 \delta - \mu\,\mu'^2 (1 + 3\tan^2 \delta)\right] t^3 + \&c. \\
\delta' &= \delta + \mu' t - \tfrac{1}{4}\mu^2 \sin 2\delta.\ t^2 - \tfrac{1}{6}\mu^2 \mu' (1 + 2\sin^2 \delta) t^3 + \&c.
\end{aligned}
\right\} \quad (10)
$$

3. In order to have the combined effect of precession and proper motion, a' and δ' should be substituted for a and δ in the series which give the effect of precession. Hence we obtain

$$
\left.
\begin{aligned}
\frac{da}{dt} &= m + n \sin a \tan \delta + \mu, \\
\frac{d\delta}{dt} &= n \cos a + \mu';
\end{aligned}
\right\} \quad (11)
$$

and, μ and μ' being considered as variable quantities,

$$
\left.
\begin{aligned}
\frac{d\mu}{dt} &= n\,\mu \cos a \tan \delta + n\,\mu' \sin a \sec^2 \delta + 2\,\mu\,\mu' \tan \delta, \\
\frac{d\mu'}{dt} &= -n\,\mu \sin a - \tfrac{1}{2}\,\mu^2 \sin 2\,\delta.
\end{aligned}
\right\} \quad (12)
$$

By differentiating the values of $\frac{da}{dt}$ and $\frac{d\delta}{dt}$, and eliminating $\frac{da}{dt}$, $\frac{d\delta}{dt}$, $\frac{d\mu}{dt}$ and $\frac{d\mu'}{dt}$, by means of their values just given, we obtain

$$\frac{d^2a}{dt^2} = \frac{dm}{dt} + \frac{n^2}{2}\sin 2a + 2n\mu'\sin a$$
$$+ \left\{ \frac{dn}{dt}\sin a + (m+2\mu)n\cos a + 2\mu\mu' \right\}\tan\delta$$
$$+ 2n\sin a\,(n\cos a + \mu')\tan^2\delta;$$

$$\frac{d^3a}{dt^3} = \frac{mn^2}{2} + 2\mu\mu'^2 + 3\frac{dn}{dt}\mu'\sin a + 3n\mu'(m+2\mu)\cos a + \tfrac{3}{2}(m+2\mu)n^2\cos 2a$$
$$+ \tfrac{3}{2}n\frac{dn}{dt}\sin 2a - 2\mu^3\sin^2\delta$$
$$+ \left\{ \begin{array}{l} (2n^2 - m^2 - 6\mu^2 + 6\mu'^2 - 3m\mu + 3n^2\cos 2a)n\sin a \\ + (2m\frac{dn}{dt} + n\frac{dm}{dt} + 3\frac{dn}{dt}\mu)\cos a + 6n^2\mu'\sin 2a \end{array} \right\}\tan\delta$$
$$+ \left\{ \begin{array}{l} 6\mu\mu'^2 + 3\frac{dn}{dt}\mu'\sin a + (12\mu + 3m)n\mu'\cos a \\ + 3n\frac{dn}{dt}\sin 2a + (3m+6\mu)n^2\cos 2a \end{array} \right\}\tan^2\delta$$
$$+ \left\{ (2n^2 + 6\mu'^2)n\sin a + 6n^2\mu'\sin 2a + 4n^3\sin a\cos 2a \right\}\tan^3\delta,$$

$$\frac{d^3\delta}{dt^3} = -\mu^2\mu' - (2m+3\mu)\frac{dn}{dt}\sin a - (m^2+3\mu^2+3m\mu)n\cos a$$
$$- n\frac{dm}{dt}\sin a - n^3\sin^2 a\cos a - 3n^2\mu'\sin^2 a - 2\mu^2\mu'\sin^2\delta$$
$$- \left\{ 6n\mu\mu'\sin a + \tfrac{3}{2}(m+2\mu)n^2\sin 2a + 3n\frac{dn}{dt}\sin^2 a \right\}\tan\delta$$
$$- 3n^2(n\cos a + \mu')\sin^2 a\tan^2\delta.$$

(13)

The values of a and δ computed by means of Maclaurin's theorem, using the above values of the differential coefficients, will give the mean place of the star.

For the epoch 1860, by substituting the proper numerical values of m and n, from Table V, expressing $\frac{da}{dt}$, $\frac{d^2a}{dt^2}$ and μ in seconds of time, $\frac{d\delta}{dt}$, $\frac{d^2\delta}{dt^2}$ and μ' in seconds of arc, and denoting that the logarithm of the number is expressed by writing it in [ ], we have the formulæ

$$\frac{da}{dt} = 3^s.071960 + [0.1261427]\sin a\tan\delta + \mu,$$
$$100\frac{d^2a}{dt^2} = 0^s.003221 - [6.63378]\left(\frac{da}{dt} - \mu\right) + [7.987809]\left(\frac{da}{dt} + \mu\right)\cos a\tan\delta$$
$$+ [6.811718]\left(\frac{d\delta}{dt} + \mu'\right)\sin a\sec^2\delta + [6.9866]\mu\mu'\tan\delta,$$
$$\frac{d\delta}{dt} = [1.3022340]\cos a + \mu',$$
$$100\frac{d^2\delta}{dt^2} = -[6.63378]\left(\frac{d\delta}{dt} - \mu'\right) - [9.163900]\left(\frac{da}{dt} + \mu\right)\sin a - [8.7367]\mu^2\sin 2\delta$$

(14)

By these formulæ the quantities in Table XXI have been computed.

The last term of $\frac{d^2a}{dt^2}$ and also that of $\frac{d^2\delta}{dt^2}$ are nearly always insensible.

The above expressions for $\frac{d^3a}{dt^3}$ and $\frac{d^3\delta}{dt^3}$ are too complicated for use in computation; hence if their values are wanted, it will be much easier to compute the values of the second differential coefficients for 50 years before and after the epoch, and divide the differences of these by 100 for the values of the third differential coefficients at the epoch.

4. We have next to consider the effect of nutation. Resuming the equations .

After line 10, insert
$$\frac{d^2\delta}{dt^2} = -(m+2\mu)n\sin a + \frac{dn}{dt}\cos a - \tfrac{1}{2}\mu^2\sin 2\delta - n^2\sin^2 a\tan\delta$$

$$\frac{dx}{dt} = by + cz,$$
$$\frac{dy}{dt} = -bx + c'z,$$
$$\frac{dz}{dt} = -cx - c'y,$$
(5)

putting for x, y and z their values from (1) in terms of a and δ, and writing $\triangle a$ and $\triangle \delta$ instead of $\frac{da}{dt}$ and $\frac{d\delta}{dt}$ we obtain

$$\triangle a = -b - c \sin a \tan \delta + c' \cos a \tan \delta,$$
$$\triangle \delta = -c \cos a - c' \sin a.$$
(15)

We may make

$$b = -m A' - E,$$
$$c = -n A',$$
$$c' = B,$$
(16)

where B and E denote the same quantities, as on pages iv and v, and A' is the quantity A, with the term τ omitted. Then

$$\triangle a = (m + n \sin a \tan \delta) A' + B \cos a \tan \delta + E,$$
$$\triangle \delta = A'n \cos a - B \sin a.$$
(17)

These formulæ give the effect of nutation when terms multiplied by the squares and products of A', B and E are neglected.

The following formulæ contain those which involve the squares and products of A' and B, still neglecting the square of E and its products with A' and B as of no moment:

$$\triangle^2 a = \frac{1}{2} \frac{d^2.\triangle a}{dA'^2} A'^2 + \frac{d^2.\triangle a}{dA'dB} A'B + \frac{1}{2} \frac{d^2.\triangle a}{dB^2} B^2,$$
$$\triangle^2 \delta = \frac{1}{2} \frac{d^2\triangle \delta}{dA'^2} A'^2 + \frac{d^2.\triangle \delta}{dA'dB} A'B + \frac{1}{2} \frac{d^2.\triangle \delta}{dB^2} B^2.$$
(18)

We have from (17)

$$\frac{d.\triangle a}{d.A'} = m + n \sin a \tan \delta, \qquad \frac{d.\triangle \delta}{dA'} = n \cos a,$$
$$\frac{d.\triangle a}{dB} = \cos a \tan \delta, \qquad \frac{d.\triangle \delta}{dB} = -\sin a.$$
(19)

Differentiating these again with respect to A' and B, and eliminating $\frac{da}{dA'}$, $\frac{da}{dB}$, &c., which are the same as $\frac{d.\triangle a}{dA'}$, $\frac{d.\triangle a}{dB}$, &c., we obtain

$$\frac{d^2.\triangle a}{dA'^2} = \frac{n^2}{2} \sin 2 a + mn \cos a \tan \delta + n^2 \sin 2 a \tan^2 \delta,$$
$$\frac{d^2.\triangle a}{dA'dB} = n \cos^2 a + n \cos 2 a \tan^2 \delta - m \sin a \tan \delta$$
$$\frac{d^2.\triangle a}{dB^2} = -\frac{1}{2} \sin 2 a - \sin 2 a \tan^2 \delta,$$
$$\frac{d^2.\triangle \delta}{dA'^2} = -mn \sin a - n^2 \sin^2 a \tan \delta,$$
$$\frac{d^2.\triangle \delta}{dA'dB} = -\frac{n}{2} \sin 2 a \tan \delta - m \cos a,$$
$$\frac{d^2.\triangle \delta}{dB^2} = -\cos^2 a \tan \delta.$$
(20)

It will be sufficient to retain in $\triangle^2 a$ only the terms multiplied by $\tan^2 \delta$, and in $\triangle^2 \delta$ those multiplied by $\tan \delta$, and to put $A' = -0.34236 \sin \Omega = -\frac{v}{n} \sin \Omega$, and $B = -9''.2235 \cos \Omega = -u \cos \Omega$. Thus we get

$$\Delta^2 a = \left[\frac{uv}{2}\cos 2\,a \sin 2\,\Omega - \frac{u^2+v^2}{4}\sin 2\,a \cos 2\,\Omega\right]\tan^2 \delta,$$

$$\Delta^2 \delta = -\left[\frac{uv}{4}\sin 2\,a \sin 2\,\Omega + \left(\frac{u^2-v^2}{8}+\frac{u^2+v^2}{8}\cos 2\,a\right)\cos 2\,\Omega\right]\tan\delta. \quad (21)$$

Hence if we put, as on page v,

$$a = \tfrac{1}{15}(m + n\sin a \tan \delta,) \qquad a' = n\cos a,$$
$$b = \tfrac{1}{15}\cos a \tan \delta, \qquad b' = -\sin a, \qquad (22)$$

the formulæ for the whole effect of nutation will be

$$\Delta a = aA' + bB + E$$
$$\quad + [0^s.0000103 \cos 2\,a \sin 2\Omega - 0^s.0000107 \sin 2\,a \cos 2\,\Omega]\tan^2 \delta,$$
$$\Delta \delta = a'A' + b'B$$
$$\quad - [0''.000077 \sin 2\,a \sin 2\,\Omega + (0''.000023 + 0''.000080\cos 2\,a)\cos 2\,\Omega]\tan\delta. \quad (23)$$

5. The effect of aberration is next to be considered. If a' and δ' denote the right ascension and declination of the star as affected by aberration, while a and δ denote the same unaffected by aberration, and $\frac{dX}{dt}$, $\frac{dY}{dt}$ and $\frac{dZ}{dt}$ denote the velocity of the earth projected on the three axes of equatorial co-ordinates, and k denote the velocity of light, we have, R' being a fictitious distance to be eliminated,

$$R'\cos\delta'\cos a' = \cos\delta\cos a + \frac{1}{k}\frac{dX}{dt},$$
$$R'\cos\delta'\sin a' = \cos\delta\sin a + \frac{1}{k}\frac{dY}{dt}, \qquad (24)$$
$$R'\sin\delta' = \sin\delta + \frac{1}{k}\frac{dZ}{dt}.$$

Whence are derived

$$R'\cos\delta'\sin(a'-a) = -\frac{1}{k}\left[\frac{dX}{dt}\sin a - \frac{dY}{dt}\cos a\right],$$
$$R'\cos\delta'\cos(a'-a) = \cos\delta + \frac{1}{k}\left[\frac{dX}{dt}\cos a + \frac{dY}{dt}\sin a\right],$$
$$R'\sin(\delta'-\delta) = -\frac{1}{k}\left[\frac{dX}{dt}\sin\delta\cos a + \frac{dY}{dt}\sin\delta\sin a - \frac{dZ}{dt}\cos\delta\right]$$
$$\quad - \frac{1}{2k^2}\tan\delta\left[\frac{dX}{dt}\sin a - \frac{dY}{dt}\cos a\right]^2,$$
$$R'\cos(\delta'-\delta) = 1 + \frac{1}{k}\left[\frac{dX}{dt}\cos\delta\cos a + \frac{dY}{dt}\cos\delta\sin a + \frac{dZ}{dt}\sin\delta\right]$$
$$\quad + \frac{1}{2k^2}\left[\frac{dX}{dt}\sin a - \frac{dY}{dt}\cos a\right]^2; \qquad (25)$$

from which, to quantities of the second order, we have

$$a'-a = -\frac{1}{k}\sec\delta\left[\frac{dX}{dt}\sin a - \frac{dY}{dt}\cos a\right]$$
$$\quad + \frac{1}{k^2}\sec^2\delta\left(\frac{dX}{dt}\sin a - \frac{dY}{dt}\cos a\right)\left(\frac{dX}{dt}\cos a + \frac{dY}{dt}\sin a\right),$$
$$\delta'-\delta = -\frac{1}{k}\left[\frac{dX}{dt}\sin\delta\cos a + \frac{dY}{dt}\sin\delta\sin a - \frac{dZ}{dt}\cos\delta\right]$$
$$\quad - \frac{1}{2k^2}\tan\delta\left[\frac{dX}{dt}\sin a - \frac{dY}{dt}\cos a\right]^2$$
$$\quad + \frac{1}{k^2}\left(\frac{dX}{dt}\sin\delta\cos a + \frac{dY}{dt}\sin\delta\sin a - \frac{dZ}{dt}\cos\delta\right)\times$$
$$\quad \left(\frac{dX}{dt}\cos\delta\cos a + \frac{dY}{dt}\cos\delta\sin a + \frac{dZ}{dt}\sin\delta\right). \qquad (26)$$

If r is the radius vector of the earth, and ω the obliquity of the ecliptic;

$$\left.\begin{array}{l} X = - r \cos \odot, \\ Y = - r \sin \odot \cos \omega, \\ Z = - r \sin \odot \sin \omega. \end{array}\right\} \quad (27)$$

And, if e denote the eccentricity of the earth's orbit, Γ the longitude of the solar perigee, and n the mean sidereal motion of the sun,

$$\left.\begin{array}{l} \dfrac{dr}{dt} = \dfrac{an}{\sqrt{(1-e^2)}}\, e \sin (\odot - \Gamma), \\[2mm] r\dfrac{d\odot}{dt} = \dfrac{an}{\sqrt{(1-e^2)}}\, [1 + e \cos(\odot - \Gamma)]. \end{array}\right\} \quad (28)$$

Whence we derive

$$\left.\begin{array}{l} \dfrac{dX}{dt} = \dfrac{an}{\sqrt{(1-e^2)}}\, [\sin \odot + e \sin \Gamma], \\[2mm] \dfrac{dY}{dt} = -\dfrac{an}{\sqrt{(1-e^2)}}\, \cos \omega\, [\cos \odot + e \cos \Gamma], \\[2mm] \dfrac{dZ}{dt} = -\dfrac{an}{\sqrt{(1-e^2)}}\, \sin \omega\, [\cos \odot + e \cos \Gamma], \end{array}\right\} \quad (29)$$

By substituting these values in the expressions (26) for $a' - a$ and $\delta' - \delta$, making $\dfrac{an}{k\sqrt{(1-e^2)}} = \varkappa$, and omitting the terms which are independent of $\odot$, we have

$$a' - a = -\varkappa \sec \delta \quad [\sin a \sin \odot + \cos a \cos \omega \cos \odot]$$
$$-\frac{\varkappa^2}{4}\sec^2 \delta\, [(1 + \cos^2 \omega) \sin 2 a \cos 2 \odot - 2 \cos \omega \cos 2 a \sin 2 \odot],$$

$$\delta' - \delta = -\varkappa \quad [\sin \delta \cos a \sin \odot - (\cos \omega \sin \delta \sin a - \sin \omega \cos \delta) \cos \odot]$$
$$-\frac{\varkappa^2}{8}\tan \delta\, [((1 + \cos^2 \omega) \cos 2 a - \sin^2 \omega) \cos 2 \odot + 2 \cos \omega \sin 2 a \sin 2 \odot].$$

In these formulæ terms multiplied by $\varkappa^2 e$ have been neglected, as also the terms in $\delta' - \delta$ multiplied by $\varkappa^2$ which are not also multiplied by $\tan \delta$. Substituting for $\varkappa$ STRUVE's value $20''.4451$, these formulæ become

$$\left.\begin{array}{l} a' - a = -20''.4451 \sec \delta\, [\sin a \sin \odot + \cos a \cos \omega \cos \odot] \\ \qquad - 0''.0009329 \sec^2 \delta \sin 2 a \cos 2 \odot \\ \qquad + 0''.0009295 \sec^2 \delta \cos 2 a \sin 2 \odot, \\ \delta' - \delta = -20''.4451 \sin \delta \cos a \sin \odot \\ \qquad + 20''.4451 \cos \odot\, [\sin \delta \sin a \cos \omega - \cos \delta \sin \omega] \\ \qquad - 0''.0004648 \tan \delta \sin 2 a \sin 2 \odot \\ \qquad + [0''.0000402 - 0''.0004665 \cos 2 a] \tan \delta \cos 2 \odot. \end{array}\right\} (30)$$

6. The values of a, δ, $\odot$ and ω to be employed here are those affected by nutation. Hence if we use values referred to the mean equinox of date, we must add to $a' - a$ the terms

$$\left.\begin{array}{l} \dfrac{d\,(a'-a)}{da}\, \triangle a + \dfrac{d\,(a'-a)}{d\delta}\, \triangle \delta + \dfrac{d\,(a'-a)}{d\odot}\, \triangle \odot + \dfrac{d\,(a'-a)}{d\omega}\, \triangle \omega; \\[3mm] \text{and to } \delta' - \delta \\[1mm] \dfrac{d\,(\delta'-\delta)}{da}\, \triangle a + \dfrac{d\,(\delta'-\delta)}{d\delta}\, \triangle \delta + \dfrac{d\,(\delta'-\delta)}{d\odot}\, \triangle \odot + \dfrac{d\,(\delta'-\delta)}{d\omega}\, \triangle \omega. \end{array}\right\} (31)$$

The terms multiplied by $\triangle \odot$ and $\triangle \omega$ are of no importance, and it will be sufficient to put

$$\left.\begin{array}{l} \triangle a = -[b \sin a \sin \Omega + a \cos a \cos \Omega] \tan \delta, \\ \triangle \delta = -b \cos a \sin \Omega + a \sin a \cos \Omega, \end{array}\right\} (32)$$

where $b = 6''.865$ and $a = 9''.2235$.

Then the terms, to add to $a' - a$, will be

$$\frac{20''.4451}{2} \tan \delta \sec \delta \begin{Bmatrix} -(b + a \cos \omega) \sin 2\,a \cos (\odot + \Omega) \\ +(b \cos \omega + a) \cos 2\,a \sin (\odot + \Omega) \\ +(b - a \cos \omega) \sin 2\,a \cos (\odot - \Omega) \\ -(b \cos \omega - a) \cos 2\,a \sin (\odot - \Omega) \end{Bmatrix};$$

and to $\delta' - \delta$ $\qquad\qquad\qquad\qquad\qquad\qquad\qquad$ (33)

$$\frac{20''.4451}{4} \sin \delta \tan \delta \begin{Bmatrix} -(b + a \cos \omega) \cos 2\,a \cos (\odot + \Omega) \\ -(b \cos \omega + a) \sin 2\,a \sin (\odot + \Omega) \\ +(b - a \cos \omega) \cos 2\,a \cos (\odot - \Omega) \\ +(b \cos \omega - a) \sin 2\,a \sin (\odot - \Omega) \\ +(b - a \cos \omega) \cos (\odot + \Omega) \\ -(b + a \cos \omega) \cos (\odot - \Omega) \end{Bmatrix};$$

Or, the numerical values of a, b and ω being substituted, we have, as on page vi, for the terms to add to $a' - a$, expressed in time,

$$\begin{Bmatrix} -0.00005065 \sin 2\,a \cos (\odot + \Omega) \\ +0.00005129 \cos 2\,a \sin (\odot + \Omega) \\ -0.00000527 \sin 2\,a \cos (\odot - \Omega) \\ +0.00000966 \cos 2\,a \sin (\odot - \Omega) \end{Bmatrix} \tan \delta \sec \delta,$$

and to $\delta' - \delta$ $\qquad\qquad\qquad\qquad\qquad\qquad\qquad$ (34)

$$\begin{Bmatrix} -0''.0003799 \cos 2\,a \cos (\odot + \Omega) \\ -0.0003847 \sin 2\,a \sin (\odot + \Omega) \\ -0.0000395 \cos 2\,a \cos (\odot - \Omega) \\ -0.0000725 \sin 2\,a \sin (\odot - \Omega) \\ -0.0000391 \cos (\odot + \Omega) \\ -0.0003799 \cos (\odot - \Omega) \end{Bmatrix} \sin \delta \tan \delta,$$

7. If now we make, as on page v,

$$\begin{rcases} C = -20''.4451 \cos \omega \cos \odot, \\ D = -20''.4451 \sin \odot, \\ c = \tfrac{1}{15} \cos a \sec \delta, \\ d = \tfrac{1}{15} \sin a \sec \delta, \\ c' = \tan \omega \cos \delta - \sin a \sin \delta, \\ d' = \cos a \sin \delta, \end{rcases} \qquad (35)$$

we shall have the combined effect of nutation and aberration on the place of the star, terms of the second order being omitted, by the formulæ

$$\begin{rcases} a' - a = aA' + bB + cC + dD + E, \\ \delta' - \delta = a'A' + b'B + c'C + d'D. \end{rcases} \qquad (37)$$

If we wish to include the mean motion of the star from the beginning of the year, we must add, respectively, to these expressions the terms $(a + \mu)\,\tau$ and $(a' + \mu')\,\tau$, where for a, a', μ and μ' should be taken their values, not for date, but for the time $\frac{\tau}{2}$. Hence if we make $A' + \tau = A$, the formulæ become in this case,

$$\begin{rcases} a' - a = aA + bB + cC + dD + E + \mu\tau, \\ \delta' - \delta = a'A + b'B + c'C + d'D + \mu'\tau; \end{rcases} \qquad (38)$$

and to our terms of the second order must be added in right ascension $-\tfrac{1}{2} \dfrac{da}{d\tau}\tau^2$ and in declination $-\tfrac{1}{2} \dfrac{da'}{d\tau}\tau^2$; or better, if μ and μ' in the last two equations denote their values at the beginning of the year, these terms will be $-\tfrac{1}{2} \dfrac{d^2 a}{d\tau^2}\tau^2$ and $-\tfrac{1}{2} \dfrac{d^2 \delta}{d\tau^2}\tau^2$ where $\dfrac{d^2 a}{d\tau^2}$ and $\dfrac{d^2 \delta}{d\tau^2}$ have the values given on page xix. Neglecting the variation of m and n, and the terms not multiplied by $\tan \delta$ or $\tan^2 \delta$, these terms of the second order are, as on page vi,

$$\begin{aligned} \Delta\,(a' - a) = &+ 0^s.000003\ \tau^2 \sin a \tan \delta \\ &- 0^s.000149\ \tau^2 \cos a \tan \delta \\ &- 0^s.0000650\ \tau^2 \sin 2a \tan^2 \delta, \end{aligned} \qquad\qquad (39)$$

$$\Delta\,(\delta' - \delta') = + 0''.000975\ \tau^2 \sin^2 a \tan \delta.$$

8. In order that the subject of star reductions may be complete, it is necessary to consider the effect of orbital motion in double stars. The corrections of the right ascension and declination have always this form

$$\Delta a = a + bt + k \sin (u + K),$$
$$\Delta \delta = a' + b't + k' \sin (u + K'),$$
$$\qquad \qquad (40)$$

where u is derived from the equation

$$u - e \sin u = n (t - T). \qquad (41)$$

Construction of Table XXIV.

9. It will be convenient to divide the quantities A and B each into two parts, so that $A = A_\odot + A_\Omega$, and $B = B_\odot + B_\Omega$, where for the epoch 1870 the values of $A_\odot$, A_Ω, $B_\odot$, B_Ω are

$$\begin{aligned}
A_\odot &= \tau + [6.5942] \sin \odot + [7.4644] \cos \odot - [8.4012] \sin 2 \odot, \\
B_\odot &= -[7.9609] \sin \odot - [7.2370] \cos \odot - [9.7410] \cos 2 \odot, \\
C &= -[1.27313] \cos \odot, \\
D &= -[1.31059] \sin \odot, \\
A_\Omega &= -[9.53457 + 0.4t] \sin \Omega + [7.6128] \sin 2 \Omega, \\
B_\Omega &= -[0.96490] \cos \Omega + [8.9518] \cos 2 \Omega, \\
E_\Omega &= -[7.4951 - 6.6t] \sin \Omega.
\end{aligned} \qquad (42)$$

And we write, the term $E_\odot$ being neglected,

$$\begin{aligned}
\Delta_\odot a &= a A_\odot + b B_\odot + c C + d D + \mu \tau, \\
\Delta_\odot \delta &= a' A_\odot + b' B_\odot + c' C + d' D + \mu' \tau, \\
\Delta_\Omega a &= a A_\Omega + b B_\Omega + E_\Omega, \\
\Delta_\Omega \delta &= a' A_\Omega + b' B_\Omega.
\end{aligned} \qquad (43)$$

To $\Delta_\odot a$ and $\Delta_\odot \delta$ are added the terms of the second order in aberration, given on pages xxii and xxiii, and to $\Delta_\Omega a$ and $\Delta_\Omega \delta$ the terms of the second order in nutation given on page xxi, whenever they are sensible.

If now we make

$$\begin{aligned}
p_\odot &= -[1.31059] d + [6.5942] a - [7.9609] b, \\
q_\odot &= -[1.27313] c + [7.4644] a - [7.2370] b, \\
p_{2\odot} &= -[8.4012] a + [5.7922] \sec^2 \delta \cos 2 a, \\
q_{2\odot} &= -[9.7410] b - [5.7938] \sec^2 \delta \sin 2 a, \\
p'_\odot &= -[1.31059] d' + [6.5942] a' - [7.9609] b', \\
q'_\odot &= -[1.27313] c' + [7.4644] a' - [7.2370] b', \\
p'_{2\odot} &= -[8.4012] a' - [6.6673] \tan \delta \sin 2 a, \\
q'_{2\odot} &= -[9.7410] b' - [6.6688] \tan \delta \cos 2 a + [5.6042] \tan \delta,
\end{aligned} \qquad (44)$$

we shall have, terms of the second order included,

$$\begin{aligned}
\Delta_\odot a &= p_\odot \sin \odot + q_\odot \cos \odot + p_{2\odot} \sin 2 \odot + q_{2\odot} \cos 2 \odot + \frac{da}{d\tau}\tau + \tfrac{1}{2}\frac{d^2 a}{d\tau^2}\tau^2, \\
\Delta_\odot \delta &= p'_\odot \sin \odot + q'_\odot \cos \odot + p'_{2\odot} \sin 2 \odot + q'_{2\odot} \cos 2 \odot + \frac{d\delta}{d\tau}\tau + \tfrac{1}{2}\frac{d^2 \delta}{d\tau^2}\tau^2.
\end{aligned} \qquad (45)$$

Let us make

$$
\begin{aligned}
p_\odot &= k_\odot \cos K_\odot, & p'_\odot &= k'_\odot \cos K'_\odot, \\
q_\odot &= k_\odot \sin K_\odot. & q'_\odot &= k'_\odot \sin K'_\odot, \\
p_{2\odot} &= k_{2\odot} \cos K_{2\odot}, & p'_{2\odot} &= k'_{2\odot} \cos K'_{2\odot}, \\
q_{2\odot} &= k_{2\odot} \sin K_{2\odot}, & q'_{2\odot} &= k'_{2\odot} \sin K'_{2\odot}.
\end{aligned} \tag{46}
$$

The above equations take the form

$$
\begin{aligned}
\triangle_\odot a &= \frac{da}{d\tau}\tau + \tfrac{1}{2}\frac{d^2 a}{d\tau^2}\tau^2 + k_\odot \sin(\odot + K_\odot) + k_{2\odot} \sin(2\odot + K_{2\odot}), \\
\triangle_\odot \delta &= \frac{d\delta}{d\tau}\tau + \tfrac{1}{2}\frac{d^2\delta}{d\tau^2}\tau^2 + k'_\odot \sin(\odot + K'_\odot) + k'_{2\odot} \sin(2\odot + K'_{2\odot}),
\end{aligned} \tag{47}
$$

10. To compute the variations of $\triangle_\odot a$ and $\triangle_\odot \delta$ in 10 years, which are given in Table XXIV, we compute values of $p_\odot$, $q_\odot$, &c., for 1880, and subtract from them the values for 1870; calling the remainders $\delta p_\odot$, $\delta q_\odot$, &c.; then, certain very small terms being neglected, we have evidently these equations:

$$
\begin{aligned}
\delta.\triangle_\odot a = {}&\delta p_\odot.\ \sin\odot + \delta q_\odot.\cos\odot + \delta p_{2\odot}.\ \sin 2\odot + \delta q_{2\odot}.\ \cos 2\odot \\
&+ 10\frac{d^2 a}{d\tau^2}\tau + k_\odot \cos(\odot + K_\odot).\ \delta\odot, \\
\delta.\triangle_\odot \delta = {}&\delta p'_\odot.\ \sin\odot + \delta q'_\odot.\cos\odot + \delta p'_{2\odot}.\ \sin 2\odot + \delta q'_{2\odot}.\ \cos 2\odot \\
&+ 10\frac{d^2\delta}{d\tau^2}\tau + k'_\odot \cos(\odot + K'_\odot)\ \delta\odot.
\end{aligned} \tag{48}
$$

The value of $\delta\odot$ is $[6.0057] \sin(\odot - 15°)$; substituting this, we have

$$
\begin{aligned}
\delta.\triangle_\odot a = {}&10\frac{d^2 a}{d\tau^2}\tau - [5.7047]\ k_\odot \sin(K_\odot + 15°) + \delta p_\odot.\ \sin\odot + \delta q_\odot.\cos\odot \\
&+ [\delta p_{2\odot} + [5.7047]\ k_\odot \cos(K_\odot - 15°)] \sin 2\odot \\
&+ [\delta q_{2\odot} + [5.7047]\ k_\odot \sin(K_\odot - 15°)] \cos 2\odot, \\
\delta.\triangle_\odot \delta = {}&10\frac{d^2\delta}{d\tau^2}\tau - [5.7047]\ k'_\odot \sin(K'_\odot + 15°) + \delta p'_\odot.\ \sin\odot + \delta q'_\odot.\cos\odot \\
&+ [\delta p'_{2\odot} + [5.7047]\ k'_\odot \cos(K'_\odot - 15°)] \sin 2\odot \\
&+ [\delta q'_{2\odot} + [5.7047]\ k'_\odot \sin(K'_\odot - 15°)] \cos 2\odot.
\end{aligned} \tag{49}
$$

As in the case of $\triangle_\odot a$ and $\triangle_\odot \delta$ these quantities can be made to take the form

$$
\begin{aligned}
\delta.\triangle_\odot a &= a + b\tau + h_\odot \sin(\odot + H_\odot) + h_{2\odot} \sin(2\odot + H_{2\odot}), \\
\delta.\triangle_\odot \delta &= a' + b'\tau + h'_\odot \sin(\odot + H'_\odot) + h'_{2\odot} \sin(2\odot + H'_{2\odot}).
\end{aligned} \tag{50}
$$

Except for stars near the pole, the first and last terms of these equations may be neglected, and regard be had in computing $\delta p_\odot$, $\delta q_\odot$, &c., only to the variations of c, d, c' and d' in the formulæ for $p_\odot$, $q_\odot$, &c. Then

$$
\begin{aligned}
\delta.\triangle_\odot a &= 10\frac{d^2 a}{d\tau^2}\tau + h_\odot \sin(\odot + H_\odot), \\
\delta.\triangle_\odot \delta &= 10\frac{d^2\delta}{d\tau^2}\tau + h'_\odot \sin(\odot + H'_\odot).
\end{aligned} \tag{51}
$$

11. In computing $\triangle_\odot a$ and $\triangle_\odot \delta$, we may either suppose $k_\odot$, $K_\odot$, $k'_\odot$ and $K'_\odot$ constant throughout the year, and afterwards add to $\triangle_\odot a$ and $\triangle_\odot \delta$ thus obtained, the proper fractional part of $h_\odot \sin(\odot + H_\odot)$ and $h'_\odot \sin(\odot + H'_\odot)$ for the fraction of the year; or we may make them to vary from date to date. For stars, whose declination is within the limits $\pm 65°$, there is, however, no need to attend to this correction.

Having formed a table of $\odot$ for every 10 sidereal days, beginning with the fictitious year, we can readily get $\odot$ for the time of the star's transit over the fictitious meridian with the constant interpolation factor $\dfrac{a - 18^{\text{h}}\,40^{\text{m}}}{240^{\text{h}}}$, and thus form the arguments $\odot + K_\odot$, $2\odot + K_{2\odot}$, $\odot + H_\odot$, &c.

Terms with small coefficients can be most readily formed by means of a Traverse Table.

12. We can reduce $\triangle_\Omega a$ and $\triangle_\Omega \delta$ to the forms, terms of the second order included,

$$\begin{aligned}
\triangle_\Omega a &= k_\Omega \sin(\Omega + K_\Omega) + k_{2\Omega} \sin(2\,\Omega + K_{2\Omega}),\\
\triangle_\Omega \delta &= k'_\Omega \sin(\Omega + K'_\Omega) + k'_{2\Omega} \sin(2\,\Omega + K'_{2\Omega}),
\end{aligned} \Bigg\}$$

by making

$$\left.\begin{aligned}
k_\Omega \cos K_\Omega &= -\lfloor 9.53457 + 0.4t\rfloor\, a - 0^{\text{s}}.0031,\\
k'_\Omega \sin K_\Omega &= -[0.96490]\, b,\\
k_{2\Omega} \cos K_{2\Omega} &= [7.6128]\, a + [5.0114]\cos 2\,a \tan^2 \delta,\\
k_{2\Omega} \sin K_{2\Omega} &= [8.9518]\, b - [5.0294]\sin 2\,a \tan^2 \delta,\\
k'_\Omega \cos K'_\Omega &= -[9.53457 + 0.4t]\, a',\\
k'_\Omega \sin K'_\Omega &= -[0.96490]\, b',\\
k'_{2\Omega} \cos K'_{2\Omega} &= [7.6128]\, a' - [5.8865]\sin 2\,a \tan \delta,\\
k'_{2\Omega} \sin K'_{2\Omega} &= [8.9518]\, b' - [5.9031]\cos 2\,a \tan \delta - [5.3617]\tan \delta.
\end{aligned}\right\} (52)$$

But perhaps it will be as well to adopt the formulæ

$$\left.\begin{aligned}
\triangle_\Omega a &= aA_\Omega + bB_\Omega + E_\Omega,\\
\triangle_\Omega \delta &= a'A_\Omega + b'B_\Omega,
\end{aligned}\right\} (53)$$

or,

$$\left.\begin{aligned}
\triangle_\Omega a &= f_\Omega + g_\Omega \sin(G_\Omega + a)\tan \delta,\\
\triangle_\Omega \delta &= g_\Omega \cos(G_\Omega + a).
\end{aligned}\right\} (54)$$

Tables A to E, pages xxx–xxxv, give all the data needed for the computation of equations (45) to (54), for the period embraced in Table XXIV.

13. Table XXVII. For stars near the pole it will be well to construct tables giving, with the arguments $\odot + \Omega$ and $\odot - \Omega$, the values of small terms given on page xxiii. These will be most readily computed with the aid of a Traverse Table, when they have been reduced to the forms

$$\left.\begin{aligned}
\triangle_{\odot + \Omega} a &= k_{\odot + \Omega} \sin(\odot + \Omega + K_{\odot + \Omega}),\\
\triangle_{\odot + \Omega} \delta &= k'_{\odot + \Omega} \sin(\odot + \Omega + K'_{\odot + \Omega}),\\
\triangle_{\odot - \Omega} a &= k_{\odot - \Omega} \sin(\odot - \Omega + K_{\odot - \Omega}),\\
\triangle_{\odot - \Omega} \delta &= k'_{\odot - \Omega} \sin(\odot - \Omega + K'_{\odot - \Omega}),
\end{aligned}\right\} (55)$$

14. Table XXVIII. Tables for $\triangle_{\mathbb{C}} a$ and $\triangle_{\mathbb{C}} \delta$ may be computed in the same way. For by making

$$\left.\begin{aligned}
k_{\mathbb{C}} \cos K_{\mathbb{C}} &= -[7.6075]\, a,\\
k_{\mathbb{C}} \sin K_{\mathbb{C}} &= -[8.9474]\, b,\\
k'_{\mathbb{C}} \cos K'_{\mathbb{C}} &= -[7.6075]\, a',\\
k'_{\mathbb{C}} \sin K'_{\mathbb{C}} &= -[8.9474]\, b',
\end{aligned}\right\} (56)$$

these quantities take the form

$$\left.\begin{aligned}
\triangle_{\mathbb{C}} a &= k_{\mathbb{C}} \sin(2\,\mathbb{C} + K_{\mathbb{C}}),\\
\triangle_{\mathbb{C}} \delta &= k'_{\mathbb{C}} \sin(2\,\mathbb{C} + K'_{\mathbb{C}}).
\end{aligned}\right\} (57)$$

In tabulating these quantities it will be better to make sidereal time the argument rather than $\mathbb{C}$; and if they are to be tabulated for several stars, they should be interpolated forwards a time equal to $a - 18^{\text{h}}\,40^{\text{m}}$, so that the argument may be the same for the transits of all the stars on the same sidereal day.

If these quantities are tabulated for every tenth of a sidereal day throughout the period of the argument, we may take advantage of the fact that this period is almost exactly 13.7 sidereal days, to arrange the Table so that there will be an interval of a sidereal day between successive values of the argument.

Example.

We will illustrate the preceding formulæ by computing $\triangle_\odot a$ and its *Variation in* 10 years for β Hydri.

	For 1870.	For 1880.
$a =$	$0^h\ 18^m\ 52^s.61$	$0^h\ 19^m\ 25^s.13$
$\delta =$	$- 77°\ 59'\ 14''$	$- 77°\ 55'\ 52''$
$\log a =$	0.40744	0.40538
$\log b =$	$9.49449n$	$9.49232n$
$\log c =$	9.50411	9.50202
$\log d =$	8.42083	8.43110

In this case it is not necessary to compute the terms of $p_{2\odot}$, $q_{2\odot}$, &c., which are of the order of the square of aberration, since they are altogether insensible. Deriving the values of $\frac{da}{d\tau}$ and $\frac{d^2a'}{d\tau^2}$ from Table XXI, we have in formula (45)

$$\triangle_\odot a = 3^s.2594\ \tau - 0^s.0008\ \tau^2 - 0^s.5349\ \sin \odot - 5^s.9794\ \cos \odot$$
$$478 \qquad\qquad 507$$
$$- 0^s.0644\ \sin 2 \odot + 0^s.1720\ \cos 2 \odot$$
$$41 \qquad\qquad 11$$

The figures written below the coefficients are those which belong to the values for 1880. To facilitate computation we give to $\triangle_\odot a$ the following form, in which the unit of τ is 10 sidereal days instead of a year, and it is counted from the first transit of the star over the fictitious meridian. This is done by substituting .027304 τ for τ, and adding the change of $\triangle_\odot a$ in the time $a - 18^h\ 40^m$ or $- 0^d.765$.

$$\triangle_\odot a = - 0^s.00681 + 0^s.088994\ \tau - 0^s.0000006\tau^2$$
$$+ [0.77839]\ \sin (\odot + 264°\ 53'.3) + [9.2639]\ \sin (2\odot + 110°\ 31'.)$$
$$641 \qquad\qquad 44'.4 \qquad\qquad 18 \qquad\qquad 31$$

Also by formula (49) we have the *Variation* of $\triangle_\odot a$ in 10 years,

$$\delta . \triangle_\odot a = + 0^s.00033 - 0^s.000439\ \tau + 0^s.0315 \sin(\odot + 114.°2) + 0^s.0012 \sin(2\odot + 279°).$$

From Table A we obtain $\odot$ with the interpolating factor $a - 18^h\ 40^m = - 0^d.765$, and thus form the arguments $\odot + K_\odot$, &c., interpolating $K_\odot$ &c., to date by means of the values obtained for 1870 and 1880.

Sid.Day.	Motion of $\odot$ for $- 0^d.765$.	$\odot$.	$2\odot$.	$\odot + K_\odot$.	$2\odot + K_{2\odot}$.	$\odot + II_\odot$.
0	-46.7	279 12.3	198 25	184 5.6	308 56	33.4
10	46.7	289 22.1	218 42	194 15.4	329 13	43.6
20	46.6	299 31.5	239 3	204 24.8	349 34	53.7
30	46.5	309 39.8	259 20	214 33.0	9 51	63.9
40	46.3	319 46.3	279 33	224 39.5	30 4	74.0
50	46.1	329 50.6	299 41	234 43.8	50 12	84.0
60	45.9	339 52.2	319 44	244 45.3	70 15	94.1
70	45.7	349 50.9	339 42	254 44.0	90 13	104.0
80	45.5	359 46.3	359 33	264 39.3	110 4	114.0
90	45.2	9 38.4	19 17	274 31.4	129 48	123.8
100	44.9	19 27.1	38 54	284 20.1	149 25	133.6
110	44.7	29 12.5	58 25	294 5.4	168 56	143 4
120	44.5	38 54.7	77 49	303 47.6	188 20	153.1
130	-44.2	48 34.1	97 8	313 27.0	207 39	162.8

Sid. Day.	Motion of ⊙ for − 0d.765.	⊙.	2 ⊙.	⊙ + $K_⊙$.	2⊙ + $K_{2⊙}$.	⊙ + $II_⊙$.
140	−44′.0	58° 10′.8	116° 22′	323° 3′.7	226° 53′	172°.4
150	43.8	67 45.3	135 31	332 38.2	246 2	161.9
160	43.8	77 18.0	154 36	342 10.8	265 7	191.5
170	43.7	86 49.4	173 39	351 42.2	284 10	201.0
180	43.6	96 20.2	192 40	1 13.0	303 11	210.5
190	43.7	105 50.5	211 41	10 43.3	322 12	220.0
200	43.7	115 21.3	230 43	20 14.0	341 14	229.5
210	43.8	124 52.8	249 46	29 45.5	0 17	239.1
220	43.9	134 25.7	268 51	39 18.4	19 22	248.6
230	44.1	144 0.3	288 1	48 53.0	38 32	258.2
240	44.2	153 37.3	307 15	58 30.0	57 46	267.8
250	44.4	163 16.8	326 34	68 9.5	77 5	277.5
260	44.7	172 59.2	345 58	77 51.9	96 29	287.2
270	45.0	182 44.8	5 30	87 37.4	116 1	296.9
280	45.2	192 33.8	25 8	97 26.4	135 39	306.8
290	45.4	202 26.2	44 52	107 18.8	155 23	316.6
300	45.7	212 21.9	64 44	117 14.4	175 15	326.6
310	45.9	222 20.8	84 42	127 13.3	195 13	336.5
320	46.1	232 22.7	104 45	137 15.2	215 16	346.6
330	46.3	242 27.3	124 55	147 19.8	235 26	356.6
340	46.4	252 33.9	145 8	157 26.4	255 39	6.8
350	46.6	262 42.1	165 24	167 34.5	275 55	16.9
360	46.7	272 51.5	185 43	177 43.9	296 14	27.0
370	−46.7	283 1.4	206 3	187 53.8	316 34	37.2

Sid. Day.	Log. sin (⊙ + $K_⊙$)	Log. $k_⊙$ sin (⊙ + $K_⊙$)	Log. sin (2 ⊙ + $K_{2⊙}$)	Log. $k_{2⊙}$ sin (2 ⊙ + $K_{2⊙}$)	Prec. + Prop. Mot.
0	8.85358n	9.63197n	9.8909n	9.1548n	−0.0068
10	9.39141	0.16980	9.7091	8.9730	+0.0822
20	61628	39466	9.2579n	8.5218n	0.1712
30	75368	53206	9.2331p	8.4970p	0.2602
40	84688	62525	9.6999	8.9638	0.3492
50	91192	69029	9.8855	9.1494	0.4381
60	95641	73477	9.9736	9.2375	0.5271
70	98440	76276	0.0000	9.2639	0.6161
80	99811	77646	9.9728	9.2367	0.7051
90	99865	77700	9.8855	9.1494	0.7941
100	98627	76461	9.7065	8.9704	0.8831
110	96043	73877	9.2832p	8.5471p	0.9721
120	91963	69796	9.1612n	8.4251n	1.0610
130	86092	63925	9.6666	8.9305	1.1500
140	77884	55717	9.8633	9.1272	1.2390
150	66241	44073	9.9608	9.2247	1.3280
160	48576	0.26407	9.9984	9.2623	1.4169
170	9.15927n	9.93758n	9.9866	9.2505	1.5059
180	8.32702p	9.10542p	9.9227	9.1866	1.5949
190	9.26960	0.04790	9.7874	9.0513	1.6839
200	53888	31717	9.5075n	8.7714n	1.7728
210	69578	47407	7.6942p	6.9581p	1.8618
220	80172	58000	9.5206	8.7845	1.9508
230	87701	65529	9.7944	9.0583	2.0397
240	93077	70904	9.9273	9.1912	2.1287
250	96764	74591	9.9888	9.2527	2.2177
260	9.99019	0.76845	9.9972	9.2611	2.3066

Sid. Day.	Log. sin $(\odot + K_\odot)$	Log. $k_\odot$ sin $(\odot + K_\odot)$	Log. sin $(2\odot + K_{2\odot})$	Log. $k_{2\odot}$ sin $(2\odot + K_{2\odot})$	Prec. + Prop. Mot.
270	9.99962	0.77787	9.9536	9.2175	+2.3956
280	99633	77458	9.8445	9.1084	2.4846
290	97987	75812	9.6197	8.8836	2.5735
300	. 94895	72719	8.9181p	8.1820p	2.6625
310	90108	67931	9.4191n	8.6830n	2.7514
320	83171	60994	9.7615	9.0254	2.8404
330	73223	51046	9.9156	9.1795	2.9293
340	58394	36216	9.9863	9.2502	3.0183
350	9.33276	0.11097	9.9976	9.2615	3.1072
360	8.59747p	9.37567p	9.9528	9.2167	3.1962
370	9.13795n	9.91614n	9.8373n	9.1012n	+3.2851

Sid. Day.	$k_\odot$ sin $(\odot + K_\odot)$	$k_{2\odot}$ sin $(2\odot + K_{2\odot})$	$\triangle_\odot a.$	$+0^s.00033$ $+10 \frac{d^2a}{dr^2}\tau$	$h_\odot$ sin $(\odot + H_\odot)$	$h_{2\odot}$ sin $(2\odot + H_{2\odot})$	Var. in 10 years.
0	−0.4285	−0.1428	−0.5781	+0.0003	+0.0173	+0.0011	+0.0187
10	1.4784	0.0940	1.4902	− 1	217	8	224
20	2.4812	−0.0333	2.3433	5	254	+ 4	253
30	3.4045	+0.0314	3.1129	10	282	0	272
40	4.2194	0.0920	3.7782	14	302	− 4	284
50	4.9011	0.1411	4.3219	19	313	8	286
60	5.4296	0.1728	4.7297	23	314	10	281
70	5.7911	0.1836	4.9914	27	305	12	266
80	5.9767	0.1725	5.0991	32	287	12	243
90	5.9841	0.1411	5.0489	36	261	11	214
100	5.8159	0.0934	4.8394	41	228	8	179
110	5.4799	+0.0352	4.4726	45	188	5	138
120	4.9884	−0.0266	3.9540	49	142	− 1	92
130	4.3576	0.0852	3.2928	54	93	+ 3	+ 42
140	3.6072	0.1310	2.5022	58	+ 42	7	− 9
150	2.7589	0.1678	1.5987	63	− 11	10	64
160	1.8368	0.1829	−0.6028	67	63	11	119
170	−0.8661	0.1780	+0.4618	71	113	12	172
180	+0.1275	0.1537	1.5687	76	160	11	225
190	1.1166	0.1125	2.6880	80	202	9	273
200	2.0757	−0.0591	3.7894	84	239	6	317
210	2.9790	+0.0009	4.8417	89	270	+ 2	357
220	3.8019	0.0608	5.8136	93	293	− 2	388
230	4.5216	0.1144	6.6757	98	308	5	411
240	5.1173	0.1553	7.4013	102	314	9	425
250	5.5707	0.1789	7.9673	106	312	11	429
260	5.8674	0.1824	8.3564	111	301	12	424
270	5.9961	0.1650	8.5567	115	281	12	408
280	5.9509	0.1284	8.5639	120	252	10	382
290	5.7296	0.0765	8.3796	124	216	7	347
300	5.3357	+0.0152	8.0134	128	173	− 3	304
310	4.7787	−0.0482	7.4819	133	125	+ 1	257
320	4.0733	0.1060	6.8077	137	73	5	205
330	3.2394	0.1512	6.0175	142	− 18	8	152
340	2.3023	0.1779	5.1427	146	+ 37	11	98
350	1.2911	0.1826	4.2157	150	91	12	− 47
360	+0.2275	0.1647	3.2690	155	143	12	0
370	−0.8244	−0.1262	+2.3345	−0.0159	+0.0190	+0.0010	+0.0041

TABLE A.

The sidereal days are reckoned from the beginning of each fictitious year.

Sid. day.	☉ 1860.	1870.	1880.	τ	Sid. days of fictitious year		Ω	Sid. days of fictitious year		Ω
— 10	269 48 87.8	67.8	47.9	—0.02730	1865	0	216 6 15	1873	0	61 22 36
+ 0	279 5* 78.7	58.2	37.6	0.00000		100	210 49 24		100	56 5 45
10	290 8 71.8	51.2	30.5	+0.02730		200	205 32 32		200	50 48 53
20	300 17 89.0	69.0	49.0	0.05461		300	200 15 41		300	45 32 2
30	310 25 94.5	75.8	57.0	0.08191		400	194 58 50		400	40 15 11
40	320 32 54.0	37.1	20.2	0.10922	1866	0	196 45 47	1874	0	42 2 9
50	330 36 58.0	43.5	28.9	0.13652		100	191 28 56		100	36 45 17
60	340 37 80.9	69.3	57.6	0.16382		200	186 12 5		200	31 28 26
70	350 36 43.3	34.8	26.3	0.19113		300	180 55 14		300	26 11 35
80	0 31 51.5	46.3	41.1	0.21843		400	175 38 22		400	20 54 44
90	10 23 37.7	36.1	34.4	0.24574	1867	0	177 25 20	1875	0	22 41 42
100	20 12 0.6	2.5	4 5	0.27304		100	172 8 29		100	17 24 50
110	29 57 4 8	10.2	15.7	0.30034		200	166 51 38		200	12 7 59
120	39 39 0.6	9.3	18.0	0.32765		300	161 34 46		300	6 51 8
130	49 18 3.0	14.7	26.5	0.35495		400	156 17 55		400	1 34 16
140	58 54 31.9	46.3	60.8	0.38225	1868	0	158 4 53	1876	0	3 21 14
150	68 28 50.6	67.3	81.0	0.40985		100	152 48 2		100	358 4 23
160	78 1 26.1	44.6	63.2	0.43686		200	147 31 10		200	352 47 31
170	87 32 47.0	66 9	86.9	0.46417		300	142 14 19		300	347 30 40
180	97 3 24.8	45.4	66.1	0.49147		400	136 57 28		400	342 13 49
190	106 33 50.5	71.3	92.2	0.51877	1869	0	138 44 26	1877	0	344 0 47
200	116 4 36.9	57.3	77.8	0.54608		100	133 27 34		100	338 43 55
210	125 35 14.8	34.3	53.9	0.57338		200	128 10 43		200	333 27 4
220	135 9 15.1	33.2	51.4	0.60068		300	122 53 52		300	328 10 13
230	144 44 6.1	22.3	38.5	0.62799		400	117 37 0		400	322 53 22
240	154 21 13.9	27.7	41.5	0.65529	1870	0	119 23 58	1878	0	324 40 20
250	164 1 0.8	11.8	22.8	0.68259		100	114 7 7		100	319 23 28
260	173 43 45.6	53.5	61.5	0.70990		200	108 50 16		200	314 6 37
270	183 29 41.9	46.6	51.3	0.73720		300	103 33 24		300	308 49 46
280	193 18 59.2	60.2	61.3	0.76451		400	98 16 33		400	303 32 54
290	203 11 39.7	37.2	34.7	0.79181	1871	0	100 3 31	1879	0	305 19 52
300	213 7 40.6	34.5	28.5	0.81911		100	94 46 39		100	300 3 1
310	223 6 52.9	43.4	34.0	0 84642		200	89 29 48		200	294 46 10
320	233 8 60.5	48.4	36.0	0.87372		300	84 12 57		300	289 29 18
330	243 13 43.9	28 5	13 2	0.90102		400	78 56 5		400	284 12 27
340	253 19 94 7	77.2	59.7	0.92833	1872	0	80 43 3	1880	0	285 59 25
350	263 28 62.8	43.5	24.2	0.95563		100	75 26 12		100	280 42 33
360	273 37 93 2	73.0	52.8	0.98294		200	70 9 21		200	275 25 42
370	283 47 89.7	68.7	47.9	1.01024		300	64 52 29		300	270 8 51
380	293 57 73.5	53.0	32.5	+1.03754		400	59 35 38		400	264 52 0

TABLE B.

The sidereal days are reckoned from the beginning of each fictitious year.

Sid. day.	log. $A_{\odot}$. 1870.	log. $B_{\odot}$. 1870.	log. C. 1860.	log. C. 1880.	log. D. 1860.	log. D. 1880.
− 10	−8.44498	+9.7480	+8.75956	+8.78615	+1.31059	+1.31059
0	+7.94052	9.7213	−0.51230	−0.51182	1.30395	1.30397
+ 10	8.64572	9.6315	0.81036	0.81013	1.28315	1.28318
20	8.89042	9.4430	0.97612	0.97598	1.24677	1.24681
30	9.03495	+8.9692	1.08517	1.08508	1.19201	1.19207
40	9.13338	−9.0062	1.16084	1.16079	1.11365	1.11374
50	9.20523	9.4510	1.21333	1.21330	1.00137	1.00148
60	9.26055	9.6317	1.24785	1.24784	0.83110	0.83123
70	9.30545	9.7173	1.26727	1.26728	+0.52310	+0.52331
80	9.34414	9.7423	1.27311	1.27312	−9.27753	−9.27508
90	9.37972	9.7145	1.26595	1.26596	0.56685	0.56682
100	9.41427	9.6275	1.24556	1.24557	0.84878	0.84881
110	9.44911	9.4565	1.21087	1.21087	1.00892	1.00896
120	9.48484	−9.0389	1.15960	1.15958	1.11548	1.11553
130	9.52143	+8.8714	1.08743	1.08739	1.19034	1.19038
140	9.55847	9.3950	0.98612	0.98603	1.24324	1.24328
150	9.59527	9.5049	0.83758	0.83741	1.27921	1.22924
160	9.63106	9.6937	0.59015	0.58980	1.30103	1.30105
170	9.66515	9.7320	−9.90468	−9.90273	1.31019	1.31019
180	9.69692	9.7203	+0.36252	+0.36323	1.30729	1.30728
190	9.72599	9.6659	0.72810	0.72841	1.29218	1.29216
200	9.75209	9.5189	0.91616	0.91635	1.26396	1.26392
210	9.77515	+9.2327	1.03918	1.03831	1.22071	1.22065
220	9.79524	−7.9180	1.12378	1.12386	1.15891	1.15883
230	9.81265	9.2730	1.18508	1.18514	1.07203	1.07194
240	9.82769	9.5401	1.22908	1.22912	0.94669	0.94677
250	9.84088	9.6703	1.25601	1.25603	0.75048	0.75032
260	9.85280	9.7298	1.27053	1.27054	−0.34892	−0.34861
270	9.86404	9.7359	1.27232	1.27233	+0.09564	+0.09597
280	9.87523	9.6889	1.26120	1.26130	0.67294	0.67296
290	9.88690	9.5737	1.23653	1.23654	0.90592	0.90590
300	9.89949	9.3331	1.19609	1.19612	1.04819	1.04815
310	9.91323	−8.4589	1.13644	1.13649	1.14530	1.14526
320	9.92812	+9.2118	1.05108	1.05116	1.21379	1.21375
330	9.94403	9.5265	0.92676	0.92692	1.26135	1.26132
340	9.96060	9.6715	0.73047	0.73072	1.29197	1.29195
350	9.97737	9.7370	+0.32805	+0.32877	1.30777	1.30776
360	9.99384	9.7445	−0.07612	−0.07479	1.30971	1.30972
370	0.00955	9.6959	0.65093	0.65050	1.29786	1.29788
380	+0.02410	+9.5759	−0.88195	−0.88176	+1.27142	+1.27146

$A_{\odot} = \tau - 0.02519 \sin 2\odot + 0.00294 \sin(\odot + 82° 19')$. $C = -18''.7556 \cos \odot$.

$B_{\odot} = -0''.55069 \cos 2\odot - 0''.0092 \cos(\odot + 280° 42')$. $D = -20''.4451 \sin \odot$.

$$\Delta_{\odot} a = aA_{\odot} + bB_{\odot} + cC + dD + \mu \tau.$$
$$\Delta_{\odot} \delta = a'A_{\odot} + b'B_{\odot} + c'C + d'D + \mu' \tau.$$

TABLE C.

The sidereal days are reckoned from the beginning of each fictitious year.

Sid. days of fictitious year.	log. A_Ω.	log. B_Ω.	E_Ω.	Sid. days of fictitious year.	log. A_Ω.	log. B_Ω.	E_Ω.
1865 0	+9.31317	+0.87388	+0.0019	1873 0	−9.47296	−0.65004	−0.0027
100	9.25299	0.90110	0.0016	100	9.44780	0.71424	0.0026
200	9.17848	0.92317	0.0014	200	9.41732	0.76686	0.0024
300	9.08366	0.94056	0.0011	300	9.38074	0.81042	0.0022
400	8.95692	0.95365	0.0008	400	9.33693	0.84664	0.0020
1866 0	+9.00441	+0.94970	+0.0009	1874 0	−9.35261	−0.83515	−0.0021
100	8.84362	0.96007	0.0006	100	9.30317	0.86716	0.0019
200	8.57830	0.96648	0.0003	200	9.24333	0.89355	0.0016
300	+7.75078	0.96904	+0.0001	300	9.16999	0.91498	0.0014
400	−8.42582	0.96780	−0.0002	400	9.07736	0.93193	0.0011
1867 0	−8.19779	+0.96865	−0.0001	1875 0	−9.11128	−0.92669	−0.0012
100	8.68058	0.96488	0.0004	100	9.00062	9.94090	0.0009
200	8.90122	0.95725	0.0007	200	8.84691	0.95115	0.0007
300	9.04398	0.94560	0.0010	300	8.60081	0.95766	0.0004
400	9.14817	0.92974	0.0013	400	7.96209	0.96051	0.0001
1868 0	−9.11615	+0.93558	−0.0012	1876 0	−8.29126	−0.95995	−0.0002
100	9.20372	0.91676	0.0014	100	+8.05073	0.96043	+0.0001
200	9.27324	0.89313	0.0017	200	8.62270	0.95733	0.0004
300	9.32972	0.86416	0.0019	300	8.85929	0.95058	0.0007
400	9.37623	0.82912	0.0021	400	9.00915	0.94006	0.0009
1869 0	−9.36151	+0.84169	−0.0021	1877 0	+8.96449	−0.94404	+0.0009
100	9.40252	0.80206	0.0023	100	9.08439	0.93093	0.0011
200	9.43642	0.75435	0.0025	200	9.17546	0.91366	0.0014
300	9.46427	0.69662	0.0026	300	9.24781	0.89193	0.0016
400	9.48683	0.62579	0.0028	400	9.30679	0.86520	0.0019
1870 0	−9.47977	+0.65142	−0.0027	1878 0	+9.28815	−0.87480	+0.0018
100	9.49913	0.56929	0.0029	100	9.34014	0.84441	0.0020
200	9.51400	0.46351	0.0030	200	9.38343	0.80774	0.0022
300	9.52473	0.31856	0.0030	300	9.41958	0.76382	0.0024
400	9.53152	0.09405	0.0031	400	9.44970	0.71031	0.0026
1871 0	−9.52965	+0.18381	−0.0031	1879 0	+9.44014	−0.72948	+0.0025
100	9.53393	+9.83245	0.0031	100	9.46668	0.66872	0.0027
200	9.53447	−9.23198	0.0031	200	9.48332	0.59357	0.0028
300	9.53132	0.00749	0.0031	300	9.50551	0.49787	0.0029
400	9.52443	0.26795	0.0031	400	9.51856	0.36970	0.0030
1872 0	−9.52717	−0.19648	−0.0031	1880 0	+9.51460	−0.41778	+0.0030
100	9.51778	0.37978	0.0030	100	9.52504	0.25465	0.0030
200	9.50445	0.50516	0.0029	200	9.53168	9.93254	0.0031
300	9.48697	0.59921	0.0028	300	9.53458	−9.05423	0.0031
400	−9.46503	−0.67322	−0.0027	400	+9.53379	+9.86753	+0.0031

$$A_\Omega = -0.342\,{}^{40}_{46}\sin\Omega + 0.00410\sin 2\Omega. \qquad {}^{1860.}_{1880.}$$

$$B_\Omega = -9''.22\,{}^{36}_{38}\cos\Omega + 0''.0895\cos 2\Omega. \qquad {}^{1860.}_{1880.}$$

$$E_\Omega = -0^s.003\,{}^{18}_{09}\sin\Omega. \qquad {}^{1860.}_{1880.}$$

$$\Delta_\Omega a = aA_\Omega + bB_\Omega + E_\Omega,$$

$$\Delta_\Omega \delta = a'A_\Omega + b'B_\Omega,$$

TABLE D.

The sidereal days are reckoned from the beginning of the fictitious year.

Sid. Day.	$f_\odot$ 1870.	Log. $g_\odot$ 1870.	$G_\odot$ 1870.	Log. h. 1870.	H. 1860.	1880.	Log. i. 1870.
− 10	−0.0855	9.89809	+134 57.0	1.31059	0 9.6	0 10.3	+8.4102
0	+0.0268	9.74411	71 37.5	1.30955	350 49.2	350 50.0	−0.1494
+ 10	0.1358	9.99341	25 45.8	1.30646	341 23.5	341 24.2	0.4476
20	0.2387	0.19941	10 5.6	1.30165	331 48.1	331 48.5	0.6134
30	0.3329	0.33757	+ 2 27.2	1.29562	321 58.7	321 59.2	0.7225
40	0.4176	0.43590	− 2 7.8	1.28905	311 53.6	311 54.2	0.7982
50	0.4928	0.50912	5 1.1	1.28277	301 32.5	301 33.0	0.8507
60	0.5597	0.56573	6 41.0	1.27758	290 57.5	290 57.9	0.8852
70	0.6207	0.61124	7 20.0	1.27422	280 13.0	280 13.3	0.9046
80	0.6785	0.64971	7 6.5	1.27314	269 25.3	269 25.5	0.9105
90	0.7364	0.68445	6 9.2	1.27447	258 41.6	258 41.7	0.9033
100	0.7974	0.71792	4 39.4	1.27796	248 8.8	248 8.7	0.8829
110	0.8640	0.75187	2 51.8	1.28309	237 52.0	237 51.9	0.8482
120	0.9381	0.78713	− 1 1.4	1.28918	227 54.3	227 54.0	0.7970
130	1.0206	0.82368	+ 0 38.4	1.29544	218 16.5	218 16.2	0.7248
140	1.1115	0.86095	1 57.6	1.30123	208 57.1	208 56.7	0.6234
150	1.2098	0.89803	2 51.1	1.30591	199 53.1	199 52.5	0.4749
160	1.3137	0.93400	3 17.7	1.30910	191 0.7	191 0.1	0.2273
170	1.4210	0.96811	3 19.7	1.31052	182 15.0	182 14.5	−9.5411
180	1.5288	0.99974	3 0.8	1.31007	173 31.3	173 30.6	+0.0003
190	1.6347	1.02860	2 25.8	1.30778	164 44.3	164 43.6	0.3656
200	1.7359	1.05449	1 40.2	1.30383	155 49.3	155 43.6	0.5536
210	1.8305	1.07741	+ 0 49.2	1.29860	146 42.0	146 41.3	0.6756
220	1.9172	1.09746	− 0 2.3	1.29256	137 18.9	137 18.3	0.7612
230	1.9957	1.11491	0 49.4	1.28635	127 37.5	127 37.0	0.8225
240	2.0660	1.13006	1 28.4	1.28065	117 37.3	117 36.9	0.8655
250	2.1297	1.14335	1 55.7	1.27621	107 20.3	107 20.0	0.8934
260	2.1890	1.15533	2 9.1	1.27363	96 49.8	96 49.5	0.9079
270	2.2461	1.16656	2 7.5	1.27329	86 11.4	86 11.2	0.9097
280	2.3050	1.17768	1 51.6	1.27529	75 31.9	75 31.9	0.8986
290	2.3678	1.18925	1 23.3	1.27938	64 57.8	64 57.9	0.8739
300	2.4374	1.20175	0 46.5	1.28501	54 34.4	54 34.6	0.8325
310	2.5157	1.21545	− 0 6.0	1.29144	44 25.0	41 25.3	0.7738
320	2.6035	· 1.23036	+ 0 32.9	1.29784	34 30.6	34 31.0	0.6885
330	2.7007	1.24633	1 5.5	1.30350	24 50.1	24 50.7	0.5642
340	2.8057	1.26296	1 28.1	1.30774	15 20.9	15 21.4	0.3680
350	2.9161	1.27977	1 38.6	1.31014	5 58.9	5 59.5	+9.9658
360	3.0289	1.29623	1 36.5	1.31046	356 39.4	356 40.1	−9.7128
370	3.1404	1.31190	1 23.2	1.30863	347 17.3	347 18.2	0.2880
380	+3.2474	1.32639	+ 1 1.1	1.30485	337 48.6	337 49.2	−0.5190

$$\triangle_\odot a = f_\odot + \mu\,\tau + g_\odot \sin(G_\odot + a)\,\frac{\tan\delta}{15} + h\sin(H + a)\,\frac{\sec\delta}{15}.$$
$$\triangle_\odot \delta = \mu'\tau + g_\odot \cos(G_\odot + a) + h\cos(H + a)\sin\delta + i\cos\delta.$$

TABLE E.

The sidereal days are reckoned from the beginning of each fictitious year.

Sid. days of fictitious year.		f_Ω	$\log. g_\Omega$	G_Ω	Sid. days of fictitious year.		f_Ω	$\log. g_\Omega$	G_Ω
1865	0	+0.6337	0.93153	61 7.5	1873	0	−0.9155	0.87202	216 51.4
	100	0.5517	0.94130	65 43.7		100	0.8641	0.88337	222 39.5
	200	0.4648	0.94977	70 9.0		200	0.8055	0.89500	228 6.9
	300	0.3736	0.95682	74 25.2		300	0.7404	0.90642	233 17.4
	400	0.2790	0.96234	78 34.6		400	0.6694	0.91731	238 11.5
1866	0	0.3113	0.96066	77 11.1	1874	0	0.6940	0.91371	236 34.0
	100	0.2149	0.96512	81 16.8		100	0.6194	0.92406	241 18.5
	200	0.1166	0.96793	85 18.6		200	0.5396	0.93339	245 49.8
	300	+0.0174	0.96907	89 18.3		300	0.4558	0.94155	250 9.7
	400	−0.0821	0.96852	93 17.7		400	0.3682	0.94836	254 20.5
1867	0	0.0485	0.96890	91 56.8	1875	0	0.3981	0.94622	252 56.7
	100	0.1476	0.96723	95 57.0		100	0.3085	0.95211	257 2.5
	200	0.2454	0.96390	99 50.8		200	0.2167	0.95649	261 2.1
	300	0.3410	0.95892	104 6.9		300	0.1230	0.95934	264 57.6
	400	0.4334	0.95239	108 20.8		400	0.0283	0.96060	268 50.8
1868	0	0.4026	0.95477	106 54.4	1876	0	−0.0603	0.96035	267 32.3
	100	0.4925	0.94725	111 13.3		100	+0.0346	0.96056	271 24.9
	200	0.5780	0.93836	115 41.8		200	0.1293	0.95919	275 18.2
	300	0.6583	0.92823	120 21.8		300	0.2229	0.95624	279 13.9
	400	0.7327	0.91712	125 15.3		400	0.3147	0.95175	283 13.9
1869	0	0.7083	0.92097	123 34.6	1877	0	0.2840	0.95313	281 52.3
	100	0.7785	0.90932	128 38.0		100	0.3742	0.94795	285 56.2
	200	0.8417	0.89716	133 57.9		200	0.4616	0.94102	290 7.5
	300	0.8974	0.88487	139 35.4		300	0.5452	0.93290	294 28.2
	400	0.9453	0.87293	145 31.4		400	0.6246	0.92339	299 0.2
1870	0	0.9300	0.87689	143 29.1	1878	0	0.5983	0.92667	297 27.0
	100	0.9725	0.86547	149 37.6		100	0.6744	0.91660	302 7.7
	200	1.0063	0.85528	156 3.8		200	0.7450	0.90568	307 3.0
	300	1.0314	0.84690	162 46.0		300	0.8097	0.89423	312 14.7
	400	1.0477	0.84082	169 40.8		400	0.8679	0.88266	317 44.2
1871	0	1.0431	0.84258	167 19.6	1879	0	0.8489	0.88653	315 51.0
	100	1.0535	0.83828	174 20.2		100	0.9025	0.87505	321 33.0
	200	1.0548	0.83682	181 25.4		200	0.9486	0.86418	327 34.1
	300	1.0473	0.83833	188 29.4		300	0.9868	0.85445	333 53.9
	400	1.0308	0.84261	195 26.4		400	1.0170	0.84641	340 30.6
1872	0	1.0373	0.84085	193 6.5	1880	0	1.0077	0.84889	338 14.9
	100	1.0151	0.84687	199 56.7		100	1.0322	0.84227	345 1.3
	200	0.9844	0.85503	206 32.4		200	1.0481	0.83816	351 59.1
	300	0.9456	0.86496	212 51.0		300	1.0551	0.83686	359 3.3
	400	−0.8990	0.87580	218 50.7		400	+1.0532	0.83850	6 8.2

$$\Delta_\Omega a = f_\Omega + g_\Omega \sin(G_\Omega + a)\,\frac{\tan \delta}{15}.$$
$$\Delta_\Omega \delta = g_\Omega \cos(G_\Omega + a).$$

ON THE PLACES AND PROPER MOTION OF β^1 SCORPII, β AND η DRACONIS AND 61¹ CYGNI.

From a report prepared by Mr. G. W. Hill.

In this discussion almost all the materials to be derived from the well known collections of reduced observations have been employed. To accord with Dr. Gould's *Standard Places of Fundamental Stars*, the right ascensions as given in these collections have been reduced to the equinoctial points of Argelander's *DLX Stellarum Positiones Mediæ*. Also the systematic corrections given by Dr. Auwer's, in the *Astronomische Nachrichten*, Vol. LXV, 370, 377–382, have been applied to the declinations.

β^1 Scorpii.

Adopting for a provisional mean place of this star that of the *Greenwich Seven-Year Catalogue* for 1860, we have for any time, with a proper motion *zero* in both co-ordinates,

$$a = 15^h\ 57^m\ 18^s.08 + 3^s.47735\ (t - 1860) + 0^s.0000711\ (t - 1860)^2,$$
$$\delta = -19°\ 25'\ 8''.37 - 10''.2316\ (t - 1860) + 0''.002203\ (t - 1860)^2.$$

Constructing an ephemeris from these formulæ and comparing it with the observations, both as published and corrected, we obtain the differences in columns I and II of the following table. From those in column II are derived, by the method of least squares, the following normal equations, in which Δa and $\Delta \delta$ denote the corrections of the provisional mean right ascension and declination, and μ and μ' are the proper motions in right ascension and declination for 1860:

$$37.5\ \Delta a - 810\ \mu = +\ 1^s.0865$$
$$-810\ \Delta a + 40379\ \mu = -\ 64^s.793$$
$$34\ \Delta \delta - 746\ \mu' = +\ 38''.685$$
$$-746\ \Delta \delta + 39090\ \mu' = -\ 1279''.485.$$

Whence

$$\Delta a = -0^s.010, \qquad \mu = -0^s.00180$$
$$\Delta \delta = +0''.72, \qquad \mu' = -0''.0189;$$

and the corrected formulæ for the mean place of the star will be

$$a = 15^h\ 57^m\ 18^s.070 + 3^s.47555\ (t - 1860) + 0^s.0000712\ (t - 1860)^2$$
$$\delta = -19°\ 25'\ 7''.65 - 10''.2505\ (t - 1860) + 0''.002200\ (t - 1860)^2.$$

The differences of these and the corrected observations constitute column III of the table.

Authority.	RIGHT ASCENSION.						DECLINATION.					
	Mean year.	No. of obs.	Weight.	Obs. — Cal. I.	II.	III.	Mean year.	No. of obs.	Weight.	Obs. — Cal. I.	II.	III.
Bradley, (*Fund. Astr.*)	1755	10	2	+.118	+.118	—.062	1755	8	2	+2.36	+2.36	—0.31
Piazzi	1800	44	2	+.145	+.206	+.108	1800	28	2	+4.54	+2.51	+0.67
Airy, *Camb. Cat.*	1829	12	2	+.037	+.037	—.009	1829	22	2	+2.17	+0.80	—0.50
Pond	1830	13	2	+.137	+.137	+.093	1830	12	2	+4.04	+1.76	+0.48
Struve, *Cat. Gen.*	1830	5	2	+.107	+.067	+.023	1830	5	2	+1.74	+0.76	—0.52
Johnson, *St. Helena*	1830	9	2	+.047	+.007	—.037	1830	14	2	+1.74	+1.94	+0.66
Robinson, *Arm. Cat.*	1834	4	½	—.081	—.051	—.088	1833	2	½	+1.57	+1.27	+0.42
Taylor, *Madras*	1837	14	1	+.090	+.010	—.020	1837	3	½	+1.02	+0.66	—0.49
Greenwich, 12 year Cat.	1838	51	} 3	—.061	} +.022	—.001 }	1838	37	} 3	+0.49	} +1.07	—0.00
Greenwich, 12 year Cat.	1845	57		+.025			1844	41		+1.01		
Gilliss, *Washington*	1840	30	1	+.020	+.020	—.006						
Edinburgh	1844	34	3	+.014	+.014	—.205	1842	15	3	+1.40	+0.22	—0.84
Radcliffe Cat.	1848	18	3	+.055	—.025	—.037	1850	5	1	+1.30	+2.05	+1.14
Greenwich	1851	54	4	+.007	—.016	—.022	1851	47	4	+0.93	+1.02	+0.13
Brussels							1856	24	3	+0.64	+0.64	—0.15
Greenwich	1857	40	4	+.003	—.008	—.003	1857	32	4	+0.06	+0.45	—0.32
Greenwich	1862	12	2	—.008	—.021	—.007	1862	8	2	+0.11	+0.50	—3.18
Paris	1860	115	4	—.005	+.011	+.022	1860	93	4	+0.46	+0.57	—0.15

η **Draconis.**

Deriving a provisional place from the same authority as for the previous star, with no proper motion, we obtain the formulæ:

$$a = 16^h\ 22^m\ 6^s.23 + 0^s.79943\ (t - 1860) + 0^s.0000943\ (t - 1860)^2,$$
$$\delta = + 61°\ 49'\ 54''.16 - 8''.3086\ (t - 1860) + 0''.000548\ (t - 1860)^2.$$

Comparing these with the published and corrected observations we have columns I and II of the following table, and we find from the latter the normal equations,

$$36\ \Delta a - 647\ \mu = - 4^s.983$$
$$- 647\ \Delta a + 21146\ \mu = + 112^s.538$$
$$39\ \Delta\delta - 766\ \mu' = - 35''.23$$
$$- 766\ \Delta\delta + 38618\ \mu' = + 2293''.37.$$

Whence

$$\Delta a = - 0^s.095, \qquad\qquad \mu = + 0^s.00242$$
$$\Delta\delta = + 0''.43, \qquad\qquad \mu' = + 0''.0679;$$

and the corrected formulæ for the mean place of the star will be

$$a = 16^h\ 22^m\ 6^s.135 + 0^s.80185\ (t - 1860) + 0^s.0000924\ (t - 1860)^2,$$
$$\delta = + 61°\ 49'\ 54''.59 - 8''.2407\ (t - 1860) + 0''.000551\ (t - 1860).^2$$

The differences of these and the corrected observations constitute column III of the table.

Authority.	RIGHT ASCENSION.					DECLINATION.				
	Mean year.	No. of obs.	Weight.	Obs. — Cal. I.	II.	III.	Mean year.	No. of obs.	Weight.	Obs. — Cal. I.	II.	III.
Bradley, (*Fund. Astr.*)	1755						1755	5	2	−7.41	−7.41	−0.74
Piazzi	1800	56	2	−.804	−.417	−.170	1800	9	1	−3.65	−2.85	+0.79
Groombridge	1810	15	2	−.295	−.049	+.172	1810	81	2	−2.96	−2.51	+0.45
Struve, *Cat. Gen.*	1830	8	3	−.022	−.062	+.108	1830	8	3	−1.41	−1.47	+0.14
Pond	1830	10	2	−.182	−.182	−.012	1830	10	2	−1.01	−0.94	+0.67
Robinson. *Arm. Cat.* . . .	1833	2	½	−.409	−.469	−.306	1832	7	2	−0.86	−0.82	−0.71
Taylor, *Madras*	1835	3	½	−.123	−.203	−.046	1835	5	1	−2.03	−1.49	−0.29
Greenwich, 12 *year Cat's* . . .	1841	80	4	−.059	−.118	+.024	1841	269	4	−0.38	−0.60	+0.26
Gilliss, *Washington*	1841	22	2	−.488	−.188	−.046						
Henderson	1841	5	1	−.045	−.045	+.097	1842	19	2	−0.49	−0.76	+0.03
Radcliffe	1842	18	3	−.070	−.150	−.010	1848	6	2	−.045	−0.05	+0.34
Washington	1853	13	1	−.108	−.168	+.005	1850	7	1	+0.51	+0.34	+0.59
Greenwich	1851	43	4	−.080	−.123	−.005	1851	71	4	+0.26	−0.13	+0.05
Brussels	1856	37	2	−.074	−.074	+.031	1855	14	2	−0.02	−0.02	−0.11
Paris	1857	14	2	−.223	−.207	−.105	1858	54	4	+0.75	+0.32	+0.03
Greenwich	1858	39	4	−.044	−.057	+.043	1858	41	4	−0.15	−0.27	−3.56
Radcliffe	1859	8	2	−.043	−.123	−.025	1860	6	2	+0.41	−0.30	−0.13
Greenwich	1863	7	1	−.173	−.186	−.098	1863	7	1	+0.44	+0.32	−0.32

β **Draconis.**

The provisional place of this star derived from the same source, with no proper motion, is

$$a = 17^h\ 27^m\ 16^s.32 + 1^s.35307\ (t - 1860) + 0^s.0000256\ (t - 1860)^2,$$
$$\delta = + 52°\ 24'\ 22''.71 - 2''.8543\ (t - 1860) + 0''.000983\ (t - 1860)^2.$$

The comparisons of these with the published and corrected observations are given in columns I and II of the following table. From column II we find the normal equations,

$$35.6 \ \Delta a - \ 744 \ \mu \ = - \ 1^{s}.635$$
$$- 744 \ \Delta a + 39800 \ \mu \ = - \ 32^{s}.231$$
$$43 \ \Delta \delta - \ 944 \ \mu' = + \ 15''.34$$
$$- 944 \ \Delta \delta + 45848 \ \mu' = - \ 440''.33.$$

Whence

$$\Delta a = - \ 0^{s}.103, \qquad\qquad \mu = - \ 0^{s}.00273$$
$$\Delta \delta = + \ 0''.27, \qquad\qquad \mu' = - \ 0''.0041;$$

and the corrected formulæ for the mean place of the star become,

$$a = 17^{h} \ 27^{m} \ 16^{s}.217 + 1^{s}.35034 \ (t - 1860) + 0^{s}.0000257 \ (t - 1860)^{2},$$
$$\delta = + 52° \ 24' \ 22''.98 - 2''.8584 \ (t - 1860) + 0''.000979 \ (t - 1860)^{2}.$$

Comparisons of which, with the corrected observations, constitute column III of the table.

Authority.	RIGHT ASCENSION.						DECLINATION.					
	Mean year.	No. of obs.	Weight	Obs. — Cal.			Mean year.	No. of obs.	Weight	Obs. — Cal.		
				I.	II.	III.				I.	II.	III.
				s	s	s				''	''	''
Bradley, (*Fund. Astr.*)	1755	10	2	+.197	+.197	+.012	1755	39	2	+0.05	+0.05	—0.61
Piazzi	1800	44	2	—.188	+.121	+.060	1800	18	2	+1.19	+1.40	+0.51
Groombridge	1810	11	1	—.220	—.067	—.101	1810	163	2	+0.61	+1.01	+0.55
Pond	1830	26	2	+.039	+.039	+.060	1830	133	3	+0.57	+0.31	—0.08
Argelander	1830	101	4	—.051	—.051	—.030	1830	103	4	+0.57	+0.44	+0.05
Taylor.	1835	3	½	+.201	+.121	+.156	1835	5	1	+0.70	+1.21	+0.84
Henderson							1839	11	2	+0.41	+0.05	—0.30
Greenwich, *12 year Cat's* . . .	1842	79	4	—.075	—.114	—.061	1840	143	4	+0.30	+0.18	—0.17
Robinson, *Arm. Cat.*	1842	1	½	—.469	—.499	—.446	1838	11	2	+0.87	—0.06	—0.42
Radcliffe Cat.	1844	9	2	—.030	—.110	—.051	1844	7	2	+0.46	+0.44	+0.11
Washington	1847	24	2	—.121	—.121	—.053	1847	34	2	+0.36	+0.36	+0.04
Greenwich	1851	29	3	—.032	—.045	+.034	1851	37	4	+0.43	+0.06	—0.25
Brussels	1856	60	2	—.032	—.032	+.060	1857	11	1	+0.49	+0.48	+0.20
Radcliffe	1857	12	2	—.135	—.135	—.040	1857	15	2	+1.15	+1.00	+0.72
Greenwich	1859	45	4	+.004	—.009	+.091	1859	44	4	0.00	+0.02	—0.25
Paris	1860	17	3	—.143	—.127	—.024	1858	44	4	+0.57	+0.36	+0.08
Greenwich	1861	7	2	—.123	—.136	—.030	1861	7	2	—0.03	—0.01	—0.08

61¹ Cygni.

From Dr. AUWERS' elements of the position of this star in the *Astronomische Nachrichten*, Vol. LIX, p. 354, we have

$$a = 21^{h} \ 0^{m} \ 37^{s}.396 + 2^{s}.67878 \ (t - 1860) + 0^{s}.0000207 \ (t - 1860)^{2},$$
$$\delta = + 38° \ 3' \ 46''.86 + 17''.4510 \ (t - 1860) + 0''.001493 \ (t - 1860)^{2},$$

including the proper motion in R. A., $\mu = + \ 0^{s}.34512$, and in Dec., $\mu' = + \ 3''.2311$.

On account of the importance of BRADLEY'S two transit observations in determining the proper motion of this star, they have been reduced anew. With the equatorial intervals of the wires, as given in the Preface to the Observations, and the clock corrections and the constants of the instrumental corrections given by BESSEL, in the *Fundamenta Astronomiæ*, the resulting mean right ascensions differ more than $0^{s}.5$. If, however, for 1753, October 8, we derive the clock correction from the observations of a Bootis, a Aquilæ, a Cygni, and a Piscis Australis, using Dr. GOULD'S well determined values of their right ascensions, we have for Oct. 8, $18^{h} \ 5^{m}$, $+ 23^{s}.13$, instead of BESSEL'S value $+ 23^{s}.58$, or a correction of BESSEL'S clock correction for that night of $- \ 0^{s}.43$.

Making this correction we have for the apparent R. A. for the time of transit at Greenwich,

	h	m	s	Wires.
1753, Sept. 25	20	55	54.54	1
Oct. 8	20	55	54.38	3

Reducing these to mean place at date with the constants derived from these tables, the effect of the two terms depending on ☾ being added, and taking the annual variation in mean R. A. at the epoch 1754 to be $+ 2^s.6695$, which is sufficiently accurate, we have as the mean R. A. for 1755.0,

	h	m	s
Sept. 25	20	55	56.23
Oct. 8	20	55	56.32

and, combined by giving double weight to the latter,

	h	m	s
	20	55	56.29

as the mean result from BRADLEY's observations.

Comparing the provisional formulæ with the different authorities and the corrected values as for the other stars, we have columns I and II of the following table. For the declinations the normal equations resulting from column II, are

$$54\, \Delta\delta - 1092\, \Delta\, \mu' = -\ 4''.59,$$
$$- 1092\, \Delta\delta + 48478\, \Delta\, \mu' = +\ 381''.45;$$

from which,

$$\Delta\delta = +\ 0''.14, \qquad \Delta\mu' = +\ 0''.0109.$$

With regard to the right ascensions, it has been found more convenient to plot the residuals and draw a parabolic curve so as most nearly to represent them. Thus the correction of AUWERS' formula is found to be

$$+ 0^s.041 + 0^s.00653\,(t - 1860) + 0^s.000054\,(t - 1860)^2.$$

Then the formulæ for the corrected place are,

$$a = 21^h\ 0^m\ 37^s.437\ + 2^s.68531\ (t - 1860) + 0^s.0000747\,(t - 1860)^2$$
$$\delta = +\ 38°\ 3'\ 47''.00 + 17''.4619\ (t - 1860) + 0''.001493\,(t - 1860)^2,$$

in which the right ascension includes the term $+ 0^s.0000536\,(t - 1860)^2$ due to variability of proper motion.

Column III of the table shows how nearly these represent the several authorities.

Authority.	RIGHT ASCENSION.						DECLINATION.					
	Mean year.	No. of obs.	Weight.	Obs. — Cal.			Mean year.	No. of obs.	Weight.	Obs. — Cal.		
				I.	II.	III.				I.	II.	III.
				s	s	s				''	''	''
Bradley, (corrected)	1755	2	1	—.062	—.062	—.013	1754	4	2	—1.27	—1.15	—0.12
Piazzi	1805	28	2	—.384	—.169	—.014	1805	21	2	+2.32	+0.29	+0.76
Bessel . . . . . . ، . . .	1816	65	2	—.131	—.131	+.011	1816	20	2	—0.29	—0 79	—0.45
Struve	1824	4	2	—.021	—.061	+.063	1824	4	2	+0.42	+0.12	+0.38
Argelander	1830	62	4	—.091	—.091	+.015	1830	32	4	+0.12	—0.22	—0.03
Pond	1830	80	0	+ 349			1830	242	4	+0.92	+0.10	+0.20
Taylor	1837	5	0	+.381			1835	7	2	—1.06	—0.52	—0.37
Greenwich	1839	55	4	—.089	—.098	—.026	1838	57	4	—0.73	—0.67	—0.57
Henderson	1841	27	3	—.053	—.053	+.011	1841	19	3	0.00	— 0. 37	—0.29
Greenwich	1844	50	4	—.059	—.068	—.018	1844	53	4	—0.13	—0.19	—0.15
Washington	1847	152	2	—.020	—.020	+.015	1847	102	3	—0.06	—0.22	—0.21
Radcliffe	1850	28	3	+.071	—.009	+.010	1853	20	3	+1.47	+0.94	+0.88
Greenwich	1851	62	4	+.010	—.013	—.000	1852	52	4	+0.18	+0.14	+0.09
Brussels	1856	78	3	—.052	—.052	—.068	1857	26	3	+0.32	+0.32	+0.22
Greenwich	1857	51	4	+.034	+.021	—.001	1857	53	4	—0.36	+0.24	+0.14
Radcliffe	1858	13	2	+.030	+.030	+.001	1858	9	2	+0.57	+0.20	+0.09
Paris . ،	1860	91	4	+.017	+.033	—.008	1860	62	4	+0.01	+0.02	—0.12
Greenwich	1863	14	2	+.082	+.069	+.038	1863	16	2	—0.59	—0.29	—0.46

GENERAL TABLES.

TABLE I.—Longitudes of the principal Observatories from Washington.

Place.	In Time. *d*	In decimals of a Day. *d'*	Year. *d''*	Place.	In Time. *d*	In decimals of a Day. *d'*	Year. *d''*
	h m s	d	y		h m s	d	y
Abo.....	—6 37 20.32	—.27593	—.00076	Leipsic...	— 5 57 46.87	—.24846	—.00068
Albany....	—0 13 12.87	—.00918	—.00002	Leyden...	— 5 26 8.57	—.22649	—.00062
Altona....	—5 47 58.54	—.24165	—.00066	Liverpool.	— 4 56 12.34	—.20570	—.00056
Ann Arbor...	+0 26 42.67	+.01855	+.00005	Madras...	—10 29 9.67	—.43692	—.00120
Armagh...	—4 41 36.92	—.19557	—.00053	Mannheim.	— 5 42 3.06	—.23753	—.00065
Athens....	—6 43 7.58	—.27995	—.00077	Markree...	— 4 34 24.00	—.19056	—.00052
Berlin....	—6 1 47.77	—.25125	—.00069	Marseilles.	— 5 29 40.55	—.22894	—.00063
Bilk..\...	—5 35 17.77	—.23284	—.00064	Milan....	— 5 44 58.20	—.23956	—.00066
Bonn....	—5 36 36.02	—.23375	—.00064	Modena...	— 5 51 55.53	—.24439	—.00067
Breslau...	—6 16 22.19	—.26137	—.00071	Moscow...	— 7 38 29.29	—.31839	—.00087
Brussels..	—5 25 41.29	—.22617	—.00062	Munich...	— 5 54 38.00	—.24627	—.00067
Cambridge, Eng..	—5 8 35.08	—.21429	—.00060	Naples...	— 6 5 10.95	—.25360	—.00070
Cambridge, Mass..	—0 23 41.54	—.01645	—.00004	New York.	— 0 12 15.47	—.00851	—.00002
Cape of Good Hope.	—6 22 8.09	—.26537	—.00073	Nicolajew.	— 7 16 6.53	—.30285	—.00083
Chicago..	+0 42 14.26	+.02933	+.00008	Olmütz...	— 6 17 15.43	—.26198	—.00072
Christiania..	—5 51 6.69	—.24383	—.00067	Oxford...	— 5 3 9.79	—.21053	—.00058
Cincinnati..	+0 29 46.90	+.02068	+.00006	Padua...	— 5 55 41.17	—.24700	—.00068
Clinton....	—0 6 35.08	—.00457	—.00001	Palermo...	— 6 1 37.00	—.25112	—.00069
Copenhagen..	—5 58 31.05	—.24897	—.00068	Paramatta.	—15 12 18.64	—.63353	—.00173
Cracow...	—6 28 2.80	—.26948	—.00074	Paris...	— 5 17 33.02	—.22052	—.00061
Dorpat....	—6 55 6.02	—.28826	—.00079	Philadelphia.	— 0 7 33.64	—.00525	—.00001
Dublin....	—4 42 50.39	—.19642	—.00054	Prague...	— 6 5 53.52	—.25409	—.00070
Durham...	—5 1 52.64	—.20964	—.00057	Pulkowa.	— 7 9 31.06	—.29828	—.00082
Edinburgh.	—4 55 29.34	—.20520	—.00056	Rome....	— 5 58 8.53	—.24871	—.00068
Florence..	—5 53 15.10	—.24531	—.00067	San Fernando.	— 4 43 22.42	—.19679	—.00054
Geneva....	—5 32 49.24	—.23113	—.00063	Santiago.	— 0 25 30.00	—.01771	—.00005
Georgetown	+0 0 6.20	+.00007	.00000	Senftenberg.	— 6 14 3.00	—.25976	—.00071
Göttingen..	—5 47 58.49	—.24165	—.00066	Speyer...	— 5 41 58.00	—.23748	—.00065
Gotha....	—5 51 3.39	—.24379	—.00067	Stockholm.	— 6 20 26.35	—.26419	—.00072
Greenwich.	—5 8 12.39	—.21403	—.00059	St. Petersburg.	— 7 9 25.87	—.29822	—.00082
Hamburg..	—5 48 5.95	—.24174	—.00066	Upsala...	— 6 18 42.70	—.26299	— 00072
Helsingfors	—6 48 1.32	—.28335	—.00078	Utrecht...	— 5 28 43.67	—.22828	—.00063
Hudson..	+0 17 32.06	+.01218	+.00003	Vienna...	— 6 13 44.09	—.25954	—.00071
Kasan...	—8 24 41.14	—.35048	—.00096	Washington.	0 0 0.00	.00000	.00000
Königsberg	—6 30 11.87	—.27097	—.00074	Wilna...	— 6 49 23.33	—.28430	—.00078
Kremsmünster.	—6 4 45.03	—.25330	—.00069				

TABLE II.—Number of days from Jan. 0 in common years, and from Jan. 1 in bissextile years.

Day of month	JANUARY. Common year.	JANUARY. Bissextile year.	FEBRUARY. Common year.	FEBRUARY. Bissextile year.	MARCH.	APRIL.	MAY.	JUNE.	JULY.	AUGUST.	SEPTEMBER.	OCTOBER.	NOVEMBER.	DECEMBER.
1	1	0	32	31	60	91	121	152	182	213	244	274	305	335
2	2	1	33	32	61	92	122	153	183	214	245	275	306	336
3	3	2	34	33	62	93	123	154	184	215	246	276	307	337
4	4	3	35	34	63	94	124	155	185	216	247	277	308	338
5	5	4	36	35	64	95	125	156	186	217	248	278	309	339
6	6	5	37	36	65	96	126	157	187	218	249	279	310	340
7	7	6	38	37	66	97	127	158	188	219	250	280	311	341
8	8	7	39	38	67	98	128	159	189	220	251	281	312	342
9	9	8	40	39	68	99	129	160	190	221	252	282	313	343
10	10	9	41	40	69	100	130	161	191	222	253	283	314	344
11	11	10	42	41	70	101	131	162	192	223	254	284	315	345
12	12	11	43	42	71	102	132	163	193	224	255	285	316	346
13	13	12	44	43	72	103	133	164	194	225	256	286	317	347
14	14	13	45	44	73	104	134	165	195	226	257	287	318	348
15	15	14	46	45	74	105	135	166	196	227	258	288	319	349
16	16	15	47	46	75	106	136	167	197	228	259	289	320	350
17	17	16	48	47	76	107	137	168	198	229	260	290	321	351
18	18	17	49	48	77	108	138	169	199	230	261	291	322	352
19	19	18	50	49	78	109	139	170	200	231	262	292	323	353
20	20	19	51	50	79	110	140	171	201	232	263	293	324	354
21	21	20	52	51	80	111	141	172	202	233	264	294	325	355
22	22	21	53	52	81	112	142	173	203	234	265	295	326	356
23	23	22	54	53	82	113	143	174	204	235	266	296	327	357
24	24	23	55	54	83	114	144	175	205	236	267	297	328	358
25	25	24	56	55	84	115	145	176	206	237	268	298	329	359
26	26	25	57	56	85	116	146	177	207	238	269	299	330	360
27	27	26	58	57	86	117	147	178	208	239	270	300	331	361
28	28	27	59	58	87	118	148	179	209	240	271	301	332	362
29	29	28		59	88	119	149	180	210	241	272	302	333	363
30	30	29			89	120	150	181	211	242	273	303	334	364
31	31	30			90		151		212	243		304		365

TABLE III.—Reduction of hours and minutes to decimals of a day and year.

Hours.	Decimal of a day.	Decimal of a year.	Minutes.	Decimal of a day.	Decimal of a year.	Minutes.	Decimal of a day.	Decimal of a year.
	d	y		d	y		d	y
1	0.042	0.00011	1	0.001	0.00000	31	0 022	0.00006
2	.083	.00023	2	.001	.00000	32	.022	.00006
3	.125	.00034	3	.002	.00001	33	.023	.00006
4	.167	.00046	4	.003	.00001	34	.024	.00006
5	.208	.00057	5	.003	.00001	35	.024	.00007
6	.250	.00068	6	.004	.00001	36	.025	.00007
7	.292	.00080	7	.005	.00001	37	.026	.00007
8	.333	.00091	8	.006	.00002	38	.026	.00007
9	.375	.00103	9	.006	.00002	39	.027	.00007
10	.417	.00114	10	.007	.00002	40	.028	.00008
11	.458	.00125	11	.008	.00002	41	.028	.00008
12	.500	.00137	12	.008	.00002	42	.029	.00008
13	.542	.00148	13	.009	.00002	43	.030	.00008
14	.583	.00160	14	.009	.00003	44	.031	.00008
15	.625	.00171	15	.010	.00003	45	.031	.00009
16	.667	.00183	16	.010	.00003	46	.032	.00009
17	.708	.00194	17	.011	.00003	47	.033	.00009
18	.750	.00205	18	.012	.00003	48	.033	.00009
19	.792	.00217	19	.013	.00004	49	.034	.00009
20	.833	.00228	20	.014	.00004	50	.035	.00010
21	.875	.00240	21	.015	.00004	51	.035	.00010
22	.917	.00251	22	.015	.00004	52	.036	.00010
23	0.958	.00262	23	.016	.00005	53	.037	.00010
24	1.000	0.00274	24	.017	.00005	54	.038	.00010
			25	.017	.00005	55	.038	.00010
			26	.018	.00005	56	.039	.00011
			27	.019	.00005	57	.040	.00011
			28	.019	.00005	58	.040	.00011
			29	.020	.00006	59	.041	.00011
			30	0.021	0.00006	60	0.042	0.00011

TABLE IV.—Fraction of the year elapsed from Jan. 0 in common years, Jan. 1 in bissextile years, to the midnight of each day of the year.

DAY.		Fraction of year.	DAY.		Fraction of year.	Day.	Fraction of year.
Com. year.	Bis. year.		Com. year.	Bis. year.			
Jan. 0	Jan. 1	0.00137	Feb. 22	Feb. 23	0.14648	Apr. 16	0.29159
1	2	.00411	23	24	.14922	17	.29433
2	3	.00684	24	25	.15195	18	.29706
3	4	.00958	25	26	.15469	19	.29980
4	5	.01232	26	27	.15743	20	.30254
5	6	.01506	27	28	.16017	21	.30528
6	7	.01780	28	29	.16291	22	.30801
7	8	.02053	Mar. 1		.16564	23	.31075
8	9	.02327	2		.16838	24	.31349
9	10	.02601	3		.17112	25	.31623
10	11	.02875	4		.17386	26	.31897
11	12	.03149	5		.17660	27	.32170
12	13	.03422	6		.17933	28	.32444
13	14	.03696	7		.18207	29	.32718
14	15	.03970	8		.18481	30	.32992
15	16	.04244	9		.18755	May 1	.33266
16	17	.04518	10		.19028	2	.33539
17	18	.04791	11		.19302	3	.33813
18	19	.05065	12		.19576	4	.34087
19	20	.05339	13		.19850	5	.34361
20	21	.05613	14		.20124	6	.34635
21	22	.05887	15		.20397	7	.34908
22	23	.06160	16		.20671	8	.35182
23	24	.06434	17		.20945	9	.35456
24	25	.06708	18		.21219	10	.35730
25	26	.06982	19		.21493	11	.36004
26	27	.07255	20		.21766	12	.36277
27	28	.07529	21		.22040	13	.36551
28	29	.07803	22		.22314	14	.36825
29	30	.08077	23		.22588	15	.37099
30	31	.08351	24		.22862	16	.37372
31	Feb. 1	.08624	25		.23135	17	.37646
Feb. 1	2	.08898	26		.23409	18	.37920
2	3	.09172	27		.23683	19	.38194
3	4	.09446	28		.23957	20	.38468
4	5	.09720	29		.24230	21	.38741
5	6	.09993	30		.24504	22	.39015
6	7	.10267	31		.24778	23	.39289
7	8	.10541	Apr. 1		.25052	24	.39563
8	9	.10815	2		.25326	25	.39837
9	10	.11089	3		.25599	26	.40110
10	11	.11362	4		.25873	27	.40384
11	12	.11636	5		.26147	28	.40658
12	13	.11910	6		.26421	29	.40932
13	14	.12184	7		.26695	30	.41206
14	15	.12457	8		.26968	31	.41479
15	16	.12731	9		.27242	June 1	.41753
16	17	.13005	10		.27516	2	.42027
17	18	.13279	11		.27790	3	.42301
18	19	.13553	12		.28064	4	.42574
19	20	.13826	13		.28337	5	.42848
20	21	.14100	14		.28611	6	.43122
21	22	0.14374	15		0.28885	7	0.43396

For noon subtract 0.00137.

TABLE IV.—Fraction of the year elapsed from Jan. 0 in common years, Jan. 1 in bis-sextile years, to the midnight of each day of the year.

Day.	Fraction of year.	Day.	Fraction of year.	Day.	Fraction of year.	Day.	Fraction of year.
June 8	0.43670	July 30	0.57907	Sept. 20	0.72144	Nov. 11	0.86381
9	.43943	31	.58181	21	.72418	12	.86655
10	.44217	Aug. 1	.58454	22	.72691	13	.86929
11	.44491	2	.58728	23	.72965	14	.87202
12	.44765	3	.59002	24	.73239	15	.87476
13	.45039	4	.59276	25	.73513	16	.87750
14	.45312	5	.59550	26	.73787	17	.88024
15	.45586	6	.59823	27	.74060	18	.88298
16	.45860	7	.60097	28	.74334	19	.88571
17	.46134	8	.60371	29	.74608	20	.88845
18	.46408	9	.60645	30	.74882	21	.89119
19	.46681	10	.60918	Oct. 1	.75156	22	.89393
20	.46955	11	.61192	2	.75429	23	.89667
21	.47229	12	.61466	3	.75703	24	.89940
22	.47503	13	.61740	4	.75977	25	.90214
23	.47777	14	.62014	5	.76251	26	.90488
24	.48050	15	.62287	6	.76525	27	.90762
25	.48324	16	.62561	7	.76798	28	.91035
26	.48599	17	.62835	8	.77072	29	.91309
27	.48872	18	.63109	9	.77346	30	.91583
28	.49145	19	.63383	10	.77620	Dec. 1	.91857
29	.49419	20	.63656	11	.77894	2	.92131
30	.49693	21	.63930	12	.78167	3	.92404
July 1	.49967	22	.64204	13	.78441	4	.92678
2	.50241	23	.64478	14	.78715	5	.92952
3	.50514	24	.64752	15	.78989	6	.93226
4	.50788	25	.65025	16	.79262	7	.93500
5	.51062	26	.65299	17	.79536	8	.93773
6	.51336	27	.65573	18	.79810	9	.94047
7	.51610	28	.65847	19	.80084	10	.94321
8	.51883	29	.66121	20	.80358	11	.94595
9	.52157	30	.66394	21	.80631	12	.94869
10	.52431	31	.66668	22	.80905	13	.95142
11	.52705	Sept. 1	.66942	23	.81179	14	.95416
12	.52979	2	.67216	24	.81453	15	.95690
13	.53252	3	.67489	25	.81727	16	.95964
14	.53526	4	.67763	26	.82000	17	.96238
15	.53800	5	.68037	27	.82274	18	.96511
16	.54074	6	.68311	28	.82548	19	.96785
17	.54348	7	.68585	29	.82822	20	.97059
18	.54621	8	.68858	30	.83096	21	.97333
19	.54895	9	.69132	31	.83369	22	.97606
20	.55169	10	.69406	Nov. 1	.83643	23	.97880
21	.55443	11	.69680	2	.83917	24	.98154
22	.55716	12	.69954	3	.84191	25	.98428
23	.55990	13	.70227	4	.84465	26	.98702
24	.56264	14	.70501	5	.84738	27	.98975
25	.56538	15	.70775	6	.85012	28	.99249
26	.56812	16	.71049	7	.85286	29	.99523
27	.57085	17	.71323	8	.85560	30	0.99797
28	.57359	18	.71596	9	.85833	31	1.00071
29	0.57633	19	0.71870	10	0.86107	32	1.00344

For noon subtract 0.00137.

TABLE V.—Precession. Motion of Ecliptic.

Year.	ANNUAL PRECESSION.		m	m	n	$\log n$	π	M
	Lunisolar.	General.						
	''	''	''	s.	''		''	o ' ''
1750	50.3906	50.2298	46.0480	3.06987	20.0650	1.302439	0.4779	172 17 50
55	.3896	.2309	.0495	.06997	.0646	430	79	20 33
60	.3885	.2320	.0509	.07006	.0641	421	79	23 22
65	.3874	.2332	.0523	.07016	.0637	411	78	26 8
70	.3863	.2343	.0537	.07025	.0633	402	78	28 54
1775	50.3852	50.2354	46.0552	3.07035	20.0629	1.302393	0.4778	172 31 40
80	.3841	.2366	.0566	.07044	.0624	383	77	34 26
85	.3830	.2377	.0580	.07054	.0620	374	77	37 13
90	.3820	.2388	.0594	.07063	.0616	365	77	39 59
95	.3809	.2400	.0609	.07073	.0611	355	76	42 45
1800	50.3798	50.2411	46.0623	3.07082	20.0607	1.302346	0 4776	172 45 31
05	.3787	.2422	.0637	.07091	.0603	337	76	48 17
10	.3776	.2434	.0651	.07101	.0598	327	75	51 3
15	.3765	.2445	.0666	.07110	.0594	318	75	53 49
20	.3755	.2456	.0680	.07120	.0590	309	75	56 36
1825	50.3744	50.2468	46.0694	3.07129	20.0585	1.302299	0.4774	172 59 22
30	.3733	.2479	.0708	.07139	.0581	290	74	173 2 8
35	.3722	.2490	.6723	.07148	.0577	281	74	4 54
40	.3711	.2502	.0737	.07158	.0572	271	73	7 40
45	.3700	.2513	.0751	.07167	.0568	262	73	10 26
1850	50.3690	50.2524	46.0765	3.07177	20.0564	1.302253	0.4772	173 13 12
55	.3679	.2536	.0780	.07187	.0559	244	72	15 59
60	.3668	.2547	.0794	.07196	.0555	234	72	18 45
65	.3657	.2559	.0808	.07206	.0551	225	71	21 31
70	.3646	.2570	.0822	.07215	.0547	216	71	24 17
1875	50.3635	50.2581	46.0837	3.07225	20.0542	1.302206	0.4771	173 27 3
80	.3624	.2593	.0851	.07234	.0538	197	70	29 49
85	.3614	.2604	.0865	.07244	.0534	187	70	32 35
90	.3603	.2615	.0879	.07253	.0529	178	70	35 22
95	.3592	.2627	.0894	.07263	.0525	169	69	38 8
1900	50.3581	50.2638	46.0908	3.07272	20.0521	1.302159	0.4769	173 40 54

MOTION.

Yr.								
	''	''	''	s	''			' ''
1	−0.0002.2	+0.0002.3	+0.0002.8	+0.00001.9	−0.0000.9	−0.000002		+0 33
2	04.3	04.5	05.7	3.8	1.7	04		1 6
3	06.5	06.8	08.5	5.7	2.6	06		1 40
4	08.7	09.1	11.4	7.6	3.5	08		2 13
5	10.8	11.3	14.2	9.5	4.3	09		2 46
10	0.0021.7	0.0022.7	0.0028.5	0.00019.0	0.0008.6	0.000019		5 32

ANNUAL PRECESSION OF FIXED STARS.

In Right Ascension, $\Delta a = m + n \sin a \tan \delta$

In Declination, $\Delta \delta = n \cos a$

In Longitude, $\Delta \lambda = $ Gen. Prec. $+ \pi \cos (\lambda - M) \tan \beta$

In Latitude, $\Delta \beta = - \pi \sin (\lambda - M)$

TABLE VI.—Arguments of Aberration and Nutation; Mean Obliquity of the Ecliptic; Time from beginning of Fictitious year.

For Washington Mean Noon of Jan. 0 in common years, Jan. 1 in bissextile years.

Year.	Arguments—			Mean Ob'lquity of Ecliptic.	Time from beginning of fictitious year.		
	I.	II.	III.		In hours, &c. k	In days. k'	In years. k'
	d	d	d	o ' "	h m s	d	y
1750	1.921	2.0	+1505.09	23 28 17.44	+ 5 31 58.0	+0.231	+0.00063
1751	1.679	2 0	1370.09	16.98	— 0 16 50.1	—0.012	—0.00003
1752 B	2.436	2.0	2236.09	16.51	+17 54 21.8	+0.746	+0.00204
1753	2.193	2.1	2601.09	16.05	12 5 33.7	0.504	.00138
1754	1.950	2.1	2966.09	15.58	6 16 45.6	0.262	.00072
1755	1.707	2.1	+3331.09	23 28 15.12	0 27 57.6	0.019	.00005
1756 B	2.465	2.1	—3101.30	14.65	18 39 9.5	0.777	.00213
1757	2.222	2.1	2736.30	14.19	12 50 21.4	0.535	.00146
1758	1.979	2.1	2371.30	13.72	7 1 33.3	0.293	.00080
1759	1.736	2.1	2006.30	13.26	1 12 45.3	0.051	.00014
1760 B	2.493	2.1	1640.30	23 28 12.80	19 23 57.2	0.808	.00222
1761	2.251	2.1	1275.30	12.34	13 35 9.2	0.566	.00155
1762	2.008	2.1	910.30	11.87	7 46 21.1	0.324	.00089
1763	1.765	2.1	545.30	11.41	1 57 33.1	0.082	.00022
1764 B	2.522	2.1	— 179.30 ·	10.94	20 8 45.1	0.839	.00230
1765	2.279	2.1	+ 185.70	23 28 10.48	14 19 57.1	0.597	.00164
1766	2.037	2.1	550.70	10.01	8 31 9.0	0.355	.00097
1767	1.794	2.1	915.70	9.55	2 42 21.0	0.113	.00031
1768 B	2.551	2.1	1281.70	9.08	20 53 33.0	0.871	.00238
1769	2.308	2.1	1646.70	8.62	15 4 45.0	0.628	.00172
1770	2.065	2.1	2011.70	23 28 8.15	9 15 57.0	0.386	.00106
1771	1.823	2.1	2376.70	7.69	3 27 9.0	0.144	.00039
1772 B	2.580	2.2	2742.70	7.22	21 38 21.1	0.902	.00247
1773	2.337	2.2	+3107.70	6.76	15 49 33.1	0.659	.00181
1774	2.094	2.2	—3325.69	6.29	10 0 45.1	0.417	.00114
1775	1.851	2.2	2960.69	23 28 5.63	4 11 57.2	0.175	.00048
1776 B	2.609	2.2	2594.69	5.36	22 23 9.2	0.933	.00255
1777	2.366	2.2	2229.69	4.90	16 34 21.2	0.691	.00189
1778	2.123	2.2	1864.69	4.43	10 45 33.3	0.448	.00123
1779	1.880	2.2	1499.69	3.97	4 56 45.4	0.206	.00057
1780 B	2.637	2.2	1133.69	23 28 3.51	23 7 57.4	0 964	.00264
1781	2.395	2.2	768.69	3.05	17 19 9.5	0.722	.00198
1782	2.152	2.2	403.69	2.58	11 30 21.6	0.479	.00131
1783	1.909	2.2	— 38.69	2.12	5 41 33.7	0.237	.00065
1784 B	2.666	2.2	+ 327.31	1.65	23 52 45.8	0.995	.00272
1785	2.423	2.2	692.31	23 28 1.19	18 3 57.8	0.753	.00206
1786	2.181	2.2	1057.31	0.72	12 15 9.9	0.511	.00140
1787	1.938	2.2	1422.31	23 28 0.26	6 26 22.1	0.268	.00074
1788 B	2.695	2.2	1788.31	23 27 50.79	24 37 34.2	1.026	.00281
1789	2.452	2.2	2153.31	59.33	18 48 46.3	0.784	.00215
1790	2.209	2.2	2518.31	23 27 58.86	12 59 58.4	0.542	.00148
1791	1.967	2.3	2883.31	58.40	7 11 10.5	0.299	.00082
1792 B	2.724	2.3	+3249.31	57.93	25 22 22.7	1.057	.00290
1793	2.481	2.3	—3184.08	57.47	19 33 34.8	0.815	.00223
1794	2.238	2.3	2819.08	57.00	13 44 47.0	0.573	.00157
1795	1.995	2.3	2454.08	23 27 56.54	7 55 59.1	0.331	.00091
1796 B	2.753	2.3	2089.08	56.07	26 7 11.3	1.088	.00208
1797	2.510	2.3	1723.08	55.61	20 18 23.5	0.846	.00232
1798	2.267	2.3	1358.08	55.14	14 29 35.6	0.604	.00165
1799	2.024	2.3	— 993.08	23 27 54.63	+ 8 40 47.8	+0.362	+0.00099

TABLE VI.—Arguments of Aberration and Nutation; Mean Obliquity of the Ecliptic; Time from beginning of Fictitious year.

For Washington Mean Noon of Jan. 0 in common years, Jan. 1 in bissextile years.

Year.	Arguments—			Mean Obliquity of Ecliptic.	Time from beginning of fictitious year.		
	I.	II.	III.		In hours, &c. k	In days. k'	In years. k''
	d	d	d	° ′ ″	h m s	d	y
1800	1.781	2.3	− 628.08	23 27 54.22	+ 2 52 0.0	+0.119	+0.00033
1801	1.539	2.3	− 263.08	53.76	− 2 56 47.8	−0.123	− .00033
1802	1.296	2.3	+ 101.93	53.29	− 8 45 35.6	−0.365	− .00100
1803	1.053	2.3	466.93	52.83	−14 34 23.4	−0.607	− .00166
1804 B	1.810	2.3	832.93	52.36	+ 3 36 48.8	+0.151	+ .00041
1805	1.568	2.3	1197.93	23 27 51.90	− 2 11 59.0	−0.092	− .00025
1806	1.325	2.3	1562.93	51.43	− 8 0 46.8	−0.334	− .00091
1807	1.082	2.3	1927.93	50.97	−13 49 34.5	−0.576	− .00158
1808 B	1.839	2.3	2293.93	50.50	+ 4 21 37.7	+0.182	+ .00050
1809	1.596	2.4	2658.93	50.04	− 1 27 10.1	−0.061	− .00016
1810	1.354	2.4	3023.93	23 27 49.58	− 7 15 57.8	−0.303	− .00083
1811	1.111	2.4	+3388.93	49.12	−13 4 45.6	−0.545	− .00149
1812 B	1.868	2.4	−3043.46	48.65	+ 5 6 26.7	+0.213	+ .00058
1813	1.625	2.4	2678.46	48.19	− 0 42 21.1	−0.029	− .00008
1814	1.382	2.4	2313.46	47.72	− 6 31 8.8	−0.272	− .00074
1815	1.140	2.4	1948.46	23 27 47.26	−12 19 56.5	−0.514	− .00140
1816 B	1.897	2.4	1582.46	46.79	+ 5 51 15.8	+0.244	+ .00067
1817	1.654	2.4	1217.46	46.33	+ 0 2 28.1	+0.002	+ .00001
1818	1.411	2.4	852.46	45.86	− 5 46 19.6	−0.241	− .00066
1819	1.168	2.4	487.46	45.40	−11 35 7.3	−0.483	− .00132
1820 B	1.926	2.4	− 121.46	23 27 44.93	+ 6 36 5.0	+0.275	+ .00076
1821	1.683	2.4	+ 243.55	44.46	+ 0 47 17.3	+0.033	+ .00009
1822	1.440	2.4	608.55	44.00	− 5 1 30.4	−0.209	− .00057
1823	1.197	2.4	973.55	43.54	−10 50 18.1	−0.452	− .00124
1824 B	1.955	2.4	1339.55	43.07	+ 7 20 54.2	+0.306	+ .00084
1825	1.712	2.4	1704.55	23 27 42.61	+ 1 32 6.6	+0.064	+ .00017
1826	1.469	2.4	2069.55	42.14	− 4 16 41.1	−0.178	− .00049
1827	1.226	2.4	2434.55	41.68	−10 5 28.7	−0.420	− .00115
1828 B	1.984	2.5	2800.55	41.21	+ 8 5 43.6	+0.337	+ .00092
1829	1.741	2.5	+3165.55	40.75	+ 2 16 56.0	+0.095	+ .00026
1830	1.498	2.5	−3267.84	23 27 40.29	− 3 31 51.7	−0.147	− .00040
1831	1.255	2.5	2902.84	39.83	− 9 20 39.3	−0.389	− .00107
1832 B	2.012	2.5	2536.84	39.36	+ 8 50 33.1	+0.368	+ .00101
1833	1.770	2.5	2171.84	38.90	+ 3 1 45.5	+0.126	+ .00035
1834	1.527	2.5	1806.84	38.43	− 2 47 2.1	−0.116	− .00032
1835	1.284	2.5	1441.84	23 27 37.97	− 8 35 49.8	−0.358	− .00098
1836 B	2.041	2.5	1075.84	37.50	+ 9 35 22.6	+0.400	+ .00109
1837	1.799	2.5	710.84	37.04	+ 3 46 35.0	+0.157	+ .00043
1838	1.556	2.5	− 345.84	36.57	− 2 2 12.6	−0.085	− .00023
1839	1.313	2.5	+ 19.17	36.11	− 7 51 0.1	−0.327	− .00090
1840 B	2.070	2.5	385.17	23 27 35.64	+10 20 12.3	+0.431	+ .00118
1841	1.827	2.5	750.17	35.18	+ 4 31 24.7	+0.188	+ .00052
1842	1.585	2.5	1115.17	34.71	− 1 17 22.9	−0.054	− .00015
1843	1.342	2.5	1480.17	34.25	− 7 6 10.4	−0.296	− .00081
1844 B	2.099	2.5	1846.17	33.78	+11 5 2.0	+0.462	+ .00126
1845	1.856	2.5	2211.17	23 27 33.32	+ 5 16 14.5	+0.220	+ .00060
1846	1.614	2.5	2576.17	32.85	− 0 32 33.1	−0.023	− .00006
1847	1.371	2.6	2941.17	32 39	− 6 21 20.6	−0.265	− .00072
1848 B	2.128	2.6	+3307.17	31.92	+11 49 51.9	+0.493	+ .00135
1849	1.885	2.6	−3126.22	23 27 31.46	+ 6 1 4.4	+0.251	+0.00069

TABLE VI.—Arguments of Aberration and Nutation; Mean Obliquity of the Ecliptic; Time from beginning of Fictitious year.

For Washington Mean Noon of Jan. 0 in common years, Jan. 1 in bissextile years.

Year.	Arguments—			Mean Obliquity of Ecliptic.	Time from beginning of fictitious year.		
	I.	II.	III.		In hours, &c. k	In days. k'	In years. k''
	d	d	d	° ′ ″	h m s	d	y
1850	1.642	2.6	−2761.22	23 27 31.00	+ 0 12 16.8	+0.009	+0.00002
1851	1.400	2.6	2396.22	30.54	− 5 36 30.7	−0.234	− .00064
1852 B	2.157	2.6	2030.22	30.07	+12 34 41.8	+0.524	+ .00144
1853	1.914	2.6	1665.22	29.61	+ 6 45 54.3	+0.282	+ .00077
1854	1.671	2.6	1300.22	29.14	+ 0 57 6.7	+0.040	+ .00011
1855	1.429	2.6	935.22	23 27 28.68	− 4 51 40.7	−0.203	− .00055
1856 B	2.186	2.6	569.22	28.21	+13 19 31.9	+0.555	+ .00152
1857	1.943	2.6	− 204.22	27.75	+ 7 30 44.4	+0.313	+ .00086
1858	1.700	2.6	+ 160.78	27.28	+ 1 41 56.9	+0.071	+ .00019
1859	1.457	2.6	525.78	26.82	− 4 6 50.6	−0.171	− .00047
1860 B	2.215	2.6	891.78	23 27 26.35	+14 4 22.0	+0.586	+ .00161
1861	1.972	2.6	1256.78	25.89	+ 8 15 34.5	+0.344	+ .00094
1862	1.729	2.6	1621.78	25.42	+ 2 26 47.1	+0.102	+ .00028
1863	1.486	2.6	1986.78	24.96	− 3 22 0.4	−0.140	− .00038
1864 B	2.244	2.6	2352.78	24.49	+14 49 12.2	+0.618	+ .00169
1865	2.001	2.6	2717.78	23 27 24.03	+ 9 0 24.8	+0.375	+ .00103
1866	1.758	2.7	+3082.78	23.56	+ 3 11 37.4	+0.133	+ .00036
1867	1.515	2.7	−3350.61	23.10	− 2 37 10.1	−0.109	− .00030
1868 B	2.273	2.7	2984.61	22.63	+15 34 2.5	+0.649	+ .00178
1869	2.030	2.7	2619.61	22.17	+ 9 45 15.1	+0.406	+ .00111
1870	1.787	2.7	2254.61	23 27 21.71	+ 3 56 27.7	+0.164	+ .00045
1871	1.544	2.7	1889.61	21.25	− 1 52 19.7	−0.078	− .00021
1872 B	2.301	2.7	1523.61	20.78	+16 18 53.0	+0.680	+ .00186
1873	2.059	2.7	1158.61	20.32	+10 30 5.6	+0.438	+ .00120
1874	1.816	2.7	793.61	19.85	+ 4 41 18.2	+0.195	+ .00054
1875	1.573	2.7	428.61	23 27 19.39	− 1 7 29.2	−0.047	− .00013
1876 B	2.330	2.7	− 62.61	18.92	+17 3 43.5	+0.711	+ .00195
1877	2.088	2.7	+ 302.40	18.46	+11 14 56.1	+0.469	+ .00128
1878	1.845	2.7	667.40	17.99	+ 5 26 8.8	+0.226	+ .00062
1879	1.602	2.7	1032.40	17.53	− 0 22 38.6	−0.016	− .00004
1880 B	2.359	2.7	1398.40	23 27 17.06	+17 48 34.1	+0.742	+ .00203
1881	2.117	2.7	1763.40	16.60	+11 59 46.7	+0.500	+ .00137
1882	1.874	2.7	2128.40	16.13	+ 6 10 59.4	+0.258	+ .00071
1883	1.631	2.7	2493.40	15.67	+ 0 22 12.1	+0.015	+ .00004
1884 B	2.388	2.7	2859.40	15.20	+18 33 24.8	+0.773	+ .00212
1885	2 145	2.8	+3224.40	23 27 14.74	+12 44 37.5	+0.531	+ .00145
1886	1.903	2.8	−3208.99	14.27	+ 6 55 50.2	+0.289	+ .00079
1887	1.660	2.8	2843.99	13.81	+ 1 7 2.9	+0.047	+ .00013
1888 B	2.417	2.8	2477.99	13.34	+19 18 15.6	+0.804	+ .00220
1889	2.174	2.8	2112.99	12.88	+13 29 28.3	+0.562	+ .00154
1890	1.931	2.8	1747.99	23 27 12.42	+ 7 40 41.0	+0.320	+ .00088
1891	1.689	2.8	1382.99	11.96	+ 1 51 53.7	+0.078	+ .00022
1892 B	2.446	2.8	1016.99	11.49	+20 3 6.5	+0.835	+ .00229
1893	2.203	2.8	651.99	11.03	+14 14 19.2	+0.593	+ .00163
1894	1.960	2.8	− 286.99	10.56	+ 8 25 32.0	+0.351	+ .00096
1895	1.718	2.8	+ 78.00	23 27 10.10	+ 2 36 44.7	+0.109	+ .00030
1896 B	2.475	2.8	444.00	9.63	+20 47 57.5	+0.867	+ .00237
1897	2 232	2.8	809.00	9.17	+14 59 10.2	+0.624	+ .00171
1898	1.989	2.8	1174.00	8.70	+ 9 10 23.0	+0.382	+ .00105
1899	1.747	2.8	1539.00	8.24	+ 3 21 35.8	+0.140	+ .00039
1900	1.504	2.8	+1904.00	23 27 7.77	− 2 27 11.5	−0.102	− 0.00028

TABLE VII.—1850.

Secular Inequality of Arg. I: . . . . Arg. = Arg. II + d' + day of year.

Precession for each 10 days: . . . . Arg. = Number of days.

Aberration of the Sun's Longitude: · } Arg. = Arg. I + d' + Sec. Ineq. + day of year.
Solar Nutation: . . . . }

Days.	Sec. Ineq. of Arg. I.	Precession.	Aberration of the Sun in Long.	Solar Nutation.					
				In Long.	Diff. for 10 d.	In R. As'n.	Diff. for 10 d.	Variation of Obliquity.	Diff. for 10 d.
		''	''	''	''	s	s	''	''
0	.000,01	0.000	—20.79	+0.37	+.44	+0.022	+.027	—0.54	+.05
10	,00	1.376	.78	0.79	.38	.048	23	.46	.10
20	,02	2.752	.77	1.12	.27	.060	16	.33	.15
30	,05	4.128	.75	1.32	+.12	.081	+ 7	—0.16	.18
40	,10	5.503	.71	1.35	—.04	.083	— 3	+0.02	.17
50	.000,16	6.879	—20.67	+1.23	.19	+0.076	12	+0.19	.15
60	,23	8.255	.62	0.97	.31	.060	20	.33	.11
70	,32	9.631	.57	0.61	.39	.037	25	.42	+.06
80	,41	11.007	.51	+0.19	.42	+0.011	26	.45	.00
90	,51	12.383	.45	—0.24	.41	—0.015	25	.41	—.07
100	.000,61	13.758	—20.39	0.63	.35	—0.039	21	+0.31	.12
110	,71	15.134	.34	0.93	.24	.057	15	+0.16	.16
120	,81	16.510	.28	1.11	—.11	.068	— 6	—0.02	.19
130	,90	17.886	.24	1.15	+.03	.070	+ 2	.22	.20
140	,98	19.262	.19	1.05	.16	.064	10	.41	.18
150	.001,04	20.638	—20.16	—0.83	.27	—0.051	17	—0.57	.14
160	1,10	22.013	.13	0.51	.35	.031	21	.69	.09
170	1,14	23.389	.11	—0.13	.39	—0.008	23	.75	—.03
180	1,16	24.765	.10	+0.27	.38	+0.016	23	.76	+.02
190	1,17	26.141	.10	0.63	.33	.039	20	.71	.08
200	.001,16	27.517	—20.11	+0.93	.25	+0.057	15	—0.60	.12
210	1.14	28.893	.13	1.12	+.13	.068	+ 8	.46	.15
220	1,09	30.268	.16	1.18	—.01	.072	0	.29	.17
230	1,04	31.644	.20	1.10	.14	.067	— 8	—0.12	.16
240	0,97	33.020	.24	0.89	.26	.055	16	+0.03	.13
250	.000,89	34.396	—20.29	+0.57	.36	+0.035	22	+0.14	.08
260	,80	35.772	.31	+0.17	.41	+0.010	26	.20	+.03
270	,70	37.148	.40	—0.26	.42	—0.016	26	.20	—.03
280	,60	38.524	.46	0.68	.39	.042	23	.14	.09
290	,50	39.899	.52	1.04	.30	.063	18	+0.02	.14
300	.000,40	41.275	—20.58	—1.28	.18	—0.078	11	—0.15	.18
310	,31	42.651	.63	1.38	—.03	.085	— 2	.35	.20
320	,23	44.027	.68	1.33	+.13	.081	+ 8	.56	.19
330	,15	45.403	.72	1.12	.27	.069	16	.74	.16
340	,09	46.779	.75	0.78	.38	.048	23	.89	.12
350	.000,05	48.154	—20.77	—0.35	.45	—0.022	27	—0.99	—.06
360	,02	49.530	.79	+0.12	.47	+0.007	28	1.01	+.01
370	.000,00	50.906	—20.79	+0.58	+.43	+0.035	+.026	—0.97	+.07

The secular Inequality of Arg. I is to be multiplied by (t — 1850).

The variation of the mean Obliquity, — 0.4645 τ, is combined with the nutation.

TABLE VIII.—Lunar Nutation.—1850.0

$$\text{Arg} = \text{Arg. III} + d' + \text{day of year} - 6793.39.^{*}$$

Days	In Long.	Diff. for 100 d.	In R. A.	Diff. for 100 d.	Of Obliquity	Diff. for 100 d.
	$''$	$''$	s	s	$''$	$''$
0	+0.00	+1.55	+0.000	+.095	+9.13	−.00
100	1.55	1.55	0.095	94	9.10	.08
200	3.10	1.53	0.189	94	8.95	.15
300	4.61	1.50	0.282	92	8.80	.23
400	6.09	1.46	0.373	89	8.53	.30
500	7.53	1.41	0.460	86	8.20	.37
600	8.90	1.34	0.544	82	7.80	.43
700	10.20	1.26	0.624	77	7.34	.50
800	11.42	1.17	0.698	72	6.81	.56
900	12.54	1.08	0.767	66	6.22	.62
1000	13.57	0.97	0.830	60	5.58	.67
1100	14.48	0.85	0.886	52	4.89	.71
1200	15.27	0.74	0.934	45	4.16	.75
1300	15.95	0.61	0.975	37	3.40	.78
1400	16.48	0.47	1.008	29	2.60	.81
1500	16.83	0.33	1.033	20	1.78	.83
1600	17.14	0.19	1.048	11	0.94	.84
1700	17.25	+0.04	1.055	+ 2	+0.09	.85
1800	17.21	−0.11	1.053	− 7	−0.77	.85
1900	17.03	0.26	1.041	16	1.62	.84
2000	16.70	0.41	1.021	25	2.45	.83
2100	16.22	0.55	0.992	34	3.27	.81
2200	15.60	0.69	0.954	42	4.06	.78
2300	14.85	0.82	0.908	50	4.82	.74
2400	13.96	0.95	0.854	58	5.54	.70
2500	12.95	1.07	0.792	66	6.21	.65
2600	11.82	1.18	0.723	73	6.83	.59
2700	10.59	1.28	0.647	79	7.39	.53
2800	9.26	1.38	0.566	84	7.89	.46
2900	7.84	1.45	0.480	88	8.31	.39
3000	6.36	1.51	0.389	92	8.67	.32
3100	4.82	1.57	0.295	96	8.95	.24
3200	3.23	1.60	0.198	98	9.15	.16
3300	+1.62	1.62	+0.099	99	9.27	.08
3400	−0.01	1.63	−0.001	.100	9.31	−.00
3500	1.64	1.63	0.100	.099	9.27	+.08
3600	3.26	1.60	0.199	98	9.15	.16
3700	4.84	1.57	0.296	96	8.95	.24
3800	6.39	1.52	0.391	92	8.66	.32
3900	−7.88	−1.45	−0.482	−.088	−8.30	+.39

When the Arg. is negative the sign of the nutation in Long. and R. A. must be changed; the sign of the nutation of the Obliquity remains the same.

TABLE IX.—Coefficients and Auxiliaries for computing A, B and E.

Year	For A		For B	
	Coef. of sin Ω	K	Coef. of cos Ω	K'.
		$°$ $'$		$°$ $'$
1750	−.34106	83 45	−9.2226	278 37
1760	109	83 38	27	278 48
1770	112	83 31	28	278 58
1780	115	83 24	29	279 9
1790	118	83 17	30	279 19
1800	221	83 10	−9.2231	279 29
1810	224	83 2	32	279 40
1820	227	82 55	33	279 50
1830	230	82 48	33	280 0
1840	233	82 41	34	280 11
1850	236	82 34	−9.2235	280 21
1860	239	82 27	36	280 31
1870	242	82 19	37	280 42
1880	246	82 12	38	280 52
1890	249	82 4	39	281 3
1900	−.34252	81 57	−9.2240	281 13

Year	Coef. of sin 2Ω	Coef. of sin (☉ + K)	Coef. of cos 2Ω	Coef. of cos (☉ + K')
		$''$	$''$	
1750		+.00296	+0.0897	−0.0693
1800	+.00410	205	96	93
1850		294	96	93
1900		293	95	92

Year	Coef. of sin 2☉	Coef. of sin 2☽	Coef. of cos 2☉	Coef. of cos 2☽
			$''$	$''$
1750			−0.5510	−0.0886
1800	−.02519	−.00405	09	86
1850			08	85
1900			06	85

Year	For E			For A
	Coef. of sin Ω	Coef. of sin 2Ω	Coef. of sin 2☉	Coef. of sin (☽ − Γ')
	$''$	$''$	$''$	
1750	−0.0553	+0.0015	−0.0040	+.0135
1800	518	15	37	
1850	483	14	35	
1900	449	14	32	

* The last term is used when Arg. > 3900/d.

14 GENERAL TABLES.

TABLE X.—The Quantities A☉ and B☉.—1850.0.

$$A_\odot = -0.02519 \sin 2\,\odot + 0.00294 \sin (\odot + 82°\,34').$$
$$B_\odot = -0''.5508 \cos 2\,\odot - 0''.0093 \cos (\odot + 280°\,21').$$

Arg. = Arg. I + d' + Inequal. + day of year.

Arg.	A☉	B☉	Arg.	A☉	B☉	Arg.	A☉	B☉	Arg.	A☉	B☉
0	+.00726	+0″.5364	55	+.02223	−0″.3388	110	−.01845	−0″.3034	165	−.00644	+0″.5183
1	.00817	.5304	56	.02171	.3538	111	.01892	.2876	166	.00567	.5233
2	.00907	.5238	57	.02114	.3636	112	.01937	.2714	167	.00491	.5277
3	.00995	.5165	58	.02056	.3827	113	.01979	.2549	168	.00414	.5315
4	.01082	.5085	59	.01996	.3965	114	.02018	.2382	169	.00336	.5346
5	.01168	.4998	60	.01934	.4096	115	.02055	.2212	170	.00258	.5372
6	.01253	.4906	61	.01869	.4224	116	.02090	.2040	171	.00179	.5392
7	.01336	.4808	62	.01802	.4346	117	.02121	.1866	172	.00100	.5407
8	.01417	.4703	63	.01735	.4463	118	.02149	.1689	173	−.00021	.5415
9	.01496	.4592	64	.01663	.4574	119	.02176	.1511	174	+.00058	.5417
10	.01574	.4477	65	.01592	.4680	120	.02199	.1331	175	.00137	.5413
11	.01649	.4355	66	.01518	.4779	121	.02220	.1149	176	.00216	.5402
12	.01724	.4228	67	.01442	.4873	122	.02237	.0967	177	.00294	.5386
13	.01795	.4096	68	.01365	.4961	123	.02253	.0784	178	.00373	.5362
14	.01863	.3958	69	.01287	.5043	124	.02266	.0600	179	.00451	.5335
15	.01931	.3816	70	.01209	.5118	125	.02276	.0415	180	.00528	.5300
16	.01996	.3669	71	.01128	.5188	126	.02282	.0230	181	.00604	.5259
17	.02058	.3517	72	.01047	.5251	127	.02286	−0.0045	182	.00680	.5213
18	.02118	.3362	73	.00964	.5307	128	.02287	+0.0140	183	.00756	.5160
19	.02175	.3202	74	.00880	.5357	129	.02286	.0324	184	.00830	.5103
20	.02229	.3038	75	.00797	.5401	130	.02282	.0509	185	.00904	.5039
21	.02280	.2870	76	.00712	.5438	131	.02274	.0692	186	.00976	.4970
22	.02330	.2699	77	.00627	.5468	132	.02264	.0874	187	.01048	.4895
23	.02375	.2525	78	.00541	.5493	133	.02252	.1056	188	.01118	.4815
24	.02419	.2346	79	.00454	.5511	134	.02236	.1237	189	.01188	.4729
25	.02459	.2166	80	.00368	.5522	135	.02217	.1414	190	.01256	.4637
26	.02497	.1983	81	.00282	.5525	136	.02196	.1591	191	.01321	.4541
27	.02530	.1798	82	.00195	.5522	137	.02173	.1765	192	.01386	.4440
28	.02562	.1610	83	.00108	.5513	138	.02147	.1938	193	.01450	.4331
29	.02590	.1421	84	+.00022	.5497	139	.02117	.2108	194	.01511	.4222
30	.02615	.1229	85	−.00064	.5475	140	.02087	.2277	195	.01571	.4106
31	.02636	.1036	86	.00149	.5446	141	.02053	.2442	196	.01630	.3986
32	.02655	.0844	87	.00235	.5411	142	.02017	.2604	197	.01686	.3851
33	.02671	.0648	88	.00319	.5370	143	.01978	.2763	198	.01739	.3732
34	.02683	.0452	89	.00403	.5322	144	.01938	.2919	199	.01792	.3599
35	.02692	.0257	90	.00486	.5267	145	.01895	.3071	200	.01843	.3460
36	.02698	+0.0061	91	.00568	.5207	146	.01849	.3220	201	.01890	.3319
37	.02700	−0.0135	92	.00650	.5141	147	.01801	.3365	202	.01936	.3174
38	.02700	.0331	93	.00730	.5068	148	.01752	.3506	203	.01979	.3024
39	.02696	.0526	94	.00808	.4991	149	.01700	.3644	204	.02021	.2872
40	.02689	.0721	95	.00886	.4905	150	.01646	.3776	205	.02060	.2716
41	.02679	.0914	96	.00963	.4816	151	.01590	.3905	206	.02097	.2557
42	.02666	.1106	97	.01038	.4720	152	.01532	.4029	207	.02131	.2395
43	.02649	.1299	98	.01111	.4618	153	.01472	.4148	208	.02162	.2230
44	.02630	.1486	99	.01183	.4512	154	.01410	.4234	209	.02191	.2062
45	.02607	.1674	100	.01253	.4400	155	.01349	.4374	210	.02219	.1893
46	.02583	.1859	101	.01321	.4284	156	.01284	.4479	211	.02243	.1721
47	.02553	.2041	102	.01388	.4163	157	.01219	.4589	212	.02264	.1517
48	.02521	.2221	103	.01452	.4036	158	.01151	.4674	213	.02284	.1372
49	.02487	.2399	104	.01514	.3906	159	.01081	.4763	214	.02301	.1196
50	.02451	.2572	105	.01575	.3771	160	.01010	.4848	215	.02314	.1016
51	.02410	.2743	106	.01635	.3631	161	.00939	.4926	216	.02325	.0836
52	.02367	.2910	107	.01690	.3487	162	.00867	.4999	217	.02333	.0655
53	.02322	.3073	108	.01744	.3340	163	.00793	.5066	218	.02339	.0474
54	.02274	.3233	109	.01796	.3188	164	.00719	.5127	219	.02342	.0291
55	+.02223	−0.3388	110	−.01845	−0.3034	165	−.00644	+0.5183	220	+.02342	+0.0108

TABLE X.—The Quantities A☉ and B☉.—1850.0.

$$A_\odot = -\,0.02519 \sin 2\odot + 0.00294 \sin (\odot + 82°\,34').$$
$$B_\odot = -\,0''.5508 \cos 2\odot - 0''.0093 \cos (\odot + 280°\,21').$$

Arg. = Arg. I + d' + Inequal. + day of year.

Arg.	A☉	B☉	Arg.	A☉	B☉	Arg.	A☉	B☉	Arg.	A☉	B☉
220	+.02342	+0″.0108	259	+.00423	−0″.5283	298	−.02465	−0″.2640	337	−.01784	+0″.4259
221	.02339	−0.0075	260	.00339	.5330	299	.02505	.2470	338	.01710	.4334
222	.02335	.0258	261	.00255	.5372	300	.02542	.2297	339	.01635	.4503
223	.02326	.0441	262	.00169	.5407	301	.02575	.2121	340	.01558	.4617
224	.02314	.0624	263	+.00083	.5437	302	.02606	.1942	341	.01479	.4726
225	.02300	.0807	264	−.00003	.5460	303	.02635	.1761	342	.01399	.4829
226	.02283	.0986	265	.00089	.5477	304	.02661	.1577	343	.01316	.4925
227	.02263	.1167	266	.00176	.5487	305	.02683	.1391	344	.01232	.5016
228	.02242	.1346	267	.00263	.5490	306	.02703	.1204	345	.01146	.5101
229	.02216	.1523	268	.00350	.5488	307	.02719	.1015	346	.01060	.5179
230	.02188	.1699	269	.00437	.5479	308	.02732	.0824	347	.00971	.5250
231	.02158	.1873	270	.00522	.5463	309	.02742	.0633	348	.00882	.5315
232	.02125	.2045	271	.00609	.5441	310	.02749	.0440	349	.00792	.5374
233	.02089	.2215	272	.00695	.5413	311	.02752	.0246	350	.00700	.5426
234	.02052	.2382	273	.00780	.5379	312	.02753	−0.0052	351	.00609	.5472
235	.02012	.2547	274	.00864	.5337	313	.02750	+0.0142	352	.00515	.5510
236	.01968	.2709	275	.00948	.5290	314	.02745	.0336	353	.00422	.5542
237	.01923	.2868	276	.01031	.5236	315	.02736	.0530	354	.00328	.5567
238	.01875	.3024	277	.01113	.5176	316	.02723	.0724	355	.00234	.5585
239	.01825	.3177	278	.01195	.5110	317	.02707	.0916	356	.00140	.5595
240	.01772	.3326	279	.01275	.5037	318	.02687	.1107	357	−.00045	.5599
241	.01718	.3471	280	.01354	.4959	319	.02668	.1297	358	+.00050	.5595
242	.01661	.3613	281	.01432	.4874	320	.02643	.1487	359	.00145	.5585
243	.01601	.3750	282	.01508	.4784	321	.02615	.1674	360	.00239	.5568
244	.01540	.3884	283	.01583	.4688	322	.02584	.1860	361	.00333	.5544
245	.01478	.4012	284	.01656	.4586	323	.02550	.2043	362	.00426	.5512
246	.01413	.4137	285	.01727	.4480	324	.02513	.2223	363	.00521	.5475
247	.01345	.4256	286	.01797	.4367	325	.02474	.2402	364	.00613	.5430
248	.01276	.4371	287	.01864	.4248	326	.02431	.2577	365	.00704	.5378
249	.01206	.4482	288	.01931	.4125	327	.02386	.2750	366	.00795	.5320
250	.01133	.4586	289	.01995	.3997	328	.02337	.2918	367	.00885	.5255
251	.01060	.4686	290	.02056	.3864	329	.02286	.3084	368	.00974	.5183
252	.00985	.4781	291	.02115	.3725	330	.02232	.3246	369	.01061	.5105
253	.00908	.4869	292	.02173	.3583	331	.02175	.3404	370	.01148	.5019
254	.00830	.4954	293	.02228	.3436	332	.02117	.3557	371	.01233	.4929
255	.00751	.5031	294	.02281	.3284	333	.02055	.3707	372	.01316	.4832
256	.00671	.5102	295	.02331	.3130	334	.01990	.3853	373	.01398	.4729
257	.00589	.5168	296	.02378	.2970	335	.01923	.3993	374	+.01477	+0.4619
258	.00506	.5227	297	.02423	.2806	336	.01855	.4128			
259	+.00423	−0.5283	298	−.02465	−0.2640	337	−.01784	+0.4259			

TABLE XI.

Secular Variation of A☉ and B☉, to be multiplied by $\dfrac{t-1850}{100}$. Argument the same as for Table X.

Arg.	δA☉	δB☉	Arg.	δA☉	δB☉	Arg.	δA☉	δB☉	Arg.	δA☉	δB☉
0	−.00006	−0″.0005	100	−.00001	0″.0000	200	+.00007	+0″.0001	300	−.00001	+0″.0003
10	7	5	110	0	0	210	7	2	310	2	+0.0001
20	7	4	120	+.00002	0	220	6	3	320	3	0
30	6	3	130	3	−0.0001	230	6	4	330	4	−0.0002
40	6	3	140	4	1	240	5	5	340	5	3
50	5	2	150	5	2	250	4	5	350	6	4
60	5	−0.0001	160	5	2	260	3	6	360	6	5
70	4	0	170	6	2	270	3	6	370	−.00006	−0.0005
80	3	0	180	6	−0.0001	280	+.00001	5			
90	−.00002	+0.0001	190	+.00007	0.0000	290	.00000	+0.0004			

16 GENERAL TABLES.

TABLE XII.—The Quantities A_Ω and B_Ω.—1850.0.

$$A_\Omega = -0.34236 \sin \Omega + 0.00410 \sin 2\Omega. \qquad B_\Omega = -9''.22355 \cos \Omega + 0''.08955 \cos 2\Omega.$$

Arg. = Arg. III + d' + day of year—6798.39.*

	0		100		200		300	
	A_Ω	B_Ω	A_Ω	B_Ω	A_Ω	B_Ω	A_Ω	B_Ω
		''		''		''		''
0	+.00000	−9.1340	+.03085	−9.0962	+.06145	−8.9830	+.09156	−8.7952
1	00031	1340	03116	(954	06175	9815	09186	7929
2	00062	1340	03147	(947	06206	9800	09216	7907
3	00092	1339	03177	0939	06236	9785	09245	7884
4	00123	1339	03208	(931	06267	9769	09275	7862
5	00154	1339	03239	0923	06297	9754	09305	7839
6	00185	1339	03270	0915	06327	9738	09335	7816
7	00216	1338	03300	0907	06358	9723	09365	7793
8	00247	1338	03331	0899	06388	9707	09394	7770
9	00278	1337	03361	0890	06419	9692	09424	7747
10	00309	1336	03392	0882	06449	9676	09454	7724
11	00340	1335	03423	0874	06479	9660	09484	7701
12	00371	1334	03454	0865	06509	9644	09513	7677
13	00401	1333	03484	0857	06540	9628	09543	7654
14	00432	1332	03515	0848	06570	9612	09572	7630
15	00463	1331	03546	0840	06600	9596	09602	7607
16	00494	1330	03577	0831	06630	9580	09632	7583
17	00525	1329	03607	0823	06661	9563	09661	7560
18	00556	1328	03638	0814	06691	9547	09691	7536
19	00587	1326	03668	0805	06722	9530	09720	7512
20	00618	1325	03699	0796	06752	9514	09750	7488
21	00649	1324	03730	0787	06782	9497	09780	7464
22	00680	1322	03761	0778	06812	9481	09809	7440
23	00710	1321	03791	0769	06843	9464	09839	7416
24	00741	1319	03822	0759	06873	9447	09868	7392
25	00772	1317	03853	0750	06903	9430	09898	7368
26	00803	1315	03884	0740	06933	9413	09928	7344
27	00834	1313	03914	0731	06963	9396	09957	7319
28	00864	1311	03945	0721	06994	9379	09987	7295
29	00895	1309	03975	0712	07024	9361	10016	7270
30	00926	1307	04006	0702	07054	9314	10046	7246
31	00957	1305	04037	0692	07084	9326	10076	7221
32	00988	1303	04068	0682	07114	9309	10105	7197
33	01019	1300	04098	0672	07145	9291	10135	7172
34	01050	1298	04129	0662	07175	9274	10164	7147
35	01081	1295	04160	0652	07205	9256	10194	7122
36	01112	1292	04191	(642	07235	9238	10224	7097
37	01143	1290	04221	0631	07265	9221	10253	7072
38	01173	1287	04252	0621	07296	9203	10283	7047
39	01204	1284	04282	0610	07326	9185	10312	7021
40	01235	1281	04313	0600	07356	9167	10342	6996
41	01266	1278	04344	0589	07386	9149	10371	6970
42	01297	1275	04375	0579	07416	9131	10401	6945
43	01328	1272	04405	0568	07447	9113	10430	6919
44	01359	1268	04436	0557	07477	9094	10460	6894
45	01390	1265	04467	0546	07507	9076	10489	6868
46	01421	1261	04498	0535	07537	9057	10518	6842
47	01452	1259	04528	0524	07567	9039	10548	6816
48	01482	1254	04559	0513	07598	9020	10577	6790
49	01513	1250	04589	0501	07628	9002	10607	6764
50	+.01544	−9.1246	+.04620	−9.0490	+.07658	−8.8983	+.10636	−8.6738

* The last term is used when the Argument exceeds 340°. When the Argument is negative the sign of A_Ω must be reversed, but the sign of B_Ω remains the same.

TABLE XII.—The Quantities A_Ω and B_Ω.—1850.0.

$$\text{Argument} = \text{Arg. III} \cdot | \cdot d' + \overset{d}{\text{day of year}} - 6798.39.$$

	0		100		200		300	
	A_Ω	B_Ω	A_Ω	B_Ω	A_Ω	B_Ω	A_Ω	B_Ω
		$''$		$''$		$''$		$''$
50	+.01544	−9.1246	+.04620	−9.0490	+.07658	−8.8983	+.10636	−8 6738
51	01575	1242	04651	0476	07688	8964	10665	6712
52	01606	1238	04681	0467	07718	8945	10695	6685
53	01636	1234	04712	0455	07749	8926	10724	6659
54	01667	1230	04742	0444	07779	8907	10754	6632
55	01698	1226	04773	0432	07809	8888	10783	6605
56	01729	1222	04804	0420	07839	8869	10812	6579
57	01760	1218	04834	0408	07869	8849	10842	6553
58	01791	1213	04865	0396	07899	8830	10871	6526
59	01822	1209	04895	0384	07929	8810	10901	6500
60	01853	1204	04926	0372	07959	8791	10930	6473
61	01884	1199	04957	0360	07989	8771	10959	6446
62	01915	1195	04987	0348	08019	8752	10988	6419
63	01945	1190	05018	0336	08049	8732	11 18	6392
64	01976	1185	05048	0323	08079	8712	11047	6365
65	02007	1180	05079	0311	08109	8692	11076	6338
66	02038	1175	05109	0299	09139	8673	11105	6311
67	02069	1170	05140	0286	08169	8652	11134	6283
68	02099	1165	05170	0273	08199	8632	11164	6256
69	02130	1160	05201	0261	08229	8612	11193	6228
70	02161	1155	05231	0248	08259	8592	11222	6201
71	02192	1150	05262	0235	08289	8572	11251	6173
72	02223	1144	05292	0222	08319	8551	11280	6146
73	02253	1139	05323	0209	08349	8531	11310	6118
74	02284	1133	05353	0196	08379	8510	11339	6090
75	02315	1128	05384	0183	08409	8490	11368	6062
76	02346	1122	05414	0170	08439	8469	11397	6034
77	02377	1117	05445	0156	08469	8449	11426	6006
78	02407	1111	05475	0143	08499	8428	11456	5978
79	02438	1105	05506	0129	08529	8407	11485	5950
80	02469	1099	05536	0116	08559	8386	11514	5922
81	02500	1093	05567	0102	08589	8365	11543	5894
82	02531	1087	05597	0089	08619	8344	11572	5865
83	02561	1081	05628	0075	08649	8323	11602	5837
84	02592	1074	05658	0061	08679	8301	11631	5808
85	02623	1068	05689	0047	08709	8280	11660	5780
86	02654	1061	05719	0033	08739	8258	11689	5751
87	02685	1055	05750	0019	08769	8237	11718	5723
88	02715	1048	05780	9.0005	08798	8215	11747	5694
89	02746	1042	05811	8.9990	08828	8194	11776	5665
90	02777	1035	05841	9976	08858	8172	11805	5636
91	02808	1028	05871	9962	08888	8150	11834	5607
92	02839	1021	05902	9947	08918	8129	11863	5578
93	02869	1014	05932	9933	08947	8107	11892	5549
94	02900	1007	05963	9918	08977	8085	11921	5519
95	02931	1000	05993	9904	09007	8063	11950	5490
96	02962	0993	06023	9889	09037	8041	11979	5460
97	02993	0985	06054	9875	09067	8019	12008	5431
98	03023	0978	06084	9860	09096	7997	12037	5401
99	03054	0970	06115	9845	09126	7974	12066	5372
100	+.03085	−9.0962	+.06145	−8.9830	+.09156	−8.7952	+.12095	−8.5342

*The last term is used when the Argument exceeds 3400. When the Argument is negative the sign of A_Ω must be reversed, but the sign of B_Ω remains the same.

TABLE XII.—The Quantities A_Ω and B_Ω.—1850.0.

Argument = III + d' + $\overset{d}{\text{day}}$ of year—6798.39.*

	400		500		600		700	
	A_Ω	B_Ω	A_Ω	B_Ω	A_Ω	B_Ω	A_Ω	B_Ω
		"		"		"		"
0	+.12095	−8.5342	+.14937	−8.2021	+.17661	−7.8015	+.20243	−7.3352
1	12124	5312	14965	1984	17688	7971	20268	3302
2	12153	5283	14993	1948	17714	7928	20293	3253
3	12181	5253	15020	1911	17741	7884	20318	3203
4	12210	5223	15048	1874	17767	7841	20343	3153
5	12239	5193	15076	1837	17794	7797	20368	3103
6	12268	5163	15104	1800	17820	7753	20393	3053
7	12297	5133	15132	1763	17847	7710	20418	3003
8	12325	5103	15159	1726	17873	7666	20442	2953
9	12354	5072	15187	1688	17900	7622	20467	2902
10	12383	5042	15215	1651	17926	7578	20492	2852
11	12412	5011	15243	1613	17952	7534	20517	2801
12	12441	4981	15271	1576	17979	7490	20542	2751
13	12469	4950	15298	1538	18005	7446	20566	2700
14	12498	4920	15326	1501	18032	7401	20591	2650
15	12527	4889	15354	1463	18058	7357	20616	2599
16	12556	4858	15382	1425	18084	7312	20641	2548
17	12585	4827	15409	1388	18111	7268	20666	2497
18	12613	4796	15437	1350	18137	7223	20690	2446
19	12642	4765	15464	1312	18164	7179	20715	2395
20	12671	4734	15492	1274	18190	7134	20740	2344
21	12700	4703	15520	1236	18216	7089	20765	2293
22	12729	4671	15547	1198	18242	7044	20789	2242
23	12757	4640	15575	1160	18269	6999	20814	2191
24	12786	4608	15602	1121	18295	6954	20838	2139
25	12815	4577	15630	1083	18321	6909	20863	2088
26	12844	4545	15658	1045	18347	6864	20888	2037
27	12872	4514	15685	1006	18373	6819	20912	1985
28	12901	4482	15713	0968	18400	6774	20937	1934
29	12929	4451	15740	0929	18426	6728	20961	1882
30	12958	4419	15768	0891	18452	6683	20986	1831
31	12987	4387	15795	0852	18478	6638	21011	1779
32	13015	4355	15823	0814	18504	6592	21035	1728
33	13044	4323	15850	0775	18530	6547	21060	1676
34	13072	4291	15878	0736	18556	6501	21084	1624
35	13101	4259	15905	0697	18582	6456	21109	1572
36	13130	4227	15932	0658	18608	6410	21133	1520
37	13158	4194	15960	0619	18634	6365	21158	1468
38	13187	4162	15987	0580	18660	6319	21182	1416
39	13215	4129	16015	0540	18686	6273	21207	1364
40	13244	4097	16042	0501	18712	6227	21231	1312
41	13273	4064	16069	0461	18738	6181	21255	1260
42	13301	4031	16097	0422	18764	6135	21280	1207
43	13330	3998	16124	0382	18790	6089	21304	1155
44	13358	3966	16152	0343	18816	6042	21329	1102
45	13387	3933	16179	0303	18842	5996	21353	1050
46	13416	3900	16206	0263	18868	5949	21377	0997
47	13444	3867	16233	0223	18894	5903	21401	0944
48	13473	3834	16261	0183	18919	5856	21426	0891
49	13501	3801	16288	0143	18945	5810	21450	0839
50	+.13530	−8.3768	+.16315	−8.0103	+.18971	−7.5763	+.21474	−7.0786

* The last term is used when the Argument exceeds 3400. When the Argument is negative the sign of A_Ω must be reversed, but the sign of B_Ω remains the same.

TABLE XII.—The Quantities A_Ω and B_Ω.—1850.0.

Argument $= III + d' + $ day of year—$6798.39.$ *

	400		500		600		700	
	A_Ω	B_Ω	A_Ω	B_Ω	A_Ω	B_Ω	A_Ω	B_Ω
		"		"		"		"
50	+.13530	—8.3768	+.16315	—8.0103	+.18971	—7.5763	+.21474	—7.0786
51	13558	3735	16342	0063	18997	5716	21498	0733
52	13587	3701	16369	8.0023	19023	5670	21522	0680
53	13615	3668	16397	7.9983	19048	5623	21547	0627
54	13644	3634	16424	9942	19074	5576	21571	0574
55	13672	3601	16451	9902	19100	5529	21595	0521
56	13700	3567	16478	9861	19126	5482	21619	0468
57	13729	3533	16505	9821	19152	5435	21643	0414
58	13757	3499	16533	9780	19177	5388	21667	0361
59	13786	3466	16560	9740	19203	5341	21691	0307
60	13814	3432	16587	9699	19229	5294	21715	0254
61	13842	3398	16614	9658	19255	5247	21739	0200
62	13870	3364	16641	9617	19280	5199	21763	0147
63	13899	3330	16668	9576	19306	5152	21787	0093
64	13927	3296	16695	9535	19331	5104	21811	7.0040
65	13955	3262	16722	9494	19357	5057	21835	6.9986
66	13983	3228	16749	9453	19383	5009	21859	9932
67	14011	3193	16776	9412	19408	4962	21883	9879
68	14040	3159	16803	9371	19434	4914	21907	9825
69	14068	3124	16830	9329	19459	4866	21931	9771
70	14096	3090	16857	9288	19485	4818	21955	9717
71	14124	3055	16884	9246	19510	4770	21979	9663
72	14152	3020	16911	9205	19536	4722	22003	9609
73	14181	2985	16938	9163	19561	4674	22026	9555
74	14209	2951	16965	9122	19587	4625	22050	9500
75	14237	2916	16992	9080	19612	4577	22074	9446
76	14265	2881	17019	9038	19637	4528	22098	9392
77	14293	2846	17046	8997	19663	4480	22121	9337
78	14321	2811	17072	8955	19688	4431	22145	9283
79	14349	2776	17099	8913	19714	4383	22168	9228
80	14377	2741	17126	8871	19739	4334	22192	9174
81	14405	2706	17153	8829	19764	4285	22216	9119
82	14433	2670	17180	8787	19790	4237	22239	9065
83	14461	2635	17206	8745	19815	4188	22263	9010
84	14489	2599	17233	8702	19841	4139	22286	8955
85	14517	2564	17260	8660	19866	4090	23310	8900
86	14545	2528	17287	8617	19891	4041	22334	8845
87	14573	2493	17314	8575	19916	3992	22357	8790
88	14601	2457	17340	8532	19942	3943	22381	8735
89	14629	2421	17367	8490	19967	3894	22404	8680
90	14657	2385	17394	8447	19992	3845	22428	8625
91	14685	2349	17421	8404	20017	3796	22451	8570
92	14713	2313	17448	8361	20042	3747	22475	8514
93	14741	2277	17474	8318	20068	3698	22498	8459
94	14769	2240	17501	8275	20093	3648	22522	8403
95	14797	2204	17528	8232	20118	3599	22545	8348
96	14825	2167	17555	8189	20143	3550	22568	8292
97	14853	2131	17581	8145	20168	3500	22592	8237
98	14881	2094	17608	8102	20193	3451	22615	8181
99	14909	2058	17634	8058	20218	3401	22639	8125
100	+.14937	—8.2021	+.17661	—7.8015	+.20243	—7.3352	+.22662	—6.8069

* The last term is used when the Argument exceeds 3400. When the Argument is negative the sign of A_Ω must be reversed, but the sign of B_Ω remains the same.

TABLE XII.—The Quantities A_Ω and B_Ω.—1850.0.

Argument = Arg. III + d' + $\dfrac{d}{\text{day of year}}$—6798.39."

	800		900		1000		1100	
	A_Ω	B_Ω	A_Ω	B_Ω	A_Ω	B_Ω	A_Ω	B_Ω
		"		"		"		"
0	+.22662	−6.8069	+.24898	−6.2207	+.26933	−5.5813	+.28747	−4.8936
1	22685	8013	24919	2146	26052	5746	28764	8865
2	22708	7958	24941	2084	26971	5680	28761	8794
3	22732	7902	24962	2023	26991	5613	28798	8723
4	22755	7847	24984	1961	27010	5547	28815	8651
5	22778	7791	25005	1900	27029	5490	28832	8580
6	22801	7735	25026	1838	27048	5413	28849	8509
7	22824	7679	25047	1777	27067	5347	28866	8437
8	22848	7623	25069	1715	27087	5280	28882	8366
9	22871	*7566	25090	1654	27106	5213	28899	8294
10	22894	7510	25111	1592	27125	5146	28916	8223
11	22917	7453	25132	1530	27144	5079	28933	8151
12	22940	7397	25153	1468	27163	5012	28949	8080
13	22963	7340	25175	1406	27182	4945	28966	8008
14	22986	7284	25196	1344	27201	4878	28982	7937
15	23009	7227	25217	1282	27220	4811	28999	7865
16	23032	7170	25238	1220	27239	4744	29016	7793
17	23055	7113	25259	1157	27258	4677	29032	7721
18	23078	7056	25280	1095	27276	4610	29049	7650
19	23101	6999	25301	1032	27295	4542	29065	7578
20	23124	6942	25322	0970	27314	4475	29082	7506
21	23147	6885	25343	0907	27333	4407	29098	7434
22	23170	6828	25364	0845	27352	4340	29115	7363
23	23193	6771	25385	0782	27370	4272	29131	7291
24	23216	6713	25406	0720	27389	4205	29148	7219
25	23239	6656	25427	0657	27408	4137	29164	7147
26	23262	6599	25448	0594	27427	4069	29180	7075
27	23285	6541	25469	0532	27445	4002	29197	7003
28	23307	6484	25489	0469	27464	3934	29213	6931
29	23330	6426	25510	0406	27482	3866	29230	6859
30	23353	6369	25531	0343	27501	3798	29246	6787
31	23376	6311	25552	0280	27520	3730	29262	6715
32	23399	6254	25573	0217	27538	3662	29278	6643
33	23421	6196	25593	0154	27557	3594	29295	6570
34	23444	6138	25614	0091	27575	3526	29311	6497
35	23467	6080	25635	6.0028	27594	3458	29327	6425
36	23490	6022	25656	5.9965	27612	3390	29343	6352
37	23512	5964	25676	9901	27631	3322	29359	6280
38	23535	5906	25697	9838	27649	3254	29375	6207
39	23557	5848	25717	9774	27668	3185	29391	6135
40	23580	5790	25738	9711	27686	3117	29407	6062
41	23602	5732	25758	9647	27704	3049	29423	5989
42	23625	5674	25779	9584	27723	2980	29439	5917
43	23647	5616	25799	9520	27741	2912	29455	5844
44	23670	5557	25820	9457	27760	2843	29471	5771
45	23692	5499	25840	9393	27778	2775	29487	5698
46	23714	5441	25860	9329	27796	2706	29503	5625
47	23737	5382	25881	9265	27814	2638	29519	5552
48	23759	5324	25901	9202	27833	2569	29534	5479
49	23782	5265	25922	9138	27851	2501	29550	5406
50	+.23804	−6.5207	+.25942	−5.9074	+.27869	−5.2432	+.29566	−4.5333

* The last term is used when the Argument exceeds 3400. When the Argument is negative the sign of A_Ω must be reversed; the sign of B_Ω remains the same.

TABLE XII.—The Quantities A_Ω and B_Ω.—1850.0.

Argument $=$ Arg. III $+ d' +$ day of year$-6799\overset{d}{.}39.$*

	800		900		1000		1100	
	A_Ω	B_Ω	A_Ω	B_Ω	A_Ω	B_Ω	A_Ω	B_Ω
		"	.	"		"	.	"
50	+.23804	−6.5207	+.25942	−5.9074	+.27869	−5.2432	+.29565	−4.5333
51	23826	5146	25962	9010	27887	2363	29582	5260
52	23848	5090	25982	8946	27905	2295	29598	5187
53	23871	5031	26003	8882	27923	2226	29613	5114
54	23893	4973	26023	8818	27941	2157	29629	5041
55	23915	4914	26043	8754	27959	2088	29645	4968
56	23937	4855	26063	8690	27977	2019	29661	4895
57	23959	4796	26083	8626	27995	1950	29676	4821
58	23982	4737	26104	8562	28013	1881	29692	4748
59	24004	4678	26124	8497	28031	1811	29707	4674
60	24026	4619	26144	8434	28049	1742	29723	4601
61	24048	4560	26164	8368	28067	1673	29738	4527
62	24070	4500	26184	8304	28085	1603	29754	4454
63	24093	4441	26204	8239	28102	1534	29769	4380
64	24115	4381	26224	8175	28120	1464	29785	4307
65	24137	4322	26244	8110	28138	1395	29800	4233
66	24159	4262	26264	8045	28156	1325	29815	4159
67	24181	4202	26284	7980	28174	1256	29831	4086
68	24203	4143	26304	7915	28191	1186	29846	4012
69	24225	4084	26324	7850	28209	1117	29862	3938
70	24247	4024	26344	7785	28227	1047	29877	3864
71	24269	3964	26364	7720	28245	0977	29892	3790
72	24291	3904	26384	7655	28262	0908	29907	3716
73	24313	3844	26404	7590	28280	0838	29923	3642
74	24335	3784	26424	7524	28297	0768	29938	3568
75	24357	3724	26444	7459	28315	0698	29953	3494
76	24379	3664	26464	7394	28332	0628	29968	3420
77	24401	3604	26484	7328	28350	0558	29983	3346
78	24422	3544	26503	7263	28367	0488	29999	3272
79	24444	3483	26523	7197	28385	0418	30014	3198
80	24466	3423	26543	7132	28402	0348	30029	3124
81	24488	3363	26563	7066	28419	0278	30044	3050
82	24510	3302	26582	7001	28437	0208	30059	2975
83	24531	3242	26602	6935	28454	0138	30074	2901
84	24553	3181	26621	6870	28472	5.0067	30089	2826
85	24575	3121	26641	6804	28489	4.9997	30104	2752
86	24597	3060	26661	6738	28506	9927	30119	2677
87	24618	3000	26680	6673	28523	9856	30134	2603
88	24640	2939	26700	6607	28541	9786	30148	2528
89	24661	2879	26719	6541	28558	9715	30163	2454
90	24683	2818	26739	6475	28575	9645	30178	2379
91	24705	2757	26758	6409	28592	9574	30193	2304
92	24726	2696	26778	6343	28609	9504	30208	2229
93	24748	2635	26797	6277	28627	9433	30222	2155
94	24769	2574	26817	6211	28644	9362	30237	2080
95	24791	2513	26836	6145	28661	9291	30252	2005
96	24812	2452	26855	6079	28678	9220	30267	1930
97	24834	2391	26875	6012	28695	9149	30281	1855
98	24855	2330	26894	5946	28713	9078	30296	1780
99	24877	2268	26914	5879	28730	9007	30310	1705
100	+.24898	−6.2207	+.26933	−5.5813	+.28747	−4.8936	+.30325	−4.1630

* The last term is used when the Argument exceeds 3400. When the Argument is negative the sign of A_Ω must be reversed, but the sign of B_Ω remains the same.

TABLE XII.—The Quantities A_Ω and B_Ω.—1850.0.

Argument $= $ Arg. III $+ d' + \overset{d}{\text{day of year}} - 6798.39.$ *

	1200		1300		1400		1500	
	A_Ω	B_Ω	A_Ω	B_Ω	A_Ω	B_Ω	A_Ω	B_Ω
		"		"		"		"
0	+.30325	−4.1630	+.31653	−3.3955	+.32718	−2.5974	+.33509	−1.7752
1	30339	1557	31665	3877	32727	5893	33515	7669
2	30354	1482	31677	3798	32736	5812	33522	7586
3	30368	1406	31688	3720	32746	5730	33528	7502
4	30383	1331	31700	3641	32755	5649	33535	7419
5	30397	1254	31712	3563	32764	5568	33541	7336
6	30411	1179	31724	3484	32773	5487	33547	7253
7	30426	1103	31736	3406	32782	5405	33553	7169
8	30440	1028	31747	3327	32791	5324	33560	7086
9	30455	0952	31759	3249	32800	5242	33566	7002
10	30469	0877	31771	3170	32809	5161	33572	6919
11	30483	0802	31783	3091	32818	5080	33578	6836
12	30497	0726	31794	3012	32827	4998	33584	6752
13	30512	0651	31806	2934	32836	4917	33591	6669
14	30526	0575	31817	2855	32845	4835	33597	6585
15	30540	0500	31829	2776	32854	4754	33603	6502
16	30554	0424	31841	2697	32863	4672	33609	6418
17	30568	0349	31852	2618	32872	4591	33615	6335
18	30583	0273	31864	2539	32880	4509	33621	6251
19	30597	0198	31875	2460	32889	4428	33627	6167
20	30611	0122	31887	2381	32898	4346	33633	6084
21	30625	4.0046	31898	2302	32907	4264	33639	6000
22	30639	3.9971	31910	2223	32916	4183	33645	5917
23	30653	9895	31921	2144	32924	4101	33651	5833
24	30667	9819	31933	2065	32933	4020	33657	5750
25	30681	9743	31944	1986	32942	3938	33663	5666
26	30695	9667	31955	1907	32951	3856	33669	5582
27	30709	9591	31966	1828	32959	3774	33675	5499
28	30722	9515	31978	1748	32968	3693	33680	5415
29	30736	9439	31989	1669	32976	3611	33686	5332
30	30750	9363	32000	1590	32985	3529	33692	5248
31	30764	9287	32011	1511	32993	3447	33698	5164
32	30778	9211	32022	1431	33002	3365	33703	5080
33	30791	9135	32034	1352	33010	3284	33709	4997
34	30805	9058	32045	1272	33019	3202	33714	4913
35	30819	8982	32056	1193	33027	3120	33720	4829
36	30833	8906	32067	1114	33035	3038	33725	4745
37	30846	8829	32078	1034	33043	2956	33731	4661
38	30860	8753	32089	0955	33052	2874	33736	4578
39	30873	8676	32100	0875	33060	2792	33742	4494
40	30887	8600	32110	.0796	33068	2710	33747	4410
41	30900	8524	32122	0716	33076	2628	33752	4326
42	30914	8447	32133	0637	33084	2546	33757	4242
43	30927	8371	32143	0557	33092	2464	33763	4159
44	30941	8294	32154	0478	33100	2382	33768	4075
45	30954	8218	32165	0398	33108	2300	33773	3991
46	30967	8141	32176	0318	33116	2218	33778	3907
47	30981	8065	32187	0238	33124	2136	33783	3823
48	30994	7938	32197	0158	33132	2053	33789	3739
49	31008	7912	32208	3.0078	33140	1971	33794	3655
50	+.31021	−3.7835	+.32219	−2.9999	+.33148	−2.1889	+.33799	−1.3571

* The last term is used when the Argument exceeds 3400. When the Argument is negative the sign of A_Ω must be reversed, but the sign of B_Ω remains the same.

TABLE XII.—The Quantities A_Ω and B_Ω.—1850.0.

Argument $=$ Arg. III $+ d' +$ day of year$-6798\ \overset{d}{39}.$ *

	1200		1300		1400		1500	
	A_Ω	B_Ω	A_Ω	B_Ω	A_Ω	B_Ω	A_Ω	B_Ω
		"		"		"		"
50	+.31021	−3.7835	+.32219	−2.9909	+.33148	−2.1889	+.33799	−1.3571
51	31034	7758	32230	9919	33156	1807	33804	3487
52	31047	7682	32240	9840	33164	1725	33809	3403
53	31061	7605	32251	9760	33171	1642	33814	3319
54	31074	7528	32261	9680	33179	1560	33819	3235
55	31087	7451	32272	9000	33187	1478	33824	3151
56	31100	7374	32282	9520	33195	1396	33829	3067
57	31113	7297	32293	9440	33202	1313	33834	2983
58	31126	7220	32303	9360	33210	1231	33838	2899
59	31139	7143	32314	9280	33217	1148	33843	2815
60	31152	7066	32324	9200	33225	1066	33848	2731
61	31165	6989	32334	9120	33233	0984	33853	2647
62	31178	6912	32345	9040	33240	0901	33858	2563
63	31191	6835	32355	8959	33248	0819	33862	2478
64	31204	6757	32366	8879	33255	0736	33867	2394
65	31217	6680	32376	8799	33263	0654	33872	2310
66	31230	6603	32386	8719	33270	0571	33877	2226
67	31243	6525	32396	9638	33278	0489	33881	2142
68	31255	6448	32407	8558	33285	0406	33886	2057
69	31268	6370	32417	8477	33293	0324	33890	1973
70	31281	6293	32427	8397	33300	0241	33895	1889
71	31294	6215	32437	8317	33307	0158	33899	1805
72	31307	6138	32447	8236	33315	2.0075	33904	1720
73	31319	6060	32457	8156	33322	1.9993	33908	1636
74	31332	5983	32467	8075	33330	9910	33913	1551
75	31345	5905	32477	7995	33337	9827	33917	1467
76	31358	5827	32487	7914	33344	9744	33921	1383
77	31370	5750	32497	7834	33351	9661	33925	1298
78	31383	5672	32506	7753	33359	9579	33930	1214
79	31395	5595	32516	7673	33366	9496	33934	1129
80	31408	5517	32526	7592	33373	9413	33938	1045
81	31420	5439	32536	7511	33380	9330	33942	0961
82	31433	5362	32546	7431	33387	9247	33946	0876
83	41445	5284	32555	7350	33394	9164	33951	0792
84	31458	5206	32565	7270	33401	9081	33955	0707
85	31470	5128	32575	7189	33408	8998	33959	0623
86	31482	5050	32585	7108	33415	8915	33963	0539
87	31495	4972	32594	7027	33422	8832	33967	0454
88	31507	4894	32604	6947	33428	8749	33971	0370
89	31520	4816	32613	6866	33435	8666	33975	0285
90	31532	4738	32623	6785	33442	8583	33979	0201
91	31544	4660	32633	6704	33449	8500	33983	0116
92	31556	4582	32642	6623	33456	8417	33987	1.0032
93	31569	4504	32652	6542	33462	8334	33990	0.9947
94	31581	4425	32661	6461	33469	8251	32994	9863
95	31593	4347	32671	6380	33476	8168	33998	9778
96	31605	4269	32680	6299	33483	8085	34002	9694
97	21617	4190	32690	6218	33489	8002	34006	9609
98	31629	4112	32699	6136	33496	7918	34009	9525
99	31641	4033	32709	6055	33502	7835	34013	9440
100	+.31653	−3.3955	+.32718	−2.5974	+.33509	−1.7752	+.34017	−0.9356

*The last term is used when the Argument exceeds 3400. When the Argument is negative the sign of A_Ω must be reversed; the sign of B_Ω remains the same.

TABLE XII.—The Quantities A_Ω and B_Ω.—1850.0.

$$\text{Argument} = \text{Arg. III} + d' + \overset{d}{\text{day of year}} - 6798.39.^{*}$$

	1600		1700		1800		1900	
	A_Ω	B_Ω	A_Ω	B_Ω	A_Ω	B_Ω	A_Ω	B_Ω
		''		''		''		''
0	+.34017	−0.9356	+.34237	−0.0858	+.34165	+0.7669	+.33799	−1.6153
1	34021	9271	34238	0773	34163	7754	33794	6237
2	34024	9187	34239	0688	34161	7839	33789	6322
3	34028	9102	34239	0602	34158	7925	33783	6406
4	34031	9018	34240	0517	34156	8010	33778	6491
5	34035	8933	34241	0432	34154	8095	33773	6575
6	34038	8848	34242	0347	34152	8180	33768	6659
7	34042	8764	34242	0261	34149	8265	33762	6743
8	34045	8679	34243	0176	34147	8351	33757	6828
9	24049	8595	34243	0090	34144	8436	33751	6912
10	34052	8510	34244	−0.0005	34142	8521	33746	6996
11	34055	8425	34244	+0.0080	34139	8606	33741	7080
12	34058	8340	34245	0165	34137	8691	33735	7164
13	34062	8256	34245	0251	34134	8776	33730	7249
14	34065	8171	34246	0336	34132	8861	33724	7333
15	34068	8086	34246	0421	34129	8946	33719	7417
16	34071	8001	34246	0506	34126	9031	33713	7501
17	34074	7916	34246	0592	34123	9116	33708	7585
18	34078	7832	34247	0677	35121	9202	33702	7670
19	34081	7747	34247	0763	34118	9287	33697	7754
20	34084	7662	34247	0848	34115	9372	33691	7838
21	34087	7577	34247	0933	34112	9457	33685	7922
22	34090	7492	34247	1018	34109	9542	33679	8006
23	34093	7408	34247	1104	34107	9627	33674	8091
24	34096	7323	34247	1189	34104	9712	33668	8175
25	34099	7238	34247	1274	34101	9797	33662	8259
26	34102	7153	34247	1359	34098	9882	33656	8343
27	34105	7068	34247	1444	34095	0.9967	33650	8427
28	34107	6984	34247	1530	34092	1.0052	33644	8511
29	34110	6899	34247	1615	34089	0137	33638	8595
30	34113	6814	34247	1700	34086	0222	33632	8679
31	34116	6729	34247	1785	34083	0307	33626	8763
32	34119	6644	34247	1871	34080	0392	33620	8847
33	34121	6560	34246	1956	34076	0477'	33614	8931
34	24124	6475	34246	2042	34073	0562	33608	9015
35	34127	6390	34246	2127	34070	0647	33602	9099
36	34130	6305	34246	2212	34067	0732	33595	9183
37	34132	6220	34245	2297	34063	0817	33590	9267
38	34135	6135	34245	2383	34060	0902	33583	9351
39	34137	6050	34244	2468	34056	0987	33577	9435
40	34140	5965	34244	2553	34053	1072	33571	9519
41	34142	5880	34243	2638	34050	1157	33565	9603
42	34145	5795	34243	2724	34046	1242	33558	9687
43	34147	5710	34242	2809	34043	1326	33552	9770
44	34150	5625	34242	2895	34039	1411	33545	9854
45	34152	5540	34241	2980	34036	1496	33539	1.9938
46	34154	5455	34240	3065	34032	1581	33533	2.0022
47	34156	5370	34240	3150	34029	1666	33526	0106
48	34159	5285	34239	3236	34025	1751	33520	0189
49	34161	5200	34239	3321	34022	1836	33513	0273
50	+.34163	−0.5115	+.34238	+0.3406	+.34018	+1.1921	+.33507	+2.0357

* The last term is used when the Argument exceeds 3400. When the Argument is negative the sign of A_Ω must be reversed, but the sign of B_Ω remains the same.

TABLE XII.—The Quantities A_Ω and B_Ω.—1850.0.

Argument = Arg. III + d' + day of year—6798.39.*

	1600		1700		1800		1900	
	A_Ω	B_Ω	A_Ω	B_Ω	A_Ω	B_Ω	A_Ω	B_Ω
		"		"		"		"
50	+.34163	−0.5115	+.34238	+0.3406	+.34018	+1.1921	+.33507	+2.0357
51	34165	5030	34237	3491	34014	2006	33500	0441
52	34167	4945	34236	3576	34010	2091	33494	0524
53	34170	4860	34236	3662	34007	2175	33487	0608
54	34172	4775	34235	3747	34003	2260	33481	0691
55	34174	4690	34234	3832	33999	2345	33474	0775
56	34176	4605	34233	3917	33995	2430	33467	0859
57	34178	4520	34232	4003	33991	2515	33460	0942
58	34180	4435	34231	4088	33988	2599	33454	1026
59	34182	4350	34230	4174	33984	2684	33447	1109
60	34184	4265	34229	4259	33980	2769	33440	1193
61	34186	4180	34228	4344	33976	2854	33433	1277
62	34188	4095	34227	4429	33972	2939	33426	1360
63	34189	4010	34226	4515	33968	3023	33419	1444
64	34191	3925	34225	4600	33964	3108	33412	1527
65	34193	3840	34224	4685	33960	3193	33405	1611
66	34195	3755	34223	4770	33956	3278	33398	1694
67	34196	3670	34222	4856	33952	3362	33391	1778
68	34198	3584	34220	4941	33947	3447	33384	1861
69	34199	3499	34219	5027	33943	3531	33377	1945
70	34201	3414	34218	5112	33939	3616	33370	2028
71	34203	3328	34217	5197	33935	3701	33363	2111
72	34204	3243	34215	5282	33930	3786	33356	2195
73	34206	3157	34214	5368	33926	3870	33348	2278
74	34207	3072	34212	5453	33921	3955	33341	2362
75	34209	2988	34211	5538	33917	4040	33334	2445
76	34210	2903	34209	5623	33913	4125	33327	2528
77	34212	2818	34208	5708	33908	4209	33319	2611
78	34213	2732	34206	5794	33904	4294	33312	2695
79	34215	2647	34205	5879	33899	4378	33304	2778
80	34216	2562	34203	5964	33895	4463	33297	2861
81	34217	2477	34201	6049	33890	4548	33289	2944
82	34218	2392	34200	6135	33886	4632	33282	3027
83	34220	2306	34198	6220	33881	4717	33274	3111
84	34221	2221	34197	6306	33877	4801	33267	3194
85	34222	2136	34195	6391	33872	4886	33259	3277
86	34223	2051	34193	6476	33867	4970	33251	3360
87	34224	1966	34191	6561	33862	5055	33244	3443
88	34226	1880	34190	6647	33858	5139	33236	3526
89	34227	1795	34188	6732	33853	5224	33229	3609
90	34228	1710	34186	6817	33848	5308	33221	3692
91	34229	1625	34184	6902	33843	5393	33213	3775
92	34230	1540	34182	6987	33838	5477	33205	3858
93	34231	1454	34180	7073	33834	5562	33198	3941
94	34232	1369	34178	7158	33829	5646	33190	4024
95	34233	1284	34176	7243	33824	5731	33182	4107
96	34234	1199	34174	7328	33819	5815	33174	4190
97	34235	1114	34172	7413	33814	5900	33166	4273
98	34235	1028	34169	7499	33809	5984	33158	4356
99	34236	0943	34167	7584	33804	6069	33150	4439
1.0	+.34237	−0.0858	+.34165	+0.7669	+.33799	+1.6153	+.33142	+2.4522

* The last term is used when the Argument exceeds 3400. When the Argument is negative the sign of A_Ω must be reversed, but the sign of B_Ω remains the same.

TABLE XII.—The Quantities A_Ω and B_Ω.—1850.0.

$$\text{Argument} = \text{Arg. III} + d' + \text{day of year} - 6798\overset{d}{\cdot}39.*$$

	2000		2100		2200		2300	
	A_Ω	B_Ω	A_Ω	B_Ω	A_Ω	B_Ω	A_Ω	B_Ω
		"		"		"		"
0	+.33142	+2.4522	+.32196	+3.2701	+.30967	+4.0617	+.29466	+4.8200
1	33134	4605	32185	2781	30953	0695	29450	8274
2	33126	4688	32174	2862	30939	0772	29433	8348
3	33117	4770	32163	2942	30926	0850	29417	8422
4	33109	4853	32152	3023	30912	0927	29400	8495
5	33101	4936	32141	3103	30898	1005	29384	8569
6	33093	5019	32130	3183	30884	1082	29367	8643
7	33085	5102	32119	3264	30870	1160	29351	8716
8	33076	5184	32107	3344	30857	1237	29334	8790
9	33068	5267	32096	3425	30843	1315	29318	8863
10	33060	5350	32085	3505	30829	1392	29301	8937
11	33052	5433	32074	3585	30815	1469	29284	9010
12	33043	5515	32063	3665	30801	1547	29268	9084
13	33035	5598	32051	3746	30787	1624	29251	9157
14	33026	5680	32040	3826	30773	1701	29235	9231
15	33018	5763	32029	3906	30759	1778	29218	9304
16	33009	5845	32018	3986	30745	1855	29201	9377
17	33001	5928	32006	4067	30731	1932	29184	9451
18	32992	6010	31995	4147	30716	2009	29168	9524
19	32984	6093	31983	4227	30702	2086	29151	9597
20	32975	6175	31972	4307	30688	2163	29134	9670
21	32966	6257	31961	4387	30674	2240	29117	9743
22	32958	6340	31949	4467	30660	2317	29100	9816
23	32949	6422	31938	4547	30645	2394	29084	9889
24	32941	6505	31926	4627	30631	2470	29067	4.9962
25	32932	6587	31915	4707	30617	2547	29050	5.0035
26	32923	6669	31903	4787	30603	2624	29033	0108
27	32914	6751	31892	4867	30588	2700	29016	0181
28	32906	6834	31880	4946	30574	2777	28999	0254
29	32897	6916	31869	5026	30559	2853	28982	0326
30	32887	6998	31857	5106	30545	2930	28965	0399
31	32879	7080	31845	5186	30530	3006	28948	0472
32	32870	7162	31833	5265	30516	3083	28931	0544
33	32861	7245	31822	5345	30501	3159	28913	0617
34	32852	7327	31810	5425	30487	3236	28896	0689
35	32843	7409	31798	5505	30472	3312	28879	0762
36	32834	7491	31786	5585	30457	3388	28862	0834
37	32825	7573	31774	5661	30443	3465	28844	0907
38	32816	7656	31762	5744	30428	3541	28827	0979
39	32807	7738	31750	5823	30414	3618	28809	1052
40	32798	7820	31738	5903	30399	3694	28792	1124
41	32789	7902	31726	5982	30384	3770	28775	1196
42	32780	7984	31714	6062	30369	3847	28757	1269
43	32770	8066	31701	6141	30355	3923	28740	1311
44	32761	8148	31689	6221	30340	3999	28722	1413
45	32752	8230	31677	6300	30325	4075	28705	1485
46	32743	8312	31665	6379	30310	4151	28687	1557
47	32733	8394	31653	6459	30295	4227	28670	1629
48	32724	8476	31640	6538	30280	4303	28652	1701
49	32714	8558	31628	6617	30265	4379	28635	1773
50	+.32705	+2.8640	+.31616	+3.6696	+.30250	+4.4455	+.28617	+5.1815

*The last term is used when the Argument exceeds 3400. When the Argument is negative the sign of A_Ω must be reversed, but the sign of B_Ω remains the same.

TABLE XII.—The Quantities A_Ω and B_Ω.—1850.0.

Argument = Arg. III + d' + day of year—6798.39.[*]

	2000		2100		2200		2300	
	A_Ω	B_Ω	A_Ω	B_Ω	A_Ω	B_Ω	A_Ω	B_Ω
		"		"		"		"
50	+.32705	+2.8640	+.31616	+3.6696	+.30250	+4.4455	+.28617	+5.1815
51	32695	8722	31604	6775	30235	4531	28599	1917
52	32686	8804	31591	6854	30220	4607	28581	1989
53	32676	8885	31579	6933	30204	4683	28564	2061
54	32666	8967	31566	7012	30189	4758	28546	2132
55	32657	9049	31554	7091	30174	4834	28528	2204
56	32647	9131	31541	7170	30159	4910	28510	2276
57	32638	9212	31529	7249	30144	4985	28492	2347
58	32628	9294	31516	7328	30128	5061	28475	2419
59	32619	9375	31504	7407	30113	5136	28457	2490
60	32609	9457	31491	7486	30098	5212	28439	2562
61	32599	9539	31478	7565	30083	5287	28421	2633
62	32589	9620	31466	7643	30067	5363	28403	2705
63	32580	9702	31453	7722	30052	5438	28385	2776
64	32570	9783	31441	7801	30036	5514	28367	2847
65	32560	9865	31428	7880	30021	5589	28349	2918
66	32550	2.9946	31415	7959	30006	5664	28331	2989
67	32540	3.0028	31402	8037	29991	5740	28313	3060
68	32530	0109	31390	8116	29975	5815	28295	3131
69	32520	0191	31377	8194	29960	5890	28277	3202
70	32510	0272	31364	8273	29944	5965	28259	3273
71	32500	0353	31351	8352	29928	6040	28241	3344
72	32490	0435	31338	8430	29913	6115	28223	3415
73	32480	0516	31326	8509	29897	6189	28204	3486
74	32470	0597	31313	8587	29882	6264	28186	3556
75	32460	0678	31300	8666	29866	6339	28168	3627
76	32450	0759	31287	8744	29850	6414	28150	3698
77	32440	0841	31274	8823	29834	6489	28131	3768
78	32429	0922	31261	8901	29819	6563	28113	3839
79	32419	1003	31248	8980	29803	6638	28094	3909
80	32409	1084	31235	9058	29787	6713	28076	3980
81	32399	1165	31222	9136	29771	6788	28058	4050
82	32388	1246	31209	9215	29755	6862	28039	4121
83	32378	1327	31195	9293	29740	6937	28021	4191
84	32367	1408	31182	9371	29724	7011	28002	4062
85	32357	1489	31169	9449	29708	7086	27984	4332
86	32346	1570	31156	9527	29692	7160	27965	4402
87	32336	1651	31142	9605	29676	7235	27947	4473
88	32325	1732	31129	9683	29660	7309	27928	4543
89	32315	1813	31115	9761	29644	7384	27910	4613
90	32304	1894	31102	9839	29628	7458	27891	4683
91	32293	1975	31088	9917	29612	7532	27872	4753
92	32282	2056	31075	3.9995	29596	7606	27854	4823
93	32272	2137	31062	4.0072	29579	7681	27835	4893
94	32261	2217	31048	0150	29563	7755	27817	4963
95	32250	2298	31035	0228	29547	7829	27798	5033
96	32239	2379	31021	0306	29531	7903	27779	5103
97	32228	2459	31008	0384	29515	7978	27760	5173
98	32218	2540	30994	0461	29498	8052	27742	5243
99	32207	2620	30981	0539	29482	8126	27723	5312
100	+.32196	+3.2701	+.30967	+4.0617	+.29466	+4.8200	+.27704	+5.5382

[*] The last term is used when the Argument exceeds 3400. When the Argument is negative the sign of A_Ω must be reversed, but the sign of B_Ω remains the same.

TABLE XII.—The Quantities A_Ω and B_Ω.—1850.0.

Argument = Arg. III + d' + $\overset{a}{\text{day}}$ of year—6798.39.*

	2400		2500		2600		2700	
	A_Ω	B_Ω	A_Ω	B_Ω	A_Ω	B_Ω	A_Ω	B_Ω
		"		"		"		"
0	+.27704	+5.5382	+.25696	+6.2098	+.23458	+6.8285	+.21009	+7.3387
1	27685	5452	25675	2162	23434	8344	20984	3940
2	27666	5521	25653	2227	23411	8402	20958	3993
3	27647	5591	25632	2291	23387	8461	20933	4046
4	27628	5660	25610	2356	23364	8520	20907	4098
5	27609	5730	25580	2420	23340	8579	20882	4151
6	27590	5799	25568	2484	23316	8638	20856	4203
7	27571	5869	25546	2549	23293	8696	20831	4256
8	27552	5938	25525	2613	23269	8755	20805	4308
9	27533	6008	25503	2677	23246	8813	20780	4361
10	27514	6077	25482	2741	23222	8872	20754	4413
11	27495	6146	25460	2805	23198	8930	20728	4465
12	27476	6215	25439	2869	23174	8989	20703	4518
13	27456	6284	25417	2933	23151	9047	20677	4570
14	27437	6353	25396	2997	23127	9106	20652	4622
15	27418	6422	25374	3061	23103	9164	20626	4674
16	27399	6491	25352	3125	23079	9222	20600	4726
17	27379	6559	25331	3188	23055	9280	20574	4778
18	27360	6628	25309	3252	23032	9338	20549	4830
19	27340	6696	25288	3315	23008	9396	20523	4881
20	27321	6765	25266	3379	22984	9454	20497	4933
21	27302	6833	25244	3442	22960	9512	20471	4984
22	27282	6902	25222	3506	22936	9570	20445	5036
23	27263	6970	25201	3569	22912	9628	20419	5087
24	27243	7039	25179	3633	22888	9685	20393	5139
25	27224	7107	25157	3696	22864	9743	20367	5190
26	27204	7175	25135	3759	22840	9801	20341	5241
27	27185	7244	25113	3823	22816	9858	20315	5293
28	27165	7312	25092	3886	22792	9916	20289	5344
29	27146	7380	25070	3949	22768	6.9973	20263	5395
30	27126	7448	25048	4012	22744	7.0031	20237	5446
31	27106	7516	25026	4075	22720	0088	20211	5497
32	27087	7584	25004	4138	22696	0146	20185	5548
33	27067	7652	24982	4201	22671	0203	20158	5599
34	27048	7720	24960	4264	22647	0260	20132	5649
35	27028	7788	24938	4327	22623	0317	20106	5700
36	27009	7856	24916	4390	22599	0374	20080	5750
37	26988	7924	24894	4452	22575	0431	20054	5801
38	26969	7992	24872	4515	22550	0488	20027	5851
39	26949	8059	24850	4577	22526	0544	20001	5902
40	26929	8127	24828	4640	22502	0601	19975	5952
41	26909	8195	24806	4702	22478	0657	19949	6002
42	26890	8262	24784	4765	22453	0714	19923	6053
43	26870	8330	24761	4827	22429	0770	19896	6103
44	26850	8397	24739	4889	22404	0827	19870	6153
45	26830	8465	24717	4951	22380	0883	19844	6203
46	26810	8532	24695	5013	22356	0939	19818	6253
47	26790	8600	24672	5075	22331	0995	19791	6303
48	26770	8667	24650	5137	22307	1051	19765	6353
49	26750	8735	24627	5199	22282	1107	19738	6402
50	+.26730	+5.8802	+.24605	+6.5261	+.22258	+7.1163	+.19712	+7.6452

* The last term is used when the Argument exceeds 3400. When the Argument is negative the sign of A_Ω must be reversed, but the sign of B_Ω remains the same.

TABLE XII.—The Quantities A_Ω and B_Ω.—1850.0.

Argument $= $ Arg. III $+ d' + \dfrac{d}{\text{day of year}}-6798.39,$*

	2400		2500		2600		2700	
	A_Ω	B_Ω	A_Ω	B_Ω	A_Ω	B_Ω	A_Ω	B_Ω
		"		"		"		"
50	+.26730	+5.8802	+.24605	+6.5261	+.22258	+7.1163	+.19712	+7.6452
51	26710	8869	24583	5323	22233	1219	19686	6502
52	26690	8937	24560	5385	22209	1275	19659	6551
53	26669	9004	24538	5447	22184	1331	19633	6601
54	26649	9071	24515	5508	22160	1386	19606	6650
55	26629	9138	24493	5570	22135	1442	19580	6700
56	26609	9205	24470	5632	22110	1498	19553	6749
57	26589	9272	24448	5693	22086	1553	19527	6799
58	26568	9339	24425	5755	22061	1609	19500	6848
59	26548	9405	24403	5816	22037	1664	19474	6897
60	26528	9472	24380	5878	22012	1720	19447	6946
61	26508	9539	24357	5939	21987	1775	19420	6995
62	26487	9605	24335	6001	21962	1831	19394	7044
63	26467	9672	24312	6062	21938	1886	19367	7093
64	26446	9738	24290	6123	21913	1941	19341	7141
65	26426	9805	24267	6184	21888	1996	19314	7190
66	26405	9871	24244	6245	21863	2051	19287	7238
67	26385	5.9938	24221	6306	21838	2106	19260	7287
68	26364	6.0004	24199	6367	21814	2161	19234	7335
69	26344	0070	24176	6427	21789	2216	19207	7384
70	26323	0136	24153	6488	21764	2271	19180	7432
71	26302	0202	24130	6549	21739	2326	19153	7480
72	26282	0268	24107	6609	21714	2380	19126	7529
73	26261	0334	24085	6670	21689	2435	19100	7577
74	26241	0400	24062	6730	21664	2489	19073	7625
75	26220	0466	24039	6791	21639	2544	19046	7673
76	26199	0532	24016	6851	21614	2598	19019	7721
77	26178	0598	23993	6912	21589	2653	18992	7769
78	26158	0664	23970	6972	21564	2707	18966	7817
79	26137	0729	23947	7033	21539	2761	18939	7864
80	26116	0795	23921	7093	21514	2815	18912	7912
81	26095	0861	23901	7153	21489	2869	18885	7960
82	26074	0926	23878	7213	21464	2923	18858	8007
83	26054	0992	23854	7273	21438	2977	18831	8055
84	26033	1057	23831	7333	21413	3031	18804	8102
85	26012	1123	23808	7393	21388	3085	18777	8150
86	25991	1188	23785	7453	21363	3139	18750	8197
87	25970	1254	23762	7513	21338	3193	18723	8245
88	25949	1319	23738	7573	21312	3247	18696	8292
89	25928	1384	23715	7632	21287	3300	18669	8339
90	25907	1449	23692	7692	21262	3351	18642	8386
91	25886	1514	23669	7751	21237	3407	18615	8433
92	25865	1579	23645	7811	21212	3461	18588	8480
93	25844	1644	23622	7870	21186	3514	18561	8527
94	25823	1709	23598	7930	21161	3568	18534	8573
95	25802	1774	23575	7989	21136	3621	18507	8620
96	25781	1839	23552	8048	21111	3674	18480	8666
97	25760	1904	23528	8108	21085	3728	18453	8713
98	25738	1969	23505	8167	21060	3781	18425	8759
99	25717	2033	23491	8226	21034	3834	18398	8806
100	+.25696	+6.2098	+.23458	+6.8285	+.21009	+7.3887	+.18371	+7.8852

* The last term is used when the Argument exceeds 3400. When the Argument is negative the sign of A_Ω must be reversed, but the sign of B_Ω remains the same.

TABLE XII.—The Quantities A_Ω and B_Ω.—1850.0.

Argument = Arg. III + d' + day of year—6798.39.*

	2800		2900		3000		3100	
	A_Ω	B_Ω	A_Ω	B_Ω	A_Ω	B_Ω	A_Ω	B_Ω
		"		"		"		"
0	+.18371	+7.8852	+.15567	+8.3135	+.12622	+8.6694	+.09562	+8.9495
1	18344	8898	15538	3174	12592	6726	09531	9519
2	18316	8945	15509	3213	12562	6757	09500	9542
3	18289	8991	15481	3252	12531	6789	09468	9566
4	18261	9037	15452	3291	12501	6820	09437	9590
5	18234	9083	15423	3330	12471	6852	09406	9614
6	18207	9129	15394	3369	12441	6883	09375	9638
7	18179	9175	15365	3408	12411	6915	09344	9661
8	18152	9221	15337	3447	12380	6946	09312	9685
9	18124	9266	15308	3485	12350	6977	09281	9708
10	18097	9312	15279	3524	12320	7008	09250	9732
11	18070	9357	15250	3562	12290	7039	09219	9755
12	18042	9403	15221	3601	12260	7070	09188	9779
13	18015	9448	15192	3639	12229	7101	09156	9802
14	17987	9494	15163	3678	12199	7131	09125	9825
15	17960	9539	15134	3716	12169	7162	09094	9848
16	17932	9584	15104	3754	12139	7193	09063	9871
17	17905	9629	15076	3792	12109	7223	09032	9894
18	17877	9674	15047	3830	12079	7254	09000	9917
19	17850	9719	15018	3868	12049	7284	08969	9939
20	17822	9764	14989	3906	12018	7315	08938	9962
21	17794	9809	14960	3944	11988	7345	08907	8,9984
22	17767	9854	14931	3981	11957	7376	08876	9,0007
23	17739	9899	14901	4019	11927	7406	08844	0029
24	17712	9943	14872	4056	11896	7436	08813	0052
25	17684	7.9998	14843	4094	11866	7466	08782	0074
26	17656	8.0032	14814	4131	11836	7496	08751	0096
27	17629	0077	14785	4169	11805	7526	08719	0118
28	17601	0121	14755	4206	11775	7556	08688	0140
29	17574	0166	14726	4243	11744	7585	08656	0162
30	17546	0210	14697	4280	11714	7615	08625	0184
31	17518	0254	14668	4317	11684	7644	08594	0206
32	17490	0298	14639	4354	11653	7674	08562	0227
33	17463	0342	14609	4391	11623	7703	08531	0249
34	17435	0386	14580	4428	11592	7733	08499	0270
35	17407	0430	14551	4465	11562	7762	08468	0292
36	17379	0474	14522	4502	11532	7791	08437	0313
37	17351	0518	14493	4538	11501	7820	08405	0335
38	17324	0562	14463	4575	11471	7849	08374	0356
39	17296	0605	14434	4611	11440	7878	08342	0377
40	17268	0649	14405	4648	11410	7907	08311	0398
41	17240	0692	14376	4684	11380	7936	08280	0419
42	17212	0736	14346	4721	11349	7964	08248	0440
43	17184	0779	14317	4757	11319	7993	08217	0461
44	17156	0823	14287	4793	11288	8021	08185	0481
45	17128	0866	14258	4829	11258	8050	08154	0502
46	17100	0909	14229	4865	11227	8078	08123	0522
47	17072	0952	14199	4901	11197	8107	08091	0542
48	17044	0995	14170	4937	11166	8135	08060	0563
49	17016	1038	14140	4972	11136	8163	08028	0584
50	+.16988	+8.1031	+.14111	+8.5008	+.11105	+8.8191	+.07997	+9.0604

* The last term is used when the Argument exceeds 3400. When the Argument is negative the sign of A_Ω must be reversed, but the sign of B_Ω remains the same.

TABLE XII.—The Quantities A_Ω and B_Ω.—1850.0.

$$\text{Argument} = \text{Arg. III} + d' + \overset{d}{\text{day of year}} - 6798\ 39.^*$$

	2800		2900		3000		3100	
	A_Ω	B_Ω	A_Ω	B_Ω	A_Ω	B_Ω	A_Ω	B_Ω
		"		"		"		"
50	+.16988	+8.1081	+.14111	+8.5008	+.11105	+8.8191	+.07997	+9.0604
51	16960	1124	14082	5043	11074	8219	07966	0624
52	16932	1166	14052	5079	11044	8247	07934	0644
53	16904	1209	14023	5114	11013	8275	07903	0664
54	16876	1251	13993	5150	10983	8302	07871	0684
55	16848	1294	13964	5185	10952	8330	07840	0704
56	16820	1336	13934	5220	10921	8357	07808	0724
57	16792	1379	13905	5255	10891	8385	07777	0743
58	16763	1421	13875	5290	10860	8412	07745	0763
59	16735	1464	13846	5325	10830	8440	07714	0782
60	16707	1506	13816	5360	10799	8467	07682	0802
61	16679	1548	13786	5395	10768	8494	07650	0821
62	16651	1590	13757	5429	10737	8521	07619	0841
63	16622	1632	13727	5464	10707	8548	07587	0861
64	16594	1674	13698	5498	10676	8575	07556	0879
65	16566	1716	13668	5533	10645	8602	07524	0898
66	16538	1758	13638	5567	10614	8629	07492	0917
67	16509	1799	13609	5602	10583	8655	07461	0936
68	16481	1841	13579	5636	10553	8682	07429	0955
69	16452	1882	13550	5671	10522	8708	07398	0973
70	16424	1924	13520	5705	10491	8735	07366	0992
71	16396	1965	13490	5739	10460	8761	07334	1010
72	16367	2007	13460	5773	10429	8788	07303	1029
73	16339	2048	13431	5807	10399	8814	07271	1047
74	16310	2089	13401	5841	10368	8841	07240	1066
75	16282	2130	13371	5875	10337	8867	07208	1084
76	16254	2171	13341	5909	10306	8893	07176	1102
77	16225	2212	13311	5942	10275	8919	07145	1120
78	16197	2253	13282	5976	10244	8945	07113	1138
79	16168	2294	13252	6009	10213	8971	07082	1156
80	16140	2335	13222	6043	10182	8997	07050	1174
81	16111	2376	13192	6076	10151	9023	07018	1192
82	16083	2416	13162	6110	10120	9048	06986	1209
83	16054	2457	13133	6143	10089	9074	06955	1227
84	16026	2497	13103	6176	10058	9099	06923	1244
85	15997	2538	13073	6209	10027	9125	06891	1262
86	15968	2578	13043	6242	09996	9150	06859	1279
87	15940	2619	13013	6275	09965	9176	06827	1297
88	15911	2659	12983	6308	09934	9201	06796	1314
89	15883	2699	12953	6340	09903	9226	06764	1331
90	15854	2739	12923	6373	09872	9251	06732	1348
91	15825	2779	12893	6405	09841	9276	06700	1365
92	15797	2819	12863	6438	09810	9300	06668	1382
93	15768	2859	12833	6470	09779	9325	06637	1399
94	15740	2899	12803	6503	09748	9349	06605	1415
95	15711	2938	12773	6535	09717	9374	06573	1432
96	15682	2977	12743	6567	09686	9398	06541	1448
97	15653	3017	12713	6599	09655	9423	06509	1465
98	15625	3056	12682	6631	09624	9447	06478	1481
99	15596	3096	12652	6662	09593	9471	06446	1498
100	+.15567	+8.3135	+.12622	+8.6694	+.09562	+8.9495	+.06414	+9.1514

*The last term is used when the Argument exceeds 3400. When the Argument is negative the sign of A_Ω must be reversed, but the sign of B_Ω remains the same.

TABLE XII.—The Quantities A_Ω and B_Ω.—1850.0.

Argument $=$ Arg. III $+ d' +$ day of year$-6798.39.$*

No.	3200 A_Ω	3200 B_Ω	3300 A_Ω	3300 B_Ω		No.	3200 A_Ω	3200 B_Ω	3300 A_Ω	3300 B_Ω
0	+.06414	+9.1514″	+.03208	+9.2730″		50	+.04816	+9.2223″	+.01592	+9.3033″
1	06382	1530	03176	2738		51	04784	2235	01560	3037
2	06350	1546	03144	2746		52	04752	2247	01527	3041
3	06319	1562	03111	2754		53	04720	2259	01495	3045
4	06287	1578	03079	2761		54	04688	2271	01462	3048
5	06255	1594	03047	2769		55	04656	2283	01430	3052
6	06223	1610	03015	2776		56	04624	2295	01398	3055
7	06191	1625	02983	2784		57	04592	2306	01365	3059
8	06160	1641	02950	2791		58	04560	2318	01333	3062
9	06128	1656	02918	2799		59	04528	2329	01300	3066
10	06096	1672	02886	2806		60	04496	2341	01268	3069
11	06064	1687	02854	2813		61	04464	2352	01236	3072
12	06032	1703	02821	2820		62	04432	2364	01203	3075
13	06000	1718	02789	2827		63	04399	2375	01171	3078
14	05968	1733	02756	2834		64	04367	2386	01138	3081
15	05936	1748	02724	2841		65	04335	2397	01106	3084
16	05904	1763	02692	2848		66	04303	2408	01074	3087
17	05872	1778	02660	2854		67	04271	2419	01041	3089
18	05840	1793	02627	2861		68	04238	2430	01009	3092
19	05808	1807	02595	2868		69	04206	2440	00976	3094
20	05776	1822	02563	2875		70	04174	2451	00944	3097
21	05744	1836	02531	2881		71	04142	2461	00912	3099
22	05712	1851	02498	2888		72	04110	2472	00879	3101
23	05680	1865	02466	2894		73	04077	2482	00847	3103
24	05648	1879	02433	2901		74	04045	2492	00814	3105
25	05616	1893	02401	2907		75	04013	2502	00782	3107
26	05584	1907	02369	2913		76	03981	2512	00750	3109
27	05552	1921	02336	2919		77	03949	2522	00717	3110
28	05520	1935	02304	2925		78	03916	2532	00685	3112
29	05488	1949	02271	2931		79	03884	2542	00652	3113
30	05456	1963	02239	2937		80	03852	2552	00620	3115
31	05424	1977	02207	2942		81	03820	2562	00588	3116
32	05392	1990	02175	2948		82	03788	2571	00555	3118
33	05360	2004	02142	2953		83	03755	2581	00523	3119
34	05328	2017	02110	2959		84	03723	2590	00490	3120
35	05296	2031	02078	2964		85	03691	2600	00458	3121
36	05264	2044	02046	2969		86	03659	2609	00426	3122
37	05232	2058	02013	2974		87	03627	2619	00393	3123
38	05200	2071	01981	2979		88	03594	2628	00361	3124
39	05168	2084	01948	2984		89	03562	2637	00328	3125
40	05136	2097	01916	2989		90	03530	2646	00296	3126
41	05104	2110	01884	2994		91	03498	2655	00264	3127
42	05072	2123	01851	2998		92	03466	2663	00231	3127
43	05040	2136	01819	3003		93	03433	2672	00199	3128
44	05008	2148	01786	3007		94	03401	2680	00166	3128
45	04976	2161	01754	3012		95	03369	2689	00134	3129
46	04944	2173	01722	3016		96	03337	2697	00102	3129
47	04912	2186	01689	3021		97	03305	2706	00069	3130
48	04880	2198	01657	3025		98	03272	2714	00037	3130
49	04848	2211	01624	3029		99	03240	2722	+.00004	3130
50	+.04816	+9.2223	+.01592	+9.3033		100	+.03208	+9.2730	−.00028	+9.3130

* The last term is used when the Argument exceeds 3400. When the Argument is negative the sign of A_Ω must be reversed, but the sign of B_Ω remains the same.

TABLE XIII.—Secular Variation of A_Ω and B_Ω.

$$\delta A_\Omega = -0.00031 \sin \Omega. \quad \delta B_\Omega = -0''.0009 \cos \Omega - 0''.0001 \cos 2\,\Omega.$$

Argument = Arg. III + d' + day of year − 6798.4.*

Arg.	δA_Ω	δB_Ω	Arg.	δA_Ω	δB_Ω	Arg.	δA_Ω	δB_Ω	Arg.	δA_Ω	δB_Ω
0	+.00000	−10	900	+.00023	−6	1800	+.00031	+2	2700	+.00019	+7
100	03	10	1000	25	5	1900	31	3	2800	16	8
200	06	10	1100	26	4	2000	30	3	2900	14	8
300	08	10	1200	28	3	2100	29	4	3000	11	8
400	11	9	1300	29	3	2200	28	5	3100	08	8
500	14	9	1400	30	2	2300	26	5	3200	06	8
600	16	8	1500	31	−1	2400	25	6	3300	03	8
700	19	8	1600	31	0	2500	23	6	3400	+.00000	+8
800	+.00021	−7	1700	+.00031	+1	2600	+.00021	+7			

When the Argument is negative the sign of δA_Ω must be reversed, but the sign of δB_Ω remains the same.

TABLE XIV.—$E_\odot$ and its Secular Variation.—1850.0.

$$E_\odot = -0''.0035 \sin 2\,\odot. \quad \delta E_\odot = +0''.0005 \sin 2\,\odot.$$

Argument = Arg I + d' + Sec. In. + day of year.

Arg.	$E_\odot$	$\delta E_\odot$	Arg.	$E_\odot$	$\delta E_\odot$	Arg.	$E_\odot$	$\delta E_\odot$	Arg.	$E_\odot$	$\delta E_\odot$
0	+0.0010	−2	100	−0.0021	+3	200	+0.0027	−4	300	−0.0032	+5
10	21	3	110	29	4	210	33	5	310	0035	5
20	29	4	120	34	5	220	35	5	320	0034	5
30	31	5	130	35	5	230	33	5	330	0029	4
40	35	5	140	32	5	240	28	4	340	0020	3
50	31	4	150	25	4	250	20	3	350	−0.0009	+1
60	23	3	160	15	2	260	+0.0009	−1	360	+0.0004	−1
70	13	−2	170	−0.0004	+1	270	−0.0003	0	370	+0.0016	−2
80	+0.0001	0	180	+0.0007	−1	280	15	+2			
90	−0.0011	+2	190	+0.0018	−3	290	−0.0025	+4			

TABLE XV.—E_Ω and its Secular Variation.—1850.0.

$$E_\Omega = -0''.0483 \sin \Omega + 0''.0015 \sin 2\,\Omega. \quad \delta E_\Omega = +0''.0069 \sin \Omega - 0''.0001 \sin 2\,\Omega.$$

Argument = Arg. III + d' + day of year − 6798.4.*

Arg.	E_Ω	δE_Ω	Arg	E_Ω	δE_Ω	Arg.	E_Ω	δE_Ω	Arg.	E_Ω	δE_Ω
0	+0.0000	−0	900	+0.0342	−50	1800	+0.0484	−69	2700	+0.0305	−43
100	42	6	1000	371	54	1900	490	68	2800	267	37
200	83	12	1100	397	58	2000	472	67	2900	227	32
300	124	18	1200	420	61	2100	460	65	3000	184	26
400	164	24	1300	440	64	2200	444	63	3100	140	19
500	203	30	1400	457	66	2300	424	60	3200	94	13
600	241	35	1500	469	67	2400	400	56	3300	47	·7
700	277	41	1600	478	69	2500	372	52	3400	+0.0000	−0
800	+0.0311	−46	1700	+0.0483	−69	2600	+0.0340	−48			

When the argument is negative the signs of the quantities in this table must be reversed.

δA_Ω, δB_Ω, $\delta E_\odot$ and δE_Ω are to be multiplied by $\dfrac{t-1850}{100}$. The last three are in units of the fourth decimal.

* The last term is used when the Argument exceeds 3400.

TABLE XVI.

Argument IV, for terms in A and B, depending on 2 ☽:
Argument V, for terms in A, depending on ☽ — Γ'.

For Washington Mean Noon of Jan. 0 in common years, Jan. 1 in bissextile years.

Year	IV	V	Year	IV	V	Year	IV	V
	d	d		d	d		d	d
1750	0.849	15.33	1800	12.033	8.66	1850	9.555	1.99
1751	10.669	22.12	1801	8.191	15.45	1851	5.714	8.78
1752 B	7.827	2.35	1802	4.350	22.24	1852 B	2.872	16.57
1753	3.986	9.14	1803	0.509	1.47	1853	12.692	23.36
1754	0.145	15.93	1804 B	11.328	9.27	1854	8.851	2.60
1755	9.964	22.72	1805	7.487	16.06	1855	5.009	9.39
1756 B	7.123	2 96	1806	3.645	22.85	1856 B	2.168	17.18
1757	3.281	9.75	1807	13.465	2 08	1857	11.987	23.97
1758	13.101	16.54	1808 B	10.623	9.87	1858	8.146	3.21
1759	9.259	23.33	1809	6.782	16.66	1859	4.335	10.00
1760 B	6.418	3.57	1810	2.941	23.46	1860 B	1.463	17.79
1761	2.577	10.36	1811	12.760	2.69	1861	11.283	24.58
1762	12.396	17.15	1812 B	9.919	10.48	1862	7.441	3.81
1763	8.555	23.94	1813	6.077	17.27	1863	3.600	10.61
1764 B	5.713	4.18	1814	2.236	24.06	1864 B	0.759	18.40
1765	1.872	10.97	1815	12.055	3.30	1865	10.578	25.19
1766	11.692	17.76	1816 B	9.214	11.09	1866	6.737	4.42
1767	7.850	21.55	1817	5.373	17.88	1867	2.895	11.21
1768 B	5.009	4.79	1818	1.531	24.67	1868 B	0.054	19 01
1769	1.167	11.58	1819	11.351	3.91	1869	9.873	25.80
1770	10.987	18.37	1820 B	8.509	11.70	1870	6.032	5.03
1771	7.146	25.16	1821	4.668	18.49	1871	2.191	11.82
1772 B	4.304	5.40	1822	0.827	25.28	1872 B	13.010	19.61
1773	0.463	12 19	1823	10.646	4.59	1873	9.169	26.40
1774	10.282	18.98	1824 B	7.805	12.31	1874	5.327	5.64
1775	6.441	25.77	1825	3 964	19.10	1875	1.486	12.43
1776 B	3 600	6.00	1826	0.122	25.89	1876 B	12.306	20.22
1777	13 419	12.80	1827	9.942	5.13	1877	8.464	27.01
1778	9.578	19 59	1828 B	7.100	12.92	1878	4.623	6.25
1779	5.736	26.33	1829	3.259	19.71	1879	0.781	13.04
1780 B	2 895	6.61	1830	13.078	26.50	1880 B	11.601	20.83
1781	12.714	13.40	1831	9.237	5.74	1881	7.760	0.07
1782	8.873	20.19	1832 B	6.006	13.53	1882	3.918	6.86
1783	5.032	26.99	1833	2.554	20.32	1883	0.077	13.65
1784 B	2.190	7.22	1834	12.374	27.11	1884 B	10.896	21.44
1785	12.010	14.01	1835	8.532	6.34	1885	7.055	0.68
1786	8.168	20.80	1836 B	5.691	14.13	1886	3.214	7.47
1787	4.327	27.59	1837	1.850	20.93	1887	13 033	14.26
1788 B	1.486	7.83	1838	11.639	0.16	1888 B	10.192	22.05
1789	11.305	14.62	1839	7.828	6.95	1889	6.350	1.29
1790	7.464	21.41	1840 B	4.986	14.74	1890	2.509	8.08
1791	3.622	0.65	1841	1.145	21.53	1891	12.318	14.87
1792 B	0.781	8.44	1842	10.964	0.77	1892 B	9.487	22.66
1793	10.601	15.23	1843	7.123	7.56	1893	5.646	1.89
1794	6.759	22.02	1844 B	4.282	15.35	1894	1.804	8.69
1795	2.918	1.26	1845	0.440	22.14	1895	11.624	15.48
1796 B	0.076	9.05	1846	10.260	1.38	1896 B	8.782	23.27
1797	9.896	15.84	1847	6.418	8.17	1897	4.941	2.50
1798	6.055	22.63	1848 B	3.577	15.96	1898	1.100	9.29
1799	2.213	1.87	1849	13.397	22.75	1899	10.919	16.08
1800	12.033	8.66	1850	9.555	1.99	1900	7.078	22.88

Multiples of the Period of Arg. IV.

	d
1	13.661
2	27.322
3	40.982
4	54.643
5	68.304
6	81.965
7	95.626
8	109.286
9	122.947
10	136.608
11	150.269
12	163.929
13	177.590
14	191.251
15	204.912
16	218.573
17	232.233
18	245.894
19	259.555
20	273.216
21	286.877
22	300.537
23	314.198
24	327.859
25	341.520
26	355.181
27	368.841

Multiples of the Period of Arg. V.

	d
1	27.55
2	55.11
3	82.66
4	110.22
5	137.77
6	165.33
7	192.88
8	220.44
9	247.99
10	275.55
11	303.10
12	330.65
13	358.21
14	385 76

TABLE XVII.—A☾, B☾, A'☾.

$$A_☾ = -\,0.00405 \sin 2\,☾ \quad \cdots \quad \Big\} \; \text{Arg.} = \text{Arg. IV} + \text{day} + d' - \text{multiple of period.}$$
$$B_☾ = -\,0\overset{''}{.}0886 \cos 2\,☾ \quad \cdots$$
$$A'_☾ = +\,0.00135 \sin (☾ - \Gamma') \; . \quad \text{Arg.} = \text{Arg. V} + \text{day} + d' - \text{multiple of period.}$$

In units of the fifth decimal for A, and of the fourth for B.

Arg. IV.	A☾	B☾	Arg. IV.	A☾	B☾	Arg. IV.	A☾	B☾	Arg. V.	A'☾
0.0	− 0	−886	4.6	−347	+459	9.2	+359	+410	0	+ 0
0.1	19	835	4.7	337	493	9.3	367	374	1	30
0.2	37	882	4.8	326	526	9.4	374	335	2	59
0.3	55	877	4.9	314	558	9.5	381	298	3	85
0.4	74	870	5.0	302	589	9.6	387	259	4	106
0.5	92	862	5.1	289	619	9.7	392	221	5	122
0.6	111	852	5.2	277	648	9.8	396	180	6	132
0.7	128	841	5.3	263	675	9.9	400	140	7	135
0.8	145	827	5.4	248	701	10.0	403	101	8	130
0.9	163	811	5.5	232	725	10.1	404	59	9	119
1.0	180	793	5.6	217	748	10.2	405	+ 19	10	102
1.1	196	775	5.7	201	769	10.3	405	− 22	11	80
1.2	212	754	5.8	185	788	10.4	404	62	12	53
1.3	228	732	5.9	168	806	10.5	402	103	13	+ 23
1.4	243	707	6.0	151	822	10.6	400	143	14	− 7
1.5	258	682	6.1	133	837	10.7	396	183	15	37
1.6	272	657	6.2	116	849	10.8	392	224	16	66
1.7	285	628	6.3	98	859	10.9	387	263	17	90
1.8	298	598	6.4	79	862	11.0	380	301	18	110
1.9	310	569	6.5	61	875	11.1	374	338	19	125
2.0	322	537	6.6	42	831	11.2	367	376	20	134
2.1	333	503	6.7	24	884	11.3	359	412	21	134
2.2	344	470	6.8	− 6	886	11.4	350	449	22	129
2.3	353	435	6.9	+ 13	885	11.5	340	483	23	116
2.4	362	399	7.0	32	883	11.6	329	516	24	97
2.5	370	362	7.1	49	879	11.7	317	549	25	74
2.6	376	324	7.2	68	873	11.8	306	581	26	47
2.7	383	285	7.3	86	865	11.9	293	610	27	− 17
2.8	389	247	7.4	105	855	12.0	281	640	28	+ 13
2.9	394	209	7.5	123	844	12.1	267	667	29	+ 43
3.0	398	169	7.6	140	831	12.2	252	693		
3.1	401	129	7.7	158	815	12.3	237	717		
3.2	403	88	7.8	175	799	12.4	221	741		
3.3	404	46	7.9	191	781	12.5	206	762		
3.4	405	− 6	8.0	207	761	12.6	190	782		
3.5	405	+ 35	8.1	223	738	12.7	174	800		
3.6	404	76	8.2	239	715	12.8	156	817		
3.7	402	116	8.3	254	691	12.9	138	833		
3.8	399	155	8.4	268	665	13.0	121	845		
3.9	395	196	8.5	282	637	13.1	104	856		
4.0	390	235	8.6	294	607	13.2	85	866		
4.1	385	274	8.7	306	578	13.3	67	873		
4.2	378	312	8.8	319	546	13.4	48	879		
4.3	372	350	8.9	330	514	13.5	30	883		
4.4	364	388	9.0	341	480	13.6	+ 11	885		
4.5	−356	+424	9.1	+350	+446	13.7	− 7	−885		

GENERAL TABLES.

TABLE XVIII.—The Quantities Log. C and Log. D.—1850.

Log. C = n 1.27312,32 + log. cos ☉; Sec. Var. = + 0.00004,25.

Argument = Arg. I + d' + Inequalities + day of year.

Log. C.

Arg.	0.0	0.1	0.2	0.3	0.4	0.5	0.6	0.7	0.8	0.9
0	n 0.43403	43927	44446	44956	45462	45962	46456	46945	47427	47905
1	.48378	48844	49305	49762	50214	50661	51103	51541	51975	52403
2	.52829	53250	53666	54078	54486	54890	55290	55686	56079	56468
3	.56553	57235	57614	57989	58361	58729	59094	59456	59815	60171
4	.60523	60873	61220	61564	61905	62243	62579	62912	63243	63572
5	n 0.63898	64221	64541	64859	65174	65486	65796	66104	66409	66711
6	.67010	67308	67604	67898	68191	68482	68770	69056	69340	69622
7	.69903	70181	70457	70731	71004	71275	71544	71811	72077	72342
8	.72604	72864	73123	73380	73635	73889	74141	74391	74640	74887
9	.75133	75377	75619	75860	76100	76338	76575	76810	77044	77277
10	n 0.77508	77738	77966	78193	78419	78645	78869	79091	79312	79531
11	.79749	79966	80182	80397	80610	80822	81033	81243	81452	81659
12	.81865	82070	82274	82477	82680	82881	83081	83280	83478	83675
13	.83870	84065	84259	84452	84644	84834	85024	85213	85401	85588
14	.85773	85958	86142	86325	86507	86689	86870	87050	87229	87407
15	n 0.87583	87759	87934	88108	88282	88455	88627	88798	88968	89138
16	.89307	89475	89642	89808	89974	90139	90303	90466	90628	90790
17	.90952	91112	91272	91431	91589	91746	91903	92059	92214	92369
18	.92523	92676	92829	92981	93132	93283	93433	93582	93731	93879
19	.94026	94173	94319	94465	94610	94754	94897	95040	95182	95324
20	n 0.95466	95607	95747	95886	96025	96163	96301	96438	96574	96710
21	.96845	96980	97114	97248	97381	97513	97645	97777	97908	98038
22	.98168	98298	98427	98555	98683	98810	98937	99063	99189	99314
23	0.99439	99563	99687	99810	99933	: 00056	: 00178	: 00299	: 00420	: 00540
24	1.00660	00780	00899	01018	01136	01253	01370	01487	01603	01719
25	n 1.01834	01949	02063	02177	02291	02404	02517	02629	02741	02853
26	.02964	03075	03185	03295	03404	03513	03621	03729	03837	03941
27	.04051	04157	04263	04369	04474	04579	04683	04787	04891	04995
28	.05098	05201	05303	05405	05506	05607	05708	05808	05908	06008
29	.06107	06206	06304	06402	06500	06598	06695	06792	06888	06984
30	n 1.07080	07175	07270	07365	07459	07553	07646	07739	07832	07925
31	.08017	08109	08200	08291	08382	08473	08563	08653	08743	08832
32	.08921	09010	09098	09186	09274	09361	09448	09535	09621	09707
33	.09793	09879	09964	10049	10134	10218	10302	10386	10469	10552
34	.10633	10717	10799	10881	10963	11044	11125	11206	11286	11366
35	n 1.11446	11525	11604	11683	11762	11841	11919	11997	12075	12153
36	.12230	12307	12383	12459	12535	12611	12686	12761	12836	12911
37	.12985	13059	13133	13207	13280	13353	13426	13499	13571	13643
38	.13715	13786	13857	13928	13999	14070	14140	14210	14280	14349
39	.14418	14487	14556	14624	14692	14760	14828	14896	14963	15030
40	n 1.15097	15163	15229	15295	15361	15427	15492	15557	15622	15687
41	.15752	15816	15880	15944	16007	16070	16133	16196	16259	16321
42	.16383	16445	16507	16568	16629	16690	16751	16812	16872	16933
43	.16992	17052	17111	17170	17229	17288	17347	17405	17463	17521
44	.17579	17636	17693	17750	17807	17864	17920	17976	18032	18088
45	n 1.18144	18199	18254	18309	18364	18419	18473	18527	18581	18635
46	.18689	18742	18795	18848	18901	18953	19005	19057	19109	19161
47	.19213	19264	19315	19366	19417	19468	19518	19568	19618	19668
48	.19718	19767	19816	19865	19914	19963	20011	20059	20107	20155
49	.20203	20250	20297	20344	20391	20438	20485	20531	20577	20623
50	n 1.20669	20715	20760	20805	20850	20895	20940	20985	21029	21073
51	.21117	21161	21205	21248	21291	21334	21377	21420	21463	21505
52	.21547	21589	21631	21673	21714	21755	21796	21837	21878	21919
53	.21959	21999	22039	22079	22119	22159	22198	22237	22276	22315
54	.22354	22393	22431	22469	22507	22545	22583	22621	22658	22695
55	n 1.22732	22769	22806	22843	22879	22915	22951	22987	23023	23059

TABLE XVIII.—The Quantities Log. C and Log. D.—1850.

Log. D = n 1.31058,92 + log. sin ☉.

Argument = Arg. I + d' + Inequalities + day of year.

Log. D.

Arg.	0.0	0.1	0.2	0.3	0.4	0.5	0.6	0.7	0.8	0.9
0	1.30598	30587	30575	30563	30551	30539	30527	30514	30502	30489
1	.30476	30464	30451	30438	30425	30412	30398	30385	30371	30358
2	.30344	30330	30316	30301	30287	30272	30257	30242	30227	30212
3	.30196	30181	30165	30149	30133	30116	30100	30083	30067	30050
4	.30033	30016	29998	29981	29963	29946	29928	29910	29892	29874
5	1.29856	29837	29819	29800	29781	29762	29743	29723	29704	29684
6	.29664	29644	29624	29604	29583	29563	29542	29521	29500	29479
7	.29458	29436	29415	29393	29371	29349	29327	29304	29282	29259
8	.29236	29213	29190	29167	29143	29120	29096	29073	29049	29025
9	.29000	28976	28951	28926	28901	28876	28851	28825	28800	28774
10	1.28749	28723	28697	28671	28645	28618	28592	28565	28538	28511
11	.28483	28456	28428	28400	28372	28344	28315	28287	28258	28230
12	.28201	28172	28143	28113	28084	28054	28025	27995	27965	27934
13	.27903	27873	27842	27811	27780	27749	27717	27685	27654	27622
14	.27590	27558	27525	27493	27460	27427	27394	27360	27327	27294
15	1.27260	27226	27192	27158	27124	27089	27055	27020	26985	26950
16	.26915	26879	26844	26808	26772	26736	26700	26663	26627	26590
17	.26553	26516	26478	26441	26403	26365	26327	26288	26250	26211
18	.26173	26134	26095	26055	26016	25977	25937	25897	25857	25817
19	.25777	25736	25695	25654	25613	25572	25531	25489	25447	25405
20	1.25363	25320	25278	25235	25193	25150	25107	25063	25020	24976
21	.24932	24888	24843	24799	24754	24710	24665	24620	24574	24529
22	.24483	24437	24391	24344	24298	24251	24204	24157	24110	24062
23	.24015	23967	23919	23871	23822	23774	23725	23676	23627	23578
24	.23528	23478	23428	23378	23328	23277	23226	23175	23124	23073
25	1.23022	22970	22918	22866	22814	22762	22709	22656	22603	22549
26	.22496	22442	22388	22334	22280	22226	22171	22116	22061	22006
27	.21951	21895	21839	21783	21727	21670	21613	21556	21499	21442
28	.21384	21326	21268	21210	21152	21093	21034	20975	20916	20857
29	.20797	20737	20677	20616	20556	20495	20434	20373	20311	20249
30	1.20187	20125	20062	20000	19937	19874	19811	19747	19684	19620
31	.19556	19491	19426	19361	19296	19231	19165	19099	19033	18967
32	.18901	18834	18767	18700	18633	18565	18497	18429	18360	18292
33	.18223	18154	18084	18015	17945	17875	17804	17733	17662	17591
34	.17520	17448	17376	17304	17232	17159	17086	17013	16939	16866
35	1.16792	16718	16643	16569	16494	16419	16341	16268	16192	16116
36	.16039	15962	15885	15807	15730	15652	15574	15496	15417	15338
37	.15258	15179	15099	15019	14938	14857	14776	14695	14613	14531
38	.14449	14367	14284	14201	14118	14034	13950	13866	13781	13697
39	.13612	13527	13441	13355	13269	13182	13095	13007	12920	12832
40	1.12744	12656	12567	12478	12389	12299	12209	12119	12028	11937
41	.11846	11754	11662	11570	11478	11385	11292	11198	11104	11010
42	.10915	10820	10724	10629	10533	10437	10340	10243	10145	10048
43	.09950	09852	09753	09654	09555	09455	09355	09254	09153	09052
44	.08950	08848	08746	08643	08540	08436	08332	08228	08123	08018
45	1.07912	07806	07700	07593	07486	07379	07271	07163	07054	06946
46	.06836	06726	06616	06505	06394	06283	06171	06058	05945	05832
47	.05719	05605	05491	05376	05261	05145	05029	04912	04795	04678
48	.04560	04441	04322	04202	04083	03963	03842	03721	03599	03477
49	.03355	03232	03108	02984	02860	02735	02610	02484	02358	02231
50	1.02103	01975	01846	01717	01588	01458	01327	01196	01064	00932
51	1.00800	00667	00533	00399	00264	00128	:99992	:99855	:99718	:99581
52	0.99443	99304	99165	99025	98885	98744	98602	98460	98317	98174
53	.98030	97885	97740	97594	97448	97301	97153	97004	96855	96706
54	.96556	96405	96253	96101	95948	95795	95641	95486	95330	95174
55	0.95017	94859	94700	94541	94381	94222	94061	93899	93736	93573

TABLE XVIII.—The Quantities Log. C and Log. D.—1850.

Argument = Arg. I + d' + Inequalities + day of year.

Log. C.

Arg.	0.0	0.1	0.2	0.3	0.4	0.5	0.6	0.7	0.8	0.9
55	n 1.22732	22769	22806	22843	22879	22915	22951	22987	23023	23058
56	.23093	23128	23163	23198	23233	23268	23302	23336	23370	23404
57	.23438	23472	23505	23538	23571	23604	23637	23670	23702	23734
58	.23766	23798	23830	23862	23893	23924	23955	23986	24017	24048
59	.24079	24109	24139	24169	24199	24229	24259	24289	24318	24347
60	n 1 24376	24405	24434	24463	24491	24519	24547	24575	24603	24631
61	.24658	24685	24712	24739	24766	24793	24820	24846	24872	24898
62	.24924	24950	24976	25002	25027	25052	25077	25102	25127	25152
63	.25176	25200	25224	25248	25272	25296	25320	25344	25367	25390
64	.25413	25436	25459	25482	25504	25526	25548	25570	25592	25614
65	n 1.25635	25657	25678	25699	25720	25741	25762	25783	25803	25823
66	.25843	25863	25883	25903	25922	25941	25960	25979	25998	26017
67	.26036	26055	26074	26092	26110	26128	26146	26164	26182	26199
68	.26216	26233	26250	26267	26284	26300	26317	26333	26349	26365
69	.26381	26397	26413	26429	26444	26459	26474	26489	26504	26519
70	n 1.26533	26547	26561	26575	26589	26603	26617	26631	26644	26657
71	.26670	26683	26696	26709	26722	26734	26747	26759	26771	26783
72	.26795	26807	26819	26830	26841	26852	26863	26874	26885	26895
73	.26905	26915	26925	26935	26945	26955	26965	26975	26984	26993
74	.27002	27011	27020	27029	27038	27046	27054	27062	27070	27078
75	n 1.27086	27094	27102	27109	27116	27123	27130	27137	27144	27151
76	.27157	27163	27169	27175	27181	27187	27193	27198	27204	27209
77	.27214	27219	27224	27229	27234	27238	27242	27246	27250	27254
78	.27258	27262	27266	27269	27272	27275	27278	27281	27284	27287
79	.27289	27292	27294	27296	27298	27300	27302	27304	27305	27306
80	n 1.27307	27308	27309	27310	27311	27311	27311	27312	27312	27312
81	.27312	27312	27312	27311	27311	27310	27309	27308	27307	27306
82	.27304	27303	27301	27299	27297	27295	27293	27291	27289	27286
83	.27283	27280	27277	27274	27271	27268	27265	27261	27257	27253
84	.27249	27245	27241	27237	27232	27227	27222	27217	27212	27207
85	n 1.27202	27197	27192	27186	27180	27174	27168	27162	27156	27140
86	.27142	27135	27128	27121	27114	27107	27100	27093	27085	27077
87	.27069	27061	27053	27045	27037	27028	27019	27010	27001	26992
88	.26983	26974	26965	26955	26945	26935	26925	26915	26905	26895
89	.26884	26873	26862	26851	26840	26829	26818	26807	26795	26783
90	n 1.26771	26759	26747	26735	26723	26710	26698	26685	26672	26659
91	.26646	26633	26620	26606	26592	26578	26564	26550	26536	26522
92	.26507	26493	26478	26463	26448	26433	26418	26403	26388	26372
93	.26356	26340	26324	26308	26292	26275	26258	26241	26224	26207
94	.26190	26173	26156	26139	26121	26103	26085	26067	26049	26031
95	n 1.26012	25994	25975	25956	25937	25918	25899	25880	25860	25840
96	.25820	25800	25780	25760	25740	25719	25698	25677	25656	25635
97	.25614	25593	25572	25550	25528	25506	25484	25462	25440	25418
98	.25395	25372	25349	25326	25303	25280	25257	25234	25210	25186
99	.25162	25138	25114	25090	25065	25040	25015	24990	24965	24940
100	n 1.24915	24890	24864	24838	24812	24786	24760	24734	24707	24680
101	.24653	24626	24599	24572	24545	24517	24490	24462	24434	24406
102	.24378	24350	24322	24293	24264	24235	24206	24177	24148	24118
103	.24088	24058	24028	23998	23968	23938	23908	23877	23846	23815
104	.23784	23753	23722	23690	23658	23626	23594	23562	23530	23498
105	n 1.23465	23432	23399	23366	23333	23300	23267	23233	23199	23165
106	.23131	23097	23063	23028	22993	22958	22923	22888	22853	22817
107	.22781	22745	22709	22673	22637	22601	22565	22528	22491	22454
108	.22417	22380	22343	22305	22267	22229	22191	22153	22115	22076
109	.22037	21998	21959	21920	21881	21841	21801	21761	21721	21681
110	n 1.21641	21601	21560	21519	21478	21437	21396	21355	21313	21271

TABLE XVIII.—The Quantities Log. C and Log D.—1850.

Argument = Arg. I + d' + Inequalities + day of year..

Log. D.

Arg.	0.0	0.1	0.2	0.3	0.4	0.5	0.6	0.7	0.8	0.9
55	0.95017	94859	94700	94541	94391	94222	94061	93899	93736	93573
56	.93408	93243	93077	92911	92744	92576	92408	92239	92069	91897
57	.91724	91551	91377	91203	91028	90852	90675	90497	90318	90139
58	.89959	89778	89596	89413	89229	89044	88859	88673	88485	88297
59	.88107	87916	87724	87532	87339	87146	86951	86755	86558	86359
60	.86159	85959	85758	85556	85352	85147	84941	84734	84526	84317
61	.84107	83896	83683	83469	83254	83039	82822	82604	82384	82163
62	.81940	81716	81491	81265	81038	80810	80580	80349	80116	79882
63	.79646	79409	79171	78931	78690	78448	78204	77959	77712	77464
64	.77212	76960	76706	76451	76195	75937	75677	75416	75153	74888
65	.74620	74351	74080	73808	73534	73259	72982	72703	72421	72137
66	.71851	71563	71273	70981	70687	70393	70096	69796	69494	69189
67	.68982	68572	68260	67946	67630	67313	66993	66670	66341	66015
68	.65681	65347	65010	64670	64328	63983	63635	63284	62929	62572
69	.62213	61850	61483	61113	60740	60365	59986	59603	59216	58826
70	.58432	58034	57633	57228	56819	56407	55989	55567	55141	54711
71	.54278	53839	53395	52947	52495	52038	51575	51107	50634	50156
72	.49672	49183	48689	48188	47682	47169	46649	46123	45591	45053
73	.44507	43954	43397	42828	42253	41671	41080	40491	39874	39258
74	.38633	38000	37356	36703	36039	35365	34680	33984	33277	32558
75	.31827	31084	30326	29556	28772	27974	27158	26329	25484	24622
76	.23742	22843	21926	20989	20028	19048	18046	17019	15958	14803
77	.13788	12654	11489	10293	09062	07795	06490	05148	03759	02324
78	0.00840	:99308	:97715	:96061	:94346	:92556	:90694	:88743	:86700	:84562
79	9.82307	79931	77418	74754	71908	68870	65600	62062	58216	53986
80	9.49308	44066	38100	31171	22941	12768	:99466	:80200	:44700	n7 87('2
81	n 8.63165	89324	:05535	:17312	:26567	:34192	:40676	:46317	:51308	:55784
82	9.59841	63552	66970	70136	73097	75849	78448	80901	83215	85419
83	9.87516	89517	91424	93255	95008	96697	98322	99885	:01397	:02854
84	0.04268	05634	06061	08245	09495	10708	11887	13038	14156	15245
85	n 0.16311	17349	18362	19352	20322	21269	22195	23101	23989	24859
86	.25714	26551	27371	28176	28966	29742	30504	31253	31989	32711
87	.33423	34123	34812	35490	36157	36813	37460	38096	38726	39344
88	.39954	40556	41148	41733	42311	42879	43441	43995	44543	45082
89	.45616	46142	46663	47177	47684	48187	48682	49173	49657	50136
90	n 0.50609	51077	51540	51998	52452	52901	53345	53784	54219	54649
91	.55074	55496	55914	56327	56735	57140	57542	57940	58334	58724
92	.59108	59491	59870	60246	60618	60987	61353	61716	62075	62431
93	.62784	63134	63481	63826	64168	64507	64843	65176	65507	65835
94	.66161	66484	66804	67122	67437	67750	68060	68369	68675	68978
95	n 0.69279	69578	69875	70170	70463	70754	71042	71328	71612	71894
96	.72176	72455	72732	73007	73279	73549	73818	74085	74351	74615
97	.74877	75137	75396	75653	75908	76162	76414	76664	76913	77160
98	.77407	77651	77893	78134	78374	78614	78851	79087	79321	79553
99	.79784	80014	80243	80470	80696	80920	81144	81367	81588	81807
100	n 0.82024	82241	82457	82672	82885	83097	83308	83518	83727	83935
101	.84141	84346	84550	84753	84955	85157	85357	85556	85754	85951
102	.86146	86341	86535	86728	86920	87110	87300	87489	87677	87864
103	.88050	88235	88419	88602	88785	88967	89148	89328	89507	89685
104	.89861	90037	90212	90387	90561	90734	90906	91077	91247	91417
105	n 0.91586	91754	91921	92097	92253	92418	92582	92745	92907	93069
106	.93231	93392	93552	93711	93869	94026	94183	94339	94495	94650
107	.94804	94958	95111	95263	95414	95565	95715	95864	96013	96161
108	.96309	96456	96603	96749	96894	97038	97182	97326	97469	97611
109	.97751	97892	98032	98172	98311	98449	98585	98723	98860	98996
110	n 0.99132	99267	99401	99535	99669	99802	99934	:00066	:00197	:00328

40 GENERAL TABLES.

TABLE XVIII.—The Quantities Log. C and Log. D.—1850.

Argument = Arg. I + d' + Inequalities + day of year.

Log. C.

Arg.	0.0	0.1	0.2	0.3	0.4	0.5	0.6	0.7	0.8	0.9
110	n 1.21641	21601	21560	21519	21478	21437	21396	21355	21313	21271
111	.21229	21187	21145	21102	21059	21016	20973	20930	20887	20843
112	.20799	20755	20711	20667	20623	20579	20535	20490	20445	20400
113	.20355	20310	20264	20218	20172	20126	20080	20033	19986	19939
114	.19892	19845	19798	19751	19703	19655	19607	19559	19511	19462
115	n 1.19413	19364	19315	19266	19216	19166	19116	19066	19016	18966
116	.18915	18864	18813	18762	18711	18659	18607	18555	18503	18451
117	.18399	18346	18293	18240	18187	18134	18081	18027	17973	17919
118	.17865	17811	17756	17701	17646	17591	17536	17480	17424	17368
119	.17312	17256	17199	17142	17085	17028	16971	16913	16855	16797
120	n 1.16739	16681	16622	16563	16504	16445	16386	16326	16266	16206
121	.16146	16086	16025	15964	15903	15842	15781	15719	15657	15595
122	.15533	15470	15407	15344	15281	15218	15154	15090	15026	14962
123	.14898	14833	14768	14703	14638	14573	14507	14441	14375	14309
124	.14242	14175	14108	14041	13974	13906	13838	13770	13702	13633
125	n 1.13564	13495	13426	13357	13287	13217	13147	13076	13005	12934
126	.12863	12791	12719	12647	12575	12503	12430	12357	12284	12211
127	.12137	12063	11989	11915	11840	11765	11690	11615	11539	11463
128	.11387	11311	11234	11157	11080	11003	10925	10847	10769	10691
129	.10612	10533	10454	10375	10295	10215	10135	10054	09973	09892
130	n 1.09811	09729	09647	09565	09483	09400	09317	09234	09150	09066
131	.08982	08897	08812	08727	08642	08557	08471	08385	08299	08212
132	.08125	08038	07950	07862	07774	07685	07596	07507	07418	07328
133	.07238	07148	07057	06966	06875	06783	06691	06599	06507	06414
134	.06321	06228	06134	06040	05946	05851	05756	05660	05564	05468
135	n 1.05372	05275	05178	05081	04983	04885	04787	04688	04589	04490
136	.04390	04290	04189	04088	03987	03886	03784	03682	03579	03476
137	.03373	03269	03165	03061	02956	02851	02745	02639	02533	02426
138	.02319	02211	02103	01995	01896	01777	01668	01558	01448	01337
139	.01226	01114	01002	00890	00778	00665	00552	00438	00324	00209
140	n 1.00094	:99978	:99862	:99746	:99629	:99512	:99394	:99276	:99157	:99038
141	0.98919	98799	98679	98558	98437	98315	98193	98070	97947	97823
142	.97699	97575	97450	97325	97199	97072	96945	96817	96689	96560
143	.96432	96303	96173	96043	95912	95780	95648	95515	95382	95249
144	.95115	94980	94845	94709	94573	94436	94299	94161	94023	93884
145	n 0.93744	93604	93463	93322	93180	93038	92895	92751	92607	92462
146	.92317	92171	92024	91877	91729	91581	91432	91282	91132	90981
147	.90829	90677	90524	90370	90216	90061	89905	89748	89591	89434
148	.89276	89118	88959	88799	88639	88474	88311	88147	87983	87818
149	.87653	87487	87320	87152	86983	86814	86644	86473	86301	86129
150	n 0.85956	85782	85607	85431	85254	85077	84899	84720	84540	84359
151	.84177	83995	83812	83628	83442	83255	83068	82880	82691	82501
152	.82310	82118	81925	81731	81536	81341	81145	80948	80749	80549
153	.80347	80145	79942	79738	79533	79327	79119	78910	78700	78490
154	.78279	78067	77854	77639	77422	77203	76984	76764	76543	76320
155	n 0.76096	75871	75644	75416	75187	74957	74725	74492	74257	74021
156	.73784	73545	73305	73063	72820	72576	72330	72083	71834	71583
157	.71331	71077	70821	70564	70306	70046	69785	69522	69257	68989
158	.68719	68448	68175	67901	67625	67347	67067	66785	66501	66215
159	.65927	65637	65345	65051	64755	64456	64155	63852	63547	63240
160	n 0.62931	62619	62305	61988	61669	61347	61023	60696	60367	60035
161	.59701	59364	59024	58681	58335	57987	57635	57280	56922	56561
162	.56199	55833	55464	55091	54714	54332	53948	53561	53170	52775
163	.52377	51975	51569	51159	50745	50328	49906	49479	49048	48613
164	.48173	47729	47280	46826	46367	45904	45435	44961	44481	43996
165	n 0.43506	43010	42508	42000	41485	40964	40437	39903	39363	38817

TABLE XVIII.—The Quantities Log. C and Log. D.—1850.

Argument = Arg. I + d' + Inequalities + day of year.

Log. D.

Arg.	0.0	0.1	0.2	0.3	0.4	0.5	0.6	0.7	0.8	0.9
110	n 0.99132	99267	99401	99535	99669	99802	99934	: 00066	: 00197	: 00328
111	1.00459	00588	00717	00845	00974	01102	01229	01356	01482	01608
112	.01733	01858	01982	02106	02229	02351	02473	02595	02716	02837
113	.02958	03078	03197	03316	03435	03553	03671	03788	03905	04021
114	.04137	04253	04368	04483	04597	04710	04823	04936	05048	05160
115	n 1.05272	05383	05494	05604	05714	05824	05933	06042	06150	06259
116	.06365	06472	06579	06685	06791	06896	07001	07106	07210	07314
117	.07418	07521	07624	07727	07829	07931	08033	08134	08235	08335
118	.08434	08534	08633	08732	08830	08928	09026	09124	09221	09318
119	.09414	09510	09606	09701	09796	09891	09986	10080	10174	10267
120	n 1.10359	10452	10545	10637	10729	10820	10911	11002	11092	11182
121	.11272	11362	11451	11540	11628	11716	11804	11892	11979	12066
122	.12153	12240	12326	12412	12498	12583	12668	12753	12837	12921
123	.13005	13089	13172	13255	13338	13420	13502	13584	13665	13746
124	.13827	13908	13988	14068	14148	14227	14307	14386	14465	14543
125	n 1.14621	14699	14777	14854	14931	15008	15085	15161	15237	15313
126	.15389	15464	15539	15614	15689	15763	15837	15911	15984	16057
127	.16130	16203	16276	16348	16420	16492	16564	16635	16706	16777
128	.16847	16917	16987	17057	17127	17196	17265	17334	17403	17471
129	.17539	17607	17675	17743	17810	17877	17944	18011	18077	18143
130	n 1.18209	18275	18340	18405	18470	18535	18600	18664	18728	18792
131	.18855	18919	18982	19045	19108	19170	19233	19295	19357	19419
132	.19480	19541	19602	19663	19724	19785	19845	19905	19965	20025
133	.20084	20143	20202	20261	20320	20378	20436	20494	20552	20610
134	.20667	20724	20781	20837	20894	20950	21006	21062	21118	21174
135	n 1.21229	21284	21339	21394	21449	21503	21557	21611	21665	21719
136	.21772	21825	21878	21931	21984	22036	22088	22140	22192	22244
137	.22296	22347	22398	22449	22500	22551	22602	22652	22702	22752
138	.22802	22852	22901	22950	22999	23048	23097	23145	23193	23241
139	.23289	23337	23385	23432	23479	23526	23573	23620	23667	23713
140	n 1.23759	23805	23851	23897	23942	23987	24032	24077	24121	24166
141	.24211	24255	24299	24343	24387	24431	24474	24517	24560	24603
142	.24646	24688	24731	24773	24815	24857	24899	24941	24982	25024
143	.25065	25106	25147	25188	25229	25269	25309	25349	25389	25429
144	.25468	25507	25546	25585	25624	25663	25701	25740	25778	25816
145	n 1.25854	25892	25929	25967	26004	26041	26078	26115	26152	26189
146	.26225	26261	26297	26333	26369	26405	26441	26476	26511	26546
147	.26581	26616	26650	26684	26719	26753	26787	26820	26854	26887
148	.26921	26954	26987	27020	27053	27086	27119	27151	27183	27215
149	.27247	27278	27310	27341	27373	27404	27435	27466	27497	27528
150	n 1.27559	27588	27618	27648	27678	27708	27738	27767	27796	27826
151	.27855	27884	27912	27941	27969	27998	28026	28054	28082	28110
152	.28138	28165	28193	28220	28247	28274	28301	28327	28354	28380
153	.28406	28432	28458	28484	28510	28535	28560	28585	28610	28635
154	.28660	28684	28709	28733	28758	28782	28806	28830	28854	28878
155	n 1.28902	28925	28949	28972	·28995	29018	29041	29063	29086	29108
156	.29130	29152	29174	29196	29218	29239	29260	29281	29302	29323
157	.29344	29365	29385	29406	29426	29446	29466	29486	29506	29526
158	.29546	29565	29584	29604	29623	29642	29661	29680	29698	29716
159	.29734	29752	29770	29788	29806	29823	29841	29858	29875	29892
160	n 1.29909	29926	29942	29959	29975	29992	30008	30024	30040	30056
161	.30072	30088	30103	30119	30134	30149	30164	30178	30193	30207
162	.30222	30236	30250	30264	30278	30292	30305	30319	30332	30346
163	.30359	30372	30385	30398	30411	30423	30436	30448	30461	30472
164	.30484	30496	30507	30519	30530	30542	30553	30564	30575	30586
165	n 1.30596	30606	30617	30627	30637	30647	30657	30667	30676	30686

TABLE XVIII.—The Quantities Log. C and Log. D.—1850.

Argument = Arg. I + d' + Inequalities + day of year.

Log. C.

Arg.	0.0	0.1	0.2	0.3	0.4	0.5	0.6	0.7	0.8	0.9
165	n 0.43506	43010	42508	42000	41485	40964	40437	39903	39363	38817
166	.38264	37702	37132	36557	35972	35379	34779	34170	33551	32925
167	.32288	31641	30987	30320	29643	28956	28257	27546	26826	26091
168	.25343	24584	23809	23022	22219	21400	20567	19718	18850	17954
169	.17059	16138	15194	14231	13244	12236	11202	10145	09058	07944
170	n 0.06803	05628	04424	03181	01906	00588	: 99233	: 97829	: 96383	: 94883
171	9.93333	91722	90053	88317	86503	84616	82637	80569	78392	76106
172	9.73686	71131	68415	65510	62400	59052	55428	51462	47110	42263
173	n 9.36811	30582	23285	14537	03560	: 88812	: 66371	n 17354	p 21397	: 67720
174	p 8.89621	: 04148	: 14987	: 23676	: 30894	: 37081	: 42511	: 47323	: 51654	: 55604
175	9.59214	62546	65650	68538	71246	73802	76209	78489	80656	82725
176	9.84694	86578	88389	90122	91788	93393	94945	96439	97883	99285
177	0.00638	01951	03225	04466	05669	06840	07980	09093	10176	11232
178	.12263	13273	14257	15219	16160	17083	17985	18868	19734	20584
179	.21416	22233	23034	23820	24595	25354	26099	26832	27554	28263
180	0.28960	29646	30322	30938	31643	32298	32923	33549	34169	34776
181	.35376	35967	36550	37127	37695	38255	38808	39354	39895	40427
182	.40953	41473	41987	42495	42996	43491	43981	44465	44944	45418
183	.45885	46348	46806	47259	47708	48152	48591	49026	49456	49881
184	.50302	50719	51132	51541	51946	52348	52745	53139	53529	53916
185	0.54290	54679	55056	55429	55798	56164	56527	56887	57244	57598
186	.57949	58297	58642	58984	59324	59661	59995	60326	60655	60981
187	.61305	61626	61944	62260	62574	62886	63195	63502	63807	64109
188	.64409	64707	65003	65297	65589	65877	66164	66449	66732	67014
189	.67294	67572	67848	68122	68394	68664	68932	69198	69463	69727
190	0.69989	70249	70507	70763	71018	71271	71523	71773	72022	72269
191	.72514	72758	73000	73241	73481	73720	73957	74193	74427	74659
192	.74890	75120	75318	75575	75801	76026	76250	76472	76693	76913
193	.77131	77348	77564	77779	77993	78205	78416	78626	78835	79043
194	.79251	79457	79662	79866	80068	80269	80469	80668	80866	81064
195	0.81261	81456	81650	81843	82036	82228	82419	82609	82798	82985
196	.83171	83357	83542	83726	83909	84091	84272	84452	84631	84810
197	.84988	85165	85341	85516	85691	85865	86038	86210	86381	86552
198	.86722	86891	87059	87226	87393	87559	87725	87890	88054	88216
199	.88377	88538	88698	88858	89018	89177	89335	89492	89649	89805
200	0.89960	90115	90269	90422	90575	90727	90878	91029	91179	91328
201	.91477	91625	91772	91919	92065	92211	92356	92501	92645	92788
202	.92930	93072	93213	93354	93495	93635	93774	93913	94051	94188
203	.94325	94462	94594	94733	94868	95002	95136	95270	95403	95535
204	.95666	95797	95927	96057	96187	96316	96445	96573	96701	96828
205	0.96954	97080	97206	97331	97456	97580	97704	97827	97950	98072
206	.98194	98315	98436	98557	98677	98797	98916	99034	99152	99270
207	0.99388	99505	99622	99738	99854	99969	: 00084	: 00198	: 00312	: 00426
208	1.00539	00652	00764	00876	00988	01099	01210	01320	01430	01539
209	.01648	01757	01865	01973	02081	02188	02295	02401	02507	02613
210	1.02718	02823	02928	03032	03136	03239	03342	03445	03547	03649
211	.03751	03852	03953	04054	04154	04254	04353	04452	04551	04650
212	.04748	04846	04943	05040	05137	05234	05330	05426	05521	05616
213	.05711	05805	05899	05993	06087	06180	06273	06366	06458	06550
214	.06642	06733	06824	06915	07006	07096	07186	07275	07364	07453
215	1.07542	07630	07718	07806	07893	07980	08067	08153	08239	08325
216	.08411	08496	08581	08666	08751	08835	08919	09003	09086	09169
217	.09252	09335	09417	09499	09581	09662	09743	09824	09905	09986
218	.10066	10146	10225	10304	10383	10462	10540	10618	10696	10774
219	.10852	10929	11006	11083	11160	11236	11312	11388	11463	11538
220	1.11613	11688	11762	11835	11910	11984	12058	12131	12204	12277

TABLE XVIII.—The Quantities Log. C and Log. D.—1850.

Argument = Arg. I + d' + Inequalities + day of year.

Log. D.

Arg.	0.0	0.1	0.2	0.3	0.4	0.5	0.6	0.7	0.8	0.9
165	n 1.30590	30606	30617	30627	30637	30647	30657	30667	30676	30686
166	.30696	30705	30714	30724	30733	30742	30751	30759	30768	30776
167	.30784	30792	30800	30808	30816	30823	30831	30838	30846	30853
168	.30860	30867	30873	30880	30886	30893	30899	30905	30911	30917
169	.30923	30928	30934	30939	30945	30950	30955	30960	30965	30970
170	n 1.30974	30978	30983	30987	30991	30995	30999	31002	31006	31010
171	.31013	31016	31019	31022	31025	31028	31031	31033	31036	31038
172	.31041	31043	31045	31047	31049	31050	31052	31053	31054	31055
173	.31056	31057	31057	31058	31058	31059	31059	31059	31059	31059
174	.31059	31059	31058	31058	31057	31056	31055	31055	31053	31050
175	n 1.31049	31047	31046	31044	31042	31040	31038	31036	31033	31031
176	.31028	31025	31022	31019	31016	31013	31009	31006	31002	30999
177	.30995	30991	30987	30983	30979	30974	30969	30965	30960	30955
178	.30950	30945	30939	30934	30928	30923	30917	30911	30905	30899
179	.30893	30886	30880	30873	30867	30860	30853	30845	30838	30831
180	n 1.30823	30816	30808	30800	30792	30784	30776	30767	30759	30750
181	.30742	30733	30724	30715	30706	30697	30688	30678	30668	30658
182	.30648	30638	30627	30617	30606	30596	30585	30575	30564	30553
183	.30542	30531	30519	30508	30496	30485	30473	30461	30449	30437
184	.30424	30411	30399	30386	30373	30360	30347	30334	30321	30307
185	n 1.30293	30279	30265	30251	30237	30223	30209	30194	30180	30165
186	.30150	30135	30120	30104	30089	30074	30058	30042	30026	30010
187	.29994	29978	29961	29945	29928	29911	29894	29877	29860	29843
188	.29826	29808	29791	29773	29755	29737	29719	29700	29682	29663
189	.29645	29626	29607	29588	29569	29550	29530	29511	29491	29471
190	n 1.29451	29431	29410	29390	29369	29349	29328	29307	29286	29265
191	.29244	29223	29201	29180	29158	29136	29114	29091	29069	29046
192	.29024	29001	28978	28955	28932	28909	28885	28862	28838	28815
193	.28791	28767	28743	28719	28695	28670	28645	28620	28595	28570
194	.28545	28519	28494	28468	28442	28416	28390	28363	28337	28310
195	n 1.28284	28257	28230	28203	28176	28149	28121	28094	28066	28039
196	.28011	27983	27954	27926	27897	27869	27840	27811	27782	27753
197	.27723	27694	27664	27634	27604	27574	27543	27513	27482	27452
198	.27421	27390	27359	27327	27296	27265	27233	27201	27169	27137
199	.27105	27072	27040	27007	26975	26942	26909	26875	26842	26808
200	n 1.26775	26741	26707	26672	26638	26604	26569	26534	26499	26464
201	.26429	26393	26358	26322	26287	26251	26215	26179	26142	26106
202	.26070	26033	25996	25958	25921	25884	25846	25808	25770	25732
203	.25694	25655	25617	25579	25539	25500	25461	25421	25382	25342
204	.25303	25263	25223	25183	25143	25102	25061	25020	24979	24938
205	n 1.24896	24854	24813	24771	24729	24687	24644	24602	24559	24517
206	.24474	24430	24387	24343	24300	24256	24212	24167	24123	24078
207	.24034	23989	23944	23899	23854	23808	23762	23716	23670	23624
208	.23578	23531	23485	23438	23391	23344	23296	23249	23201	23153
209	.23105	23056	23008	22959	22911	22862	22812	22763	22713	22664
210	n 1.22614	22564	22513	22463	22412	22362	22311	22260	22208	22157
211	.22106	22054	22002	21949	21897	21845	21792	21738	21685	21631
212	.21578	21524	21470	21416	21362	21307	21252	21197	21142	21087
213	.21032	20976	20920	20864	20808	20752	20695	20638	20581	20524
214	.20467	20409	20351	20293	20235	20177	20118	20059	20000	19941
215	n 1.19882	19822	19762	19702	19642	19582	19521	19460	19399	19338
216	.19276	19214	19152	19090	19028	18965	18902	18839	18776	18713
217	.18649	18585	18521	18457	18393	18328	18263	18197	18132	18066
218	.18001	17934	17868	17801	17735	17668	17600	17533	17465	17398
219	.17330	17261	17193	17124	17055	16986	16916	16846	16776	16706
220	n 1.16636	16565	16494	16422	16351	16280	16208	16135	16063	15990

TABLE XVIII.—The Quantities Log. C and Log. D.—1850.

Argument = Arg. I + d' + Inequalities + day of year.

Log. C.

Arg.	0.0	0.1	0.2	0.3	0.4	0.5	0.6	0.7	0.8	0.9
220	1.11613	11688	11762	11836	11910	11984	12058	12131	12204	12277
221	.12350	12422	12494	12566	12638	12709	12780	12851	12922	12992
222	.13062	13132	13202	13271	13340	13409	13478	13546	13614	13682
223	.13750	13818	13885	13952	14019	14086	14153	14219	14285	14351
224	.14417	14482	14547	14612	14677	14742	14806	14870	14934	14998
225	1.15061	15124	15187	15250	15313	15376	15438	15500	15562	15624
226	.15685	15746	15807	15868	15929	15989	16049	16109	16169	16228
227	.16287	16346	16405	16464	16523	16581	16639	16697	16755	16813
228	.16870	16927	16984	17041	17098	17154	17210	17266	17322	17378
229	.17433	17488	17543	17598	17653	17707	17761	17815	17869	17923
230	1.17977	18030	18083	18136	18189	18242	18294	18346	18398	18450
231	.18502	18554	18605	18656	18707	18758	18809	18859	18909	18959
232	.19009	19059	19109	19158	19207	19256	19305	19354	19402	19450
233	.19498	19546	19594	19642	19689	19736	19783	19830	19877	19924
234	.19970	20016	20062	20108	20154	20200	20245	20290	20335	20380
235	1.20425	20470	20514	20558	20602	20646	20690	20734	20777	20820
236	.20863	20906	20949	20992	21034	21076	21118	21160	21202	21244
237	.21285	21326	21367	21408	21449	21490	21531	21571	21611	21651
238	.21691	21731	21771	21810	21849	21888	21927	21966	22005	22043
239	.22081	22119	22157	22195	22233	22270	22307	22344	22381	22418
240	1.22455	22492	22528	22564	22600	22636	22672	22708	22744	22779
241	.22814	22849	22884	22919	22954	22988	23022	23056	23090	23124
242	.23158	23192	23226	23259	23292	23325	23358	23391	23424	23457
243	.23488	23520	23552	23584	23616	23647	23678	23709	23740	23771
244	.23802	23833	23864	23894	23924	23954	23984	24014	24044	24073
245	1.24102	24131	24160	24189	24218	24247	24276	24304	24332	24360
246	.24388	24416	24444	24472	24499	24526	24553	24580	24607	24634
247	.24660	24687	24713	24739	24765	24791	24817	24843	24868	24893
248	.24918	24943	24968	24993	25018	25042	25066	25090	25114	25138
249	.25162	25186	25210	25233	25256	25279	25302	25325	25348	25371
250	1.25393	25415	25437	25459	25481	25503	25525	25547	25568	25589
251	.25610	25631	25652	25673	25693	25713	25733	25753	25773	25793
252	.25813	25833	25853	25872	25891	25910	25929	25948	25967	25986
253	.26004	26022	26040	26058	26076	26094	26112	26130	26147	26164
254	.26181	26198	26215	26232	26249	26265	26281	26297	26313	26329
255	1.26345	26361	26377	26392	26407	26422	26437	26452	26467	26482
256	.26496	26511	26525	26539	26553	26567	26581	26595	26608	26621
257	.26634	26647	26660	26673	26686	26698	26711	26723	26735	26747
258	.26759	26771	26783	26795	26806	26817	26828	26839	26850	26861
259	.26871	26882	26893	26903	26913	26923	26933	26943	26953	26962
260	1.26971	26980	26989	26998	27007	27016	27025	27034	27042	27050
261	.27058	27066	27074	27082	27090	27097	27104	27111	27118	27125
262	.27132	27139	27146	27152	27158	27164	27170	27176	27182	27188
263	.27193	27199	27204	27209	27214	27219	27224	27229	27234	27238
264	.27242	27246	27250	27254	27258	27262	27266	27269	27272	27275
265	1.27278	27281	27284	27287	27289	27291	27293	27295	27297	27299
266	.27301	27303	27305	27306	27307	27308	27309	27310	27311	27312
267	.27312	27312	27312	27313	27313	27313	27313	27313	27312	27311
268	.27310	27309	27308	27307	27306	27304	27303	27301	27299	27297
269	.27295	27293	27291	27289	27286	27283	27280	27277	27274	27271
270	1.27267	27264	27261	27257	27253	27249	27245	27241	27237	27232

TABLE XVIII.—The Quantities Log. C and Log. D.—1850.

Argument = Arg. I + d' + Inequalities + day of year.

Log. D.

Arg.	0.0	0.1	0.2	0.3	0.4	0.5	0.6	0.7	0.8	0.9
220	n 1.16636	16565	16494	16422	16351	16280	16208	16135	16063	15990
221	.15918	15845	15771	15698	15624	15550	15476	15401	15326	15251
222	.15176	15100	15024	14948	14872	14795	14718	14640	14563	14486
223	.14408	14330	14251	14173	14094	14015	13935	13855	13775	13695
224	.13614	13533	13452	13370	13288	13206	13123	13040	12957	12874
225	n 1.12791	12707	12623	12539	12455	12370	12285	12199	12113	12027
226	.11941	11854	11767	11679	11592	11504	11416	11327	11238	11149
227	.11060	10970	10880	10790	10699	10608	10517	10425	10333	10241
228	.10149	10056	09963	09869	09775	09681	09586	09491	09396	09301
229	.09205	09109	09012	08915	08818	08721	08623	08525	08426	08327
230	n 1.08228	08128	08028	07928	07827	07726	07625	07523	07421	07318
231	.07215	07112	07008	06904	06799	06694	06589	06483	06377	06271
232	.06164	06057	05950	05842	05734	05625	05516	05406	05296	05286
233	.05075	04964	04852	04740	04628	04515	04402	04288	04174	04059
234	.03944	03829	03713	03597	03480	03363	03245	03127	03009	02890
235	n 1.02771	02651	02531	02410	02289	02167	02045	01922	01799	01675
236	.01551	01426	01301	01175	01049	00923	00796	00668	00540	00412
237	1.00283	00153	00023	: 99892	: 99761	: 99630	: 99498	: 99365	: 99232	: 99098
238	0.98964	98829	98694	98558	98421	98284	98146	98008	97869	97730
239	.97590	97449	97308	97166	97024	96881	96737	96593	96448	96303
240	n 0.96157	96010	95863	95715	95566	95417	95267	95117	94966	94814
241	.94662	94509	94355	94201	94046	93890	93733	93575	93417	93259
242	.93101	92941	92780	92618	92456	92293	92129	91964	91799	91633
243	.91467	91300	91132	90963	90793	90622	90451	90279	90106	89932
244	.89756	89580	89403	89225	89047	88869	88689	88508	88326	88144
245	n 0.87961	87777	87592	87406	87219	87030	86841	86651	86460	86268
246	.86075	85881	85686	85490	85293	85095	84896	84696	84495	84293
247	.84089	83885	83680	83473	83265	83056	82847	82636	82424	82210
248	.81994	81778	81561	81343	81123	80902	80680	80456	80231	80005
249	.79778	79550	79320	79089	78856	78621	78386	78149	77911	77671
250	n 0.77429	77186	76941	76695	76448	76200	75949	75697	75443	75188
251	.74931	74673	74413	74151	73887	73621	73354	73085	72814	72541
252	.72266	71990	71712	71432	71149	70864	70577	70288	69997	69705
253	.69411	69114	68815	68514	68210	67904	67596	67286	66974	66659
254	.66342	66022	65700	65375	65048	64716	64383	64047	63708	63366
255	n 0.63022	62675	62325	61972	61616	61256	60894	60529	60160	59787
256	.59411	59032	58650	58264	57875	57482	57085	56684	56279	55870
257	.55458	55042	54622	54197	53767	53331	52892	52448	52000	51548
258	.51093	50631	50164	49691	49213	48730	48240	47744	47242	46735
259	.46222	45701	45174	44640	44100	43554	43001	42441	41874	41300
260	n 0.40717	40124	39525	38917	38298	37673	37036	36391	35735	35070
261	.34393	33705	33008	32298	31575	30843	30095	29334	28562	27773
262	.26970	26151	25317	24468	23600	22714	21809	20886	19941	18976
263	.17989	16979	15944	14884	13798	12683	11542	10364	09156	07969
264	0.06630	05311	03951	02547	01002	: 99591	: 98035	: 96422	: 94741	: 92998
265	n 9.91182	89280	87298	85214	83031	80727	78299	75721	72987	70061
266	9.66933	63554	59896	55891	51479	46578	41046	34698	27275	18367
267	n 9.06988	: 91639	: 67680	n 00797	p 35127	: 75904	: 96568	10510	21049	29523
268	p 9.36611	42703	48045	52801	57087	60987	64566	67872	70944	73813
269	9.76504	79045	81438	83707	85862	87921	89892	91758	93560	95287
270	9.96946	98550	: 00091	: 01580	: 03020	: 04416	: 05769	: 07078	: 08351	: 09585

TABLE XVIII.—The Quantities Log. C and Log. D.—1850.

Argument = Arg. I + d' + Inequalities + day of year.

Log. C.

Arg.	0.0	0.1	0.2	0.3	0.4	0.5	0.6	0.7	0.8	0.9
270	1.27267	27264	27261	27257	27253	27249	27245	27241	27237	27232
271	.27227	27222	27217	27212	27207	27202	27197	27192	27186	27180
272	.27174	27168	27162	27156	27149	27142	27135	27128	27121	27114
273	.27107	27100	27093	27085	27077	27069	27061	27053	27045	27037
274	.27028	27020	27011	27002	26993	26984	26975	26966	26956	26946
275	1.26936	26926	26916	26906	26896	26885	26875	26864	26853	26842
276	.26831	26820	26809	26798	26786	26774	26762	26750	26738	26726
277	.26713	26701	26688	26675	26662	26649	26636	26623	26609	26595
278	.26581	26567	26553	26539	26525	26510	26496	26481	26466	26451
279	.26436	26421	26406	26391	26375	26359	26343	26327	26311	26295
280	1.26278	26261	26244	26227	26210	26193	26176	26159	26141	26123
281	.26105	26087	26069	26051	26033	26014	25996	25977	25958	25939
282	.25920	25901	25882	25862	25842	25822	25802	25782	25762	25741
283	.25720	25699	25678	25657	25636	25615	25594	25572	25550	25528
284	.25506	25484	25462	25440	25417	25394	25371	25348	25325	25302
285	1.25278	25254	25230	25206	25182	25158	25134	25110	25085	25060
286	.25035	25010	24985	24960	24935	24909	24883	24857	24831	24805
287	.24779	24753	24726	24699	24672	24645	24618	24591	24563	24535
288	.24507	24479	24451	24423	24394	24365	24336	24307	24278	24249
289	.24220	24191	24161	24131	24101	24071	24041	24011	23980	23949
290	1.23918	23887	23856	23825	23793	23761	23729	23697	23665	23633
291	.23601	23569	23536	23503	23470	23437	23404	23370	23336	23302
292	.23268	23234	23200	23166	23131	23096	23061	23026	22991	22955
293	.22919	22883	22847	22811	22775	22739	22702	22665	22628	22591
294	.22554	22516	22479	22441	22403	22365	22327	22289	22250	22211
295	1.22172	22133	22094	22055	22015	21975	21935	21895	21855	21814
296	.21773	21732	21691	21650	21609	21568	21526	21484	21442	21400
297	.21358	21316	21273	21230	21187	21144	21101	21057	21013	20969
298	.20925	20881	20836	20791	20746	20701	20656	20611	20565	20519
299	.20473	20427	20381	20335	20288	20241	20194	20147	20100	20052
300	1.20004	19956	19908	19860	19811	19762	19713	19664	19615	19566
301	.19516	19466	19416	19366	19315	19264	19213	19162	19111	19060
302	.19008	18956	18904	18852	18800	18747	18694	18641	18588	18535
303	.18482	18428	18374	18320	18266	18211	18156	18101	18046	17990
304	.17934	17878	17822	17766	17710	17653	17596	17539	17482	17424
305	1.17366	17308	17250	17192	17134	17075	17016	16957	16898	16838
306	.16778	16718	16658	16597	16536	16475	16414	16352	16290	16229
307	.16166	16104	16041	15978	15915	15852	15789	15725	15661	15597
308	.15533	15468	15403	15338	15273	15208	15142	15076	15010	14943
309	.14876	14809	14742	14675	14607	14539	14471	14402	14333	14264
310	1.14195	14126	14056	13986	13916	13846	13775	13704	13633	13562
311	.13490	13418	13346	13274	13201	13128	13055	12981	12907	12833
312	.12759	12684	12609	12534	12459	12384	12308	12232	12156	12079
313	.12002	11925	11847	11769	11691	11613	11534	11455	11376	11297
314	.11217	11137	11057	10976	10895	10814	10733	10651	10569	10487
315	1.10404	10321	10238	10154	10070	09986	09902	09817	09732	09647
316	.09561	09475	09389	09302	09215	09128	09040	08952	08864	08776
317	.08687	08598	08509	08419	08329	08239	08148	08057	07966	07874
318	.07782	07690	07597	07504	07410	07316	07222	07127	07032	06937
319	.06842	06746	06650	06553	06456	06359	06262	06164	06066	05967
320	1.05868	05769	05669	05569	05469	05368	05267	05165	05063	04961

TABLE XVIII.—The Quantities Log. C and Log. D.—1850.

Argument = Arg. I + d' + Inequalities + day of year.

Log. D.

Arg.	0.0	0.1	0.2	0.3	0.4	0.5	0.6	0.7	0.8	0.9
270	9.96946	98550	:00091	:01580	:03020	:04416	:05769	:07078	:08351	:09585
271	0.10788	11958	13095	14205	15285	16341	17372	18379	19360	20322
272	.21263	22184	23084	23967	24833	25681	26513	27330	28131	28918
273	.29690	30449	31195	31928	32649	33357	34055	34741	35416	36081
274	.36736	37382	38018	38644	39260	39871	40470	41062	41647	42222
275	0.42790	43351	43905	44452	44992	45526	46052	46572	47086	47594
276	.48095	48591	49081	49566	50046	50520	50988	51451	51909	52363
277	.52812	53256	53696	54131	54562	54998	55410	55828	56242	56652
278	.57057	57459	57857	58252	58643	59031	59415	59796	60173	60546
279	.60915	61282	61646	62007	62365	62719	63070	63418	63764	64107
280	0.64447	64784	65118	65450	65780	66107	66431	66752	67071	67388
281	.67703	68015	68325	68632	68937	69240	69540	69838	70134	70429
282	.70722	71012	71300	71586	71870	72152	72432	72710	72986	73261
283	.73534	73805	74074	74341	74607	74871	75133	75393	75652	75909
284	.76165	76419	76671	76922	77171	77419	77665	77909	78152	78394
285	0.78634	78873	79111	79347	79581	79814	80046	80276	80505	80733
286	.80960	81186	81410	81633	81854	82074	82293	82510	82726	82941
287	.83156	83369	83580	83791	84001	84209	84416	84622	84827	85031
288	.85234	85436	85637	85837	86036	86233	86430	86626	86821	87015
289	.87207	87399	87590	87780	87969	88157	88344	88530	88715	88899
290	0.89083	89265	89446	89627	89807	89987	90165	90342	90518	90694
291	.90869	91043	91216	91388	91560	91731	91901	92070	92239	92407
292	.92574	92740	92905	93070	93234	93397	93559	93721	93882	94042
293	.94202	94361	94519	94676	94833	94989	95144	95299	95453	95606
294	.95759	95911	96063	96214	96364	96513	96662	96810	96958	97105
295	0.97251	97397	97542	97687	97831	97974	98117	98259	98401	98542
296	0.98682	98822	98961	99100	99238	99376	99513	99650	99786	99921
297	1.00055	00189	00322	00455	00588	00721	00853	00984	01114	01244
298	.01373	01502	01630	01758	01886	02013	02140	02266	02392	02517
299	.02641	02765	02889	03012	03134	03256	03378	03499	03620	03740
300	1.03860	03980	04099	04218	04336	04453	04570	04687	04803	04919
301	.05035	05150	05264	05378	05492	05605	05718	05830	05942	06054
302	.06165	06276	06386	06496	06606	06715	06824	06932	07040	07148
303	.07255	07362	07468	07574	07680	07785	07890	07995	08099	08202
304	.08306	08409	08512	08614	08716	08817	08918	09019	09120	09220
305	1.09320	09420	09519	09618	09716	09813	09911	10008	10105	10202
306	.10298	10394	10490	10585	10680	10774	10868	10962	11056	11149
307	.11242	11335	11427	11519	11611	11702	11793	11884	11974	12064
308	.12153	12242	12331	12420	12509	12597	12685	12772	12859	12946
309	.13033	13119	13205	13291	13377	13462	13547	13631	13715	13799
310	1.13883	13966	14049	14132	14215	14297	14379	14461	14542	14623
311	.14704	14784	14864	14944	15024	15104	15183	15262	15341	15419
312	.15497	15575	15652	15729	15806	15883	15959	16035	16111	16187
313	.16263	16338	16413	16488	16562	16636	16710	16784	16857	16930
314	.17003	17076	17148	17220	17292	17364	17435	17506	17577	17648
315	1.17718	17788	17858	17928	17998	18067	18136	18205	18273	18341
316	.18409	18477	18544	18611	18678	18745	18811	18877	18943	19009
317	.19075	19140	19205	19270	19335	19400	19464	19528	19592	19656
318	.19719	19782	19845	19908	19970	20032	20094	20156	20218	20279
319	.20340	20401	20462	20523	20583	20643	20703	20763	20822	20881
320	1.20940	20999	21058	21116	21174	21232	21290	21347	21404	21461

TABLE XVIII.—The Quantities Log. C and Log. D.—1850.

Argument = Arg. I + d' + Inequalities + day of year.

Log. C.

Arg.	0.0	0.1	0.2	0.3	0.4	0.5	0.6	0.7	0.8	0.9
320	1.05868	05769	05669	05569	05469	05368	05267	05165	05063	04961
321	.04858	04755	04651	04547	04443	04338	04233	04127	04021	03915
322	.03809	03702	03595	03487	03379	03270	03161	03051	02941	02831
323	.02720	02609	02497	02385	02273	02160	02046	01932	01818	01704
324	.01589	01473	01357	01241	01124	01007	00889	00771	00652	00533
325	1.00413	00293	00172	00051	:99929	:99807	:99684	:99561	:99437	:99313
326	0.99189	99064	98938	98812	98686	98559	98431	98303	98175	98046
327	.97917	97787	97656	97525	97393	97260	97127	96993	96859	96725
328	.96590	96454	96318	96181	96044	95906	95767	95628	95488	95348
329	.95208	95067	94925	94782	94639	94495	94350	94205	94059	93913
330	0.93766	93618	93470	93321	93171	93021	92870	92718	92566	92413
331	.92260	92106	91951	91795	91638	91481	91323	91164	91005	90845
332	.90685	90524	90362	90199	90035	89870	89705	89539	89372	89204
333	.89036	88867	88697	88526	88354	88182	88009	87835	87660	87484
334	.87308	87130	86951	86772	86592	86411	86229	86046	85862	85677
335	0.85492	85306	85119	84931	84741	84550	84359	84167	83974	83779
336	.83583	83386	83188	82989	82790	82590	82388	82185	81981	81776
337	.81571	81364	81156	80947	80736	80524	80311	80097	79882	79665
338	.79447	79228	79008	78786	78563	78338	78113	77886	77658	77428
339	.77197	76965	76731	76496	76260	76022	75783	75542	75300	75056
340	0.74811	74564	74315	74065	73813	73560	73306	73050	72792	72532
341	.72269	72006	71741	71474	71206	70936	70664	70399	70114	69836
342	.69556	69274	68990	68704	68416	68127	67835	67541	67245	66946
343	.66645	66342	66037	65730	65420	65108	64793	64476	64156	63834
344	.63510	63183	62853	62520	62185	61847	61506	61162	60816	60467
345	0.60115	59760	59402	59040	58675	58306	57935	57561	57183	56801
346	.56416	56028	55636	55240	54840	54436	54029	53616	53200	52780
347	.52357	51929	51496	51059	50617	50170	49719	49263	48802	48335
348	.47863	47386	46904	46416	45922	45422	44916	44404	43886	43362
349	.42834	42297	41753	41202	40644	40078	39504	38922	38332	37734
350	0.37127	36513	35888	35256	34614	33960	33298	32624	31941	31245
351	.30540	29821	29091	28347	27592	26821	26039	25239	24427	23597
352	.22753	21890	21011	20112	19193	18257	17298	16319	15316	14288
353	.13238	12159	11055	09919	08753	07558	06325	05000	03753	02405
354	0.01017	:99580	:98094	:96559	:94963	:93306	:91588	:89794	:87923	:85972
355	9.83924	81775	79513	77134	74609	71929	69080	66022	62733	59173
356	9.55306	51049	46329	41032	35015	28008	19649	09287	:95652	:75735
357	8.37700	n7.9791	:63224	:88204	:03973	:15515	:24620	:32145	:38559	:44141
358	n9.49092	53536	57567	61255	64645	67798	70738	73490	76079	78521
359	9.80834	83024	85113	87107	89013	90839	92591	94275	95896	97454
360	n9.98063	:00420	:01830	:03196	:04520	:05804	:07052	:08261	:09440	:10538
361	0.11707	12797	13861	14895	15912	16902	17870	18817	19744	20651
362	.21539	22409	23260	24097	24917	25723	26513	27289	28052	28801
363	.29537	30261	30973	31673	32362	33041	33708	34366	35013	35651
364	.36279	36897	37507	38109	38703	39288	39865	40436	40999	41554
365	n0.42102	42644	43179	43707	44228	44741	45250	45753	46249	46739
366	.47223	47703	48177	48646	49110	49570	50024	50473	50917	51356
367	.51791	52222	52648	53070	53488	53902	54312	54718	55120	55518
368	.55911	56302	56689	57073	57453	57829	58202	58571	58937	59300
369	.59661	60018	60372	60723	61072	61418	61761	62101	62438	62771
370	n0.63100	63429	63755	64078	64399	64717	65033	65346	65657	65966

TABLE XVIII.—The Quantities Log. C and Log. D.—1850.

Argument = Arg. I + d' + Inequalities + day of year.

Log. D.

Arg.	0.0	0.1	0.2	0.3	0.4	0.5	0.6	0.7	0 8	0.9
320	1.20940	20999	21058	21116	21174	21232	21290	21347	21404	21461
321	.21518	21575	21632	21688	21744	21800	21856	21911	21966	22021
322	.22076	22131	22185	22239	22293	22347	22401	22454	22507	22560
323	.22613	22666	22718	22770	22822	22874	22926	22978	23029	23080
324	.23131	23182	23233	23283	23333	23383	23433	23483	23532	23581
325	1.23630	23679	23728	23776	23824	23872	23920	23968	24016	24063
326	.24110	24157	24204	24251	24297	24343	24389	24435	24481	24526
327	.24571	24616	24661	24706	24751	24795	24839	24883	24927	24971
328	.25014	25057	25100	25143	25186	25229	25272	25314	25356	25398
329	.25440	25482	25523	25564	25605	25646	25687	25728	25768	25808
330	1.25848	25888	25928	25968	26007	26046	26085	26124	26163	26201
331	.26239	26277	26315	26353	26391	26429	26466	26503	26540	26577
332	.26614	26651	26687	26723	26759	26795	26831	26866	26901	26936
333	.26971	27006	27041	27076	27110	27144	27178	27212	27246	27280
334	.27313	27346	27379	27412	27445	27477	27510	27542	27574	27606
335	1.27638	27670	27702	27733	27764	27795	27826	27857	27888	27918
336	.27948	27978	28008	28038	28068	28097	28126	28155	28184	28213
337	.28242	28271	28299	28327	28355	28383	28411	28439	28466	28493
338	.28520	28547	28574	28601	28628	28654	28680	28706	28732	28758
339	.28784	28810	28835	28860	28885	28910	28935	28960	28984	29008
340	1.29032	29056	29080	29104	29127	29150	29173	29196	29219	29242
341	.29265	29288	29310	29332	29354	29376	29398	29420	29442	29463
342	.29484	29505	29526	29547	29568	29588	29608	29628	29648	29668
343	.29688	29708	29727	29746	29765	29784	29803	29822	29841	29859
344	.29877	29895	29913	29931	29949	29966	29984	30001	30018	30035
345	1.30052	30069	30086	30102	30118	30134	30150	30166	30182	30198
346	.30213	30228	30243	30258	30273	30288	30303	30318	30332	30346
347	.30360	30374	30388	30402	30415	30428	30441	30454	30467	30480
348	.30492	30505	30517	30529	30541	30553	30565	30577	30589	30600
349	.30611	30622	30633	30644	30655	30665	30675	30685	30695	30705
350	1.30715	30725	30735	30744	30753	30762	30771	30780	30789	30798
351	.30806	30814	30822	30830	30838	30846	30854	30861	30868	30875
352	.30882	30889	30896	30903	30909	30915	30921	30927	30933	30939
353	.30945	30951	30956	30961	30966	30971	30976	30981	30986	30990
354	.30994	30998	31002	31006	31010	31013	31017	31020	31023	31026
355	1.31029	31032	31035	31038	31040	31042	31044	31046	31048	31050
356	.31051	31053	31054	31055	31056	31057	31058	31058	31059	31059
357	.31059	31059	31059	31058	31058	31058	31057	31055	31055	31054
358	.31053	31052	31051	31051	31049	31047	31045	31043	31041	31036
359	.31033	31030	31027	31024	31021	31018	31015	31012	31008	31004
360	1.31000	30996	30992	30988	30983	30978	30973	30968	30963	30958
361	.30953	30948	30942	30936	30930	30924	30918	30912	30906	30899
362	.30892	30885	30878	30871	30864	30856	30849	30841	30833	30825
363	.30817	30809	30801	30792	30783	30774	30765	30756	30747	30738
364	.30728	30719	30709	30699	30689	30679	30669	30659	30648	30637
365	1.30626	30615	30604	30593	30581	30569	30557	30545	30533	30521
366	.30509	30497	30484	30471	30458	30445	30432	30419	30406	30392
367	.30378	30364	30350	30336	30322	30307	30293	30278	30263	30248
368	.30233	30218	30203	30187	30171	30155	30139	30123	30107	30091
369	.30074	30057	30040	30023	30006	29989	29972	29955	29936	29918
370	1.29900	29882	29864	29846	29827	29808	29789	29770	29751	29732

TABLE XIX.—The Quantities Log. h, II and Log. i.—1850.

Argument = Arg. I + d' + Inequalities + day of year.

Arg.	Log. h.	H.	Log. i.	Arg.	Log. h.	II.	Log. i.
		° '				° '	
0	1.30986	352 21.1	n 0.0715	51	1.28304	302 3.7	n 0.8486
1	.30967	351 24.7	.1212	52	.28245	301 0.6	.8529
2	.30947	350 28.4	.1657	53	.28188	299 57.4	.8570
3	.30925	349 32.0	.2060	54	.28132	298 54.1	.8610
4	.30900	348 35.5	.2427	55	.28076	297 50.7	.8648
5	1.30873	347 38.9	n 0.2764	56	1.28022	296 47.2	n 0.8684
6	.30844	346 42.3	.3075	57	.27970	295 43.5	.8718
7	.30813	345 45.6	.3365	58	.27920	294 39.7	.8751
8	.30780	344 48.8	.3635	59	.27872	293 35.7	.8782
9	.30745	343 51.9	.3888	60	.27827	292 31.6	.8812
10	1.30709	342 55.0	n 0.4125	61	1.27782	291 27.5	n 0.8840
11	.30671	341 58.0	.4349	62	.27738	290 23.3	.8867
12	.30631	341 0.8	.4561	63	.27695	289 19.0	.8892
13	.30589	340 3.6	.4761	64	.27654	288 14.6	.8916
14	.30545	339 6.2	.4952	65	.27614	287 10.0	.8938
15	1.30499	338 8.7	n 0.5133	66	1.27577	286 5.5	n 0.8959
16	.30453	337 11.2	.5305	67	.27543	285 0.9	.8978
17	.30405	336 13.5	.5470	68	.27511	283 56.2	.8996
18	.30354	335 15.6	.5627	69	.27482	282 51.4	.9013
19	.30303	334 17.7	.5777	70	.27456	281 46.5	.9028
20	1.30250	333 19.6	n 0.5921	71	1.27431	280 41.7	n 0.9041
21	.30196	332 21.4	.6059	72	.27408	279 36.8	.9054
22	.30141	331 23.0	.6191	73	.27388	278 31.9	.9065
23	.30085	330 24.5	.6318	74	.27370	277 26.9	.9075
24	.30027	329 25.9	.6440	75	.27355	276 21.8	.9083
25	1.29968	328 27.2	n 0.6558	76	1.27342	275 16.8	n 0.9090
26	.29908	327 28.3	.6671	77	.27332	274 11.8	.9096
27	.29847	326 29.2	.6780	78	.27324	273 6.8	.9100
28	.29785	325 30.0	.6884	79	.27318	272 1.9	.9103
29	.29723	324 30.6	.6985	80	.27313	270 57.0	.9105
30	1.29660	323 31.0	n 0.7082	81	1.27312	269 52.1	n 0.9106
31	.29596	322 31.3	.7176	82	.27314	268 47.2	.9105
32	.29532	321 31.4	.7267	83	.27318	267 42.4	.9103
33	.29467	320 31.4	.7354	84	.27324	266 37.7	.9099
34	.29401	319 31.3	.7438	85	.27333	265 33.0	.9095
35	1.29335	318 31.0	n 0.7519	86	1.27344	264 28.4	n 0.9089
36	.29269	317 30.5	.7597	87	.27358	263 23.8	.9081
37	.29202	316 29.9	.7673	88	.27374	262 19.3	.9073
38	.29136	315 29.1	.7746	89	.27392	261 14.9	.9063
39	.29070	314 28.1	.7816	90	.27413	260 10.7	.9052
40	1.29004	313 26.9	n 0.7884	91	1.27436	259 6.5	n 0.9039
41	.28938	312 25.6	.7950	92	.27461	258 2.4	.9025
42	.28872	311 24.2	.8013	93	.27488	256 58.4	.9010
43	.28806	310 22.6	.8074	94	.27517	255 54.5	.8993
44	.28741	309 20.8	.8132	95	.27549	254 50.8	.8976
45	1.28676	308 18 7	n 0.8189	96	1.27582	253 47.2	n 0.8956
46	.28612	307 16.6	.8243	97	.27617	252 43.7	.8936
47	.28549	306 14.3	.8296	98	.27654	251 40.4	.8914
48	.28486	305 11.9	.8346	99	.27694	250 37.3	.8891
49	.28424	304 9.3	.8395	100	.27736	249 34.3	.8866
50	1.28364	303 6.6	n 0.8441	101	1.27779	248 31.5	n 0.8840

TABLE XIX.—The Quantities Log. h, H and Log. i.—1850.

Argument = Arg. I + d' + Inequalities + day of year.

Arg.	Log. h.	H. (o /)	Log. i.	Arg.	Log. h.	H. (o /)	Log. i.
102	1.27824	247 28.8	n 0.8912	153	1.30658	198 17.8	n 0.4409
103	.27870	246 26.3	.8783	154	.30695	197 24.2	.4202
104	.27918	245 23.9	.8753	155	.30731	196 30.7	.3984
105	.27967	244 21.6	.8721	156	.30765	195 37.3	.3753
106	.28017	243 19.6	.8687	157	.30797	194 44.0	.3508
107	1.28069	242 17.8	n 0.8653	158	1.30827	193 50.8	n 0.3246
108	.28122	241 16.2	.8616	159	.30855	192 57.6	.2967
109	.28176	240 14.8	.8578	160	.30880	192 4.5	.2668
110	.28232	239 13.5	.8539	161	.30904	191 11.5	.2345
111	.28289	238 12.4	.8497	162	.30926	190 18.5	.1994
112	1.28347	237 11.5	n 0.8454	163	1.30947	189 25.6	n 0.1612
113	.28406	236 10.8	.8410	164	.30967	188 32 8	.1192
114	.28466	235 10.3	.8364	165	.30986	187 40 0	.0725
115	.28526	234 10.0	.8316	166	.31002	186 47.3	0.0201
116	.28587	233 9.9	.8266	167	.31016	185 54.6	9.9603
117	·1.28648	232 10.0	n 0.8214	168	1.31028	185 2.0	n 9.8909
118	.28710	231 10.3	.8161	169	.31038	184 9.4	.8090
119	.28772	230 10.8	.8106	170	.31045	183 16.8	.7055
120	.28834	229 11.6	.8048	171	.31051	182 24.2	.5708
121	.28897	228 12.5	.7989	172	.31055	181 31.7	.3743
122	1.28960	227 13.6	n 0.7928	173	1.31057	180 39.2	n 9.0056
123	.29023	226 14.9	.7864	174	.31058	179 46.7	p 8.5337
124	.29086	225 16.4	.7799	175	.31057	178 54.2	9.2296
125	.29150	224 18.2	.7731	176	.31055	178 1.7	.4844
126	.29214	223 20.1	.7661	177	.31050	177 9.2	.6438
127	1.29277	222 22.2	n 0.7588	178	1.31043	176 16.7	9.7601
128	.29340	221 24.5	.7513	179	.31033	175 24.2	9.8516
129	.29403	220 27.0	.7436	180	.31021	174 31.6	.9270
130	.29465	219 29.7	.7356	181	.31008	173 39.0	9.9912
131	.29527	218 32.5	.7273	182	.30994	172 46.4	0.0470
132	1.29589	217 35.5	n 0.7187	183	1.30978	171 53.7	.0.0963
133	.29649	216 38.7	.7098	184	.30960	171 1.1	.1405
134	.29709	215 42.1	.7007	185	.30939	170 8.4	.1804
135	.29768	214 45.9	.6912	186	.30917	169 15.7	.2169
136	.29826	213 49.7	.6813	187	.30893	168 22.9	.2505
137	1.29884	212 53.6	n 0.6712	188	1.30867	167 30.0	0.2815
138	.29941	211 57.7	.6606	189	.30840	166 37.0	.3104
139	.29998	211 2.0	.6497	190	.30811	165 43 9	.3373
140	.30054	210 6.6	.6384	191	.30781	164 50.8	.3626
141	.30108	209 11.2	.6266	192	.30749	163 57.6	.3863
142	1.30161	208 16.0	n 0.6144	193	1.30715	163 4.3	0.4088
143	.30213	207 20.9	.6018	194	.30679	162 10.9	.4300
144	.30263	206 26.0	.5886	195	.30642	161 17.4	.4501
145	.30313	205 31.2	.5749	196	.30604	160 23.8	.4692
146	.30361	204 36.6	.5606	197	.30564	159 30.1	.4873
147	1.30408	203 42.1	n 0.5457	198	1.30522	158 36.3	0.5047
148	.30453	202 47.8	.5302	199	.30479	157 42.5	.5212
149	.30497	201 53.6	.5140	200	.30434	156 48.6	.5370
150	.30540	200 59.5	.4970	201	.30389	155 54.3	.5522
151	.30581	200 5.5	.4792	202	.30342	154 59.9	.5667
152	1.30620	199 11.6	n 0.4605	203	1.30294	154 5.3	0.5807

TABLE XIX.—The Quantities Log. h, II and Log. i.—1850.

Argument = Arg. I + d' + Inequalities + day of year.

Arg.	Log. h.	H.	Log. i.	Arg.	Log. h.	H.	Log. i.
		° '				° '	
204	1 30244	153 10 5	0.5941	255	1.27490	103 5.9	0.9009
205	.30192	152 16.6	.6070	256	.27463	102 2.7	.9024
206	.30140	151 21.8	.6194	257	.27438	100 59.4	.9038
207	.30087	150 26.8	.6313	258	.27415	99 56.0	.9050
208	.30033	149 31.7	.6428	259	.27394	98 52.5	.9062
209	1.29077	148 36.5	0.6539	260	1.27376	97 48.8	0.9072
210	.29021	147 41.3	.6646	261	.27360	96 45.2	.9080
211	.29864	146 45.8	.6750	262	.27346	95 41.5	.9088
212	.29806	145 50.1	.6849	263	.27335	94 37.7	.9094
213	.29747	144 54.2	.6946	264	.27326	93 33.7	.9099
214	1.29688	143 58.2	0.7039	265	1.27319	92 29.7	0.9102
215	.29628	143 2.0	.7129	266	.27315	91 25.6	.9105
216	.29568	142 5.6	.7216	267	.27313	90 21.5	.9106
217	.29507	141 9.1	.7300	268	.27313	89 17.3	.9105
218	.29446	140 12.4	.7381	269	.27316	88 13.2	.9104
219	1.29384	139 15 5	0.7460	270	1.27321	87 9.1	0.9101
220	.29321	138 18 4	.7536	271	.27328	86 4.9	.9097
221	.29259	137 21.2	.7609	272	.27337	85 0.7	.9092
222	.29197	136 23.8	.7681	273	.27349	83 56.5	.9085
223	.29134	135 26.2	.7749	274	.27364	82 52.3	.9077
224	1 29071	134 28 3	0.7816	275	1.27382	81 48.2	0.9068
225	.29007	133 30 2	.7881	276	.27402	80 44.0	.9058
226	.28944	132 32.0	.7943	277	.27424	79 30.9	.9046
227	.28881	131 33.6	.8003	278	.27448	78 35.8	.9033
228	.28819	130 35.0	.8061	279	.27474	77 31.7	.9018
229	1.28757	129 36.2	0.8118	280	1.27502	76 27.6	0.9002
230	.28696	128 37.3	.8172	281	.27532	75 23.6	.8985
231	.28635	127 38.2	.8225	282	.27565	74 19.7	.8966
232	.28574	126 38.9	.8275	283	.27600	73 15.8	.8946
233	.28514	125 39.4	.8324	284	.27637	72 12.0	.8925
234	1.28455	124 39 7	0.8371	285	1.27675	71 8.3	0.8902
235	.28396	123 39.8	.8417	286	.27715	70 4.7	.8878
236	.28338	122 39.7	.8461	287	.27757	69 1.2	.8852
237	.28281	121 39.4	.8503	288	.27801	67 57.7	.8825
238	.28225	120 38 9	.8544	289	.27847	66 54.3	.8796
239	1.28170	119 38.3	0.8583	290	1.27896	65 51.0	0.8766
240	.28116	118 37.5	.8620	291	.27945	64 47.9	.8735
241	.28063	117 36.5	.8656	292	.27996	63 44.9	.8701
242	.28011	116 35 3	.8690	293	.28048	62 42.0	.8666
243	.27961	115 33.9	.8723	294	.28102	61 39.1	.8630
244	1 27913	114 32 4	0.8755	295	1.28158	60 36.3	0.8592
245	.27867	113 30 8	.8785	296	.28214	59 33.7	.8552
246	.27822	112 29.0	.8813	297	.28271	58 31.3	.8510
247	.27778	111 27.1	.8840	298	.28329	57 29.0	.8467
248	.27736	110 25.0	.8866	299	.28389	56 26.8	.8422
249	1.27695	109 22 6	0.8891	300	1.28450	55 24.7	0.8375
250	.27655	108 20.1	.8914	301	.28512	54 22 8	.8326
251	.27618	107 17 5	.8935	302	.28574	53 21 0	.8275
252	.27583	106 14.8	.8956	303	.28637	52 19 4	.8223
253	.27550	105 12 0	.8975	304	.287 1	51 18 0	.8168
254	1.27519	104 9.0	0.8993	305	1.28765	50 16.7	0 8111

TABLE XIX.—The Quantities Log. h, H and Log. l.—1850.

Argument = Arg. I + d' + Inequalities + day of year.

Arg.	Log. h.	H.	Log. l.	Arg.	Log. h.	H.	Log. l.
		° ′				° ′	
306	1.28829	49 15.5	0.8052	338	1.30676	17 54.1	0.4319
307	.28894	48 14.5	.7991	339	.30714	16 57.3	.4094
308	.28959	47 13.6	.7928	340	.30750	16 0.6	.3856
309	.29025	46 12.9	.7862	341	.30784	15 3.9	.3601
310	.29091	45 12.4	.7794	342	.30816	14 7.3	.3330
311	1.29157	44 12.0	0.7723	343	1.30846	13 10.8	0.3039
312	.29223	43 11.7	.7650	344	.30875	12 14.4	.2725
313	.29289	42 11.6	.7575	345	.30902	11 18.0	.2386
314	.29354	41 11.7	.7496	346	.30927	10 21.6	.2016
315	.29419	40 11.9	.7415	347	.30950	9 25.3	.1610
316	1.29484	39 12.2	0.7331	348	1.30971	8 29.0	0.1161
317	.29549	38 12.7	.7243	349	.30989	7 32.8	.0658
318	.29613	37 13.3	.7153	350	.31005	6 36.6	0.0087
319	.29676	36 14.1	.7059	351	.31019	5 40.4	9.9428
320	.29738	35 15.1	.6961	352	.31031	4 44.3	.8650
321	1.29800	34 16.2	0.6860	353	1.31041	3 48.2	9.7698
322	.29861	33 17.4	.6755	354	.31049	2 52.1	.6476
323	.29921	32 18.8	.6646	355	.31054	1 56.1	.4767
324	.29980	31 20.3	.6533	356	.31057	1 0.1	9.1905
325	.30039	30 22.0	.64 6	357	.31058	0 4,0	8.0144
326	1.30097	29 23.7	0.6293	358	1.31057	359 7.9	π 9.1284
327	.30153	28 25.6	.6166	359	.31054	358 11.8	.4458
328	.30208	27 27.6	.6033	360	.31049	357 15.7	.6271
329	.30261	26 29.8	.5895	361	.31042	356 19.6	.7545
330	.30312	25 32.1	.5751	362	.31033	355 23.4	.8528
331	.30363	24 34.5	.5600	363	.31022	354 27.2	9.9328
332	1.30412	23 37.0	0.5443	364	1.31008	353 31.0	π 0.0002
333	.30460	22 39.6	.5278	365	.30992	352 34.7	.0585
334	.30507	21 42.3	.5105	366	.30974	351 38.4	.1097
335	.30552	20 45.1	.4924	367	.30954	350 42.1	.1554
336	.30595	19 48.0	.4733	368	.30931	349 45.7	.1966
337	1.30636	18 51.0	0.4532	369	1.30906	348 49.2	π 0.2341

TABLE XX.—For Annual Precessions in Right Ascension.—1850.0.

log. $\Delta_0\,a = 0.12616,2$ + log. sin a — $0.00000,187\,(t — 1850)$. Arg. = Star's Mean Right Ascension.

0ʰ + 12ʰ —	Diff. for 10ˢ	0ˢ	10ˢ	20ˢ	30ˢ	40ˢ	50ˢ	
0ᵐ	+ 97	0.00000	0.00097	0.00195	0.00292	0.00389	0.00486	59ᵐ
1	97	0583	0681	0778	0875	0972	1070	58
2	97	1167	1264	1361	1458	1556	1653	57
3	97	1750	1847	1945	2042	2139	2236	56
4	97	2334	2431	2528	2625	2723	2820	55
5	97	2917	3014	3111	3208	3306	3403	54
6	97	3500	3597	3695	3792	3889	3986	53
7	97	4083	4181	4278	4375	4472	4569	52
8	97	4666	4764	4861	4958	5055	5152	51
9	97	5249	5347	5444	5541	5638	5735	50
10	+723	8.76584	8.77301	8.78007	8.78701	8.79355	8.80058	49
11	659	86721	81373	82016	82650	83274	83889	48
12	603	84496	85095	85685	86267	86842	87409	47
13	556	87969	88522	89067	89606	90138	90664	46
14	516	91184	91697	92204	92706	93201	93691	45
15	483	94176	94655	95129	95598	96062	96520	44
16	452	96974	97424	97869	98300	98743	99176	43
17	425	99603	9.00026	9.00445	9.00860	9.01271	9.01678	42
18	491	9.02081	02480	02876	03268	03657	04042	41
19	380	04424	04802	05177	05549	05918	06234	40
20	361	06646	07005	07362	07716	08066	08414	39
21	344	08759	09101	09441	09778	10112	10444	38
22	328	10773	11100	11425	11747	12066	12383	37
23	314	12698	13010	13321	13629	13934	14238	36
24	301	14540	14839	15136	15432	15725	16016	35
25	289	16306	16594	16879	17162	17444	17724	34
26	277	18002	18278	18553	18826	19097	19366	33
27	267	19634	19900	20164	20427	20688	20948	32
28	257	21206	21462	21717	21971	22223	22473	31
29	248	22722	22969	23215	23460	23703	23945	30
30	240	24186	24425	24663	24900	25135	25369	29
31	232	25602	25833	26063	26292	26520	26747	28
32	225	26972	27196	27419	27641	27861	28080	27
33	218	28299	28516	28733	28948	29162	29375	26
34	211	29586	29797	30007	30216	30423	30630	25
35	205	30836	31040	31244	31447	31649	31849	24
36	200	32049	32248	32446	32643	32840	33035	23
37	194	33229	33422	33615	33807	33998	34188	22
38	189	34377	34565	34753	34940	35125	35310	21
39	184	35495	35678	35861	36042	36223	36403	20
40	179	36583	36762	36940	37117	37294	37470	19
41	174	37644	37818	37992	38165	38337	38508	18
42	170	38679	38849	39019	39188	39356	39523	17
43	167	39690	39856	40021	40186	40350	40513	16
44	163	40676	40838	41000	41161	41321	41481	15
45	159	41640	41798	41956	42113	42270	42426	14
46	156	42582	42737	42891	43045	43198	43351	13
47	152	,43503	43655	43806	43956	44106	44255	12
48	149	44404	44552	44700	44847	44994	45140	11
49	145	45286	45431	45576	45720	45864	46007	10
50	142	46150	46292	46434	46575	46716	46856	9
51	140	46996	47136	47275	47413	47551	47688	8
52	137	47825	47962	48098	48234	48369	48504	7
53	134	48638	48772	48905	49038	49171	49303	6
54	132	49435	49566	49697	49828	49958	50087	5
55	129	50216	50345	50474	50602	50730	50857	4
56	127	50984	51110	51236	51362	51487	51612	3
57	125	51737	51861	51985	52109	52232	52354	2
58	122	52476	52598	52720	52841	52962	53082	1
59	+120	9.53202	9.53322	9.53442	9.53561	9.53680	9.53798	0
		60ˢ	50ˢ	40ˢ	30ˢ	20ˢ	10ˢ	11ʰ + 23ʰ —

Annual Precession, $\Delta\,a = 3.07177 + \Delta_0\,a \tan \delta + 0.00001,9\,(t — 1850)$.

TABLE XX.—Annual Precessions in Declination.—1850.0.

$\triangle \delta = 20''.0564 \cos \alpha - 0''.0000,86 \cos \alpha \ (t - 1850).$ Arg. = Star's Mean Right Ascension.

Var. in 100 yrs.	0ʰ + / 12ʰ —	Diff. for 10ˢ	0ˢ	10ˢ	20ˢ	30ˢ	40ˢ	50ˢ	
—0″.0086	0ᵐ	0	20″.0564	20″.0564	20″.0564	20″.0563	20″.0563	20″.0563	59ᵐ
86	1	0	0562	0562	0561	0560	0559	0558	58
83	2	—1	0556	0555	0554	0552	0550	0549	57
86	3	2	0547	0545	0543	0541	0538	0536	56
86	4	2	0533	0531	0528	0525	0522	0519	55
86	5	3	0516	0513	0510	0506	0503	0499	54
86	6	4	0495	0491	0487	0483	0479	0475	53
86	7	4	0470	0466	0461	0457	0452	0447	52
86	8	5	0442	0437	0432	0426	0421	0415	51
86	9	6	0409	0401	0398	0392	0386	0379	50
86	10	6	0373	0367	0360	0353	0347	0340	49
86	11	7	0333	0326	0319	0311	0304	0297	48
86	12	8	0299	0281	0274	0266	0258	0250	47
86	13	8	0241	0233	0225	0216	0207	0199	46
86	14	9	0190	0181	0172	0163	0153	0144	45
86	15	10	0135	0125	0115	0105	0095	0085	44
86	16	10	0075	0065	20.0055	20.0044	20.0034	20.0023	43
86	17	11	20.0012	20.0002	19.9991	19.9980	19.9968	19.9957	42
86	18	12	19.9946	19.9934	9923	9911	9899	9887	41
86	19	12	9875	9863	9851	9838	9826	9813	40
86	20	13	9801	9788	9775	9762	9749	9736	39
86	21	13	9723	9709	9696	9682	9668	9655	38
86	22	14	9641	9627	9612	9598	9584	9569	37
86	23	15	9555	9540	9525	9511	9496	9481	36
86	24	15	9465	9450	9435	9419	9403	9388	35
85	25	16	9372	9356	9340	9324	9308	9291	34
85	26	16	9275	9258	9242	9225	9208	9191	33
85	27	17	9174	9157	9139	9122	9104	9087	32
85	28	18	9069	9051	9033	9015	8997	8979	31
85	29	18	8960	8942	8923	8905	8886	8867	30
85	30	19	8848	8829	8810	8791	8771	8752	29
85	31	20	8732	8712	8692	8672	8652	8632	28
85	32	20	8612	8592	8571	8551	8530	8509	27
85	33	21	8488	8467	8446	8425	8404	8383	26
85	34	22	8361	8339	8318	8296	8274	8252	25
85	35	22	8230	8207	8185	8163	8140	8117	24
85	36	23	8095	8072	8049	8026	8003	7979	23
85	37	23	7956	7933	7909	7885	7861	—7837	22
85	38	24	7813	7789	7765	7741	7716	7692	21
85	39	25	7667	7642	7617	7592	7567	7542	20
85	40	25	7517	7492	7466	7440	7415	7389	19
85	41	26	7363	7337	7311	7285	7258	7232	18
85	42	26	7205	7179	7152	7125	7098	7071	17
84	43	27	7044	7017	6990	6962	6935	6907	16
84	44	28	6879	6851	6823	6795	6767	6739	15
84	45	28	6710	6682	6653	6624	6596	6567	14
84	46	29	6538	6509	6479	6450	6421	6391	13
84	47	30	6361	6332	6302	6272	6242	6212	12
84	48	30	6181	6151	6120	6090	6059	6028	11
84	49	31	5997	5966	5935	5904	5872	5841	10
84	50	31	5810	5778	5746	5715	5683	5651	9
84	51	32	5619	5586	5554	5522	5489	5456	8
84	52	33	5424	5391	5358	5325	5291	5258	7
84	53	33	5225	5191	5158	5124	5090	5056	6
84	54	34	5022	4988	4954	4920	4885	4851	5
84	55	35	4816	4782	4747	4712	4677	4642	4
83	56	35	4606	4571	4536	4500	4464	4429	3
83	57	36	4393	4357	4321	4285	4248	4212	2
83	58	36	4176	4139	4103	4066	4029	3992	1
—0″.0083	59	—37	19.3955	19.3917	19.3880	19.3843	19.3805	19.3768	0
			60ˢ	50ˢ	40ˢ	30ˢ	20ˢ	10ˢ	11ʰ— / 23ʰ+

TABLE XX.—For Annual Precessions in Right Ascension.—1850.0.

log. $\triangle_0 a = 0.12616,2 +$ log. sin $a - 0.00000,187 (t - 1850)$.   Arg. = Star's Mean Right Ascension.

$1^h +$ $13^h -$	Diff. for 10ˢ	0ˢ	10ˢ	20ˢ	30ˢ	40ˢ	50ˢ	
0ᵐ	+118	9.53916	9.54034	9.54151	9.54268	9.54385	9.54501	59ᵐ
1	116	54617	54733	54848	54963	55078	55192	58
2	114	55306	55420	55533	55646	55759	55872	57
3	112	55984	56095	56207	56318	56429	56540	56
4	110	56650	56760	56870	56979	57088	57197	55
5	108	57306	57414	57522	57629	57737	57844	54
6	106	57950	58057	58163	58269	58375	58480	53
7	105	58585	58690	58794	58899	59003	59106	52
8	104	59210	59313	59416	59518	59621	59723	51
9	102	59825	59926	60028	60129	60230	60330	50
10	100	60430	60530	60630	60730	60829	60928	49
11	98	61027	61125	61224	61322	61420	61517	48
12	97	61614	61711	61808	61905	62001	62097	47
13	96	62193	62289	62384	62480	62575	62669	46
14	95	62764	62858	62952	63046	63140	63233	45
15	93	63326	63419	63512	63604	63696	63789	44
16	91	63880	63972	64063	64155	64246	64336	43
17	90	64427	64517	64607	64697	64787	64876	42
18	89	64966	65055	65144	65232	65321	65409	41
19	88	65497	65585	65673	65760	65847	65934	40
20	87	66021	66108	66194	66281	66367	66453	39
21	85	66538	66624	66709	66794	66879	66964	38
22	84	67049	67133	67217	67301	67385	67469	37
23	83	67552	67635	67718	67801	67884	67967	36
24	82	68049	68131	68213	68295	68377	68458	35
25	81	68540	68621	68702	68782	68863	68943	34
26	80	69024	69104	69184	69263	69343	69422	33
27	79	69502	69581	69660	69738	69817	69895	32
28	78	69974	70052	70130	70207	70285	70363	31
29	77	70440	70517	70594	70671	70747	70824	30
30	76	70900	70976	71052	71128	71204	71279	29
31	75	71355	71430	71505	71580	71655	71729	28
32	74	71804	71878	71952	72027	72100	72174	27
33	73	72248	72321	72394	72467	72541	72613	26
34	73	72686	72759	72831	72903	72976	73048	25
35	72	73119	73191	73263	73334	73405	73476	24
36	71	73547	73618	73689	73760	73830	73900	23
37	70	73971	74041	74111	74180	74250	74320	22
38	69	74389	74458	74527	74596	74665	74734	21
39	+68	74802	74871	74939	75007	75075	75143	20
40	+677	752110	752787	753462	754136	754809	755480	19
41	670	756151	756820	757488	758154	758819	759483	18
42	663	760146	760808	761468	762127	762785	763441	17
43	655	764097	764751	765404	766056	766706	767356	16
44	648	768004	768651	769296	769941	770584	771227	15
45	640	771868	772507	773146	773784	774420	775055	14
46	634	775689	776322	776954	777584	778214	778842	13
47	627	779469	780095	780720	781344	781967	782588	12
48	620	783209	783828	784446	785063	785679	786294	11
49	613	786908	787520	788132	788742	789352	789960	10
50	607	790567	791174	791779	792383	792986	793587	9
51	601	794188	794788	795387	795984	796581	797177	8
52	594	797771	798365	798957	799548	800139	800728	7
53	588	801316	801904	802490	803075	803659	804242	6
54	582	804825	805406	805986	806565	807143	807721	5
55	576	808297	808872	809446	810019	810591	811163	4
56	570	811733	812302	812871	813438	814004	814570	3
57	564	815134	815698	816260	816822	817382	817942	2
58	558	818501	819058	819615	820171	820726	821280	1
59	+553	9.821833	9.822385	9.822936	9.823487	9.824036	9.824584	0
		60ˢ	50ˢ	40ˢ	30ˢ	20ˢ	10ˢ	$10^h +$ $22^h -$

Annual Precession, $\triangle a = 3.07177 + \triangle_0 a \tan \delta + 0.00001,9 (t - 1850)$.

TABLE XX.—Annual Precessions in Declination.—1850.0.

$\triangle\ \delta = 20''.0564 \cos a - 0''.0000{,}86 \cos a\ (t - 1850)$. Arg. = Star's Mean Right Ascension.

Var. in 100 yrs.	1h+ 13h−	Diff. for 10s	0s	10s	20s	30s	40s	50s	
−0.0083	0m	−38	19.3730	19.3692	19.3654	19.3616	19.3578	19.3540	59m
83	1	38	3502	3463	3425	3386	3347	3309	58
83	2	39	3270	3231	3191	3152	3113	3073	57
83	3	40	3034	2994	2955	2915	2875	2835	56
83	4	40	2794	2754	2714	2673	2633	2592	55
83	5	41	2551	2511	2470	2429	2387	2346	54
82	6	42	2305	2263	2222	2180	2138	2096	53
82	7	42	2054	2012	1970	1928	1885	1843	52
82	8	43	1800	1758	1715	1672	1629	1586	51
82	9	43	1543	1499	1456	1412	1369	1325	50
82	10	44	1281	1237	1193	1149	1105	1061	49
82	11	44	1016	0972	0927	0882	0838	0793	48
82	12	45	0748	0703	0657	0612	0567	0521	47
82	13	45	0475	0429	0384	0338	0292	19.0246	46
82	14	46	19.0200	19.0153	19.0107	19.0060	19.0013	18.9967	45
81	15	47	18.9920	18.9873	18.9826	18.9779	18.9732	9684	44
81	16	48	9637	9589	9542	9494	9446	9398	43
81	17	48	9350	9302	9254	9205	9157	9109	42
81	18	49	9060	9011	8962	8913	8864	8815	41
81	19	49	8766	8717	8667	8618	8568	8518	40
81	20	49	8469	8419	8369	8318	8268	8218	39
81	21	50	8167	8117	8066	8016	7965	7914	38
81	22	51	7863	7812	7760	7709	7658	7606	37
80	23	51	7554	7503	7451	7399	7347	7295	36
80	24	52	7243	7190	7138	7085	7033	6980	35
80	25	53	6927	6874	6821	6768	6715	6662	34
80	26	53	6608	6555	6501	6447	6394	6340	33
80	27	54	6286	6232	6178	6123	6069	6014	32
80	28	55	5960	5905	5850	5795	5740	5685	31
80	29	55	5630	5575	5519	5464	5408	5353	30
79	30	56	5297	5241	5185	5129	5073	5017	29
79	31	56	4960	4904	4847	4791	4734	4677	28
79	32	57	4620	4563	4506	4449	4391	4334	27
79	33	58	4276	4219	4161	4103	4045	3987	26
79	34	58	3929	3871	3813	3754	3696	3637	25
79	35	59	3578	3520	3461	3402	3343	3284	24
79	36	59	3224	3165	3106	3046	2986	2927	23
78	37	60	2867	2807	2747	2686	2626	2566	22
78	38	60	2505	2445	2384	2323	2263	2202	21
78	39	61	2141	2080	2018	1957	1896	1834	20
78	40	61	1773	1711	1649	1587	1525	1463	19
78	41	62	1401	1339	1276	1214	1151	1089	18
78	42	63	1026	0963	0900	0837	0774	0711	17
77	43	64	0648	0584	0521	0457	0393	18.0330	16
77	44	64	18.0266	18.0202	18.0138	18.0073	18.0009	17.9945	15
77	45	65	17.9880	17.9816	17.9751	17.9686	17.9622	9557	14
77	46	65	9492	9427	9361	9296	9230	9165	13
77	47	66	9099	9034	8968	8902	8836	8770	12
77	48	66	8704	8638	8571	8505	8438	8372	11
76	49	67	8305	8238	8171	8104	8037	7970	10
76	50	67	7902	7835	7768	7700	7632	7565	9
76	51	68	7497	7429	7361	7292	7224	7156	8
76	52	69	7087	7019	6950	6882	6813	6744	7
76	53	69	6675	6606	6537	6467	6398	6329	6
76	54	70	6259	6189	6120	6050	5980	5910	5
75	55	70	5840	5770	5699	5629	5558	5488	4
75	56	71	5417	5347	5276	5205	5134	5063	3
75	57	71	4991	4920	4849	4777	4706	4634	2
75	58	72	4562	4490	4418	4316	4274	4202	1
−0.0075	59	−72	17.4129	17.4057	17.3985	17.3912	17.3839	17.3766	0
			60s	50s	40s	30s	20s	10s	10h− 22h+

TABLE XX.—For Annual Precessions in Right Ascension.—1850.0.

log. $\Delta_0\, a = 0.12616,2$ + log. sin $a - 0.00000,187\ (t - 1850)$. Arg. = Star's Mean Right Ascension.

2^h+ 14^h-	Diff. for 10^m	0^s	10^s	20^s	30^s	40^s	50^s	
0^m	+547	9.825132	9.825678	9.826224	9.826769	9.827312	9.827855	59^m
1	542	828397	828939	829479	830018	830556	831094	58
2	536	831631	832166	832701	833235	833768	834300	57
3	531	834832	835362	835892	836420	836948	837475	56
4	526	838001	838526	839051	839574	840097	840618	55
5	521	841139	841659	842179	842697	843214	843731	54
6	516	844247	844762	845276	845789	846302	846813	53
7	511	847324	847834	848343	848851	849359	849866	52
8	505	850371	850876	851381	851884	852387	852888	51
9	500	853389	853889	854389	854887	855386	855882	50
10	496	856378	856874	857368	857862	858355	858847	49
11	491	859338	859829	860319	860808	861296	861784	48
12	486	862270	862756	863242	863726	864210	864693	47
13	482	865175	865656	866137	866616	867095	867574	46
14	477	868051	868528	869004	869479	869954	870428	45
15	472	870901	871373	871844	872315	872785	873255	44
16	468	873723	874191	874658	875125	875590	876055	43
17	464	876520	876983	877446	877908	878369	878830	42
18	460	879290	879749	880207	880665	881122	881579	41
19	455	882034	882489	882943	883397	883850	884302	40
20	451	884753	885204	885654	886103	886552	887000	39
21	447	887447	887893	888339	888784	889229	889673	38
22	443	890116	890558	891000	891441	891881	892321	37
23	439	892760	893198	893636	894073	894510	894945	36
24	435	895380	895815	896249	896682	897114	897546	35
25	431	897977	898407	898837	899266	899694	900122	34
26	427	900549	900976	901402	901827	902251	902675	33
27	423	903099	903521	903943	904365	904785	905205	32
28	420	905625	906044	906462	906879	907296	907712	31
29	416	908128	908543	908958	909371	909784	910197	30
30	412	910609	911020	911431	911841	912250	912659	29
31	408	913067	913475	913882	914288	914694	915099	28
32	405	915504	915908	916311	916714	917116	917517	27
33	401	917918	918319	918718	919117	919516	919914	26
34	397	920311	920708	921104	921500	921895	922289	25
35	394	922683	923076	923469	923861	924252	924643	24
36	390	925033	925423	925812	926201	926589	926976	23
37	387	927363	927749	928135	928520	928905	929289	22
38	383	929672	930055	930437	930819	931200	931581	21
39	380	931961	932340	932719	933097	933475	933852	20
40	377	934229	934605	934981	935356	935730	936104	19
41	373	936477	936850	937222	937594	937966	938336	18
42	370	938706	939076	939445	939813	940181	940548	17
43	367	940915	941281	941647	942012	942377	942741	16
44	364	943105	943468	943830	944192	944554	944915	15
45	360	945275	945635	945994	946353	946711	947069	14
46	357	947426	947783	948139	948495	948850	949205	13
47	354	949559	949912	950265	950618	950970	951322	12
48	351	951673	952023	952373	952723	953072	953420	11
49	348	953768	954115	954462	954809	955155	955500	10
50	345	955845	956180	956533	956877	957220	957562	9
51	342	957904	958245	958586	958927	959267	959606	8
52	339	959945	960283	960621	960959	961296	961632	7
53	336	961968	962304	962639	962973	963307	963641	6
54	333	963974	964307	964639	964970	965301	965632	5
55	330	965962	966292	966621	966950	967278	967606	4
56	327	967933	968260	968586	968912	969237	969562	3
57	325	969887	970211	970534	970857	971180	971502	2
58	322	971824	972145	972465	972785	973105	973124	1
59	+319	9.973743	9.974062	9.974380	9.974697	9.975014	9.975331	0
		60^s	50^s	40^s	30^s	20^s	10^s	9^h+ 21^h-

Annual Precession, $\Delta\, a = 3.07177 + \Delta_0\, a \tan \delta + 0.00001,9\ (t - 1850)$.

TABLE XX.—Annual Precessions in Declination.—1850.0.

$$\Delta\,\delta = 20''.0564\,\cos\alpha - 0''.0000{,}86\,\cos\alpha\,(t-1850).\quad \text{Arg. = Star's Mean Right Ascension.}$$

Var. in 100 yrs.	2^b+ 14^h-	Diff. for 10^s	0^s	10^s	20^s	30^s	40^s	50^s	
−0″.0074	0^m	− 73	17″.3693	17″.3620	17″.3547	17″.3474	17″.3401	17″.3328	59^m
74	1	74	3254	3181	3107	3033	2960	2886	58
74	2	74	2812	2738	2664	2589	2515	2440	57
74	3	75	2366	2291	2217	2142	2067	1992	56
74	4	75	1917	1842	1766	1691	1616	1540	55
74	5	76	1465	1389	1313	1237	1161	1085	54
73	6	76	1009	0933	0856	0780	0703	0627	53
73	7	77	0550	0473	17.0396	17.0319	17.0242	17.0165	52
73	8	77	17.0088	17.0011	16.9933	16.9856	16.9778	16.9700	51
73	9	78	16.9623	16.9545	9467	9389	9311	9232	50
73	10	78	9154	9075	8997	8918	8840	8761	49
72	11	79	8682	8603	8524	8445	8366	8286	48
72	12	79	8207	8127	8048	7968	7889	7809	47
72	13	80	7729	7649	7569	7489	7408	7328	46
72	14	80	7248	7167	7086	7006	6925	6844	45
72	15	81	6763	6682	6601	6519	6438	6357	44
71	16	82	6275	6193	6112	6030	5948	5866	43
71	17	82	5784	5702	5620	5537	5455	5373	42
71	18	83	5290	5207	5125	5042	4959	4876	41
71	19	83	4793	4710	4626	4543	4460	4376	40
70	20	84	4292	4209	4125	4041	3957	3873	39
70	21	84	3789	3705	3620	3536	3452	3367	38
70	22	85	3282	3198	3113	3028	2943	2858	37
70	23	85	2772	2687	2602	2516	2431	2346	36
70	24	86	2260	2174	2088	2002	1916	1830	35
69	25	86	1744	1657	1571	1485	1398	1311	34
69	26	87	1225	1138	1051	0964	0877	0790	33
69	27	87	0703	0615	0528	16.0440	16.0353	16.0265	32
68	28	88	16.0177	16.0090	16.0002	15.9914	15.9826	15.9738	31
68	29	88	15.9649	15.9561	15.9473	9384	9296	9207	30
68	30	89	9118	9029	8940	8851	8762	8673	29
68	31	89	8584	8495	8405	8316	8226	8136	28
68	32	90	8047	7957	7867	7777	7687	7597	27
68	33	90	7506	7416	7325	7235	7144	7054	26
67	34	91	6963	6872	6781	6690	6599	6508	25
67	35	91	6417	6325	6234	6142	6051	5959	24
67	36	92	5868	5776	5684	5592	5500	5408	23
67	37	92	5315	5223	5131	5038	4946	4853	22
66	38	93	4760	4667	4574	4481	4388	4295	21
66	39	93	4202	4109	4015	3922	3828	3735	20
66	40	94	3641	3547	3453	3359	3265	3171	19
66	41	94	3077	2983	2888	2794	2699	2605	18
65	42	95	2510	2415	2320	2226	2131	2035	17
65	43	95	1940	1845	1750	1654	1559	1463	16
65	44	96	1368	1272	1176	1080	0984	0888	15
65	45	96	0792	0696	0599	15.0503	15.0407	15.0310	14
64	46	97	15.0214	15.0117	15.0020	14.9923	14.9826	14.9729	13
64	47	97	14.9632	14.9535	14.9438	9341	9243	9146	12
64	48	98	9048	8951	8853	8755	8657	8559	11
64	49	98	8461	8363	8265	8167	8068	7970	10
63	50	98	7871	7773	7674	7575	7477	7378	9
63	51	99	7279	7179	7080	6981	6882	6783	8
63	52	99	6683	6584	6484	6385	6285	6185	7
63	53	100	6085	5985	5885	5785	5684	5584	6
62	54	100	5484	5384	5283	5182	5082	4981	5
62	55	101	4880	4779	4678	4577	4476	4375	4
62	56	101	4274	4172	4071	3969	3868	3766	3
62	57	102	3664	3563	3461	3359	3257	3155	2
61	58	102	3052	2950	2848	2745	2643	2540	1
−.0061	59	−103	14.2438	14.2335	14.2232	14.2129	14.2026	14.1923	0
			60^s	50^s	40^s	30^s	20^s	10^s	9^b- 21^b+

TABLE IX.—For Annual Precessions in Right Ascension.—1850.0.

log. $\triangle_0 a = 0.12616,2 + $ log. sin $a - 0.00000,187$ $(t - 1850)$.   Arg. $=$ Star's Mean Right Ascension.

3h + / 15h —	Diff. for 10s	0s	10s	20s	30s	40s	50s	
0m	+315	9.975647	9.975962	9.976277	9.976592	9.976906	9.977220	59m
1	313	977533	977846	978159	978471	978782	979093	58
2	311	979404	979714	980023	980333	980642	980950	57
3	308	981258	981565	981872	982179	982485	982791	56
4	305	983096	983401	983705	984009	984312	984615	55
5	302	984918	985220	985522	985823	986124	986424	54
6	300	986724	987023	987322	987621	987919	988217	53
7	297	988514	988811	989108	989404	989699	989994	52
8	295	990289	990583	990877	991171	991464	991756	51
9	292	992048	992340	992632	992923	993213	993503	50
10	290	993793	994082	994371	994659	994947	995234	49
11	287	995521	995808	996094	996380	996666	996951	48
12	284	997235	997519	997803	998086	9.998369	9.998652	47
13	282	9.998934	9.999216	9.999497	9.999778	0.000058	0.000338	46
14	280	0.000618	0.000897	0.001176	0.001454	001732	002010	45
15	277	002287	002564	002840	003116	003392	003667	44
16	275	003942	004216	004490	004763	005036	005309	43
17	273	005582	005854	006125	006396	006667	006937	42
18	270	007207	007477	007746	008015	008283	008551	41
19	268	008819	009086	009353	009619	009885	010151	40
20	265	010416	010681	010945	011209	011473	011736	39
21	263	011999	012261	012523	012785	013046	013307	38
22	261	013568	013828	014088	014347	014606	014865	37
23	258	015123	015381	015638	015895	016152	016408	36
24	256	016664	016920	017175	017430	017684	017938	35
25	254	018192	018445	018698	018951	019203	019455	34
26	251	019706	019957	020208	020458	020708	020958	33
27	249	021207	021456	021704	021952	022200	022447	32
28	247	022694	022940	023186	023432	023678	023923	31
29	245	024168	024412	024656	024900	025143	025386	30
30	242	025628	025870	026112	026354	026595	026836	29
31	240	027076	027316	027556	027795	028034	028272	28
32	238	028510	028748	028986	029223	029459	029696	27
33	236	029932	030168	030403	030638	030872	031106	26
34	234	031340	031574	031807	032040	032272	032504	25
35	232	032736	032968	033199	033429	033660	033890	24
36	230	034119	034349	034578	034806	035034	035262	23
37	228	035490	035717	035944	036170	036396	036622	22
38	226	036848	037073	037298	037522	037746	037970	21
39	223	038193	038416	038639	038861	039083	039305	20
40	221	039526	039747	039968	040188	040408	040628	19
41	219	040847	041066	041285	041503	041721	041938	18
42	217	042155	042372	042589	042805	043021	043237	17
43	215	043452	043667	043881	044095	044309	044523	16
44	213	044736	044949	045161	045373	045585	045797	15
45	211	046008	046219	046430	046640	046850	047059	14
46	209	047268	047477	047686	047894	048102	048309	13
47	207	048517	048724	048930	049136	049342	049548	12
48	205	049753	049958	050163	050367	050571	050775	11
49	203	050978	051181	051384	051586	051788	051990	10
50	201	052191	052392	052593	052793	052993	053193	9
51	199	053392	053591	053790	053989	054187	054385	8
52	197	054582	054779	054976	055173	055369	055565	7
53	196	055761	055956	056151	056345	056540	056734	6
54	194	056928	057121	057314	057507	057699	057891	5
55	192	058083	058275	058466	058657	058847	059037	4
56	190	059227	059417	059606	059795	059984	060172	3
57	188	060360	060548	060736	060923	061109	061296	2
58	186	061482	061668	061854	062039	062224	062408	1
59	+184	0.062593	0.062777	0.062961	0.063144	0.063327	0.063510	0
		60s	50s	40s	30s	20s	10s	8h + / 20h —

Annual Precession, $\triangle a = 3.07177 + \triangle_0 a$ tan $\delta + 0.00001,9$ $(t - 1850)$.

TABLE IX.—Annual Precessions in Declination.—1850.0.

$\triangle \delta = 20''.0564 \cos a - 0''.0000,86 \cos a\ (t - 1850)$. Arg. = Star's Mean Right Ascension.

Var. in 100 yrs.	3ᵇ + 15ʰ —	Diff. for 10ᵐ	0ˢ	10ˢ	20ˢ	30ˢ	40ˢ	50ˢ	
—0".0061	0ᵐ	—103	14".1820	14".1717	14".1614	14".1510	14".1407	14".1304	59ᵐ
61	1	104	1200	1096	0993	0889	0785	0681	58
60	2	104	14.0577	14.0473	14.0369	14.0265	14.0160	14.0056	57
60	3	104	13.9952	13.9847	13.9743	13.9638	13.9533	13.9428	56
60	4	105	9323	9218	9113	9008	8903	8798	55
59	5	106	8693	8587	8482	8376	8271	8165	54
59	6	106	8059	7953	7847	7741	7635	7529	53
59	7	106	7423	7317	7210	7104	6998	6891	52
59	8	107	6784	6678	6571	6464	6357	6250	51
58	9	107	6143	6036	5929	5821	5714	5607	50
58	10	108	5499	5392	5284	5176	5068	4961	49
58	11	108	4853	4745	4636	4528	4420	4312	48
58	12	108	4204	4095	3997	3878	3769	3661	47
57	13	109	3552	3443	3334	3225	3116	3007	46
57	14	109	2898	2788	2679	2570	2460	2351	45
57	15	110	2241	2131	2021	1912	1802	1692	44
56	16	110	1582	1472	1361	1251	1141	1031	43
56	17	111	0920	0810	0699	13.0588	13.0478	13.0367	42
56	18	111	13.0256	13.0145	13.0034	12.9923	12.9812	12.9700	41
56	19	111	12.9589	12.9478	12.9366	9255	9143	9032	40
55	20	112	8920	8808	8696	8585	8473	8360	39
55	21	112	8248	8136	8024	7912	7799	7687	38
55	22	113	7574	7462	7349	7236	7124	7011	37
54	23	113	6898	6785	6672	6559	6446	6332	36
54	24	113	6219	6106	5992	5879	5765	5651	35
54	25	114	5538	5424	5310	5196	5082	4968	34
54	26	114	4854	4740	4626	4511	4397	4282	33
53	27	115	4168	4053	3939	3824	3709	3594	32
53	28	115	3480	3365	3250	3134	3019	2904	31
53	29	116	2789	2673	2558	2442	2327	2211	30
52	30	116	2096	1980	1864	1748	1632	1516	29
52	31	116	1400	1284	1168	1052	0935	0819	28
52	32	117	0702	12.0586	12.0469	12.0353	12.0236	12.0119	27
51	33	117	12.0002	11.9886	11.9769	11.9652	11.9534	11.9417	26
51	34	117	11.9300	9183	9065	8948	8831	8713	25
51	35	118	8595	8478	8360	8242	8124	8006	24
51	36	118	7888	7770	7652	7534	7416	7298	23
50	37	119	7179	7061	6942	6824	6705	6587	22
50	38	119	6468	6349	6230	6112	5993	5874	21
50	39	119	5755	5635	5516	5397	5278	5158	20
49	40	120	5039	4919	4799	4680	4560	4411	19
49	41	120	4321	4201	4081	3961	3841	3721	18
49	42	120	3601	3480	3360	3240	3119	2999	17
48	43	120	2978	2758	2537	2517	2396	2275	16
48	44	121	2154	2033	1912	1791	1670	1549	15
48	45	121	1427	1306	1185	1063	0942	0820	14
47	46	122	11.0699	11.0577	11.0455	11.0334	11.0212	11.0090	13
47	47	122	10.9968	10.9846	10.9724	10.9602	10.9480	10.9357	12
47	48	122	9235	9113	8990	8868	8745	8623	11
47	49	123	8500	8377	8254	8132	8009	7886	10
46	50	123	7763	7640	7517	7391	7270	7147	9
46	51	124	7024	6900	6777	6653	6530	6406	8
46	52	124	6283	6159	6035	5911	5788	5664	7
45	53	124	5540	5415	5291	5167	5043	4919	6
45	54	125	4794	4670	4545	4421	4296	4172	5
45	55	125	4047	3922	3798	3673	3548	3423	4
44	56	125	3298	3173	3048	2923	2797	2672	3
44	57	125	2547	2422	2296	2171	2045	1919	2
44	58	126	1794	1668	1542	1417	1291	1165	1
—.0043	59	—126	10.1039	10.0913	10.0787	10.0661	10.0534	10.0408	0
			60ˢ	50ˢ	40ˢ	30ˢ	20ˢ	10ˢ	3ᵇ 26ᵇ+

TABLE XX.—For Annual Precessions in Right Ascension.—1850.0.

log. $\triangle_0\, a = 0.12616,2 +$ log. sin $a - 0.00000,187\ (t - 1850)$.   Arg. = Star's Mean Right Ascension.

4ʰ + 16ʰ −	Diff. for 10ˢ	0ˢ	10ˢ	20ˢ	30ˢ	40ˢ	50ˢ	
0ᵐ	+182	0.063692	0.063874	0.064056	0.064238	0.064419	0.064600	59ᵐ
1	181	064781	064961	065141	065321	065500	065679	58
2	179	065858	066037	066215	066393	066571	066748	57
3	177	066925	067102	067278	067454	067630	067806	56
4	175	067981	068156	068331	068505	068679	068853	55
5	173	069026	069199	069372	069545	069717	069889	54
6	171	070060	070232	070403	070573	070744	070914	53
7	170	071084	071254	071423	071591	071760	071929	52
8	168	072097	072264	072432	072599	072766	072933	51
9	166	073099	073265	073431	073596	073761	073926	50
10	165	074091	074255	074419	074583	074746	074909	49
11	163	075072	075234	075397	075559	075720	075882	48
12	161	076043	076204	076364	076524	076684	076844	47
13	159	077003	077162	077321	077479	077637	077795	46
14	158	077953	078110	078267	078424	078581	078737	45
15	156	078893	079048	079204	079359	079513	079668	44
16	154	079822	079976	080129	080283	080436	080539	43
17	152	080741	080893	081045	081197	081348	081499	42
18	151	081650	081800	081950	082100	082250	082400	41
19	149	082549	082698	082846	082994	083142	083290	40
20	147	083437	083584	083731	083878	084024	084170	39
21	146	084316	084462	084607	084752	084896	085041	38
22	144	085185	085328	085472	085615	085758	085901	37
23	142	086043	086185	086327	086469	086610	086751	36
24	141	086892	087032	087173	087313	087453	087592	35
25	139	087731	087869	088008	088146	088284	088422	34
26	138	088560	088697	088834	088970	089107	089243	33
27	136	089379	089514	089649	089784	089919	090054	32
28	134	090188	090322	090455	090589	090722	090855	31
29	133	090987	091120	091252	091383	091515	091646	30
30	131	091777	091908	092038	092168	092298	092428	29
31	129	092557	092686	092815	092944	093072	093200	28
32	128	093328	093455	093582	093709	093836	093962	27
33	126	094088	094214	094340	094465	094590	094715	26
34	125	094840	094964	095088	095212	095335	095458	25
35	123	095581	095704	095826	095948	096070	096192	24
36	121	096313	096434	096555	096676	096796	096916	23
37	120	097036	097156	097275	097394	097513	097631	22
38	118	097749	097867	097985	098102	098220	098337	21
39	117	098453	098570	098686	098802	098917	099032	20
40	115	099147	099262	099377	099491	099605	099719	19
41	114	099833	099946	100059	100172	100284	100396	18
42	112	100508	100620	100731	100843	100954	101064	17
43	111	101175	101285	101395	101504	101614	101723	16
44	109	101832	101940	102049	102157	102265	102372	15
45	107	102480	102587	102694	102800	102906	103012	14
46	106	103118	103224	103329	103434	103539	103644	13
47	104	103748	103852	103956	104059	104162	104265	12
48	103	104368	104471	104573	104675	104777	104878	11
49	101	104979	105080	105181	105281	105381	105481	10
50	100	105581	105681	105780	105879	105978	106076	9
51	98	106174	106272	106370	106467	106564	106661	8
52	97	106758	106854	106951	107047	107142	107238	7
53	95	107333	107428	107523	107617	107711	107805	6
54	93	107899	107992	108085	108178	108271	108363	5
55	92	108455	108547	108639	108731	108822	108913	4
56	91	109003	109094	109184	109274	109364	109453	3
57	89	109542	109631	109720	109808	109897	109985	2
58	87	110072	110160	110247	110334	110421	110507	1
59	+86	0.110593	0.110679	0.110765	0.110851	0.110936	0.111021	0
		60ˢ	50ˢ	40ˢ	30ˢ	20ˢ	10ˢ	7ʰ + 19ʰ −

Annual Precession, $\triangle a = 3.07177 + \triangle_0\, a \tan \delta + 0.00001,9\ (t - 1850)$.

TABLE XX.—AnnualPrecessions in Declination.—1850.0.

$\Delta \delta = 20''.0564 \cos a - 0''.0000{,}86 \cos a\,(t - 1850).$ Arg. = Star's Mean Right Ascension.

Var. in 100 yrs.	4ʰ + 16ʰ —	Diff. for 10ˢ	0ˢ	10ˢ	20ˢ	30ˢ	40ˢ	50ˢ	
−0″.0043	0ᵐ	−126	10″.0282	10″.0156	10″.0029	9″.9903	9″.9776	9″.9650	59ᵐ
43	1	127	9.9523	9.9396	9 9270	9143	9016	8889	58
42	2	127	8762	8635	8508	8381	8254	8127	57
42	3	127	8000	7872	7745	7618	7490	7363	56
42	4	129	7235	7108	6980	6852	6725	6597	55
41	5	128	6469	6341	6213	6085	5957	5829	54
41	6	128	5701	5573	5444	5316	5188	5059	53
41	7	129	4931	4802	4674	4545	4417	4288	52
40	8	129	4159	4030	3901	3772	3643	3514	51
40	9	129	3385	3256	3127	2998	2869	2739	50
40	10	129	2610	2481	2351	2222	2092	1963	49
39	11	130	1833	1703	1574	1444	1314	1184	48
39	12	130	1054	0924	0794	9.0664	9.0534	9.0404	47
39	13	130	9.0273	9.0143	9.0013	8.9882	8.9752	8.9622	46
38	14	131	8.9491	8.9361	8.9230	9099	8969	8838	45
38	15	131	8707	8576	8445	8315	8184	8053	44
38	16	131	7921	7790	7659	7528	7397	7265	43
37	17	131	7134	7003	6871	6740	6608	6476	42
37	18	132	6345	6213	6081	5950	5618	5486	41
37	19	132	5554	5422	5290	5158	5026	4894	40
36	20	132	4762	4630	4497	4365	4233	4100	39
36	21	132	3968	3836	3703	3570	3438	3305	38
36	22	133	3173	3040	2907	2774	2641	2508	37
35	23	133	2375	2242	2109	1976	1843	1710	36
35	24	133	1577	1444	1310	1177	1043	0910	35
35	25	133	8.0776	8.0643	8.0509	8.0376	8.0242	8.0108	34
34	26	131	7.9975	7.9841	7.9707	7.9573	7.9439	7.9305	33
34	27	134	9171	9037	8903	8769	8635	8501	32
34	28	134	8367	8232	8098	7934	7829	7695	31
33	29	134	7560	7426	7291	7157	7022	6887	30
33	30	135	6753	6618	6483	6348	6213	6078	29
33	31	135	5943	5808	5673	5538	5403	5268	28
32	32	135	5133	4997	4862	4727	4591	4456	27
32	33	136	4321	4185	4050	3914	3778	3643	26
32	34	136	3507	3371	3236	3100	2964	2828	25
31	35	136	2692	2556	2420	2284	2148	2012	24
31	36	136	1876	1739	1603	1467	1331	1194	23
30	37	137	1058	0922	7.0785	7.0649	7.0512	7.0376	22
30	38	137	7.0239	7.0102	6.9965	6.9829	6.9692	6.9555	21
30	39	137	6.9419	6.9282	9145	9008	8871	8734	20
29	40	137	8597	8460	8323	8186	8048	7911	19
29	41	137	7774	7637	7499	7362	7224	7087	18
29	42	138	6950	6812	6675	6537	6399	6262	17
28	43	138	6124	5986	5849	5711	5573	5435	16
28	44	138	5297	5159	5021	4883	4745	4607	15
28	45	138	4469	4331	4193	4055	3916	3778	14
27	46	138	3640	3502	3363	3225	3086	2948	13
27	47	139	2809	2671	2532	2394	2255	2116	12
27	48	139	1978	1839	1700	1561	1423	1284	11
26	49	139	1145	1006	0867	6.0728	6.0589	6.0450	10
26	50	139	6.0311	6.0172	6.0032	5.9893	5.9754	5.9615	9
25	51	139	5.9476	5.9336	5.9197	9058	8918	8779	8
25	52	140	8639	8500	8360	8221	8081	7941	7
25	53	140	7802	7662	7522	7383	7243	7103	6
24	54	140	6963	6823	6684	6544	6404	6264	5
24	55	140	6124	5984	5844	5703	5563	5423	4
24	56	140	5283	5143	5002	4862	4722	4582	3
23	57	141	4441	4301	4160	4020	3880	3739	2
23	58	141	3599	3458	3317	3177	3036	2895	1
−0.0023	59	−141	5.2755	5.2614	5.2473	5.2332	5.2191	5.2051	0
			60ˢ	50ˢ	40ˢ	30ˢ	20ˢ	10ˢ	7ʰ— 19ʰ+

TABLE XX.—For Annual Precessions in Right Ascension.—1850.0.

log. $\Delta_0 a = 0.12616,2 +$ log. sin $a - 0.00000,187\ (t - 1850)$.   Arg. = Star's Mean Right Ascension.

5ʰ + 17ʰ —	Diff. for 10ˢ	0ˢ	10ˢ	20ˢ	30ˢ	40ˢ	50ˢ	
0m	+84	0.111106	0.111190	0.111274	0.111358	0.111442	0.111526	59m
1	83	111609	111692	111775	111857	111939	112021	58
2	82	112103	112185	112266	112347	112428	112509	57
3	80	112589	112669	112749	112829	112908	112987	56
4	79	113066	113144	113223	113301	113379	113457	55
5	77	113534	113611	113688	113765	113841	113917	54
6	76	113993	114069	114144	114220	114295	114369	53
7	74	114444	114518	114592	114666	114739	114813	52
8	72	114886	114958	115031	115103	115175	115247	51
9	71	115319	115390	115461	115532	115603	115673	50
10	70	115743	115813	115883	115952	116021	116090	49
11	68	116159	116227	116296	116364	116431	116499	48
12	67	116566	116633	116700	116766	116833	116899	47
13	66	116965	117030	117096	117161	117225	117290	46
14	64	117354	117418	117482	117546	117610	117673	45
15	62	117736	117798	117861	117923	117985	118047	44
16	61	118108	118170	118231	118291	118352	118412	43
17	60	118472	118532	118592	118651	118710	118769	42
18	59	118828	118886	118944	119002	119060	119118	41
19	57	119175	119232	119289	119345	119401	119457	40
20	56	119513	119569	119624	119679	119734	119789	39
21	54	119843	119897	119951	120005	120058	120111	38
22	53	120164	120217	120270	120322	120374	120426	37
23	52	120477	120529	120580	120631	120681	120732	36
24	50	120782	120832	120881	120931	120980	121029	35
25	48	121078	121126	121174	121222	121270	121318	34
26	47	121365	121412	121459	121506	121552	121598	33
27	46	121644	121690	121735	121780	121825	121870	32
28	44	121915	121959	122003	122047	122090	122134	31
29	43	122177	122219	122262	122305	122347	122389	30
30	42	122430	122472	122513	122554	122595	122635	29
31	40	122676	122716	122755	122795	122834	122873	28
32	39	122912	122951	122990	123028	123066	123103	27
33	38	123141	123178	123215	123252	123289	123325	26
34	36	123361	123397	123433	123468	123503	123538	25
35	35	123573	123607	123641	123675	123709	123743	24
36	33	123776	123809	123842	123875	123907	123939	23
37	32	123971	124003	124034	124065	124096	124127	22
38	30	124155	124188	124218	124218	124278	124307	21
39	29	124336	124365	124394	124422	124450	124478	20
40	28	124506	124533	124561	124589	124615	124641	19
41	27	124668	124694	124720	124745	124771	124796	18
42	25	124821	124846	124870	124894	124918	124942	17
43	24	124966	124989	125012	125035	125058	125080	16
44	22	125103	125125	125146	125168	125189	125210	15
45	21	125231	125251	125272	125292	125312	125332	14
46	19	125351	125370	125389	125408	125426	125445	13
47	18	125463	125481	125498	125515	125532	125549	12
48	17	125566	125583	125599	125615	125631	125646	11
49	15	125661	125676	125691	125706	125720	125734	10
50	14	125748	125762	125775	125789	125802	125814	9
51	13	125827	125839	125851	125863	125875	125886	8
52	11	125897	125908	125919	125929	125939	125949	7
53	10	125959	125969	125978	125987	125996	126005	6
54	8	126013	126021	126029	126037	126044	126051	5
55	7	126058	126065	126072	126078	126084	126090	4
56	6	126096	126101	126106	126111	126116	126120	3
57	4	126125	126129	126132	126136	126139	126142	2
58	3	126145	126148	126150	126152	126154	126156	1
59	+1	126159	0.126159	0.126160	0.126161	0.126161	0.126162	0
60	0	0.126162						— 1
		60ˢ	50ˢ	40ˢ	30ˢ	20ˢ	10ˢ	6ʰ + 18ʰ —

Annual Precession, $\Delta a = 3.07177 + \Delta_0 a \tan \delta + 0.00001,9\ (t - 1850)$.

TABLE XX.—Annual Precessions in Declination.—1850.0.

$\Delta \delta = 20''.0564 \cos a - 0''.0000,86 \cos a (t - 1850)$. Arg. = Star's Mean Right Ascension.

Var. in 100 yrs.	5h+ 17h−	Diff. for 10s	0s	10s	20s	30s	40s	50s	
−0".0023	0m	−141	5".1910	5".1769	5".1628	5".1487	5".1346	5".1205	59m
22	1	141	1064	0923	5.0782	5.0641	5.0500	5.0358	58
22	2	141	5.0217	5.0076	4.9935	4.9793	4.9652	4.9511	57
21	3	141	4.9370	4.9228	90e7	8945	8804	8662	56
21	4	142	8521	8379	8238	8096	7955	7813	55
20	5	142	7671	7530	7388	7246	7104	6963	54
20	6	142	6821	6679	6537	6395	6253	6111	53
20	7	142	5969	5827	5685	5543	5401	5259	52
19	8	142	5117	4975	4833	4691	4548	4406	51
19	9	142	4264	4122	3979	3837	3695	3552	50
19	10	142	3410	3268	3125	2983	2840	2698	49
18	11	143	2555	2413	2270	2128	1985	1842	48
18	12	143	1700	1557	1414	1272	1129	0986	47
18	13 ·	143	4.0843	4.0700	4.0558	4.0415	4.0272	4.0129	46
17	14	143	3.9986	3.9843	3.9700	3.9557	3.9414	3.9271	45
17	15	143	9128	8985	8842	8699	8556	8413	44
16	16	143	8269	8126	7983	7840	7697	7553	43
16	17	143	7410	7267	7123	6980	6837	6693	42
16	18	144	6550	6406	6263	6119	5976	5833	41
15	19	144	5689	5546	5402	5258	5115	4971	40
15	20	144	4829	4684	4540	4397	4253	4109	39
15	21	144	3965	3822	3678	3534	3390	3246	38
14	22	144	3103	2959	2815	2671	2527	2383	37
14	23	144	2239	2095	1951	1807	1663	1519	36
13	24	144	1375	1231	1087	0943	3.0799	3.0655	35
13	25	144	3.0510	3.0366	3.0222	3.0078	2.9934	2.9789	34
13	26	144	2.9645	2.9501	2.9357	2.9212	9068	8924	33
12	27	144	8779	8635	8491	8346	8202	8058	32
12	28	144	7913	7769	7624	7480	7335	7191	31
12	29	144	7046	6902	6757	6613	6468	6323	30
11	30	144	6179	6034	5890	5745	5600	5456	29
11	31	145	5311	5166	5022	4877	4732	4587	28
10	32	145	4443	4298	4153	4008	3863	3719	27
10	33	145	3574	3429	3284	3139	2994	2849	26
10	34	145	2705	2560	2415	2270	2125	1980	25
9	35	145	1835	1690	1545	1400	1255	1110	24
9	36	145	0965	2.0820	2.0675	2.0529	2.0384	2.0239	23
9	37	145	2.0094	1.9949	1.9804	1.9659	1.9514	1.9368	22
8	38	145	1.9223	9078	8933	8788	8642	8497	21
8	39	145	8352	8207	8061	7916	7771	7626	20
7	40	145	7480	7335	7190	7044	6899	6754	19
7	41	145	6608	6463	6318	6172	6027	5881	18
7	42	145	5736	5591	5445	5300	5154	5009	17
6	43	145	4863	4718	4573	4427	4282	4136	16
6	44	145	3991	3845	3700	3554	3409	3263	15
6	45	146	3118	2972	2826	2681	2535	2390	14
5	46	146	2244	2099	1953	1807	1662	1516	13
5	47	146	1371	1225	1079	0934	1.0788	1.0642	12
5	48	146	1.0497	1.0351	1.0205	1.0060	0.9914	0.9768	11
4	49	146	0.9623	0.9477	0.9331	0.9186	9040	8894	10
4	50	146	8748	8603	8457	8311	8166	8020	9
3	51	146	7874	7728	7583	7437	7291	7145	8
3	52	146	7000	6854	6708	6562	6416	6271	7
3	53	146	6125	5979	5833	5688	5542	5396	6
2	54	146	5250	5104	4959	4813	4667	4521	5
2	55	146	4375	4229	4084	3938	3792	3646	4
2	56	146	3500	3354	3209	3063	2917	2771	3
1	57	146	2625	2479	2334	2188	2042	1896	2
1	58	146	1750	1604	1459	1313	1167	1021	1
0	59	146	0875	0.0729	0.0583	0.0438	0.0292	0.0146	0
−0.0000	60	−146	0.0000						− 1
			60s	50s	40s	30s	20s	10s	6h 18h +

5

SPECIAL TABLES

FOR THE STANDARD STARS OF THE AMERICAN EPHEMERIS AND NAUTICAL ALMANAC.

TABLE XXI.—Mean Right Ascensions of Standard Stars for 1860.0.

Star's name.	Mag.	Right Ascension.	An. Variation.	Sec. Variation.	Prop. Motion.
		h m s	s	s	s
α Andromedæ	2	0 1 9.427	+ 3.08590	+ 0.01820	+0.0102
γ Pegasi, (*Algenib*)	3.2	0 6 1.797	3.08157	+ 0.00995	+0.0006
* β Hydri	3	0 18 19.936	3.27548	— 0.16094	+0.7080
α Cassiopeæ	Var.	0 32 35.073	3.35801	+ 0.05503	+0.0076
*21 Cassiopeæ	6	0 36 28.192	3.81033	+ 0.15810	—0.0114
β Ceti	2	0 36 33.601	3.01414	— 0.00566	+0.0143
ε Piscium	4	0 55 40.798	3.10773	+ 0.00864	—0.0045
* α Ursæ Minoris, (*Polaris*)	2	1 8 3.195	18.78480	+12.78781	+0.1172
θ¹ Ceti	3	1 17 1.568	2.99756	+ 0.00169	—0.0053
*38 Cassiopeæ	6	1 20 52.220	4.33548	+ 0.14223	+0.0249
η Piscium	4.3	1 23 59.745	3.19737	+ 0.01423	+0.0004
α Eridani, (*Achernar*)	1	1 32 20.669	2.23616	— 0.01315	+0.0028
o Piscium	4	1 38 0.301	3.16045	+ 0.01106	+0.0061
β Arietis	3.2	1 46 54.740	3.29848	+ 0.01818	+0.0062
*50 Cassiopeæ	4	1 51 33.318	4.95626	+ 0.18464	—0.0113
α Arietis	2	1 59 17.286	3.36565	+ 0.02026	+0.0142
ξ¹ Ceti	4.5	2 5 34.978	3.16798	+ 0.01154	—0.0042
* ι Cassiopeæ	4	2 17 34.852	4.82371	+ 0.13002	—0.0079
γ Ceti	3.4	2 36 2.966	3.10142	+ 0.00018	—0.0094
α Ceti	2.3	2 54 57.857	3.12762	+ 0.00967	—0.0015
*48 Cephei, (Hev.)	6	3 2 42.022	7.30312	+ 0.35066	+0.0164
ζ Arietis	4.5	3 6 51.602	3.43481	+ 0.01764	—0.0015
α Persei	2	3 14 20.684	4.24196	+ 0.04830	+0.0018
δ Persei	3	3 32 58.207	4.23447	+ 0.04159	+0.0002
η Tauri	3	3 39 10.067	3.55181	+ 0.01730	+0.0010
ζ Persei	3	3 45 20.325	3.75354	+ 0.02220	+0 0006
γ¹ Eridani	3	3 51 29.919	2.79595	+ 0.00454	+0.0044
γ Tauri	4	4 11 49.768	3.40594	+ 0.01156	—0.0035
ε Tauri	4.3	4 20 26.703	3.49403	+ 0.01215	+0.0076
α Tauri, (*Aldebaran*)	1	4 27 53.441	3.43452	+ 0.01061	+0.0045
* 9 Camelopardalis	4	4 40 9.364	5.90462	+ 0.07036	—0.0031
ι Aurigæ	3	4 47 52.863	3.89493	+ 0.01458	—0.0008
11 Orionis	5	4 56 34.329	3.42404	+ 0.00785	+0.0025
α Aurigæ, (*Capella*)	1	5 6 21.120	4.42034	+ 0.01655	+0.0086
β Orionis, (*Rigel*)	1	5 7 48.651	2.88030	+ 0.00397	—0.0001
θ Tauri	2	5 17 26.642	3.78669	+ 0.00804	+0.0017
* Groombridge 966	6.7	5 21 1.861	7.97812	+ 0.08056	+0.0080
δ Orionis	2	5 24 51.337	3.06350	+ 0.00322	+0.0009
α Leporis	3	5 26 33.420	2.64606	+ 0.00297	+0.0020
ε Orionis	2	5 29 6.637	3.04152	+ 0.00356	—0.0005
α Columbæ	2	5 34 34.859	2.17186	+ 0.00275	+0.0013
α Orionis	Var.	5 47 35.602	3.24652	+ 0.00278	+0.0017
*22 Camelopardalis, (Hev.)	5.4	6 3 24.648	6.61942	— 0.00473	—0.0021
μ Geminorum	3	6 14 29.434	3.63280	— 0.00040	+0.0059
α Argus, (Canopus)	1	6 20 50.780	1.33010	+ 0.00100	+0.0010
γ Geminorum	2.3	6 29 37.426	3.46909	— 0.00141	+0.0040
*51 Cephei, (Hev.)	5	6 33 38.690	30.52200	— 1.77295	—0.0695
α Canis Majoris, (*Sirius*)	1	6 38 58.677	2.64513	0.00000	—0.0358
ε Canis Majoris	2.1	6 53 7.502	2.35835	+ 0.00132	+0.0013
δ Canis Majoris	2	7 2 41.998	+ 2.43958	+ 0.00118	+0.0003

* Circumpolar Stars.

TABLE XXI.—Mean Declinations of Standard Stars for 1860.0.

Star's name.	Declination.	An.Variation.	Sec.Variation.	Prop.Motion.	Authority.
α Andromedæ.	+28 19 3.11	+19.9057	—0.0109	—0.1496	Gould.
γ Pegasi	+14 24 18.85	20.0487	0.0205	+0.0001	"
β Hydri	—78 2 36.91	20.2504	0.0440	+0.2590	Brit. N. A., 1848.
α Cassiopeæ	+55 46 7.98	19.8106	0.0779	—0.0425	Gould.
21 Cassiopeæ	+74 13 17.73	19.7431	0.0963	—0.0590	"
β Ceti	—18 45 20.08	19.8402	0.0787	+0.0393	"
ε Piscium	+ 7 8 8.22	19.4918	0.1173	+0.0253	"
α Ursæ Minoris . . .	+88 33 47.08	19.1797	0.8137	+0.0019	"
θ¹ Ceti	— 8 54 23.91	18.7409	0.1520	—0.1926	"
38 Cassiopeæ	+69 32 32.03	18.7408	0.2279	—0.0791	"
η Piscium	+14 37 22.87	18.7417	0.1752	+0.0182	"
α Eridani	—57 56 55.77	18.4328	0.1360	—0.0115	Brit. N. A., 1848.
o Piscium	+ 8 27 6.29	18.2876	0.1994	+0.0381	Gould.
β Arietis	+20 7 19.99	17.8185	0.2244	—0.0941	"
50 Cassiopeæ	+71 44 27.27	17.7262	0.3450	0.0000	"
α Arietis	+22 47 55.28	17.2661	0.2527	—0.1335	"
ξ¹ Ceti	+ 8 11 17.40	17.1083	0.2485	—0.0109	"
ι Cassiopeæ	+66 46 10.70	16.5300	0.4039	—0.0190	"
γ Ceti	+ 2 38 37.59	15.4304	0.2906	—0.1531	"
α Ceti	+ 3 32 17.29	14.4003	0.3214	—0.0893	"
48 Cephei . . . . • .	+77 12 49.84	13.9492	0.7702	—0.0641	"
ζ Arietis	+20 31 23.18	13.6937	0.3704	—0.0570	"
α Persei	+49 21 33.12	13.2237	0.4699	—0.0428	"
δ Persei	+47 20 9.29	11.9518	0.5000	—0.0500	"
η Tauri	+23 40 8.69	11.5153	0.4298	—0.0476	"
ζ Persei	+31 27 51.97	11.0935	0.4604	—0.0240	"
γ¹ Eridani	—13 54 32.91	10.5765	0.3504	—0.0885	"
γ Tauri	+15 17 10.88	9.1160	0.4474	—0.0022	"
ε Tauri	+18 51 59.72	8.4329	0.4669	—0.0076	"
α Tauri	+16 13 28.29	7.6789	0.4650	—0.1662	"
9 Camelopardalis. . .	+66 5 55.38	6.8556	0.8137	+0.0090	"
ι Aurigæ	+32 56 25.77	6.1952	0.5427	—0.0123	"
11 Orionis	+15 12 20.28	5.4692	0.4632	—0.0106	"
α Aurigæ	+45 51 3.06	4.2275	0.0303	—0.4243	"
β Orionis	— 8 21 58.98	4.5290	0.4111	+0 0004	"
β Tauri	+28 29 6.43	3.5295	0.5446	—0.1731	'
Groombridge 966 . .	+74 56 32.00	3.3916	1.1494	—0.0021	"
δ Orionis	— 0 24 21.96	3.0538	0.4430	—0.0096	"
α Leporis	—17 55 30.86	2.9423	0.3433	+0.0261	"
ε Orionis	— 1 17 40.47	2.6991	0 4406	+0.0041	. "
α Columbæ	—34 9 2.81	2.1930	0.3160	—0.0217	"
α Orionis	+ 7 22 38.93	+1.1028	0.4736	+0.0175	"
22 Camelopardalis. . .	+69 21 42.78	—0.4075	0.9649	—0.1090	"
μ Geminorum . . .	+22 34 54.00	1.3743	0.5290	—0.1071	"
α Argus	—52 37 13.74	1.8215	0.1924	+0.0002	Brit. N. A., 1848.
γ Geminorum	+16 30 54.82	2.6125	0.5011	—0.0273	Gould.
51 Cephei	+87 14 54.04	2.9808	4.3835	—0.0472	"
α Canis Majoris . . .	—16 31 36.16	4.6029	0.3810	—1.2002	Wolfers.
ε Canis Majoris . . .	—28 47 2.22	4.6037	0.3330	+0.0036	Gould.
δ Canis Majoris . . .	—26 10 23.13	—5.3812	—0.3403	+0.0374	"

SPECIAL TABLES.

TABLE XXI.—Mean Right Ascensions of Standard Stars for 1860.0.

Star's name.	Mag.	Right Ascension.	An. Variation.	Sec. Variation.	Prop. Motion.
		h m s	s	s	s
δ Geminorum	3.4	7 11 45.569	+3.59161	—0.00716	—0.0004
" Piazzi vii. 67.	6	7 16 16.666	6.32323	0.08224	+0.0026
a Geminorum, (Castor) . .	2.1	7 25 39.450	3.84071	0.01310	—0.0148
a Canis Minoris, (Procyon) .	1	7 31 58.363	3.14674	0.00420	—0.0455
β Geminorum, (Polluz) . .	1.2	7 36 44.678	3.68326	0.01255	—0.0471
φ Geminorum	5	7 44 55.501	3.68595	—0.01301	—0.0004
* 3 Ursæ Majoris, (H.) . .	6	7 58 49.845	6.08409	—0.11856	+0.0056
15 Argus, (ι).	3	8 1 34.981	2.55624	+0.00138	—0.0046
ε Hydræ	3.4	8 39 21.616	3.18504	—0.00707	—0.0117
ι Ursæ Majoris	3	8 49 36.286	4.14609	0.04443	—0.0453
* σ² Ursæ Majoris	5	8 58 1.288	5.39428	—0.13444	—0.0025
κ Cancri	5	9 0 9.674	3.25653	0.00937	—0.0030·
ι Argus	2	9 13 20.530	1.60178	0.00210	—0.0090
* 1 Draconis, (H.) . . .	4.5	9 16 48.367	9.23317	0.80709	—0.0077
a Hydræ	2	9 20 42.459	2.94970	0.00142	—0.0011
*¹ d Ursæ Majoris, . . .	5.4	9 22 1.965	5.45077	—0.17036	—0.0147
θ Ursæ Majoris	3	9 23 28.286	4.05784	0.05532	—0.1064
ε Leonis	3	9 37 53.912	3.42186	0.01778	—0.0028
μ Leonis	4	9 44 47.659	3.42738	0.01967	—0.0181
a Leonis, (Regulus) . .	1.2	10 0 54.794	3.20447	0.01008	—0.0165
*32 Ursæ Majoris	6	10 7 49.327	4.45459	—0.11571	—0.0164
γ¹ Leonis	2	10 12 14.938	3.31931	0.01499	+0.0203
* υ Draconis, (H.) . . .	5.4	10 23 5.172	5.34531	0.28415	—0.0002
ρ Leonis	4	10 25 26.257	3.16725	—0.00806	+0.0005
η Argus	2	10 39 38.279	2.30708	+0.02142	—0.0021
l Leonis	5	10 41 53.734	3.16054	—0.00818	—0.0006
a Ursæ Majoris	2	10 55 3.364	3.77075	—0.08221	—0.0195
δ Leonis	2.3	11 6 39.521	3.20384	—0.01341	+0.0117
δ Crateris	3.4	11 12 20.625	2.99523	+0.00629	+0.0078
τ Leonis	5	11 20 44.232	3.08831	—0.00218	+0.0019
* λ Draconis	3.4	11 23 2.875	3.65420	—0.11285	—0.0108
υ Leonis, ...	5.4	11 29 46.889	3.07180	+0.00024	0.0000
β Leonis	2	11 41 54.983	3.06650	—0.00729	—0.0344
γ Ursæ Majoris	2.3	11 46 26.987	3.79421	—0.04400	+0.0116
o Virginis	4	11 58 4.620	3.05994	—0.00317	—0.0139
* 4 Draconis, (H.) . . .	5.4	12 5 35.671	2.92306	—0.12901	+0.0100
* β Chamæleontis . . .	5	12 10 12.636	3.32097	+0.17339	—0.0446
η Virginis	3.4	12 12 44.660	3.06812	+0.00256	—0.0037
a¹ Crucis	1	12 18 50.086	3.25791	+0.06607	—0.0233
β Corvi	2.3	12 27 2.370	3.13634	+0.01627	—0.0012
* κ Draconis	3.4	12 27 29.236	2.60780	—0.05496	—0.0109
*32 Camelopardalis, (H.) (foll.)	5.4	12 48 8.627	0.32723	+0.23160	—0.0124
12 Canum Venaticorum . .	3	12 49 28.417	2.81902	—0.01510	—0.0204
θ Virginis	4.5	13 2 42.276	3.09984	+0.00773	—0.0024
* a Virginis, (Spica). . .	1	13 17 49.316	3.15153	+0.01141	—0.0024
ζ Virginis	3.4	13 27 33.709	3.05200	+0.00631	—0.0189
η Ursæ Majoris.	2	13 42 1.238	2.37533	—0.01029	—0.0102
η Bootis	3	13 48 1.143	2.85862	—0.00047	—0.0031
β Centauri	1	13 53 58.685	4.15306	+0.08330	—0.0103
* a Draconis	3.4	14 0 36.040	+1.62222	+0.00517	—0.0066

TABLE XXI.—Mean Declinations of Standard Stars for 1860.0.

Star's name.	Declination.	An. Variation.	Sec. Variation.	Prop. Motion.	Authority.
	° ′ ″	″	″	″	
δ Geminorum	+22 14 11.64	−6.1683	−0.4956	+0.0092	Gould.
Piazzi, vii. 67 . . .	+68 44 42.08	6.6254	0.8692	−0.0730	"
α Geminorum	+32 11 29.45	7.3991	0.5270	−0.0766	Wolfers.
α Canis Minoris . . .	+ 5 34 50.54	8.8766	0.4200	−1.0425	"
β Geminorum	+28 21 39.43	8.2593	0.4803	−0.0429	Gould.
φ Geminorum	+27 7 28.79	8.6784	0.4784	−0.0140	"
3 Ursæ Majoris . . .	+68 52 49.75	9.9500	0.7672	−0.0110	"
15 Argus	−23 54 10.34	10.0747	0.3166	+0.0727	"
ε Hydræ	+ 6 55 48.21	12.6705	0.3499	−0.0221	"
ι Ursæ Majoris . . .	+48 35 17.66	13.7891	0.4359	−0.2657	"
σ² Ursæ Majoris . . .	+67 41 54.30	14.1534	0.5548	−0.0950	"
κ Cancri	+11 13 45.73	14.1708	0.3293	+0.0207	"
ι Argus	−58 41 17.84	14.9116	0.1482	+0.0709	Brit. N. A., 1848.
1 Draconis	+81 56 22.52	15.1773	0.8726	+0.0050	Gould.
α Hydræ	− 8 3 12.79	15.3589	0.2688	+0.0442	"
24 Ursæ Majoris, (d) . .	+70 26 31.53	15.4271	0.4976	+0.0501	"
θ Ursæ Majoris . . .	+52 18 46.37	16.1117	0.3570	−0.5552	"
ε Leonis	+24 25 1.40	16.3283	0.2827	−0.0060	"
μ Leonis	+26 39 52.13	16.7115	0.2695	−0.0460	"
α Leonis	+12 39 0.45	17.3868	0.2233	+0.0215	"
32 Ursæ Majoris . . .	+65 48 16.36	17.7356	0.2961	−0.0349	"
γ¹ Leonis	+20 32 54.31	17.9983	0.2130	−0.1187	"
9 Draconis	+76 25 55.14	18.3190	0.3121	−0.0300	"
ρ Leonis	+10 1 33.18	18.3711	0.1774	+0.0014	"
η Argus	−58 56 55.25	18.7435	0.1073	+0.0917	Brit. N. A.. 1848.
ι Leonis	+11 17 6.68	18.9028	0.1459	−0.0007	Gould.
α Ursæ Majoris . . .	+62 30 20.87	19.3382	0.1447	−0.0826	"
δ Leonis	+21 17 25.20	19.6398	0.0998	−0.1250	"
δ Crateris	−14 1 16.21	19.4277	0.0816	+0.1958	"
τ Leonis	+ 3 37 37.16	19.7706	0.0683	−0.0087	"
λ Draconis	+70 6 10.94	19.8544	0.0768	−0.0590	"
91 Leonis, (v)	− 0 3 3.39	19.8285	0.0503	+0.0529	"
β Leonis	+15 21 17.18	20.0855	0.0263	−0.0924	"
γ Ursæ Majoris . . .	+54 28 23.28	20.0181	−0.0190	+0.0024	"
ο Virginis	+ 9 30 39.20	20.0048	+0.0049	+0.0500	"
4 Draconis	+76 23 38.51	20.0575	0.0191	−0.0080	"
β Chamæleontis . . .	−78 32 5.54	20.0443	0.0302	−0.0087	Brit. N. A., 1848.
η Virgin's	+ 0 6 42.14	20.0369	0.0334	−0.0124	Gould.
α¹ Crucis	−62 19 18.83	19.9368	0.0462	+0.0511	Brit. N. A., 1848.
β Corvi	−22 37 17.85	19.9533	0.0624	−0.0372	Gould.
κ Draconis	+70 33 36.42	19.9355	0.0539	−0.0240	"
32 Camelopardalis . . .	+84 10 25.52	19.6356	0.0190	−0.0210	"
12 Canum Venaticorum .	+39 4 31.12	19.5247	0.0958	+0.0654	"
θ Virginis	− 4 47 25.44	19.3300	0.1305	−0.0204	"
α Virginis	−10 25 44.85	18.9290	0.1611	−0.0186	"
ζ Virginis	+ 0 7 17.18	18.5417	0.1729	+0.0678	"
η Ursæ Majoris . . .	+50 0 47.62	18.1226	0.1563	−0.0215	"
η Bootis	+19 6 4.38	18.2021	0.1968	−0.3332	"
β Centauri	−59 41 42.79	17.6953	0.2930	−0.0692	Brit. N. A., 1848.
α Draconis	+65 2 44.10	−17.3763	+0.1258	−0.0340	Gould.

TABLE XXI.—Mean Right Ascensions of Standard Stars for 1860.0.

Star's name.	Mag.	Right Ascension.	An. Variation.	Sec. Variation.	Prop. Motion.
		h m s	s	s	s
a Bootis, (*Arcturus*) . . .	1	14 9 16.600	+ 2.73406	+0.00234	—0.0790
θ Bootis	4.3	14 20 25.797	+ 2.04328	—0.00126	—0.0266
* 5 Ursæ Minoris	5.4	14 27 52.026	— 0.22573	+0.12228	+0.0051
a² Centauri	1	14 30 7.977	+ 4.02459	+0.07274	—0.4714
ε Bootis	2.3	14 38 52.388	+ 2.62154	— 0.00007	—0.0025
a² Libræ	2.3	14 43 8.343	+ 3.30497	+0.01548	—0.0085
* β Ursæ Minoris	2	14 .51 9.200	— 0.26134	0.10430	—0.0071
β Bootis	3	14 56 40.350	+ 2.25991	0.00004	—0.0038
β Libræ	2	15 9 28.642	+ 3.21866	0.01178	—0.0067
μ¹ Bootis	4.3	15 19 12.148	+ 2.26760	0.00124	—0.0102
* γ² Ursæ Minoris	3	15 20 58.742	— 0.15562	+0.07528	—0.0005
a Coronæ Borealis	2	15 28 45.665	+ 2.53905	0.00239	+0.0097
a Serpentis	2.3	15 37 22.437	+ 2.04959	0.00612	+0.0085
ε Serpentis	3.4	15 43 50.379	+ 2.98604	0 06653	+0.0091
* ζ Ursæ Minoris	4.5	15 49 8.359	— 2.31107	0.20415	+0.0127
ε Coronæ Borealis	4	15 51 47.594	+ 2.48481	+0.00297	—0.0026
δ Scorpii	2.3	15 52 3.640	+ 3.53431	0.01595	—0.0009
β¹ Scorpii	2	15 57 18.070	+ 3.47555	0.01424	—0.0018
* Groombridge 2320 . . .	6.5	16 5 57.164	+ 0.12786	0.04068	—0.0098
δ Ophiuchi	3	16 7 0.693	+ 3.13680	0.00829	—0.0037
τ Herculis	3.4	16 15 31.946	+ 1.79739	+0.00515	—0.0029
a Scorpii, (*Antares*) . . .	1.2	16 20 49.733	+ 3.66695	0.01516	—0.0001
η Draconis	3.2	16 22 6.135	+ 0.80185	0.01848	+0.0024
* A Draconis	5	16 28 16.400	— 0.14696	0.04097	+0.0008
ζ Ophiuchi	3.2	16 29 27.162	+ 3.29667	0 00787	+0.0009
* a Trianguli Australis . . .	2	16 33 52.787	+ 6.27219	+0.09346	—0.0004
η Herculis	3	16 38 5.849	+ 2.05393	0.00355	+0.0032
κ Ophiuchi	3.4	16 51 2.560	+ 2.83417	0.00433	—0.0219
d Herculis . . ✓ . . .	5	16 56 26.193	+ 2.20866	0.00324	—0.0033
* ε Ursæ Minoris	4.5	17 0 26.893	— 6.42185	0.30174	+0.0149
a¹ Herculis	Var.	17 8 15.884	+ 2.73286	+0.00316	—0.0008
44 Ophiuchi	5	17 17 49.359	+ 3 65795	0.00748	—0.0004
θ Draconis	3.2	17 27 16.217	+ 1.35034	0.00515	—0.0027
a Ophiuchi	2	17 28 26.188	+ 2.78175	0.00334	+0.0074
* ω Draconis	5	17 37 46.464	— 0.35701	0.01095	+0.0058
μ Herculis	3.4	17 40 58.841	+ 2.34439	+0.00379	—0.0249
* ψ¹ Draconis, (*pr.*) . . .	4.5	17 44 26.134	— 1.08473	0.01897	+0.0022
* σ Octantis	6	17 48 6.608	+109.01126	8.54270	0.0000
γ Draconis	2.3	17 53 21.468	+ 1.39318	0.00360	+0.0018
γ² Sagittarii	3.4	17 56 48.940	+ 3.85209	0.00249	—0.0049
μ¹ Sagittarii	4	18 5 23.480	+ 3.58601	.+0.00101	—0.0015
* δ Ursæ Minoris	4.5	18 17 30.123	— 19.35124	—0.52531	+0.0289
η Serpentis	3	18 14 3.956	+ 3.09920	+0.00185	—0.0411
l Aquilæ, (3 H. Scuti) . .	4.5	18 27 35.262	+ 3.26430	+0.00008	—0.0022
a Lyræ, (*Vega*)	1	18 32 11.897	+ 2.03143	+0.00104	+0.0184
β Lyræ	Var.	18 44 54.671	+ 2.21409	+0.00149	+0.0004
σ Sagittarii	2.3	18 46 34.982	+ 3.72419	—0.00514	+0.0003
*50 Draconis	6	18 50 52.058	— 1.89172	—0 05569	—0.0040
ζ Aquilæ	3	18 58 58.484	+ 2.75475	+0.00041	—0.0030
d Sagittarii	5	19 9 26.501	+ 3.51410	—0.00605	—0.0022

TABLE XXI.—Mean Declinations of Standard Stars for 1860.0.

Star's name.	Declination.	An.Variation.	Sec.Variation.	Prop.Motion.	Authority.
	° ′ ″	″	″	″	
α Bootis	+19 54 47.55	—18.9129	+ 0.2144	—1.9643	Gould.
θ Bootis	+52 29 57.51	16.8025	+ 0.1762	—0.3953	"
5 Ursæ Minoris . . .	+76 19 5.08	16.0445	— 0.0125	—0.0200	"
α² Centauri	—60 15 8.84	15.0808	+ 0.3329	+0.8232	Brit. N. A., 1848.
ε Bootis	+27 39 59.41	15.3967	+ 0.2502	+0.0300	Gould.
α² Libræ	—15 27 26.23	15.2415	+ 0.3206	—0.0561	"
β Ursæ Minoris . . .	+74 43 38.57	14 7471	— 0.0203	—0.0290	"
β Bootis	+40 56 40.72	14.4247	+ 0.2355	—0.0390	"
ϑ Libræ	— 8 51 48.10	13.5871	+ 0.3509	—0.0041	"
μ¹ Bootis	+37 52 12.68	12.8456	+ 0.2571	+0.0993	"
γ²Ursæ Minoris . .	+72 19 56.11	12.7977	— 0.0120	+0.0280	"
α Coronæ Borealis . .	+27 11 17.90	12.3698	+ 0.2989	—0.0750	"
α Serpentis	+ 6 52 8.21	11.6309	+ 0.3555	+0.0598	"
ε Serpentis	+ 4 54 7.07	11.1466	+ 0.3667	+0.0801	"
ζ Ursæ Minoris . . .	+78 13 23.82	10.8422	— 0.2774	—0.0029	"
ε Coronæ Borealis . .	+27 17 9.14	10.6767	+ 0.3115	—0.0336	"
δ Scorpii	—22 13 9.85	10.6214	0.4417	+0.0018	"
β¹ Scorpii	—19 25 7.65	10 2505	0.4401	—0.0189	Hill.
Groombridge 2320 . .	+68 10 44.98	9.5034	0.0194	+0.0699	Gould.
δ Ophiuchi	— 3 19 49.73	9.6195	0.4067	—0.1277	"
τ Herculis	+46 38 54.90	8.8023	+ 0.2387	+0.0263	"
α Scorpii	—26 7 2.57	8.4343	+ 0.4892	—0.0244	"
η Draconis	+61 49 54.59	8.2407	+ 0.1103	+0.0679	Hill.
λ Draconis	+69 4 15.40	7.7803	— 0.0163	+0.0340	Gould
ζ Ophiuchi	—10 16 47.33	7.6724	+ 0.4470	+0.0468	"
α Trianguli Australis .	—68 45 50.10	7.4397	+ 0.8541	—0.0796	Brit. N. A., 1848.
η Herculis	+39 11 27.23	7.0797	+ 0.2840	—0.0041	Gould.
κ Ophiuchi	+ 9 35 45.26	5.9212	+ 0.3914	+0.0227	"
d Herculis	+33 46 24.79	5.4593	+ 0.3113	+0.0315	"
ε Ursæ Minoris . . .	+82 15 41.05	5.1518	— 0.9009	+0.0011	"
α¹ Herculis	+14 33 11.01	4.4418	+ 0.3903	+0.0472	"
44 Ophiuchi	—24 2 31.07	3.7555	+ 0.5261	—0.0853	"
β Draconis	+52 24 22.98	2.8584	+ 0.1958	—0.0041	Hill.
α Ophiuchi	+12 39 54.60	2.9676	+ 0.4041	—0.2143	Gould.
ω Draconis	+68 49 18.76	1.6499	— 0.0501	+0.2920	"
μ Herculis	+27 48 19.08	2.3859	+ 0.3379	—0.7234	"
ψ¹ Draconis	+72 12 59.31	1.6220	— 0.1570	—0.2619	"
σ Octantis	—89 16 40.42	1.0400	+15.8781	0.0000	Brit. N. A., 1848.
γ Draconis	+51 30 24.48	0.6181	+ 0.2020	—0.0369	Wolfers.
γ²Sagittarii	—30 25 16.86	— 0.4984	+ 0.5610	—0.2202	Gould.
μ¹ Sagittarii	—21 5 28.68	+ 0.4743	+ 0 5224	+0.0026	"
δ Ursæ Minoris . . .	+86 36 6.96	1.5733	— 2.8099	+0.0432	"
η Serpentis	— 2 55 53.48	0.5603	+ 0.4447	—0 6698	"
λ Aquilæ	— 8 20 17.29	2.0989	+ 0.4713	—0.3095	"
α Lyræ	+38 39 30.92	3.0924	+ 0.2948	+0.2839	"
β Lyræ	+33 12 9.00	3.8926	+ 0.3151	—0.0125	"
σ Sagittarii	—26 27 58.26	3.9864	+ 0.5304	—0.0621	"
50 Draconis	+75 15 59.70	4.4729	— 0.2714	+0.0580	"
ζ Aquilæ	+13 39 30.42	5.0185	+ 0.3860	—0 0855	"
d Sagittarii	—19 11 51.51	+ 6.0243	+ 0.4863	+0.0401	"

TABLE XXI.—Mean Right Ascensions of Standard Stars for 1800.0.

Star's name.	Mag.	Right Ascension.	An. Variation.	Sec. Variation.	Prop. Motion.
		h m s	s	s	s
* δ Draconis	3	19 12 30.754	+ 0.63629	− 0.02301	+0.0192
* τ Draconis	5	19 18 13.278	− 1.09981	0.05829	−0.0264
δ Aquilæ	3.4	19 18 26.314	+ 3.02470	0.00182	+0.0152
κ Aquilæ	5	19 29 21.465	+ 3.23085	0.00438	−0.0003
γ Aquilæ	3	19 39 36.205	+ 2.85292	0.00103	+0.0008
a Aquilæ, (*Altair*)	1.2	19 43 57.103	+ 2.92851	− 0.00182	+0.0362
β Aquilæ	4	19 48 26.146	+ 2.94711	0.00144	+0.0015
* ε Draconis	4	19 48 37.643	− 0.16643	0.04326	+0.0144
τ Aquilæ	6.5	19 57 17.998	+ 2.93359	0.00201	+0.0024
* λ Ursæ Minoris	6.7	20 3 53.941	−56.17110	29.83668	−0.0731
a² Capricorni	3.4	20 10 17.032	+ 3.33419	− 0.00847	+0.0026
* κ Cephei	4.5	20 13 31.937	− 1.87463	0.16370	+0.0025
a Pavonis	2	20 14 33.200	+ 4.80157	0.05914	+0.0037
π Capricorni ,	5	20 19 18.236	+ 3.44277	0.01148	0.0000
ε Delphini	4	20 26 31.431	+ 2.86610	0.00127	−0.0006
* Groombridge 3241	6.7	20 30 34.967	− 0.26019	− 0.06643	−0.0028
a Cygni	2.1	20 36 39.578	+ 2.04369	+ 0.00216	+0.0005
μ Aquarii	5.4	20 45 5.967	+ 3.24122	− 0.00826	+0.0010
ν Cygni	4	20 51 57.277	+ 2.23340	+ 0.00368	+0.0006
* 12 Year Cat. 1879	6	20 53 48.777	− 2.45812	− 0.30440	−0.0115
61 Cygni (*pr.*)	5.6	21 0 37.437	+ 2.68531	+ 0.01494	+0.3516
ζ Cygni	3	21 6 58.728	2.54973	+ 0.00388	−0.0006
a Cephei	3.2	21 15 14.138	1.43812	− 0.00630	+0.0217
1 Pegasi	4.5	21 15 36.799	2.77387	+ 0.00183	+0.0181
β Aquarii	3	21 24 11.185	3.16505	− 0.00717	+0.0020
* β Cephei	3	21 26 50.335	+ 0.80412	− 0.03379	+0.0018
ξ Aquarii	5.4	21 30 17.778	3.19930	0.00824	+0.0062
ε Pegasi	2.3	21 37 18.600	2.94799	0.00059	+0.0028
* 11 Cephei	5	21 39 51.457	0.91065	0.03188	+0.0265
μ Capricorni	5	21 45 39.575	3.28073	0.01136	+0.0215
* 79 Draconis	6.7	21 51 7.560	+ 0.74280	− 0.04568	+0.0083
a Aquarii	3	21 58 35.522	3.08423	0.00423	+0.0005
a Gruis	2	21 59 23.576	3.81920	0.04601	+0.0108
θ Aquarii	4.5	22 9 26.628	3.17142	0.00768	+0.0070
π Aquarii	5.4	22 18 7.589	3.06565	0.00284	+0.0004
η Aquarii	4.3	22 28 9.680	+ 3.08399	− 0.00316	+0.0044
*226 Cephei (B.)	5.6	22 29 48.070	1.08725	− 0.03295	−0.0014
ζ Pegasi	3.4	22 34 28.790	2.98812	+ 0.00220	+0.0030
* ι Cephei	4.3	22 44 42.244	2.11526	+ 0.02204	−0.0116
λ Aquarii	4	22 45 18.502	3.13219	− 0.00640	−0.0024
a Pis. Aus. (*Fomalhaut*)	1.2	22 49 54.422	+ 3.33190	− 0.02136	+0.0241
a Pegasi, (*Markab*)	2	22 57 47.339	2.98386	+ 0.00558	+0.0043
* o Cephei	6.5	23 12 53.525	2.43193	+ 0.04148	+0.0138
θ Piscium	4.5	23 20 52.012	3.04044	+ 0.00257	−0.0002
ι Piscium	4.5	23 32 45.061	3.08425	+ 0.00999	+0.0258
* γ Cephei	3.4	23 33 37.821	+ 2.39398	+ 0.07122	−0.0209
* Groombridge 4163	7	23 48 3.644	2.83893	+ 0.08750	+0.0040
ω Piscium	4	23 52 7.427	+ 3.07756	+ 0.00466	+0.0105

* Circumpolar Stars.

TABLE XXI.—Mean Declinations of Standard Stars for 1850.0.

Star's name.	Declination.	An.Variation.	Sec.Variation.	Prop.Motion.	Authority.
δ Draconis	+67 24 54.74	+ 6.3082	+0.0050	+0.0681	Gould.
τ Draconis	+73 5 39.37	6.8107	−0.1487	+0.0978	"
δ Aquilæ	+ 2 50 20.12	6.8249	+0.4147	+0.0934	"
κ Aquilæ	− 7 20 6.31	7.6445	+0.4325	+0.0218	"
γ Aquilæ	+10 16 29.87	8.4508	+0.3739	+0.0064	"
α Aquilæ	+ 8 30 5.50	9.1685	+0.3849	+0.3804	"
β Aquilæ	+ 6 3 36.04	8.6686	+0.3789	−0.4704	"
ε Draconis	+69 54 39.75	9.1500	−0.0237	−0.0039	"
τ Aquilæ	+ 6 53 8.85	9.8419	+0.3691	+0.0194	"
λ Ursæ Minoris . . .	+88 53 24.30	10.3231	−7.0463	+0.0013	"
α² Capricorni	−12 58 32.33	10.8105	+0.4055	+0.0137	"
κ Cephei	+77 17 15.90	11.0342	−0.2328	−0.0010	"
α Pavonis	−57 10 44.68	11.0791	+0.5806	−0.0306	Brit. N.A., 1848.
π Capricorni	−18 40 2.24	11.4237	+0.4073	−0.0297	Gould.
ε Delphini	+10 49 48.03	11.9166	+0.3303	−0.0197	"
Groombridge 3241 . .	+72 3 25.94	12.2275	−0.0287	−0.0220	"
α Cygni	+44 46 53.99	12.6621	+0.2256	−0.0041	"
μ Aquarii	− 9 30 20.63	13.2103	+0.3497	−0.0196	"
ν Cygni	+40 37 48.25	13.6878	+0.2323	+0.0128	"
12 Year Cat. 1879 . .	+80 1 29.66	13.7443	−0.2674	−0.0491	"
61 Cygni (pr.) . . .	+38 3 47.00	17.4619	+0.2997	+3.2420	Hill.
ζ Cygni	+29 39 16.46	14.5501	0.2485	−0.0564	Gould.
α Cephei	+61 59 34.99	15.0941	0.1310	+0.0020	Wolfers.
1 Pegasi	+19 12 27.68	15.2009	0.2609	+0.0869	Gould.
β Aquarii	− 6 11 5.07	15.6040	0.2837	+0.0077	"
β Cephei	+69 56 47.01	15.7032	+0.0661	−0.0360	"
ξ Aquarii	− 8 28 47.43	15.9101	0.2772	−0.0167	"
ε Pegasi	+ 9 14 6.25	16.3005	0.2439	+0 0082	"
11 Cephei	+70 40 1.56	16.4935	0.0714	+0.0721	"
μ Capricorni	−14 12 30 51	16.7389	0.2591	+0.0312	"
79 Draconis	+73 2 24.79	16.9584	+0.0511	−0.0090	"
α Aquarii	− 0 59 53.78	17.3024	0.2199	−0.0042	"
α Gruis	−47 38 11.73	17.1610	0.2748	−0.1810	Brit. N. A., 1848
θ Aquarii	− 8 28 43.64	17.7559	0.2074	−0.0111	Gould.
π Aquarii	+ 0 40 6.26	18.1091	0.1845	+0.0025	"
η Aquarii	− 0 50 15.96	18.4168	+0.1679	−0.0499	"
226 Cephei	+75 30 18.15	18.5122	0.0528	−0.0100	"
ζ Pegasi	+10 6 6.56	18.6822	0.1510	+0.0068	"
ι Cephei	+65 27 52.60	18.8418	0.0908	−0.1410	"
λ Aquarii	− 8 19 24.06	19.0524	0.1379	+0.0526	"
α Pis. Aus.	−30 21 46.91	18.9692	+0.1392	−0.1556	"
α Pegasi	+14 27 10.67	19.3005	0.1085	−0.0206	"
ο Cephei	+67 20 44.36	19.6143	0.0644	−0.0190	"
θ Piscium	+ 5 36 38.53	19.7377	0.0666	−0.0261	"
ι Piscium	+ 4 52 4.65	19.4785	0.0452	−0.4355	"
γ Cephei	+76 51 4.05	20 0709	+0.0312	+0.1480	"
Groombridge 4163 . .	+73 37 52.29	19.9983	0.0129	−0.0300	"
ω Piscium	+ 6 5 18.21	+19.9416	+0.0069	−0.1020	"

SPECIAL TABLES.

TABLE XXII.—Mean Right Ascensions of Standard Stars, 1865—1872.

Star's name.	1865.	1866.	1867.	1868.	1869.	1870.	1871.	1872.
	h m s	s	s	s	s	s	s	s
a Andromedæ . . .	0 1 24.858	27.945	31.032	34.119	37.207	40.294	43.382	46.469
γ 1 egasi . . .	0 6 17.206	20.288	23.370	26.452	29.535	32.618	35.700	38.783
* β Hydri . . .	0 18 36.294	39.561	42.826	46.089	49.351	52.612	55.870	59.128
a Cassiopeæ . .	0 32 51.870	55.231	58.593	61.955	65.318	63.681	72.045	75.409
*21 Cassiopeæ . .	0 36 47.263	51.082	54.903	58.725	62.549	66.375	70.202	74.031
β Ceti	0 36 48.671	51.685	54.699	57.713	60.727	63.740	66.754	69.767
ε Piscium . . .	0 55 56.337	59.445	62.554	65.662	68.770	71.879	74.987	78.096
* a Ursæ Min.,(Polaris)	1 9 38.747	58.256	77.902	97.686	117.609	137.673	157.880	178.231
b¹ Ceti . . .	1 17 16.556	19.554	22.551	25.549	28.546	31.544	34.542	37.539
*38 Cassiopeæ . .	1 21 13.915	18.258	22.603	26.949	31.297	35.646	39.996	44.348
η Piscium . . .	1 24 15.734	18.933	22.130	25.329	28.527	31.727	34.925	38.125
a Eridani, (Achernar)	1 32 40.849	43.085	45.320	47.555	49.789	52.024	54.259	56.494
o Piscium . . .	1 38 16.105	19.266	22.427	25.588	28.749	31.911	35.072	38.234
β Arietis . . .	1 47 11.235	14.534	17.834	21.134	24 434	27.734	31.034	34.335
*50 Cassiopeæ . .	1 51 58.123	63.089	68.057	73.027	77.999	82.973	87.949	92.927
a Arietis . . .	1 59 34.116	37.483	40.850	44.217	47.584	50.952	54.319	57 687
ξ¹ Ceti . . .	2 5 50.820	53.989	57.157	60.326	63.495	66.664	69.833	73 002
* ι Cassiopeæ . .	2 17 58.987	63.818	68.650	73.484	78.318	83.154	87.992	92.831
γ Ceti . . .	2 36 18.474	21.576	24.678	27.780	30.882	33.985	37.087	40.189
a Ceti . . .	2 55 13.496	16.624	19.752	22.880	26.009	29.138	32.266	35.395
*48 Cephei, (H) . .	3 3 18 581	25.904	33.230	40.559	47.892	55.229	62 569	69.912
ζ Arietis . .	3 7 8.778	12.214	15.650	19.086	22.522	25.959	29.395	32.832
a Persei . . .	3 14 41.900	46.145	50.390	54.635	58.881	63.128	67.375	71.622
δ Persei . . .	3 33 19.385	23.622	27.859	32.097	36.335	40.573	44.812	49.051
η Tauri . . .	3 39 27.828	31.381	34.934	38.487	42.040	45.594	49.147	52.701
ζ Persei . . .	3 45 39.096	42.851	46.606	50.361	54.116	57.872	61.628	65 384
γ¹ Eridani . .	3 51 43.899	46.695	49.491	52.287	55.084	57.881	60.677	63 474
γ Tauri . . .	4 12 6.799	10.206	13.612	17.019	20.426	23.833	27.240	30.647
ε Tauri . . .	4 20 44.180	47.675	51.170	54.665	58.160	61.655	65.150	68.646
a Tauri, (Aldebaran).	4 28 10.615	14.050	17.485	20.921	24.356	27.792	31.227	34.663
* 9 Camelopardalis. .	4 40 38.896	44.805	50.714	56.624	62.534	68.446	74.358	80.270
ι Aurigæ . . .	4 48 12.339	16.235	20.130	24.026	27.922	31.819	35.715	39.612
11 Orionis . . .	4 56 51.450	54.874	58.299	61.724	65.148	69.573	71.998	75.423
a Aurigæ, (Capella) .	5 6 43.223	47.644	52.066	56.487	60.909	65.331	69.753	74.175
β Orionis, (Rigel) .	5 8 3.053	5.934	8.814	11.695	14.575	17.456	20.337	23.217
β Tauri . . .	5 17 45.577	49.364	53.151	56.938	60.725	64.513	68.300	72.088
* Groombridge 966	5 21 41.761	49.744	57.727	65.711	73.696	81.682	89.668	97.655
δ Orionis . . .	5 25 6.655	9.719	12.782	15.846	18.910	21.974	25.038	28.102
a Leporis . . .	5 26 46.651	49.297	51.943	54.589	57.236	59 882	62.528	65.175
ε Orionis . .	5 29 21.845	24.887	27.928	30.970	34.012	37.054	40.096	43.138
a Columbæ . .	5 31 45.719	47.891	50.063	52.235	54.408	56.580	58.752	60 924
a Orionis . . .	5 47 51.835	55.082	58.328	61.575	64.822	68.069	71.316	74 562
*22 Camelopardalis,(H.)	6 3 57.744	64.363	70.982	77.601	84 220	90.839	97.458	104.077
μ Geminorum . .	6 14 47.598	51.231	54.864	58.497	62.130	65.762	69.395	73 028
a Argus, (Canopus) .	6 20 57.430	58.760	60.090	61.420	62.750	64.081	65.411	66.741
γ Geminorum. .	6 29 54.771	58.240	61.709	65 178	68.647	72.116	75.585	79.054
*51 Cephei, (H.) .	6 36 11.074	41.496	71.900	102.285	132.650	162.996	193.322	223 629
a Canis Maj., (Sirius)	6 39 11.903	14.548	17.193	19.838	22.483	25.128	27.773	30 419
ε Canis Majoris .	6 53 19.293	21.651	24.010	26.368	28.727	31.085	33.444	35.802
δ Canis Majoris .	7 2 54.196	56.636	59.075	61.515	63.954	66.394	68.834	71.273

* Circumpolar Stars.

TABLE XXII.—Mean Declinations of Standard Stars, 1865–1872.

1865.	1866.	1867.	1868.	1869.	1870.	1871.	1872.
° ′ ″	′ ″	′ ″	′ ″	′ ″	′ ″	′ ″	′ ″
+28 20 42.64	21 2.54	21 22.45	21 42.35	22 2.26	22 22.16	22 42.07	23 1.97
+14 25 59.09	26 19.13	26 39.18	26 59.23	27 19.28	27 39.32	27 59.37	28 19.42
−77 60 55.68	60 35.43	60 15.18	59 54.93	59 34.68	59 14.43	58 54.18	58 33.93
+55 47 47.03	48 6.83	48 26.64	48 46.44	49 6.25	49 26.05	49 45.85	50 5.65
+74 14 56.43	15 16.17	15 35.91	15 55.64	16 15.38	16 35.11	16 54.84	17 14.57
−18 43 40.89	43 21.05	43 1.22	42 41.38	42 21.55	42 1.72	41 41.88	41 22.05
+ 7 9 45.67	10 5.15	10 24.64	10 44.12	11 3.60	11 23.08	11 42.56	12 2.04
+88 35 22.88	35 42.01	36 1.14	36 20.25	36 39.36	36 58.46	37 17.55	37 36.63
− 8 52 50.22	52 31.49	52 12.76	51 54.03	51 35.30	51 16.57	50 57.85	50 39.13
+69 34 5.71	34 24.44	34 43.16	35 1.89	35 20.61	35 39.33	35 58.04	36 16.76
+14 38 56.56	39 15.29	39 34.02	39 52.75	40 11.47	40 30.20	40 48.92	41 7.65
−57 55 23.62	55 5.19	54 46.77	54 28.35	54 9.93	53 51.50	53 33.08	53 14.66
+ 8 28 37.71	28 55.98	29 14.26	29 32.53	29 50.80	30 9.07	30 27.34	30 45.60
+20 8 49.05	9 6.86	9 24.67	0 42.47	10 0.27	10 18.06	10 35.86	10 53.65
+71 45 55.86	46 13.57	46 31.27	46 48.97	47 6.67	47 24.36	47 42.05	47 59.74
+22 49 21.58	49 38.83	49 56.08	50 13.33	50 30.57	50 47.82	51 5.06	51 22.29
+ 8 12 42.91	13 0.01	13 17.10	13 34.19	13 51.29	14 8.36	14 25.44	14 42.52
+66 47 33.30	47 49.81	48 6.31	48 22.81	48 39.31	48 55.80	49 12.28	49 28.77
+ 2 39 54.70	40 10.12	40 25.53	40 40.94	40 56.34	41 11.75	41 27.15	41 42.54
+ 3 33 29.25	33 43.64	33 58.01	34 12.39	34 26.76	34 41.13	34 55.50	35 9.86
+77 13 59.49	14 13.40	14 27.30	14 41.19	14 55.07	15 8.95	15 22.81	15 36.68
+20 32 31.61	32 45.29	32 58.95	33 12.62	33 26.28	33 39.94	33 53.59	34 7.24
+49 22 39.18	22 52.37	23 5.57	23 18.76	23 31.94	23 45.12	23 58.29	24 11.46
+47 21 8.99	21 20.91	21 32.83	21 44.75	21 56.66	22 8.56	22 20.46	22 32.35
+23 41 6.21	41 17.70	41 29.19	41 40.68	41 52.15	42 3.63	42 15.10	42 26.56
+31 28 47.37	28 58.44	29 9.51	29 20.57	29 31.62	29 42.67	29 53.72	30 4.76
−13 53 40.07	53 29.52	53 18.96	53 8.41	52 57.87	52 47.32	52 36.78	52 26.25
+15 17 56.40	18 5.49	18 14.58	18 23.66	18 32.74	18 41.81	18 50.88	18 59.95
+18 52 41.83	52 50.24	52 58.64	53 7.04	53 15.43	53 23.82	53 32.20	53 40.58
+16 14 6.63	14 14.29	14 21.93	14 29.57	14 37.21	14 44.85	14 52.48	15 0.10
+66 6 29.56	6 36.37	6 43.17	6 49.96	6 56.75	7 3.53	7 10.30	7 17.06
+32 56 56.68	57 2.85	57 9.01	57 15.16	57 21.31	57 27.45	57 33.59	57 39.73
+15 12 47.56	12 53.00	12 58.44	13 3.88	13 9.30	13 14.73	13 20.14	13 25.56
+45 51 24.11	51 28.31	51 32.49	51 36.67	51 40.85	51 45.02	51 49.18	51 53.33
− 8 21 36.39	21 31.88	21 27.38	21 22.89	21 18.39	21 13.90	21 9.42	21 4.94
+28 29 24.00	29 27.50	29 31.00	29 34.49	29 37.97	29 41.45	29 44.92	29 48.39
+74 56 48.82	56 52.14	56 55.46	56 58.77	57 2.06	57 5.34	57 8.62	57 11.88
− 0 24 6.74	24 3.71	24 0.69	23 57.67	23 54.65	23 51.64	23 48.63	23 45.63
−17 55 16.20	55 13.28	55 10.36	55 7.44	55 4.54	55 1.63	54 58.73	54 55.83
− 1 17 27.03	17 24.35	17 21.68	17 19.02	17 16.36	17 13.70	17 11.05	17 8.40
−34 8 51.86	8 49.68	8 47.50	8 45.33	8 43.16	8 40.99	8 38.82	8 36.66
+ 7 22 44.39	22 45.46	22 46.54	22 47.61	22 48.67	22 49.72	22 50.78	22 51.83
+69 21 40.62	21 40.16	21 39.69	21 39.21	21 38.72	21 38.23	21 37.72	21 37.20
+22 34 47.07	34 45.66	34 44.25	34 42.84	34 41.42	34 40.00	34 34.57	34 37.13
−52 37 22.87	37 24.70	37 26.54	37 28.37	37 30.21	37 32.05	37 33.89	37 35.73
+16 30 41.69	30 39.05	30 36.41	30 33.76	30 31.10	30 28.44	30 25.78	30 23.11
+87 14 38.59	14 35.37	14 32.11	14 28.80	14 25.45	14 22.05	14 18.61	14 15.13
−16 31 59.22	32 3.85	32 8.48	32 13.11	32 17.74	32 22.39	32 27.02	32 31.67
−28 47 25.28	47 29.90	47 34.52	47 39.15	47 43.78	47 48.42	47 53.06	47 57.70
−26 10 50.08	10 55.48	11 0.69	11 6.29	11 11.70	11 17.12	11 22.53	11 27.95

TABLE XXII.—Mean Right Ascensions of Standard Stars, 1865—1872.

Star's name.	1865.	1866.	1867.	1868.	1869.	1870.	1871.	1872.
	h m s	s	s	s	s	s	s	s
δ Geminorum . . .	7 12 3.526	7.117	10.708	14.299	17.890	21.481	25.072	28.663
* Piazzi vii. 67 . .	7 16 48.272	54.591	60.909	67.226	73.542	79.857	86.172	92.486
a Geminor. (*Castor*) .	7 25 58.652	62.492	66.332	70.172	74.011	77.851	81.090	85.529
a Can. Min. (*Procyon*)	7 32 14.096	17.242	20.389	23.535	26.682	29.828	32.974	36.120
β Geminor. (*Pollux*) .	7 37 3.093	6.776	10.458	14.140	17.822	21.504	25.186	28.868
φ Geminornm . . .	7 45 13.930	17.615	21.300	24.985	28.670	32.355	36.039	39.724
* 3 Ursæ Majoris, (H.) .	7 59 20.251	26.328	32.405	38.480	44.554	50.627	56.698	62.769
15 Argus, (ι) . . .	8 1 47.762	50.318	52.875	55.431	57.988	60.544	63.100	65.657
ε Hydræ	8 39 37.540	40.725	43.909	47.094	50.278	53.463	56.647	59.831
ι Ursæ Majoris . .	8 49 57.011	61.155	65.298	69.441	73.583	77.725	81.867	86.008
* σ² Ursæ Majoris . .	8 58 28.243	33.630	39.015	44.399	49.782	55.164	60.544	65.923
κ Cancri	9 0 25.955	29.211	32.467	35.723	38.979	42.234	45.490	48.745
ι Argus	9 13 28.539	30.141	31.742	33.344	34.946	36.547	38.149	39.750
* 1 Draconis,(H) . .	9 17 34.432	43.621	52.802	61.975	71.140	80.296	89.445	98.586
a Hydræ	9 20 57.207	60.157	63.106	66.056	69.006	71.955	74.905	77.854
* d Ursæ Majoris . .	9 22 29.198	34.639	40.079	45.517	50.952	56.388	61.821	67.252
θ Ursæ Majoris .	9 23 48.568	52.623	56.677	60.730	64.783	68.836	72.888	76.940
ε Leonis	9 38 11.019	14.440	17.861	21.282	24.702	28.122	31.542	34.962
μ Leonis	9 45 4.794	8.221	11.646	15.072	18.498	21.924	25.348	28.774
a Leonis, (*Regulus*) .	10 1 10.815	14.019	17.223	20.427	23.631	26.834	30.038	33.241
*32 Ursæ Majoris . .	10 8 11.586	16.034	20.481	24.927	29.372	33.815	38.258	42.699
γ¹ Leonis . . .	10 12 31.533	34.852	38.170	41.488	44.806	48.124	51.442	54.759
* 9 Draconis, (H.) .	10 23 31.863	37.193	42.520	47.844	53.165	58.483	63.799	69.112
ρ Leonis	10 25 42.092	45.259	48.425	51.592	54.759	57.925	61.092	64.258
η Argus	10 39 49.818	52.126	54.435	56.744	59.053	61.362	63.671	65.981
l Leonis	10 42 9.535	12.695	15.855	19.015	22.175	25.334	28.494	31.653
a Ursæ Majoris . .	10 55 22.207	25.973	29.739	33.503	37.267	41.030	44.792	48.553
δ Leonis	11 6 55.538	58.741	61.944	65.147	68.350	71.552	74.755	77.957
δ Crateris	11 12 35.602	38.598	41.593	44.588	47.584	50.580	53.576	56.572
τ Leonis	11 20 59.673	62.761	65.849	68.937	72.026	75.114	78.202	81.290
* λ Draconis . .	11 23 21.132	24.780	28.427	32.073	35.717	39.361	43.003	46.644
υ Leonis	11 30 2.248	5.320	8.392	11.464	14.535	17.607	20.679	23.751
β Leonis	11 42 10.315	13.381	16.447	19.513	22.579	25.645	28.710	31.776
γ Ursæ Majoris . .	11 46 42.952	46.144	49.335	52.526	55.716	58.906	62.096	65.285
o Virginis	11 58 19.919	22.979	26.039	29.099	32.158	35.218	38.278	41.337
* 4 Draconis, (H.) . .	12 5 50.271	53.187	56.101	59.015	61.927	64.838	67.747	70.656
* β Chamæleontis . .	12 10 29.263	32.593	35.925	39.259	42.595	45.933	49.272	52.613
η Virginis	12 13 0.001	3.069	6.137	9.206	12.274	15.342	18.411	21.479
a¹ Crucis	12 19 6.384	9.645	12.907	16.170	19.434	22.698	25.963	29.228
β Corvi	12 27 18.053	21.191	24.328	27.466	30.603	33.741	36.879	40.017
* κ Draconis. . . .	12 27 42.268	44.873	47.477	50.081	52.684	55.286	57.889	60.490
*32 Camelop (H.) (*foll.*)	12 48 10.292	10.632	10.974	11.318	11.665	12.014	12.365	12.719
12 Can. Venaticorum .	12 49 42.510	45.328	48.146	50.964	53.782	56.600	59.417	62.235
θ Virginis . . .	13 2 57.778	60.878	63.979	67.079	70.180	73.280	76.381	79.481
a Virginis, (*Spica*) .	13 18 5.075	8.227	11.379	14.532	17.684	20.837	23.989	27.142
ζ Virginis . . .	13 27 48.970	52.022	55.075	58.127	61.179	64.232	67.284	70.337
η Ursæ Majoris . .	13 42 13.113	15.488	17.862	20.237	22.612	24.986	27.360	29.734
η Bootis	13 48 15.436	18.295	21.153	24.012	26.871	29.729	32.588	35.446
β Centauri. . . .	13 54 19.460	23.617	27.775	31.934	36.095	40.257	44.419	48.582
a Draconis . . .	14 0 44.152	45.775	47.397	49.020	50.643	52.265	53.887	55.511

* Circumpolar Stars.

TABLE XXIII.—Mean Declinations of Standard Stars, 1865—1872.

1865.	1866.	1867.	1868.	1869.	1870.	1871.	1872.
+22 13 40.74	13 34.54	13 2&.34	13 22.14	13 15.92	13 9.71	13 3.49	12 57.26
+68 44 8.85	44 2.17	43 55.49	43 48.80	43 42.10	43 35.39	43 28.68	43 21.95
+32 10 52.39	10 44.96	10 37.53	10 30.09	10 22.64	10 15.20	10 7.74	10 0.28
+ 5 34 6.11	33 57.21	33 48.30	33 39.40	33 30.48	33 21.57	33 12.65	33 3.72
+28 20 58.08	20 49.79	20 41.50	20 33.21	20 24.91	20 16.60	20 8.29	19 59.93
+27 6 44.34	6 35.43	6 26.52	6 17.61	6 8.69	5 59.76	5 50.84	5 41.90
+68 51 59.90	51 49.91	51 39.91	51 29.90	51 19.89	51 9.86	50 59.83	50 49.79
−23 55 0.76	55 10.85	55 20.94	55 31.04	55 41.14	55 51.25	56 1.36	56 11.47
+ 6 54 43.81	54 30.93	54 18.03	54 5.14	53 52.24	53 39.33	53 26.42	53 13.51
+48 34 8.65	33 54.85	33 41.03	33 27.21	33 13.38	32 59.55	32 45.71	32 31.88
+67 40 43.47	40 29.28	40 15.09	40 0.90	39 46.70	39 32.49	39 18.28	39 4.06
+11 12 34.83	12 20.64	12 6.45	11 52.26	11 38.06	11 23.85	11 9.65	10 55.44
−58 42 32.41	42 47.33	43 2.26	43 17.18	43 32.10	43 47.03	44 1.96	44 16.89
+81 55 6.53	54 51.30	54 36.07	54 20.83	54 5.57	53 50.31	53 35.05	53 19.77
− 8 4 29.62	4 44.99	5 0.37	5 15.75	5 31.13	5 46.51	6 1.90	6 17.29
+70 25 14.33	24 58.87	24 43.42	24 27.95	24 12.48	23 57.01	23 41.53	23 26.04
+52 17 25.76	17 9.63	16 53.50	16 37.36	16 21.22	16 5.07	15 48.92	15 32.77
+24 23 39.73	23 23.38	23 7.04	22 50.69	22 34.33	22 17.98	22 1.62	21 45.26
+26 38 28.53	38 11.81	37 55.08	37 38.35	37 21 61	37 4.88	36 48.14	36 31.39
+12 37 33.49	37 16.09	36 58.69	36 41.29	36 23.88	36 6.47	35 49.06	35 31.65
+65 46 47.64	46 29.89	46 12.14	45 54.38	45 36.62	45 18.86	45 1.09	44 43.32
+20 31 24.29	31 6.28	30 48.26	30 30.25	30 12.23	29 54.22	29 36.20	29 18.17
+76 24 23.51	24 5.17	23 46.83	23 28.49	23 10.15	22 51.80	22 33.45	22 15.09
+ 9 60 1.30	59 42.92	59 24.54	59 6.15	58 47.76	58 29 38	58 10.99	57 52.60
−58 58 28.99	58 47.74	59 6.49	59 25.23	59 43.98	60 2.74	60 21.49	60 40.25
+11 15 32.15	15 13.24	14 54.33	14 35.42	14 16.50	13 57.58	13 38.67	13 19.75
+62 28 44.16	28 24.81	28 5.46	27 46.12	27 26.76	27 7.41	26 48.06	26 28.70
+21 15 46.99	15 27.35	15 7.70	14 48.05	14 28.40	14 8.76	13 49.11	13 29.45
−14 2 53.36	3 12.79	3 32.22	3 51.66	4 11.09	4 30.53	4 49.96	5 9.40
+ 3 35 58.29	35 38.52	35 18.74	34 58.97	34 39.19	34 19.42	33 59.64	33 39.86
+70 4 31.66	4 11.80	3 51.94	3 32.08	3 12.22	2 52.36	2 32.49	2 12.63
− 0 4 42.53	5 2.37	5 22.20	5 42.03	6 1.86	6 21.70	6 41.53	7 1.36
+15 19 36.74	19 16.60	18 56.57	18 36.48	18 16.40	17 56.31	17 36.22	17 16.13
+54 26 43.19	26 23.17	26 3.15	25 43.13	25 23.11	25 3.09	24 43.07	24 23.05
+ 9 28 59.17	28 39.17	28 19.16	27 59.16	27 39.15	27 19.15	26 59.15	26 39.14
+78 21 58.22	21 38.17	21 18.11	20 58.06	20 38.00	20 17.95	19 57.89	19 37.83
−78 33 45.76	34 5.80	34 25.84	34 45.89	35 5.93	35 25.97	35 46.01	36 6.05
+ 0 5 1.96	4 41.93	4 21.89	4 1.86	3 41.82	3 21.79	3 1.76	2 41.72
−62 20 58.51	21 18.45	21 38.38	21 58.31	22 18.24	22 38.17	22 58.11	23 18.04
−22 38 57.61	39 17.56	39 37.51	39 57.46	40 17.41	40 37.36	40 57.30	41 17.25
+70 31 56.74	31 36.81	31 16.88	30 56.95	30 37.02	30 17.09	29 57.16	29 37.23
+84 8 47.34	8 27.71	8 8.08	7 48.44	7 28.81	7 9.17	6 49.54	6 29.91
+39 2 53.51	2 33.99	2 14.48	1 54.96	1 35.44	1 15.93	0 56.41	0 36.90
− 4 49 2.07	49 21.39	49 40.71	50 0.03	50 19.35	50 38.67	50 57.99	51 17.30
−10 27 19.47	27 38.39	27 57.31	28 16.23	28 35.14	28 54.05	29 12.97	29 31.88
+ 0 5 44.49	5 25.96	5 7.43	4 48.90	4 30.37	4 11.85	3 53.33	3 34.80
+49 59 17.02	58 58.91	58 40.80	58 22.69	58 4.58	57 46.47	57 28.36	57 10.26
+19 4 33.40	4 15.21	3 57.02	3 38.83	3 20.65	3 2.46	2 44.28	2 26.10
−59 43 11.23	43 28.91	43 46.59	44 4.26	44 21.93	44 39 60	44 57.27	45 14.91
+64 61 17.24	60 59.87	60 42.50	60 25.13	60 7.77	59 50.40	59 33.04	59 15.68

TABLE XXII.—Mean Right Ascensions of Standard Stars, 1865—1872.

Star's name.	1865.	1866.	1867.	1868.	1869.	1870.	1871.	1872.
	h m s	s	s	s	s	s	s	s
α Bootis, (*Arcturus*) .	14 9 30.271	33.005	35.739	38.473	41.207	43.942	46.676	49.410
θ Bootis	14 20 36.013	38.056	40.099	42.142	44.186	46.229	48.272	50.315
5 Ursæ Minoris . .	14 27 50.913	50.694	50.476	50.259	50.044	49.830	49.617	49.405
α² Centauri. . .	14 30 28.109	32.138	36.168	40.198	44.229	48.260	52.293	56.326
ε Bootis . . .	14 39 5.495	8.116	10.738	13.359	15.981	18.603	21.224	23.846
α² Libræ	14 43 24.870	28.176	31.482	34.788	38.094	41.400	44 707	48.013
* β Ursæ Minoris .	14 51 7.907	7.651	7.396	7.143	6.890	6.639	6.388	6.139
β Bootis . . .	14 56 51.649	53.909	56.169	58.429	60.689	62.948	65.208	67.468
β Libræ	15 9 44.737	47.956	51.176	54.396	57.615	60.835	64.055	67.275
μ¹ Bootis . . .	15 19 23.486	25.754	28.021	30.289	32.557	34.825	37.092	39.360
* γ² Ursæ Minoris .	15 20 57.974	57.822	57.672	57.522	57.372	57.224	57.076	56.929
α Coronæ Borealis .	15 28 58.361	60.900	63.439	65.978	68.517	71.057	73.596	76.135
α Serpentis . . .	15 37 37.186	40.136	43.086	46.036	48.986	51.936	54.886	57.837
ε Serpentis . .	15 44 5.310	8.296	11.283	14.270	17.257	20.243	23.230	26.217
* ζ Ursæ Minoris .	15 48 56.829	54.529	52.232	49.936	47.642	45.350	43.061	40.773
ε Coronæ Borealis .	15 52 0.018	2.503	4.988	7.473	9.958	12.443	14.928	17.413
δ Scorpii	15 52 21.313	24.848	28.384	31.919	35.454	38.990	42.526	46.062
β¹ Scorpii . . .	15 57 35.450	38.926	42.402	45.879	49.356	52.833	56.310	59.787
Groombridge 2320 .	16 5 57.809	57.939	58.069	58 200	58.331	58.463	58.595	58.728
δ Ophiuchi . . .	16 7 16.378	19.515	22.653	25.790	28.928	32.065	35.203	38.340
τ Herculis. . . .	16 15 40.934	42.732	44.530	46.328	48.126	49.923	51.721	53.519
α Scorpii, (*Antares*) .	16 21 8.070	11.738	15.406	19.074	22.742	26.410	30.079	33.748
η Draconis . . .	16 22 10.147	10.949	11.752	12.556	13.359	14.163	14.967	15.771
* λ Draconis . . .	16 28 15.670	15.526	15.381	15.237	15.094	14.951	14.808	14.666
ζ Ophiuchi . . .	16 29 43.647	46.944	50.241	53.538	56.836	60.133	63.430	66.728
* α Trianguli Australis.	16 34 24 160	30.438	36.716	42.995	49.275	55.556	61.838	68.121
η Herculis . . .	16 38 16.119	18.173	20.227	22.281	24.336	26.390	28.444	30.499
κ Ophiuchi . . .	16 51 16.732	19.566	22.401	25.236	28.070	30.904	33.739	36 573
d Herculis . . .	16 56 37.237	39.446	41.655	43.863	46.072	48.281	50.490	52.699
* ε Ursæ Minoris . .	16 59 54.822	48.416	42.014	35.615	29.219	22.826	16.436	10.049
α¹ Herculis . . .	17 8 29.549	32.282	35.015	37.748	40.481	43.214	45.947	48.681
44 Ophiuchi . . .	17 18 7.650	11.308	14 967	18.625	22.284	25.942	29 601	33.260
β Draconis . . .	17 27 22.969	24.320	25.671	27.021	28.372	29.723	31.074	32.425
α Ophiuchi . . .	17 28 40.097	42.879	45.661	48.443	51.225	54.007	56.789	59.571
* ω Draconis . . .	17 37 44.680	44.323	43.967	43.611	43.255	42.899	42.543	42.187
μ Herculis. . . .	17 41 10.564	12.908	15.253	17.598	19 943	22.287	24.632	26.977
* ψ¹ Draconis, (*pr.*) . .	17 44 20.713	19.629	18.546	17.462	16.379	15.296	14.213	13.131
γ Draconis . . .	17 53 28.434	29 828	31.221	32.615	34.008	35.402	36.795	38 189
γ² Sagittarii . . .	17 57 8.201	12.053	15.905	19.757	23.610	27.462	31.314	35.167
* σ Octantis. . . .	17 57 12.461	121.744	231.034	340.317	449.580	558.811	667.996	777.121
μ¹ Sagittarii . . .	18 5 41.410	44.996	48.582	52.168	55.754	59.340	62.926	66.512
* δ Ursæ Minoris . .	18 13 173.303	153.925	134.542	115.154	95.762	76.364	56.963	37.558
η Serpentis . . .	18 14 19 452	22.551	25.651	28.750	31.850	34.949	38.048	41.148
1 Aquilæ, (3 H. Scuti)	18 27 51.583	54.847	58.112	61.376	64 640	67.904	71.169	74.433
α Lyræ, (*Vega*) . .	18 32 22.054	24.086	26.117	28.149	30.180	32.212	34.243	36.275
β Lyræ	18 45 5.741	7.955	10.169	12.383	14.598	16.812	19.026	21 240
σ Sagittarii . . .	18 46 53.602	57.326	61.050	64 774	68.498	72.221	75.945	79.669
* 50 Draconis . . .	18 50 42.593	40.698	38.803	36.907	35.010	33.113	31.216	29.318
ζ Aquilæ . . .	18 59 12.257	15.012	17.767	20.522	23.276	26.031	28.786	31.540
d Sagittarii , . .	19 9 44.071	47.585	51.098	54.612	58.126	61.639	65.153	68.666

* Circumpolar Stars.

TABLE XXIII.—Mean Declinations of Standard Stars, 1865—1872.

1865.	1866.	1867.	1868.	1869.	1870.	1871.	1872.
° ′ ″	′ ″	′ ″	′ ″	′ ″	′ ″	′ ″	′ ″
+19 53 13.01	52 54.11	52 35.21	52 16.31	51 57.42	51 38.53	51 19.64	51 0.75
+52 28 33.51	28 16.72	27 50.93	27 43.14	27 26.35	27 9.57	26 52.78	26 36.00
+76 17 44 86	17 28.81	17 12.76	16 56.72	16 40.67	16 24.63	16 8.58	15 52.54
−60 16 24.20	16 39.27	16 54.33	17 9.38	17 24 43	17 39.48	17 54.53	18 9 56
+27 38 42.45	38 27.07	38 11.69	37 56.31	37 40.94	37 25.56	37 10.19	36 54.83
−15 28 42.39	28 57.02	29 12.84	29 28.06	29 43.27	29 58.48	30 13.09	30 28.90
+74 42 24 63	42 10.08	41 55.33	41 40.58	41 25.84	41 11.09	40 56.34	40 41.59
+40 55 28 62	55 14.21	54 59.80	54 45.39	54 30 99	54 16.59	54 2.19	53 47.79
− 8 52 55.99	53 9.56	53 23.12	53 36.68	53 50.24	54 3.79	54 17.35	54 30 89
+37 51 8.48	50 55.65	50 42.82	50 30.00	50 17.17	50 4.35	49 51.53	49 38.72
+72 18 52.12	18 39.32	18 26.53	18 13.73	18 0.93	17 48.13	17 35.33	17 22.53
+27 10 16.49	10 3.74	9 51.39	9 39.04	9 26.70	9 14.35	9 2.02	8 49.68
+ 6 51 19.10	50 58.49	50 46.88	50 35.28	50 23 68	50 12.08	50 0.49	49 48.90
+ 4 53 11.38	53 0.26	52 49.13	52 38.02	52 26.90	52 15.79	52 4.68	51 53.58
+78 12 29.58	12 18.72	12 7.86	11 57.00	11 46.13	11 35.26	11 24.39	11 13.52
+27 16 15.79	16 5.13	15 54.48	15 43.82	15 33.17	15 22.53	15 11.88	15 1.24
−22 14 2 90	14 13.50	14 24.48	14 34.68	14 45.27	14 55.85	15 6.42	15 16.99
−19 25 58.84	26 9.07	26 19.29	26 29.51	26 39.72	26 49.93	27 0.13	27 10.33
+68 9 57.47	9 47.96	9 38.46	9 28.96	9 19.46	9 9.96	9 0 46	8 50.95
− 3 20 37.77	20 47.37	20 56.97	21 6.55	21 16.14	21 25.72	21 35.30	21 44.87
+46 38 10.92	38 2.13	37 53.34	37 44.56	37 35.78	37 27.00	37 18.22	37 9.45
−26 7 44 68	7 53.09	8 1.49	8 9.89	8 18.28	8 26.67	8 35.05	8 43.43
+61 49 13.40	49 5.17	48 56.93	48 48.70	48 40.47	48 32.24	48 24.01	48 15.78
+69 3 36 50	3 28.72	3 20.93	3 13.15	3 5.37	2 57.59	2 49.81	2 42.03
−10 17 25.63	17 33.28	17 40 93	17 48.56	17 56.20	18 3.83	18 11.45	18 19.07
−68 46 27.19	46 34.58	46 41.96	46 49.34	46 56.71	47 4.07	47 11.42	47·18.76
+39 10 51 86	10 44.80	10 37.74	10 30.68	10 23.62	10 16 57	10 9.52	10 2 47
+ 9 55 15.71	35 9.81	35 3.91	34 58.02	34 52.13	34 46.25	34 40.37	34 34.49
+33 45 57.53	45 52.09	45 46.65	45 41.21	45 35.78	45 30.35	45 24.92	45 19.50
+82 15 15.18	15 9.98	15 4.77	14 59.55	14 54.32	14 49.09	14 43.84	14 38.58
+14 32 48 85	32 44.43	32 40.02	32 35.60	32 31.19	32 26.79	32 22 39	32 17.99
−24 2 49.78	2 53.51	2 57.23	3° 0.95	3 4.66	3 8.37	3 12.07	3 15 76
+52 24 8 71	24 5.86	24 3.02	24 0.18	23 57.33	23 54.49	23 51 66	23 48.82
+12 39 39 81	39 36.87	39 33.93	39 30.99	39 28.06	39 25.13	39 22 20	39 19 28
+68 49 10.50	49 8.85	49 7.20	49 5.54	49 3.89	49 2.23	49 0.58	48 58.92
+27 48 7.19	48 4.82	48 2.46	48 0.10	47 57.74	47 55.39	47 53.04	47 50.69
+72 12 51.18	12 49.55	12 47.92	12 46.28	12 44 65	12 43.01	12 41.37	12 39.73
+51 30 21.42	30 20 81	30 20.20	30 19.60	30 19.00	30 18.40	30·17.81	30 17.21
− 30 25 19.28	25 19.75	25 20.21	25 20.67	25 21.12	25 21.57	25 22.00	25 22.44
−89 16 43.63	16 43.80	16 43.80	16 43.65	16 43.34	16 42.86	16 42.23	16 41.44
−21 5 26 25	5 25.74	5 25.24	5 24.72	5 24.20	5 23.68	5 23 15	5 22 62
+86 36 14.49	36 15.91	36 17.30	36 18.66	36 20.00	36 21.30	36 22.58	36 23.83
− 2 55 50 63	55 50.04	55 49.45	55 48.86	55 48 26	55 47.66	55 47.05	55 46.44
− 8 20 6.74	20 4.62	20 2.49	20 0.35	19 58.21	19 56.07	19 53 92	19 51.77
+38 39 35.42	39 38.53	39 41.64	39 44.76	39 47.87	39 51.00	39 54.12	39 57.25
+33 12 28.51	12 32.42	12 36.33	12 40.25	12 44.16	12 48.09	12 52.01	12 55.94
−26 27 38.27	27 34.25	27 30 23	27 26.20	27 22.17	27 18.13	27 14.09	27 10.05
+75 16 22.03	16 26.49	16 30.94	16 35.39	16 39.84	16 44.29	16 48.74	16 53.19
+13 39 55.56	40 0.60	40 5.65	40 10.70	40 15.75	40 20.80	40 25.86	40 30 92
−19 11 21.33	11 15.28	11 9.22	11 3.16	10 57.09	10 51.02	10 44.95	10 38.87

6

TABLE XXII.—Mean Right Ascensions of Standard Stars, 1865—1872.

Star's name.	1865.	1866.	1867.	1868.	1869.	1870.	1871.	1872.
	h m s	s	s	s	s	s	s	s
* δ Draconis	19 12 30.933	30.968	31.003	31.037	31.072	31.106	31.140	31.173
τ Draconis	19 18 7.772	6.669	5.565	4.461	3.356	2.251	1.145	0.039
δ Aquilæ	19 18 41.437	44.462	47.486	50.511	53.535	56.560	59.584	62.609
κ Aquilæ	19 20 37.619	40.850	44.080	47.310	50.541	53.772	57.002	60.232
γ Aquilæ	19 39 50.469	53.322	56.175	59.028	61.880	64.733	67.586	70.438
α Aquilæ, (*Altair*)	19 44 11.745	14.673	17.602	20.530	23.459	26.387	29.315	32 244
* ε Draconis	19 48 36.806	36.637	36.468	36.298	36.128	35.957	35.786	35.615
β Aquilæ	19 48 40.881	43.828	46.775	49.722	52.669	55.616	58.563	61.510
τ Aquilæ	19 57 32 666	35.599	38.533	41.466	44.400	47.333	50.266	53.200
* λ Ursæ Minoris	19 52 429.351	371.557	313.423	255.009	196.295	137.283	77.971	18.360
α² Capricorni	20 10 33.702	37.036	40.369	43.703	47.037	50.370	53.703	57.036
* κ Cephei	20 13 22.544	20.660	18.775	16.888	14.999	13.109	11.217	9.324
α Pavonis	20 14 57.200	61.998	66.795	71.592	76.389	81.185	85.980	90.775
π Capricorni	20 19 35.448	38.890	42.332	45.776	49.217	52.658	56.100	59.541
ε Delphini	20 26 45.761	48.627	51.493	54.359	57.225	60.091	62.957	65.823
* Groombridge 3241	20 30 33.958	33.754	33.550	33.345	33.139	32.932	32.725	32.517
α Cygni	20 36 49.797	51.841	53.885	55.928	57.972	60.016	62.060	64.104
μ Aquarii	20 45 22.172	25.413	28.653	31.894	35.134	38.375	41.615	44.855
ν Cygni	20 52 8.444	10.678	12.911	15.145	17.378	19.612	21 846	24.080
12 Year Cat. 1879	20 53 36.449	33.974	31.496	29.015	26.531	24.044	21.553	19.060
61 Cygni, (*pr.*)	21 0 50.865	53.552	56.238	58.924	61.611	64.298	66.984	69.671
ζ Cygni	21 7 11.477	14.027	16.577	19.127	21.677	24.227	26.777	29.327
α Cephei	21 15 21.327	22.765	24.203	25.641	27.078	28.516	29.953	31 391
1 Pegasi	21 15 50.669	53.443	56.217	58.991	61.765	64.539	67.313	70.087
β Aquarii	21 24 27.010	30.175	33.340	36.504	39.669	42.833	45.997	49.161
* β Cephei	21 26 54.351	55.153	55.955	56.757	57.558	58 359	59.160	59.960
ξ Aquarii	21 30 33.773	36.972	40.171	43.370	46.568	49.766	52.965	56 163
ε Pegasi	21 37 33.804	36.288	39.236	42.184	45.132	48.080	51.028	53 976
* 11 Cephei	21 39 56.006	56.915	57.824	58.732	59 640	60 548	61.455	62 362
μ Capricorni	21 45 55.977	59.257	62.557	65.817	69 097	72 377	75.656	78.936
* 79 Draconis	21 51 11.268	12.008	12.748	13.487	14 226	14.965	15.703	16 440
α Aquarii	21 58 50.942	54 026	57.110	60.194	63.278	66.361	69.445	72.529
α Gruis	21 59 42.666	46.483	50.299	54.115	57.930	61.745	65.559	69.373
θ Aquarii	22 9 42.484	45.655	48 826	51.997	55.167	58 338	61.509	64.679
π Aquarii	22 18 22.916	25.982	29.047	32.112	35.178	38.244	41.309	44.374
η Aquarii	22 28 25.100	28.184	31.268	34.352	37.436	40.519	43.603	46 687
*226 Cephei, (B)	22 29 53 502	54.588	55.673	56.758	57.842	58 926	60.010	61 093
ζ Pegasi	22 34 43.731	46.719	49.707	52.696	55.684	58.672	61.661	64.649
ι Cephei	22 44 52.823	54.939	57.056	59.173	61.290	63 407	65.525	67.643
* λ Aquarii	22 45 34.162	37.294	40.426	43.557	46.689	49.820	52.952	56.083
α Pis. Aus (*Fomalhaut*)	22 50 11.079	14.410	17.740	21.070	24.400	27.730	31.060	34.389
α Pegasi, (*Markab*)	22 58 2.259	5 243	8 227	11.212	14.196	17.180	20.165	23.149
* ο Cephei	23 13 5.689	8.123	10.558	12.993	15.428	17.864	20.300	22.737
θ Piscium	23 21 7.214	10.255	13.295	16.336	19.376	22.417	25.458	28 499
ι Piscium	23 33 0.482	3.567	6.651	9.736	12.820	15.905	18.989	22.074
* γ Cephei	23 33 49.800	52.198	54 596	56.996	59.396	61.797	64.198	66 600
* Groombridge 4163	23 48 17.849	20.693	23 536	26.383	29 230	32.077	34.925	37 774
ω Piscium	23 52 22.816	25.894	28.972	32.050	35.128	38.206	41.284	44.362

TABLE XXII.—Mean Declinations of Standard Stars, 1865—1872.

1865.	1866.	1867.	1868.	1869.	1870.	1871.	1872.
° ′ ″	′ ″	′ ″	′ ″	′ ″	′ ″	′ ″	′ ″
+67 25 26.28	25 32.59	25 38.90	25 45.21	25 51.52	25 57.82	26 4.13	26 10.44
+73 6 13.41	6 20.21	6 27.01	6 33.81	6 40 61	6 47.40	6 54.20	7 0.99
+ 2 50 54.30	51 1.15	51 8.00	51 14.85	51 21.71	51 28.58	51 35.45	51 42.32
− 7 19 29.03	19 20.37	19 12.69	19 5 02	18 57.34	18 49.65	18 41.96	18 34.27
+10 17 12.17	17 20.64	17 29.11	17 37.59	17 46.08	17 54.56	18 3.05	18 11.55
+ 8 30 51.39	31 0.58	31 9.78	31 18.98	31 28.18	31 37.38	31 46.59	31 55.80
+69 55 25.50	55 34.05	55 43.80	55 52.95	56 2.09	56 11.24	56 20.39	56 29.54
+ 6 4 19.43	4 28.12	4 36.81	4 45.51	4 54.21	5 2.91	5 11.62	5 20.33
+ 6 53 58.11	54 7.97	54 17.84	54 27.71	54 37.58	54 47.46	54 57.34	55 7.22
+88 54 15.02	54 24.95	54 34.80	54 44.58	54 54.29	55 3.92	55 13.47	55 22.94
−12 57 38.22	57 27.39	57 16.56	57 5.71	56 54.87	56 44.02	56 33.17	56 22.31
+77 18 11.04	18 22.06	18 33.08	18 44.10	18 55.11	19 6.13	19 17.13	19 28.14
−57 9 49.21	9 38.10	9 26.99	·9 15.87	9 4.74	8 53.60	8 42.46	8 31.31
−18 39 5.07	38 53.63	38 42.18	38 30.72	38 19.26	38 7.80	37 56.34	37 44.87
+10 50 47.81	50 59.77	51 11.74	51 23.71	51 35.68	51 47.66	51 59.64	52 11.63
+72 4 27.07	4 39.30	4 51.53	5 3.75	5 15.98	5 28.20	5·40.43	5 52.65
+44 47 57.33	48 10.01	48 22.68	48 35.36	48 48.04	49 0.73	49 13.41	49 26.10
− 9 29 14.54	29 1.31	28 48.07	28 34.84	28 21.60	28 8.35	27 55.11	27 41.86
+40 38 56.72	39 10.42	39 24.12	39 37.83	39 51.53	40 5.24	40 18.96	40 32.67
+80 2 38.34	2 52.07	3 5.80	3 19.52	3 33.24	3 46.96	4 0.68	4 14.39
+38 5 14.35	5 31.83	5 49.31	6 6.79	6 24.28	6 41.77	6 59.26	7 16.76
+29 40 29.24	40 43.80	40 58.37	41 12.94	41 27.51	41 42.08	41 56.66	42 11.24
+62 0 50.43	1 5.58	1 20.68	1 35.78	1 50.89	2 6.00	2 21.10	2 36.21
+19 13 43.72	13 58.93	14 14.15	14 29.37·	14 44.60	14 59.82	15 15.05	15 30.28
− 6 9 47.01	9 31.39	9 15.77	9 0.14	8 44.51	8 28.88	8 13.25	7 57.61
+63 58 5.53	58 21.24	58 36.95	58 52.65	59 8.36	59 24.07	59 39.78	59 55.49
− 8 27 27.85	27 11.92	26 56.00	26 40.06	26 24.13	26 8.19	25 52.26	25 36.31
+ 9 15 27.78	15 44.10	16 0.42	16 16.73	16 33.06	16 49.38	17 5.70	17 22.03
+70 41 24.03	41 40.53	41 57.03	42 13.53	42 30.03	42 46.53	43 3.03	43 19.53
−14 11 6.78	10 50.03	10 33.27	10 16.51	9 59.75	9 42.99	9 26.22	9 9.45
+73 3 49.58	4 6.55	4 23.51	4 40.47	4 57.43	5 14.39	5 31.36	5 48.32
− 0 58 27.24	58 9.92	57 52.60	57 35.29	57 17.96	57 0.64	56 43.32	56 25.99
−47 36 45.80	36 28.72	36 11.54	35 54.36	35 37.17	35 19.98	35 2.79	34 45.59
− 8 27 14.83	26 57.06	26 39.29	26 21.52	26 3.75	25 45.97	25 28.20	25 10.42
+ 0 41 36.83	41 54.95	42 13.07	42 31.19	42 49.32	43 7.45	43 25.57	43 43.70
− 0 48 43.85	48 25.43	48 7.00	47 48.57	47 30.14	47 11.71	46 53.27	46 34.83
+75 31 50.72	32 9.24	32 27.75	32 46.27	33 4.79	33 23.30	33 41.82	34 0.34
+10 7 39.99	7 58.68	8 17.37	8 36.07	8 54.76	9 13.46	9 32.16	9 50.86
+65 29 26.82	29 45.66	30 4.51	30 23.36	30 42.21	31 1.06	31 19.91	31 38.76
− 8 17 48.78	17 29.72	17 10.65	16 51.59	16 32.53	16 13.46	15 54.40	15 35.33
−30 20 12.05	19 53.07	19 34.09	19 15.11	18 56.13	18 37.15	18 18.17	17 59.18
+14 28 47.18	29 6.49	29 25.80	29 45.11	30 4.42	30 23.73	30 43.04	31 2.35
+67 22 22.44	22 42.06	23 1.68	23 21.30	23 40.92	24 0.54	24 20.16	24 39.78
+ 5 38 17.23	38 36.97	38 56.71	39 16.45	39 36.20	39 55.94	40 15.69	40 35.43
+ 4 53 42.04	54 1.53	54 21.01	54 40.49	54 59.97	55 19.45	55 38.94	55 58.42
+76 52 44.41	53 4.48	53 24.55	53 44.63	54 4.70	54 24.77	54 44.85	55 4.92
+73 39 32.28	39 52.28	40 12.28	40 32.28	40 52.28	41 12.28	41 32.28	41 52.28
+ 6 6 57.92	7 17.86	7 37.80	7 57.74	8 17.68	8 37.63	8 57.57	9 17.51

TABLE XXIII.—Mean Right Ascensions of Standard Stars, 1873—1880.

Star's name.	1873.	1874.	1875.	1876.	1877.	1878.	1879.	1880.
	h m s	s	s	s	s	s	s	s
α Andromedæ . .	0 1 49.557	52.645	55.734	58.822	61.911	65.000	68.089	71.178
γ Pegasi	0 6 41.866	44.949	48.032	51.115	54.198	57.282	60.365	63.449
* β Hydri . . .	0 19 2.384	5.638	8.890	12.141	15.391	18.638	21.885	25.129
α Cassiopeæ . .	0 33 18.774	22.140	25.506	28.872	32.239	35.607	38.975	42.344
β Ceti	0 37 12.781	15.794	18.807	21.820	24.834	27.847	30.860	33.873
*21 Cassiopeæ . . .	0 37 17.861	21.693	25.527	29.361	33.198	37.036	40.876	44.717
ε Piscium	0 56 21.205	24.314	27.423	30.532	33.641	36.751	39.860	42.970
* α Ursæ Min. (Polaris)	1 12 18.728	39.372	60.165	81.109	102.205	123.455	144.861	166.424
0¹ Ceti	1 17 40.537	43.535	46.533	49.531	52.529	55.526	58.524	61.522
*33 Cassiopeæ . . .	1 21 48.701	53.056	57.413	61.770	66.129	70.490	74.852	79.215
η Piscium	1 24 41.323	44.523	47.722	50.922	54.121	57.321	60.521	63.722
α Eridani, (Achernar).	1 32 58.728	60.963	63.196	65.431	67.665	69.899	72.133	74.366
ο Piscium	1 38 41.396	44.558	47.721	50.883	54.045	57.208	60.370	63.533
β Arietis	1 47 37.636	40.937	44.238	47.539	50 841	54.142	57.444	60.746
*50 Cassiopeæ . . .	1 52 37.906	42.888	47.871	52.856	57.842	62.831	67.822	72.814
α Arietis	2 0 1.055	4.424	7.793	11.161	14.530	17.899	21.269	24.638
ξ¹ Ceti	2 6 16.171	19.341	22.511	25.680	28.850	32.020	35.190	38.360
* ι Cassiopeæ . . .	2 18 37.671	42.512	47.354	52 198	57.043	61.890	66.738	71.587
γ Ceti	2 36 43.292	46.395	49.498	52.600	55.703	58.806	61.909	65.013
α Ceti	2 55 38.524	41.653	44.782	47.911	51.040	54.169	57.299	60.428
*48 Cephei, (H). . .	3 4 17.259	24.610	31.964	39.321	46.682	54.047	61.415	68.787
ζ Arietis	3 7 36.269	39.706	43.144	46.581	50.019	53.457	56.895	60.333
α Persei	3 15 15.869	20.118	24.368	28.618	32.868	37.118	41.369	45.621
δ Persei	3 33 53.290	57 530	61.771	66.012	70.253	74.495	78.737	82.980
η Tauri	3 39 56.255	59.809	63.364	66.918	70.473	74.028	77.583	81.138
ζ Persei	3 46 9.140	12.897	16.654	20.411	24.168	27.925	31.683	35.441
γ¹ Eridani	3 52 6.270	9.067	11.863	14.660	17.457	20.253	23.050	25.847
γ Tauri	4 12 34.054	37.462	40.870	44.277	47.685	51.093	54.501	57.909
ε Tauri	4 21 12.141	15.637	19.132	22.628	26.124	29.620	33.116	36.613
α Tauri, (Aldebaran) .	4 28 38.099	41.535	44.971	48.407	51.843	55.280	58.716	62.153
* 9 Camelopardalis . .	4 41 26.184	32.098	38.012	43.928	49.844	55.761	61.678	67.596
ι Aurigæ	4 48 43.508	47.405	51.303	55.200	59.097	62.995	66.892	70.790
11 Orionis	4 57 18.848	22.273	25.698	29.123	32.549	35.974	39.400	42 825
α Aurigæ, (Capella) .	5 7 18.598	23.020	27.443	31.866	36.289	40.712	45.136	49.559
β Orionis, (Rigel). .	5 8 26.098	28.979	31.860	34.741	37.622	40.503	43.384	46.265
β Tauri	5 18 15.876	19.664	23.452	27.240	31.028	34.816	38.604	42.393
* Groombridge 966	5 22 45.643	53.632	61.622	69.612	77.603	85.595	93.587	101.581
δ Orionis	5 25 31.166	34.230	37.294	40.358	43.422	46.486	49.551	52.615
α Leporis	5 27 7.821	10 467	13.114	15.760	18.407	21.053	23.700	26.346
ε Orionis	5 29 46.180	49.222	52.264	55.306	58.348	61.390	64.433	67.475
α Columbæ . . .	5 35 3.097	5.268	7.440	9.613	11.784	13.957	16.129	18.302
α Orionis	5 48 17.809	21.056	24.303	27.550	30.797	34.044	37.291	40.538
*22 Camelopardalis,(II)	6 4 50.096	57.314	63.933	70.552	77.170	83.789	90.407	97.025
μ Geminorum . . .	6 15 16.661	20.293	23.926	27.559	31.192	34.825	39.457	42.090
α Argus, (Canopus) .	6 21 8.071	9.401	10.731	12.062	13.392	14.722	16.052	17.383
γ Geminorum . . .	6 30 22.523	25.992	29.460	32.929	36.398	39.867	43 336	46 804
α Canis Maj. (Sirius).	6 39 33.064	35.709	38.354	40.999	43.644	26.289	48.935	51.580
*51 Cephei,(II.). . .	6 40 13.916	44.183	74.430	104.656	134.861	165.044	195.205	225.342
ε Canis Majoris . .	6 53 38.161	40.519	42.878	45.236	47.595	49 954	52.313	54.671
δ Canis Majoris . .	7 3 13.713	16.153	18.593	21.032	23.472	25.912	28.351	30.791

TABLE XXIII.—Mean Declinations of Standard Stars, 1873—1880.

1873.	1074.	1875.	1876.	1877.	1878.	1879.	1880.
° ′ ″	′ ″	′ ″	′ ″	′ ″	′ ″	′ ″	′ ″
+23 23 21.87	23 41.78	24 1.68	24 21.59	24 41.49	25 1.40	25 21.30	25 41.20
+14 28 39.46	28 59.51	29 19.55	29 39.60	29 59.64	30 19.69	30 39.74	30 59.78
—77 59 13.69	57 53.45	57 33.20	57 12.96	56 52.72	56 32.47	56 12 23	55 21.98
+55 50 25.45	50 45.25	51 5.05	51 24.85	51 44.65	52 4 45	52 24.24	52 41 04
—18 41 2.22	40 42.39	40 22.56	40 2.74	39 42.91	39 23.08	39 3.26	38 43.43
+74 17 34.31	17 54.04	18 13.76	18 33.49	18 53.22	19 12.94	19 32.67	19 52.39
+ 7 12 21.52	12 40.99	13 0.47	13 19.94	13 39.41	13 58.89	14 18.36	14 37.82
+88 37 55.70	38 14.76	38 33.81	38 52.85	39 11.88	39 30.90	39 49.92	40 8.92
— 8 50 20.40	50 1.68	49 42.96	49 24.25	49 5.53	48 46.82	48 28.11	48 9.40
+69 36 35.47	36 54.18	37 12.89	37 31.59	37 50.30	38 9.00	38 27.69	38 46.39
+14 41 26 36	41 45.08	42 3.80	42 22.51	42 41.23	42 59.94	43 18.65	43 37.36
—57 52 56.25	52 37.83	52 19.42	52 1.01	51 42.60	51 24.19	51 5.79	50 47.39
+ 8 31 3.e6	31 22.12	31 40.38	31 58.64	32 16.89	32 35.15	32 53.40	33 11.65
+20 11 11.44	11 29.23	11 47.02	12 4.80	12 22.58	12 40.36	12 58.14	13 15.91
+71 48 17.42	48 35.10	48 52.78	49 10.45	49 28.12	49 45.78	50 3.44	50 21.10
+22 51 39.53	51 56.76	52 13.99	52 31.22	52 48.44	53 5.66	53 22.88	53 40.10
+ 8 14 59.60	15 16.67	15 33.75	15 50.82	16 7.89	16 24.95	16 42.01	16 59.07
+66 49 45.25	50 1.72	50 18.19	50 34.66	50 51.12	51 7.58	51 24.04	51 40.49
+ 2 41 57.94	42 13.33	42 28.72	42 44.10	42 59.48	43 14.86	43 30.24	43 45.61
+ 3 35 24.22	35 38.58	35 52.93	36 7.28	36 21.63	36 35.98	36 50.32	37 4.65
+77 15 50.53	16 4.37	16 18.21	16 32.04	16 45.86	16 59.67	17 13.48	17 27.28
+20 34 20.89	34 34.53	34 48.17	35 1.81	35 15.44	35 29.07	35 42.70	35 56.32
+49 24 24.63	24 37.79	24 50.94	25 4.10	25 17.24	25 30.38	25 43.52	25 56.65
+47 22 41 24	22 56.13	23 8.01	23 19.88	23 31.75	23 43.61	23 55.47	24 7.33
+23 42 38.03	42 49.48	43 0.94	43 12.39	43 23.83	43 35.27	43 46.71	43 58.14
+31 30 15.79	30 26.82	30 37.85	30 48.87	30 59.89	31 10.90	31 21.91	31 32.91
—13 52 15.72	52 5.19	51 54.66	51 44.14	51 33.62	51 23.10	51 12.59	51 2.08
+15 19 9.01	19 18.06	19 27.11	19 36.16	19 45.20	19 54.24	20 3.27	20 12.30
+18 53 48.96	53 57.33	54 5.69	54 14.05	54 22.41	54 30.76	54 39.11	54 47.45
+16 15 7.73	15 15.34	15 22.95	15 30.56	15 38.16	15 45.76	15 53.35	16 0.94
+66 7 23.81	7 30.56	7 37.30	7 44.03	7 50.75	7 57.46	8 4.16	8 10.86
+32 57 45.85	57 51.98	57 58.09	58 4.20	58 10.31	58 16.41	58 22.50	58 28.59
+15 13 30.97	13 36.37	13 41.77	13 47.16	13 52.55	13 57.94	14 3.32	14 8.69
+45 51 57.48	52 1.62	52 5.76	52 9.89	52 14.01	52 18.13	52 22.24	52 26.35
— 8 21 0.46	20 55.99	20 51.52	20 47.06	20 42.60	20 38.14	20 33.69	20 29.24
+28 29 51.85	29 55.30	29 58.76	30 2.20	30 5.64	30 9.07	30 12.50	30 15.93
+74 57 15.12	57 18.36	57 21.58	57 24.80	57 28.00	57 31.19	57 34.37	57 37.54
— 0 23 42.63	23 39.64	23 36.65	23 33.66	23 30.68	23 27.71	23 24.73	23 21.77
—17 54 52.93	54 50.04	54 47.16	54 44.27	54 41.40	54 38.52	54 35 65	54 32.78
— 1 17 5.75	17 3.11	17 0.48	16 57.85	16 55.22	16 52.60	16 49.98	16 47.37
—34 8 34.50	8 32.35	8 30.20	8 28 05	8 25.90	8 23.76	8 21.62	8 19.48
+ 7 22 52.87	22 53.91	22 54.94	22 55.97	22 57.00	22 58.02	22 59.03	23 0.04
+09 21 36.67	21 36.13	21 35.58	21 35.03	21 34.46	21 33.88	21 33 30	21 32 70
+22 34 35.69	34 34.25	34 32.79	34 31.34	34 29 88	34 28.41	34 26.94	34 25.46
—52 37 37.57	37 39.42	37 41.27	37 43.12	37 44.98	37 46.84	37 48.70	37 50.56
+16 30 20.43	30 17.75	30 15.07	30 12.38	30 9.68	30 6.98	30 4.28	30 1.57
—16 32 36.32	32 40.97	32 45.63	32 50.29	32 54 96	32 59.63	33 4.30	33 8.98
+87 14 11 61	14 8.04	14 4.43	14 0.77	13 57.07	13 53.33	13 49.54	13 45.72
—28 48 2.35	48 6.99	48 11.65	48 16.30	48 20.96	48 25.62	48 30.29	48 34.96
—26 11 33.38	11 38.80	11 44.23	11 49.67	11 55.11	12 0.55	12 5.99	12 11.44

SPECIAL TABLES.

TABLE XXIII.—Mean Eight Ascensions of Standard Stars, 1873—1880.

Star's name.	1873.	1874.	1875.	1876.	1877.	1878.	1879.	1880.
	h m s	s	s	s	s	s	s	s
δ Geminorum . . .	7 12 32.253	35.844	39.435	43.025	46.616	50.206	53.797	57.387
* Piazzi, vii. 67 . .	7 17 38.799	45.111	51.422	57.732	64.042	70.351	76.658	82.965
a Geminor. (*Castor*) .	7 26 29.368	33.207	37.046	40.885	44.724	48.562	52.401	56.239
α Can. Min. (*Procyon*)	7 32 39.267	42.413	45.560	48.705	51.851	54.997	58.143	61.289
β Geminor. (*Polluz*) .	7 37 32.550	36.231	39.913	43.594	47.276	50.957	54.638	58.319
φ Geminorum . . .	7 45 43.408	47.092	50.776	54.460	58.144	61.827	65.511	69.194
* 3 Ursæ Majoris,(H.).	8 0 8.838	14.906	20.973	27.039	33.103	39.166	45.228	51.289
15 Argus, (ι) . . .	8 2 8.213	10.769	13.325	15.882	18.438	20.995	23.551	26.107
ε Hydræ	8 40 3.015	6.199	9.383	12.567	15.751	18.935	22.118	25.302
ι Ursæ Majoris . .	8 50 30.149	34.239	38.428	42.567	46.706	50.844	54.982	59.119
* σ² Ursæ Majoris . .	8 59 11.300	16.676	22.051	27.425	32.797	38.168	43.537	48.905
κ Cancri	9 0 52.001	55.256	58.511	61.766	65.021	68.276	71.531	74.785
ι Argus	9 13 41.352	42.954	44.555	46.157	47.758	49.360	50.961	52.562
* 1 Draconis,(H.) . .	9 18 47.719	56.844	65.961	75.070	84.171	93.264	102.350	111.427
α Hydræ	9 21 20.804	23.753	26.703	29.652	32.602	35.551	38.501	41.450
* d Ursæ Majoris . .	9 23 12.682	18.109	23.535	28.960	34.383	39.804	45.223	50.640
θ Ursæ Majoris . .	9 24 20.991	25.041	29.091	33.140	37.189	41.237	45.285	49.332
ε Leonis	9 38 34.381	41.801	45.220	48.639	52.058	55.477	58.895	62.314
μ Leonis	9 45 32.199	35.623	39.048	42.472	45.896	49.320	52.744	56.167
α Leonis, (*Regulus*) .	10 1 36.444	39.647	42.850	46.053	49.256	52.459	55.661	58.864
* 32 Ursæ Majoris . .	10 8 47.139	51.578	56.016	60.453	64.888	69.322	73.756	78.188
γ¹ Leonis	10 12 58.077	61.394	64.711	68.028	71.345	74.661	77.978	31.294
* 9 Draconis, (H.). .	10 24 14.422	19.729	25.033	30.335	35.633	40.929	46.223	51.514
ρ Leonis	10 26 7.424	10.590	13.756	16.922	20.088	23.253	26.419	29.585
η Argus	10 40 8.291	10.601	12.911	15.222	17.532	19.843	22.154	24.465
l Leonis	10 42 34.813	37.972	41.132	44.291	47.450	50.609	53.769	56.928
α Ursæ Majoris . .	10 55 52.314	56.073	59.832	63.590	67.347	71.103	74.859	78.614
δ Leonis	11 7 21.159	24.361	27.563	30.765	33.967	37.168	40.370	43.571
δ Crater's	11 12 59.568	62.564	65.561	68.557	71.553	74.549	77.546	80.542
τ Leonis	11 21 24.378	27.466	30.554	33.642	36.730	39.818	42.906	45.994
* λ Draconis . . .	11 23 50.285	53.924	57.561	61.198	64.834	68.468	72.102	75.735
υ Leonis	11 30 26.823	29.895	32.966	36.038	39.110	42.182	45.254	48.325
β Leonis	11 42 34.841	37.907	40.973	44.038	47.104	50.169	53.234	56.299
γ Ursæ Majoris . .	11 47 8.474	11.062	14.850	18.037	21.224	24.411	27.597	30.783
ο Virginis . . .	11 58 44.397	47.456	50.516	53.575	56.635	59.694	62.753	65.813
* 4 Draconis, (H.) . .	12 6 13.563	16.468	19.373	22.276	25.178	28.079	30.979	33.877
* β Chamæleontis . .	12 10 55.956	59.301	62.647	65.995	69.345	72.697	76.051	79.406
η Virginis . . .	12 13 24.548	27.616	30.685	33.753	36.822	39.891	42.959	46.028
α¹ Crucis . . .	12 19 32.494	35.761	39.029	42.897	45.566	48.836	52.106	55.377
β Corvi	12 27 43.156	46.294	49.433	52.572	55.711	58.850	61.989	65.129
* κ Draconis . . .	12 28 3.091	5.691	8.291	10.891	13.489	16.088	18.685	21.283
* 32 Camelop.(H.)(*foll.*)	12 48 13.074	13.432	13.792	14.155	14.519	14.886	15.255	15.626
12 Canum Venaticorum	12 50 5.052	7.869	10.685	13.502	16.318	19.135	21.951	24.767
θ Virginis . . .	13 2 22.582	25.683	28.784	31.885	34.986	38.088	41.189	44.290
α Virginis, (*Spica*) .	13 18 30.295	33.448	36.602	39.755	42.909	46.062	49.216	52.370
ζ Virginis . . .	13 28 13.390	16.443	19.496	22.549	25.602	28.655	31.708	34.762
η Ursæ Majoris . .	13 42 32.108	34.482	36.856	39.229	41.603	43.977	46.351	48.724
η Boötis	13 48 38.305	41.163	44.022	46.880	49.739	52.597	55.456	58.314
β Centauri	13 54 52.745	56.909	61.074	65.240	69.407	73.575	77.743	81 912
* α Draconis . . .	14 0 57.134	58.757	60.380	62.003	63.626	65.249	66.872	68.495

TABLE XXIII.—Mean Declinations of Standard Stars, 1873–1880.

1873.	1874.	1875.	1876.	1877.	1878.	1879.	1880.
° ′ ″	′ ″	′ ″	′ ″	′ ″	′ ″	′ ″	′ ″
+22 12 51.03	12 44.80	12 38.56	12 32.31	12 26.06	12 19.81	12 13.55	12 7.28
+68 43 15.22	43 8.47	43 1.72	42 54.96	42 48.19	42 41.42	42 34.63	42 27.84
+32 9 52.82	9 45.35	9 37.87	9 30.39	9 22.90	9 15.41	9 7.92	9 0.41
+ 5 32 54.79	32 45.86	32 36.92	32 27.98	32 19.03	32 10.08	32 1.13	31 52.17
+28 19 51.66	19 43.33	19 35.00	19 26.67	19 18.33	19 9.99	19 1.64	18 53.29
+27 5 32.96	5 24.02	5 15.07	5 6 12	4 57.16	4 48.20	4 39.23	4 30.26
+68 50 39.75	50 29.70	50 19.63	50 9.57	49 59.49	49 49.41	49 39.31	49 29.22
—23 56 21.58	56 31.70	56 41.82	56 51.94	57 2.07	57 12.20	57 22.33	57 32.47
+ 6 53 0.60	52 47.68	52 34 76	52 21.84	52 8.91	51 55.98	51 43.04	51 30.10
+48 32 18.03	32 4.18	31 50.33	31 36.48	31 22.61	31 8.75	30 54.86	30 41.00
+67 38 49 84	38 35.61	38 21.38	38 7.14	37 52.90	37 38.65	37 24.39	37 10.13
+11 10 41.23	10 27.01	10 12.79	9 58.57	9 44.35	9 30.12	9 15.89	9 1.65
—58 44 31.82	44 46.74	45 1.68	45 16.61	45 31.55	45 46 48	46 1.42	46 16.36
+81 53 4.49	52 49.19	52 33 89	52 18.58	52 3.26	51 47.93	51 32.59	51 17.25
— 8 6 32.68	6 48.08	7 3.48	7 18.88	7 34.28	7 49.60	8 5.10	8 20.51
+70 23 10.55	22 55.06	22 39.56	22 24.06	22 8.55	21 53.04	21 37.52	21 21.99
+52 15 16.61	15 0.45	14 44.29	14 28.12	14 11.95	13 55.78	13 39.60	13 23.42
+24 21 28.90	21 12.53	20 56.16	20 39.79	20 23.42	20 7.04	19 50.66	19 34.27
+26 36 14.65	35 57.90	35 41.15	35 24.40	35 7.64	34 50.88	34 34.12	34 17.36
+12 35 14.24	34 56.82	34 39.40	34 21.98	34 4.56	33 47.13	33 29.70	33 12.27
+65 44 25.55	44 7.77	43 49.99	43 32.21	43 14.43	42 56.64	42 38.85	42 21.06
+20 29 0.15	28 42 12	28 24.09	28 6.06	27 48.03	27 29.99	27 11.95	26 53.91
+76 21 56.73	21 38 37	21 20.01	21 1.64	20 43.27	20 24.90	20 6.53	19 48.15
+ 9 57 34.20	57 15.81	56 57.41	56 39.01	56 20.61	56 2.21	55 43.80	55 25.40
—59 0 59.01	1 17.77	1 36.53	1 55.29	2 14.05	2 32.81	2 51.58	3 10.34
+11 13 0.82	12 41.90	12 22 98	12 4.05	11 45.13	11 26.20	11 7.27	10 48.34
+62 26 9.35	25 49.99	25 30.63	25 11.27	24 51.91	24 32.54	24 13.18	23 53.81
+21 13 9.80	12 50.15	12 30.49	12 10.84	11 51.18	11 31.53	11 11.87	10 52.21
—14 5 28.84	5 48.28	6 7.72	6 27.16	6 46.60	7 6.04	7 25.48	7 44.93
+ 3 33 20.08	33 0.30	32 40.52	32 20.74	32 0.96	31 41.17	31 21.39	31 1.61
+69 61 52.77	61 32.90	61 13.04	60 53.17	60 33.30	60 13 44	59 53.57	59 33.70
— 0 7 21.20	7 41.03	8 0.87	8 20.71	8 40.54	9 0.38	9 20.22	9 40.06
+15 16 56.04	16 35.96	16 15.86	15 55.86	15 35.68	15 15.59	14 55.50	14 35.41
+54 24 3.03	23 43.01	23 22.99	23 2.97	22 42.95	22 22.93	22 2.90	21 42.88
+ 9 26 19.14	25 59.13	25 39.13	25 19 12	24 59.12	24 39.12	24 19.11	23 59.11
+78 19 17.78	18 57.72	18 37.67	18 17.62	17 57.56	17 37.51	17 17.45	16 57.40
—78 36 26.09	36 46.13	37 6.17	37 26.21	37 46.25	38 6.29	38 26.33	38 46.37
+ 0 2 21.69	2 1.66	1 41.62	1 21.59	1 1.56	0 41.53	0 21.50	0 1.47
—62 23 37.97	23 57.90	24 17.83	24 37.76	24 57.69	25 17 61	25 37.54	25 57.47
—22 41 37.19	41 57.14	42 17.08	42 37.03	42 56.97	43 16.91	43 36.85	43 56.80
+70 29 17.30	28 57.37	28 37.44	28 17.52	27 57.59	27 37.67	27 17.74	26 57.82
+84 6 10.27	5 50.64	5 31.01	5 11.37	4 51.74	4 32.11	4 12.48	3 52.85
+38 60 17.38	59 57.87	59 38 36	59 18.85	58 59.34	58 39.84	58 20.33	58 0.82
— 4 51 36.62	51 55.93	52 15.24	52 34.55	52 53.86	53 13.16	53 32.47	53 51.78
—10 29 50.79	30 9.69	30 28.60	30 47.50	31 6.40	31 25.31	31 44.21	32 3.10
+ 0 3 16.28	2 57.77	2 39.25	2 20.73	2 2.22	1 43.71	1 25.20	1 6.69
+49 56 52.16	56 34.05	56 15.95	55 57.86	55 39.76	55 21 66	55 3.57	54 45.48
+19 2 7.92	1 49.75	1 31.57	1 13.40	0 55.23	0 37.07	0 18.90	0 0.74
—59 45 32.59	45 50.24	46 7.89	46 25.54	46 43.18	47 0.82	47 18.47	47 36.11
+64 58 58.32	58 40.96	58 23.60	58 6.24	57 48.89	57 31.53	57 14.18	56 56.82

TABLE XXIII.—Mean Right Ascensions of Standard Stars, 1873—1880.

Star's name.	1873.	1874.	1875.	1876.	1877.	1878.	1879.	1880.
	h m s	s	s	s	s	s	s	s
α Bootis,(*Arcturus*)	14 9 52.145	54.879	57.614	60.348	63.082	65.817	68.551	71.286
θ Bootis	14 20 52.358	54.401	56.444	58.487	60.530	62.574	64.617	66 660
5 Ursæ Minoris	14 27 49.194	48.985	48.777	48.570	48.365	48.160	47.956	47.754
α² Centauri	14 31 0.360	4.394	8.430	12.466	16.503	20.540	24.579	28.617
ε Bootis	14 39 26.467	29.089	31.710	34.332	36.953	39.575	42.196	44.818
α² Libræ	14 43 51.320	54.627	57 935	61.242	64.550	67.857	71.165	74.473
* β Ursæ Minoris	14 51 5.891	5.643	5.397	5.152	4.908	4.664	4.422	4.181
β Bootis	14 57 9.728	11.988	14.248	16.508	18.768	21.028	23.288	25.548
θ Libræ	15 10 10.495	13.715	16.935	20.156	23.376	26.597	29.818	33.038
μ¹ Bootis	15 19 41.628	43.895	46.163	48.431	50.699	52.966	55.234	57.502
* γ² Ursæ Minoris	15 20 56.783	56.637	56.493	56.349	56.205	56.063	55.921	55.780
α Coronæ Borealis	15 29 18.675	21.214	23.754	26.293	28.833	31.372	33.912	36.451
α Serpentis	15 38 0.787	3.738	6.688	9.639	12.589	15.540	18.491	21.441
ε Serpentis	15 44 29.203	32.190	35.177	38.161	41.151	44.138	47.125	50.113
* ζ Ursæ Minoris	15 48 38.487	36.204	33.922	31.643	29.365	27.090	24.816	22.545
ε Coronæ Borealis	15 52 19.898	22.384	24.869	27.354	29.840	32.325	34.810	37.296
δ Scorpii	15 52 49.598	53.135	56.672	60.209	63.746	67.283	70.820	73.358
β¹ Scorpii	15 58 3.264	6.742	10.219	13.697	17.175	20.653	24 131	27.609
* Groombridge 2320	16 5 58.861	58.994	59.128	59.262	59.397	59.532	59.667	59.803
δ Ophiuchi	16 7 41.478	44.616	47.754	50.892	54.030	57.168	60.306	63.445
τ Herculis	16 15 55.317	57.115	58.913	60.711	62.509	64.307	66.106	67.904
α Scorpii,(*Antares*)	16 21 37.417	41.086	44.755	48.424	52.094	55.763	59.432	63.102
η Draconis	16 22 16.575	17.379	18.184	18.988	19.793	20.598	21.404	22.209
* A Draconis	16 28 14.524	14.383	14.242	14.101	13.961	13 821	13.082	13.543
ζ Ophiuchi	16 30 10.026	13.323	16.621	19.919	23.217	26.515	29.813	33.112
* αTrianguli Australis	16 35 14.405	20.090	26.975	33.262	39.550	45.839	52.128	58.418
η Herculis	16 38 32.553	34.608	36.662	38.717	40.771	42.826	44.880	46.935
κ Ophiuchi	16 51 39.408	42.243	45.078	47.912	50.747	53.582	56.417	59.252
d Herculis	16 56 54.968	57.117	59.326	61.535	63.744	65.953	68.162	70.372
* ε Ursæ Minoris	16 58 63.665	57.285	50.907	44.532	38.161	31.792	25.427	19.064
a¹ Herculis	17 8 51.414	54.147	56.881	59.614	62.347	65.081	67.814	70.548
44 Ophiuchi	17 18 36.919	40.578	44.237	47.896	51.555	55.214	58.873	62.533
β Draconis	17 27 33.776	35.127	36.478	37.829	39.180	40.531	41.883	43.234
α Ophiuchi	17 29 2.353	5.135	7.918	10.700	13.483	16.265	19.047	21.830
* ω Draconis	17 37 41.832	41.476	41.121	40.765	40.410	40.055	39.700	39.345
μ Herculis	17 41 29.322	31.667	34.012	36.357	38.702	41.047	43.392	45.737
* ψ Draconis,(*pr.*)	17 44 12.049	10.966	9.884	8.803	7.721	6.640	5.558	4 477
γ Draconis	17 53 39.583	40.976	42.370	43.764	45.153	46.551	47.945	49.339
γ² Sagittarii	17 57 39.019	42.872	46 724	50.577	54.429	58.282	62.131	65 987
μ¹ Sagittarii	18 6 10.098	13.684	17.271	20.857	24.443	28.029	31.616	35.202
* σ Octantis	18 11 46.173	155 139	264.004	372.758	481.388	589.883	698.230	806.417
* δ Ursæ Minoris	18 11 138.149	118.735	99.317	79.895	60.469	41.040	21.609	2.174
η Serpentis	18 14 44.247	47.346	50.445	53.545	56.644	59.744	62.843	65.943
1 Aquilæ, (3 H. Scuti)	18 28 17.697	20.962	24.226	27.490	30.755	34.019	37.284	40.548
α Lyræ,(*Vega*)	18 32 38.307	40.338	42.370	44.401	46.433	48.465	50.496	52.528
β Lyræ	18 45 23.455	25.669	27.883	30.097	32.312	34.526	36.740	38.955
σ Sagittarii	18 47 23.392	27.116	30.839	34.562	38.286	42.009	45.732	49.455
* 50 Draconis	18 50 27.419	25.520	23.620	21.720	19.819	17.917	16.015	14.113
ζ Aquilæ	18 59 34.295	37.050	39.805	42.560	45.314	48.069	51.824	54.579
d Sagittarii	19 10 12.179	15.693	19.206	22.719	26.232	29.745	33.258	36.771

* Circumpolar Stars.

TABLE XXIII.—Mean Declinations of Standard Stars, 1873—1880.

1873.	1874.	1875.	1876.	1877.	1878.	1879.	1880.
° ′ ″	′ ″	′ ″	′ ″	′ ″	′ ″	′ ″	′ ″
+19 50 41.86	50 22.98	50 4.10	49 45.22	49 26.34	49 7.46	48 48.59	48 29.72
+52 26 19.22	26 2.44	25 45.67	25 28.89	25 12.12	24 55.35	24 38.58	24 21.81
+76 15 36.49	15 20.44	15 4.40	14 48.35	14 32.31	14 16 26	14 0.21	13 44.17
−60 18 24.60	18 39.63	18 54.66	19 9.68	19 24.71	19 39.72	19 54.74	20 9.75
+27 36 39.46	36 24.10	36 8 74	35 53.38	35 38.02	35 22.67	35 7.32	34 51.97
−15 30 44.10	30 59.29	31 14.49	31 29.68	31 44.87	32 0.06	32 15.24	32 30.42
+74 40 26.84	40 12 09	39 57.34	39 42.59	39 27.84	39 13.09	38 58.34	38 43.59
+40 53 33.30	53 19 00	53 4.61	52 50.22	52 35.84	52 21.45	52 7.07	51 52.69
− 8 54 44.44	54 57.98	55 11.51	55 25.04	55 38.57	55 52.10	56 5.62	56 19.14
+37 49 25.90	49 13.09	49 0.29	48 47.48	48 34.68	48 21.88	48 9.08	47 56.28
+72 17 9.73	16 56.93	16 44.13	16 31.33	16 18.53	16 5.74	15 52.94	15 40.15
+27 8 37.35	8 25.02	8 12.69	8 0.37	7 48.05	7 35.73	7 23.42	7 11.10
+ 6 49 37.31	49 25.73	49 14.15	49 2.57	48 51.00	48 39.43	48 27.87	48 16.30
+ 4 51 42.48	51 31.38	51 20.28	51 9.20	50 58.11	50 47.03	50 35.95	50 24.87
+78 11 2.64	10 51.76	10 40.88	10 29.99	10 19.11	10 8.22	9 57.32	9 46.43
+27 14 50.00	14 39.97	14 29.34	14 18.71	14 8.08	13 57.46	13 46.84	13 36.23
−22 15 27.56	15 38 12	15 48.68	15 59.23	16 9.78	16 20.32	16 30.86	16 41.40
−19 27 20.53	27 30.72	27 40.91	27 51.09	28 1.27	28 11.44	28 21.61	28 31.77
+68 8 41.45	8 31.95	8 22.45	8 12.95	8 3.45	7 53.95	7 44.45	7 34.95
− 3 21 54.44	22 4.00	22 13.56	22 23.12	22 32.67	22 42.22	22 51.76	23 1.30
+46 37 0.67	36 51.90	36 43.14	36 34.37	36 25.61	36 16.85	36 8.09	35 59.33
−26 8 51.80	9 0.17	9 8.54	9 16.90	9 25.25	9 33.60	9 41.94	9 50.28
+61 48 7.55	47 59.33	47 51.10	47 42.88	47 34.66	47 26.44	47 18.22	47 10.00
+69 2 34.24	2 26.46	2 18.68	2 10.89	2 3.11	1 55.33	1 47.55	1 39.76
−10 18 26.69	18 34.30	18 41.91	18 49.51	18 57.11	19 4.71	19 12.30	19 19.88
−08 47 26.09	47 33.42	47 40.74	47 48.05	47 55.35	48 2.64	48 9.92	48 17.19
+39 9 55.43	9 48.39	9 41.35	9 34.31	9 27.28	9 20.25	9 13.22	9 6.20
+ 9 34 28.62	34 22.75	34 16.89	34 11.03	34 5.17	33 59.32	33 53.47	33 47.63
+33 45 14.08	45 8.66	45 3.24	44 57.83	44 52.42	44 47 02	44 41.62	44 36.22
+82 14 33.32	14 28.05	14 22.77	14 17.47	14 12.18	14 6.87	14 1.55	13 56.22
+14 32 13.60	32 9.21	32 4.82	32 0.44	31 56.07	31 51.69	31 47.32	31 42.96
−24 3 19.45	3 23.13	3 26.81	3 30.49	3 34.16	3 37.82	3 41.48	3 45.13
+52 23 45.99	23 43.15	23 40.32	23 37.50	23 34.67	23 31.85	23 29.02	23 26.20
+12 39 16.36	39 13.45	39 10.54	39 7.64	39 4.74	39 1.84	38 58.95	38 56.06
+68 48 57 27	48 55.61	48 53.95	48 52.29	48 50.64	48 48.98	48 47.32	48 45.66
+27 47 49.35	47 46.01	47 43.67	47 41.34	47 39.01	47 36.68	47 34.36	47 32.04
+72 12 38.09	12 36.43	12 34.80	12 33.16	12 31.51	12 29.86	12 28.21	12 26.56
+51 30 16 62	30 16.03	30 15.44	30 14.85	30 14.27	30 13.68	30 13.10	30 12.52
−30 25 22.87	25 23.29	25 23.71	25 24.11	25 24.52	25 24.92	25 25.32	25 25.71
−21 5 22.08	5 21.53	5 20.98	5 20.43	5 19.87	5 19.30	5 18.73	5 18.15
−89 16 40.49	16 39.38	16 38.12	16 36 69	16 35.10	16 33.36	16 31.47	16 29.41
+86 36 25.05	36 26.24	36 27.41	36 28.55	36 29.65	36 30.73	36 31.79	36 32.81
− 2 55 45.82	55 45.20	55 44.58	55 43.95	55 43.32	55 42 68	55 42.04	55 41.39
− 8 19 49.61	19 47.45	19 45.28	19 43.11	19 40.93	19 38.75	19 36.56	19 34.37
+38 40 0.38	40 3.51	40 6.64	40 9.78	40 12.92	40 16.07	40 19.21	40 22.36
+33 12 59.87	13 3.81	13 7.75	13 11.69	13 15.63	13 19.58	13 23.53	19 27.49
−26 27 5.99	27 1 93	26 57.87	26 53.80	26 49.73	26 45.65	26 41.57	26 37.48
+75 16 57.62	17 2.05	17 6.49	17 10.92	17 15.35	17 19.77	17 24.19	17 28.61
+13 40 35 99	40 41.06	40 46.14	40 51.21	40 56.30	41 1.39	41 6.47	41 11.57
−19 10 32.78	10 26.69	10 20.60	10 14.50	10 8.39	10 2.28	9 56.17	9 50.06

TABLE XXIII.—Mean Right Ascensions of Standard Stars, 1873—1880.

Star's name.	1873.	1874.	1875.	1876.	1877.	1878.	1879.	1880.
	h m s	s	s	s	s	s	s	s
" δ Draconis	19 12 31.207	31 240	31.273	31.305	31.338	31.370	31.402	31.434
* τ Draconis	19 17 58.931	57.824	56.715	55.607	54.497	53.387	52.277	51.165
δ Aquilæ	19 19 5.633	8.658	11.682	14.706	17.731	20.755	23.779	26.804
κ Aquilæ	19 30 3.463	6.693	9.923	13.153	16.383	19.613	22.843	26.073
γ Aquilæ	19 40 13.291	16.144	18.997	21.850	24.703	27.556	30.408	33.261
a Aquilæ,(Altair)	19 44 35.172	38.100	41.029	43.957	46.885	49.813	52.741	55.669
* ε Draconis	19 48 35.443	35.271	35.098	34.925	34.751	34.577	34.403	34.228
β Aquilæ	19 49 4.456	7.403	10.350	13.297	16.244	19.191	22.138	25.085
* λ Ursæ Minoris	19 44 438.451	378.244	317.739	256.936	195.836	134.440	72.747	10.758
τ Aquilæ	19 57 56.133	59.066	62.000	64.933	67.866	70.800	73.733	76.666
a² Capricorni	20 11 0.369	3.702	7.035	10.368	13.701	17.033	20.366	23.699
* κ Cephei	20 12 67.429	65.532	63.633	61.733	59.831	57.928	56.023	54.116
a Pavonis	20 15 35.569	40.363	45.156	49.948	54.740	59.531	64.322	69.113
π Capricorni	20 20 2.982	6.423	9.864	13.305	16.746	20.187	23.627	27.068
ε Delphini	20 27 8.689	11.555	14.421	17.287	20.153	23.019	25.885	28.750
' Groombridge 3241	20 30 32.309	32.099	31.889	31.679	31.468	31.256	31.043	30.830
a Cygni	20 37 6.148	8.192	10.236	12.280	14.324	16.368	18.412	20.456
μ Aquarii	20 45 48.096	51.336	54.576	57.816	61.056	64.296	67.535	70.775
ν Cygui	20 52 26.314	28.548	30.782	33.016	35.250	37.484	39.718	41.952
* 12 Year Cat. 1879	20 52 76.564	74.063	71.561	69.056	66.547	64.035	61.520	59.002
61 Cygni (pr.)	21 1 12.359	15.046	17.733	20.421	23.109	25.797	28.485	31.173
ζ Cygni	21 7 31.877	34.428	36.978	39.528	42.079	44.629	47.180	49.730
a Cephei	21 15 32.828	34.265	35.703	37.140	38.577	40.014	41.451	42.888
1 Pegasi	21 16 12.861	15.635	18.409	21.183	23.958	26.732	29.506	32.280
β Aquarii	21 24 52.326	55.490	58.654	61.818	64.982	68.146	71.309	74.473
* β Cephei	21 27 0.760	1.559	2.358	3.157	3.956	4.754	5.552	6 349
ξ Aquarii	21 30 59.361	62.560	65.758	68.956	72.154	75.352	78.550	81.747
ε Pegasi	21 37 56.924	59.871	62.819	65.767	68.715	71.663	74.611	77.559
*11 Cephei	21 40 3.269	4.175	5.081	5.987	6.892	7.797	8.702	9.606
μ Capricorni	21 46 22.215	25.494	28.773	32.052	35.331	38.610	41.888	45.167
*79 Draconis	21 51 17.177	17.914	18.650	19.386	20.121	20.856	21.590	22.324
a Aquarii	21 59 15.613	18.696	21.780	24.864	27.947	31.031	34.114	37.198
a Gruis	22 0 13.186	16.999	20.812	24.624	28.436	32.247	36.058	39.868
θ Aquarii	22 10 7 850	11.020	14.191	17.361	20.531	23.701	26.871	30.041
π Aquarii	22 18 47.440	50.505	53.570	56.635	59.700	62.766	65.831	68.896
η Aquarii	22 28 49.770	52.854	55.937	59.020	62.103	65.186	68.269	71.352
*226 Cephei,(B.).	22 30 2.177	3.259	4.342	5.424	6.506	7.587	8.668	9.749
ζ Pegasi	22 35 7.637	10.625	13.614	16.602	19.591	22.579	25.568	28.557
* ι Cephei	22 43 9.761	11.879	13.997	16.116	18.235	20.354	22.473	24.593
λ Aquarii	22 45 59.215	62.346	65.477	68.609	71.740	74.871	78.002	81.133
a Pis Aus.(Fomalhaut)	22 50 37.719	41.048	44.377	47.706	51.034	54.362	57.690	61.017
a Pegasi,(Markab)	22 58 26.134	29.119	32.103	35.088	38.073	41.057	44.042	47.027
* o Cephei	23 13 25.174	27.612	30.049	32.488	34.926	37.365	39.805	42.245
θ Piscium	23 21 31.539	34.580	37.621	40.662	43.703	46.744	49.785	52.826
ι Piscium	23 33 25.158	28.243	31.328	34.413	37.497	40.582	43.667	46.752
* γ Cephei	23 34 9.003	11.407	13.811	16.217	18.622	21.029	23.436	25.844
* Groombridge 4163	23 48 40.624	43.475	46.327	49.179	52.033	54.887	57.742	60.599
ω Piscium	23 52 47.440	50.518	53.596	56.675	59.753	62.831	65.910	68.988

' Circumpolar Stars.

TABLE XXIII.—Mean Declinations of Standard Stars, 1873—1880.

1873.	1874.	1875.	1876.	1877.	1878.	1879.	1880.
+67 26 16.75	26 23.06	26 29.37	26 35.68	26 41.99	26 48.30	26 54.60	27 0.91
+73 7 7.79	7 14.58	7 21.36	7 28.15	7 34.94	7 41.72	7 48.51	7 55.29
+ 2 51 49.20	51 56.08	52 2.96	52 9.85	52 16.74	52 23.64	52 30.54	52 37.45
− 7 18 26.57	18 18.86	18 11.16	18 3.45	17 55.73	17 48.01	17 40.29	17 32.56
+10 18 20.04	18 28.55	18 37.05	18 45.56	18 54.07	19 2.59	19 11.11	19 19.63
+ 8 32 5.02	32 14.24	32 23.46	32 32.69	32 41.93	32 51.16	33 0.40	33 9.64
+69 56 38.68	56 47.83	56 56.98	57 6.12	57 15.27	57 24.41	57 33.56	57 42.71
+ 6 5 29.05	5 37.77	5 46.49	5 55.22	6 3.95	6 12.68	6 21.42	6 30.16
+88 55 32.34	55 41.66	55 50.90	56 0.07	56 9.15	56 18.16	56 27.08	56 35.92
+ 6 55 17.11	55 27.00	55 36.90	55 46.80	55 56.70	56 6.61	56 16.52	56 26.43
−12 56 11.45	56 0.58	55 49.71	55 38.84	55 27.96	55 17.08	55 6.20	54 55.31
+77 19 39.15	19 50.15	20 1.15	20 12.15	20 23.14	20 34.14	20 45.13	20 56.12
−57 8 20.16	8 9.00	7 57.84	7 46.67	7 35.50	7 24.32	7 13.13	7 1.94
−18 37 33.39	37 21.91	37 10.43	36 58.94	36 47.45	36 35.96	36 24.46	36 12.96
+10 52 23.62	52 35.61	52 47.60	52 59.60	53 11.60	53 23.61	53 35.61	53 47.62
+72 6 4.87	6 17.10	6 29.32	6 41.54	6 53.77	7 5.99	7 18.21	7 30.43
+44 49 38.79	49 51.48	50 4.18	50 16.87	50 29.57	50 42.28	50 54.98	51 7.69
− 9 27 28.00	27 15.35	27 2.08	26 48.82	26 35.55	26 22.28	26 9.01	25 55.73
+40 40 46.39	41 0.11	41 13.83	41 27.55	41 41.28	41 55.01	42 8.74	42 22.47
+80 4 23.10	4 41.81	4 55.52	5 9.22	5 22.92	5 36.62	5 50.31	6 4.00
+38 7 34.26	7 51.76	8 9.26	8 26.77	8 44.28	9 1.80	9 19.31	9 36.84
+29 42 25.82	42 40.40	42 54.99	43 9.58	43 24.17	43 38.76	43 53.36	44 7.96
+62 2 51.32	3 6.43	3 21.55	3 36.66	3 51.78	4 6.89	4 22.01	4 37.13
+19 15 45.51	16 0.75	16 15.99	16 31.23	16 46.47	17 1.72	17 16.97	17 32.22
− 6 7 41.97	7 26.33	7 10.69	6 55.04	6 39.39	6 23.73	6 8.08	5 52.42
+70 0 11.20	0 26.92	0 42.63	0 58.34	1 14.06	1 29.77	1 45.49	2 1.20
− 8 25 20.37	25 4.42	24 48.47	24 32.52	24 16.56	24 0.60	23 44.64	23 28.69
+ 9 17 38.36	17 54.70	18 11.03	18 27.37	18 43.71	19 0.06	19 16.40	19 32.75
+70 43 36.03	43 52.54	44 9.04	44 25.55	44 42.05	44 58.56	45 15.06	45 31.57
−14 8 52.68	8 35.91	8 19.13	8 2.35	7 45.57	7 28.79	7 12.00	6 55.21
+73 6 5.29	6 22.25	6 39.22	6 56.18	7 13.15	7 30.12	7 47.09	8 4.05
− 0 56 8.66	55 51.33	55 33.99	55 16.66	54 59.32	54 41.98	54 24.63	54 7.29
−47 34 28.39	34 11.20	33 54.00	33 36.80	33 19.60	33 2.39	33 45.18	33 27.96
− 8 24 52.63	24 34.85	24 17.06	23 59.28	23 41.49	23 23.69	23 5.90	22 48.10
+ 0 44 1.84	44 19.97	44 38.11	44 56.24	45 14.38	45 32.52	45 50.67	46 8.81
− 0 46 16.40	45 57.96	45 39.52	45 21.07	45 2.63	44 44.18	44 25.73	44 7.29
+75 34 18.86	34 37.38	34 55.90	35 14.42	35 32.94	35 51.46	36 9.98	36 28.50
+10 10 9.56	10 28.26	10 46.96	11 5.67	11 24.38	11 43.09	12 1.80	12 20.51
+65 31 57.62	32 16.47	32 35.33	32 54.18	33 13.04	33 31.90	33 50.75	34 9.61
− 8 15 16.26	14 57.19	14 38.11	14 19.04	13 59.96	13 40.89	13 21.81	13 2.73
−30 17 40.19	17 21.21	17 2.22	16 43.23	16 24.23	16 5.24	15 46.24	15 27.25
+14 31 21.67	31 40.98	32 0.30	32 19.62	32 38.93	32 58.25	33 17.58	33 36.90
+67 24 59.40	25 19.03	25 38.65	25 58.27	26 17.90	26 37.52	26 57.15	27 16.78
+ 5 40 55.18	41 14.92	41 34.67	41 54.42	42 14.17	42 33.92	42 53.67	43 13.42
+ 4 56 17.91	56 37.39	56 56.88	57 16.36	57 35.85	57 55.33	58 14.82	58 34.31
+76 55 25.00	55 45.07	56 5.15	56 25.22	56 45.30	57 5.38	57 25.45	57 45.53
+73 42 12.28	42 32.28	42 52.28	43 12.28	43 32.28	43 52.28	44 12.28	44 32.28
+ 6 9 37.45	9 57.40	10 17.34	10 37.28	10 57.22	11 17.17	11 37.11	11 57.05

TABLE XXIV.—* β Hydri.

R.A. 0 18.9. (h m)　　　　　Dec. — 77 59. (° ')

Upper transit at fictitious meridian.

Sidereal Day	Mean Day	$\Delta_\odot a$ 1870.	Var.in 10y.	Diff. for 10d.	$\Delta_\odot \delta$ 1870.	Var.in 10y.	Diff. for 10d.
0, Jan. 0	− 0.76	−0.578	+17	−932	−20.11	− 0	+ 74
10	+ 9.21	1.490	21	887	19.06	1	135
20	19.18	2.343	24	815	17.43	2	192
30	29.15	3.113	26	720	15.25	3	242
Feb. 9	8.13	3.778	28	605	12.61	4	286
19	18.10	4.322	28	478	9.56	4	323
Mar. 1	0.07	4.730	28	336	6.18	5	351
11	10.04	4.991	27	185	− 2.57	5	371
21	20.02	5.099	25	− 29	+ 1.21	5	382
31	29.99	5.049	22	+130	5.05	5	385
100, Apr. 10	8.96	4.839	18	289	8.88	5	380
20	18.93	4.473	14	444	12.62	5	367
30	28.91	3.954	9	592	16.18	5	346
May 10	8.88	3.293	+ 4	729	19.50	4	317
20	18.85	2.502	− 2	851	22.51	4	282
30	28.83	1.599	7	954	25.13	3	241
June 9	7.80	−0.603	13	1035	27.31	2	193
19	17.77	+0.462	18	1091	28.99	1	142
29	27.74	1.569	24	1118	30.14	− 1	88
July 9	7.72	2.688	28	1116	30.73	0	+ 30
200, 19	17.69	3.789	33	1083	30.74	+ 1	− 28
29	27.66	4.842	37	1017	30.18	2	84
Aug. 8	6.63	5.814	39	922	29.06	3	138
18	16.61	6.676	41	798	27.43	3	189
28	26.58	7.401	43	650	25.33	4	231
Sept. 7	5.55	7.967	43	481	22.85	4	265
17	15.53	8.356	42	296	20.08	5	291
27	25.50	8.557	40	+104	17.07	5	305
Oct. 7	5.47	8.564	39	− 89	14.00	5	307
17	15.44	8.380	34	277	10.97	5	297
300, 27	25.42	8.013	30	452	8.09	4	276
Nov. 6	4.39	7.482	26	607	5.49	4	242
16	14.36	6.808	21	737	3.28	3	199
26	24.33	6.017	16	837	1.54	3	147
Dec. 6	4.31	5.143	11	906'	+ 0.35	2	90
16	14.28	4.216	6	942	− 0.24	+ 1	− 28
26	24.25	3.269	− 1	946	− 0.21	0	+ 35
36	34.22	+2.334	+ 3	−918	+ 0.46	− 1	+ 97

Sidereal Day	$\Delta_\Omega a$	$\Delta_\Omega \delta$	$\Delta_\Omega a$	$\Delta_\Omega \delta$
	1865.		**1873.**	
0	−1.811	+3.51	+0.630	−5.57
100	2.031	2.94	0.894	5.18
200	2.233	2.34	1.151	4.74
300	2.416	1.72	1.397	4.27
400	2.578	1.08	1.631	3.76
	1866.		**1874.**	
0	−2.526	+1.30	+1.554	−3.94
100	2.673	0.66	1.779	3.41
200	2.797	+0.01	1.989	2.85
300	2.897	−0.64	2.181	2.27
400	2.971	1.29	2.356	1.68
	1867.		**1875.**	
0	−2.949	−1.07	+2.299	−1.88
100	3.007	1.71	2.461	1.28
200	3.038	2.33	2.602	0.66
300	3.042	2.93	2.721	−0.04
400	3.020	3.50	2.818	+0.58
	1868 B.		**1876 B.**	
0	−3.030	−3.31	+2.788	+0.37
100	2.991	3.87	2.870	0.98
200	2.925	4.39	2.928	1.59
300	2.834	4.87	2.962	2.19
400	2.719	5.30	2.971	2.77
	1869.		**1877.**	
0	−2.760	−5.16	+2.971	+2.58
100	2.629	5.57	2.964	3.14
200	2.476	5.93	2.933	3.68
300	2.301	6.23	2.878	4.19
400	2.107	6.48	2.798	4.66
	1870.		**1878.**	
0	−2.175	−6.40	+2.828	+4.51
100	1.969	6.61	2.733	4.96
200	1.747	6.77	2.616	5.37
300	1.510	6.86	2.476	5.74
400	1.261	6.90	2.310	6.06
	1871.		**1879.**	
0	−1.346	−6.89	+2.372	+5.96
100	1.090	6.80	2.197	6.24
200	0.826	6.83	2.006	6.48
300	0.555	6.71	1.797	6.66
400	0.281	6.53	1.572	6.79
	1872 B.		**1880 B.**	
0	−0.374	−6.60	+1.649	+6.76
100	−0.098	6.39	1.415	6.85
200	+0.178	6.12	1.163	6.88
300	0.451	5.81	0.911	6.85
400	+0.720	−5.44	+0.645	+6.77

* ☌ ☉,　　　 March 25.4.
* ☌ Mean Sun, March 27.0.
* ☍ Mean Sun, Sept. 25.6.

TABLE XXIV.—β Ceti.

R.A. 0ʰ 37ᵐ.1.   Dec. −18° 42'.

Upper transit at fictitious meridian.

Sidereal Day	Mean Day	Δ☉α 1870.	Var.in 10y.	Diff.for 10d.	Δ☉δ 1870.	Var.in 10y.	Diff.for 10d.
0, Jan. 0	− 0.75	+0.025	+ 3	−123	− 7.75	+ 1	− 60
10	+ 9.22	−0.098	3	123	8.22	1	35
20	19.19	0.221	3	120	8.45	+ 1	− 11
30	29.17	0.336	3	110	8.43	0	+ 16
Feb. 9	8.14	0.440	2	96	8.13	0	43
19	18.11	0.527	2	76	7.57	0	71
Mar. 1	0.08	0.590	+ 1	51	6.72	− 1	98
11	10.06	0.627	0	− 20	5.62	1	123
21	20.03	0.629	0	+ 17	4.27	1	148
31	30.00	0.592	0	55	2.67	2	172
100, Apr.10	8.97	0.519	0	95	− 0.83	2	193
20	18.95	0.401	− 1	139	+ 1.18	2	210
30	28.92	0.242	1	180	3.36	3	225
May 10	8.89	−0.042	2	219	5.65	3	234
20	18.86	+0.195	2	254	8.02	3	238
30	28.84	0.464	2	281	10.41	3	238
June 9	7.81	0.757	3	305	12.77	3	231
19	17.78	1.072	3	320	15.01	2	218
29	27.75	1.394	3	324	17.12	2	201
July 9	7.73	1.718	4	323	19.02	2	178
200, 19	17.70	2.037	4	312	20.67	2	150
29	27.67	2.339	3	293	22.01	1	118
Aug. 8	6.65	2.621	3	269	23.03	1	85
18	16.62	2.874	3	237	23.70	1	48
28	26.59	3.093	2	201	24.00	− 1	+ 13
Sept. 7	5.56	3.276	2	164	23.96	0	− 21
17	15.54	3.420	2	124	23.59	0	53
27	25.51	3.524	1	85	22.91	+ 1	81
Oct. 7	5.48	3.591	− 1	47	21.99	1	103
17	15.45	3.619	0	+ 11	20.87	1	121
300, 27	25.43	3.615	0	− 19	19.60	2	131
Nov. 6	4.40	3.583	+ 1	47	18.26	2	135
16	14.37	3.523	2	71	16.91	2	133
26	24.34	3.442	2	88	15.61	1	126
Dec. 6	4.32	3.346	2	103	14.41	1	113
16	14.29	3.235	2	115	13 36	1	95
26	24.26	3.117	2	122	12.51	1	74
36	+34.23	+2.992	+ 2	−125	+11.88	+ 1	− 51

Sidereal Day	ΔΩα	ΔΩδ	ΔΩα	ΔΩδ
	1865.		1873.	
0	+0.452	+2.88	−0.795	−5.16
100	0.361	2.27	0.729	4.71
200	0.267	1.64	0.656	4.23
300	0.170	1.00	0.579	3.71
400	0.072	0.35	0.499	3.16
	1866.		1874.	
0	+0.105	+0.57	−0.525	−3.35
100	+0.006	−0.08	0.441	2.78
200	−0.093	0.73	0.353	2.20
300	0.191	1.38	0.263	1.59
400	0.287	2.02	0.169	0.98
	1867.		1875.	
0	−0.255	−1.80	−0.201	−1.19
100	0.350	2.43	0.107	−0.57
200	0.442	3.03	−0.013	+0.06
300	0.530	3.61	+0.082	0.68
400	0.613	4.15	0.175	1.30
	1868 B.		1876 B.	
0	−0.585	−3.97	+0.144	+1.09
100	0.665	4.49	0.237	1.70
200	0.739	4.97	0.328	2.30
300	0.806	5.40	0.416	2.83
400	0.866	5.79	0.501	3.43
	1869.		1877.	
0	−0.846	−5.67	+0.472	+3.26
100	0.901	6.02	0.555	3.79
200	0.948	6.32	0.633	4.30
300	0.987	6.57	0.705	4.77
400	1.017	6.75	0.773	5.21
	1870.		1878.	
0	−1.008	−6.70	+0.750	+5.06
100	1.032	6.84	0.813	5.47
200	1.047	6.95	0.876	5.83
300	1.053	6.96	0.919	6.15
400	1.051	6.93	0.961	6.41
	1871.		1879.	
0	−1.053	−6.95	+0.948	+6.33
100	1.044	6.88	0.98	6.56
200	1.026	6.75	1.015	6.73
300	1.000	6.56	1.035	6.85
400	0.965	6.32	1.045	6.91
	1872 B.		1880 B.	
0	−0.978	−6.41	+1.042	+6.90
100	0.938	6.13	1.046	6.92
200	0.890	5.81	1.045	6.89
300	0.835	5.43	1.035	6.79
400	−0.773	−5.02	+1.012	+6.64

✻ ☌ ☉   March 30.4.
✻ ☌ Mean Sun,   March 31.6.

TABLE XXIV.—*21 Cassiopeæ.

R.A. 0^h 37^m.1.   Dec. +74° 16′.

Upper transit at fictitious meridian.

Sidereal Day.	Mean Day.	$\Delta_\odot a$ 1870.	Var.in 10y.	Diff.for 10d.	$\Delta_\odot \delta$ 1870.	Var.in 10y.	Diff for 10d.
0, Jan. 0	− 0.75	+0.218	+15	−693	+19.32	+ 1	+ 30
10	+ 9.22	−0.485	13	706	19.31	1	− 32
20	19.19	1.184	10	688	18.69	2	92
30	29.17	1.851	6	643	17.48	3	149
Feb. 9	8.14	2.461	+ 3	572	15.74	4	198
19	18.11	2.987	− 1	475	13.54	5	240
Mar. 1	0.08	3.404	4	356	10.98	5	271
11	10 06	3.693	7	220	8.16	6	291
21	20.03	3.840	10	− 72	5.20	6	299
31	30.00	3.836	13	+ 81	+ 2.22	6	293
100, Apr 10	8 97	3.678	14	234	− 0.65	5	278
20	18.95	3.370	16	381	3.30	5	252
30	28.92	2.921	16	516	5.65	4	216
May 10	8.89	2.344	16	634	7.60	4	172
20	18.86	1.660	15	732	9.08	3	124
30	28.84	0.887	14	808	10.05	2	71
June 9	7.81	−0.052	12	860	10.49	+ 1	− 16
19	17.78	+0.824	9	887	10.36	0	+ 40
29	27.75	1.715	6	890	9.70	− 1	94
July 9	7.73	2.597	− 3	872	8.50	2	145
200, 19	17.70	3.451	+ 1	832	6.80	3	193
29	27.67	4.255	4	773	4.65	4	237
Aug. 8	6.65	4.991	8	698	− 2.09	4	275
18	16.62	5.647	12	611	+ 0.83	5	307
28	26.59	6.209	15	512	4.03	6	333
Sept. 7	5.56	6.668	18	406	7.46	6	352
17	15.54	7.018	22	294	11.05	6	364
27	25.51	7.254	26	177	14.72	6	369
Oct. 7	5.48	7.372	28	+ 58	18.39	6	365
17	15.45	7.373	32	− 58	22.00	6	355
300, 27	25.43	7.257	33	173	25.46	6	336
Nov. 6	4.40	7 029	34	284	28.69	5	309
16	14.37	6.692	35	388	31.61	5	274
26	24.34	6.256	35	482	34.14	4	232
Dec. 6	4.32	5.732	35	565	36.21	3	182
16	14.29	5.132	34	631	37.77	2	127
26	24.26	4.476	32	678	38.74	1	68
36	34.23	+3.784	+30	−703	+39.12	− 0	+ 7

* ☌ ☉,   March 30.4.
* ☌ Mean Sun,   March 31 6.
* 8 Mean Sun,   Sept. 30.2.

Sidereal Day.	$\Delta_\Omega a$	$\Delta_\Omega \delta$	$\Delta_\Omega a$	$\Delta_\Omega \delta$
	1865.		**1873.**	
0	+2.535	+2.86	−2.169	−5.16
100	2.546	2.28	2.291	4.71
200	2.535	1.63	2.374	4.23
300	2.501	1.01	2.438	3.71
400	2.446	0.36	2.481	3.16
	1866.		**1874.**	
0	+2.467	+0.58	−2.469	−3.35
100	2.398	−0.08	2.498	2.79
200	2.308	0.73	2.507	2.20
300	2.197	1.38	2 493	1.60
400	2.067	2.01	2.462	0.98
	1867.		**1875.**	
0	+2.113	−1.80	−2.476	−1.19
100	1.970	2.42	2.430	−0.57
200	1.812	3.03	2.364	+0.06
300	1.637	3.60	2 279	0.68
400	1.448	4.15	2.174	1.30
	1868 B.		**1876 B.**	
0	+1.513	−3.97	−2.212	+1.09
100	1.316	4.49	2.096	1.70
200	1.107	4.97	1 962	2.30
300	0.889	5.40	1.813	2.88
400	•0.664	5.79	1.647	3.44
	1869.		**1877.**	
0	+0.740	−5.67	−1.705	+3.25
100	0.511	6.02	1.531	3.79
200	0.278	6.32	1.344	4.30
300	+0.044	6.56	1.145	4.77
400	−0.191	6.75	0.937	5.21
	1870.		**1878.**	
0	−0.111	−6 70	−1.009	+5.06
100	0.346	6.84	0.795	5.47
200	0.577	6.93	0.574	5.83
300	0.800	6.96	0.347	6.15
400	1.017	6.93	0.117	6.41
	1871.		**1879.**	
0	−0.944	−6.95	−0.195	+6.33
100	1.156	6.88	+0.036	6 56
200	1.356	6.75	0.268	6.73
300	1.545	6.56	0.498	6.85
400	1.720	6.32	0.724	6.91
	1872 B.		**1880 B.**	
0	−1.662	−6.41	+0.648	+6.90
100	1.828	6.13	0.871	6.92
200	1.978	5.81	1.087	6.89
300	2.111	5.43	1.295	6.79
400	−2.226	−5.01	+1.492	+6.64

TABLE XXIV.—ε Piscium.

R.A. 0h 56m.2.   Dec. +7° 11'.

Upper transit at fictitious meridian.

Sidereal Day	Mean Day	$\Delta_\odot a$ 1870.	Var. in 10y.	Diff. for 10d.	$\Delta_\odot \delta$ 1870.	Var. in 10y.	Diff. for 10d.
0, Jan. 0	− 0.74	+0.155	+ 3	−112	+ 1.24	+ 1	− 66
10	+ 9.23	+0.041	3	116	+ 0.56	2	70
20	19.21	−0.076	3	118	− 0.15	2	70
30	29.18	0.193	2	115	0.84	2	68
Feb. 9	8.15	0.303	2	104	1.50	1	63
19	18.12	0.399	2	87	2.09	1	55
Mar. 1	0.10	0.475	1	65	2.58	1	42
11	10.07	0.526	1	− 35	2.92	1	26
21	20.04	0.543	+ 1	0	3.08	1	− 7
31	30.02	0.525	0	+ 39	3.04	+ 1	+ 15
100, Apr. 10	8.90	0.465	− 1	81	2.77	0	40
20	18.96	0.363	1	123	2.24	0	66
30	28.93	0.219	1	166	1.45	− 1	92
May 10	8.91	−0.032	2	206	− 0.41	· 1	117
20	18.88	+0.192	2	241	+ 0.88	2	141
30	28 85	0.449	2	271	2.40	2	161
June 9	7.82	0.732	2	294	4.09	2	177
19	17.80	1.035	2	309	5.93	2	190
29	27.77	1.348	2	316	7.88	2	197
July 9	7.74	1.663	2	315	9.86	2	200
200, 19	17.71	1.975	2	306	11.85	2	197
29	27.69	2.273	2	289	13.78	2	187
Aug. 8	6.66	2.551	1	267	15.59	3	175
18	16.63	2.806	1	240	17.29	2	159
28	26.61	3.030	1	208	18.77	2	139
Sept. 7	5.58	3.222	1	175	20.06	2	119
17	15.55	3.379	− 1	140	21.14	2	95
27	25.52	3.502	0	105	21.96	2	71
Oct. 7	5.50	3.589	+ 1	71	22.57	1	50
17	15.47	3.645	1	40	22.96	1	29
300, 27	25.44	3.670	2	+ 11	23.15	− 1	+ 9
Nov. 6	4.41	3.667	2	− 17	23.14	0	− 9
16	14 39	3.638	3	40	22.97	0	24
26	24.36	3.588	3	60	22.67	0	37
Dec. 6	4.33	3.519	3	78	22.23	0	48
16	14.30	3.432	4	94	21.71	0	56
26	24.28	3.332	4	105	21.12	0	63
36	34.25	+3.223	+ 5	−113	+20.47	+ 1	− 68

✳ ☌ ⊙,   April 4.7.
✳ ☌ Mean Sun,   April 5.4.

Sidereal Day	$\Delta_\Omega a$	$\Delta_\Omega \delta$	$\Delta_\Omega a$	$\Delta_\Omega \delta$
	1865.		**1873.**	
0	+0.703	+2.20	−0.964	−4.69
100	0.624	1.56	0.918	4.19
200	0.539	0.91	0.864	3.66
300	0.450	+0.25	0.803	3.10
400	0.356	−0.41	0.736	2.51
	1866.		**1874.**	
0	+0.389	−0.19	−0.759	−2.71
100	0.292	0.85	0.688	2.11
200	0.193	1.50	0.611	1.50
300	+0.093	2.14	0.529	0.87
400	−0.008	2.77	0.443	0.24
	1867.		**1875.**	
0	+0.027	−2.56	−0.473	−0.45
100	−0.075	3.17	0.384	+0.18
200	0.175	3.74	0.293	0.81
300	0.274	4.29	0.199	1.44
400	0.370	4.80	0.103	2.05
	1868 B.		**1876 B.**	
0	−0.338	−4.63	−0.136	+1.84
100	0.432	5.11	−0.040	2.45
200	0.522	5.55	+0.057	3.03
300	0 607	5.93	0.153	3.58
400	0.687	6.26	0.248	4.11
	1869.		**1877.**	
0	−0.661	−6.16	+0.910	+3.94
100	0.737	6.46	0.309	4.45
200	0.806	6.69	0.401	4.92
300	0.869	6.87	0.489	5.35
400	0.923	6.99	0.573	5.74
	1870.		**1878.**	
0	−0.906	−6.96	+0.545	+5.61
100	0.955	7.04	0.626	5.97
200	0.936	7.07	0 702	6.27
300	1.028	7.02	0.773	6.53
400	1.052	6.92	0.838	6.73
	1871.		**1879.**	
0	−1.045	−6.96	+0.816	+6.67
100	1.062	6.82	0.876	6.84
200	1.070	6.62	0 929	6.95
300	1.070	6.37	0.974	7.00
400	1.060	6.06	1.012	6.99
	1872 B.		**1880 B.**	
0	−1.064	−6.17	+1.000	+7.00
100	1.048	5.83	1.031	6.95
200	1.024	5.44	1.055	6.85
300	0.991	5.00	1.069	6.68
400	−0.956	−4.53	+1.074	+6.47

TABLE XXIV.—* α Ursæ Minoris. †

R.A. 1 11.3 (h m).   Dec. + 88 37 (° ').

Upper transit at fictitious meridian.

Sidereal Day	Mean Day	Δ☉α 1870.	Var. in 10y.	Diff. for 10d.	Δ☉δ 1870.	Var. in 10y.	Diff. for 10d.
0, Jan. 0	− 0.73	+10.68	+123	−858	+20.07	− 5	+113
10	+ 9.24	+ 1.90	92	893	20.88	− 1	+ 48
20	19.22	− 7.06	58	893	21.03	+ 4	− 18
30	29.19	15.85	+ 22	860	20.52	9	83
Feb. 9	8.16	24.14	− 15	793	19.39	15	143
19	18.14	31.60	51	694	17.68	18	197
Mar. 1	0.11	37.94	85	570	15.47	22	243
11	10.08	42.92	115	423	12.86	24	277
21	20.05	46.36	140	263	9.96	26	300
31	30.03	48.16	159	− 93	6.89	27	311
100, Apr. 0	9.00	48.22	172	+ 78	3.78	27	309
20	18.97	46.61	170	243	+ 0.75	26	295
30	28.94	43.40	178	397	− 2.09	24	271
May 10	8.92	38.72	170	536	4.64	21	237
20	18.89	32.74	157	655	6.82	18	196
30	28.86	25.69	137	752	8.55	15	140
June 9	7.83	17.78	112	826	9.79	11	97
19	17.81	9.26	82	876	10.49	6	−42
29	27.78	− 0.34	49	903	10.63	+ 1	+13
July 9	7.75	+ 8.72	− 14	906	10.24	− 4	67
200, 19	17.73	17.71	+ 23	889	9.30	8	120
29	27.70	26.43	63	852	7.84	13	171
Aug. 8	6.67	34.68	104	796	5.89	18	218
18	16.64	42.29	141	724	3.50	22	260
28	26.62	49.11	177	637	− 0.71	26	298
Sept. 7	5.59	54.99	212	536	+ 2.43	29	329
17	15.56	59.79	244	425	5.84	31	353
27	25.53	63.45	273	302	9.47	33	371
Oct. 7	5.51	65.82	298	172	13.24	34	382
17	15.48	66.85	317	+ 35	17.08	35	384
300, 27	25.45	66.49	331	−107	20.89	34	377
Nov. 6	4.43	64.71	339	249	21.59	33	362
16	14.40	61.51	341	389	28.10	32	337
26	24.37	56.95	337	522	31.31	30	303
Dec. 6	4.34	51.12	326	642	34.14	26	261
16	14.32	44.16	309	745	36.50	22	209
26	24.29	36.28	286	826	38.31	18	153
36	34.26	+27.74	+259	−876	+39.55	−13	+ 96

Sidereal Day	ΔΩα	ΔΩδ	ΔΩα	ΔΩδ
	1865.		**1873.**	
0	+23.31	+1.76	−17.91	−4.28
100	24.07	1.04	19.48	3.74
200	24.62	+0.37	20.89	3.17
300	24.96	−0.30	22.12	2.57
400	25.07	0.97	23.16	1.95
	1866.		**1874.**	
0	+25.06	−0.74	−23.84	−2.16
100	25.03	1.41	23.76	1.53
200	24.78	2.06	24.49	0.89
300	24.31	2.70	25.02	−0.24
400	23.63	3.31	25.33	+0.40
	1867.		**1875.**	
0	+23.87	−3.11	−25.26	+0.18
100	23.06	3.71	25.43	0.83
200	22.03	4.27	25.40	1.47
300	20.82	4.79	25.15	2.09
400	19.41	5.27	24.70	2.70
	1868 B.		**1876 B.**	
0	+19.91	−5.11	−24.87	+2.50
100	18.39	5.56	24.2-	3.09
200	16.71	5.96	23.49	3.66
300	14.89	6.31	22.56	4.20
400	12.93	6.60	21.32	4.70
	1869.		**1877.**	
0	+13.61	−6.51	−21.74	+4.53
100	11.58	6.76	20.43	5.01
200	9.45	6.95	18.95	5.45
300	7.24	7.08	17.31	5.84
400	4.96	7.15	15.52	6.19
	1870.		**1878.**	
0	+ 5.73	−7.13	−16.14	+6.07
100	3.42	7.16	14.26	6.38
200	+ 1.09	7.12	12.25	6.64
300	− 1.25	7.02	10.12	6.84
400	3.58	6.87	7.91	6.99
	1871.		**1879.**	
0	− 2.79	−6.93	− 8.60	+6.94
100	5.10	6.73	6.32	7.05
200	7.36	6.48	4.06	7.10
300	9.56	6.17	− 1.65	7.09
400	11.68	5.81	+ 0.73	7.02
	1872 B.		**1880 B.**	
0	−10.98	−5.93	− 0.09	+7.05
100	13.03	5.54	+ 2.33	6.94
200	14.97	5.10	4.73	6.77
300	16.79	4.62	7.10	6.54
400	−18.46	−4.10	+ 9.43	+6.25

* ♂ ☉, April 8.8.
*·♂ Mean Sun, April 9.2.
* ☍ Mean Sun, Oct. 8.8.

† See pages 249, 251–253 for additional corrections.

TABLE XXIV.—0ᵗ Ceti.

R.A. 1ʰ 17ᵐ.5.   Dec. − 8° 51'.

Upper transit at fictitious meridian.

Sidereal Day	Mean Day	$\Delta_\odot a$ 1870.	Var. in 10y.	Diff. for 10d.	$\Delta_\odot \delta$ 1870.	Var. in 10y.	Diff. for 10d.
0, Jan. 0	− 0.72	+0.273	+ 3	−113	4.43	+ 1	− 79
10	+ 9.25	0.156	3	121	5.16	2	64
20	19.22	+0.032	3	125	5.70	2	46
30	29.19	−0.093	3	125	6.08	1	28
Feb. 9	8.17	0.215	3	117	6.25	1	− 7
19	18.14	0.324	2	103	6.22	+ 1	+ 15
Mar. 1	0.11	0.418	2	84	5.95	0	38
11	10.08	0.489	2	57	5.45	0	61
21	20.06	0.529	1	− 23	4.71	0	86
31	30.03	0.534	+ 1	+ 14	3.73	− 1	110
100, Apr. 10	9.00	0.500	0	55	2.52	1	133
20	18.97	0.424	− 1	97	1.07	1	156
30	28.95	0.306	2	140	+ 0.59	2	176
May 10	8.92	−0.144	2	182	2.44	2	193
20	18.89	+0.057	2	220	4.44	3	206
30	28.87	0.295	2	253	6.54	3	215
June 9	7.84	0.561	3	279	8.72	3	219
19	17.81	0.851	3	300	10.91	3	217
29	27.78	1.158	3	311	13.05	3	210
July 9	7.76	1.470	3	313	15.09	3	196
200, 19	17.73	1.781	3	310	16.97	2	178
29	27.70	2.087	2	298	18.65	2	156
Aug. 8	6.67	2.374	2	278	20.08	2	129
18	16.65	2.642	2	254	21.23	1	99
28	26.62	2.821	2	225	22.06	1	67
Sept. 7	5.59	3.091	2	193	22.58	1	36
17	15.57	3.267	1	158	22.79	1	+ 5
27	25.54	3.407	1	123	22.69	− 1	− 24
Oct. 7	5.51	3.514	− 1	90	22.32	0	50
17	15.48	3.587	0	57	21.70	0	72
300, 27	25.46	3.629	0	+ 26	20.90	0	88
Nov. 6	4.43	3.640	+ 1	− 3	19.95	0	100
16	14.40	3.623	2	30	18.91	0	107
26	24.37	3.581	2	52	17.83	+ 1	108
Dec. 6	4.35	3.519	3	72	16.77	1	105
16	14.32	3.438	3	91	15.74	+ 1	98
26	24.29	3.339	3	106	14.81	0	87
36	34.27	+3.228	+ 3	−116	+14.00	0	− 74

✱ ☌ ⊙,   April 10.5.
✱ ☌ Mean Sun,   April 10.8.

Sidereal Day	$\Delta_\Omega a$	$\Delta_\Omega \delta$	$\Delta_\Omega a$	$\Delta_\Omega \delta$
	1865.		**1873.**	
0	+0.546	+1.42	−0.852	−4.13
100	0.461	0.75	0.794	3.58
200	0.372	+0.08	0.730	3.00
300	0.280	−0.59	0.661	2.39
400	0.185	1.26	0.586	1.77
	1866.		**1874.**	
0	+0.217	−1.04	−0.612	−1.98
100	0.120	1.70	0.534	1.35
200	+0.023	2.35	0.451	0.71
300	−0.074	2.98	0.365	−0.06
400	0.171	3.58	0.276	+0.59
	1867.		**1875.**	
0	−0.139	−3.38	−0.307	+0.37
100	0.235	3.96	0.216	1.01
200	0.329	4.51	0.125	1.65
300	0.420	5.02	−0.032	2.27
400	0.507	5.48	+0.062	2.87
	1868 B.		**1876 B.**	
0	−0.478	−5.33	+0.030	+2.67
100	0.562	5.76	0.123	3.25
200	0.642	6.14	0.215	3.81
300	0.715	6.47	0.305	4.34
400	0.782	6.74	0.393	4.83
	1869.		**1877.**	
0	−0.760	−6.66	+0.365	+4.68
100	0.823	6.88	0.449	5.14
200	0.879	7.05	0.531	5.57
300	0.926	7.16	0.609	5.95
400	0.966	7.21	0.682	6.28
	1870.		**1878.**	
0	−0.953	−7.20	+0.659	+6.17
100	0.987	7.20	0.727	6.47
200	1.012	7.14	0.791	6.72
300	1.029	7.02	0.848	6.90
400	1.036	6.84	0.898	7.04
	1871.		**1879.**	
0	−1.035	−6.91	+0.892	+7.00
100	1.037	6.69	0.928	7.09
200	1.030	6.42	0.965	7.13
300	1.014	6.09	0.995	7.10
400	0.990	5.71	1.017	7.02
	1872 B.		**1880 B.**	
0	−0.999	−5.85	+1.011	+7.06
100	0.909	5.44	1.027	6.93
200	0.931	4.98	1.034	6.75
300	0.886	4.49	1.033	6.51
400	−0.833	−3.95	+1.023	+6.22

TABLE XXIV.—*38 Cassiopeæ.

R.A. 1^h 21^m.6.   Dec. + 69° 36′.

Upper transit at fictitious meridian.

Sidereal Day.	Mean Day	$\Delta_\odot a$ 1870.	Var. in 10 y.	Diff. for 10 d.	$\Delta_\odot \delta$ 1870.	Var. in 10 y.	Diff. for 10 d.	Sidereal Day.	$\Delta_\Omega a$	$\Delta_\Omega \delta$	$\Delta_\Omega a$	$\Delta_\Omega \delta$
0, Jan. 0	− 0.72	+0.920	+15	−480	+18.19	− 1	+ 77		**1865.**		**1873.**	
10	+ 9.25	+0.422	14	512	18.67	0	+ 19	0	+2.145	+1.28	−2.039	−4.03
20	19.22	−0.098	13	524	18.56	+ 1	− 40	100	2.112	+0.61	2.087	3.46
30	29.20	0.619	11	515	17.87	2	96	200	2.060	−0.07	2.117	2.87
Feb. 9	8.17	1.121	9	484	16.64	3	149	300	1.989	0.74	2.129	2.26
								400	1.901	1.41	2.124	1 64
19	18.14	1.579	6	430	14.92	4	194		**1866.**		**1874.**	
Mar. 1	0.11	1.974	4	355	12.79	5	231	0	+1.933	−1.19	−2.127	−1.84
11	10.09	2.284	+ 1	263	10.33	6	259	100	1.834	1.85	2.111	1.20
21	20.06	2.495	− 1	156	7.65	6	275	200	1.719	2.50	2.076	−0.56
31	30.03	2.593	4	− 40	4.87	6	280	300	1.589	3.13	2.025	+0.09
								400	1.444	3.73	1.956	0.74
100, Apr. 10	9.01	2.574	5	+ 81	+ 2.09	6	274		**1867.**		**1875.**	
20	18.98	2.431	7	202	− 0.57	5	256	0	+1.495	−3.53	−1.981	+0.53
30	28.95	2 171	8	318	3.01	5	230	100	1.342	4.10	1.903	1.17
May 10	8.92	1.793	9	425	5.14	4	195	200	1.178	4.65	1.808	1.81
20	18.90	1.325	10	519	6.89	4	153	300	1.003	5.15	1.690	2.42
								400	0.820	5.60	1.576	3.02
30	28 87	0.765	9	598	8.19	3	107		**1868 B.**		**1876 B.**	
June 9	7.84	−0.135	9	659	9.02	2	57	0	+0.883	−5.45	−1.619	+2.82
19	17 81	+0 547	8	701	9.33	+ 1	− 6	100	0.695	5.88	1.487	3.41
29	27.79	1.261	7	725	9.13	0	+ 46	200	0.502	6.25	1.343	3.96
July 9	7.76	1.990	5	730	8.42	− 2	96	300	0.304	6.56	1.188	4.48
								400	0.104	6.82	1.022	4.97
200, 19	17.73	2.715	3	718	7.22	3	144		**1869.**		**1877.**	
29	27.71	3.420	− 1	689	5.56	4	188	0	+0.172	−6.74	−1 079	+4.81
Aug. 8	6.68	4.089	+ 2	647	3.48	4	228	100	−0.029	6.96	0.908	5.27
18	16.65	4.709	4	593	−1.02	5	263	200	0.228	7.11	0.729	5.69
28	26.62	5.270	7	527	+1.76	6	292	300	0.426	7.21	0.544	6.06
								400	0.619	7.24	0.354	6.38
Sept. 7	5 60	5.761	10	454	4.80	7	316		**1870.**		**1878.**	
17	15.57	6.175	12	374	8.05	7	333	0	−0.554	−7.24	−0.418	+6.27
27	25.54	6.508	15	290	11.44	8	343	100	0.744	7.23	0.226	6.56
Oct. 7	5.51	6.753	18	202	14.89	8	347	200	0.926	7.15	−0.031	6.79
17	15.49	6.910	20	111	18.35	8	344	300	1.100	7.02	+0.165	6.97
								400	1.264	6.83	0.366	7.09
300, 27	25.46	6.975	23	+ 20	21.74	8	333		**1871.**		**1879.**	
Nov. 6	4.43	6.950	25	− 71	24.98	7	314	0	−1.210	−6.90	+0.294	+7.06
16	14.40	6.834	27	160	27.99	7	287	100	1 367	6.67	0.487	7.14
26	24.38	6.631	28	245	30.70	6	254	200	1.512	6.35	0.677	7.16
Dec. 6	4.35	6.347	29	324	33.04	6	212	300	1.644	6.04	0.862	7.12
								400	1.762	5.64	1.040	7.02
16	14.32	5.987	29	394	34.92	5	165		**1872 B.**		**1880 B.**	
26	24.29	5.563	29	452	36.31	4	112	0	−1.723	−5.80	+0.981	+7.06
36	34.27	+5.089	+28	−494	+37.15	− 2	+ 55	100	1.831	5.36	1.153	6.92
								200	1.923	4.89	1.317	6.73
								300	1.999	4.3−	1.469	6.47
								400	−2.057	−3.84	+1.610	+3.16

✳ ☌ ☉,   April 11.6.
✳ ☌ Mean Sun,   April 11.9.
✳ ☌ Mean Sun,   Oct. 11.5.

TABLE XXIV.—η Piscium.

R.A. 1h 24.5m.   Dec. +14° 40'.

Upper transit at fictitious meridian.

Sidereal Day	Mean Day	$\Delta_\odot a$ 1870.	Var. in 10y.	Diff. for 10d.	$\Delta_\odot \delta$ 1870.	Var. in 10y.	Diff. for 10d.
0, Jan. 0	− 0.72	+0.336	+ 3	−111	+ 3.70	+ 1	− 52
10	+ 9.25	0.219	4	122	3.14	2	62
20	19 23	+0.093	4	129	2.46	2	70
30	29.20	−0.038	4	131	1.74	2	75
Feb. 9	8.17	0.166	3	125	0.96	2	79
19	18.14	0.285	2	112	+ 0.16	3	78
Mar. 1	0.12	0.389	2	91	− 0.59	3	73
11	10.09	0.465	1	62	1.28	3	63
21	20.06	0.511	1	− 28	1.83	2	48
31	30.03	0.520	+ 1	+ 12	2.23	1	31
100, Apr. 10	9.01	0.487	0	55	2.44	+ 1	− 9
20	18.98	0.410	0	100	2.39	0	+ 17
30	28.95	0.239	− 1	144	2.09	0	43
May 10	8.93	−0.122	1	189	1.53	0	69
20	18.90	+0.087	2	228	− 0.70	− 1	96
30	28.87	0.332	2	262	+ 0.39	1	122
June 9	7.84	0.608	2	289	1.73	2	144
19	17.82	0.907	2	308	3.26	3	163
29	27.79	1.222	2	319	4.97	3	177
July 9	7.76	1.543	2	323	6.79	3	187
200, 19	17.73	1.865	3	318	8.69	3	193
29	27.71	2.176	3	305	10.62	3	192
Aug. 8	6.68	2.473	2	287	12.50	3	187
18	16.65	2.749	1	262	14.34	3	179
28	26.62	2.996	1	233	16.06	3	165
Sept. 7	5.60	3.215	− 1	203	17.63	3	149
17	15.57	3.402	0	170	19.03	3	132
27	25.54	3.555	0	137	20.26	3	112
Oct. 7	5.52	3.676	+ 1	104	21.27	2	91
17	15.49	3.764	1	71	22.03	2	71
300, 27	25.46	3.819	2	41	22.69	2	51
Nov. 6	4.43	3.846	2	+ 12	23.12	2	33
16	14.41	3.844	3	− 15	23.36	1	+ 15
26	24.38	3.817	4	39	23.43	1	− 1
Dec. 6	4.35	3.767	4	62	23.34	1	17
16	14.32	3.694	4	84	23.10	− 1	31
26	24.30	3.601	5	102	22.73	0	44
36	34.27	+3.492	+ 5	−115	+22.23	0	− 56

✶ ☌ ⊙,   April 12.4.
✶ ☌ Mean Sun, April 12.6.

Sidereal Day	$\Delta_\Omega a$	$\Delta_\Omega \delta$	$\Delta_\Omega a$	$\Delta_\Omega \delta$
	1865.		1873.	
0	+0.781	+1.16	−1.026	−3.94
100	0.704	+0.49	0.984	3.37
200	0.620	−0.19	0.934	2.78
300	0.531	0.87	0.876	2.16
400	0.437	1.54	0.812	1.52
	1866.		1874.	
0	+0.469	−1.32	−0.834	−1.74
100	0.372	1.98	0.765	1.10
200	0.272	2.62	0.690	−0.44
300	0.170	3.24	0.609	+0.21
400	0.066	3.84	0.523	0.86
	1867.		1875.	
0	+0.101	−3.64	−0.552	+0.64
100	−0.004	4.22	0.464	1.28
200	0.108	4.75	0.371	1.92
300	0.211	5.25	0.270	2.53
400	0.313	5.69	0.178	3.13
	1868 B.		1876 B.	
0	−0.279	−5.55	−0.212	+2.93
100	0.378	5.96	0.113	3.51
200	0.474	6.33	−0.013	4.06
300	0.566	6.63	+0.087	4.58
400	0.653	6.88	0.186	5.06
	1869.		1877.	
0	−0.624	−6.81	+0.152	+4.91
100	0.707	7.01	0.250	5.36
200	0.784	7.16	0.347	5.77
300	0.853	7.24	0.440	6.13
400	0.915	7.26	0.531	6.45
	1870.		1878.	
0	−0.895	−7.26	+0.501	+6.35
100	0.952	7.24	0.588	6.62
200	1.000	7.16	0.671	6.85
300	1.040	7.01	0.749	7.02
400	1.071	6.81	0.820	7.12
	1871.		1879.	
0	−1.061	−6.88	+0.797	+7.09
100	1.086	6.64	0.864	7.16
200	1.101	6.34	0.924	7.18
300	1.107	5.99	0.976	7.13
400	1.103	5.59	1.021	7.02
	1872 B.		1880 B.	
0	−1.106	−5.73	+1.007	+7.06
100	1.096	5.30	1.046	6.91
200	1.077	4.82	1.073	6.71
300	1.049	4.31	1.094	6.44
400	−1.013	−3.76	+1.109	+6.12

TABLE XXIV.—α Eridani.

R.A. 1h 32m.9.   Dec. — 57° 54'.

Upper transit at fictitious meridian.

Sidereal Day	Mean Day	$\Delta_\odot a$ 1870.	Var. in 10 y.	Diff. for 10 d.	$\Delta_\odot \delta$ 1870.	Var. in 10 y.	Diff. for 10 d.
0, Jan. 0	-- 0.71	+0.611	+ 4	—321	—17.51	+ 1	— 71
10	+ 9.26	+0.285	4	331	17.94	0	— 15
20	19.23	—0.048	4	333	17.80	0	+ 43
30	29.20	0.378	4	324	17.09	0	97
Feb. 9	8.18	0.692	5	304	15.86	— 1	150
19	18.15	0.983	5	275	14.11	2	199
Mar. 1	0.12	1.239	5	236	11.90	2	241
11	10.09	1.453	4	189	9.31	2	278
21	20.07	1.615	4	133	6.37	3	309
31	30.04	1.718	3	71	— 3.16	3	333
100, Apr. 10	9.01	1.756	2	— 5	+ 0.26	3	350
20	18.99	1.727	2	+ 64	3.81	4	359
30	28.96	1.627	1	136	7.41	4	361
May 10	8.93	1.456	+ 1	205	11.00	4	355
20	18.90	1.218	0	271	14.49	4	341
30	28.89	0.916	— 1	332	17.80	3	320
June 9	7.85	0.557	1	383	20.86	3	290
19	17.82	—0.153	2	426	23.58	2	254
29	27.79	+0.291	3	459	25.91	2	212
July 9	7.77	0.760	4	476	27.79	1	163
200, 19	17.74	1.239	5	481	29.15	1	110
29	27.71	1.718	5	475	29.97	— 1	+ 55
Aug. 8	6.69	2.184	6	454	30.24	0	— 2
18	16.66	2.622	6	421	29.92	+ 1	61
28	26.63	3.022	6	377	29.03	1	115
Sept. 7	5.60	3.372	6	323	27.63	2	165
17	15.58	3.666	6	262	25.75	2	210
27	25.55	3.894	5	195	23.45	2	247
Oct. 7	5.52	4.054	5	124	20.85	2	273
17	15.49	4.142	4	+ 52	18.02	2	291
300, 27	25.47	4.150	3	— 17	15.07	2	296
Nov. 6	4.44	4.109	2	83	12.15	2	298
16	14.41	3.994	1	144	9.35	2	270
26	24.38	3.823	— 1	197	6.79	2	241
Dec. 6	4.36	3.602	0	243	4.56	+ 1	202
16	14.33	3.339	0	281	2.77	0	156
26	24.30	3.044	+ 1	309	1.46	0	105
36	34.28	+2.725	+ 2	—326	+ 0.68	0	— 49

✳ ☌ ⊙,   April 14.7.
✳ ☌ Mean Sun,   April 14.7.

Sidereal Day	$\Delta_\Omega a$	$\Delta_\Omega \delta$	$\Delta_\Omega a$	$\Delta_\Omega \delta$
	1865.		**1873.**	
0	-0.270	+0.85	-0.230	-3.71
100	0 377	+0.17	0.123	3.12
200	0.481	-0.52	-0.016	2.51
300	0.581	1.20	+0.092	1.87
400	0.676	1.87	0.199	1.23
	1866.		**1874.**	
0	-0.644	-1.64	+0.163	-1.45
100	0.735	2.30	0.268	0.79
200	0.820	2.95	0.371	0.14
300	0.898	3.56	0.470	+0.52
400	0.967	4.15	0.566	1.18
	1867.		**1875.**	
0	-0.945	-3.95	+0.534	+0.96
100	1.008	4.52	0.627	1.60
200	1.064	5.04	0.714	2.24
300	1.111	5.51	0.795	2.85
400	1.147	5.94	0.870	3.44
	1868 B.		**1876 B.**	
0	-1.135	-5.81	+0.846	+3.24
100	1.165	6.20	0.916	3.81
200	1.184	6.54	0.978	4.35
300	1.193	6.82	1.032	4.86
400	1.192	7.04	1.078	5.32
	1869.		**1877.**	
0	-1.193	-6.98	+1.063	+5.17
100	1.185	7.16	1.103	5.61
200	1.167	7.27	1.134	6.00
300	1.138	7.33	1.156	6.34
400	1.100	7.32	1.168	6.63
	1870.		**1878.**	
0	-1.114	-7.33	+1.165	+6.54
100	1.069	7.28	1.171	6.80
200	1.016	7.17	1.167	6.99
300	0.953	6.99	1.154	7.14
400	0.883	6.76	1.131	7.22
	1871.		**1879.**	
0	-0.908	-6.84	+1.140	+7.20
100	0.833	6.57	1.110	7.24
200	0.751	6.24	1.072	7.22
300	0.662	5.86	1.024	7.14
400	0.569	5.43	0.968	7.01
	1872 B.		**1880 B.**	
0	-0.601	-5.58	+0.988	+7.06
100	0.504	5.13	0.926	6.88
200	0.404	4.63	0.856	6.65
300	0.300	4.09	0.778	6.35
400	-0.194	-3.52	+0.694	+6.00

TABLE XXIV.—σ Piscium.

R.A. 1h 38.5m.　　　　Dec. +8° 30'.

Upper transit at fictitious meridian.

Sidereal Day	Mean Day	Δ☉a 1870.	Var. in 10 y.	Diff. for 10 d.	Δ☉δ 1870.	Var. in 10 y.	Diff. for 10 d.
0, Jan. 0	− 0.71	+0.407	+ 3	−104	+ 1.49	+ 2	− 59
10	+ 9.26	0.295	4	118	0.88	2	63
20	19.24	0.172	4	126	+ 0.24	2	64
30	29.21	+0.044	3	129	− 0.40	2	63
Feb. 9	8.18	−0.084	3	127	1.01	2	59
19	18.15	0.207	2	117	1.57	2	53
Mar. 1	0.13	0.315	2	98	2.06	1	43
11	10.10	0.401	2	73	2.41	1	31
21	20.07	0.459	1	40	2.63	1	− 14
31	30.04	0.480	1	− 2	2.68	+ 1	+ 7
100, Apr 10	9.02	0.461	+ 1	+ 38	2.52	0	27
20	18.99	0.402	0	82	2.13	0	51
30	28.96	0.296	0	128	1.49	0	76
May 10	8.93	−0.146	− 1	171	0.61	0	100
20	18.91	+0.046	1	211	+ 0.50	0	123
30	28.88	0.275	2	246	1.85	− 1	144
June 9	7.85	0.536	2	275	3.37	1	161
19	17.83	0.823	2	297	5.06	2	175
29	27.80	1.127	2	311	6.86	2	184
July 9	7.77	1.442	2	316	8.73	3	188
200, 19	17.74	1.756	3	313	10.62	3	187
29	27.72	2.066	2	305	12.47	3	181
Aug. 8	6.69	2.363	2	288	14.24	3	171
18	16.66	2.640	2	266	15.88	3	157
28	26.63	2.894	1	240	17.36	3	139
Sept. 7	5.61	3.120	1	211	18.65	3	118
17	15.58	3.315	− 1	180	19.72	3	97
27	25.55	3.479	0	147	20.58	3	75
Oct. 7	5.53	3.610	0	115	21.21	2	52
17	15.50	3.710	+ 1	84	21.63	2	31
300, 27	25.47	3.779	2	54	21.84	2	+ 12
Nov. 6	4.44	3.819	2	+ 25	21.88	2	− 4
16	14.42	3.830	3	− 2	21.76	1	20
26	24.39	3.815	3	27	21.50	1	32
Dec. 6	4.36	3.776	3	51	21.13	1	42
16	14.33	3.713	4	74	20.66	− 1	50
26	24.31	3.629	4	94	20.13	0	57
36	34.28	+3.527	+ 5	−109	+19.53	0	− 62

✳ ♂ ☉,　　April 16.2.
✳ ♂ Mean Sun,　April 16.2.

Sidereal Day	Δ♃a	Δ♃δ	Δ♃a	Δ♃δ
	1865.		**1873.**	
0	+0.719	+0.64	−0.981	−3.55
100	0.639	−0.05	0.935	2.95
200	0.553	0.73	0.881	2.32
300	0.463	1.41	0.820	1.68
400	0.368	2.09	0.751	1.02
	1866.		**1874.**	
0	+0.400	−1.86	−0.775	−1.24
100	0.302	2.52	0.703	−0.59
200	0.203	3.16	0.626	+0.08
300	+0.102	3.77	0.543	0.74
400	0.000	4.35	0.456	1.40
	1867.		**1875.**	
0	+0.034	−4.16	−0.486	+1.18
100	−0.068	4.71	0.396	1.82
200	0.170	5.22	0.304	2.45
300	0.270	5.69	0.209	3.06
400	0.368	6.11	0.112	3.65
	1868 B.		**1876 R.**	
0	−0.335	−5.97	−0.145	+3.46
100	0.431	6.35	−0.047	4.02
200	0.523	6.6	+0.051	4.55
300	0.610	6.94	0.148	5.05
400	0.691	7.15	0.244	5.50
	1869.		**1877.**	
0	−0.665	−7.09	+0.212	+5.26
100	0.742	7.25	0.307	5.78
200	0.813	7.35	0.400	6.16
300	0.877	7.38	0.480	6.49
400	0.953	7.35	0.575	6.76
	1870.		**1878.**	
0	−0.915	−7.37	+0.546	+6.68
100	0.965	7.30	0.629	6.91
200	1.007	7.17	0.707	7.09
300	1.041	6.97	0.779	7.22
400	1.065	6.72	0.845	7.28
	1871.		**1879.**	
0	−1.058	−6.81	+0.823	+7.26
100	1.076	6.52	0.885	7.29
200	1.085	6.17	0.939	7.25
300	1.085	5.77	0.985	7.15
400	1.076	5.32	1.023	6.99
	1872 B.		**1880 B.**	
0	−1.080	−5.48	+1.012	+7.05
100	1.064	5.01	1.044	6.85
200	1.040	4.49	1.062	6.60
300	1.007	3.94	1.083	6.28
400	−0.966	−3.35	+1.089	+5.92

TABLE XXIV.—β Arietis.

R.A. 1h 47m.5.   Dec. + 20° 10'.

Upper transit at fictitious meridian.

Sidereal Day	Mean Day	$\Delta_\odot a$ 1870.	Var. in 10 y.	Diff. for 10 d.	$\Delta_\odot \delta$ 1870.	Var. in 10 y.	Diff. for 10 d.
0, Jan. 0	− 0.70	+0.489	+ 4	−110	+ 5.32	+ 1	− 33
10	+ 9.27	0.371	4	127	4.91	1	49
20	19.24	0.238	3	137	4.35	2	62
30	29.21	+0.099	3	142	3.67	2	74
Feb. 9	8.19	−0.043	3	142	2.88	2	83
19	18.16	0.181	3	131	2.02	2	88
Mar. 1	0.13	0.303	3	112	1.13	3	89
11	10.10	0.403	2	87	+0.26	3	84
21	20.08	0.475	+ 1	52	− 0.54	2	76
31	30.05	0.507	0	− 11	1.24	2	62
100, Apr. 10	9.02	0.496	0	+ 33	1.76	2	42
20	19.00	0.440	0	79	2.08	1	22
30	28.97	0.337	− 1	127	2.17	+ 1	+ 3
May 10	8.94	−0.186	1	173	1.98	0	31
20	18.91	+0.008	1	216	1.53	0	59
30	28.89	0.245	2	254	− 0.81	0	86
June 9	7.86	0.514	2	284	+ 0.18	− 1	111
19	17.83	0.811	2	307	1.41	2	134
29	27.80	1.126	2	322	2.85	2	154
July 9	7.78	1.453	2	329	4.47	2	168
200, 19	17.75	1.782	2	328	6.20	3	179
29	27.72	2.106	2	320	8.03	3	185
Aug. 8	6.70	2.419	2	304	9.89	3	186
18	16.67	2.711	2	282	11.74	4	183
28	26.64	2.981	1	257	13.54	4	176
Sept. 7	5.61	3.223	− 1	228	15.24	4	164
17	15.59	3.436	0	197	16.81	4	151
27	25.56	3.616	+ 1	164	18.25	4	136
Oct. 7	5.53	3.764	1	131	19.53	4	119
17	15.50	3.879	2	99	20.02	4	101
300, 27	25.48	3.962	2	68	21.54	3	83
Nov. 6	4.45	4.016	3	38	22.28	3	64
16	14.42	4.038	4	+ 8	22.83	3	46
26	24.39	4.032	4	− 20	23.21	3	29
Dec. 6	4.37	3.998	5	48	23.41	2	+ 11
16	14.31	3.937	5	73	23.44	2	− 7
26	24.31	3.853	5	96	23.29	1	23
36	34.29	+3.746	+ 5	−116	+22.99	− 1	39

✴ ☌ ☉,   April 18.6.
✴ ☌ Mean Sun,   April 18.4.

Sidereal Day	$\Delta_\Omega a$ 1865.	$\Delta_\Omega \delta$ 1865.	$\Delta_\Omega a$ 1873.	$\Delta_\Omega \delta$ 1873.
0	+0.843	+0.31	−1.080	−3.29
100	0.765	−0.39	1.040	2.67
200	0.681	1.08	0.992	2.03
300	0.591	1.76	0.935	1.37
400	0.495	2.43	0.671	0.70

Sidereal Day	$\Delta_\Omega a$ 1866.	$\Delta_\Omega \delta$ 1866.	$\Delta_\Omega a$ 1874.	$\Delta_\Omega \delta$ 1874.
0	+0.528	−2.21	−0.894	−0.93
100	0.429	2.87	0.825	−0.26
200	0.327	3.50	0.750	+0.42
300	0.222	4.10	0.668	1.08
400	0.115	4.67	0.582	1.74

Sidereal Day	$\Delta_\Omega a$ 1867.	$\Delta_\Omega \delta$ 1867.	$\Delta_\Omega a$ 1875.	$\Delta_\Omega \delta$ 1875.
0	+0.151	−4.48	−0.612	+1.52
100	+0.043	5.02	0.522	2.16
200	−0.065	5.52	0.429	2.79
300	0.173	5.96	0.330	3.40
400	0.279	6.36	0.230	3.97

Sidereal Day	$\Delta_\Omega a$ 1868 B.	$\Delta_\Omega \delta$ 1868 B.	$\Delta_\Omega a$ 1876 B.	$\Delta_\Omega \delta$ 1876 B.
0	−0.243	−6.23	−0.264	+3.78
100	0.348	6.59	0.163	4.34
200	0.449	6.89	−0.060	4.96
300	0.546	7.13	+0.044	5.33
400	0.638	7.30	0.147	5.77

Sidereal Day	$\Delta_\Omega a$ 1869.	$\Delta_\Omega \delta$ 1869.	$\Delta_\Omega a$ 1877.	$\Delta_\Omega \delta$ 1877.
0	−0.608	−7.25	+0.112	+5.64
100	0.696	7.39	0.215	6.04
200	0.778	7.45	0.316	6.40
300	0.854	7.46	0.414	6.70
400	0.921	7.40	0.510	6.95

Sidereal Day	$\Delta_\Omega a$ 1870.	$\Delta_\Omega \delta$ 1870.	$\Delta_\Omega a$ 1878.	$\Delta_\Omega \delta$ 1878.
0	−0.899	−7.43	+0.478	+6.87
100	0.962	7.32	0.570	7.08
200	1.015	7.16	0.659	7.24
300	1.060	6.93	0.741	7.33
400	1.096	6.64	0.819	7.36

Sidereal Day	$\Delta_\Omega a$ 1871.	$\Delta_\Omega \delta$ 1871.	$\Delta_\Omega a$ 1879.	$\Delta_\Omega \delta$ 1879.
0	−1.085	−6.75	+0.793	+7.36
100	1.115	6.42	0.866	7.35
200	1.135	6.05	0.932	7.28
300	1.145	5.62	0.990	7.15
400	1.140	5.15	1.039	6.96

Sidereal Day	$\Delta_\Omega a$ 1872 B.	$\Delta_\Omega \delta$ 1872 B.	$\Delta_\Omega a$ 1880 B.	$\Delta_\Omega \delta$ 1880 B.
0	−1.147	−5.31	+1.024	+7.03
100	1.141	4.81	1.068	6.80
200	1.125	4.27	1.103	−6.52
300	1.101	3.69	1.129	6.17
400	−1.067	−3.09	+1.146	+5.77

TABLE XXIV.—'50 Cassiopeæ.

R.A. 1 52.4. (h m)   Dec. + 71 47. (° ')

Upper transit at fictitious meridian.

Sidereal Day	Mean Day	$\Delta_\odot a$ 1870.	Var. in 10 y.	Diff. for 10 d.	$\Delta_\odot \delta$ 1870.	Var. in 10 y.	Diff. for 10 d.
0, Jan. 0	− 0.70	+1.584	+19	−507	+17.71	− 2	+121
10	+ 9.27	1.049	19	561	18.64	− 1	64
20	19.24	+0.471	17	592	18.98	+ 1	+ 5
30	29.22	−0.128	16	600	18 75	2	− 53
Feb. 9	8.19	0.722	14	582	17.93	3	109
19	18.16	1.282	11	536	16.59	4	160
Mar. 1	0.14	1.786	8	467	14.77	5	203
11	10.11	2.209	5	375	12.55	5	238
21	20.08	2.530	+ 2	264	10.04	6	262
31	30.05	2.733	− 1	140	7.34	6	276
100, Apr. 10	9.03	2.807	4	− 7	4.56	6	278
20	19.00	2.745	6	+130	+ 1.81	6	270
30	28.97	2.548	8	263	− 0.80	6	251
May 10	8.94	2.221	10	389	3.18	5	223
20	18.92	1.774	11	503	5.24	5	188
30	28.89	1.219	11	602	6.91	4	146
June 9	7.86	−0.575	11	684	8.15	3	100
19	17.84	+0.141	10	746	8.90	+ 1	51
29	27.81	0.909	9	787	9.17	0	− 1
July 9	7.78	1.709	8	809	8.93	− 1	+ 49
200, 19	17.75	2.520	6	812	8.19	2	98
29	27.73	3.324	− 3	795	6.98	4	144
Aug. 8	6.70	4.104	0	763	5.32	5	187
18	16.67	4.845	+ 3	716	3.25	6	226
28	26.64	5.531	6	656	− 0.81	7	260
Sept. 7	5.62	6.152	10	585	+ 1.94	8	289
17	15.59	6.698	13	505	4.95	9	312
27	15 56	7.160	17	418	8.16	9	329
Oct. 7	5.53	7.532	21	324	11.52	10	340
17	15.51	7.806	24	225	14.94	10	343
300, 27	25.48	7.980	27	122	18.36	10	340
Nov. 6	4.45	8.050	30	+ 17	21.71	10	328
16	14.43	8.014	33	− 89	24.89	9	309
26	24.40	7.873	35	192	27.85	9	281
Dec. 6	4.37	7.630	36	292	30.50	8	246
16	14.34	7.291	37	384	32.75	7	203
26	24.32	6.866	38	465	34.54	6	154
36	34.29	+6.367	+38	−529	+35.81	− 5	+100

* ♂ ⊙, April 20.1.
* ♂ Mean Sun, April 19.8.
* ☍ Mean Sun, Oct. 19.4.

Sidereal Day | $\Delta_\Omega a$ | $\Delta_\Omega \delta$ | $\Delta_\Omega a$ | $\Delta_\Omega \delta$

Sidereal Day	1865. $\Delta_\Omega a$	1865. $\Delta_\Omega \delta$	1873. $\Delta_\Omega a$	1873. $\Delta_\Omega \delta$
0	+2.362	+0.14	−2 284	−3.15
100	2.316	−0.56	2.328	2.52
200	2.250	1.26	2.353	1.87
300	2.164	1.94	2.358	1.20
400	2.059	2.61	2 343	0.53
	1866.		**1874.**	
0	+2.096	−2.39	−2.350	−0.75
100	1.979	3.05	2.323	−0 08
200	1.844	3.6?	2.276	+0.60
300	1.694	4.27	2.211	1.27
400	1.522	4.83	2.128	1.92
	1867..		**1875.**	
0	+1.585	−4.65	−2.158	+1.70
100	1.411	5.18	2.063	2.35
200	1.224	5.67	1 951	2.98
300	1.026	6.11	1 823	3.58
400	0.820	6.49	1.680	4.15
	1868 B.		**1876 B.**	
0	+0.890	−6.37	−1.730	+3.97
100	0.679	6.71	1.578	4.51
200	0.462	7.00	1.413	5.03
300	0.242	7.22	1.235	5.50
400	0.020	7.38	1.048	5.91
	1869.		**1877.**	
0	+0.095	−7.34	−1.112	+5.79
100	−0.127	7.45	0.919	6.18
200	0.347	7.51	0.718	6.52
300	0.564	7.50	0.510	6.82
400	0.776	7.42	0.298	7.05
	1870.		**1878.**	
0	−0.705	−7.45	−0.370	+6.98
100	0.912	7.33	−0.155	7.17
200	1.111	7.15	+0.061	7.31
300	1.299	6.90	0.277	7.39
400	1.476	6.60	0.492	7.41
	1871.		**1879.**	
0	−1.418	−6.71	+0.420	+7.41
100	1.586	6.37	0.632	7.38
200	1.740	5.98	0.840	7.30
300	1.880	5.53	1.041	7.15
400	2.003	5.05	1.234	6.94
	1872 B.		**1880 B.**	
0	−1.964	−5.22	+1.170	+7.02
100	2.075	4.70	1.357	6.77
200	2.169	4.14	1.533	6.46
300	2.245	3.56	1.694	6.10
400	−2.302	−2.94	+1.845	+5.69

SPECIAL TABLES.

TABLE XXIV.—ξ¹ Ceti.

R.A. $2^{h}\,6.1^{m}$. Dec. $+\,8^{\circ}\,14'$.

Upper transit at fictitious meridian.

Sidereal Day	Mean Day	$\Delta_{\odot}\alpha$ 1870.	Var. in 10y.	Diff. for 10d.	$\Delta_{\odot}\delta$ 1870.	Var. in 10y.	Diff. for 10d.
0, Jan. 0	− 0.69	+0.561	+ 3	− 96	+ 1.22	+ 1	− 59
10	+ 9.28	0.457	3	114	0.62	1	60
20	19.25	0.335	3	128	+ 0.03	1	59
30	29.23	0.203	3	136	− 0.56	1	59
Feb. 9	8.20	+0.066	3	138	1.14	2	55
19	18.17	−0.070	3	132	1.65	2	48
Mar. 1	0.15	0.195	2	118	2.09	2	38
11	10.12	0.303	2	96	2.40	1	26
21	20.09	0.384	2	66	2.59	1	− 12
31	30.06	0.432	+ 1	− 30	2.63	+ 1	+ 6
100, Apr. 10	9.04	0.442	0	+ 11	2.47	0	27
20	19.01	0.408	0	55	2.08	0	49
30	28.98	0.329	− 1	102	1.49	− 1	71
May 10	8.95	0.205	1	146	− 0.66	1	94
20	18.93	−0.038	1	188	+ 0.39	1	117
30	28.90	+0.170	1	226	1.67	2	136
June 9	7.87	0.413	2	259	3.11	2	153
19	17.84	0.685	2	284	4.73	2	167
29	27.82	0.978	2	301	6.44	3	176
July 9	7.79	1.285	2	312	8.23	3	181
200, 19	17.76	1.599	3	314	10.05	3	180
29	27.74	1.910	3	308	11.82	3	173
Aug. 8	6.71	2 213	2	296	13.50	3	164
18	16.68	2.501	1	279	15.08	3	150
28	26.65	2.769	1	257	16.49	3	132
Sept. 7	5.63	3.014	1	232	17.71	3	112
17	15.60	3.232	1	203	18.73	3	90
27	25.57	3.419	− 1	173	19.51	3	67
Oct. 7	5.54	3.578	0	144	20 08	3	46
17	15.52	3.706	+ 1	112	20.43	3	25
300, 27	25.49	3.803	1	81	20.59	3	+ 7
Nov. 6	4.46	3.869	2	52	20.57	3	− 10
16	14.44	3 908	3	+ 24	20.40	3	24
26	24.41	3.917	3	− 5	20.10	2	36
Dec. 6	4.38	3.890	3	32	19.69	2	45
16	14.35	3.854	4	57	19.21	2	52
26	24.33	3.786	4	80	18.66	1	56
36	34.30	+3.694	+ 4	−102	+18.09	− 1	59

✳ ♂ ☉,　April 23.6.
✳ ♂ Mean Sun,　April 23.2.

Sidereal Day	$\Delta_{\Omega}\alpha$	$\Delta_{\Omega}\delta$	$\Delta_{\Omega}\alpha$	$\Delta_{\Omega}\delta$
	1865.		**1873.**	
0	+0.716	−0.39	−0.983	−2.74
100	0.635	1.09	0.935	2.08
200	0.549	1.79	0.880	1.40
300	0.458	2.48	0.818	0.72
400	0.362	3.14	0.749	0.03
	1866.		**1874.**	
0	+0.395	−2.92	−0.773	−0.26
100	0.297	3.57	0.701	+0.43
200	0.196	4.19	0.622	1.11
300	+0.094	4.77	0.539	1.78
400	−0.008	5.31	0.451	2.44
	1867.		**1875.**	
0	+0.026	−5.13	−0.481	+2.22
100	−0.077	5.64	0.391	2.86
200	0.179	6 10	0.298	3.48
300	0.280	6.50	0.202	4.07
400	0.378	6.85	0.105	4.63
	1868 B.		**1876 B.**	
0	−0.345	−6.74	−0.139	+4.44
100	0.441	7.05	−0.039	4.98
200	0.533	7.29	+0.059	5.46
300	0.620	7.48	0.157	5.91
400	0.701	7.50	0.253	6.31
	1869.		**1877.**	
0	−0.675	−7.56	+0.221	+6.19
100	0 752	7.64	0.316	6.55
200	0.823	7.64	0.409	6.86
300	0.886	7.58	0.499	7.11
400	0.942	7.45	0.585	7.31
	1870.		**1878.**	
0	−0.924	−7.50	+0.556	+7.25
100	0.974	7.33	0.639	7.40
200	1.016	7.10	0.717	7.50
300	1.048	6.81	0.789	7.53
400	1.072	6.46	0.854	7.50
	1871.		**1879.**	
0	−1.065	−6.59	+0.833	+7.52
100	1.083	6.20	0.894	7.45
200	1.091	5.76	0.948	7.31
300	1.090	5.28	0 994	7.12
400	1.085	4.75	1.031	6.86
	1872 B.		**1880 B.**	
0	−1.084	−4.93	+1.020	+6.96
100	1.065	4.38	1.052	6.66
200	1.043	3.79	1.075	6.31
300	1.009	3.17	1.089	5.91
400	−0.967	−2.52	+1.094	+5.45

TABLE XXIV.—ι Cassiopeæ.

R.A. 2h 18m.4.   Dec. + 66° 49'.

Upper transit at fictitious meridian.

Sidereal Day	Mean Day	Δ⊙a 1870	Var. in 10y.	Diff. for 10d.	Δ⊙δ 1870	Var. in 10y.	Diff. for 10d.
0, Jan. 0	− 0.68	+1.616	+14	−346	+16.13	− 2	+134
10	+ 9.29	1.241	14	401	17.22	− 1	83
20	19.26	0.820	14	440	17.79	0	+ 29
30	29.24	+0.368	13	460	17.80	+ 1	− 26
Feb. 9	8.21	−0.093	12	460	17.27	2	80
19	18 18	0.544	10	438	16.22	3	128
Mar. 1	0.15	0.961	9	395	14.71	4	173
11	10.13	1.326	7	331	12.79	5	209
21	20.10	1.618	4	251	10.56	5	236
31	30.07	1.823	+ 2	157	8.11	6	253
100, Apr. 10	9.05	1.928	0	− 53	5.54	6	259
20	19.02	1.927	− 2	+ 56	2.96	6	256
30	28.99	1.816	4	165	+ 0.46	5	242
May 10	8.96	1.598	5	271	− 1.85	5	219
20	18.94	1.278	6	309	3.89	4	189
30	28.91	0.864	7	456	5.61	3	152
June 9	7 88	−0.371	7	530	6.92	2	111
19	17.85	+0.190	7	589	7.81	+ 1	66
29	27.83	0.801	7	632	8.24	0	− 20
July 9	7.80	1.448	6	659	8.21	− 1	+ 27
200, 19	17.77	2.113	5	670	7.71	2	73
29	27 74	2.783	4	666	6.76	3	116
Aug. 8	6.72	3.441	3	648	5.39	4	157
18	16 69	4.075	− 1	619	3.63	5	195
28	26.66	4.675	+ 2	579	− 1.51	7	228
Sept. 7	5.63	5.229	4	529	+ 0.92	8	257
17	15.61	5.730	6	471	3.62	8	281
27	25.58	6.169	9	406	6.52	9	299
Oct. 7	5.55	6.541	11	336	9.59	9	312
17	15.53	6.840	14	261	12.74	10	318
300, 27	25.50	7.062	16	182	15.92	10	318
Nov. 27	4.47	7.203	19	100	19.07	10	310
16	14.44	7.261	21	+ 15	22.10	10	206
26	24.42	7.234	23	− 70	24.96	9	274
Dec. 6	4.39	7.122	25	153	27.55	9	244
16	14.36	6.929	26	233	29.82	8	208
26	24.33	6.639	27	306	31.68	7	164
36	34.31	+6.321	+27	−368	+33.09	− 6	+116

✱ ♂ ⊙,   April 26 9.
✱ ♂ Mean Sun,   April 26.3.
✱ ☍ Mean Sun,   Oct. 25.9.

Sidereal Day	ΔΩa	ΔΩδ	ΔΩa	ΔΩδ
	1865.		**1873.**	
0	+1.956	−0.83	−2.016	−2.36
100	1.889	1.55	2.026	1.68
200	1.806	2.25	2.019	0.99
300	1.706	2.93	1.996	−0.29
400	1.592	3.59	1.956	+0.41
	1866.		**1874.**	
0	+1.632	−3.37	−1.971	+0.17
100	1.508	4.01	1.921	0.87
200	1.371	4.62	1.854	1.56
300	1.222	5.18	1.773	2.24
400	1.062	5.70	1.677	2.89
	1867.		**1875.**	
0	+1.117	−5.53	−1.711	+2.67
100	0.951	6.02	1.606	3.31
200	0.776	6.45	1.498	3.93
300	0.595	6.83	1.357	4.51
400	0.409	7.15	1.215	5.05
	1868 B.		**1876 B.**	
0	+0.472	−7.05	−1.264	+4.87
100	0.284	7.32	1.116	5.38
200	+0.093	7.53	0.958	5.85
300	−0.098	7.68	0.793	6.27
400	0.288	7.76	0.620	6.64
	1869.		**1877.**	
0	−0.224	−7.74	−0.679	+6.53
100	0.413	7.77	0.503	6.86
200	0.597	7.73	0.323	7.14
300	0.775	7.63	−0.140	7.36
400	0.947	7.46	+0.045	7.52
	1870.		**1878.**	
0	−0.890	−7.53	−0.017	+7.47
100	1.056	7.32	+0.168	7.59
200	1.212	7.04	0.352	7.65
300	1.357	6 71	0.534	7.64
400	1.491	6.32	0.712	7.57
	1871.		**1879.**	
0	−1.447	−6.46	+0.652	+7.60
100	1.572	6.03	0.827	7.49
200	1.684	5.56	0.995	7.31
300	1.780	5.03	1.154	7.07
400	1.862	4.47	1.305	6.77
	1872 B.		**1880 B.**	
0	−1.836	−4.67	+1.256	+6.88
100	1.907	4.08	1.399	6.54
200	1.962	3.46	1.532	6.15
300	2.000	2.81	1.652	5.71
400	2.021	−2.14	+1.758	+5.21

TABLE XXIV.—γ Ceti.

R.A. 2h 36m.6.　　　　　Dec. +2° 41'.

Upper transit at fictitious meridian.

Sidereal Day	Mean Day	Δ☉α 1870	Var. in 10 y.	Diff. for 10 d.	Δ☉δ 1870	Var. in 10 y.	Diff. for 10 d.
0, Jan. 0	− 0.67	+0.713	+ 3	− 82	0.72	+ 1	− 75
10	+ 9.30	0.620	3	105	1.45	1	70
20	19.28	0.504	3	125	2.12	1	63
30	29.25	0.371	3	138	2.70	1	54
Feb. 9	8.22	0.230	3	145	3.19	1	44
19	18.19	+0.084	3	146	3.56	1	31
Mar. 1	0.17	−0.058	2	136	3.80	1	17
11	10.14	0.184	2	116	3.90	1	− 2
21	20.11	0.288	2	91	3.84	+ 1	+ 15
31	30.08	0.364	1	59	3.59	0	35
100, Apr. 10	9.06	0.404	1	− 20	3.14	0	55
20	19.03	0.402	+ 1	+ 25	2.48	0	77
30	29.00	0.354	0	70	1.60	0	98
May 10	8.98	0.263	− 1	114	− 0.52	0	119
20	18.95	−0.127	1	158	+ 0.77	− 1	139
30	28.92	+0.052	1	198	2 25	2	155
June 9	7.89	0.268	1	234	3.86	2	169
19	17.87	0.517	2	262	5.61	3	178
29	27.84	0.790	2	284	7.41	3	182
July 9	7.81	1.082	2	300	9.23	3	182
200, 19	17.78	1.388	3	307	11.04	3	177
29	27.76	1.694	3	305	12.76	4	167
Aug. 8	6.73	1.997	2	298	14.37	4	152
18	16.70	2.291	2	286	15.79	4	132
28	26.67	2.570	2	270	17.01	4	110
Sept. 7	5.65	2.830	2	248	17.99	4	86
17	15.62	3.065	1	224	18.73	4	60
27	25.59	3.276	− 1	197	19.19	3	32
Oct. 7	5.57	3.458	0	163	19.39	3	+ 9
17	15.54	3.612	0	140	19.38	3	− 14
300, 27	25.51	3.737	+ 1	111	19.12	3	35
Nov. 6	4.48	3.853	1	'80	18.70	3	51
16	14.46	3.897	2	50	18.12	3	63
26	24.43	3.933	2	+ 21	17.46	3	72
Dec. 6	4.40	3.938	2	− 9	16.70	2	77
16	14.37	3.914	3	38	15.93	2	78
26	24.35	3.863	4	65	15.15	2	77
36	34.32	+3.784	+ 4	− 91	+14.40	− 2	− 73

✷ ♂ ☉, May 1.7.
✷ ♂ Mean Sun, April 30.9.

Sidereal Day	ΔΩα	ΔΩδ	ΔΩα	ΔΩδ
	1865.		**1873.**	
0	+0.660	−1.51	−0.938	−1.79
100	0.578	2.23	0.888	1.08
200	0.491	2.93	0.830	−0.37
300	0.400	3.61	0.766	+0.35
400	0.304	4.26	0.696	1.06
	1866.		**1874.**	
0	+0.337	−4.05	−0.720	+0.83
100	0.240	4.67	0.646	1.53
200	0.140	5.25	0.566	2.23
300	+0.040	5.78	0.483	2.90
400	−0.061	6.27	0.394	3 55
	1867.		**1875.**	
0	−0.027	−6.11	−0.424	+3.33
100	0.127	6.56	0.334	3.96
200	0.227	6.96	0.241	4.56
300	0.224	7.29	0.147	5.11
400	0.418	7.55	0.051	5.63
	1868 B.		**1876 B.**	
0	−0.387	−7.47	−0.083	+5.46
100	0.479	7.70	+0 013	5.95
200	0.567	7.85	0.109	6.38
300	0.649	7.94	0.204	6.77
400	0.726	7.96	0.297	7.09
	1869.		**1877.**	
0	−0.701	−7.96	+0.263	+6.99
100	0.773	7.94	0.358	7.28
200	0.839	7.83	0.445	7.51
300	0.897	7.67	0.533	7.68
400	0.947	7.44	0.615	7.79
	1870.		**1878.**	
0	−0.931	−7.53	+0.588	+7.76
100	0.976	7.25	0.666	7.82
200	1.012	6.92	0.739	7.82
300	1.040	6.52	0.806	7.75
400	1.058	6.07	0.867	7.62
	1871.		**1879.**	
0	−1.053	−6.23	+0.847	+7.67
100	1.065	5.75	0.903	7.50
200	1.069	5.22	0.951	7.26
300	1.063	4.64	0.992	6.96
400	1.049	4.03	1.025	6.61
	1872 B.		**1880 B.**	
0	−1.055	−4.24	1.015	+6.73
100	1.034	3.61	1.041	6.34
200	1.005	2.95	1.060	5.89
300	0.967	2.26	1.069	5.39
400	−0.922	−1.58	+1.069	+4.84

TABLE XXIV.— 48 Cephei (II,)

R.A. 3^h 3^m.9.   Dec. + 77° 15'.

Upper transit at fictitious meridian.

Sidereal Day.	Mean Day.	$\Delta_\odot a$ 1870.	Var. in 10 y.	Diff. for 10 d.	$\Delta_\odot \delta$ 1870.	Var. in 10 y.	Diff. for 10 d.
0, Jan. 0	− 0.65	+3.901	+38	−564	+15.22	− 6	+214
10	+ 9.32	3.271	39	691	17.12	5	165
20	19.29	2.527	39	792	18.50	4	111
30	29.27	1.697	38	861	19.32	− 2	+ 52
Feb. 9	8.24	+0.817	36	892	19.54	0	− .8
19	18.21	−0.073	34	884	19.17	+ 2	66
Mar. 1	0.19	0.938	28	837	18.23	3	122
11	10.16	1.736	23	752	16.76	5	171
21	20.13	2.430	18	632	14.83	6	213
31	30.10	2.990	12	484	12.53	7	245
100, Apr. 10	9.08	3.391	6	315	9.96	8	268
20	19.05	3 615	+ 1	−132	7.21	8	260
30	29.02	3.652	− 4	+ 59	4.40	8	290
May 10	8.99	3.498	10	247	1.63	8	271
20	18.97	3.160	13	428	0.99	7	253
30	28.94	2.646	16	597	3.40	6	227
June 9	7.91	1.973	18	747	5.50	6	193
19	17.89	1.160	19	875	7.23	4	153
29	27.86	−0.230	19	980	8.55	2	110
July 9	7.83	+0.792	19	1060	9.42	+ 1	61
200, 19	17.80	1.882	17	1115	9.83	− 1	− 17
29	27.78	3.013	14	1144	9.76	3	+ 31
Aug. 8	6.75	4.162	10	1150	9.22	5	78
18	16.72	5.305	6	1132	8.21	7	123
28	26.69	6.419	− 1	1094	6.77	8	165
Sept. 7	5.67	7.486	+ 5	1036	4.92	10	204
17	15.64	8.496	12	960	2.70	12	240
27	25.61	9.400	18	866	− 0.14	13	270
Oct. 7	5.58	10.213	25	757	+ 2.69	15	296
17	15.56	10.909	32	633	5.76	16	316
300, 27	25.53	11.474	39	495	8.99	17	330
Nov. 6	4.50	11.895	46	345	12.33	17	336
16	14.48	12.160	53	185	15.68	17	334
26	24.45	12.263	59	+ 19	18.98	17	324
Dec. 6	4.42	12.197	64	−150	22.14	17	305
16	14.39	11.964	68	316	25.06	16	277
26	24.37	11.568	71	473	27.66	15	241
36	34.34	+11.023	+74	−609	+29.85	−14	+197

✶ ♂ ⊙,   May 8.7.
✶ ♂ Mean Sun,   May 7.8.
✶ ☍ Mean Sun,   Nov. 6.4.

Sidereal Day.	$\Delta_\Omega a$	$\Delta_\Omega \delta$	$\Delta_\Omega a$	$\Delta_\Omega \delta$
	1865.		**1873.**	
0	+3.038	−2.49	−3.095	−0.92
100	2.943	3.21	3.119	−0.18
200	2.822	3.90	3.116	+0.57
300	2.676	4.56	3.087	1.31
400	2.506	5.18	3.033	2.04
	1866.		**1874.**	
0	+2.566	−4.98	−3.054	+1.79
100	2.381	5.58	2.984	2.51
200	2.176	6.12	2.888	3.20
300	1.951	6.61	2.769	3.87
400	1.708	7.04	2.628	4.50
	1867.		**1875.**	
0	+1.793	−6.90	−2.678	+4.29
100	1.541	7.29	2.522	4.90
200	1.275	7.62	2.345	5.46
300	0.999	7.88	2.150	5.99
400	0.714	8.07	1.936	6.46
	1868 B.		**1876 B.**	
0	+0.811	−8.02	−2.010	+6.30
100	0.522	8.16	1.786	6.74
200	+0.229	8.23	1.546	7.12
300	−0.066	8.24	1.294	7.44
400	0.359	8.17	1.031	7.70
	1869.		**1877.**	
0	−0.260	−8.20	−1.121	+7.62
100	0.551	8.08	0.852	7.84
200	0.837	7.89	0.575	7.99
300	1.115	7.64	0.293	8.08
400	1.383	7.32	0.010	8.11
	1870.		**1878.**	
0	−1.293	−7.43	−0.105	+8.11
100	1.553	7.07	+0.181	8.08
200	1.798	6.64	0.465	7.99
300	2 027	6.16	0.747	7.84
400	2.238	5.63	1.024	7.61
	1871.		**1879.**	
0	−2.169	−5.82	+0.931	+7.70
100	2.368	5.25	1.204	7.43
200	2.545	4.65	1 464	7.10
300	2.701	4.00	1.715	6.72
400	2.833	3.33	1.951	6.29
	1872 B.		**1880 B.**	
0	−2.791	−3.56	+1.873	+6.43
100	2.907	2.86	2.099	5.94
200	2.999	2.15	2.309	5.41
300	3.066	1.41	2 499	4.83
400	−3.106	−0.67	+2.669	+4.21

TABLE XXIV.—ζ Arietis.

R.A. 3^h 7^m.4.   Dec. + 20° 34'.

Upper transit at fictitious meridian.

Sidereal Day	Mean Day	$\Delta_\odot a$			$\Delta_\odot \delta$		
		1870.	Var. in 10 y.	Diff. for 10 d.	1870.	Var. in 10 y.	Diff. for 10 d.
0, Jan. 0	− 0.65	+0.931	+ 3	− 68	+ 4.09	0	− 10
10	+ 9.32	0.848	3	98	3.94	0	20
20	19.30	0.736	3	125	3.70	0	30
30	29.27	0.600	4	146	3.35	+ 1	40
Feb. 9	8.24	0.446	4	161	2.91	1	48
19	18.21	0.282	4	165	2.39	1	55
Mar. 1	0.19	+0.120	3	159	1.81	1	60
11	10.16	−0.033	3	141	1.20	1	62
21	20.13	0.166	2	119	0.59	1	59
31	30.11	0.269	2	86	+ 0.03	1	52
100, Apr. 10	9.08	0.336	1	− 46	− 0.46	1	43
20	19.05	0.359	+ 1	0	0.83	1	29
30	29.02	0.336	0	+ 48	1.04	+ 1	− 13
May 10	9.00	0.263	0	97	1.09	0	+ 6
20	18.97	−0.142	0	144	0.92	0	27
30	28.94	+0.024	− 1	188	− 0.54	0	49
June 9	7.91	0.233	1	230	+ 0.05	0	71
19	17.89	0.482	2	264	0.85	− 1	89
29	27.86	0.758	2	290	1.82	2	106
July 9	7.83	1.059	2	310	2.96	2	121
200, 19	17.81	1.375	2	321	4.22	3	131
29	27.78	1.698	2	325	5.57	3	138
Aug. 8	6.75	2.023	2	322	6.97	4	141
18	16.72	2.341	2	314	8.38	4	141
28	26.70	2.649	2	301	9.77	4	136
Sept. 7	5.67	2.942	1	283	11.08	5	127
17	15.64	3.214	1	263	12.30	5	118
27	25.61	3.466	− 1	238	13.43	5	106
Oct. 7	5.59	3.690	0	211	14.42	5	92
17	15.56	3.888	0	185	15.27	5	78
300, 27	25.53	4.059	0	156	15.99	5	65
Nov. 6	4.50	4.199	+ 1	124	16.58	5	52
16	14.48	4.307	2	92	17.03	5	40
26	24.45	4.383	2	59	17.39	5	30
Dec. 6	4.42	4.425	3	+ 25	17.63	5	18
16	14.40	4.432	4	− 11	17.75	5	+ 7
26	24.37	4.403	5	46	17.78	4	− 3
36	34.34	+4.340	+ 6	− 79	+17.70	− 4	− 14

Sidereal Day	$\Delta_\Omega a$	$\Delta_\Omega \delta$	$\Delta_\Omega a$	$\Delta_\Omega \delta$
	1865.		**1873.**	
0	+0.837	−2.63	−1.101	−0.81
100	0.753	3.35	1.056	−0.06
200	0.663	4 04	1.001	+0.69
300	0.567	4.69	0.939	1.43
400	0.466	5.31	0.869	2.16
	1866.		**1874.**	
0	+0.500	−5.11	−0.894	+1.91
100	0.396	5.69	0.819	2.63
200	0.289	6.23	0.738	3.32
300	0.179	6.71	0.651	3.98
400	0.067	7.13	0.558	4.61
	1867.		**1875.**	
0	+0.105	−7.00	−0.590	+4.40
100	−0.007	7.38	0.494	5.00
200	0.119	7.70	0.396	5.56
300	0.230	7.95	0.293	6.08
400	0.339	8.13	0.188	6.55
	1868 B.		**1876 B.**	
0	−0.303	−8.08	−0.223	+6.39
100	0.410	8.21	0.117	6.82
200	0.513	8.28	−0.010	7.20
300	0.611	8.27	+0.097	7.51
400	0.704	8.13	0.203	7.76
	1869.		**1877.**	
0	−0.674	−8.22	+0.168	+7.69
100	0.763	8.09	0.273	7.90
200	0.845	7 89	0.377	8.04
300	0.919	7.62	0.477	8.12
400	0.985	7.29	0.574	8.13
	1870.		**1878.**	
0	−0.964	−7.41	+0.542	+8.14
100	1.025	7.03	0.635	8.10
200	1.077	6.60	0.724	8 01
300	1.118	6.11	0.807	7.84
400	1.151	5.57	0.884	7 61
	1871.		**1879.**	
0	−1.141	−5.76	+0.859	+7.69
100	1.167	5.18	0.930	7.42
200	1.183	4.57	0.995	7.08
300	1.189	3.92	1.051	6.68
400	1.185	3.23	1.093	6.23
	1872 B.		**1880 B.**	
0	−1.188	−3.47	+1.083	+6.39
100	1.177	2.77	1.125	5.90
200	1.156	2.04	1.157	5.36
300	1.126	1.31	1.181	4.77
400	−1.087	−0.56	+1.191	+4.14

✳ ☌ ☉,   May 9.7.
✳ ☌ Mean Sun,   May 8.7.

TABLE XXIV.—δ Persei.

R.A. 3 33.7 (h m).   Dec. + 47 22 (° ').

Upper transit at fictitious meridian.

Sidereal Day	Mean Day.	Δ⊙α 1870.	Var. in 10 y.	Diff. for 10 d.	Δ⊙δ 1870.	Var. in 10 y.	Diff for 10 d.
0, Jan. 0	− 0.63	+1.467	+ 5	− 89	+ 9.40	− 3	+120
10	+ 9.34	1.353	5	138	10.47	2	92
20	19.31	1.193	6	181	11.22	2	59
30	29.29	0.994	7	216	11.64	− 1	+ 25
Feb. 9	8.26	0.765	7	240	11.71	+ 1	− 11
19	18.23	0.518	6	251	11.42	1	46
Mar. 1	0.21	0.267	6	245	10.79	2	79
11	10.18	+0.027	6	231	9.85	2	108
21	20.15	−0.191	5	201	8.64	2	132
31	30.12	0.370	4	157	7.22	3	150
100, Apr 10	9.10	0.502	3	105	5.67	3	161
20	19.07	0.578	2	− 45	4.03	3	165
30	29.04	0.591	+ 1	+ 20	2.39	3	162
May 10	9.01	0.538	0	87	+ 0.82	2	151
20	18.99	0.417	− 1	152	− 0.61	2	134
30	28.96	−0.235	1	213	1.85	2	114
June 9	7.93	+0.007	2	270	2.87	+ 1	89
19	17.91	0.302	3	318	3.61	0	60
29	27.88	0.641	3	358	4.06	0	− 30
July 9	7.85	1.016	3	388	4.21	− 1	+ 1
200, 19	17.82	1.415	3	410	4.05	1	30
29	27.80	1.833	3	423	3.62	2	59
Aug. 8	6.77	2.258	3	427	2.88	3	86
18	16.74	2.684	3	423	1.91	4	109
28	26.71	3.102	2	413	− 0.70	5	131
Sept. 7	5.69	3 507	2	395	+ 0.71	6	150
17	15.66	3.891	− 1	371	2.29	6	166
27	25.63	4.250	0	358	4.02	7	179
Oct. 7	5.61	4.582	+ 1	316	5.85	7	188
17	15.58	4.881	2	282	7.76	8	195
300, 27	25.55	5.144	3	243	9.73	9	198
Nov. 6	4.52	5.365	4	200	11.71	9	198
16	14.50	5.542	5	155	13 67	9	193
26	24.47	5.673	6	106	15.56	9	186
Dec. 6	4.44	5.752	7	+ 53	17.37	8	175
16	14 41	5.779	8	− 2	19.03	8	158
26	24.39	5.749	9	55	20.50	8	136
36	34.36	+5.669	+10	−106	+21.74	− 8	+110

Sidereal Day	Δ_Ω α	Δ_Ω δ	Δ_Ω α	Δ_Ω δ
	1865.		**1873.**	
0	+1.197	−3.54	−1.455	+0 05
100	1.105	4.24	1.415	0.82
200	1.003	4.91	1.362	1.58
300	0.892	5.54	·1.300	2.33
400	0.773	6.13	1.226	3.06
	1866.		**1874.**	
0	+0.814	−5.94	−1 252	+2.81
100	0.690	6.48	1.172	3.52
200	0.561	6.97	1.082	4.20
300	0.426	7.40	0.983	4.85
400	0.288	7.77	0.876	5.45
	1867.		**1875.**	
0	+0.335	−7.66	−0.913	+5.25
100	0.195	7.98	0.802	5.82
200	+0.053	8.23	0.684	6.35
300	−0.089	8.40	0.560	6.82
400	0.230	8.51	0.433	7.23
	1868 B.		**1876 D.**	
0	−0.183	−8.48	−0.476	+7.10
100	0.322	8.54	0 346	7.47
200	0.459	8.52	0.212	7 79
300	0.592	8 43	−0.077	8.04
400	0.719	8.26	+0 059	8.22
	1869.		**1877.**	
0	−0.677	−8.32	+0.013	+8.17
100	0.800	8.11	0.149	8 31
200	0.915	7.83	0.284	8.38
300	1.023	7.47	0.417	8.38
400	1.121	7.06	0.546	8.31
	1870.		**1878.**	
0	−1.089	−7.21	+0.503	+8.34
100	1.181	6.75	0.630	8.23
200	1.262	6.24	0.751	8.05
300	1.332	5.67	0.867	7.80
400	1.391	5.06	0.977	7.48
	1871.		**1879.**	
0	−1.372	−5.27	+0.940	+7.60
100	1.423	4.63	1.044	7.24
200	1.462	3.95	1.142	6.82
300	1.488	3.24	1.226	6.35
400	1.501	2.51	1.302	5.82
	1872 B.		**1880 B.**	
0	−1.498	−2.76	+1.378	+6.00
100	1.503	2.01	1.347	5.44
200	1.495	1.25	1.405	4.82
300	1.475	−0.47	1.451	4.17
400	−1.443	+0.30	+1.485	+3.48

✳ δ ⊙,   May 16.3.
✳ δ Mean Sun,   May 15.4.

TABLE XXIV.—η Tauri.

R.A. 3h 39.8m.   Dec. + 23° 42′.

Upper transit at fictitious meridian.

Sidereal Day	Mean Day	$\Delta_\odot a$ 1870.	Var. in 10 y.	Diff. for 10 d.	$\Delta_\odot \delta$ 1870.	Var. in 10 y.	Diff. for 10 d.
0, Jan. 0	− 0.63	+1.107	+ 3	− 45	+ 4.09	0	+ 11
10	+ 9.35	1.043	4	82	4.15	0	0
20	19.32	0.945	4	115	4.10	0	− 11
30	29.29	0.814	4	143	3.94	0	22
Feb. 9	8.26	0.660	.4	163	3.67	+ 1	33
19	18.24	0.490	4	174	3.29	1	42
Mar. 1	0.21	0.315	4	175	2.83	1	50
11	10.18	+0.143	4	164	2.30	1	57
21	20.16	−0.011	3	143	1.70	1	61
31	30.13	0.141	3	114	1.10	1	60
100, Apr. 10	9.10	0.237	2	76	0.52	1	55
20	19.07	0.291	2	− 32	+ 0.01	1	46
30	29.05	0.300	+ 1	+ 16	− 0.39	1	34
May 10	9.02	0.258	0	67	0.66	+ 1	19
20	18.99	0.166	0	116	0.76	0	− 1
30	28.96	−0.026	0	164	0.68	0	+ 17
June 9	7.94	+0.160	− 1	207	− 0.40	0	36
19	17.91	0.386	1	245	+ 0.06	0	55
29	27.88	0.647	2	276	0.70	− 1	73
July 9	7.86	0.935	2	300	1.52	1	89
200, 19	17.83	1.245	2	316	2.47	2	102
29	27.80	1.565	3	325	3.54	3	111
Aug. 8	6.77	1.894	3	329	4.67	3	116
18	16.75	2.222	3	326	5.85	4	119
28	26.72	2.545	2	318	7.04	4	118
Sept. 7	5.69	2.856	2	304	8.20	5	114
17	15.66	3.152	1	287	9.31	5	107
27	25.64	3.429	1	268	10.34	5	99
Oct. 7	5.61	3.688	−.1	246	11.28	6	90
17	15.58	3.921	0	220	12.14	6	81
300, 27	25.55	4.127	0	192	12.89	6	70
Nov. 6	4.53	4.305	+ 1	163	13.54	6	61
16	14.50	4.452	2	131	14.11	6	52
26	24.47	4.566	2	95	14.58	7	42
Dec. 6	4.45	4.642	3	58	14.96	6	33
16	14.42	4.681	4	+ 19	15.25	5	25
26	24.39	4.680	5	− 20	15.47	5	18
36	34.36	+4.641	+ 5	− 59	+15.60	− 5	+ 7

Sidereal Day	$\Delta_\Omega a$	$\Delta_\Omega \delta$	$\Delta_\Omega a$	$\Delta_\Omega \delta$
	1865.		**1873.**	
0	+0.859	−3.74	−1.134	+0.24
100	0.772	4.45	1.086	1.02
200	0.678	5.11	1.030	1.78
300	0.579	5.73	0.965	2.53
400	0.474	6.31	0.892	3.26
	1866.		**1874.**	
0	+0.509	−6.12	−0.917	+3.02
100	0.402	6.66	0.840	3.72
200	0.291	7.14	0.755	4.40
300	0.177	7.55	0.665	5.04
400	0.061	7.90	0.569	5.63
	1867.		**1875.**	
0	+0.100	−7.79	+0.602	+5.43
100	−0.016	8.10	0.503	6.00
200	0.131	8.33	0.401	6.51
300	0.246	8.49	0.294	6.97
400	0.358	8.58	0.186	7.38
	1868 B.		**1876 B.**	
0	−0.320	−8.56	−0.223	+7.25
100	0.430	8.60	0.113	7.61
200	0.537	8.56	−0.003	7.91
300	0.638	8.45	+0.106	8.31
400	0.733	8.26	0.218	8.31
	1869.		**1877.**	
0	−0.702	−8.33	+0.181	+8.27
100	0.793	8.10	0.290	8.39
200	0.878	7.80	0.396	8.44
300	0.954	7.43	0.500	8.42
400	1.022	6.99	0.599	8.33
	1870.		**1878.**	
0	−1.000	−7.15	+0.566	+8.38
100	1.062	6.67	0.663	8.24
200	1.114	6.14	0.754	8.04
300	1.158	5.56	0.839	7.78
400	1.190	4.93	0.918	7.45
	1871.		**1879.**	
0	−1.180	−5.15	+0.892	+7.56
100	1.207	4.49	0.965	7.19
200	1.222	3.80	1.031	6.75
300	1.228	3.08	1.098	6.26
400	1.223	2.34	1.137	5.71
	1872 B.		**1880 B.**	
0	−1.226	−2.59	+1.121	+5.90
100	1.214	1.83	1.164	5.32
200	1.192	1.06	1.196	4.69
300	1.160	−0.28	1.218	4.03
400	−1.119	+0.50	+1.230	+3.32

✷ ☌ ☉,   May 17.9.
✷ ☌ Mean Sun,   May 16.9.

TABLE XXIV.—ζ Persei.

R.A. 3^h 46^m.0.   Dec. + 31° 30′.

Upper transit at fictitious meridian.

Sidereal Day	Mean Day	$\Delta_\odot\alpha$ 1870.	Var. in 10y.	Diff. for 10d.	$\Delta_\odot\delta$ 1870.	Var. in 10y.	Diff. for 10d.
0, Jan. 0	− 0.62	+1.220	+ 3	− 46	+ 5.66	− 2	+ 49
10	+ 9.35	1.153	4	87	6.08	1	34
20	19.32	1.048	4	123	6.33	− 1	+ 16
30	29.30	0.909	4	155	6.40	0	− 1
Feb. 9	8.27	0.741	4	178	6.30	0	21
19	18.24	0.557	4	190	5.99	+ 1	39
Mar. 1	0.21	0.364	4	192	5.52	1	55
11	10.19	0.176	4	181	4.89	1	69
21	20.16	+0.006	4	159	4.15	1	81
31	30.13	−0.140	3	130	3.29	1	88
100, Apr. 10	9.11	0.250	3	89	2.40	1	89
20	19.08	0.315	2	− 41	1.52	2	86
30	29.05	0.330	+ 1	+ 11	+ 0.70	2	78
May 10	9.02	0.293	0	63	− 0.02	2	66
20	19.00	0.203	0	117	0.60	2	49
30	28.97	−0.060	− 1	168	1.00	+ 1	30
June 9	7.94	+0.132	1	214	1.20	0	− 10
19	17.91	0.367	2	255	1.19	0	+ 12
29	27.89	0.639	2	289	0.96	0	35
July 9	7.86	0.942	2	315	− 0.53	− 1	52
200, 19	17.83	1.267	2	335	+ 0.08	1	70
29	27.80	1.609	2	346	0.87	2	87
Aug. 8	6.78	1.956	2	350	1.82	3	99
18	16.75	2.306	2	347	2.85	3	109
28	26.72	2.648	2	340	3.99	4	116
Sept. 7	5.70	2.984	2	329	5.17	5	119
17	15.67	3.304	2	311	6 37	5	121
27	25.64	3.605	1	291	7.59	6	121
Oct. 7	5.61	3.885	− 1	269	8.78	6	118
17	15.59	4.141	0	243	9.94	6	115
300, 27	25.56	4.369	+ 1	213	11.07	7	110
Nov. 6	4.53	4.566	2	181	12.13	7	104
16	14.50	4.730	2	146	13.14	7	97
26	24.48	4.857	2	108	14.07	7	90
Dec. 6	4.45	4.946	3	68	14.93	6	82
16	14.42	4.993	4	+ 24	15.71	6	71
26	24.40	4.995	5	− 19	16.38	6	58
36	34.37	+4.956	+ 6	− 60	+16.88	− 6	+ 44

✳ ☌ ⊙,   May 19.4.
✳ ☌ Mean Sun,   May 18.5.

Sidereal Day	$\Delta_\Omega\alpha$	$\Delta_\Omega\delta$	$\Delta_\Omega\alpha$	$\Delta_\Omega\delta$
	1865.		**1873.**	
0	+0.943	−3.95	−1.219	+0.45
100	0.854	4.65	1.173	1.22
200	0.757	5.31	1.116	1.99
300	0.053	5.92	1.050	2.74
400	0.544	6.48	0.976	3.46
	1866.		**1874.**	
0	+0.581	−6.30	−1.002	+3.22
100	0.468	6.83	0.923	3.93
200	0.351	7.29	0.836	4.60
300	0.231	7.70	0.742	5.23
400	0.109	8.04	0.643	5.82
	1867.		**1875.**	
0	+0.151	−7.93	−0.677	+5.62
100	−0.028	8.22	0.574	6.18
200	−0.095	8.44	0.466	6.68
300	0.217	8.58	0.355	7.13
400	0.337	8.65	0.240	7.52
	1868 B.		**1876 B.**	
0	−0.297	−8.63	−0.279	+7.39
100	0.415	8.65	0.163	7.74
200	0.530	8.60	−0.046	8 03
300	0.639	8.46	+0.071	8.25
400	0.743	8.26	0.188	8.40
	1869.		**1877.**	
0	−0.709	−8.34	+0.149	+8 36
100	0.808	8.08	0.266	8.46
200	0.900	7.76	0.390	8.50
300	0.984	7.37	0.491	8.46
400	1.060	6.92	0.598	8.36
	1870.		**1878.**	
0	−1.035	−7.08	+0.563	+8.40
100	1.105	6.58	0.667	8.25
200	1.164	6.04	0.766	8.03
300	1.213	5.44	0.859	7.74
400	1.252	4.80	0.945	7.39
	1871.		**1879.**	
0	−1.240	−5.02	+0.917	+7.52
100	1.272	4.35	0.998	7 13
200	1.293	3.65	1.071	6.67
300	1.302	2.91	1.135	6.16
400	1.301	2.16	1.190	5.60
	1872 B.		**1880 B.**	
0	−1.303	−2.42	+1.173	+5.79
100	1.294	1.65	1.221	5.20
200	1.273	0.87	1.260	4.55
300	1.245	−0.08	1.287	3.87
400	−1.205	+0.70	+1.304	+3.16

TABLE XXIV.—γ¹ Eridani.

R.A. 3^h 52^m.0   Dec. −13° 53′

Upper transit at fictitious meridian.

Sidereal Day	Mean Day	$\Delta_\odot a$ 1870.	Var.in 10 y.	Diff. for 10 d.	$\Delta_\odot \delta$ 1870.	Var.in 10 y.	Diff. for 10 d.
0, Jan. 0	− 0.62	+1.076	+ 2	− 52	− 4.85	+ 1	−154
10	+ 9.35	1.007	3	85	6.29	1	133
20	19.33	0.906	3	117	7.50	1	109
30	29.30	0.775	3	144	8.47	+ 1	82
Feb. 9	8.27	0.621	3	163	9.14	0	54
19	18.25	0.451	3	174	9.55	0	− 26
Mar. 1	0.22	0.275	2	177	9.64	0	+ 6
11	10.19	+0.100	2	169	9.43	0	35
21	20.16	−0.061	2	153	8.94	0	65
31	30.14	0.204	2	129	8.14	− 1	94
100, Apr. 10	9.11	0.317	2	96	7.07	1	120
20	19.08	0.394	2	57	5.75	1	146
30	29.05	0.430	1	− 14	4.16	2	170
May 10	9.03	0.422	+ 1	+ 31	2.35	2	190
20	19.00	0.367	0	77	− 0.36	3	208
30	28.97	0.268	0	122	+ 1.80	3	222
June 9	7.95	−0.124	− 1	163	4.06	3	229
19	17.92	+0.057	1	200	6.36	3	232
29	27.89	0.275	1	233	8.69	3	228
July 9	7.86	0.521	1	259	10.92	3	218
200, 19	17.84	0.791	2	279	13.04	3	203
29	27.81	1.077	2	292	14.96	3	181
Aug. 8	6.78	1.372	2	297	16.64	3	153
18	16.75	1.670	2	297	18.00	3	120
28	26.73	1.965	2	293	19.02	3	84
Sept. 7	5.70	2.254	3	283	19.66	3	44
17	15.67	2.530	2	268	19.89	3	+ 3
27	25.65	2.788	2	249	19.72	3	− 37
Oct. 7	5.62	3.027	1	227	19.16	3	75
17	15.59	3.242	1	203	18.24	2	108
300, 27	25.56	3.432	− 1	177	17.02	2	137
Nov. 6	4.54	3.594	0	147	15.52	2	159
16	14.51	3.725	0	114	13.86	2	173
26	24.48	3.822	+ 1	80	12.06	2	184
Dec. 6	4.45	3.884	2	44	10.21	2	184
16	14.43	3.909	2	+ 7	8.40	2	177
26	24.40	3.899	2	− 28	6.69	2	165
36	34.37	+3.852	+ 3	− 64	+ 5.12	− 2	−148

✷ ♂ ⊙,   May 20 9.
✷ ♂ Mean Sun,   May 20.0.

Sidereal Day	$\Delta_\Omega a$	$\Delta_\Omega \delta$	$\Delta_\Omega a$	$\Delta_\Omega \delta$
	1865.		**1873.**	
0	+0.511	−4.15	−0 794	+0.64
100	0.432	4.84	0.741	1.42
200	0.349	5.49	0.681	2.19
300	0.263	6.10	0.617	2.93
400	0.175	6.65	0.547	3.66
	1866.		**1874.**	
0	+0.206	−6.47	−0.571	+3.42
100	0.116	6.99	0.499	4.12
200	+0.025	7.44	0 423	4.78
300	−0.066	7.83	0.343	5.41
400	0.156	8.15	0.260	5.99
	1867.		**1875.**	
0	−0.125	−8.05	−0.288	+5.80
100	0.215	8.33	0 205	6.34
200	0.302	8.53	0.119	6.84
300	0.387	8.66	−0.033	7.27
400	0.468	8.71	+0.054	7.65
	1868 B.		**1876 B.**	
0	−0.411	−8.70	+0.025	+7.53
100	0.520	8.70	0.111	7.87
200	0.594	8.62	0.196	8.14
300	0.662	8.47	0.280	8.34
400	0.725	8.25	0.362	8.48
	1869.		**1877.**	
0	−0.705	−8.33	+0.335	+8.44
100	0.763	8.06	0.414	8.53
200	0.815	7.72	0.491	8.55
300	0.859	7.31	0.564	8.49
400	0.896	6.84	0.632	8.37
	1870.		**1878.**	
0	−0.885	−7.01	+0.609	+8.42
100	0.916	6.50	0.674	8.25
200	0.940	5.94	0.733	8 02
300	0.956	5 34	0.787	7.71
400	0.963	4.67	0.834	7.34
	1871.		**1879.**	
0	−0.962	−4.89	+0.818	+7.47
100	0.964	4.21	0.861	7.06
200	0.958	3.49	0.807	6.59
300	0.943	2.75	0.925	6.07
400	0.921	1.98	0.945	5.49
	1872 B.		**1880 B.**	
0	−0.929	−2.24	+0.939	+5.69
100	0.902	1.47	0.954	5.08
200	0.867	−0.68	0.961	4.42
300	0 825	+0.11	0.960	3.73
400	−0.776	+0.90	+0.951	+3.00

TABLE XXIV.—γ Tauri.

R.A. 4h 12m.4.   Dec. + 15° 19'.

Upper transit at fictitious meridian.

Sidereal Day.	Mean Day.	$\Delta_{\odot}a$ 1870.	Var. in 10 y.	Diff. for 10 d.	$\Delta_{\odot}\delta$ 1870.	Var. in 10 y.	Diff. for 10 d.
0, Jan. 0	− 0.60	+1.175	+ 2	− 17	+ 1.44	0	− 28
10	+ 9.37	1.138	3	56	1.15	0	29
20	19.34	1.065	4	92	0.85	0	30
30	29.31	0.936	3	124	0.55	0	30
Feb. 9	8.29	0.819	3	149	+ 0.25	0	31
19	18.26	0.660	3	165	− 0.07	0	32
Mar. 1	0.23	0.492	3	171	0.38	0	31
11	10.20	0.321	3	168	0.67	+ 1	28
21	20.18	0.158	3	154	0.94	1	25
31	30 15	+0.016	3	130	1.16	1	19
100, Apr. 10	9.12	−0.099	2	98	1.32	1	12
20	19.10	0.178	2	58	1.40	1	− 1
30	29.07	0.214	2	− 15	1.33	+ 1	+ 12
May 10	9.04	0.207	+ 1	+ 31	1.16	0	25
20	19.01	0.152	0	79	0.82	0	41
30	28.99	−0.050	0	125	− 0.34	0	55
June 9	7.96	+0.097	− 1	167	+ 0.29	− 1	71
19	17.93	0.283	1	205	1.07	1	85
29	27.90	0.506	1	210	1.98	2	96
July 9	7.88	0.760	2	267	2.99	2	105
200, 19	17.85	1.037	2	286	4.08	3	111
29	27.82	1.330	3	300	5.20	3	112
Aug. 8	6.80	1.635	3	308	6.31	3	110
18	16.77	1.944	2	310	7.39	4	104
28	26.74	2.254	2	307	8.39	4	95
Sept. 7	5.71	2.557	2	299	9.29	4	83
17	15.69	2.851	2	289	10.05	5	69
27	25.66	3 133	1	274	10.66	5	54
Oct. 7	5.63	3.398	1	257	11.12	5	38
17	15.60	3.645	− 1	237	11.43	5	23
300, 27	25.58	3.870	0	212	11.59	6	+ 10
Nov. 6	4.55	4.068	0	185	11.63	6	− 2
16	14.52	4.239	+ 1	157	11.56	6	11
26	24.50	4.380	1	124	11.42	6	18
Dec. 6	4.47	4.486	2	88	11.21	6	23
16	14.44	4.555	2	50	10.96	6	26
26	24.41	4.585	3	+ 9	10.69	6	28
36	34.39	+4.573	+ 4	− 32	+10.40	− 6	− 29

✳ ♂ ☉,   May 26.0.
✳ ♂ Mean Sun, May 25.2.

Sidereal Day	$\Delta_{\Omega}a$	$\Delta_{\Omega}\delta$	$\Delta_{\Omega}a$	$\Delta_{\Omega}\delta$
1865.	s.	"	s.	"
0	+0.763	−4.80	−1.050	+1.30
100	0.676	5.47	0.999	2.08
200	0.583	6.10	0.939	2.85
300	0.485	6.67	0.872	3.59
400	0.383	7.19	0.798	4.30
1866.			**1874.**	
0	+0.418	−7.02	−0.824	+4.07
100	0.313	7.50	0.746	4.75
200	0.205	7.91	0.661	5.40
300	+0.096	8.25	0.572	6.00
400	−0.014	8.52	0.478	6.55
1867.			**1875.**	
0	+0.023	−8.44	−0.510	+6.37
100	−0.087	8.66	0.413	6.88
200	0.196	8.80	0.313	7.34
300	0.304	8.87	0.211	7.73
400	0.409	8.86	0.109	8.07
1868 B.			**1876 B.**	
0	−0.374	−8.87	−0.142	+7.96
100	0.477	8.81	−0.037	8.25
200	0.575	8.67	+0.065	8.47
300	0.668	8.46	0.173	8.62
400	0.755	8.18	0.276	8.70
1869.			**1877.**	
0	−0.726	−8.23	+0.242	+8.68
100	0.809	7.95	0.314	8.71
200	0.884	7.54	0.443	8.67
300	0.951	7.08	0.539	8.56
400	1.011	6.55	0.631	8.38
1870.			**1878.**	
0	−0.992	−6.73	+0.600	+8.45
100	1.045	6.17	0.680	8.22
200	1.089	5.56	0.771	7.92
300	1.124	4.89	0.843	7.55
400	1.149	4.19	0.918	7.13
1871.			**1879.**	
0	−1.141	−4.43	+0.895	+7.28
100	1.160	3.71	0.960	6.81
200	1.168	2.95	1.017	6.28
300	1.167	2.18	1.066	5.70
400	1.155	1.38	1.106	5.07
1872 B.			**1880 B.**	
0	−1.160	−1.65	+1.093	+5.29
100	1.143	0.85	1.127	4.63
200	1.115	−0.04	1.152	3.93
300	1.079	+0.76	1.166	3.19
400	−1.033	+1.56	+1.171	+2.43

TABLE XXIV.—ε Tauri.

R.A. 4 21.0. (h m)   Dec. + 18 53. (° ′)

Upper transit at fictitious meridian.

Sidereal Day	Mean Day	$\Delta_\odot a$ 1870.	Var. in 10 y.	Diff. for 10 d.	$\Delta_\odot \delta$ 1870.	Var. in 10 y.	Diff. for 10 d.
0, Jan. 0	− 0.60	+1.229	+ 2	− 10	+ 1.95	− 1	− 11
10	+ 9.38	1.199	3	51	1.83	1	12
20	19.35	1.129	3	89	1.70	1	15
30	29.32	1.023	3	122	1.52	1	20
Feb. 9	8.29	0.887	3	149	1.31	1	23
19	18.27	0.727	4	168	1.07	− 1	27
Mar. 1	0.24	0.554	4	176	0.78	0	30
11	10.21	0.378	4	173	0.48	0	32
21	20.18	0.211	3	160	+ 0.15	+ 1	33
31	30.16	+0.061	3	137	− 0.15	1	29
100, Apr. 10	9.13	−0.061	3	103	0.42	1	25
20	19.10	0.149	2	65	0.65	1	18
30	29.08	0.193	1	− 23	0.78	1	− 8
May 10	9.05	0.193	+ 1	+ 24	0.81	+ 1	+ 4
20	19.02	0.144	0	73	0.70	0	18
30	28.99	−0.047	0	121	0.45	0	33
June 9	7.97	+0.096	− 1	164	− 0.05	0	47
19	17.94	0.279	1	203	+ 0.49	− 1	61
29	27.91	0.500	2	235	1.17	1	74
July 9	7.88	0.753	2	265	1.96	2	84
200, 19	17.86	1.028	2	286	2 85	2	92
29	27.83	1.324	2	303	3.80	3	97
Aug. 8	6.80	1.632	3	312	4.78	3	97
18	16.77	1.946	3	315	5.74	4	95
28	26.75	2.261	3	314	6.67	4	89
Sept. 7	5.72	2.572	3	307	7.52	4	81
17	15 09	2.874	2	298	8.30	4	70
27	25 67	3.166	2	284	8.94	5	58
Oct. 7	5.64	3.441	2	267	9.47	5	47
17	15.61	3.699	1	248	9.89	6	35
300, 27	25.58	3.936	− 1	225	10.18	6	24
Nov. 6	4.56	4.148	0	199	10.38	6	15
16	14.53	4.333	0	169	10.48	6	7
26	24.50	4.485	+ 1	135	10.52	6	+ 1
Dec. 6	4.47	4.602	2	98	10.51	6	− 3
16	14.45	4.681	3	60	10.46	6	6
26	24.42	4.721	4	+ 19	10.39	6	9
36	34.39	+4.718	+ 5	− 24	+10.29	− 6	11

Sidereal Day	$\Delta_\Omega a$	$\Delta_\Omega \delta$	$\Delta_\Omega a$	$\Delta_\Omega \delta$
	1865.		**1873.**	
0	+0.791	−5.06	−1.082	+1.57
100	0.702	5.72	1.030	2.36
200	0.608	6.34	0.970	3.13
300	0.507	6.90	0.902	3.86
400	0.403	7.40	0.827	4.57
	1866.		**1874.**	
0	+0.438	−7.24	−0.853	+4.33
100	0.331	7.69	0.773	5.01
200	0.221	8.09	0.687	5.65
300	+0.109	8.41	0.596	6.23
400	−0.004	8.65	0.500	6.77
	1867.		**1875.**	
0	+0.034	−8.58	−0.532	+6.60
100	−0.079	8 78	0.433	7.09
200	0.192	8 90	0.331	7.53
300	0.303	8.94	0.226	7.91
400	0.410	8.91	0.119	8.22
	1868 B.		**1876 B.**	
0	−0.374	−8.93	−0.155	+8.12
100	0.480	8.84	−0.048	8.39
200	0.581	8.68	+0.060	8.59
300	0.677	8.44	0.168	8.72
400	0.767	8.12	0.274	8.77
	1869.		**1877.**	
0	−0.738	−8.24	+0.239	+8.76
100	0.823	7.88	0.344	8.77
200	0 901	7.45	0.446	8.70
300	0.971	6.96	0.545	8.57
400	1.031	6.41	0.639	8.36
	1870.		**1878.**	
0	−1.013	−6.60	+0.608	+8.44
100	1.068	6.02	0.699	8.18
200	1.114	5.38	0.785	7.86
300	1.151	4.70	0.864	7.47
400	1.177	3.98	0.936	7.02
	1871.		**1879.**	
0	−1.169	−4.23	+0.913	+7.18
100	1.189	3.49	0.980	6.69
200	1.199	2.72	1.040	6.14
300	1.198	1.93	1.090	5.54
400	1.188	1.12	1.132	4.89
	1872 B.		**1880 B.**	
0	−1.192	−1.40	+1.119	+5.11
100	1.175	−0.59	1.155	4.43
200	1.148	+0.23	1.181	3.71
300	1.111	1.04	1.197	2.96
400	−1.065	+1.83	+1.203	+2.19

✱ ☌ ☉, May 28.1.
✱ ☌ Mean Sun, May 27.4.

TABLE XXIV.—* 9 Camelopardalis.

R.A. 4h 41m.1.   Dec. +66° 7'.

Upper transit at fictitious meridian.

Sidereal Day	Mean Day	Δ☉α 1870.	Var. in 10 y.	Diff. for 10 d.	Δ☉δ 1870.	Var. in 10 y.	Diff for 10 d.
0, Jan. 0	− 0.58	+3.023	+ 9	− 63	+ 7.86	− 7	+237
10	+ 9.39	2.909	11	163	10.12	7	212
20	19.36	2.699	13	256	12.09	6	180
30	29.33	2.402	14	336	13.70	5	141
Feb. 9	8.31	2.032	15	400	14.89	4	96
19	18.28	1.608	15	444	15.62	2	+ 48
Mar. 1	0.25	1.151	15	465	15.85	− 1	− 1
11	10.23	0.685	15	463	15.60	0	50
21	20 20	+0.232	14	437	14.86	+ 1	96
31	30.17	−0.183	12	390	13.69	2	136
100, Apr 10	9.14	0.540	11	323	12.14	3	172
20	19.12	0.823	9	240	10.27	4	200
30	29 09	1.016	7	146	8.17	5	219
May 10	9.06	1.112	4	− 44	5.92	5	230
20	19.03	1.104	+ 2	+ 60	3.59	5	233
30	29.01	0.993	0	163	+ 1.28	5	228
June 9	7.98	0.779	− 2	262	− 0.94	4	215
19	17.95	0.470	4	354	3.01	4	197
29	27.92	−0.075	5	436	4.86	3	173
July 9	7.90	+0.398	7	507	6.45	2	144
200, 19	17.87	0.935	8	565	7.73	+ 1	113
29	27.84	1.525	8	612	8.69	− 1	79
Aug. 8	6.82	2.155	9	646	9.30	2	43
18	16.79	2.812	9	667	9.55	3	− 7
28	26.76	3.486	9	678	9.45	5	+ 28
Sept. 7	5.73	4.164	8	676	8.99	6	63
17	15.71	4.835	7	665	8.19	8	97
27	25.68	5.490	6	643	7.06	9	129
Oct. 7	5.65	6 118	4	611	5.61	11	160
17	15.62	6.709	2	570	3.87	12	187
300, 27	25.60	7.254	− 1	517	− 1.87	13	212
Nov. 6	4.57	7.740	+ 2	453	+ 0.36	14	233
16	14.54	8.157	4	380	2.77	15	249
26	24.52	8 496	7	296	5.32	15	259
Dec. 6	4.49	8.747	10	204	7.94	16	263
16	14.46	8.901	12	104	10.56	16	260
26	24.43	8.954	15	+ 2	13.11	15	249
36	34.41	+8.905	+16	−101	+15.50	−15	+229

* ♂ ☉, June 2.1.
* ♂ Mean Sun, June 1 5.
* ☍ Mean Sun, Dec. 1.1.

Sidereal Day	ΔΩα	ΔΩδ	ΔΩα	ΔΩδ
	1865.		**1873.**	
0	+1.600	−5 63	−1.987	+2.20
100	1.468	6 27	1.924	2.98
200	1.321	6.85	1.845	3.74
300	1.164	7.38	1.752	4.47
400	0.996	7.84	1.643	5.15
	1866.		**1874.**	
0	+1.054	−7.69	−1.681	+4.92
100	0.879	8.11	1.564	5.58
200	0.697	8.45	1.434	6.19
300	0.509	8.72	1.293	6.75
400	0.316	8.92	1.141	7.25
	1867.		**1875.**	
0	+0.382	−8.86	−1.193	+7.09
100	+0.187	9.00	1.035	7.55
200	−0 009	9.07	0.869	7.95
300	0.205	9.05	0.690	8.28
400	0.399	8.96	0.516	8.54
	1868 B.		**1876 B.**	
0	−0.334	−9.00	−0.577	+8.46
100	0.525	8.85	0.395	8.68
200	0.712	8.63	0 209	8.82
300	0.893	8.33	−0.022	8.89
400	1.065	7.96	+0.165	8.89
	1869.		**1877.**	
0	−1.007	−8.10	+0.102	+8.90
100	1.173	7.68	0.289	8.85
200	1.329	7.20	0.474	8.73
300	1.472	6.65	0.655	8.54
400	1.602	6.06	0.832	8.27
	1870.		**1878.**	
0	−1.560	−6.26	+0.773	+8.36
100	1.681	5.63	0.945	8.06
200	1.787	4.95	1.110	7.68
300	1.877	4.23	1.266	7.23
400	1.951	3.47	1.411	6.74
	1871.		**1879.**	
0	−1.928	−3.73	+1.363	+6.90
100	1.991	2.95	1.502	6.36
200	2.037	2.15	1.628	5.76
300	2.065	1.34	1.741	5.11
400	2.076	0.52	1.839	4.42
	1872 B.		**1880 B.**	
0	−2.074	−0.80	+1.808	+4.66
100	2.074	+0.03	1.896	3.94
200	2.055	0.85	1.969	3.18
300	2.020	1.67	2.025	2.40
400	−1.968	+2.47	+2.064	+1.59

TABLE XXIV.— ι Aurigae.

R.A. 4 h 48.5 m.　　　Dec. + 32° 57′.

Upper transit at fictitious meridian.

Sidereal Day	Mean Day	Δ⊙a 1870	Var.in 10y	Diff. for 10d	Δ⊙δ 1870	Var.in 10y	Diff. for 10d
0, Jan. 0	− 0.58	+1.483	+ 2	+ 16	+ 3.37	− 3	+ 69
10	+ 9.39	1.474	3	− 34	4.03	3	61
20	19.37	1.416	3	82	4.59	2	50
30	29.34	1.311	4	125	5.03	2	37
Feb. 9	8.31	1.168	4	161	5.32	1	21
19	18.28	0.992	4	188	5.44	1	+ 4
Mar. 1	0.26	0.796	4	201	5.39	− 1	15
11	10.23	0.594	5	204	5.15	0	32
21	20.20	0.394	5	195	4.76	0	47
31	30.18	0.208	4	173	4.22	+ 1	60
100, Apr. 10	9.15	+0.051	3	141	3.56	1	70
20	19.12	−0.072	2	100	2.83	1	75
30	29.09	0.148	2	52	2.06	2	77
May 10	9.07	0.175	1	− 1	1.30	2	74
20	19.04	0.150	+ 1	+ 52	+ 0.59	2	67
30	29.01	−0.072	0	104	− 0.04	1	58
June 9	7.98	+0.056	− 1	154	0.56	+ 1	46
19	17.96	0.234	1	200	0.95	0	31
29	27.93	0.454	2	240	1.18	− 1	15
July 9	7.90	0.712	2	275	1.26	1	0
200, 19	17.88	1.001	2	302	1.18	2	+ 14
29	27.85	1.314	2	323	0.98	2	27
Aug. 8	6.82	1.645	3	339	0.64	2	40
18	16.79	1.989	3	348	− 0.18	3	50
28	26.77	2.339	3	351	+ 0.36	3	57
Sept. 7	5.74	2.689	3	349	0.96	4	63
17	15.71	3.035	3	342	1.62	5	68
27	25.68	3.372	2	333	2.31	6	70
Oct. 7	5.66	3.700	2	320	3.02	6	72
17	15.63	4.010	− 1	301	3.74	6	73
300, 27	25.60	4.300	0	279	4.48	7	75
Nov. 6	4.57	4.567	0	252	5.24	7	77
16	14.55	4.803	0	220	6.00	8	77
26	24.52	5.006	+ 1	184	6.78	8	78
Dec. 6	4.49	5.1t9	2	142	7.56	8	78
16	14.47	5.289	3	97	8.33	8	76
26	24.44	5.361	4	+ 47	9.07	8	72
36	34.41	+5.382	+ 4	− 4	+ 9.77	− 8	+ 66

✻ ♂ ⊙,　　June 3.9.
✻ ♂ Mean Sun,　June 3.4.

Sidereal Day	ΔΩa	ΔΩδ	ΔΩa	ΔΩδ
	1865.		**1873.**	
0	+0.903	−5.85	−1.220	+2.43
100	0.805	6.47	1.164	3.21
200	0.701	7.04	1.099	3.97
300	0.590	7.55	1.024	4.68
400	0.473	7.99	0.942	5.36
	1866.		**1874.**	
0	+0.513	−7.85	−0.970	+5.14
100	0.394	8.25	0.883	5.78
200	0.271	8.57	0.788	6.38
300	0.146	8.83	0.687	6.92
400	0.019	9.00	0.580	7.41
	1867.		**1875.**	
0	+0.062	−8.95	−0.616	+7.25
100	−0.065	9.07	0.506	7.70
200	0.191	9.11	0.393	8.08
300	0.315	9.08	0.276	8.39
400	0.436	8.96	0.156	8.64
	1868 B.		**1876 B.**	
0	−0.396	−9.01	−0.197	+8.56
100	0.515	8.84	−0.077	8.76
200	0.629	8.60	+0.044	8.89
300	0 737	8.28	0.165	8.94
400	0.839	7.89	0.284	8.92
	1869.		**1877.**	
0	−0.806	−8.02	+0.245	+8.94
100	0.903	7.59	0.362	8.87
200	0.992	7.09	0.477	8.72
300	1.072	6.52	0.589	8.51
400	1.142	5.91	0.696	8.22
	1870.		**1878.**	
0	−1.120	−6.12	+0.660	+8.33
100	1.184	5.47	0.763	7.99
200	1.237	4.78	0.860	7.59
300	1.280	4.04	0.950	7.13
400	1.312	3.27	1.033	6.61
	1871.		**1879.**	
0	−1.302	−3.53	+1.006	+6.79
100	1.327	2.75	1.083	6.23
200	1.340	1.94	1.151	5.62
300	1.341	1.12	1 2 0	4.95
400	1.332	0.30	1.259	4.25
	1872 B.		**1880 B.**	
0	−1.336	−0.57	+1.244	+1.49
100	1.319	+0.26	1.285	3.76
200	1.290	1.08	1.317	2.99
300	1.251	1.89	1.337	2.20
400	−1.202	+2.69	+1.345	+1.38

TABLE XXIV.—11 Orionis.

R.A. 4 57.1 (h m)　　　　Dec. + 15 13 (° ')

Upper transit at fictitious meridian.

Sidereal Day	Mean Day	$\Delta_{\odot}\alpha$ 1870	Var. in 10 y.	Diff. for 10 d.	$\Delta_{\odot}\delta$ 1870	Var. in 10 y.	Diff. for 10 d.
0, Jan. 0	− 0.57	+1.311	+ 2	+ 21	+ 0.45	− 1	− 32
10	+ 9.40	1.309	2	− 23	+ 0.14	1	29
20	19.37	1.267	2	63	− 0.14	1	27
30	29.35	1.184	3	102	0.40	1	24
Feb. 9	8.32	1.065	3	134	0.63	1	22
19	18.29	0.919	4	159	0.84	0	20
Mar. 1	0.26	0.751	4	174	1.04	0	19
11	10.24	0.575	4	177	1.22	0	18
21	20.21	0.400	3	171	1.39	0	15
31	30.18	0.237	3	154	1.52	0	11
100, Apr. 10	9.15	+0.096	3	127	1.60	0	− 6
20	19.13	−0.015	2	92	1.63	0	+ 1
30	29.10	0.090	2	54	1.57	0	11
May 10	9.07	0.121	1	− 9	1.41	0	21
20	19.05	0.107	+ 1	+ 36	1.14	0	32
30	29.02	−0.048	0	82	0.76	0	44
June 9	7.99	+0.057	0	127	− 0.26	1	57
19	17.96	0.204	− 1	167	+ 0.37	1	67
29	27.94	0.389	1	203	1.08	1	76
July 9	7.91	0 609	1	234	1.89	1	84
200, 19	17.88	0.855	2	259	2.75	2	88
29	27.85	1.125	2	279	3.65	2	89
Aug. 8	6.83	1.411	2	292	4.52	3	85
18	16.80	1.708	2	301	5.35	3	80
28	26.77	2.012	3	305	6.11	4	71
Sept. 7	5.74	2.317	3	305	6.76	4	59
17	15.72	2.621	3	301	7.28	4	46
27	25.69	2.918	2	293	7.67	4	31
Oct. 7	5.66	3.206	2	282	7.89	5	15
17	15.64	3.480	2	267	7.97	5	+ 1
300, 27	25.61	3.739	2	249	7.92	5	− 12
Nov. 6	4.58	3.977	− 1	226	7.75	5	23
16	14.55	4.190	0	200	7.47	5	30
26	24.53	4.375	+ 1	169	7.16	6	33
Dec. 6	4.50	4.526	1	133	6.81	6	36
16	14.47	4.640	2	93	6.44	6	37
26	24.44	4.711	2	50	6.08	6	35
36	34.42	+4.739	+ 3	+ 7	+ 5.74	− 6	− 32

✳ ♂ ⊙,　June 6.0.
✳ ♂ Mean Sun,　June 5.5.

Sidereal Day	$\Delta_{\Omega}\alpha$	$\Delta_{\Omega}\delta$	$\Delta_{\Omega}\alpha$	$\Delta_{\Omega}\delta$
	1865.		**1873.**	
0	+0.743	−6.08	−1.042	+2.69
100	0.654	6.69	0.988	3.47
200	0.559	7.24	0.926	4.22
300	0.459	7.73	0.856	4.92
400	0.355	8.16	0.786	5.59
	1866.		**1874.**	
0	+0.390	−8.02	−0.807	+5.37
100	0.284	8.40	0.726	6.01
200	0.175	8.70	0.639	6.59
300	+0.065	8.93	0.548	7.12
400	−0.046	9.08	0.452	7.59
	1867.		**1875.**	
0	−0.008	−9.04	−0.485	+7.44
100	0.119	9.14	0.386	7.86
200	0.229	9.16	0.285	8.23
300	0.336	9.09	0.181	8.53
400	0.441	8.95	0.076	8.74
	1868 B.		**1876 B.**	
0	−0.406	−9.01	−0.112	+8.68
100	0.508	8.82	−0.006	8.85
200	0.605	8.55	+0.100	8.96
300	0.697	8.20	0.205	8 99
400	0.783	7.79	0.308	8.94
	1869.		**1877.**	
0	−0.755	−7.93	+0.273	+8.97
100	0.836	7.47	0.375	8.87
200	0.910	6.95	0.474	8.70
300	0.975	6.37	0.568	8.46
400	1.034	5.74	0.660	8.15
	1870.		**1878.**	
0	−1.014	−5.95	+0.630	+8.27
100	1.065	5.28	0.717	7.91
200	1.106	4.57	0.799	7.49
300	1.139	3.82	0.874	7.01
400	1.161	3.04	0.942	6.46
	1871.		**1879.**	
0	−1.154	−3.31	+0.950	+6.65
100	1.170	2.51	0.983	6.07
200	1.176	1.69	1.037	5.44
300	1.171	0.87	1.084	4.76
400	1.157	0.03	1.121	4.03
	1872 B.		**1880 B.**	
0	−1.163	−0.31	+1.110	+4.28
100	1.142	+0.52	1.141	3.54
200	1.112	1.35	1.163	2.76
300	1.073	2.16	1.175	1.95
400	−1.024	+2.95	+1.177	+1.13

TABLE XXIV.—" 74 Camelopardalis (B); Groombridge 966.

R.A. 5h 22m.4.   Dec. + 74° 57'.

Upper transit at fictitious meridian.

Sidereal Day	Mean Day	$\Delta_\odot\alpha$ 1870	Var. in 10y.	Diff. for 10d.	$\Delta_\odot\delta$ 1870	Var. in 10y.	Diff. for 10d.
0, Jan. 0	− 0.55	+ 5.055	+12	− 1	+ 5.26	−11	+296
10	+ 9.42	4.971	17	167	8.03	11	267
20	19.39	4.724	21	325	10.58	10	241
30	29.36	4.327	25	467	12.83	9	206
Feb. 9	8.34	3.798	28	587	14.67	7	162
19	18.31	3.163	30	677	16.05	6	113
Mar. 1	0.28	2.453	30	736	16.92	4	60
11	10.25	1.703	31	758	17.25	2	+ 5
21	20.23	0.949	29	745	17.02	− 1	− 49
31	30.20	+ 0.224	28	698	16.27	+ 1	101
100, Apr. 10	9.17	− 0.436	25	619	15.03	3	147
20	19.15	1.004	22	513	13.35	4	187
30	29.12	1.455	18	385	11.30	5	220
May 10	9.09	1.770	14	242	8.98	6	244
20	19.06	1.937	10	− 90	6.46	6	259
30	29.04	1.949	5	+ 65	3.83	7	266
June 9	8.01	1.807	+ 1	219	+ 1.18	6	264
19	17.98	1.513	− 4	367	− 1.42	6	255
29	27.95	1.076	8	505	3.89	5	238
July 9	7.93	+ 0.508	12	630	6.17	4	216
200, 19	17.89	+ 0.178	15	739	8.20	3	188
29	27.87	0.966	18	833	9.92	+ 1	157
Aug. 8	6.84	1.838	20	909	11.33	− 1	123
18	16.82	2.778	21	968	12.37	3	86
28	26.79	3.768	22	1008	13.03	5	47
Sept. 7	5.76	4.789	22	1032	13.30	7	− 7
17	15.74	5.826	21	1039	13.17	9	+ 33
27	25.71	6.861	20	1027	12.64	11	73
Oct. 7	5.68	7.874	18	997	11.72	13	112
17	15.65	8.849	15	950	10.41	15	150
300, 27	25.63	9.767	12	883	8.73	17	185
Nov. 6	4.60	10.608	8	796	6.72	19	217
16	14.57	11.332	− 4	690	4.40	20	245
26	24.54	11.981	+ 1	565	− 1.83	21	268
Dec. 6	4.52	12.477	6	423	+ 0.93	22	283
16	14.49	12.823	11	268	3.81	23	291
26	24.46	13.010	16	+104	6.73	23	290
36	34.44	+13.030	+22	− 63	+ 9.58	−23	+279

☀ ♂ ⊙,   June 12.1.
☀ ♂ Mean Sun, June 12.0.
☀ ☍ Mean Sun, Dec. 11.6.

Sidereal Day	$\Delta_\Omega\alpha$	$\Delta_\Omega\delta$	$\Delta_\Omega\alpha$	$\Delta_\Omega\delta$
	1865.		**1873.**	
0	+1.951	−6.69	−2.553	+3.44
100	1.758	7.25	2.449	4.20
200	1.550	7.76	2.323	4.92
300	1.328	8.19	2.179	5.60
400	1.093	8.56	2.017	6.23
	1866.		**1874.**	
0	+1.174	−8.45	−2.074	+6.02
100	0.933	8.76	1 901	6.62
200	0.683	9.00	1.713	7.16
300	0.428	9.16	1.511	7.64
400	0.169	9.25	1.297	8.05
	1867.		**1875.**	
0	+0.256	−9.23	−1.370	+7.92
100	−0.004	9.25	1.149	8.29
200	0.264	9.20	0.918	8.59
300	0.522	9.07	0.680	8.82
400	0.775	8.85	0.437	8.98
	1868 B.		**1876 B.**	
0	−0.690	−8.94	−0.520	+8.94
100	0.939	8.67	0.274	9.05
200	1.179	8.33	−0.025	9.08
300	1.408	7.92	+0.224	9 04
400	1.624	7.44	0.470	8.93
	1869.		**1877.**	
0	−1.552	−7.61	+0.387	+8.97
100	1.759	7.09	0.632	8.81
200	1.950	6.50	0.872	8.57
300	2.124	5.86	1.105	8.26
400	2.278	5.18	1.330	7.89
	1870.		**1878.**	
0	−2.228	−5.41	+1.256	+8.02
100	2.370	4.69	1.473	7.60
200	2.490	3.94	1.679	7.11
300	2 589	3.15	1.872	6.57
400	2.666	2.34	2.049	5.96
	1871.		**1879.**	
0	−2.643	−2.62	+1.991	+6.17
100	2.704	1.79	2.157	5.54
200	2.742	0.95	2.306	4.85
300	2.756	−0.11	2.436	4.12
400	2.747	+0.74	2.546	3.36
	1872 B.		**1880 B.**	
0	−2.753	+0.45	+2.512	+3.62
100	2.728	1.29	2.607	2.84
200	2.681	2.12	2.682	2 03
300	2.612	2.92	2.733	1.20
400	−2.521	+3.70	+2.762	+0.35

TABLE XXIV.—δ Orionis.

R.A. 5 25.4. (h m)   Dec. — 0 24. (° ')

Upper transit at fictitious meridian.

Sidereal Day	Mean Day	Δ⊙a 1870	Var. in 10 y	Diff. for 10 d	Δ⊙δ 1870	Var. in 10 y	Diff. for 10 d
0, Jan. 0	− 0.55	+1.319	+ 1	+ 38	− 1.87	0	−128
10	+ 9.42	1.336	1	− 5	3.10	0	115
20	19.39	1.309	2	48	4.17	− 1	100
30	29.37	1.240	2	88	5.10	1	84
Feb. 9	8.34	1.134	2	122	5.85	1	67
19	18.31	0.997	2	150	6.43	0	49
Mar. 1	0.28	0.837	3	169	6.83	0	30
11	10.26	0.663	3	177	7.02	0	− 11
21	20.23	0.486	3	176	7.04	0	+ 5
31	30.20	0.315	3	164	6.91	1	23
100, Apr. 10	9.17	0.161	3	143	6.57	1	43
20	19.15	+0.032	2	115	6.06	1	61
30	29.12	−0.066	2	79	5.36	1	79
May 10	9.09	0.125	1	49	4.49	2	95
20	19.06	0.143	. 1	+ 3	3.47	2	110
30	29.04	0.119	1	46	2.29	2	125
June 9	8.01	−0.052	+ 1	87	− 0.98	2	137
19	17.98	+0.055	0	126	+ 0.45	2	146
29	27.96	0.200	0	163	1.93	2	150
July 9	7.93	0.381	− 1	196	3.45	2	151
200, 19	17.90	0.591	1	224	4.95	3	149
29	27.87	0.827	1	246	6.39	3	138
Aug. 8	6.85	1.081	1	263	7.70	3	123
18	16.82	1.351	2	276	8.84	3	105
28	26.79	1.632	2	284	9.79	3	82
Sept. 7	5.76	1.918	3	289	10.47	3	54
17	15.74	2.208	3	289	10.87	3	+ 26
27	25.71	2.495	3	285	10.99	3	− 4
Oct. 7	5.68	2.777	3	279	10.79	3	34
17	15.66	3.051	2	268	10.31	4	62
300, 27	25.63	3.311	2	253	9.56	4	87
Nov. 6	4.60	3.555	1	234	8.58	4	109
16	14.57	3.777	1	209	7.40	4	125
26	24.55	3.972	− 1	180	6.09	4	135
Dec. 6	4.52	4.135	0	146	4.72	4	140
16	14.49	4.263	0	108	3.31	4	140
26	24.46	4 350	+ 1	66	1.94	4	133
36	34.44	+4.394	+ 2	+ 22	+ 0.66	− 4	−123

✱ δ ⊙,   June 12 8.
✱ δ Mean Sun, June 12.7.

Sidereal Day	ΔΩa	ΔΩδ	ΔΩa	ΔΩδ
	1865.		**1873.**	
0	+0.632	−6.77	−0.913	+3.53
100	0.550	7.33	0.861	4.28
200	0.463	7.82	0.803	5.00
300	0.372	8.25	0 738	5.67
400	0.278	8.61	0.667	6.30
	1866.		**1874.**	
0	+0.310	−8 50	−0.691	+6.09
100	0.214	8.81	0.617	6.68
200	0.116	9.04	0.538	7.21
300	+0.017	9.19	0.454	7.69
400	−0.082	9.26	0.367	8.10
	1867.		**1875.**	
0	−0.049	−9.24	−0.396	+7.97
100	0.148	9.26	0.307	8.33
200	0.245	9.20	0.215	8.63
300	0.340	9.06	0.122	8.85
400	0.433	8.84	0.028	9.00
	1868 B.		**1876 B.**	
0	−0.402	−8.92	−0.060	+8.96
100	0.492	8.65	+0.035	9.06
200	0.577	8.30	0.130	9.09
300	0.657	7.88	0.223	9.04
400	0.731	7.39	0.315	8.92
	1869.		**1877.**	
0	−0.707	−7.56	+0.284	+8.97
100	0.777	7.03	0.374	8.80
200	0.840	6.44	0.461	8.55
300	0.895	5.79	0.544	8.24
400	0.943	5.10	0.623	7.85
	1870.		**1878.**	
0	−0 928	−5.34	+0.597	+7.99
100	0.970	4.64	0.673	7.56
200	1.004	3.86	0.743	7.07
300	1.029	3.07	0.808	6.52
400	1.045	2.25	0.866	5.91
	1871.		**1879.**	
0	−1.040	−2.53	+0.847	+6.13
100	1.050	1.70	0 900	5.49
200	1.052	0.86	0.946	4.80
300	1.044	−0.02	0.984	4 07
400	1.028	+0.82	1.014	3.30
	1872 B.		**1880 B.**	
0	−1.034	+0.54	+1.005	+3.56
100	1.012	1.38	1.029	2.78
200	0.981	2.20	1.045	1.96
300	0.943	3.00	1.052	1.13
400	−0.890	+3.78	+1.050	+0.29

TABLE XXIV.—a Leporis.

R.A. 5h 27.0m   Dec. — 17° 55′

Upper transit at fictitious meridian.

Sidereal Day	Mean Day	Δ☉a 1870.	Var. in 10y.	Diff. for 10d.	Δ☉δ 1870.	Var. in 10y.	Diff. for 10d.
0, Jan. 0	− 0.55	+1.383	+ 1	+ 22	− 3.60	+ 1	−216
10	+ 9.42	1.383	1	− 23	5.67	1	197
20	19.39	1.337	1	67	7.52	+ 1	173
30	29.37	1.250	2	108	9.12	0	145
Feb. 9	8.34	1.122	2	143	10.41	0	113
19	18.31	0.966	2	169	11.38	0	81
Mar. 1	0.28	0.786	2	189	12.03	0	46
11	10.26	0.591	2	197	12.31	− 1	12
21	20.23	0.395	2	195	12.26	1	+ 21
31	30.20	0.204	2	183	11.89	1	54
100, Apr. 10	9.17	+0.031	2	162	11.18	2	86
20	19.15	−0.119	2	134	10.17	2	116
30	29 12	0.236	2	99	8.86	2	144
May 10	9.09	0.315	2	58	7.29	2	169
20	19.07	0.353	1	− 17	5.48	3	192
30	29.04	0.348	+ 1	+ 26	3.46	3	211
June 9	8.01	0.301	0	70	1.28	3	224
19	17.98	0.208	0	112	+ 1.01	3	232
29	27.96	−0.077	0	150	3.35	3	234
July 9	7.93	+0.092	− 1	185	5.67	3	229
200, 19	17.90	0.292	1	215	7.91	3	218
29	27.87	0.521	1	240	10.01	3	200
Aug. 8	6.85	0.770	1	260	11.90	3	174
18	16.82	1.040	2	276	13.49	3	144
28	26.79	1.320	2	286	14.76	3	108
Sept. 7	5.77	1.611	2	293	15.63	3	65
17	15.74	1.904	2	293	16.06	2	+ 21
27	25.71	2 196	2	290	16.05	2	− 24
Oct. 7	5.68	2.482	2	282	15.58	2	68
17	15.66	2.758	2	270	14.69	2	111
300, 27	25.63	3.020	2	253	13.37	2	150
Nov. 6	4.60	3.262	2	230	11.71	2	182
16	14.57	3.478	1	203	9.76	2	207
26	24.55	3.667	1	172	7.60	2	224
Dec. 6	4.52	3.820	− 1	135	5.31	2	232
16	14.49	3.935	0	94	2.98	2	233
26	24.47	4.007	0	50	+ 0.69	2	225
36	34.44	+4.035	+ 1	+ 5	− 1.49	− 2	−210

Sidereal Day	ΔΩa	ΔΩδ	ΔΩa	ΔΩδ
	1865.		**1873.**	
0	+0.523	−6.81	−0 775	+3.57
100	0.450	7.36	0.728	4.32
200	0.374	7.85	0.676	5.04
300	0.295	8.28	0.618	5.71
400	0.212	8.63	0.555	6.33
	1866.		**1874.**	
0	+0.240	−8.52	−0.577	+6.13
100	0.157	8.82	0.511	6.72
200	+0.072	9.05	0.441	7.25
300	−0.014	9.20	0.367	7.72
400	0.100	9.26	0.291	8.12
	1867.		**1875.**	
0	−0.071	−9.25	−0.317	+7.99
100	0.156	9.26	0.239	8.35
200	0.240	9.20	0.159	8.64
300	0.321	9.05	−0.078	8.86
400	0.400	8.82	+0.004	9.01
	1868 B.		**1876 B.**	
0	−0.373	−8.91	−0.024	+8.97
100	0.450	8.63	+0.058	9.07
200	0.522	8.28	0.139	9.09
300	0.590	7.85	0.219	9.04
400	0.652	7.36	0.298	8.91
	1869.		**1877.**	
0	−0.632	−7.53	+0.272	+8.96
100	0.690	7.00	0.348	8.79
200	0.742	6.41	0.423	8.54
300	0.788	5.76	0.493	8.22
400	0.827	5.06	0.560	7.83
	1870.		**1878.**	
0	−0.815	−5.30	+0.538	+7.97
100	0.849	4.58	0.602	7.54
200	0.876	3.82	0.661	7.05
300	0.895	3.02	0.715	6.49
400	0.906	2.21	0.763	5.88
	1871.		**1879.**	
0	−0.903	−2.48	+0.748	+6.09
100	0.909	1.66	0.792	5.45
200	0.908	−0.82	0.829	4.76
300	0.899	+0.03	0.860	4.03
400	0.882	0.87	0.883	3.26
	1872 B.		**1880 B.**	
0	−0.888	+0.59	+0.876	+3.52
100	0.867	1.43	0.894	2.73
200	0.838	2.25	0.90?	1.92
300	0.802	3.05	0.90?	1.09
400	−0.759	+3.83	+0.905	+0.24

✳ ♂ ☉,   June 13.2.
✳ ♂ Mean Sun,   June 13.1.

TABLE XXIV.—ε Orionis.

R.A. 5ʰ 23ᵐ.6.   Dec. — 1° 17′.

Upper transit at fictitious meridian.

Sidereal Day	Mean Day	Δ☉α 1870.	Var.in 10y.	Diff. for 10 d.	Δ☉δ 1870.	Var.in 10y.	Diff. for 10 d.
0, Jan. 0	— 0.55	+1.327	+ 1	+ 42	— 1.97	0	—133
10	+ 9.42	1.347	1	— 3	3.24	0	121
20	19.39	1.322	2	46	4.34	0	106
30	29.37	1.256	2	86	5.36	0	89
Feb. 9	8.34	1.151	2	120	6.15	0	70
19	18.31	1.015	3	149	6.75	0	51
Mar. 1	0.29	0.855	3	168	7.17	—1	·32
11	10.26	0.682	3	177	7.39	1	— 12
21	20.23	0.504	3	177	7.41	1	+ 6
31	30.20	0.331	3	166	7.27	1	24
100, Apr 10	9.18	0.175	2	145	6.92	1	44
20	19.15	+0.044	2	116	6.39	.1	62
30	29.12	—0.056	2	82	5.63	1	81
May 10	9.09	0.119	1	43	4.78	2	98
20	19.09	0.142	+ 1	— 2	3.71	2	114
30	29.04	0.123	0	+ 41	2.49	2	129
June 9	8.01	—0.060	0	83	— 1.14	2	141
19	17.99	+0.043	0	123	+ 0.32	2	149
29	27.96	0.185	— 1	159	1.83	2	154
July 9	7.93	0.360	1	191	3.38	2	154
200, 19	17.90	0.566	2	220	4.90	2	150
29	27.87	0.798	2	242	6.36	3	141
Aug. 8	6.85	1.049	2	260	7.70	3	126
18	16.82	1.316	2	273	8.87	3	107
28	26.79	1.594	2	283	9.82	3	83
Sept. 7	5.77	1.890	3	298	10.52	3	56
17	15.74	2.169	3	288	10.93	3	+ 25
27	25.71	2.455	3	286	11.02	3	— 6
Oct. 7	5.69	2.739	3	280	10.81	3	36
17	15.66	3.013	2	270	10.30	4	65
300, 27	25.63	3.277	2	256	9 51	4	92
Nov. 6	4.60	3.524	1	236	8.47	4	114
16	14.58	3.747	— 1	212	7.24	4	131
26	24.55	3.945	0	183	5.87	4	141
Dec. 6	4.52	4.111	0	150	4.43	4	146
16	14.49	4 243	+ 1	112	2.96	4	145
26	24.46	4.333	1	70	1.54	4	140
36	34.44	+4.381	+ 1	+ 26	+ 0.18	— 4	—130

* ♂ ☉, June 13.8.
* ♂ Mean Sun, June 13.8.

Sidereal Day	Δ☊α	Δ☊δ	Δ☊α	Δ☊δ
	1865.		**1873.**	
0	+0.626	—6.86	—0.906	+3.65
100	0.545	7.41	0.855	4.40
200	0.459	7.90	0.797	5.11
300	0.368	8.32	0.732	5.78
400	0.275	8.67	0.662	6.39
	1866.		**1874.**	
0	+0.306	—8.56	—0.686	+6.19
100	0.211	8.85	0.612	6.77
200	0.114	9.07	0.533	7.30
300	+0.015	9.21	0.450	7.76
400	—0.083	9.27	0.363	8.16
	1867.		**1875.**	
0	—0.050	—9.26	—0.393	+8.03
100	0.148	9.27	0.304	8.39
200	0.245	9.19	0.213	8.67
300	0.339	9.04	0.120	8.89
400	0.431	8.81	0.026	9.03
	1868 B.		**1876 B.**	
0	—0.399	—8.89	—0.058	+8.99
100	0.489	8.61	+0.036	9.08
200	0.574	8.25	0.130	9.10
300	0.653	7.82	0.223	9.04
400	0.727	7.32	0.313	8.90
	1869.		**1877.**	
0	—0.703	—7.49	+0.283	+8.96
100	0.772	6.95	0.372	8.77
200	0.835	6.35	0.459	8.52
300	0.890	5.70	0.541	8.19
400	0.937	5.00	0.620	7.80
	1870.		**1878.**	
0	—0.922	—5.24	+0.594	+7.94
100	0.964	4.51	0.669	7.50
200	0.997	3.75	0.739	7.00
300	1.022	2.95	0.803	6.44
400	1.038	2.13	0.861	5.82
	1871.		**1879.**	
0	—1.034	—2.41	+0.842	+6.04
100	1.044	1 58	0.895	5.39
200	1.045	—0.74	0.940	4.69
300	1.037	+0.11	0.978	3.96
400	1.020	0.95	1.008	3.19
	1872 B.		**1880 B.**	
0	—1.027	+0.67	+0.939	+3.45
100	1.005	1.51	1.023	2.66
200	0.974	2.33	1.038	1.84
300	0.936	3.13	1.045	1.01
400	—0.890	+3.90	+1.043	+0.16

TABLE XXIV.—α Columbæ.

R.A. 5h 34.9m.   Dec. — 34° 9'.

Upper transit at fictitious meridian.

Sidereal Day	Mean Day	$\Delta_\odot \alpha$ 1870.	Var. in 10 y.	Diff. for 10 d.	$\Delta_\odot \delta$ 1870.	Var. in 10 y.	Diff. for 10 d.
0, Jan. 0	— 0.55	+1.600	0	+ 2	— 4.56	+ 2	—284
10	+ 9.43	1.577	+ 1	— 48	7.29	2	261
20	19.40	1.504	1	98	9.75	2	229
30	29.37	1.392	1	144	11.86	1	193
Feb. 9	8.34	1.219	2	182	13.60	+ 1	153
19	18.32	1.021	2	211	14.91	0	110
Mar. 1	0.29	0.799	2	232	15.79	0	65
11	10.26	0.560	2	243	16.20	0	— 19
21	20.24	0.316	3	242	16.17	0	+ 26
31	30.21	+0.078	3	230	15.69	— 1	70
100, Apr. 10	9.18	—0.142	3	209	14.79	1	112
20	19.15	0.338	2	180	13.47	1	152
30	29.13	0.500	2	143	11.77	2	188
May 10	9.10	0.622	1	100	9.73	2	219
20	19.07	0.699	+ 1	54	7.41	2	246
30	29.04	0.730	0	— 6	4.83	3	269
June 9	8.02	0.712	0	+ 42	— 2.06	3	284
19	17.99	0.646	0	89	+ 0.82	3	292
29	27.96	0.534	0	134	3.76	3	293
July 9	7.93	0.379	— 1	175	6.66	3	285
200, 19	17.91	—0.185	1	213	9.43	3	268
29	27.88	+0.045	1	246	12.01	3	246
Aug. 8	6.85	0.304	2	269	14.34	3	214
18	16.83	0.585	2	290	16.28	3	173
28	26.80	0.886	2	308	17.78	3	127
Sept. 7	5.77	1.198	3	317	18.81	2	77
17	15.74	1.518	3	321	19.29	2	+ 22
27	25.72	1.838	2	318	19.23	2	— 33
Oct. 7	5.69	2.152	2	311	18.62	2	90
17	15.66	2.457	2	297	17.43	2	144
300, 27	25.63	2.743	1	275	15.76	1	191
Nov. 6	4.61	3.004	1	248	13.64	1	233
16	14.58	3.237	— 1	216	11.13	1	265
26	24.55	3.435	0	177	8.37	1	288
Dec. 6	4.53	3.590	0	134	5.40	1	301
16	14.50	3.701	0	86	+ 2.39	1	301
26	24.47	3.761	+ 1	+ 35	— 0.59	1	294
36	34.44	+3.770	+ 1	— 17	— 3.45	— 1	—276

✶ ☌ ☉, June 15.1.
✶ ☌ Mean Sun, June 15.1.

Sidereal Day	$\Delta_\Omega \alpha$	$\Delta_\Omega \delta$	$\Delta_\Omega \alpha$	$\Delta_\Omega \delta$
	1865.		**1873.**	
0	+0.411	—6.98	—0.626	+3.80
100	0.351	7.52	0.586	4.54
200	0.287	8.00	0.541	5.24
300	0.221	8.40	0.492	5.90
400	0.153	8.73	0.439	6.52
	1866.		**1874.**	
0	+0.176	—8.63	—0.458	+6.31
100	0.107	8.91	0.402	6.88
200	+0.037	9.12	0.344	7.40
300	—0.034	9.24	0.282	7.85
400	0.104	9.29	0.219	8.24
	1867.		**1875.**	
0	—0.080	—9.28	—0.240	+8.12
100	0.150	9.27	0.176	8.46
200	0.218	9.18	0.110	8.73
300	0.285	9.01	—0.043	8.93
400	0.349	8.77	+0.023	9.06
	1868 B.		**1876 B.**	
0	—0.327	—8.86	+0.002	+9.02
100	0.389	8.56	0.069	9.10
200	0.448	8.18	0.136	9.10
300	0.502	7.74	0.201	9.03
400	0.552	7.23	0.265	8.88
	1869.		**1877.**	
0	—0.535	—7.41	+0.244	+8.94
100	0.582	6.85	0.306	8.74
200	0.624	6.24	0.367	8.47
300	0.659	5.58	0.424	8.13
400	0.690	4.87	0.478	7.73
	1870.		**1878.**	
0	—0.680	—5.11	+0.460	+7.87
100	0.706	4.38	0.511	7.42
200	0.726	3.60	0.558	6.91
300	0.740	2.80	0.601	6.34
400	0.747	1.98	0.639	5.71
	1871.		**1879.**	
0	—0.746	—2.26	+0.627	+5.93
100	0.749	1.42	0.661	5.27
200	0.746	—0.58	0.690	4.57
300	0.736	+0.27	0.714	3.82
400	0.720	1.11	0.731	3.04
	1872 B.		**1880 B.**	
0	0.726	+0.83	+0.726	+3.31
100	0.706	1.66	0.739	2.51
200	0.681	2.48	0.746	1.69
300	0.649	3.25	0.747	0.85
400	—0.613	+4.05	+0.742	+0.01

TABLE XXIV.—* 22 Camelopardalis (II.)

R.A. 6h 4.5m   Dec. +69° 22′

Upper transit at fictitious meridian.

Sidereal Day	Mean Day	$\Delta_\odot\alpha$ 1870	Var.in 10y	Diff.for 10d	$\Delta_\odot\delta$ 1870	Var.in 10y	Diff.for 10d
0, Jan. 0	− 0.52	+3.868	+ 2	+140	+ 1.51	− 9	+263
10	+ 9.45	3.944	5	+ 12	4.12	9	258
20	19.42	3.893	8	−115	6.64	9	244
30	29.39	3.718	11	234	8.97	8	221
Feb. 9	8.37	3.429	13	340	11.03	7	189
19	18.34	3.044	15	428	12.73	6	150
Mar. 1	0.31	2.582	16	492	14.01	5	105
11	10.28	2.067	17	532	14.81	4	56
21	20.26	1.527	18	544	15.12	2	+ 6
31	30.23	0.988	17	530	14.93	− 1	− 44
100, Apr. 10	9.20	0.476	16	490	14.25	0	91
20	19.18	+0.016	15	428	13.12	+ 2	134
30	29.15	−0.373	13	347	11.59	3	171
May 10	9.12	0.674	11	252	9.72	4	201
20	19.09	0.873	9	146	7.59	4	224
30	29.07	0.964	6	− 35	5.27	5	239
June 9	8.04	0 943	3	+ 78	2.83	5	247
19	18.01	0.810	+ 1	188	+ 0.36	5	247
29	27.98	0.569	− 2	293	− 2.08	4	240
July 9	7.96	−0.226	5	391	4.42	4	228
200, 19	17.93	+0.210	7	480	6.62	3	210
29	27.90	0.730	10	558	8.61	2	188
Aug. 8	6.87	1.322	12	625	10.36	+ 1	162
18	16.85	1.975	14	630	11.84	− 1	133
28	26.82	2.677	15	724	13.01	2	101
Sept. 7	5.79	3.418	16	755	13.86	4	67
17	15.77	4.184	18	776	14.36	6	− 33
27	25.74	4.965	17	785	14.51	7	+ 3
Oct. 7	5.71	5.748	17	779	14.29	9	40
17	15.68	6.520	16	762	13.71	11	77
300, 27	25.66	7.267	15	730	12.76	13	113
Nov. 6	4.63	7.974	14	683	11.45	14	148
16	14.60	8.627	12	620	9.81	16	180
26	24.57	9.208	9	541	7.86	17	209
Dec. 6	4.55	9.703	7	446	5.64	18	233
16	14.52	10.096	4	338	3.22	18	250
26	24.49	10.375	− 1	219	− 0.66	19	261
36	34.47	+10.531	+ 2	+ 93	+ 1.97	−19	+262

✳ ♂ ☉, June 22.0.
✳ ♂ Mean Sun, June 22.4.
✳ ☌ Mean Sun, Dec. 22.0.

Sidereal Day	$\Delta_\Omega\alpha$	$\Delta_\Omega\delta$	$\Delta_\Omega\alpha$	$\Delta_\Omega\delta$
	1865.		**1873.**	
0	+1.335	−7.55	−1.956	+4.59
100	1.157	8.02	1.843	5.29
200	0.969	8.43	1.715	5 95
300	0.771	8.76	1.573	6.56
400	0.567	9.02	1.419	7.11
	1866.		**1874.**	
0	+0.637	−8.94	−1.473	+6.94
100	0.429	9.14	1.310	7.45
200	0.217	9.27	1.138	7.90
300	+0.004	9.31	0.956	8.28
400	−0.210	9.28	0.767	8.60
	1867.		**1875.**	
0	−0.138	−9.30	−0.832	+8.50
100	0.351	9.20	0 63e	8.77
200	0.561	9.03	0.440	8.96
300	0.765	8.78	0.238	9.09
400	0.963	8.45	0.035	9.13
	1868 B.		**1876 B.**	
0	−0.897	−8.57	−0.104	+9.13
100	1.089	8.20	+0.100	9.12
200	1.271	7.75	0.305	9.04
300	1.442	7.23	0.505	8.89
400	1.600	6.66	0.701	8.66
	1869.		**1877.**	
0	−1.548	−6.86	+0.635	+8.75
100	1 697	6.24	0.829	8.47
200	1.830	5.58	1.015	8.13
300	1.948	4.86	1.194	7.71
400	2.04e	4.11	1.364	7.24
	1870.		**1878.**	
0	−2.016	−4.37	+1.308	+7.40
100	2.105	3.59	1.470	6.89
200	2.175	2.78	1.620	6.31
300	2.226	1.95	1.757	5.68
400	2.259	1.11	1.881	5.00
	1871.		**1879.**	
0	−2.250	−1.39	+1.841	+5.23
100	2.269	−0.55	1.954	4.52
200	2.269	+0.31	2.051	3.77
300	2.250	1.15	2.131	2.99
400	2.212	1.99	2.194	2.18
	1872 B.		**1880 B.**	
0	−2.227	+1.71	+2.175	+2.46
100	2.177	2.53	2 225	1.64
200	2.108	3.33	2.258	+0.80
300	2.022	4.10	2.270	−0.05
400	−1.920	+4.83	+2.264	−0.90

TABLE XXIV.—μ Geminorum.

R.A. 6h 15.1.   Dec. +22° 35'.

Upper transit at fictitious meridian.

Sidereal Day	Mean Day.	$\Delta_\odot a$ 1870.	Var.in 10y.	Diff.for 10d.	$\Delta_\odot \delta$ 1870.	Var.in 10y.	Diff.for 10d.
0, Jan. 0	− 0.52	+1.492	0	+104	− 1.10	− 2	− 3
10	+ 9.45	1.570	+ 1	53	1.09	2	+ 5
20	19.43	1.598	2	+ 2	1.01	2	12
30	29.40	1.575	2	− 48	0.86	2	16
Feb. 9	8.37	1.504	3	91	0.69	2	18
19	18.34	1.391	3	131	0.49	2	18
Mar. 1	0.32	1.244	3	161	0.31	2	15
11	10.29	1.072	3	180	0.18	2	11
21	20.26	0.888	3	186	0.09	1	6
31	30.24	0.703	3	183	0.05	1	+ 1
100, Apr. 10	9 21	0.526	3	168	0.07	1	− 5
20	19.18	0.371	3	142	0.14	1	9
30	29 15	0.244	2	110	0.25	1	11
May 10	9.13	0.152	2	73	0.36	1	12
20	19.10	0.100	2	− 31	0.49	0	12
30	29.07	0.091	2	+ 13	0.60	0	9
June 9	8.04	0.127	1	58	0.66	0	5
19	18 02	0.207	+ 1	100	0.60	0	− 1
29	27.99	0.327	0	139	0.68	1	+ 3
July 9	7.96	0.485	0	177	0.62	1	7
200, 19	17.94	0.679	− 1	209	0.54	1	10
29	27.91	0.902	1	237	0.42	1	13
Aug. 8	6.88	1.152	2	259	0.29	2	13
18	16.85	1 422	2	280	0.17	2	10
28	26.83	1.711	3	296	0.10	2	+ 6
Sept. 7	5.80	2.012	3	307	0.06	3	0
17	15.77	2.323	3	315	0.09	3	− 7
27	25.74	2.642	4	320	0.20	4	14
Oct. 7	5.72	2.964	4	321	0.38	4	22
17	15.69	3.283	3	318	0.62	4	28
300, 27	25.66	3.596	3	310	0.91	5	31
Nov. 6	4 63	3.902	3	298	1.24	5	33
16	14.61	4.190	3	277	1.56	6	32
26	24 58	4.454	2	252	1.88	7	30
Dec. 6	4.55	4.691	2	220	2.16	7	24
16	14.53	4.891	− 1	180	2.36	7	17
26	24.50	5.050	0	135	2.50	7	− 9
36	34.47	+5.160	0	+ 85	− 2.55	− 7	0

✱ ♂ ☉,   June 24.7.
✱ ♂ Mean Sun, June 25.3.

Sidereal Day	$\Delta_\Omega a$	$\Delta_\Omega \delta$	$\Delta_\Omega a$	$\Delta_\Omega \delta$
	1865.		**1873.**	
0	+0.735	−7.73	−1.072	+4.86
100	0.637	8.18	1.010	6.18
200	0.534	8.56	0.940	6.18
300	0.425	8.86	0.862	6.77
400	0.313	9.09	0.777	7.30
	1866.		**1874.**	
0	+0.351	−9.02	−0.806	+7.13
100	0.237	9.19	0.717	7.62
200	0.121	9.29	0.622	8.04
300	+0.004	9.30	0.523	8.40
400	−0.114	9.23	0.419	8.69
	1867.		**1875.**	
0	−0.074	−9.26	−0.454	+8.60
100	0.191	9.14	0.348	8.84
200	0.306	8.94	0.239	9.01
300	0.418	8.66	0.128	9.10
400	0.527	8.30	0.016	9.12
	1868 B.		**1876 B.**	
0	−0.491	−8.43	−0.054	+9.13
100	0.596	8.03	+0.058	9.09
200	0.696	7.56	0.170	8.99
300	0.790	7.02	0.280	8.81
400	0.877	6.42	0.388	8.55
	1869.		**1877.**	
0	−0.847	−6.63	+0.352	+8.65
100	0.930	5.90	0.458	8.34
200	1.004	5.31	0.560	7.97
300	1.068	4.58	0.655	7.54
400	1.123	3.81	0.751	7.04
	1870.		**1878.**	
0	−1.106	−4.07	+0.720	+7.21
100	1.154	3.28	0.809	6.67
200	1.193	2.47	0.891	6.08
300	1.221	1.63	0.966	5.43
400	1.239	0.78	1.034	4.74
	1871.		**1879.**	
0	−1.234	−1.07	+1.012	+4.97
100	1.244	−0.23	1.074	4.25
200	1.245	+0.62	1.127	3.49
300	1.254	1.47	1.176	2.70
400	1.213	2.29	1.204	1.89
	1872 B.		**1880 B.**	
0	−1.221	+2.02	+1.194	+2.16
100	1.193	2.83	1.221	1.34
200	1.156	3.62	1.239	+0.49
300	1.109	4.37	1.245	−0.36
400	−1.052	+5.09	+1.245	−1.20

TABLE XXIV.—α Argus.

R.A. 6 21.1.   Dec. — 52 38.

Upper transit at fictitious meridian.

Sidereal Day	Mean Day	$\Delta_\odot\alpha$ 1870.	Var.in 10y.	Diff. for 10 d.	$\Delta_\odot\delta$ 1870.	Var.in 10y.	Diff. for 10 d.
0, Jan. 0	− 0.51	+2.250	+ 1	+ 15	− 2.33	+ 1	−350
10	+ 9.46	2.229	1	− 57	5.75	1	333
20	19.43	2.137	1	126	8.96	1	306
30	29.40	1.979	2	190	11.85	1	271
Feb. 9	8.38	1.760	2	247	14.36	1	230
19	18.35	1.488	2	294	16.43	+ 1	183
Mar. 1	0.32	1.175	2	329	18.01	0	133
11	10.29	0.835	2	352	19.09	0	81
21	20.27	0.476	2	362	19.63	0	− 28
31	30.24	+0.116	2	358	19.66	0	+ 23
100, Apr. 10	9 21	−0.235	2	342	19.18	− 1	74
20	19.19	0 564	2	315	18.19	1	123
30	29.16	0.862	1	278	16.73	1	169
May 10	9.13	1.117	1	232	14.82	1	211
20	19.10	1.324	1	181	12.53	2	247
30	29.08	1.478	+ 1	125	9.90	2	278
June 9	8.05	1.573	0	64	6.99	2	302
19	18.02	1.606	0	− 3	3.89	3	318
29	27.99	1.579	0	+ 57	− 0.66	3	327
July 9	7.97	1.492	− 1	117	+ 2.62	3	326
200, 19	17.94	1.346	1	174	5.82	2	315
29	27.91	1.146	1	226	8.89	2	296
Aug. 8	6 88	0.895	1	275	11.71	2	266
18	16.86	0.599	1	317	14.17	2	226
28	26.83	−0.264	2	351	16.20	2	180
Sept. 7	5.80	+0.101	2	379	17.74	2	125
17	15.78	0.491	2	293	18.69	2	65
27	25.75	0.894	2	408	19.03	1	+ 3
Oct. 7	5.72	1.304	2	409	18.74	1	− 62
17	15.69	1.709	2	398	17.79	1	126
300, 27	25.67	2.097	1	378	16.23	− 1	185
Nov. 6	4.64	2.462	1	347	14.11	0	238
16	14 61	2.788	1	305	11.49	0	284
26	24 58	3.070	1	255	8.46	0	320
Dec. 6	4.56	3.297	− 1	196	5.12	0	343
16	14 53	3.460	0	130	+ 1.63	0	355
26	24.50	3.556	0	+ 62	− 1.95	0	357
36	34.48	+3.582	+ 1	− 10	− 5.47	0	−346

✱ ♂ ☉,   June 26.2.
✱ ♂ Mean Sun,   June 26.8.

Sidereal Day	$\Delta_\Omega\alpha$	$\Delta_\Omega\delta$	$\Delta_\Omega\alpha$	$\Delta_\Omega\delta$
	1865.		1873.	
0	+0.365	−7.83	−0.434	+5.00
100	0.303	8.26	0.417	5.68
200	0.269	8.62	0.307	6.31
300	0.232	8.91	0.374	6.88
400	0.193	9.12	0.347	7.40
	1866.		1874.	
0	+0.206	−9.05	−0.357	+7.23
100	0.166	9.21	0.328	7 71
200	0.124	9.29	0.297	8.12
300	0.082	9.28	0.264	8.46
400	0.039	9.20	0.229	8.73
	1867.		1875.	
0	+0.053	−9.24	−0.241	+8.65
100	+0.010	9.10	0.204	8.88
200	−0.034	8.88	0.166	9.03
300	0.078	8.58	0.126	9.11
400	0.120	8.21	0.086	9.11
	1868 B.		1876 B.	
0	−0.106	−8.35	−0.100	+9.12
100	0.148	7.93	0.059	9.07
200	0.189	7.44	−0.017	8.95
300	0.227	6.89	+0 025	8.75
400	0.264	6.28	0.066	8.49
	1869.		1877.	
0	−0.252	−6.49	+0.052	+8.58
100	0.287	5.85	0.094	8.27
200	0.320	5.15	0.134	7.88
300	0.350	4.42	0.174	7.44
400	0.377	3 64	0.212	6.92
	1870.		1878.	
0	−0.368	−3 91	+0.199	+7.10
100	0.392	3.11	0.236	6.55
200	0.414	2 29	0.272	5.95
300	0.431	1.46	0.305	5.29
400	0.445	0.62	0.336	4.59
	1871.		1879.	
0	−0.441	−0.90	+0.325	+4.83
100	0.452	−0.05	0.354	4.10
200	0.460	+0.80	0.386	3.33
300	0.463	1.64	0.403	2.54
400	0.463	2.46	0.423	1.72
	1872 B.		1880 B.	
0	−0.463	+2.19	+0.417	+2.00
100	0.460	3.00	0.454	1.17
200	0.453	3.78	0 448	+0.32
300	0.443	4.52	0.437	−0.52
400	−0.428	+5.23	+0.464	−1.37

TABLE XXIV.—γ Geminorum.

R.A. 6 30.2 (h m).   Dec. + 16 30 (° ′).

Upper transit at fictitious meridian.

Sidereal Day	Mean Day	$\Delta_\odot a$ 1870.	Var. in 10 y.	Diff. for 10 d.	$\Delta_\odot \delta$ 1870.	Var. in 10 y.	Diff. for 10 d.
0, Jan. 0	− 0.51	+1.441	0	+114	− 1.71	− 2	− 45
10	+ 9.46	1.530	0	64	2.11	2	34
20	19.44	1.570	+ 1	+ 15	2.40	2	24
30	29 41	1.561	1	− 34	2.58	2	15
Feb. 9	8.38	1.504	2	80	2.69	2	− 7
19	18.36	1.404	2	119	2.72	2	0
Mar. 1	0.33	1.269	2	149	2.70	2	+ 5
11	10.30	1.110	3	169	2.63	2	7
21	20 28	0.934	3	179	2.55	1	8
31	30.25	0.756	3	177	2.47	1	8
100, Apr. 10	9.22	0.584	3	165	2.38	1	9
20	19.19	0.429	3	144	2.29	1	10
30	29.16	0.298	3	116	2.17	1	12
May 10	9.14	0.199	2	81	2.04	1	15
20	19.11	0.138	1	40	1.87	1	18
30	29.08	0.118	1	− 1	1.67	1	22
June 9	8.06	0.137	+ 1	+ 40	1.42	0	27
19	18.03	0.198	0	81	1.13	0	31
29	28.00	0.299	0	120	0.80	1	35
July 9	7.97	0.438	0	155	0.43	1	38
200, 19	17.95	0.608	− 1	185	− 0.05	1	38
29	27.92	0.808	1	215	+ 0.32	2	36
Aug. 8	6.89	1.038	2	240	0.66	2	31
18	16.86	1.287	2	259	0.94	2	25
28	26.84	1.555	3	276	1.15	2	16
Sept. 7	5.81	1.838	3	290	1.26	3	+ 4
17	15.78	2.133	3	300	1.23	3	− 9
27	25.75	2.436	3	307	1.07	3	23
Oct. 7	5.73	2.745	4	311	0.78	4	36
17	15.70	3.056	4	310	+ 0.35	4	48
300, 27	25.67	3.364	3	305	− 0.18	4	58
Nov. 6	4.65	3.664	3	294	0.80	5	66
16	14.62	3.951	2	277	1.49	5	70
26	24.59	4.217	2	254	2.19	5	70
Dec. 6	4.56	4.457	1	224	2.88	5	66
16	14.54	4.663	1	187	3.51	6	60
26	24.51	4.829	− 1	144	4.08	6	52
36	34.48	+4.950	0	+ 96	− 4.54	− 7	− 41

✳ ☌ ⊙,   June 28.4.
✳ ☌ Mean Sun,   June 29.1.

Sidereal Day	$\Delta_\Omega a$	$\Delta_\Omega \delta$	$\Delta_\Omega a$	$\Delta_\Omega \delta$
	1865.		**1873.**	
0	+0.695	−7.95	−1.021	+5.22
100	0.602	8.36	0.961	5.88
200	0.503	8.70	0.893	6.49
300	0.399	8.96	0.818	7.04
400	0.292	9.15	0.736	7.54
	1866.		**1874.**	
0	+0.328	−9.09	−0.765	+7.38
100	0.219	9.23	0.679	7.84
200	+0.108	9.28	0.588	8.22
300	−0.004	9.25	0.492	8.54
400	0.116	9.14	0.392	8.79
	1867.		**1875.**	
0	−0.079	−9.18	−0.427	+8.72
100	0.190	9.02	0.325	8.92
200	0.300	8.78	0.221	9.04
300	0.407	8.46	0.115	9.10
400	0.511	8.06	0.008	9.07
	1868 B.		**1876 B.**	
0	−0.476	−8.20	−0.044	+9.09
100	0.577	7.76	+0.063	9.02
200	0.672	7.26	0.169	8.87
300	0.761	6.69	0.275	8.65
400	0.844	6.06	0.378	8.36
	1869.		**1877.**	
0	−0.817	−6.28	+0.343	+8.47
100	0.894	5.62	0.444	8.13
200	0.964	4.91	0.542	7.72
300	1.025	4.17	0.635	7.25
400	1.077	3.38	0.723	6.72
	1870.		**1878.**	
0	−1.060	−3.65	+0.694	+6.91
100	1.106	2.84	0.779	6.34
200	1.142	2.02	0.857	5.72
300	1.168	1.18	0.928	5.05
400	1.185	0.33	0.992	4.33
	1871.		**1879.**	
0	−1.180	−0.62	+0.971	+4.58
100	1.190	+0.23	1.030	3.84
200	1.189	1.07	1.080	3.06
300	1.178	1.91	1.121	2.26
400	1.157	2.72	1.153	1.44
	1872 B.		**1880 B.**	
0	−1.165	+2.45	+1.143	+1.72
100	1.138	3.25	1.168	0.88
200	1.102	4.02	1.184	+0.04
300	1.056	4.75	1.190	−0.81
400	−1.001	+5.44	+1.186	−1.65

TABLE XXIV.—*51 Cephei (Hev.)†

R.A. 6 33.7.   Dec. + 87 14.

Upper transit at fictitious meridian.

Sidereal Day.	Mean Day.	Δ☉a 1870.	Var. in 10y.	Diff. for 10d.	Δ☉δ 1870.	Var. in 10y.	Diff. for 10d.
0, Jan. 0	− 0.51	+28.32	−12	+107	− 0.96	−46	+320
10	+ 9.46	28.93	− 2	+ 15	+ 2.27	46	323
20	19.44	28.62	+ 8	− 76	5.46	45	314
30	29.41	27.42	18	164	8.51	43	293
Feb. 9	8.38	25.38	27	243	11.27	40	261
19	18.36	22.59	36	312	13.67	35	219
Mar. 1	0.33	19.20	43	366	15.63	30	169
11	10.30	15.33	48	404	17.04	24	113
21	20 28	11.17	52	425	17.87	17	+ 53
31	30.25	6.89	54	428	18.09	10	− 8
100, Apr. 10	9.22	+ 2.66	55	414	17.72	− 3	68
20	19.19	− 1.34	53	384	16.76	+ 3	123
30	29 16	4.97	49	340	15.26	9	174
May 10	9.14	8.09	44	283	13.29	14	218
20	19.11	10.60	38	218	10.93	18	254
30	29.08	12.42	30	145	8.24	21	282
June 9	8.06	13.49	21	− 69	5.32	23	301
19	18.03	13.78	12	+ 10	+ 2 26	24	310
29	28.00	13 29	+ 2	88	− 0.86	23	313
July 9	7.97	12.04	− 8	163	3.96	21	306
200, 19	17.95	10.04	18	236	6 96	18	292
29	27.92	7.35	27	302	9.79	14	272
Aug. 8	6.89	4.04	37	362	12.39	9	246
18	16.86	− 0.16	45	413	14.70	+ 3	215
28	26.84	+ 4.21	53	458	16.67	− 4	179
Sept. 7	5.81	8.97	59	493	18.27	11	139
17	15.78	14.05	64	520	19.45	19	97
27	25.75	19.33	68	535	20.19	27	51
Oct. 7	5.73	24.74	71	541	20.48	36	− 5
17	15.70	30.13	72	535	20.28	44	+ 44
300, 27	25.67	35.40	72	517	19.59	53	93
Nov. 6	4.65	40.43	70	487	18.42	61	140
16	14.62	45.10	66	445	16.78	68	186
26	24.59	49.29	61	390	14.70	74	227
Dec. 6	4.56	52.86	54	324	12.24	80	264
16	14.54	55.73	46	248	9.46	84	293
26	24.51	57.79	38	163	6.42	87	313
36	34.48	+58.97	−28	+ 73	− 3.23	−89	+323

Sidereal Day / ΔΩa / ΔΩδ / ΔΩa / ΔΩδ

Sidereal Day	1865. ΔΩa	ΔΩδ	1873. ΔΩa	ΔΩδ
0	+ 4.65	−8.03	− 7.95	+5.44
100	3.72	8.43	7.26	6.08
200	2.76	8.75	6.52	6.67
300	1.78	8.99	5.72	7.21
400	0.78	9.16	4.88	7.68

	1866.		1874.	
0	+ 1.12	−9.11	− 5.17	+7.53
100	+ 0.11	9.22	4.30	7.96
200	− 0.90	9.26	3.40	8.32
300	1.90	9.21	2.46	8.62
400	2.88	9.08	1.51	8.84

	1867.		1875.	
0	− 2.55	−9.13	− 1.84	+8.77
100	3.52	8.95	− 0.88	8.95
200	4.46	8.68	+ 0.09	9.05
300	5.35	8.34	1.05	9.07
400	6.20	7.93	2.00	9.01

	1868 B.		1876 B.	
0	− 5.92	−8.06	+ 1.68	+9.04
100	6.73	7.62	2.63	8.94
200	7.48	7.09	3.55	8.76
300	8.17	6.51	4.44	8.51
400	8.78	5.86	5.30	8.19

	1869.		1877.	
0	− 8.58	−6.09	+ 5.01	+8.30
100	9.14	5.41	5.84	7.94
200	9.61	4.69	6.62	7.50
300	10.00	3.93	7.34	7.01
400	10.31	3.13	8.01	6.45

	1870.		1878.	
0	−10.21	−3.41	+ 7.79	+6.65
100	10.46	2.59	8.41	6.06
200	10.60	1.76	8.96	5.41
300	10.66	0.92	9.44	4.72
400	10.62	0.07	9.84	3.98

	1871.		1879.	
0	−10.65	−0.35	+ 9.72	+4.24
100	10.55	+0.50	10.06	3.48
200	10.36	1.34	10.3.	2.69
300	10.08	2.17	10.50	1.88
400	9.72	2.98	10.58	1.05

	1872 B.		1880 B.	
0	− 9.85	+2.71	+10.56	+1.33
100	9.43	3.50	10.59	+0.49
200	8.94	4.26	10.52	−0.35
300	8.36	4.98	10.37	1.20
400	7.72	+5.66	+10.12	−2.03

✳ ♂ ☉,   June 30 5.
✳ ♂ Mean Sun,   July 1.3.
✳ ☍ Mean Sun,   Dec. 30.9.

† See pages 248, 249, 251-253 for additional corrections.

TABLE XXIV.—ε Canis Majoris.

R.A. 6ʰ 53ᵐ.5.   Dec. — 28° 48′.

Upper transit at fictitious meridian.

Sidereal Day	Mean Day	Δ☉a 1870	Var. in 10 y.	Diff. for 10 d.	Δ☉δ 1870	Var. in 10 y.	Diff. for 10 d.
0, Jan. 0	− 0.49	+1.568	0	+ 98	− 0.92	+ 2	−296
10	+ 9.48	1.640	0	+ 45	3.83	2	284
20	19.45	1.658	+ 1	− 8	6.57	2	263
30	29.43	1.625	1	59	9.07	1	236
Feb. 9	8.40	1.541	2	106	11.28	+ 1	204
19	18.37	1.414	2	148	13.14	0	168
Mar. 1	0.34	1.248	2	182	14.63	0	129
11	10.32	1.054	2	203	15.72	− 1	89
21	20.29	0.844	2	216	16.40	1	48
31	30.26	0.623	2	219	16 67	1	− 6
100, Apr. 10	9.23	0.407	2	212	16.53	1	+ 34
20	19.21	0.201	2	197	16.00	1	72
30	29.18	+0.015	2	172	15.09	2	111
May 10	9.15	−0.141	2	140	13.79	2	146
20	19.13	0.264	2	105	12.18	2	176
30	29.10	0.351	1	67	10.27	3	204
June 9	8.07	0.398	1	− 26	8.11	3	228
19	18.04	0.403	+ 1	+ 16	5.74	3	245
29	28.02	0.367	0	56	3.24	4	254
July 9	7.99	0.291	0	96	− 0.68	4	258
200, 19	17.96	0.175	0	134	+ 1.89	4	253
29	27.93	−0.023	− 1	168	4.36	3	241
Aug. 8	6.91	+0.161	1	199	6.69	3	221
18	16.88	0.375	2	229	8.76	3	192
28	26.85	0.618	2	255	10.52	3	157
Sept. 7	5.83	0.883	2	276	11.88	3	113
17	15.80	1.168	2	293	12.77	3	65
27	25.77	1.468	2	305	13.17	3	+ 14
Oct. 7	5.74	1.777	2	313	13.04	2	− 41
17	15.72	2.092	2	315	12.36	2	94
300, 27	25.69	2.405	2	310	11.18	2	144
Nov. 6	4.66	2.710	1	298	9.50	2	190
16	14.63	2.999	1	279	7.40	2	230
26	24.61	3.265	1	253	4.93	2	262
Dec. 6	4.58	3.502	1	219	+ 2.19	2	284
16	14.55	3.702	− 1	177	− 0.71	2	297
26	24.53	3.855	0	129	3.70	2	300
36	34.50	+3.960	0	+ 79	− 6.67	− 2	−293

Sidereal Day	ΔΩa	ΔΩδ	ΔΩa	ΔΩδ
	1865.		**1873.**	
0	+0.550	−8.23	−0.741	+5.73
100	0.491	8.58	0.708	6.34
200	0.428	8.85	0.66~	6.90
300	0.361	9.05	0.624	7.41
400	0.290	9.14	0.574	7.84
	1866.		**1874.**	
0	+0.314	−9.13	−0.591	+7.70
100	0 242	9.20	0.538	8.10
200	0.168	9.18	0.481	8.43
300	0.092	9.09	0.420	8.69
400	0.015	8.92	0.356	8.87
	1867.		**1875.**	
0	+0.041	−8.98	−0.378	+8.82
100	−0.035	8.75	0.311	8.96
200	0.112	8.45	0.243	9.02
300	0.187	8.07	0.172	9.01
400	0.261	7.62	0.100	8.92
	1868 B.		**1876 B.**	
0	−0.236	−7.78	−0.124	+8 96
100	0.306	7.29	−0.051	8.83
200	0.378	6.74	+0.022	8.62
300	0.444	6.13	0 095	8.34
400	0.506	5.46	0.168	8.00
	1869.		**1877.**	
0	−0.485	−5.60	+0.143	+8.12
100	0.544	4.99	0.215	7.73
200	0.598	4.26	0.285	7.27
300	0.647	3.49	0.352	6.76
400	0.690	2.69	0.417	6.18
	1870.		**1878.**	
0	−0.676	−2.96	+0.396	+6.38
100	0.715	2.14	0.458	5.78
200	0.748	1.31	0.518	5.12
300	0.774	−0.47	0.572	4.42
400	0.794	+0.37	0.623	3.68
	1871.		**1879.**	
0	−0.788	+0.09	+0.606	+3.93
100	0.803	0.93	0.653	3.17
200	0.811	1.76	0.695	2.38
300	0.813	2.56	0.731	1.56
400	0.807	3.36	0.761	0.74
	1872 B.		**1880 B.**	
0	−0.810	+3.09	+0.752	+1.02
100	0.800	3.86	0.777	+0.18
200	0.783	4.60	0 797	−0.66
300	0.760	5.29	0.809	1.49
400	−0.731	+5.94	+0.815	−2.31

✳ ☌ ☉,   July 4.0.
✳ ☌ Mean Sun,   July 5.1.

TABLE XXIV.—δ Canis Majoris.

R.A. 7h 3.1m. Dec. − 26° 11′.

Upper transit at fictitious meridian.

Sidereal Day	Mean Day	Δ☉α 1870.	Δ☉α Var. in 10 y.	Δ☉α Diff. for 10 d.	Δ☉δ 1870.	Δ☉δ Var. in 10 y.	Δ☉δ Diff. for 10 d.
0, Jan. 0	− 0.49	+1.526	0	+111	− 0.66	+ 2	−287
10	+ 9.49	1.612	0	60	3.47	2	276
20	19.46	1.645	0	+ 6	6.16	2	258
30	29.43	1.625	+ 1	− 45	8.61	2	232
Feb. 9	8.41	1.557	1	92	10.78	+ 1	201
19	18.38	1.442	2	134	12.62	0	167
Mar. 1	0.35	1.291	2	168	14.11	0	131
11	10.32	1.109	2	192	15.23	0	92
21	20.30	0.909	3	206	15.93	0	52
31	30.27	0.699	2	211	16.26	− 1	− 12
100, Apr. 10	9 24	0.489	2	205	16.18	1	+ 27
20	19.21	0.291	2	190	15.73	1	63
30	29.19	+0.111	2	168	14.92	2	99
May 10	9.16	−0.044	2	139	13.75	2	134
20	19.13	0.166	2	104	12.26	2	164
30	29.11	0.252	1	68	10.49	2	190
June 9	8.08	0.302	+ 1	− 30	8 47	3	213
19	18.05	0.312	0	+ 11	6.25	3	231
29	28.02	0.281	0	50	3.88	3	242
July 9	8.00	0.212	0	89	− 1.44	3	246
200, 19	17.97	−0.104	− 1	126	+ 1.01	3	243
29	27.94	+0.039	1	159	3.40	4	232
Aug. 8	6.91	0.214	1	191	5 63	4	213
18	16.89	0.421	1	219	7.63	3	186
28	26.86	0.652	2	.243	9.33	3	152
Sept. 7	5.83	0.907	2	266	10.65	3	113
17	15.80	1.183	2	234	11.54	3	67
27	25.78	1.474	2	300	11.95	2	+ 16
Oct. 7	5.75	1.780	2	309	11.85	2	− 36
17	15.72	2.089	2	311	11.23	2	87
300, 27	25.70	2.400	2	310	10.11	2	137
Nov. 6	4.67	2.706	1	300	8.51	2	183
16	14.64	2.937	1	283	6.48	2	221
26	24.61	3.269	1	259	4.11	2	252
Dec. 6	4.59	3.513	− 1	227	+ 1.47	2	275
16	14.56	3.721	0	187	− 1.36	2	288
26	24.53	3.883	0	143	4.25	2	290
36	34.50	+4.005	0	+ 93	− 7.14	− 2	−285

✳ δ ☉, July 6.4.
✳ δ Mean Sun, July 7.5.

Sidereal Day	Δ☊α	Δ☊δ	Δ☊α	Δ☊δ
	1865.		**1873.**	
0	+0.570	−8.32	−0.768	+5 93
100	0.509	8.64	0.733	6 52
200	0.444	8.88	0.692	7 05
300	0 375	9 05	0 646	7 53
400	0.302	9.14	0.595	7.95
	1866.		**1874.**	
0	+0.327	−9.12	−0.613	+7 81
100	0 252	9.16	0 558	8 18
200	0.175	9.12	0.499	8.49
300	0.097	8 99	0 436	8 72
400	0.017	8.79	0.369	8.88
	1867.		**1875.**	
0	+0.044	−8.87	−0.392	+8.83
100	−0.035	8.62	0.323	8.95
200	0.114	8.29	0.252	8 98
300	0.192	7.89	0.179	8 95
400	0.269	7.42	0.104	8.83
	1868 B.		**1876 B.**	
0	−0.243	−7 59	−0.130	+8.88
100	0 318	7.07	−0.054	8.72
200	0.390	6.50	+0.022	8.49
300	0.458	5.87	0.097	8 19
400	0.522	5.20	0.172	7.82
	1869.		**1877.**	
0	−0.501	−5 43	+0.147	+7 95
100	0.562	4 72	0.221	7.54
200	0.618	3 98	0.293	7.06
300	0.669	3.20	0 363	6.53
400	0.713	2.39	0.431	5.94
	1870.		**1878.**	
0	−0.700	2.67	+0.408	+6.15
100	0.740	1.85	0.473	5.52
200	0.774	1.02	0 534	4.85
300	0.801	−0.18	0 591	4.14
400	0.822	+0.66	0.644	3.39
	1871.		**1879.**	
0	−0.815	+0.38	+0.627	+3.65
100	0.831	1.21	0.675	2 88
200	0 840	2.03	0.719	2.09
300	0.841	2.83	0.756	1.27
400	0.836	.3.61	0.787	0.44
	1872 B.		**1880 B.**	
0	−0.838	+3.35	+0.777	+0.72
100	0.828	4.11	0.804	−0.11
200	0.811	4.82	0.824	0.94
300	0.787	5.50	0.838	1.77
400	−0.756	+6.13	+0.844	−2.58

TABLE XXIV.—δ Geminorum.

R.A. 7 12.4. (h m)　　　　Dec. + 22 13. (° ')

Upper transit at fictitious meridian.

Sidereal Day	Mean Day	Δ☉α 1870.	Var.in 10y.	Diff.for 10d.	Δ☉δ 1870.	Var.in 10y.	Diff.for 10d.
0, Jan. 0	− 0.48	+1.469	0	+163	− 3.04	− 2	− 24
10	+ 9.49	1.608	0	113	3.21	2	− 9
20	19 47	1.694	0	58	3.23	2	+ 5
30	29.44	1.725	+ 1	+ 5	3.11	3	17
Feb. 9	8.41	1.704	2	− 46	2.89	3	25
19	18.38	1.634	2	91	2 62	3	30
Mar. 1	0.36	1.524	3	129	2.29	2	33
11	10.33	1.379	3	158	1.94	2	33
21	20.30	1.212	4	174	1.63	2	30
31	30.28	1.034	4	181	1.35	1	25
100, Apr. 10	9.25	0.854	4	176	1.13	1	19
20	19.22	0.685	3	161	0.98	1.	13
30	29.19	0.534	3	139	0.89	1	7
May 10	9.17	0.410	3	109	0.83	1	+ 2
20	19.14	0.318	2	73	0.84	0	− 2
30	29.11	0.265	2	− 35	0.87	0	5
June 9	8.08	0.249	2	+ 4	0.94	0	7
19	18.06	0.273	+ 1	44	1.02	0	8
29	28.03	0.337	0	84	1.10	0	9
July 9	8.00	0.440	0	121	1.21	0	11
200, 19	17.97	0.578	− 1	154	1.31	1	12
29	27.95	0.747	1	185	1.44	1	15
Aug. 8	6.92	0.947	2	213	1.61	1	18
18	16.89	1.172	2	237	1.80	2	23
28	26.87	1.421	3	260	2.08	2	30
Sept. 7	5.84	1.692	3	279	2.41	2	38
17	15.81	1.979	3	295	2.84	2	47
27	25.78	2.281	4	310	3.36	2	56
Oct. 7	5.76	2.598	4	321	3.96	3	63
17	15.73	2.921	4	326	4.62	3	70
300, 27	25.70	3.249	4	328	5.35	3	74
Nov. 6	4.67	3.576	4	323	6.09	4	75
16	14.65	3.894	4	313	6.84	4	73
26	24.62	4.201	4	296	7.54	5	67
Dec. 6	4.59	4.484	3	269	8.16	5	58
16	14.57	4.736	3	234	8.60	6	47
26	24.54	4.950	2	192	9.02	6	33
36	34.51	+5.118	− 1	+143	9.34	− 6	− 18

✱ δ ☉, July 8.6.
✱ δ Mean Sun, July 9.8.

Sidereal Day	Δ☊α	Δ☊δ	Δ☊α	Δ☊δ
	1865.		**1873.**	
0	+0.678	−8.39	−1.032	+6.10
100	0.578	8.68	0.966	6.67
200	0.473	8.90	0.892	7.19
300	0.363	9.04	0.810	7.64
400	0.250	9.11	0.722	8.03
	1866.		**1874.**	
0	+0.289	−9.10	−0.753	+7.91
100	0.174	9.11	0.661	8.25
200	+0.058	9.04	0.564	8.53
300	−0.058	8.89	0.463	8.74
400	0.174	8.66	0.358	8.87
	1867.		**1875.**	
0	−0.135	−8.75	−0.394	+8.83
100	0.250	8.47	0.286	8.92
200	0.363	8.12	0.177	8.93
300	0.473	7.70	−0.067	8.87
400	0.578	7 21	+0.045	8 73
	1868 B.		**1876 B.**	
0	−0.543	−7.38	+0.007	+8.79
100	0.645	6.85	0.118	8.35
200	0.741	6.27	0.228	8.35
300	0.831	5.62	0.336	8.03
400	0.913	4.94	0.442	7.64
	1869.		**1877.**	
0	−0.886	−5.17	+0.406	+7.77
100	0.963	4 45	0.510	7.34
200	1.032	3.70	0.609	6.85
300	1.091	2.91	0.703	6.30
400	1.140	2.10	0.794	5.69
	1870.		**1878.**	
0	−1.125	−2.38	+0.763	+5.90
100	1.168	1.56	0.847	5.27
200	1.201	−0.73	0.925	4.59
300	1.223	+0.11	0.997	3.86
400	1.235	+0.94	1.058	3.11
	1871.		**1879.**	
0	−1.232	+0.66	+1.037	+3.37
100	1.237	1.49	1.094	2.59
200	1.231	2 30	1.142	1.80
300	1.215	3.09	1.180	0.98
400	1.189	3.85	1.208	0.16
	1872 B.		**1880 B.**	
0	−1.199	+3.59	+1.200	+0.44
100	1.166	4.33	1.221	−0.39
200	1.123	5.03	1.233	1.22
300	1.071	5.69	1.234	2.04
400	−1.011	+6.30	+1.224	−2.84

TABLE XXIV.—* 143 Camelopardalis (B): Piazzi VII. 67.

R.A. 7h 17m.3.   Dec. + 68° 44'.

Upper transit at fictitious meridian.

Sidereal Day.	Mean Day.	$\Delta_\odot \alpha$ 1870.	Var. in 10y.	Diff. for 10d.	$\Delta_\odot \delta$ 1870.	Var. in 10y.	Diff. for 10d.
0, Jan. 0	− 0.47	+ 3.699	− 7	+329	− 4.53	− 9	+237
10	+ 9.50	3.966	4	205	− 2.08	9	252
20	19.47	4.10?	− 1	+ 77	+ 0.48	9	258
30	29.44	4.120	+ 2	− 52	3.05	9	253
Feb. 9	8.42	4.006	4	174	5.52	9	239
19	18.39	3.776	7	284	7.79	8	214
Mar. 1	0.36	3.445	9	377	9.78	7	182
11	10.33	3.030	11	447	11.40	6	141
21	20.31	2.558	13	494	12.59	5	95
31	30.28	2.051	14	516	13.31	4	+ 48
100, Apr. 10	9.25	1.535	14	512	13 54	2	− 2
20	19.23	1.034	14	485	13.28	− 1	50
30	29.20	0.572	13	436	12.55	0	96
May 10	9.17	+ 0.168	13	370	11.38	+ 1	138
20	19.14	− 0.162	11	288	9.81	2	174
30	29.12	0.405	10	197	7.92	3	204
June 9	8 09	0.554	7	− 99	5.78	4	228
19	18.06	0.602	5	+ 2	3.39	4	245
29	28.03	0.550	+ 3	103	+ 0.88	4	255
July 9	8.01	0.39?	0	201	− 1.69	4	258
200, 19	17.98	− 0.150	− 3	295	4.27	4	256
29	27.95	+ 0.189	6	392	6.80	3	249
Aug. 8	6.92	0.611	9	461	9.22	2	235
18	16.90	1.109	11	534	11.49	+ 1	218
28	26.87	1.675	14	597	13.57	0	197
Sept. 7	5.84	2.300	16	651	15.41	− 1	171
17	15.82	2.975	18	697	16.98	2	142
27	25.79	3.690	20	732	18.24	4	110
Oct. 7	5.76	4.435	21	756	19.17	5	75
17	15.73	5.19?	23	768	19.74	7	− 38
300, 27	25.71	5.966	23	767	19.92	9	+ 2
Nov. 6	4.68	6.726	23	749	19.70	10	43
16	14.65	7.459	25	715	19.06	12	84
26	24.62	8.15?	22	664	18.02	14	124
Dec. 6	4.60	8.78?	20	593	16.59	15	162
16	14 57	9.331	19	505	14.80	16	196
26	24.54	9.785	16	401	12.70	17	223
36	34.52	+10.12?	− 14	+283	−10.36	− 18	+244

Sidereal Day. — $\Delta_\Omega \alpha \quad \Delta_\Omega \delta \quad \Delta_\Omega \alpha \quad \Delta_\Omega \delta$

Sid. Day	1865. $\Delta_\Omega\alpha$	$\Delta_\Omega\delta$	1873. $\Delta_\Omega\alpha$	$\Delta_\Omega\delta$
0	+0.881	−8.42	−1.624	+6.19
100	0.685	8.70	1.478	6.75
200	0.483	8.91	1.320	7.25
300	0 276	9.03	1.151	7 70
400	0.067	9.08	0.973	8.07

Sid. Day	1866.		1874.	
0	+0.138	−9.08	−1.034	+7.95
100	−0.073	9.07	0.851	8.29
200	0.282	8.99	0.661	8.55
300	0.489	8.83	0.467	8.74
400	0.692	8.59	0.268	8.86

Sid. Day	1867.		1875.	
0	−0.624	−8.66	−0.336	+8.83
100	0.823	8.39	−0.136	8.90
200	1.015	8.03	+0.065	8.90
300	1.19?	7.60	0.26?	8.82
400	1.37?	7.10	0.463	8.67

Sid. Day	1868 B.		1876 B.	
0	−1.313	−7.28	+0.396	+8.73
100	1.477	6.74	0.592	8.53
200	1.62?	6.14	0.782	8.26
300	1.76?	5.49	0.966	7.93
400	1.885	4.79	1.14?	7.53

Sid. Day	1869.		1877.	
0	−1.846	−5.03	+1.084	+7.67
100	1.956	4.31	1.254	7.23
200	2.04?	3.55	1.414	6.72
300	2.123	2.76	1.56?	6.16
400	2.179	1.95	1.099	5.55

Sid. Day	1870.		1878.	
0	−2.162	−2.23	+1.656	+5.76
100	2.205	1.41	1.781	5.12
200	2.229	−0.58	1.894	4.43
300	2.234	+0.26	1.991	3.71
400	2.220	1.09	2.072	2.95

Sid. Day	1871.		1879.	
0	−2.227	+0.81	+2.047	+3.21
100	2.200	1.63	2.116	2.43
200	2 154	2.43	2.16?	1.63
300	2.091	3.22	2.202	+0.81
400	2.009	3.97	2.218	−0.01

Sid. Day	1872 B.		1880 B.	
0	−2.039	+3.72	+2.215	+0.27
100	1.946	4.45	2.218	−0.56
200	1.837	5.14	2.203	1.38
300	1.714	5.79	2.16?	2 20
400	−1.576	+6.39	+2.116	−2.39

* ♂ ☉,   July 9.8.
* ♂ Mean Sun,   July 11.1.
* ☌ Mean Sun,   Jan. 9.5.

SPECIAL TABLES.

TABLE XXIV.—φ Geminorum.

R. A. 7h 45.5m.   Dec. +27° 6'.

Upper transit at fictitious meridian.

Sidereal Day.	Mean Day.	$\Delta_\odot\alpha$ 1870.	Var. in 10 y.	Diff. for 10 d.	$\Delta_\odot\delta$ 1870.	Var. in 10 y.	Diff. for 10 d.
0, Jan. 0	− 0.46	+1.474	− 2	+203	− 4.55	− 2	− 7
10	+ 9.52	1.652	− 1	152	4.53	3	+ 12
20	19.49	1.777	0	97	4.32	3	20
30	29.46	1.845	0	+ 39	3.96	3	43
Feb. 9	8.43	1.856	+ 1	− 16	3.47	3	54
19	18.41	1.815	2	66	2.89	3	60
Mar. 1	0.38	1.726	2	109	2.26	3	63
11	10.35	1.599	2	144	1.63	3	61
21	20.33	1.441	3	168	1.05	3	54
31	30.30	1.266	3	181	0.55	2	46
100, Apr. 10	9.27	1.083	3	183	− 0.14	2	36
20	19.24	0.904	3	173	+ 0.15	2	23
30	29.22	0.739	3	155	0.32	2	+ 10
May 10	9.19	0.596	3	130	0.36	1	− 1
20	19.16	0.481	3	98	0.30	1	11
30	29.13	0.401	2	63	+ 0.14	1	21
June 9	8.11	0.356	2	− 24	− 0.10	1	29
19	18.08	0.353	1	+ 15	0.43	1	37
29	28.05	0.386	+ 1	52	0.83	1	43
July 9	8.03	0.457	0	90	1.29	0	48
200, 19	18.00	0.565	0	126	1.78	0	52
29	27.97	0.708	− 1	158	2.32	0	56
Aug. 8	6.94	0.881	1	189	2.90	1	61
18	16.92	1.085	2	217	3.54	1	67
28	26.89	1.315	2	244	4.24	1	73
Sept. 7	5.86	1.572	3	268	5.00	2	79
17	15.83	1.850	4	289	5.80	2	84
27	25.81	2.150	4	308	6.66	2	89
Oct. 7	5.78	2.465	5	323	7.57	2	93
17	15.75	2.796	5	337	8.51	3	94
300, 27	25.72	3.138	5	345	9.45	3	93
Nov. 6	4.70	3.484	5	346	10.37	4	89
16	14.67	3.828	5	340	11.23	4	82
26	24.64	4.162	5	327	12.00	5	71
Dec. 6	4.62	4.480	5	304	12.64	5	56
16	14.59	4.768	4	272	13.11	6	38
26	24.56	5.022	3	233	13.40	7	− 20
36	34.53	+5.232	− 2	+185	−13.49	− 8	0

Sidereal Day	$\Delta_\Omega\alpha$	$\Delta_\Omega\delta$	$\Delta_\Omega\alpha$	$\Delta_\Omega\delta$
	1865.		**1873.**	
0	+0.647	−8.53	−1.030	+6.66
100	0.541	8.73	0.957	7.14
200	0.431	8.85	0.876	7.57
300	0.316	8.89	0.789	7.93
400	0.199	8.96	0.696	8.23
	1866.		**1874.**	
0	+0.238	−8.88	−0.728	+8.14
100	+0.120	8.80	0.631	8.39
200	0.000	8.63	0.528	8.57
300	−0.120	8.40	0.422	8.68
400	0.239	8.09	0.312	8.72
	1867.		**1875.**	
0	−0.199	−8.20	−0.349	+8.71
100	0.317	7.84	0.237	8.71
200	0.432	7.41	0.124	8.63
300	0.543	6.92	−0.010	8.48
400	0.649	6.37	+0.105	8.26
	1868 B.		**1876 B.**	
0	−0.613	−6.56	+0.066	+8.34
100	0.716	5.97	0.180	8.07
200	0.812	5.33	0.293	7.74
300	0.900	4.65	0.403	7.34
400	0.981	3.93	0.510	6.89
	1869.		**1877.**	
0	−0.954	−4.17	+0.474	+7.04
100	1.030	3.43	0.578	6.55
200	1.095	2.65	0.678	5.99
300	1.151	1.86	0.772	5.39
400	1.197	1.05	0.860	4.75
	1870.		**1878.**	
0	−1.183	−1.32	+0.831	+4.97
100	1.222	−0.51	0.915	4.29
200	1.251	+0.31	0.991	3.58
300	1.269	1.12	1.059	2.84
400	1.275	1.92	1.118	2.07
	1871.		**1879.**	
0	−1.274	+1.65	+1.099	+2.33
100	1.273	2.44	1.153	1.55
200	1.262	3.21	1.197	+0.75
300	1.240	3.94	1.231	−0.05
400	1.208	4.61	1.255	0.83
	1872 B.		**1880 B.**	
0	−1.220	+4.41	+1.248	−0.59
100	1.181	5.09	1.265	1.39
200	1.132	5.72	1.271	2.19
300	1.073	6.30	1.260	2.97
400	−1.006	+6.82	+1.251	−3.72

✻ ☌ ☉,   July 16.8.
✻ ☌ Mean Sun,   July 18.2.

TABLE XXIV.—'3 Ursæ Majoris (H).

R.A. 7 59.8. Dec. + 68 51.

Upper transit at fictitious meridian.

Sidereal Day	Mean Day	Δ⊙α 1870.	Var. in 10y.	Diff. for 10d.	Δ⊙δ 1870.	Var. in 10y.	Diff. for 10d.
0, Jan. 0	− 0.44	+3.512	−11	+433	− 7.90	− 8	+211
10	+ 9.53	3.887	9	315	5.65	9	237
20	19.50	4.139	6	183	3.19	9	254
30	29.47	4.262	4	+ 57	− 0.61	9	261
Feb. 9	8.45	4.254	− 1	− 71	+ 1.99	9	257
19	18.42	4.122	+ 2	192	4 50	9	243
Mar. 1	0.39	3.875	5	298	6.82	8	219
11	10 36	3.531	7	396	8.84	7	186
21	20.34	3.110	9	452	10.51	6	145
31	30.31	2.635	11	494	11.74	5	100
100, Apr. 10	9.28	2.130	12	511	12.50	4	52
20	19.26	1.621	13	504	12.76	3	+ 2
30	29.23	1.129	13	475	12.54	− 1	− 47
May 10	9.20	0.677	13	426	11.84	0	93
20	19.17	+0.283	12	361	10.69	+ 1	136
30	29.15	−0 040	11	283	9.13	2	174
June 9	8.12	0.280	9	196	7.23	3	206
19	18.09	0.429	7	103	5.04	3	232
29	28.06	0.484	5	− 7	2.62	4	251
July 9	8.04	0.443	+ 2	+ 89	+ 0.04	4	264
200, 19	18.01	0.306	− 1	183	− 2.65	4	271
29	27.98	−0.078	4	273	5.37	4	273
Aug. 8	6.95	+0.238	6	359	8.08	3	268
18	16.93	0.638	10	438	10.71	3	258
28	26.90	1.113	12	511	13.23	2	244
Sept. 7	5.87	1.658	15	578	15.57	+ 1	224
17	15.85	2.266	18	636	17.70	0	200
27	25.82	2.927	20	686	19.56	− 2	172
Oct. 7	5.79	3.634	22	726	21.13	3	140
17	15.76	4.375	24	755	22.34	5	103
300, 27	25.74	5.139	26	771	23.18	6	64
Nov. 6	4.71	5.912	27	772	23.61	8	− 21
16	14.68	6.678	27	756	23.61	9	+ 23
26	24.65	7.418	27	721	23.15	11	68
Dec. 6	4.63	8.113	26	667	22.25	12	112
16	14.60	8.744	26	592	20.92	14	154
26	24.57	9.291	24	499	19.20	15	191
36	34.55	+9.737	−22	+391	−17.13	−16	+222

✱ δ Mean Sun, Jan. 20.3.
✱ δ ⊙, July 20 3.
✱ δ Mean Sun, July 21.9.

Sidereal Day	ΔΩα	ΔΩδ	ΔΩα	ΔΩδ
	1865.		**1873.**	
0	+0.610	−8.54	−1.420	+6.85
100	0.406	8.69	1.257	7.30
200	+0.199	8.77	1.084	7.68
300	−0.011	8.77	0.902	8.01
400	0.220	8.70	0.713	8.26
	1866.		**1874.**	
0	−0.148	−8.73	−0.778	+8.18
100	0.358	8.61	0.586	8.39
200	0.564	8.41	0.389	8.53
300	0.765	8.13	−0.189	8.60
400	0.959	7.79	+0.012	8.60
	1867.		**1875.**	
0	−0.894	−7.91	−0.056	+8.61
100	1.083	7.52	+0.145	8.56
200	1.262	7.06	0.344	8.44
300	1.430	6.54	0.541	8.25
400	1.585	5.97	0.732	7.99
	1868 B.		**1876 B.**	
0	−1.535	−6.17	+0.660	+8.09
100	1.681	5.56	0.856	7.78
200	1.812	4.96	1.037	7.42
300	1.927	4 20	1.210	6.99
400	2.025	3.47	1.372	6.51
	1869.		**1877.**	
0	−1.994	−3.72	+1.318	+6.68
100	2.080	2.97	1.474	6.16
200	2.148	2.19	1.617	5.58
300	2.197	1.40	1.747	4.96
400	2.227	0.59	1.863	4.30
	1870.		**1878.**	
0	−2.219	−0.86	+1.826	+4.52
100	2.237	−0.06	1.932	3.84
200	2.235	+0.75	2.022	3.12
300	2.213	1.55	2.096	2 37
400	2.173	2.33	2.152	1.60
	1871.		**1879.**	
0	−2.188	+2.07	+2.135	+1.86
100	2.136	2.84	2.186	1.08
200	2.065	3 58	2.206	+0.29
300	1.977	4.29	2.213	−0.51
400	1.873	4.96	2.204	1.30
	1872 B.		**1880 B.**	
0	−1.910	+4.74	+2.210	−1.04
100	1.795	5.38	2.187	1.83
200	1.665	5.97	2.146	2.60
300	1.522	6.52	2.086	3.36
400	−1.366	+7.01	+2.009	−4.09

TABLE XXIV.—15 Argus.

R.A. 8h 2.0m.　　　　Dec. — 23° 56'.

Upper transit at fictitious meridian.

Sidereal Day	Mean Day	$\Delta_\odot\alpha$ 1870.	Var. in 10 y.	Diff. for 10 d.	$\Delta_\odot\delta$ 1870.	Var. in 10 y.	Diff for 10 d.
0, Jan. 0	− 0.44	+1.409	0	+174	+ 1.31	+ 2	—288
10	+ 9.53	1.559	0	125	— 1.56	2	284
20	19.50	1.659	0	74	4.34	2	270
30	29.47	1.707	+ 1	+ 20	6.94	2	250
Feb. 9	8.45	1.700	1	— 32	9.32	1	225
19	18.42	1.645	2	78	11.42	+ 1	195
Mar. 1	0.39	1.546	2	119	13.21	0	162
11	10.36	1.409	2	151	14.66	0	128
21	20.34	1.247	2	174	15.76	— 1	91
31	30.31	1.064	2	188	16.48	1	53
100, Apr. 10	9.28	0.873	3	192	16.83	2	— 17
20	19.26	0.683	3	187	16.83	2	+ 18
30	29.23	0.501	3	174	16.48	2	53
May 10	9.20	0.336	3	155	15.78	2	87
20	19.17	0.192	3	131	14.75	2	117
30	29.15	+0.075	2	101	13.43	2	145
June 9	8.12	—0.010	1	68	11.84	3	171
19	18.09	0.061	1	35	10.02	3	191
29	28.06	0.079	+ 1	— 1	8.03	3	206
July 9	8.04	0.064	0	+ 33	5.91	3	217
200, 19	18.01	—0.013	0	68	3.71	4	220
29	27.98	+0.072	0	102	— 1.54	3	215
Aug. 8	6.95	0.191	0	135	+ 0.57	3	204
15	16.93	0.341	— 1	166	2.52	3	185
28	26.90	0.523	1	197	4.24	3	157
Sept. 7	5.87	0.734	2	225	5.64	3	122
17	15.85	0.972	2	250	6.67	3	83
27	25.82	1.234	2	273	7.28	3	+ 39
Oct. 7	5.79	1.518	2	293	7.44	3	— 10
17	15.76	1.819	2	308	7.03	2	69
300, 27	25.74	2.132	2	317	6.24	2	109
Nov. 6	4.71	2.450	3	318	4.91	1	156
16	14.68	2.766	2	313	3.14	1	198
26	24.65	3.073	2	299	+ 0.98	1	232
Dec. 6	4.63	3.361	2	275	— 1.48	1	259
16	14.60	3.621	1	244	4.17	1	278
26	24.57	3.846	— 1	204	7.01	1	288
36	34.55	+4.026	0	+157	— 9.90	— 1	—287

Sidereal Day	$\Delta_\Omega\alpha$	$\Delta_\Omega\delta$	$\Delta_\Omega\alpha$	$\Delta_\Omega\delta$
	1865.		**1873.**	
0	+0.641	—8.54	—0.831	+6.88
100	0.580	8.68	0.799	7.32
200	0.513	8.76	0.760	7.70
300	0.442	8.75	0.715	8.02
400	0.368	8.67	0.664	8.26
	1866.		**1874.**	
0	+0.393	—8.70	—0.682	+8.19
100	0.316	8.57	0.627	8.39
200	0.236	8.36	0.568	8.52
300	0.154	8.08	0.504	8.59
400	0.071	7.73	0.436	8.58
	1867.		**1875.**	
0	+0.099	—7.86	—0.459	+8.59
100	+0.015	7.46	0.389	8.54
200	—0.069	7.00	0.315	8.41
300	0.152	6.48	0.239	8 22
400	0.234	5.90	0.161	7.96
	1868 B.		**1876 B.**	
0	—0.206	—6.10	—0.188	+8.05
100	0.287	5.49	0.109	7.75
200	0.365	4.83	—0.029	7.38
300	0.439	4.13	+0 053	6.95
400	0.510	3 39	0.131	6.46
	1869.		**1877.**	
0	—0.487	—3.64	+0.104	+6.63
100	0.554	2.89	0.184	6.10
200	0.617	2.11	0.261	5.53
300	0.674	1.32	0.337	4.91
400	0.725	0.52	0.410	4.24
	1870.		**1878.**	
0	—0.708	—0.79	+0.386	+4.47
100	0.755	+0.02	0.457	3.78
200	0.796	0.82	0.525	3.06
300	0.829	1.61	0.588	2.31
400	0.855	2.39	0.647	1.54
	1871.		**1879.**	
0	—0.847	+2.13	+0.627	+1.81
100	0.869	2.90	0.683	1.03
200	0.882	3.63	0.732	+0.23
300	0.889	4.34	0.776	—0.56
400	0.888	5.00	0.813	1.35
	1872 B.		**1880 B.**	
0	—0.889	+4.78	+0.801	—1.09
100	0.883	5.42	0.834	1.87
200	0.869	6.01	0.860	2.65
300	0.848	6.55	0.878	3.40
400	—0.821	+7.03	+0.890	—4.12

✱ ♂ ☉, July 20.9.
✱ ♂ Mean Sun, July 22.4.

TABLE XXIV.—ε Hydræ.

R.A. 8^h 39.9^m. Dec. + 6° 54′.

Upper transit at fictitious meridian.

Sidereal Day	Mean Day	$\Delta_\odot\alpha$ 1870.	Var. in 10 y.	Diff. for 10 d.	$\Delta_\odot\delta$ 1870.	Var. in 10 y.	Diff. for 10 d.
0, Jan. 0	− 0.42	+1.193	− 2	+225	− 3.10	0	−148
10	+ 9.55	1.307	2	192	4.51	0	132
20	19.53	1.556	− 1	135	5.73	− 1	112
30	29.50	1.666	0	85	6.75	1	92
Feb. 9	8.47	1.725	0	+ 34	7.56	1	70
19	18.45	1.734	+ 1	− 15	8.15	1	49
Mar. 1	0.42	1.696	1	58	8.53	2	29
11	10.39	1.619	2	94	8.74	2	− 12
21	20.36	1.510	2	122	8.78	2	+ 4
31	30.34	1.378	2	141	8.67	2	16
100, Apr. 10	9.31	1.230	2	151	8.46	3	26
20	19.28	1.079	3	151	8.14	3	35
30	29.25	0.930	3	144	7.76	3	42
May 10	9.23	0.793	3	130	7.31	3	48
20	19.20	0.672	3	111	6.81	2	52
30	29.17	0.573	2	87	6.27	2	56
June 9	8.14	0.500	2	59	5.69	2	59
19	18.12	0.456	.1	31	5.10	2	60
29	28.09	0.439	1	− 2	4.50	2	60
July 9	8.06	0.452	1	+ 27	3.91	2	58
200, 19	18.04	0.494	+ 1	57	3.35	2	53
29	28.01	0.566	0	87	2.85	2	46
Aug. 8	6.98	0.668	0	115	2.44	2	35
18	16.95	0.796	− 1	142	2.15	1	22
28	26.93	0.952	1	169	2.01	1	+ 6
Sept. 7	5.90	1.134	2	196	2.04	1	− 14
17	15.87	1.344	3	222	2.29	1	36
27	25.84	1.577	3	246	2.76	2	58
Oct. 7	5.82	1.836	4	269	3.46	2	82
17	15.79	2.114	4	289	4.40	2	106
300, 27	25.76	2.412	4	305	5.57	2	127
Nov. 6	4.74	2.723	4	315	6.91	2	145
16	14.71	3.041	4	319	8.44	2	159
26	24.68	3.359	4	315	10.07	2	167
Dec. 6	4.65	3.669	3	302	11.76	3	169
16	14.63	3.961	3	280	13.44	3	166
26	24.60	4.228	3	251	15.06	3	156
36	34.57	+4.460	− 2	+212	−16.55	− 4	−142

✳ ♂ ☉, July 30.5.
✳ ♂ Mean Sun, Aug. 1.0.

Sidereal Day	$\Delta_\Omega\alpha$	$\Delta_\Omega\delta$	$\Delta_\Omega\alpha$	$\Delta_\Omega\delta$
	1865.		**1873.**	
0	+0.621	−8.39	−0.929	+7.25
100	0.533	8.41	0.872	7.54
200	0.440	8.37	0.809	7.85
300	0.344	8.25	0.737	8.05
400	0.244	8.06	0.660	8.18
	1866.		**1874.**	
0	+0.278	−8.13	−0.686	+8.14
100	0.176	7.89	0.606	8.23
200	+0.073	7.58	0.521	8.25
300	−0.030	7.21	0.432	8.20
400	0.133	6.78	0.339	8.09
	1867.		**1875.**	
0	−0.099	−6.93	−0.370	+8.13
100	0.201	6.45	0.275	7.97
200	0.302	5.92	0.179	7.75
300	0.400	5.34	−0.081	7.46
400	0.495	4.71	+0.018	7.11
	1868 B.		**1876 B.**	
0	−0.463	−4.93	−0.016	+7.23
100	0.555	4.27	+0.083	6.84
200	0.642	3.58	0.181	6.40
300	0.723	2.86	0.278	5.90
400	0.797	2.11	0.372	5.35
	1869.		**1877.**	
0	−0.773	−2.36	+0.341	+5.54
100	0.843	1.60	0.433	4.96
200	0.905	0.84	0.522	4.34
300	0.959	−0.06	0.607	3.69
400	1.005	+0.72	0.688	2.99
	1870.		**1878.**	
0	−0.991	+0.46	+0.661	+3.23
100	1.031	1.23	0.738	2.52
200	1.062	1.98	0.808	1.79
300	1.084	2.72	0.872	1.05
400	1.096	3.43	0.925	0.29
	1871.		**1879.**	
0	−1.093	+3.19	+0.911	+0.55
100	1.099	3.89	0.963	−0.21
200	1.096	4.54	1.007	0.98
300	1.084	5.16	1.043	1.73
400	1.063	5.73	1.070	2.47
	1872 B.		**1880 B.**	
0	−1.071	+5.54	+1.061	−2.22
100	1.044	6.06	1.083	2.95
200	1.007	6.57	1.095	3.66
300	0.963	7.00	1.09?	4.34
400	−0.911	+7.37	+1.092	−4.98

TABLE XXIV.—ι Ursæ Majoris.

R.A. 8h 50.3m   Dec. + 48° 33′.

Upper transit at fictitious meridian.

Sidereal Day	Mean Day	Δ☉a 1870.	Var. in 10 y.	Diff. for 10 d.	Δ☉δ 1870.	Var. in 10 y.	Diff. for 10 d.
0, Jan. 0	− 0.41	+1.711	− 5	+332	− 9.89	− 4	+ 73
10	+ 9.56	2.015	4	.273	8.99	4	107
20	19.53	2.254	3	205	7.77	5	136
30	29.51	2.423	3	132	6.29	5	159
Feb. 9	8.48	2.517	2	+ 57	4.63	5	174
19	18.45	2.538	− 1	− 15	2.84	5	181
Mar. 1	0.42	2.489	+ 1	81	− 1.03	5	180
11	10.40	2.378	2	139	+ 0.73	6	170
21	20.37	2.214	2	186	2.35	5	153
31	30.34	2.010	3	218	3.77	4	129
100, Apr. 10	9.32	1.781	3	237	4.91	4	100
20	19.29	1.539	4	245	5.76	4	68
30	29.26	1.295	4	239	6.27	3	+ 34
May 10	9.23	1.064	5	222	6.44	2	− 1
20	19.21	0.854	5	196	6.27	2	34
30	29.18	0.674	4	162	5.77	− 1	67
June 9	8.15	0.532	3	123	4.94	0	98
19	18.12	0.430	3	80	3.83	0	124
29	28.10	0.373	2	− 34	2.48	+ 1	147
July 9	8.07	0.362	2	+ 13	+ 0.90	1	167
200, 19	18.04	0.398	+ 1	59	− 0.84	1	183
29	28.02	0.480	0	104	2.74	1	196
Aug. 8	6.99	0.605	− 1	147	4.74	2	205
18	16.96	0.774	2	190	6.82	2	210
28	26.93	0.985	3	232	8.93	1	214
Sept. 7	5.91	1.238	4	273	11.08	+ 1	213
17	15.88	1.530	5	310	13.18	0	208
27	25.85	1.858	6	346	15.22	0	200
Oct. 7	5.82	2.221	7	379	17.16	0	188
17	15.80	2.615	8	409	18.97	− 1	172
300, 27	25.77	3.037	9	433	20.59	2	151
Nov. 6	4.74	3.478	10	448	21.98	3	125
16	14.72	3.930	10	454	23.08	4	96
26	24.69	4.383	10	450	23.89	5	63
Dec. 6	4.66	4.826	11	435	24.33	6	− 26
16	14.63	5.248	10	407	24.41	7	+ 12
26	24.61	5.635	9	365	24.10	8	50
36	34.58	+5.974	− 8	+311	−23.42	− 8	+ 85

✱ ♂ ☉,   Aug. 2.2.
✱ ♂ Mean Sun,   Aug. 3.7.

Sidereal Day	ΔΩa	ΔΩδ	ΔΩa	ΔΩδ
	1865.		**1873.**	
0	+0.482	−8.30	−1.018	+7.32
100	0.346	8.30	0.911	7.62
200	0.206	8.22	0.798	7.85
300	+0.064	8.07	0.677	8.02
400	−0.078	7.85	0.552	8.12
	1866.		**1874.**	
0	−0.030	−7.94	−0.595	+8.09
100	0.173	7.67	0.467	8.15
200	0.313	7.34	0.335	8.14
300	0.451	6.94	0.200	8.06
400	0.586	6.48	0.064	7.91
	1867.		**1875.**	
0	−0.541	−6.64	−0.110	+7.97
100	0.672	6.15	+0.026	7.78
200	0.797	5.60	0.162	7.53
300	0.915	5.00	0.296	7.21
400	1.025	4.36	0.428	6.84
	1868 B.		**1876 B.**	
0	−0.989	−4.58	+0.384	+6.97
100	1.092	3.91	0.514	6.56
200	1.186	3.22	0.639	6.10
300	1.270	2.49	0.760	5.58
400	1.342	1.75	0.874	5.02
	1869.		**1877.**	
0	−1.319	−1.99	+0.836	+5.20
100	1.384	1.24	0.946	4.61
200	1.436	−0.47	1.047	3.98
300	1.476	+0.29	1.141	3.32
400	1.503	1.05	1.225	2.63
	1870.		**1878.**	
0	−1.495	+0.80	+1.197	+2.86
100	1.514	1.55	1.273	2.16
200	1.519	2.29	1.342	1.43
300	1.511	3.01	1.399	+0.69
400	1.490	3.70	1.443	−0.06
	1871.		**1879.**	
0	−1.499	+3.47	+1.430	+0.19
100	1.469	4.14	1.406	−0.56
200	1.428	4.77	1.491	1.31
300	1.374	5.36	1.504	2.05
400	1.309	5.91	1.503	2.77
	1872 B.		**1880 B.**	
0	−1.332	+5.73	+1.505	−2.53
100	1.260	6.24	1.496	3.24
200	1.177	6.69	1.475	3.92
300	1.085	7.09	1.441	4.58
400	−0.984	+7.43	+1.395	−5.19

TABLE XXIV.—'σ² Ursæ Majoris.

R.A. 8h 58m.9.   Dec. + 67° 40'.

Upper transit at fictitious meridian.

Sidereal Day	Mean Day	Δ⊙a			Δ⊙δ		
		1870.	Var. in 10 y.	Diff. for 10 d.	1870.	Var. in 10 y.	Diff. for 10 d.
0, Jan. 0	− 0.40	+2.876	−13	+533	−12.07	− 6	+154
10	+ 9.57	3.361	12	435	10.33	7	194
20	19.54	3.741	11	323	8.22	7	226
30	29.51	4.005	9	203	5.85	8	248
Feb. 9	8.49	4.146	7	+ 79	3.30	9	261
19	18.46	4.164	4	− 42	− 0.67	8	262
Mar. 1	0.43	4.065	− 2	156	+ 1.91	8	252
11	10.40	3.857	+ 1	257	4.34	8	232
21	20.38	3.557	3	340	6.53	7	203
31	30.35	3.183	5	404	8.38	6	166
100, Apr. 10	9.32	2.756	6	446	9.82	5	123
20	19.30	2.299	8	466	10.81	4	76
30	29.27	1.832	9	465	11.33	3	+ 26
May 10	9.24	1.375	9	444	11.34	− 2	− 23
20	19.21	0.949	10	406	10.87	0	71
30	29.19	0.568	9	354	9.94	0	115
June 9	8.16	+0.245	9	290	8.57	+ 1	157
19	18.13	−0.010	8	218	6.82	2	193
29	28.10	0.189	7	140	4.72	3	224
July 9	8.08	0.288	5	− 58	+ 2.35	4	250
200, 19	18.05	0.304	+ 3	+ 26	− 0.26	4	270
29	28.02	0.236	0	109	3.02	4	283
Aug. 8	6.99	−0.086	− 2	191	5.90	4	291
18	16.97	+0.145	5	271	8.83	4	293
28	26.94	0.455	7	348	11.75	3	290
Sept. 7	5.91	0.839	10	421	14.61	3	281
17	15.89	1.296	13	490	17.36	2	267
27	25.86	1.818	16	554	19.93	+ 1	247
Oct. 7	5.83	2.401	18	611	22.27	0	221
17	15.80	3.038	21	660	24.34	− 1	190
300, 27	25.78	3.718	23	698	26.06	3	154
Nov. 6	4.75	4.430	25	723	27.41	4	114
16	14.72	5.160	26	734	28.32	5	69
26	24.69	5.892	27	727	28.77	7	− 21
Dec. 6	4.67	6.607	28	700	28.73	8	+ 29
16	14.64	7.285	28	652	28.19	9	79
26	24.61	7.905	27	585	27.16	11	126
36	34.59	+8.448	−26	+496	−25.68	−11	+169

Sidereal Day	ΔΩa	ΔΩδ	ΔΩa	ΔΩδ
	1865.		**1873.**	
0	+0.258	−8.22	−1.092	+7.37
100	+0.059	8.19	0.920	7.64
200	−0.141	8.09	0.741	7.84
300	0.339	7.91	0.557	7.98
400	0.536	7.67	0.360	8.05
	1866.		**1874.**	
0	−0.470	−7.76	−0.433	+8.04
100	0.663	7.47	0.242	8 06
200	0.851	7.12	−0.050	8.03
300	1.031	6.70	+0.142	7.92
400	1.203	6.23	0.333	7.75
	1867.		**1875.**	
0	−1.146	−6.40	+0.269	+7.82
100	1.310	5.89	0.457	7.61
200	1.463	5.32	0.642	7.33
300	1.603	4.71	0.821	7.00
400	1.729	4.07	0.994	6.60
	1868 B.		**1876 B.**	
0	−1.689	−4.29	−0.936	+6.74
100	1.804	3.62	1.103	6.31
200	1.904	2.91	1.261	5.83
300	1.987	2.19	1.409	5.30
400	2.052	1.44	1.545	4.73
	1869.		**1877.**	
0	−2.032	−1.70	+1.501	+4.93
100	2.086	0.94	1.628	4.33
200	2.122	−0.18	1.743	3.69
300	2.138	+0.57	1.843	3.02
400	2.137	1.33	1.929	2.33
	1870.		**1878.**	
0	−2.139	+1.07	+1.902	+2.56
100	2.125	1.82	1.977	1.85
200	2.093	2.54	2.035	1.13
300	2.043	3.24	2.077	+0.39
400	1.975	3.92	2.102	−0.35
	1871.		**1879.**	
0	−2.000	+3.69	+2.096	−0.10
100	1.921	4.34	2.109	0.84
200	1.826	4.95	2.105	1.58
300	1.716	5.52	2.083	2.31
400	1.592	6.04	2.043	3.02
	1872 B.		**1880 B.**	
0	−1.635	+5.87	+2.059	−2.78
100	1.502	6.35	2.008	3.47
200	1.357	6.78	1.940	4.14
300	1.200	7.15	1.855	4.77
400	−1.035	+7.47	+1.754	−5.36

* δ Mean Sun, Feb. 4.3.
* δ ⊙, Aug. 4 4.
* δ Mean Sun, Aug. 5.9.

TABLE XXIV.—κ Cancri.

R.A. 9h 0.7m.   Dec. + 11° 11'.

Upper transit at fictitious meridian.

Sidereal Day.	Mean Day.	Δ⊙a 1870.	Var. in 10 y.	Diff. for 10 d.	Δ⊙δ 1870.	Var. in 10 y.	Diff. for 10 d.
0, Jan. 0	− 0.40	+1.134	− 2	+248	− 4.15	0	−133
10	+ 9.57	1.363	2	207	5.39	0	114
20	19.54	1.546	− 1	159	6.43	− 1	93
30	29.51	1.680	0	108	7.24	1	69
Feb. 9	8.49	1.762	0	56	7.82	1	46
19	18 46	1.793	0	+ 6	8.16	2	26
Mar. 1	0.43	1.776	− 0	− 39	8.33	2	− 7
11	10.40	1.717	+ 1	78	8.30	2	+ 10
21	20.38	1.623	1	108	8.13	2	22
31	30.35	1.503	2	130	7.86	3	31
100, Apr. 10	9.32	1.365	3	143	7.52	3	38
20	19.30	1.220	3	148	7.10	3	44
30	29.27	1.072	3	145	6.65	3	46
May 10	9.24	0.933	3	133	6.19	3	47
20	19.21	0.809	3	117	5.71	2	47
30	29.19	0.702	3	95	5.26	2	45
June 9	8.16	0.619	2	69	4.81	2	44
19	18.13	0.564	2	43	4.38	2	41
29	28 10	0.533	2	− 16	3 98	2	36
July 9	8.08	0.532	1	+ 12	3.65	2	31
200, 19	18.05	0.558	+ 1	40	3.37	2	25
29	28 02	0.613	0	69	3.15	2	17
Aug. 8	7.00	0.696	0	97	3.04	1	+ 6
18	16.97	0.808	− 1	125	3.04	1	− 7
28	26.94	0.947	1	153	3.19	1	24
Sept. 7	5.91	1.114	2	182	3.52	1	42
17	15.89	1.310	3	210	4.03	1	64
27	25.86	1.534	3	236	4.74	0	81
Oct. 7	5.83	1.782	3	261	5.65	1	102
17	15.80	2.056	3	285	6.77	1	121
300, 27	25.78	2.351	4	305	8.06	1	138
Nov. 6	4.75	2.664	4	319	9.52	1	152
16	14.72	2.986	4	326	11.09	1	161
26	24.69	3.313	4	326	12.73	1	165
Dec. 6	4.67	3.635	4	317	14.38	2	163
16	14.64	3.944	4	298	15.98	2	155
26	24.61	4.229	3	269	17.48	3	144
36	34.59	+4.480	− 3	+232	−18.85	− 3	−127

Sidereal Day.	ΔΩa	ΔΩδ	ΔΩa	ΔΩδ
	1865.		**1873.**	
0	+0.602	−8.20	−0.929	+7.38
100	0.511	8.16	0.808	7.64
200	0.415	8.06	0.800	7.84
300	0.315	7.88	0.725	7.97
400	0.212	7.63	0.644	8.04
	1866.		**1874.**	
0	+0.247	−7.72	−0.672	+8.02
100	0.142	7.43	0.588	8.05
200	−0.037	7.07	0.499	8.01
300	−0.069	6.65	0.406	7.90
400	0.174	6.17	0.311	7.72
	1867.		**1875.**	
0	−0.130	−6.34	−0.343	+7.79
100	0.243	5.82	0.246	7.57
200	0.345	5.26	0.146	7.29
300	0.444	4.65	−0.046	6.96
400	0.530	4.00	+0.055	6.56
	1868 B.		**1876 B.**	
0	−0.508	−4.22	+0.021	+6.70
100	0.600	3.55	0.122	6.27
200	0.686	2.85	0.222	5.79
300	0.766	2.12	0.320	5.25
400	0.840	1.38	0.415	4.68
	1869.		**1877.**	
0	−0.816	−1.62	+0.383	+4.87
100	0.885	0.87	0.474	4.27
200	0.946	−0.12	0.566	3.63
300	0.998	+0.64	0.651	2.96
400	1.042	1.39	0.731	2.27
	1870.		**1878.**	
0	−1.028	+1.14	+0.704	2.51
100	1.066	1.88	0.780	1.80
200	1.094	2.60	0.850	1.07
300	1.113	3.30	0.913	+0.34
400	1.123	3.96	0.968	−0.40
	1871.		**1879.**	
0	−1.121	+3.74	+0.950	−0.15
100	1.124	4.39	1.000	0.90
200	1.117	4.99	1.042	1.63
300	1.101	5.55	1.076	2.35
400	1.076	6.07	1.100	3.06
	1872 B.		**1880 B.**	
0	−1.085	+5.90	+1.093	−2.82
100	1.054	6.38	1.111	3.51
200	1.014	6.80	1.120	4.17
300	0.966	7.17	1.120	4.80
400	−0.909	+7.47	+1.110	−5.39

✳ ☌ ⊙,   Aug. 4.9.
✳ ☌ Mean Sun,   Aug. 6.3.

TABLE XXIV.—ι Argus.

R.A. 9^h 13.6^m Dec. —58° 44'

Upper transit at fictitious meridian.

Sidereal Day	Mean Day	$\Delta_\odot\alpha$ 1870.	Var. in 10 y.	Diff. for 10 d.	$\Delta_\odot\delta$ 1870.	Var. in 10 y.	Diff. for 10 d.
0, Jan. 0	− 0.40	+2.074	0	+316	+ 9.95	+ 2	−349
10	+ 9.58	2.354	+ 1	241	6.35	2	370
20	19.55	2.555	2	160	+ 2.59	2	381
30	29.52	2.674	2	+ 77	− 1.23	2	391
Feb. 9	8.50	2.709	3	− 7	4.99	2	370
19	18.47	2.662	3	86	8.61	2	352
Mar. 1	0.44	2.540	3	158	12.01	1	325
11	10.41	2.350	4	220	15.09	1	291
21	20.39	2.104	4	271	17.82	+ 1	253
31	30.36	1.811	4	312	20.13	0	210
100, Apr. 10	9.33	1.483	4	341	22.00	0	162
20	19.30	1.132	3	359	23.37	0	113
30	29.28	0.768	3	365	24.25	0	62
May 10	9.25	0.405	3	360	24.60	− 1	− 10
20	19.22	+0.051	2	347	24.45	1	+ 41
30	29.20	−0.286	2	324	23.79	2	91
June 9	8.17	0.595	+ 1	293	22.63	2	139
19	18.14	0.870	0	255	21.02	2	182
29	28.11	1.103	− 1	220	19.00	2	221
July 9	8.09	1.289	1	160	16.62	3	253
200, 19	18.06	1.422	1	104	13.97	3	277
29	28.03	1.496	2	− 43	11.10	3	295
Aug. 8	7.00	1.508	3	+ 20	8.10	3	302
18	16.98	1.456	3	86	5.09	3	298
28	26.95	1.336	4	154	− 2.17	3	284
Sept. 7	5.92	1.149	5	221	+ 0.56	3	259
17	15.89	0.895	5	286	2.98	2	224
27	25.87	0.579	5	346	5.02	2	180
Oct. 7	5.84	−0.206	5	400	6.56	2	127
17	15.81	+0.217	5	444	7.54	1	67
300, 27	25.79	0.678	4	476	7.89	1	+ 4
Nov. 6	4.76	1.165	4	496	7.61	− 1	− 62
16	14.73	1.665	3	501	6.66	0	126
26	24.70	2.162	2	488	5.10	0	186
Dec. 6	4.68	2.637	1	459	2.95	0	243
16	14.65	3.076	− 1	416	+ 0.26	0	292
26	24.62	3.466	0	358	− 2.86	+ 1	331
36	34.59	+3.789	+ 1	+288	− 6.30	+ 1	−358

✻ ♂ ☉, Aug. 8.2.
✻ ♂ Mean Sun, Aug. 9.6.

Sidereal Day	$\Delta_\Omega\alpha$	$\Delta_\Omega\delta$	$\Delta_\Omega\alpha$	$\Delta_\Omega\delta$
1865.			**1873.**	
0	+0.947	−8.05	−0.849	+7.42
100	0.943	7.97	0.881	7.64
200	0.932	7.83	0.905	7.80
300	0.912	7.61	0.922	7.89
400	0.884	7.33	0.931	7.92
1866.			**1874.**	
0	+0.894	−7.43	−0.929	+7.92
100	0.861	7.10	0.932	7.90
200	0.820	6.72	0.929	7.82
300	0.773	6.27	0.917	7.67
400	0.719	5.77	0.898	7.47
1867.			**1875.**	
0	+0.738	−5.94	−0.905	+7.54
100	0.679	5.41	0.881	7.29
200	0.614	4.82	0.850	6.98
300	0.545	4.20	0.812	6.62
400	0.470	3.54	0.767	6.20
1868 B.			**1876 B.**	
0	+0.496	−3.77	−0.783	+6.34
100	0.419	3.09	0.734	5.89
200	0.338	2.38	0.679	5.39
300	0.254	1.65	0.618	4.84
400	0.169	0.91	0.552	4.25
1869.			**1877.**	
0	+0.198	−1.16	−0.574	+4.45
100	0.111	−0.42	0.505	3.83
200	+0.024	+0.33	0.432	3.19
300	−0.063	1.07	0.355	2.51
400	0.150	1.80	0.275	1.82
1870.			**1878.**	
0	−0.121	+1.55	−0.302	+2.06
100	0.207	2.27	0.221	1.35
200	0.290	2.97	0.137	+0.63
300	0.371	3.64	−0.052	−0.10
400	0.449	4.28	+0.034	0.83
1871.			**1879.**	
0	−0.423	+4.07	+0.005	−0.58
100	0.498	4.68	0.091	1.30
200	0.569	5.25	0.176	2.02
300	0.634	5.77	0.260	2.72
400	0.694	6.25	0.342	3.40
1872 B.			**1880 B.**	
0	−0.674	+6.09	+0.314	−3.17
100	0.730	6.53	0.395	3.84
200	0.780	6.92	0.472	4.47
300	0.823	7.24	0.545	5 07
400	−0.860	+7.50	+0.614	−5.62

TABLE XXIV.—* 1 Draconis (H.)

R.A. 9h 18.3m   Dec. +81° 54'

Upper transit at fictitious meridian.

Sidereal Day	Mean Day	Δ☉a 1870	Var. in 10 y.	Diff. for 10 d.	Δ☉δ 1870	Var. in 10 y.	Diff. for 10 d.
0, Jan. 0	− 0.39	+ 7.186	− 81	+1352	−13.84	−10	+185
10	+ 9.58	8.422	79	1113	11.76	12	229
20	19.55	9.401	75	839	9.28	13	265
30	29.53	10.091	68	538	6.49	14	290
Feb. 9	8.50	10.470	59	+ 222	3.51	15	304
19	18.47	10.534	49	− 95	− 0.46	15	305
Mar. 1	0.45	10.287	38	397	+ 2.55	14	294
11	10.42	9.748	25	674	5.38	13	271
21	20.39	8.950	− 13	914	7.93	12	237
31	30.36	7.935	0	1109	10.09	11	195
100, Apr. 10	9.34	6.750	+ 11	1251	11.80	9	146
20	19.31	5.450	21	1340	12.98	7	91
30	29.28	4.088	30	1374	13.61	5	+ 35
May 10	9.25	2.719	37	1355	13.68	3	− 22
20	19.23	1.393	42	1288	13.17	− 1	79
30	29.20	+ 0.156	45	1179	12.12	+ 1	131
June 9	8.17	− 0.952	45	1032	10.56	3	180
19	18.15	1.898	44	856	8.54	4	223
29	28.12	2.657	40	657	6.12	6	260
July 9	8.09	3.207	34	441	3.37	7	290
200, 19	18.06	3.536	26	− 215	+ 0.34	7	314
29	28.04	3.635	16	+ 16	− 2.89	8	330
Aug. 8	7.01	3.503	− 5	249	6.24	8	340
18	16.98	3.139	− 8	478	9.65	7	342
28	26.95	2.550	22	700	13.05	7	337
Sept. 7	5.93	1.743	36	912	16.37	6	326
17	15.90	− 0.730	51	1112	19.55	4	308
27	25.87	+ 0.475	67	1295	22.51	3	283
Oct. 7	5.84	1.853	82	1458	25.18	+ 1	252
17	15.81	3.382	97	1597	27.52	− 1	214
300, 27	25.79	5.036	111	1707	29.45	3	171
Nov. 6	4.76	6.783	124	1781	30.92	6	122
16	14.74	8.586	135	1817	31.89	8	70
26	24.71	10.402	145	1807	32.30	11	− 14
Dec. 6	4.68	12.184	153	1748	32.16	13	+ 43
16	14.65	13.881	158	1638	31.44	15	100
26	24.63	15.443	160	1477	30.18	18	154
36	34.60	+16.819	−160	+1268	−28.39	−20	+202

Sidereal Day	Δ☊a	Δ☊δ	Δ☊a	Δ☊δ
	1865.		**1873.**	
0	−0.770	−8.00	−1.127	+7.43
100	1.188	7.91	0.719	7.64
200	1.596	7.75	−0.307	7.78
300	1.991	7.52	+0.107	7.85
400	2.369	7.23	0.518	7.86
	1866.		**1874.**	
0	−2.244	−7.33	+0.380	+7.87
100	2.608	7.00	0.788	7.84
200	2.950	6.60	1.190	7.74
300	3.266	6.14	1.580	7.57
400	3.554	5.63	1.956	7.35
	1867.		**1875.**	
0	−3.460	−5.81	+1.831	+7.43
100	3.727	5.26	2.197	7.17
200	3.962	4.68	2.544	6.85
300	4.161	4.05	2.870	6.47
400	4.324	3.38	3.171	6.03
	1868 B.		**1876 B.**	
0	−4.273	−3.61	+3.072	+6.18
100	4.411	2.92	3.357	5.72
200	4.509	2.22	3.614	5.20
300	4.569	1.49	3.841	4.65
400	4.588	0.75	4.036	4.05
	1869.		**1877.**	
0	−4.586	−1.00	+3.974	+4.26
100	4.578	−0.26	4.148	3.64
200	4.531	+0.48	4.287	2.99
300	4.444	1.22	4.392	2.31
400	4.320	1.94	4.460	1.62
	1870.		**1878.**	
0	−4.366	+1.70	+4.441	+1.85
100	4.216	2.41	4.485	1.15
200	4.026	3.10	4.492	0.43
300	3.811	3.76	4.461	−0.29
400	3.559	4.39	4.393	1.02
	1871.		**1879.**	
0	−3.648	+4.18	+4.420	−0.77
100	3.375	4.78	4.328	1.49
200	3.076	5.34	4.199	2.20
300	2.750	5.85	4.035	2.89
400	2.403	6.31	3.833	3.56
	1872 B.		**1880 B.**	
0	−2.523	+6.16	+3.907	−3.34
100	2.162	6.59	3.686	3.99
200	1.784	6.95	3.434	4.60
300	1.392	7.26	3.152	5.18
400	−0.990	+7.51	+2.843	−5.72

✱ ☉ Mean Sun, Feb. 9.2.
✱ ☌ ☉, Aug. 9.4.
✱ ☌ Mean Sun, Aug. 10.8.

TABLE XXIV.—*d Ursæ Majoris.

R.A. 9h 22m.9.   Dec. +70° 24'.

Upper transit at fictitious meridian.

Sidereal Day	Mean Day	$\Delta_\odot a$ 1870.	Var. in 10 y.	Diff. for 10 d.	$\Delta_\odot \delta$ 1870.	Var. in 10 y.	Diff. for 10 d.
0, Jan. 0	− 0.39	+2.980	−18	+635	−13.75	− 5	+139
10	+ 9.59	3.566	17	534	12.12	6	185
20	19.56	4.043	15	416	10.08	7	222
30	29.53	4.394	13	285	7.70	8	251
Feb. 9	8.50	4.610	11	148	5.10	8	269
19	18.48	4.689	9	+ 10	− 2.36	9	275
Mar. 1	0.45	4.632	6	−122	+ 0.37	9	271
11	10.42	4.450	− 3	241	3.02	8	255
21	20.40	4.155	0	344	5.43	8	228
31	30 37	3.769	+ 3	426	7.54	7	193
100, Apr. 10	9.34	3.311	5	486	9.27	6	151
20	19.31	2.806	7	521	10.56	5	104
30	29.29	2.277	9	533	11.35	4	54
May 10	9.26	1.747	10	523	11.63	2	+ 3
20	19.23	1.237	11	493	11.40	− 1	− 48
30	29.20	0.766	11	446	10.67	0	97
June 9	8.18	0.350	11	384	9.47	+ 1	143
19	18.15	+0.002	10	311	7.83	3	184
29	28.12	−0.270	9	230	5.81	3	220
July 9	8.09	0.456	7	142	3.46	3	250
200, 19	18.07	0.553	5	− 52	+ 0.83	4	275
29	28.04	0.559	+ 3	+ 40	− 2.02	4	293
Aug. 8	7.01	0.472	0	134	5.01	4	305
18	16.99	0.292	− 4	225	8 10	4	312
28	26.96	−0.022	7	315	11.23	4	313
Sept. 7	5.93	+0.337	10	402	14.33	4	307
17	15.90	0.781	13	486	17.35	3	295
27	25.88	1.306	17	564	20.21	2	277
Oct. 7	5.85	1.906	20	635	22.86	+ 1	253
17	15.82	2.574	23	699	25.25	0	223
300, 27	25.79	3.300	26	751	27.30	− 1	187
Nov. 6	4.77	4.072	29	790	28.96	2	145
16	14.74	4.874	31	812	30.19	4	93
26	24.71	5.690	33	815	30.93	5	− 43
Dec. 6	4.69	6.497	34	796	31.15	7	+ 4
16	14.66	7.274	35	754	30.84	8	57
26	24.63	7 997	35	688	30.01	10	109
36	34.60	+8.643	−34	+600	−28.68	−10	+157

Sidereal Day	$\Delta_\Omega a$	$\Delta_\Omega \delta$	$\Delta_\Omega a$	$\Delta_\Omega \delta$
	1865.		1873.	
0	+0.041	−7.93	−0.973	+7.44
100	−0.174	7.83	0.779	7.63
200	0.389	7.65	0.578	7.76
300	0.600	7.41	0.374	7 82
400	0.807	7.10	0.166	7.81
	1866.		1874.	
0	−0.738	−7.22	−0.237	+7.82
100	0.940	6.87	−0.029	7.78
200	1.134	6.46	+0.180	7.67
300	1.318	5.99	0.385	7.49
400	1.490	5.47	0.588	7.26
	1867.		1875.	
0	−1.434	−5.65	+0.520	+7.34
100	1.598	5.10	0.719	7.06
200	1.748	4.51	0.912	6.73
300	1.882	3.88	1.097	6.35
400	2.000	3.21	1.273	5.91
	1868 B.		1876 B.	
0	−1.963	−3.44	+1.215	+6.06
100	2.068	2.75	1.385	5.59
200	2.157	2.04	1.542	5.07
300	2.226	1.32	1.688	4.51
400	2.276	0.58	1.819	3.91
	1869.		1877.	
0	−2.261	−0.83	+1.776	+4.11
100	2.298	−0.09	1 89c	3.49
200	2.314	+0.64	2.004	2.84
300	2.311	1.37	2.094	2.16
400	2.287	2.09	2.166	1.47
	1870.		1878.	
0	−2 297	+1.85	+2.144	+1.71
100	2.260	2.55	2.205	1.00
200	2.204	3 23	2.247	+0.29
300	2.129	3.88	2.272	−0.43
400	2.036	4.49	2.277	1.15
	1871.		1879.	
0	−2.069	+4.29	+2.277	−0.91
100	1.964	4.85	2.270	1.62
200	1.843	5.42	2.244	2.32
300	1.707	5.92	2.199	3 00
400	1.556	6.37	2.136	3.66
	1872 B.		1880 B.	
0	−1.609	+6.22	+2.159	−3.44
100	1.450	6.63	2.084	4.18
200	1.279	6.99	1.990	4.69
300	1.095	7 28	1.879	5.26
400	−0.908	+7.51	+1.753	−5.79

✳ 8 Mean Sun,   Feb. 11.6.
✳ ♂ ⊙,   Aug. 10.6.
✳ ♂ Mean Sun,   Aug. 12.2.

TABLE XXIV.—θ Ursæ Majoris.

R.A. 9 24.1 (h m)   Dec. + 52 16. (° ')

Upper transit at fictitious meridian.

Sidereal Day	Mean Day	$\Delta_\odot a$ 1870	Var. in 10 y.	Diff. for 10 d.	$\Delta_\odot \delta$ 1870	Var. in 10 y.	Diff. for 10 d.
0, Jan. 0	− 0.39	+1.641	− 6	+389	−12.12	− 3	+ 59
10	+ 9.58	2.002	6	331	11.32	3	101
20	19.56	2.300	5	263	10.12	4	136
30	29.53	2.525	4	187	8.61	5	166
Feb. 9	8.50	2.673	3	108	6.82	5	189
19	18.48	2.741	2	+ 30	4.86	5	202
Mar. 1	0.45	2.734	− 1	− 45	2.81	6	206
11	10.42	2.654	0	111	− 0.77	6	200
21	20.39	2.515	+ 1	167	+ 1.17	5	186
31	30.37	2.324	2	212	2.92	5	164
100, Apr. 10	9.34	2.095	3	243	4.43	4	136
20	19.31	1.843	3	259	5.63	4	103
30	29.28	1.582	4	262	6.47	3	65
May 10	9.26	1.322	4	254	6.94	2	+ 27
20	19.23	1.077	4	235	7.02	1	− 12
30	29 20	0.855	4	207	6.70	− 1	50
June 9	8.18	0.635	4	173	6.02	0	86
19	18.15	0.511	3	134	4.99	0	120
29	28.12	0.399	2	89	3.64	0	150
July 9	8.09	0.333	2	− 43	2.01	+ 1	176
200, 19	18.07	0.313	1	+ 4	+ 0.14	1	198
29	28.04	0.340	+ 1	51	− 1.94	2	217
Aug. 8	7.01	0.415	− 1	98	4.18	2	232
18	16.98	0.536	2	145	6.56	3	242
28	26.96	0.704	3	192	9.01	2	246
Sept. 7	5.93	0.919	4	238	11.51	2	252
17	15.90	1.180	5	284	14.03	2	250
27	25.87	1.486	6	328	16.49	2	242
Oct. 7	5.85	1.834	7	369	18.86	+ 1	231
17	15.82	2.222	8	407	21.09	0	214
300, 27	25.79	2.645	10	439	23.13	0	193
Nov. 6	4.77	3.097	11	464	24.93	− 1	165
16	14.74	3.570	11	480	26.42	2	133
26	24.71	4.053	11	485	27.57	3	96
Dec. 6	4.68	4.536	12	478	28.33	4	55
16	14.66	5.004	12	455	28.66	5	− 12
26	24.63	5.441	12	418	28.56	6	+ 32
36	34.60	+5.835	−12	+368	−28.01	− 7	+ 74

✳ ☌ ☉,   Aug. 11.0.
✳ ☌ Mean Sun,   Aug. 12.3.

Sidereal Day / $\Delta_\Omega a$, $\Delta_\Omega \delta$

Sidereal Day	1865 $\Delta_\Omega a$	1865 $\Delta_\Omega \delta$	1873 $\Delta_\Omega a$	1873 $\Delta_\Omega \delta$
0	+0.357	−7.91	−0.938	+7.44
100	0.214	7.81	0.821	7.63
200	+0.068	7.63	0.607	7.75
300	−0.078	7.38	0.568	7.81
400	0.224	7.07	0.434	7.80

Sidereal Day	1866 $\Delta_\Omega a$	1866 $\Delta_\Omega \delta$	1874 $\Delta_\Omega a$	1874 $\Delta_\Omega \delta$
0	−0.175	−7.18	−0.480	+7.81
100	0.320	6.83	0.344	7.76
200	0.462	6.42	0.205	7.65
300	0.600	5.95	−0.065	7.47
400	0.733	5.43	+0.075	7.23

Sidereal Day	1867 $\Delta_\Omega a$	1867 $\Delta_\Omega \delta$	1875 $\Delta_\Omega a$	1875 $\Delta_\Omega \delta$
0	−0.689	−5.61	+0.028	+7.32
100	0.817	5.06	0.168	7.04
200	0.939	4.46	0.306	6.71
300	1.052	3.83	0.442	6.32
400	1.156	3.16	0.574	5.88

Sidereal Day	1868 B. $\Delta_\Omega a$	1868 B. $\Delta_\Omega \delta$	1876 B. $\Delta_\Omega a$	1876 B. $\Delta_\Omega \delta$
0	−1.122	−3.39	+0.530	+6.03
100	1.219	2.70	0.659	5.56
200	1.306	1.99	0.782	5.04
300	1.381	1.27	0.899	4.47
400	1.443	0.54	1.009	3.87

Sidereal Day	1869 $\Delta_\Omega a$	1869 $\Delta_\Omega \delta$	1877 $\Delta_\Omega a$	1877 $\Delta_\Omega \delta$
0	−1.423	−0.78	+0.973	+4.07
100	1.478	−0.04	1.077	3.45
200	1.519	+0.69	1 173	2.80
300	1.547	1.42	1.250	2.12
400	1.561	2.13	1.335	1.43

Sidereal Day	1870 $\Delta_\Omega a$	1870 $\Delta_\Omega \delta$	1878 $\Delta_\Omega a$	1878 $\Delta_\Omega \delta$
0	−1.558	+1.89	1.311	+1.66
100	1.564	2.59	1.380	0.96
200	1.556	3.27	1.437	+0.25
300	1.535	3.91	1.483	−0.47
400	1.500	4.52	1.516	1.18

Sidereal Day	1871 $\Delta_\Omega a$	1871 $\Delta_\Omega \delta$	1879 $\Delta_\Omega a$	1879 $\Delta_\Omega \delta$
0	−1.513	+4.32	+1.506	−0.94
100	1.470	4.91	1.532	1.65
200	1.415	5.45	1.544	2.35
300	1.348	5.94	1.544	3.03
400	1.270	6.38	1.531	3.69

Sidereal Day	1872 B. $\Delta_\Omega a$	1872 B. $\Delta_\Omega \delta$	1880 B. $\Delta_\Omega a$	1880 B. $\Delta_\Omega \delta$
0	−1.298	+6.24	+1.537	−3.47
100	1.212	6.65	1.515	4.11
200	1.117	7.00	1.480	4.71
300	1.013	7.28	1.433	5.28
400	−0.900	+7.51	+1.373	−5.80

TABLE XXIV.—ε Leonis.

R.A. 9h 38m.5.   Dec. + 24° 22′

Upper transit at fictitious meridian.

Sidereal Day.	Mean Day.	Δ☉α 1870.	Var. in 10y.	Diff. for 10 d.	Δ☉δ 1870.	Var. in 10y.	Diff. for 10 d.
0, Jan. 0	− 0.38	+1.053	− 4	+296	− 7.68	0	− 87
10	+ 9.59	1.330	3	257	8.42	− 1	58
20	19.57	1.564	2	210	8.84	1	26
30	29.54	1.748	1	158	8.95	2	+ 2
Feb. 9	8.51	1.879	− 1	104	8.81	2	27
19	18.49	1.955	0	+ 49	8.42	3	51
Mar. 1	0.46	1.977	0	− 3	7.80	3	69
11	10.43	1.951	+ 1	48	7.05	3	81
21	20.40	1.883	1	86	6.20	3	88
31	30.38	1.781	2	115	5.30	4	90
100, Apr. 10	9.35	1.655	2	136	4.41	3	87
20	19 32	1.511	2	148	3.58	3	80
30	29.29	1.362	3	150	2.83	3	69
May 10	9.27	1.213	3	146	2.20	2	57
20	19.24	1.073	3	135	1.70	2	43
30	29.21	0.946	3	118	1.35	1	27
June 9	8.19	0.839	2	97	1.15	1	+ 11
19	18.16	0.753	2	73	1.13	1	− 5
29	28.13	0.693	2	47	1.24	1	20
July 9	8.10	0.659	2	− 20	1.53	1	35
200, 19	18.08	0.654	1	+ 8	1.94	1	50
29	28.05	0.676	1	36	2.52	0	65
Aug. 8	7.02	0.726	+ 1	66	3.24	0	80
18	16.99	0.809	− 1	97	4.11	0	95
28	26.97	0.921	1	127	5.13	0	110
Sept 7	5.94	1.063	2	158	6.31	0	124
17	15.91	1.236	2	190	7.62	0	138
27	25.88	1.442	3	222	9.08	0	151
Oct. 7	5.86	1.679	3	253	10.64	0	163
17	15.83	1.947	4	283	12.34	0	173
300, 27	25.80	2.213	4	309	14.09	0	177
Nov. 6	4.78	2.503	5	332	15.87	0	178
16	14.75	2 904	5	347	17.64	1	174
26	24.72	3.255	6	353	19.31	1	164
Dec. 6	4.69	3.608	6	351	20.91	1	149
16	14.67	3.954	6	339	22.30	2	128
26	24.64	4.283	5	316	23.46	2	104
36	34.61	+4.582	− 5	+282	−24.37	− 3	− 77

Sidereal Day.	Δ☊α	Δ☊δ	Δ☊α	Δ☊δ
	1865.		**1873.**	
0	+0.522	−7.79	−0.910	+7.44
100	0.419	7.54	0.835	7.58
200	0.312	7.32	0.753	7.66
300	0.202	7.04	0.665	7.07
400	0.090	6.69	0.572	7.62
	1866.		**1874.**	
0	+0.127	−6.81	−0.604	+7.64
100	+0.015	6.43	0.508	7.55
200	−0.098	5.99	0.408	7.39
300	0.210	5.49	0.305	7 17
400	0.320	4.93	0.200	6.90
	1867.		**1875.**	
0	−0.283	−5.13	−0.235	+7.00
100	0.392	4.56	0.129	6.68
200	0.497	3 95	−0.021	6.32
300	0.597	3.30	+0.087	5 90
400	0.692	2.62	0.193	5.43
	1868 B.		**1876 B.**	
0	−0.661	−2.86	+0.157	+5.59
100	0.752	2.17	0.263	5.09
200	0.836	1.46	0.367	4.55
300	0.913	0.74	0.468	3.97
400	0.982	0.02	0.565	3.36
	1869.		**1877.**	
0	−0.960	−0.26	+0.533	+3.57
100	1.023	+0.46	0.627	2.95
200	1.077	1.18	0.716	2.28
300	1.122	1.89	0.799	1.60
400	1.157	2.57	0.876	0.91
	1870.		**1878.**	
0	−1 146	+2.34	+0.851	+1.15
100	1.174	3.01	0.923	+0.45
200	1.192	3.66	0.968	−0.25
300	1.200	4.27	1.044	0.95
400	1.198	4.84	1.093	1.65
	1871.		**1879.**	
0	−1.200	+4.65	+1.077	−1.42
100	1.190	5.20	1.120	2.10
200	1.171	5.70	1.153	2.78
300	1.141	6.15	1.176	3.43
400	1.103	6.54	1.190	4.05
	1872 B.		**1880 B.**	
0	−1.117	+6.42	+1.186	−3.85
100	1.072	6.78	1.193	4.45
200	1.018	7.08	1.191	5.02
300	0.955	7.32	1.178	5.54
400	−0.885	+7.50	+1.154	−6.02

* ♂ ☉,   Aug. 14.8.
* ♂ Mean Sun,   Aug. 15.9.

SPECIAL TABLES.

TABLE XXIV.—μ Leonis.

R.A. 9 45.4.   Dec. +26 37.

Upper transit at fictitious meridian.

Sidereal Day.	Mean Day.	Δ☉α			Δ☉δ			Sidereal Day.	ΔΩα	ΔΩδ	ΔΩα	ΔΩδ
		1870.	Var. in 10 y.	Diff. for 10 d.	1870.	Var. in 10 y.	Diff. for 10 d.		1865.		1873.	
								0	+0.502	−7.58	−0.901	+7.44
								100	0.307	7.41	0.824	7.55
								200	0.288	7.17	0.740	7.60
		s			"			300	0.176	6.86	0.658	7.59
0, Jan. 0	− 0.37	+1.038	− 3	+305	− 8.38	0	− 80	400	0.063	6.50	0.555	7.52
10	+ 9.60	1.325	− 3	266	9.02	− 1	48					
20	19.57	1.567	2	219	9.34	2	− 17		1866.		1874.	
30	29.55	1.761	2	168	9.37	2	+ 12	0	+0.101	−6.63	−0.587	+7.55
Feb. 9	8.52	1.901	1	111	9.10	2	40	100	−0.013	6.23	0.489	7.43
19	18.49	1.984	− 1	56	8.57	3	63	200	0.127	5.77	0.387	7.26
Mar. 1	0.46	2.015	0	+ 4	7.85	3	82	300	0.239	5.26	0.282	7.02
11	10.44	1.994	0	− 43	6.95	3	94	400	0.350	4.71	0.175	6.73
21	20.41	1.931	+ 1	82	5.98	4	100					
31	30.38	1.833	2	114	4.96	4	101		1867.		1875.	
100, Apr. 10	9.35	1.706	2	137	3.97	3	97	0	−0.313	−4.90	−0.211	+6.83
20	19.33	1.562	3	149	3.04	3	88	100	0.422	4.32	−0.103	6.50
30	29.30	1.411	3	152	2.23	3	75	200	0.527	3.70	+0 006	6.12
May 10	9.27	1.260	3	150	1.55	2	60	300	0.627	3.05	0.115	5 68
20	19.24	1.114	3	140	1.03	2	43	400	0.722	2.37	0.222	5.20
30	29.22	0.982	3	123	0.68	2	26		1868 B.		1876 B.	
June 9	8.19	0.869	3	103	0.52	1	+ 8	0	−0.691	−2.60	−0.186	+5.37
19	18.16	0.777	2	80	0.53	1	− 10	100	0.781	1.91	0.293	4.86
29	28.14	0.710	2	54	0.71	1	28	200	0.865	1.20	0.397	4.31
July 9	8.11	0.669	1	− 28	1.08	− 1	46	300	0.941	−0.49	0.493	3.73
200, 19	18.08	0.655	1	0	1.63	0	62	400	1.009	+0.23	0.595	3.11
29	28.05	0.670	+ 1	+ 30	2.31	0	77		1869.		1877.	
Aug. 8	7.03	0.715	0	59	3.16	+ 1	94	0	−0.987	−0.01	+0.502	+3.32
18	17.00	0.788	0	89	4.19	1	110	100	1.049	+0.71	0 656	2.68
28	26.97	0.893	− 1	121	5.36	1	124	200	1.101	1.41	0.745	2 02
Sept. 7	5.94	1.030	2	153	6.67	+ 1	139	300	1.144	2.11	0.827	1.35
17	15.92	1.199	2	185	8.13	0	153	400	1.177	2.78	0.903	0.66
27	25.89	1.401	3	218	9.73	0	166		1870.		1878.	
Oct. 7	5.86	1.636	3	251	11.45	0	175	0	−1.167	+2.56	+0.878	+0 89
17	15.84	1.903	4	282	13.22	0	181	100	1.193	3.21	0.95	+0.20
300, 27	25.81	2.199	4	309	15.07	0	185	200	1.209	3.84	1.013	−0.49
Nov. 6	4.78	2.520	5	333	16 92	0	184	300	1.214	4.44	1.068	1.10
16	14.75	2.863	6	351	18.74	0	178	400	1.206	4.99	1.115	1.87
26	24.73	3.219	6	360	20 47	− 1	166		1871.		1879.	
Dec. 6	4.70	3.579	6	358	22.05	1	149	0	−1.211	+4.81	+1.100	−1.64
16	14.67	3.932	5	346	23.43	2	126	100	1.199	5 33	1.140	2.32
26	24.64	4.269	5	323	24.55	3	99	200	1.177	5.81	1.171	2.98
36	34.62	+4.575	− 5	+290	−25.40	− 3	− 70	300	1.145	6.24	1.193	3.62
								400	1.104	6.61	1.204	4.22
									1872 B.		1880 B.	
								0	−1.119	+6.49	+1.201	−4.02
								100	1.071	6.83	1.206	4.61
								200	1.014	7.11	1.201	5.16
								300	0.949	7.33	1.187	5.66
								400	−0.876	+7.46	+1.159	−6 12

✳ ♂ ☉,   Aug. 16 6.
✳ ♂ Mean Sun,   Aug. 17.6.

TABLE XXIV.—'32 Ursæ Majoris.

R.A. 10^h 8.6^m Dec. + 65° 45'.

Upper transit at fictitious meridian.

Sidereal Day	Mean Day	Δ⊙α 1870	Var.in 10y	Diff. for 10d	Δ⊙δ 1870	Var.in 10y	Diff. for 10d
0, Jan. 0	− 0.36	+1.943	−13	+ 595	−15.85	− 3	+ 69
10	+ 9.62	2.506	13	527	14.90	4	121
20	19.59	2.991	12	442	13.45	5	168
30	29.56	3.384	11	343	11.57	6	207
Feb. 9	8.54	3.674	10	235	9.34	6	238
19	18.51	3.853	9	123	6.85	7	258
Mar. 1	0.48	3.919	7	+ 12	4.21	7	267
11	10.45	3.878	5	− 93	−1.54	7	265
21	20.43	3.738	3	186	+1.04	7	251
31	30.40	3.510	−1	266	3.45	6	228
100, Apr. 10	9.37	3.211	+1	329	5.57	6	196
20	19.34	2.858	2	375	7.34	5	156
30	29.32	2.468	4	402	8.68	4	112
May 10	9.29	2.060	5	411	9.57	3	64
20	19.26	1.651	6	404	9.97	2	+ 15
30	29.24	1.256	7	383	9.87	− 1	− 34
June 9	8.21	0.889	7	350	9.29	0	82
19	18.18	0.561	7	305	8.24	+ 1	127
29	28.15	0.281	7	252	6.76	1	169
July 9	8.13	+0.058	6	194	4.88	2	206
200, 19	18.10	−0.104	5	130	2.65	3	239
29	28.07	0.201	4	− 62	+ 0.13	3	266
Aug. 8	7.04	0.228	+ 2	− 7	− 2.65	4	288
18	17.02	0.185	0	79	5.62	4	305
28	26.99	−0.070	− 2	152	8.73	4	316
Sept. 7	5.96	+0.118	4	225	11.91	4	320
17	15.94	0.380	6	298	15.11	4	319
27	25.91	0.714	9	370	18.28	3	311
Oct. 7	5.88	1.119	11	439	21.32	3	296
17	15.85	1.591	13	504	24.18	2	276
300, 27	25.83	2.125	16	563	26.81	+ 1	248
Nov. 6	4.80	2.714	18	613	29.12	0	213
16	14.77	3.346	20	650	31.05	− 1	172
26	24.74	4.008	21	672	32.54	2	126
Dec. 6	4.72	4.684	23	677	33.55	3	74
16	14.69	5.356	23	663	34.02	4	− 20
26	24.66	6.002	24	627	33.95	5	+ 35
36	34.64	+6.604	−24	+ 572	−33.33	−7	+ 89

Sidereal Day	Δ_Ωα	Δ_Ωδ	Δ_Ωα	Δ_Ωδ
	1865.		**1873.**	
0	−0.058	−7.15	−0.743	+7.35
100	0.241	6.90	0.575	7.39
200	0.421	6.60	0.403	7.36
300	0.599	6.24	0.228	7.28
400	0.771	5.82	0.051	7.13
	1866.		**1874.**	
0	−0.713	−5.96	−0.111	+7.19
100	0.882	5.51	+0.066	7.00
200	1.042	5.01	0.242	6.76
300	1.193	4.46	0.415	6.46
400	1.334	3.88	0.585	6.10
	1867.		**1875.**	
0	−1.288	−4.08	+0.528	+6.23
100	1.421	3.47	0.694	5.84
200	1.542	2.83	0.855	5.41
300	1.649	2.17	1.008	4.93
400	1.742	1.49	1.153	4.42
	1868 B.		**1876 B.**	
0	−1.712	−1.72	+1.105	+4.59
100	1.795	1.03	1.244	4.05
200	1.862	−0.33	1.373	3.48
300	1.912	+0.36	1.490	2.87
400	1.946	1.06	1.595	2.24
	1869.		**1877.**	
0	−1.936	+0.83	+1.561	+2.46
100	1.958	1.51	1.657	1.81
200	1.964	2.19	1.740	1.16
300	1.953	2.84	1.809	+0.49
400	1.924	3.46	1.863	−0.19
	1870.		**1878.**	
0	−1.935	+3.26	+1.846	+0.04
100	1.896	3.86	1.890	−0.63
200	1.840	4.43	1.918	1.30
300	1.768	4.96	1.931	1.97
400	1.682	5.45	1.927	2.61
	1871.		**1879.**	
0	−1.713	+5.29	+1.930	−2.40
100	1.617	5.75	1.915	3.03
200	1.507	6.15	1.885	3.64
300	1.386	6.50	1.839	4.23
400	1.252	6.80	1.778	4.77
	1872 B.		**1880 B.**	
0	−1.298	+6.70	+1.800	−4.59
100	1.158	6.96	1.728	5.11
200	1.009	7.16	1.642	5.59
300	0.851	7.30	1.541	6.03
400	−0.697	+7.37	+1.427	−6.41

✳ ♂ Mean Sun, Feb. 21.9.
✳ ☌⊙, Aug. 22 9.
✳ ☌ Mean Sun, Aug. 23.5.

TABLE XXIV.— γ¹Leonis.

R.A. $10^h 12^m.8$.   Dec. $+ 20° 30'$.

Upper transit at fictitious meridian.

Sidereal Day.	Mean Day.	$\Delta_\odot a$			$\Delta_\odot d$			Sidereal Day	$\Delta_\Omega a$	$\Delta_\Omega d$	$\Delta_\Omega a$	$\Delta_\Omega d$
		1870.	Var. in 10 y.	Diff. for 10 d.	1870.	Var. in 10 y.	Diff. for 10 d.		1865.		1873.	
		s			"			0	+0.514	−7.06	−0.883	+7.33
								100	0.415	6.80	0.812	7.35
								200	0.312	6.48	0.734	7 31
		s						300	0.207	6.11	0.651	7.21
0, Jan. 0	− 0.35	+0.859	− 3	+311	− 7.46	0	−124	400	0.099	5.66	0.56.	7.05
10	+ 9.62	1.154	3	277	8.56	0	95		1866.		1874.	
20	19.59	1.410	3	235	9.36	0	66					
30	29.56	1.623	2	188	9.87	− 1	36	0	+0.136	−5.83	−0.593	+7.11
Feb. 9	8.54	1.785	1	137	10.07	2	− 4	100	+0.028	5.37	0.501	6.91
19	18.51	1.896	− 1	84	9.96	2	+ 22	200	−0.081	4.86	0.40c	6.66
Mar. 1	0.48	1.954	0	+ 34	9.62	2	45	300	0.189	4.31	0.30c	6.35
11	10.45	1.965	0	− 12	9.16	3	64	400	0.295	3.72	0.20:	5.99
21	20.43	1.932	0	52	8.36	3	76		1867.		1875.	
31	30.40	1.864	+ 1	84	7.56	3	84					
								0	−0.259	3.92	−0.239	+6.11
100, Apr. 10	9.37	1.766	2	109	6.69	3	88	100	0.364	3.31	0.157	5.72
20	19.35	1.648	2	125	5.82	3	85	200	0.465	2.67	−0.034	5.28
30	29.32	1.519	2	132	5.00	3	79	300	0.562	2.00	+0.076	4.79
May 10	9.29	1.386	3	133	4.24	2	71	400	0.654	1.32	0.175	4.27
20	19.26	1.253	3	129	3.59	2	59		1868 B.		1876 B.	
30	29.24	1.129	3	119	3.06	2	47					
June 9	8.21	1.017	3	105	2.66	2	33	0	−0.624	−1.55	+0.138	+4.45
19	18.18	0.921	3	87	2.40	2	18	100	0.712	0.86	0.24c	3.91
29	28.15	0.844	2	67	2.29	1	+ 3	200	0.794	−0.17	0.34c	3.33
July 9	8.13	0.788	2	45	2.33	1	− 12	300	0.869	+0.5.	0.43c	2.72
200, 19	18.10	0.755	1	− 22	2.53	− 1	28	400	0.936	1.21	0.531	2.09
29	28.07	0.745	+ 1	+ 3	2.89	0	44		1869.		1877.	
Aug. 8	7.05	0.761	0	30	3.41	0	60					
18	17.02	0.801	0	58	4.09	0	77	0	−0.915	+0.96	+0.500	+2.30
28	26.99	0.877	0	87	4.96	0	95	100	0.976	1.67	0.590	1.65
								200	1.030	2.33	0.677	1.00
Sept. 7	5.96	0.979	− 1	119	6.00	0	114	300	1.074	2.97	0.757	+0.33
17	15.94	1.115	2	152	7.23	+ 1	131	400	1.108	3.59	0.833	−0.34
27	25.91	1.282	2	185	8.63	1	148		1870.		1878.	
Oct. 7	5.88	1.484	3	219	10.19	1	164					
17	15.85	1.720	4	252	11.89	1	178	0	−1.098	+3.39	+0.808	−0.11
								100	1.126	3.9c	0.879	0.78
300, 27	25.83	1.988	4	284	13 73	1	188	200	1.145	4.54	0.942	1.45
Nov. 6	4.80	2.286	5	311	15.64	+ 1	194	300	1.153	5.0c	0.997	2.10
16	14 77	2.608	5	332	17.59	0	196	400	1.152	5.5:	1.045	2.75
26	24.74	2.947	5	344	19.54	0	191		1871.		1879.	
Dec. 6	4.72	3.294	5	349	21.39	− 1	179					
								0	−1.154	+5.37	+1.030	−2.53
16	14.69	3.641	5	344	23.11	1	163	100	1.146	5.8.	1.072	3.15
26	24.66	3.978	5	326	24.64	2	141	200	1.128	6.21	1.105	3.76
36	34.64	+4.290	− 5	+298	−25.92	− 2	−114	300	1.101	6.54	1.129	4.33
								400	1.065	6.82	1.143	4.86
									1872 B.		1880 B.	
								0	−1.078	+6.74	+1.130	−4.69
								100	1.016	6 9c	1.147	5.20
								200	0.985	7 1c	1.14c	5.67
								300	0.926	7.2:	1.13:	6.09
								400	−0.860	+7.3:	+1.113	−6.46

✳ ♂ ☉,   Aug. 24.0.
✳ ♂ Mean Sun,   Aug. 24.6.

TABLE XXIV.—" θ Draconis (II.)

R.A. 10h 24m.0.   Dec. + 76° 23'.

Upper transit at fictitious meridian.

Sidereal Day	Mean Day	ΔΘα 1870.	Var. in 10y.	Diff. for 10d.	ΔΘδ 1870.	Var. in 10y.	Diff. for 10d.
0, Jan. 0	− 0.34	+3.040	−31	+988	−17.33	− 4	+ 86
10	+ 9 63	3.979	32	884	16.18	5	142
20	19.60	4.799	32	750	14.50	6	193
30	29.57	5.471	31	592	12.36	7	235
Feb. 9	8.55	5.976	30	415	9.83	8	268
19	18.52	6.298	27	228	7.04	8	280
Mar. 1	0.49	6.432	24	+ 40	4.10	9	298
11	10.46	6.380	20	−142	1.13	9	294
21	20.44	6.153	16	310	+ 1.74	8	279
31	30.41	5.767	11	458	4.41	8	253
100, Apr. 10	9.38	5.246	6	580	6.76	7	217
20	19.36	4.617	− 2	674	8.71	7	174
30	29.33	3.909	+ 2	737	10.21	5	125
May 10	9.30	3.152	6	771	11.20	4	72
20	19.27	2.377	10	776	11.64	2	+ 17
30	29.25	1.610	12	749	11.53	− 1	− 38
June 9	8.22	0.877	14	708	10.88	0	91
19	18.19	+0.201	15	641	9.71	+ 1	142
29	28.16	−0.399	16	557	8.06	2	188
July 9	8.14	0.908	15	459	5.96	3	230
200, 19	18.11	1.313	14	350	3.48	4	267
29	28.08	1.605	12	232	+ 0.65	.4	297
Aug. 8	7.06	1.775	10	−108	− 2.44	5	320
18	17.03	1.819	6	+ 20	5.74	5	338
28	27.00	1.734	+ 2	151	9.18	5	349
Sept. 7	5.97	1.517	− 2	282	12.70	5	353
17	15.95	1.170	8	413	16.22	5	350
27	25.92	0.692	13	541	19.67	4	340
Oct. 7	5.89	−0.089	19	664	22.99	4	322
17	15.86	+0.633	25	779	26.09	3	297
300, 27	25.84	1.466	30	883	28.91	2	265
Nov. 6	4.81	2.394	36	971	31.36	+ 1	225
16	14.78	3.402	42	1040	33.38	0	179
26	24.76	4.467	47	1085	34.91	− 2	127
Dec. 6	4.73	5.562	51	1191	35.90	3	70
16	14.70	6.658	55	1085	36.30	5	− 11
26	24.67	7.721	57	1036	36.11	6	+ 49
36	34.65	+8.718	−59	+952	35.32	− 7	+108

Sidereal Day	ΔΩα	ΔΩδ	ΔΩα	ΔΩδ
	1865.		1873.	
0	−0.783	−6.82	−0.463	+7.26
100	1.047	6.53	−0.191	7.24
200	1.302	6.18	+0.078	7.16
300	1.546	5.78	0.345	7.03
400	1.777	5.33	0.609	6.83
	1866.		1874.	
0	−1.701	−5.49	+0.520	+6.90
100	1.922	5.00	0.780	6.67
200	2.126	4.47	1.034	6.38
300	2.312	3.90	1.278	6.04
400	2.477	3.30	1.511	5.66
	1867.		1875.	
0	−2.424	−3.51	+1.434	+5.79
100	2.575	2.89	1.659	5.37
200	2.704	2 24	1.869	4.91
300	2.809	1.57	2.066	4.40
400	2.889	0.89	2.243	3.86
	1868 B.		1876 B.	
0	−2.865	−1.12	+2.185	+4.05
100	2.928	−0.44	2.351	3.49
200	2.966	+0.23	2.498	2.90
300	2.978	0.93	2.624	2.29
400	2.964	1.61	2.728	1.65
	1869.		1877.	
0	−2.971	+1.38	+2.695	+1.87
100	2.939	2.04	2.785	1.22
200	2.883	2.69	2.852	+0.57
300	2.802	3.31	2.895	−0.09
400	2.696	3.90	2.915	0.75
	1870.		1878.	
0	−2.735	+3.70	+2.911	−0.53
100	2.614	4.27	2.915	1.19
200	2.470	4.80	2.894	1.84
300	2.306	5.29	2.849	2.48
400	2.123	5.72	2.781	3.10
	1871.		1879.	
0	−2.187	+5.58	+2.807	−2.89
100	1.992	5.99	2.723	3.49
200	1.780	6.34	2.616	4.07
300	1.554	6.64	2.497	4.60
400	1.315	6.88	2.337	5.11
	1872 B.		1880 B.	
0	−1.397	+6.81	+2.390	−4.94
100	1.151	7.01	2.226	5 42
200	0.896	7.15	2.043	5.85
300	0.635	7.21	1.842	6.24
400	−0 369	+7.26	+1.626	−6.57

✳ δ Mean Sun, Feb. 25 8.
✳ δ ☉, Aug. 27.1.
✳ δ Mean Sun, Aug. 27.4.

TABLE XXIV.—ρ Leonis.

R.A. 10^h 26^m.0. Dec. + 9° 58′

Upper transit at fictitious meridian

Sidereal Day	Mean Day	$\Delta_\odot\alpha$ 1870.	Var. in 10 y.	Diff. for 10 d.	$\Delta_\odot\delta$ 1870.	Var. in 10 y.	Diff. for 10 d.
0, Jan. 0	− 0 34	+0.758	− 3	+302	− 4.67	+ 1	−172
10	+ 9.63	1.045	3	272	6.29	+ 1	151
20	19.60	1.299	2	234	7.69	0	127
30	29.57	1.511	2	189	8.83	0	100
Feb. 9	8.55	1.676	1	140	9.69	0	72
19	18.52	1.792	− 1	92	10.27	− 1	45
Mar. 1	0.49	1.861	0	46	10.58	1	− 20
11	10 46	1.885	0	+ 2	10.66	2	+ 2
21	20.44	1.866	0	− 37	10.54	2	22
31	30.41	1.813	+ 1	69	10.23	2	37
100, Apr. 10	9 38	1.731	2	93	9.80	2	48
20	19.35	1.630	2	108	9.28	2	55
30	29.33	1.517	2	118	8.70	3	60
May 10	9.30	1.396	3	121	8.08	3	62
20	19.27	1.276	3	119	7.47	3	61
30	29.25	1.160	3	112	6.87	2	59
June 9	8.22	1.053	3	101	6.30	2	55
19	18.19	0.960	2	86	5.78	2	49
29	28.16	0.882	2	70	5.31	2	42
July 9	8.14	0.820	2	52	4.94	1	33
200, 19	18.11	0.779	2	31	4.67	1	24
29	28.08	0.758	1	− 10	4.47	1	+ 12
Aug. 8	7.05	0.760	+ 1	+ 15	4.42	− 1	− 2
18	17.03	0.788	0	40	4.51	0	17
28	27.00	0.841	0	68	4.76	0	34
Sept. 7	5.97	0.925	− 1	99	5.19	0	53
17	15.95	1 039	1	130	5.83	0	75
27	25.92	1.186	2	164	6.69	0	97
Oct. 7	5.89	1.368	2	198	7.76	0	120
17	15.86	1.583	3	232	9.08	0	142
300, 27	25.84	1.832	3	264	10.58	0	162
Nov. 6	4.81	2.110	3	292	12.30	+ 1	180
16	14.78	2.414	4	315	14.16	1	191
26	24.75	2 737	4	330	16.10	1	198
Dec. 6	4.73	3.071	4	336	18.09	+ 1	200
16	14.70	3.405	4	331	20.07	0	195
26	24.67	3.730	3	317	21.96	− 1	183
36	34.64	+4.036	− 3	+293	−23.70	− 1	−165

* ☌ ☉, Aug. 27.6.
* ☌ Mean Sun, Aug. 27.9.

Sidereal Day	$\Delta_\Omega\alpha$	$\Delta_\Omega\delta$	$\Delta_\Omega\alpha$	$\Delta_\Omega\delta$
1865.			**1873.**	
0	+0.573	−6.77	−0.896	+7.24
100	0.483	6.48	0.835	7.22
200	0.389	6.12	0.767	7.14
300	0.291	5.72	0.694	6.99
400	0.191	5.26	0.614	6.79
1866.			**1874.**	
0	+0.225	−5.42	−0.642	+6.87
100	0.123	4.93	0.559	6.63
200	+0.020	4.40	0.472	6.34
300	−0.082	3.83	0.381	5.99
400	0.185	3.22	0.288	5.60
1867.			**1875.**	
0	−0.150	−3.43	−0.320	+5.74
100	0.251	2.80	0.221	5 32
200	0.350	2.15	0.127	4.85
300	0.446	1.49	−0.029	4.34
400	0.538	0.81	+0.069	3.80
1868 B.			**1876 B.**	
0	−0.508	−1.04	+0.036	+3.99
100	0.596	−0.36	0.134	3.43
200	0.680	+0.33	0.230	2.83
300	0.757	1.01	0.325	2.22
400	0.828	1.68	0.418	1.58
1869.			**1877.**	
0	−0.805	+1.46	+0.387	+1.79
100	0.870	2.12	0.477	1 15
200	0.928	2.76	0.563	+0.50
300	0.978	3.37	0.645	−0.16
400	1.019	3.96	0.722	0.82
1870.			**1878.**	
0	−1.006	+3.77	+0.697	−0.60
100	1.042	4.33	0.770	1.25
200	1.068	4.85	0.836	1.90
300	1.085	5.33	0.896	2.53
400	1.093	5.76	0.949	3.15
1871.			**1879.**	
0	−1.091	+5.62	+0.932	−2.94
100	1.093	6.02	0.980	3.54
200	1.085	6.36	1.019	4.11
300	1.068	6.66	1.050	4 65
400	1.042	6.89	1.073	5.15
1872 B.			**1880 B.**	
0	−1.052	+6.82	+1.066	−4.98
100	1.020	7.01	1.083	5.45
200	0.980	7.15	1.090	5.88
300	0.932	7.23	1.088	6.26
400	−0.876	+7.24	1.077	6.58

TABLE XXIV.—η Argus.

R.A. 10h 40.0.   Dec. − 59° 0'.

Upper transit at fictitious meridian.

Sidereal Day.	Mean Day.	Δ⊙α 1870.	Var. in 10y.	Diff. for 10 d.	Δ⊙δ 1870.	Var. in 10y.	Diff. for 10 d.
0, Jan. 0	− 0.34	+1.347	− 2	+447	+14.30	+ 3	−286
10	+ 9.64	1.768	− 1	393	11.25	3	322
20	19.61	2.130	0	327	7.89	3	349
30	29.58	2.420	+ 1	253	4.31	3	357
Feb. 9	8.56	2.634	2	175	+ 0.59	3	375
19	18.53	2.769	3	97	− 3.15	3	373
Mar. 1	0.50	2.828	4	+ 21	6.83	3	363
11	10.47	2.812	5	− 50	10.38	3	344
21	.20.45	2.730	6	114	13.09	3	318
31	30.42	2.587	6	171	16.72	3	287
100, Apr 10	9.39	2.391	6	219	19.42	2	251
20	19.36	2.153	7	256	21.72	1	210
30	29.34	1.882	6	284	23.61	+ 1	165
May 10	9.31	1.587	6	305	25.02	0	118
20	19.28	1.274	5	317	25.96	0	69
30	29.26	0.955	5	320	26.39	− 1	− 18
June 9	8.23	0.637	5	315	26.32	1	+ 32
19	18.20	0.327	4	302	25.76	1	81
29	28.17	+0.035	3	292	24.71	2	128
July 9	8.15	−0.234	2	254	23.21	3	171
200, 19	18.12	.470	+ 1	216	21.31	4	207
29	28.09	0.664	0	172	19.08	4	240
Aug. 8	7 06	0.812	0	121	16.53	4	264
18	17.04	0.903	− 1	− 61	13.82	4	279
28	27.01	0.932	2	+ 4	10.98	4	285
Sept. 7	5.98	0.893	2	74	8.16	4	279
17	15.95	0.782	3	147	5.44	4	263
27	25.93	0.598	3	222	2.93	4	236
Oct. 7	5.90	0.339	4	294	− 0.75	4	199
17	15.87	−0.012	4	361	+ 1.02	3	153
300, 27	25.85	+0.380	4	420	2.28	2	98
Nov. 6	4.82	0.825	3	468	2.97	2	+ 38
16	14.79	1.312	3	503	3.04	− 1	− 24
26	24.76	1.827	3	523	2.49	0	86
Dec. 6	4.74	2.353	3	525	+ 1.32	0	148
16	14.71	2.872	2	510	− 0.46	+ 1	206
26	24.68	3.367	− 1	477	2.78	1	257
36	34.65	+3.821	0	+429	− 5.57	+ 2	−289

✳ ☾ Mean Sun, Aug. 31.5.
✳ ♂ ⊙, Aug. 31.5.

Sidereal Day.	Δ☊α	Δ☊δ	Δ☊α	Δ☊δ
	1865.		**1873.**	
0	+1.256	−6.44	−1.156	+7.13
100	1.245	6.10	1.192	7.05
200	1.223	5.71	1.217	6.92
300	1.190	5.27	1.233	6.74
400	1.146	4.79	1.238	6.49
	1866.		**1874.**	
0	+1.162	−4 95	−1.237	+6.58
100	1.112	4.44	1.236	6 30
200	1.052	3.89	1.234	5.97
300	0.983	3.30	1.202	5.59
400	0.906	2.65	1.170	5.17
	1867.		**1875.**	
0	+0.933	−2.89	−1.182	+5.32
100	0.850	2.25	1.144	4.87
200	0.760	1.60	1.096	4.37
300	0.663	0.94	1.040	3.85
400	0.560	0.26	0.975	3.29
	1868 II.		**1876 II.**	
0	+0.595	−0.49	−0.998	+3.48
100	0.490	+0.19	0.927	2.90
200	0.380	0.86	0.849	2.30
300	0.267	1.52	0.764	1 69
400	0.152	2.17	0.673	1.05
	1869.		**1877.**	
0	+0.191	+1.96	−0.705	+1.26
100	+0.075	2.60	0.619	+0.61
200	−0.042	3.21	0.509	−0.03
300	0.157	3.80	0.404	0.68
400	0.271	4.34	0.296	1.32
	1870.		**1878.**	
0	−0.233	+4.16	−0.333	−1.11
100	0.346	4.68	0.222	1.75
200	0.455	5.16	0.110	2.37
300	0.560	5.60	+0.004	2.98
400	0.660	5.98	0.116	3.56
	1871.		**1879.**	
0	−0.627	+5.86	+0.079	−3.37
100	0.723	6.21	0.193	3.93
200	0.812	6.51	0.305	4.47
300	0.895	6.75	0.415	4.97
400	0.970	6.94	0.522	5.43
	1872 B.		**1880 B.**	
0	−0.945	+6.89	+0.486	−5.28
100	1.015	7.03	0.591	5.71
200	1.075	7.11	0.689	6.09
300	1.127	7.14	0.783	6.42
400	−1.169	+7.11	+0.871	−6.70

TABLE XXIV.—ι Leonis.

R.A. 10ʰ 42.4ᵐ   Dec. + 11° 14′

Upper transit at fictitious meridian.

Sidereal Day.	Mean Day.	$\Delta_\odot a$ 1870.	Var. in 10y.	Diff. for 10d.	$\Delta_\odot \delta$ 1870.	Var. in 10y.	Diff. for 10d.
0, Jan. 0	− 0.33	+0.673	− 3	+312	− 5.16	+ 1	−174
10	+ .64	0.973	3	285	6.79	1	152
20	19.61	1.240	2	247	8.18	+ 1	126
30	29.58	1.466	2	204	9 30	0	98
Feb. 9	8.56	1.047	2	158	10.14	0	69
19	18.53	1.781	1	109	10.68	− 1	39
Mar. 1	0.50	1.866	− 1	62	10.93	1	12
11	10.47	1.906	0	+ 18	10.94	1	+ 10
21	20.45	1.904	+ 1	− 22	10.74	1	30
·31	30.42	1.865	1	54	10.35	2	45
100, Apr. 10	9.39	1.798	1	81	9.85	2	56
20	19.37	1.706	2	100	9.24	2	65
30	29.34	1.600	2	110	8.57	2	68
May 10	9.31	1.488	2	116	7.89	2	67
20	19.28	1.370	2	117	7.23	2	65
30	29.26	1.255	2	112	6.59	2	62
June 9	8.23	1.147	3	104	6.00	2	56
19	18.20	1.048	3	93	5.48	2	48
29	28.18	0.962	3	78	5.05	2	39
July 9	8.15	0.892	2	61	4.70	2	30
200, 19	18.12	0.840	2	43	4.46	2	18
29	28.09	0.806	1	− 24	4.34	1	+ 6
Aug. 8	7.07	0.793	+ 1	0	4.35	1	− 9
18	17.04	0.806	0	+ 25	4.52	1	26
28	27.01	0.844	0	52	4.87	− 1	44
Sept. 7	5.98	0.911	− 1	82	5.40	0	63
17	15.96	1.008	1	114	6.14	0	84
27	25.93	1.139	1	149	7.09	0	106
Oct. 7	5.90	1.307	2	185	8.27	+ 1	129
17	15.87	1.509	2	220	9.67	1	150
300, 27	25.85	1.746	3	254	11.26	1	170
Nov. 6	4.82	2.016	3	285	13.05	1	186
16	14.79	2.313	4	310	14.96	1	197
26	24.77	2.633	4	328	16.98	+ 1	204
Dec. 6	4.74	2.966	4	337	19.02	0	203
16	14.71	3.303	4	336	21.03	0	197
26	24.68	3.634	4	324	22.95	0	185
36	34.66	+3.948	− 4	+303	−24.71	0	−166

⁂ δ ☉, Sept. 1.9.
⁂ δ Mean Sun, Sept. 1.1.

Sidereal Day.	$\Delta_\Omega a$	$\Delta_\Omega \delta$	$\Delta_\Omega a$	$\Delta_\Omega \delta$
	1865.		**1873.**	
0	+0.558	−6.38	−0.886	+7.10
100	0.468	6.04	0.824	7.02
200	0.374	5.64	0.756	6.88
300	0.275	5.20	0.681	6.09
400	0.175	4.71	0.601	6.44
	1866.		**1874.**	
0	+0.209	−4.88	−0.629	+6.53
100	0.107	4.36	0.545	6.24
200	−0.004	3.80	0.458	5.90
300	−0.098	3.21	0.366	5.52
400	0.201	2.59	0.272	5.09
	1867.		**1875.**	
0	−0.166	−2.80	−0.304	+5.24
100	0.267	2.16	0.209	4.78
200	0.366	1.51	0.111	4.29
300	0.461	0.84	−0.013	3.76
400	0.552	0.17	+0.085	3.20
	1868 B.		**1876 B.**	
0	−0.522	−0.39	+0.052	+3.39
100	0.610	+0.28	0.149	2.81
200	0.692	0.95	0.246	2.21
300	0.769	1.61	0.341	1.59
400	0.838	2.26	0.432	0.95
	1869.		**1877.**	
0	−0.815	+2.04	+0.402	+1.16
100	0.880	2.68	0.491	0.52
200	0.937	3.28	0.577	−0.13
300	0.985	3.86	0.658	0.78
400	1.025	4.40	0.734	1.42
	1870.		**1878.**	
0	−1.013	+4.22	+0.709	−1.20
100	1.047	4.74	0.781	1.84
200	1.071	5.21	0.846	2.46
300	1.087	5.64	0.905	3.06
400	1.053	6.02	0.956	3.64
	1871.		**1879.**	
0	−1.092	+5.90	+0.940	−3.44
100	1.092	6.24	0.986	4.00
200	1.083	6.53	1.024	4.53
300	1.065	6.77	1.054	5.02
400	1.037	6.94	1.075	5.48
	1872 B.		**1880 B.**	
0	−1.047	+6.89	+1.069	−5.33
100	1.014	7.03	1.084	5.75
200	0.973	7.11	1.090	6.12
300	0.922	7.12	1.087	6.45
400	−0.866	+7.08	+1.074	−6.71

TABLE XXIV.—δ Leonis.

R.A. 11^h 7.2^m.   Dec. +21° 14′.

Upper transit at fictitious meridian.

Sidereal Day	Mean Day	$\Delta_\odot\alpha$ 1870.	Var. in 10 y.	Diff. for 10 d.	$\Delta_\odot\delta$ 1870.	Var. in 10 y.	Diff. for 10 d.
0, Jan. 0	− 0.32	+0.560	− 3	+336	− 8.39	0	−153
10	+ 9.66	0.885	3	311	9.77	0	123
20	19.63	1.180	3	278	10.83	0	89
30	29.60	1.439	2	237	11.54	− 1	56
Feb. 9	8.57	1.652	2	191	11.89	1	− 17
19	18.55	1.819	2	142	11.89	2	+ 16
Mar. 1	0.52	1.935	1	91	11.58	2	45
11	10.49	2.001	− 1	43	11.00	2	70
21	20.47	2.023	0	+ 2	10.20	2	88
31	30.44	2.006	+ 1	− 35	9.26	3	100
100, Apr. 10	9.41	1.955	1	66	8.22	3	107
20	19.38	1.876	1	90	7.13	3	109
30	29.36	1.778	2	107	6.06	3	105
May 10	9.33	1.664	2	118	5.04	3	97
20	19.30	1.544	2	121	4.13	3	85
30	29.27	1.424	3	120	3.36	3	71
June 9	8.25	1.3.5	3	116	2.72	2	54
19	18.22	1.194	3	107	2.27	2	36
29	28.19	1.092	3	96	2.00	1	+ 17
July 9	8.16	1.003	2	82	1.93	− 1	− 3
200, 19	18.14	0.929	2	66	2.05	0	22
29	28.11	0.872	1	46	2.36	0	42
Aug. 8	7.08	0.837	+ 1	− 24	2.88	0	63
18	17.06	0.825	0	+ 1	3.62	+ 1	83
28	27.03	0.839	0	29	4.54	1	104
Sept. 7	6.00	0.883	− 1	59	5.69	1	125
17	15.97	0.958	1	92	7.05	1	146
27	25.95	1.068	2	123	8.61	1	166
Oct. 7	5.92	1.215	2	167	10.37	1	184
17	15.89	1.403	3	206	12.29	1	200
300, 27	25.86	1.627	3	244	14.37	1	213
Nov. 6	4.84	1.890	4	279	16.55	1	221
16	14.81	2.184	4	309	18.78	1	224
26	24.78	2.506	5	333	21.01	2	221
Dec. 6	4.76	2.848	5	348	23.17	2	211
16	14.73	3.199	5	352	25.20	1	194
26	24.70	3.549	5	346	27.03	+ 1	171
36	34.67	+3.857	− 5	+328	−28.59	0	−143

Sidereal Day	$\Delta_\Omega\alpha$	$\Delta_\Omega\delta$	$\Delta_\Omega\alpha$	$\Delta_\Omega\delta$
	1865.		**1873.**	
0	+0.470	−5.73	−0.839	+6.82
100	0.372	5.32	0.767	6.65
200	0.271	4.87	0.699	6.43
300	0.168	4.37	0.606	6.16
400	0.063	3.83	0.518	5.84
	1866.		**1874.**	
0	+0.099	−4.01	−0.548	+5.95
100	−0.007	3.45	0.458	5.60
200	0.112	2.86	0.363	5.20
300	0.217	2.24	0.266	4.76
400	0.320	1.61	0.167	4.28
	1867.		**1875.**	
0	−0.283	−1.82	−0.201	+4.44
100	0.386	1.18	−0.101	3.94
200	0.484	−0.52	0.000	3.40
300	0.577	+0.14	+0.101	2.84
400	0.665	0.80	0.201	2.25
	1868 B.		**1876 B.**	
0	−0.636	+0.58	+0.167	+2.45
100	0.720	1.23	0.266	1.86
200	0.797	1.87	0.363	1.24
300	0.868	2.50	0.456	+0.62
400	0.931	3.10	0.546	−0.01
	1869.		**1877.**	
0	−0.911	+2.90	+0.516	+0.19
100	0.964	3.49	0.603	−0.44
200	1.017	4.04	0.685	1.07
300	1.057	4.55	0.762	1.69
400	1.088	5.03	0.833	2.30
	1870.		**1878.**	
0	−1.079	+5.37	+0.810	−2.10
100	1.103	5.32	0.876	2.69
200	1.118	5.71	0.935	3.27
300	1.124	6.05	0.987	3.82
400	1.119	6.36	1.030	4.34
	1871.		**1879.**	
0	−1.122	+5.96	+1.016	−4.17
100	1.111	6.52	1.054	4 67
200	1.091	6.72	1.083	5.13
300	1.062	6.87	1.104	5.54
400	1.024	6.96	1.115	5.92
	1872 B.		**1880 B.**	
0	−1.038	+6.93	+1.112	−5.80
100	0.994	6.93	1.117	6.14
200	0.942	6.97	1.112	6.43
300	0.882	6.90	1.09+	6.66
400	−0.815	+6.77	+1.075	−6.84

✳ δ ⊙,   Sept. 8.0.
✳ δ Mean Sun,   Sept. 7.4.

TABLE XXIV.—δ Crateris.

R.A. 11h 12.8m   Dec. — 14° 5′

Upper transit at fictitious meridian.

Sidereal Day	Mean Day	$\Delta_\odot a$ 1870	Var.in 10y	Diff.for 10d	$\Delta_\odot \delta$ 1870	Var.in 10y	Diff.for 10d
0, Jan. 0	− 0.31	+0.527	− 3	+320	+ 3.05	+ 2	−239
10	+ 9.66	0.835	2	294	+ 0.64	2	241
20	19.63	1.113	2	262	− 1.76	2	237
30	29.61	1.357	1	223	4.09	3	227
Feb. 9	8.58	1.557	1	178	6.29	3	212
19	18.55	1.712	− 1	132	8.31	2	192
Mar. 1	0.52	1.822	0	88	10.12	1	170
11	10.50	1.888	0	45	11.70	+ 1	145
21	20.47	1.912	+ 1	+ 5	13.02	1	119
31	30.44	1.900	1	− 29	14.08	0	94
100, Apr. 10	9.41	1.857	2	56	14.90	− 1	69
20	19.39	1.790	2	77	15.47	1	45
30	29.36	1.704	3	94	15.80	1	− 22
May 10	9.33	1.604	3	104	15.91	2	0
20	19.31	1.497	3	110	15.81	2	+ 21
30	29.28	1.385	3	113	15.50	2	40
June 9	8.25	1.273	3	111	15.01	2	57
19	18.22	1.165	3	106	14.36	2	73
29	28.20	1.063	3	99	13.55	2	88
July 9	8.17	0.969	3	88	12.61	2	99
200, 19	18.14	0.888	2	74	11.58	2	108
29	28.11	0.822	2	58	10.47	2	112
Aug. 8	7.09	0.774	2	38	9.35	2	113
18	17.06	0.748	1	− 15	8.23	2	109
28	27.03	0.746	+ 1	+ 13	7.19	2	99
Sept. 7	6.00	0.776	0	45	6.27	2	84
17	15.98	0.838	0	79	5.52	1	64
27	25.95	0.935	− 1	117	5.01	1	39
Oct. 7	5.92	1.073	1	157	4.76	1	+ 8
17	15.90	1.250	1	196	4.87	− 1	− 27
300, 27	25.87	1.465	2	235	5.31	0	61
Nov. 6	4.84	1.719	2	271	6.10	0	98
16	14.81	2.005	3	300	7.27	0	135
26	24.79	2.317	3	322	8.79	0	167
Dec. 6	4.76	2.647	2	335	10.60	+ 1	194
16	14.73	2.984	2	338	12.65	1	216
26	24.70	3.319	2	330	14.90	1	232
36	34.68	+3.641	− 2	+312	−17.27	+ 2	−240

Sidereal Day / $\Delta_\Omega a$, $\Delta_\Omega \delta$

Sidereal Day	$\Delta_\Omega a$	$\Delta_\Omega \delta$	$\Delta_\Omega a$	$\Delta_\Omega \delta$
	1865.		**1873.**	
0	+0.742	−5.57	−0.969	+6.74
100	0.669	5.15	0.930	6.56
200	0.591	4.68	0.883	6.32
300	0.508	4.17	0.830	6.03
400	0.420	3.62	0.770	5.69
	1866.		**1874.**	
0	+0.449	−3.81	−0.791	+5.81
100	0.359	3.24	0.726	5.44
200	0.265	2.64	0.656	5.03
300	0.169	2.02	0.581	4.58
400	0.072	1.38	0.500	4.08
	1867.		**1875.**	
0	+0.105	−1.60	−0.528	+4.25
100	+0.006	0.95	0.445	3.74
200	−0.092	−0.29	0.358	3.20
300	0.189	+0.36	0.269	2.63
400	0.285	1.02	0.177	2.04
	1868 B.		**1876 B.**	
0	−0.253	+0.80	−0.208	+2.24
100	0.346	1.45	0.116	1.64
200	0.437	2.08	−0.022	1.02
300	0.524	2.70	+0.072	+0.39
400	0.606	3.29	0.165	−0.24
	1869.		**1877.**	
0	−0.579	+3.10	+0.133	−0.03
100	0.657	3.67	0.226	0.66
200	0.730	4.20	0.317	1.28
300	0.796	4.70	0.405	1.90
400	0.855	5.16	0.490	2.50
	1870.		**1878.**	
0	−0.836	+5.01	+0.462	−2.30
100	0.890	5.44	0.545	2.88
200	0.936	5.82	0.623	3.45
300	0.974	6.15	0.697	3.99
400	1.004	6.42	0.764	4.49
	1871.		**1879.**	
0	−0.995	+6.34	+0.742	−4.33
100	1.019	6.57	0.806	4.81
200	1.034	6.76	0.863	5.25
300	1.041	6.88	0.913	5.65
400	1.038	6.95	0.956	6.05
	1872 B.		**1880 B.**	
0	−1.040	+6.94	−0.943	−5.80
100	1.032	6.96	0.980	6.22
200	1.015	6.93	1.009	6.49
300	0.990	6.84	1.030	6.70
400	−0.956	+6.69	+1.042	−6.86

✱ ☌ ☉,   Sept. 9.6.
✱ ☌ Mean Sun, Sept. 8.8.

TABLE XXIV.—τ Leonis.

R.A. 11h 21m.3.   Dec. + 3° 34′.

Upper transit at fictitious meridian.

Sidereal Day	Mean Day	Δ☉a 1870.	Var. in 10 y.	Diff. for 10 d.	Δ☉δ 1870.	Var. in 10 y.	Diff. for 10 d.
0, Jan. 0	− 0.31	+0.455	− 3	+322	− 2.81	+ 2	−205
10	+ 9.67	0.767	3	300	4.79	2	191
20	19.64	1.052	2	269	6 62	2	172
30	29.61	1.303	2	232	8.21	1	147
Feb. 9	8.58	1.515	1	189	9.55	+ 1	121
19	18.56	1.681	1	143	10.62	0	93
Mar. 1	0.53	1.802	1	99	11.40	0	65
11	10.50	1.880	− 1	57	11.92	− 1	39
21	20.47	1.917	0	+ 18	12.19	1	− 15
31	30.45	1.917	+ 1	− 17	12.23	1	+ 6
100, Apr. 10	9.42	1.884	1	45	12.08	1	24
20	19.39	1.828	2	68	11.77	1	37
30	29.37	1.750	2	85	11.35	2	48
May 10	9.34	1.650	2	95	10.82	2	56
20	19.31	1.561	2	102	10.24	2	60
30	29.28	1.456	3	105	9.62	2	64
June 9	8.26	1.353	3	102	8.97	2	64
19	18.23	1.253	3	98	8.34	2	62
29	28 20	1.158	3	92	7.72	1	60
July 9	8.17	1.071	3	81	7.15	1	55
200, 19	18.15	0.996	2	68	6.63	1	48
29	28.12	0.935	2	53	6.19	1	40
Aug. 8	7.09	0.890	1	35	5.84	1	30
18	17.07	0.865	+ 1	− 13	5.61	− 1	+ 16
28	27.04	0.865	0	+ 12	5.54	0	− 2
Sept. 7	6 01	0.891	0	41	5 66	0	22
17	15.98	0.948	0	73	5.98	0	42
27	25.96	1.038	− 1	108	6.51	0	66
Oct. 7	5.93	1.165	2	146	7.30	+ 1	92
17	15.90	1.331	2	185	8.35	1	118
300, 27	25.87	1.535	3	223	9.66	1	143
Nov. 6	4.85	1.776	3	258	11.21	1	166
16	14.82	2.050	3	289	12.96	2	187
26	24 79	2.352	3	313	14.94	2	202
Dec. 6	4.77	2.674	3	329	17.01	2	212
16	14.74	3.007	3	335	19.15	2	215
26	24.71	3.340	3	330	21.28	1	210
36	34.68	+3.663	− 3	+314	−23.34	+ 1	−200

✳ ☌ ☉,   Sept. 11.9.
✳ ☌ Mean Sun, Sept. 11.0.

Sidereal Day	ΔΩa	ΔΩδ	ΔΩa	ΔΩδ
	1865.		**1873.**	
0	+0.606	−5.33	−0.902	+6.62
100	0.521	4.89	0.847	6.41
200	0.432	4.40	0.785	6.15
300	0.339	3.87	0.717	5.83
400	0.243	3.31	0.644	5.47
	1866.		**1874.**	
0	+0.276	−3.50	−0.669	+5.60
100	0.178	2.92	0.592	5.21
200	+0.079	2.31	0.510	4.77
300	−0.021	1.68	0.424	4.30
400	0.121	1.04	0.335	3.79
	1867.		**1875.**	
0	−0.087	−1.26	−0.366	+3.97
100	0.186	−0.61	0.274	3.44
200	0.284	+0.04	0.181	2.88
300	0.379	0.70	−0.087	2.31
400	0.470	1.34	+0.009	1.71
	1868 B.		**1876 B.**	
0	−0.440	+1.13	−0.023	+1.91
100	0.529	1.77	+0.072	1.30
200	0.613	2.39	0.167	0.69
300	0.691	2.99	0.260	+0.06
400	0.764	3.56	0.352	−0.56
	1869.		**1877.**	
0	−0.740	+3.38	+0.321	−0.36
100	0.808	3.93	0.410	0.98
200	0.869	4 45	0.497	1.60
300	0.924	4.92	0.579	2.20
400	0.967	5.36	0.65?	2.79
	1870.		**1878.**	
0	−0.953	+5.21	+0.631	−2.59
100	0.992	5.62	0.706	3.17
200	1.023	5.97	0.774	3.71
300	1.045	6.27	0.837	4.23
400	1.058	6.51	0.893	4.72
	1871.		**1879.**	
0	−1.054	+6.44	+0.874	−4.56
100	1.061	6.65	0.925	5.02
200	1.059	6.80	0.969	5.44
300	1.048	6.89	1.004	5.81
400	1.028	6.92	1.031	6.14
	1872 B.		**1880 B.**	
0	−1.036	+6.92	+1.023	−6.03
100	1.010	6.92	1.044	6.33
200	0.976	6.85	1.057	6.57
300	0.934	6.73	1.060	6.75
400	−0.884	+6.56	+1.055	−6.88

TABLE XXIV.—* λ Draconis.

R.A. 11h 23m.7. Dec. +70° 3'.

Upper transit at fictitious meridian.

Sidereal Day	Mean Day.	$\Delta_{\odot}\alpha$ 1870.	Var.in 10y.	Diff. for 10 d.	$\Delta_{\odot}\delta$ 1870.	Var.in 10y.	Diff. for 10 d.
0, Jan. 0	− 0.30	+1.162	−14	+758	−18.94	− 1	− 15
10	+ 9.67	1.901	15	715	18.78	2	+ 48
20	19.64	2.584	16	647	18.00	3	107
30	29.61	3.188	16	558	16.65	4	161
Feb. 9	8.59	3.695	16	452	14.80	4	208
19	18.56	4.088	15	333	12.52	5	246
Mar. 1	0.53	4.358	14	207	9.92	5	273
11	10.51	4.501	12	+ 79	7.11	6	288
21	20.48	4.518	11	− 43	4.21	6	291
31	30.45	4.117	9	157	− 1.33	6	282
100, Apr. 10	9.42	4.208	7	258	+ 1.39	5	262
20	19.40	3.900	4	343	3.87	5	232
30	29.37	3.528	− 2	419	6.01	4	194
May 10	9.34	3.092	0	459	7.73	4	150
20	19.32	2.616	+ 2	489	9.00	3	102
30	29.29	2.119	4	502	9.76	2	+ 50
June 9	8.26	1.617	5	499	9.99	− 1	− 3
19	18.23	1.126	6	480	9.70	0	55
29	28.20	0.661	7	449	8.90	+ 1	106
July 9	8.18	+0.233	8	406	7.60	1	154
200, 19	18.15	−0.147	8	353	5.83	2	199
29	28.12	0.470	8	292	3.64	3	239
Aug. 8	7.10	0.728	7	223	+ 1.07	3	274
18	17.07	0.913	6	146	− 1.83	4	304
28	27.04	1.019	5	− 65	4.99	4	328
Sept. 7	6.01	1.042	3	+ 21	8.37	4	346
17	15.99	0.976	+ 1	112	11.89	5	357
27	25.96	0.817	− 1	206	15.49	5	361
Oct. 7	5.93	0.563	4	302	19.09	5	358
17	15.90	−0.214	6	396	22.62	4	347
300, 27	25.88	+0.228	9	488	26.00	4	327
Nov. 6	4.85	0.760	12	573	29.14	3	300
16	14.82	1.372	14	648	31.97	3	264
26	24.80	2.052	17	710	34.39	2	220
Dec. 6	4.77	2.786	20	753	36.34	+ 1	169
16	14.74	3.550	22	773	37.76	0	113
26	24.71	4.325	24	772	38.59	− 1	− 53
36	34.69	+5.085	−25	+745	−38.81	− 2	+ 9

* ☌ Mean Sun, Mar. 12.9.
* ☌ ☉, Sept. 12.5.
* ☌ Mean Sun, Sept. 11.5.

Sidereal Day	$\Delta_{\Omega}\alpha$	$\Delta_{\Omega}\delta$	$\Delta_{\Omega}\alpha$	$\Delta_{\Omega}\delta$
	1865.		**1873.**	
0	−0.603	−5.26	−0.279	+6.59
100	0.789	4.81	−0.088	6.37
200	0.967	4.32	+0.102	6.10
300	1.138	3.79	0.291	5.77
400	1.299	3.22	0.477	5.40
	1866.		**1874.**	
0	−1.246	−3.42	+0.415	+5.53
100	1.400	2.83	0.598	5.14
200	1.541	2.22	0.777	4.70
300	1.669	1.59	0.948	4.22
400	1.783	0.95	1.111	3.71
	1867.		**1875.**	
0	−1.746	−1.17	+1.057	+3.88
100	1.849	−0.52	1.214	3.35
200	1.936	+0.14	1.361	2.79
300	2.006	0.79	1.496	2.21
400	2.059	1.44	1.619	1.61
	1868 B.		**1876 B.**	
0	−2.043	+1.22	+1.579	+1.81
100	2.085	1.86	1.694	1.21
200	2.107	2.49	1.794	+0.59
300	2.111	3.07	1.880	−0.04
400	2.097	3.64	1.950	0.66
	1869.		**1877.**	
0	−2.101	+3.46	+1.928	−0.45
100	2.076	4.00	1.988	1.07
200	2.031	4.51	2.031	1.69
300	1.969	4.98	2.058	2.29
400	1.889	5.41	2.067	2.87
	1870.		**1878.**	
0	−1.918	+5.27	+2.066	−2.68
100	1.829	5.67	2.064	3.25
200	1.724	6.01	2.046	3.79
300	1.604	6.30	2.010	4.30
400	1.471	6.54	1.958	4.78
	1871.		**1879.**	
0	−1.517	+6.46	+1.977	−4.62
100	1.376	6.66	1.914	5.08
200	1.223	6.81	1.834	5.49
300	1.060	6.89	1.739	5.85
400	0.889	6.92	1.629	6.17
	1872 B.		**1880 B.**	
0	−0.948	+6.91	+1.669	−6.07
100	0.772	6.90	1.549	6.36
200	0.590	6.83	1.416	6.59
300	0.404	6.70	1.271	6.77
400	−0.215	+6.52	+1.116	−6.89

TABLE XXIV.—v Leonis.

R.A. 11h 30m.3.   Dec. — 0° 6'.

Upper transit at fictitious meridian.

Sidereal Day	Mean Day	Δ☉α 1870.	Var.in 10y.	Diff. for 10 d.	Δ☉δ 1870.	Var.in 10y.	Diff for 10 d.
0, Jan. 0	− 0.30	+0.406	− 3	+324	− 1.55	+ 2	−213
10	+ 9.67	0.720	3	303	3.64	2	203
20	19.65	1.009	2	273	5.60	1	187
30	29.62	1.264	2	237	7.37	1	166
Feb. 9	8.59	1.482	2	196	8.91	1	141
19	18.56	1.655	− 1	151	10.19	+ 1	115
Mar. 1	0.54	1.784	0	108	11.20	0	88
11	10.51	1.871	0	66	11.96	0	62
21	20.48	1.916	0	+ 26	12.44	0	37
31	30.45	1.924	+ 1	− 8	12.70	− 1	− 15
100, Apr. 10	9.43	1.901	1	36	12.74	1	+ 4
20	19.40	1.853	2	60	12.62	2	20
30	29.37	1.782	2	78	12.35	2	34
May 10	9.34	1.699	3	90	11.95	2	45
20	19.32	1.604	3	98	11.46	2	53
30	29.29	1.504	3	102	10.90	2	59
June 9	8.26	1.401	3	102	10.29	2	63
19	18.24	1.301	3	99	9.65	2	65
29	28.21	1.204	3	94	9.00	2	66
July 9	8.18	1.115	3	85	8.34	2	64
200, 19	18.15	1.035	2	75	7.72	2	60
29	28 13	0.966	2	61	7.15	2	54
Aug. 8	7.10	0.915	2	43	6.65	1	45
18	17.07	0.882	1	− 23	6.25	1	33
28	27.04	0.871	+ 1	+ 2	5.99	1	19
Sept. 7	6.02	0.888	0	31	5.87	− 1	+ 1
17	15.99	0.935	0	63	5.96	0	− 21
27	25.96	1.016	0	100	6.29	0	45
Oct. 7	5.94	1.135	− 1	138	6.87	+ 1	70
17	15.91	1.292	2	177	7.70	1	98
300, 27	25.88	1.489	2	217	8.83	1	126
Nov. 6	4.85	1.724	2	252	10.22	1	152
16	14.83	1.992	2	284	11.96	1	176
26	24.80	2.290	3	310	13.72	1	196
Dec. 6	4.77	2.609	3	327	15.74	1	208
16	14.74	2.940	3	334	17 87	2	216
26	24.72	3.274	3	331	20.04	2	216
36	34.69	+3.599	− 3	+317	−22.18	+ 2	−211

✻ ☌ Mean Sun, Sept. 14.4.
✻ ☌ ☉, Sept. 13.3.

Sidereal Day	ΔΩα	ΔΩδ	ΔΩα	ΔΩδ
	1865.		**1873.**	
0	+0.635	−5.06	−0.916	+6.48
100	0.553	4.60	0.865	6.24
200	0.466	4.09	0.806	5.95
300	0.375	3.55	0.741	5.61
400	0.280	2.97	0.670	5.22
	1866.		**1874.**	
0	+0.312	−3.17	−0.695	+5.36
100	0.216	2.57	0.621	4.94
200	0.117	1.96	0.541	4.49
300	+0.018	1.32	0.457	4.00
400	−0.081	0.68	0.370	3.47
	1867.		**1875.**	
0	−0.048	−0.89	−0.399	+3.65
100	0.147	−0.24	0.310	3.11
200	0.244	+0.41	0.218	2.54
300	0.340	1.06	0.124	1.96
400	0.433	1.69	0.030	1.35
	1868 B.		**1876 B.**	
0	−0.402	+1.48	−0.062	+1.56
100	0.492	2.11	+0.033	0.95
200	0.577	2.72	0.128	+0.33
300	0.657	3.30	0.221	−0.30
400	0.732	3.85	0.313	0.92
	1869.		**1877.**	
0	−0.707	+3.68	+0.282	−0.72
100	0.778	4.21	0.373	1.33
200	0.841	4.70	0.460	1.94
300	0.897	5.15	0.544	2.53
400	0.945	5.56	0.623	3.10
	1870.		**1878.**	
0	−0.929	+5.43	+0.597	−2.91
100	0.972	5.80	0.673	3.47
200	1.006	6.12	0.744	3.99
300	1.031	6.39	0.809	4.49
400	1.047	6.60	0.867	4.95
	1871.		**1879.**	
0	−1.043	+6.54	+0.818	−4.80
100	1.053	6.71	0.902	5.23
200	1.055	6.83	0.948	5.62
300	1.047	6.89	0.986	5.97
400	1.031	6.89	1.016	6.27
	1872 B.		**1880 B.**	
0	−1.037	+6.90	+1.007	−6.17
100	1.015	6.86	1.032	6.44
200	0.985	6.77	1.048	6.64
300	0.946	6.62	1.055	6.80
400	−0.990	+6.41	+1.053	−6.89

TABLE XXIV.—o Virginis.

R.A. 11ʰ 58.6ᵐ   Dec. + 9° 27′.

Upper transit at fictitious meridian.

Sidereal Day	Mean Day	Δ⊙α 1870.	Var. in 10 y.	Diff. for 10 d.	Δ⊙δ 1870.	Var. in 10 y.	Diff. for 10 d.
0, Jan. 0	− 0.28	+0.240	− 3	+334	4.81	+ 2	−203
10	+ 9.69	0.567	3	319	6.75	2	183
20	19.66	0.874	3	294	8.46	2	157
30	29.64	1.152	2	262	9.88	1	128
Feb. 9	8.61	1.396	2	224	11.02	+ 1	98
19	18.58	1.598	2	181	11.83	0	64
Mar. 1	0.56	1.758	1	137	12.31	0	32
11	10.53	1.873	− 1	95	12.48	0	− 4
21	20.50	1.948	0	55	12.40	0	+ 21
31	30.47	1.984	0	+ 18	12.08	− 1	43
100, Apr. 10	9.45	1.986	+ 1	− 14	11.56	1	60
20	19.42	1.958	1	40	10.90	2	72
30	29.39	1.908	2	61	10.14	2	79
May 10	9.36	1.838	2	78	9.34	2	82
20	19.34	1.753	2	89	8.52	2	81
30	29.31	1.661	2	96	7.72	2	78
June 9	8.28	1.561	3	102	6.96	2	73
19	18.26	1.457	3	103	6.26	2	65
29	28.23	1.356	3	100	5.66	2	56
July 9	8.20	1.257	2	96	5.14	2	44
200, 19	18.17	1.164	2	89	4.77	1	31
29	28.15	1.079	2	79	4.53	− 1	17
Aug. 8	7.12	1.006	2	65	4.44	0	+ 1
18	17.09	0.951	1	46	4.51	0	− 17
28	27.06	0.915	1	− 24	4.78	0	36
Sept. 7	6.04	0.905	+ 1	+ 4	5.22	+ 1	57
17	16.01	0.924	0	35	5.91	1	79
27	25.98	0.976	− 1	70	6.81	1	102
Oct. 7	5.95	1.066	1	110	7.95	1	126
17	15.93	1.196	2	150	9.33	2	150
300, 27	25.90	1.367	2	192	10.95	2	173
Nov. 6	4.87	1.580	2	232	12.77	2	192
16	14.85	1.830	3	268	14.77	2	208
26	24.82	2.114	3	299	16.92	2	218
Dec. 6	4.79	2.425	3	321	19.12	2	222
16	14.76	2.753	3	334	21.35	2	221
26	24.74	3.090	4	337	23.52	2	212
36	34.71	+3.424	− 4	+329	−25.57	+ 2	−196

* ☌ ⊙,   Sept. 22.3.
* ☌ Mean Sun,   Sept. 20.4.

Sidereal Day	ΔΩα	ΔΩδ	ΔΩα	ΔΩδ
	1865.		**1873.**	
0	+0.551	−4.18	−0.867	+5.98
100	0.463	3.65	0.807	5.65
200	0.372	3.08	0.741	5.27
300	0.277	2.49	0.669	4.85
400	0.179	1.88	0.592	4.39
	1866.		**1874.**	
0	+0.212	−2.09	−0.619	+4.55
100	0.113	1.46	0.538	4.07
200	+0.014	0.82	0.453	3.55
300	−0.086	−0.18	0.365	3.01
400	0.185	+0.47	0.274	2.44
	1867.		**1875.**	
0	−0.152	+0.25	−0.305	+2.63
100	0.250	0.90	0.212	2.05
200	0.346	1.54	0.118	1.45
300	0.439	2.16	−0.023	0.85
400	0.528	2.76	+0.073	+0.23
	1868 B.		**1876 B.**	
0	−0.499	+2.56	+0.041	−0.44
100	0.584	3.15	0.136	−0.18
200	0.665	3.71	0.230	0.80
300	0.740	4.24	0.322	1.41
400	0.808	4.73	0.411	2.00
	1869.		**1877.**	
0	−0.786	+4.57	+0.381	−1.81
100	0.849	5.03	0.469	2.40
200	0.905	5.44	0.552	2.97
300	0.953	5.81	0.632	3.52
400	0.993	6.13	0.706	4.03
	1870.		**1878.**	
0	−0.980	+6.03	+0.681	−3.86
100	1.014	6.31	0.752	4.36
200	1.039	6.53	0.816	4.82
300	1.055	6.70	0.874	5.25
400	1.062	6.81	0.925	5.63
	1871.		**1879.**	
0	−1.061	+6.76	+0.908	−5.50
100	1.062	6.85	0.954	5.85
200	1.053	6.87	0.992	6.16
300	1.036	6.82	1.022	6.41
400	1.011	6.72	1.043	6.61
	1872 B.		**1880 B.**	
0	−1.020	+6.76	+1.037	−6.55
100	0.989	6.62	1.052	6.71
200	0.949	6.43	1.059	6.82
300	0.902	6.18	1.057	6.87
400	−0.847	+5.88	+1.046	−6.86

TABLE XXIV.—* 4 Draconis (H.)

R.A. 12h 6m.1.   Dec. + 78° 20'.

Upper transit at fictitious meridian.

Sidereal Day	Mean Day	$\Delta_\odot a$ 1870.	Var. in 10y.	Diff. for 10 d.	$\Delta_\odot \delta$ 1870.	Var. in 10y.	Diff. for 10 d.
0, Jan. 0	− 0.27	+0.718	−18	+1214	−20.23	0	− 50
10	+ 9.70	1.920	23	1184	20.41	− 1	+ 15
20	19.67	3.072	27	1113	19.93	2	79
30	29.64	4.132	31	1005	18.83	3	140
Feb. 9	8.62	5.065	33	856	17.15	3	194
19	18.59	5.839	35	685	14.97	4	240
Mar. 1	0.56	6.429	35	492	12.39	4	275
11	10.54	6.820	35	288	9.52	5	298
21	20.51	7.004	33	+ 81	6.48	5	308
31	30.48	6.983	30	− 121	3.39	5	306
100, Apr. 10	9.45	6.766	27	310	− 0.39	5	293
20	19.43	6.370	23	479	+ 2.42	4	268
30	29.40	5.816	18	624	4.94	4	234
May 10	9.37	5.131	13	742	7.07	3	192
20	19.34	4.342	8	831	8.75	3	143
30	29.32	3.478	− 3	892	9.93	2	91
June 9	8.29	2.568	+ 2	923	10.56	1	+ 36
19	18.26	1.641	7	925	10.65	− 1	− 19
29	28.23	+0.721	11	907	10.18	0	74
July 9	8.21	−0.165	15	863	9.17	+ 1	128
200, 19	18.18	0.993	18	798	7.64	2	178
29	28.15	1.755	20	715	5.63	2	224
Aug. 8	7.13	2.422	22	615	3.19	3	265
18	17.10	2.960	23	506	+ 0.35	3	301
28	27.07	3.416	23	371	− 2.82	4	331
Sept. 7	6.04	3.719	22	232	6.26	4	355
17	16.02	3.877	21	82	9.89	5	372
27	25.99	3.890	18	+ 76	13.66	5	381
Oct. 7	5.96	3.722	15	240	17.49	5	382
17	15.93	3.400	12	405	21.28	5	376
300, 27	25.91	2.912	7	569	24.97	4	360
Nov. 6	4.88	2.263	+ 2	727	28.45	4	335
16	14.85	1.462	− 4	873	31.64	4	302
26	24.83	−0.523	10	1000	34.46	3	260
Dec. 6	4 80	+0.531	16	1103	36.81	2	209
16	14.77	1.673	22	1175	38.63	2	153
26	24.74	2.869	27	1210	39.84	+ 1	91
36	34.72	+4.081	−33	+1206	−40.43	0	− 26

Sidereal Day	$\Delta_\Omega a$	$\Delta_\Omega \delta$	$\Delta_\Omega a$	$\Delta_\Omega \delta$
	1865.		**1873.**	
0	−1.821	−3.93	+0.576	+5.84
100	2.055	3.39	0.854	5.48
200	2.271	2.81	1.124	5.08
300	2.468	2.21	1.384	4.64
400	2.644	1.59	1.632	4.16
	1866.		**1874.**	
0	−2.587	−1.86	+1.550	+4.33
100	2.747	1.17	1.789	3.83
200	2.884	−0.52	2.012	3.30
300	2.995	+0.13	2.219	2.74
400	3.080	0.77	2.406	2.16
	1867.		**1875.**	
0	−3.054	+0.55	+2.345	+2.36
100	3.122	1.20	2.520	1.77
200	3.162	1.83	2.673	1.16
300	3.174	2.45	2.805	+0.55
400	3.159	3.04	2.913	−0.07
	1868 B.		**1876 B.**	
0	−3.167	+2.84	+2.879	+0.14
100	3.134	3.42	2.971	−0.48
200	3.073	3.96	3.039	1.09
300	2 985	4.47	3.082	1.70
400	2.872	4.94	3.099	2.29
	1869.		**1877.**	
0	−2 913	+4.79	+3.096	−2.09
100	2.784	5.25	3.097	2.67
200	2.630	5.62	3.072	3.23
300	2.454	5.97	3.021	3.77
400	2.257	6.28	2.946	4.27
	1870.		**1878.**	
0	−2.326	+6.17	+2.977	−4.10
100	2.116	6.42	2.882	4.58
200	1.889	6.62	2.766	5.03
300	1.647	6.77	2.627	5.43
400	1.390	6.85	2.466	5.79
	1871.		**1879.**	
0	−1.478	+6.83	+2.523	−5.67
100	1.214	6.87	2.348	6.00
200	0.941	6.86	2.153	6.28
300	0.661	6.79	1.940	6.51
400	0.376	6.66	1.709	6.63
	1872 B.		**1880 B.**	
0	−0.472	+6.71	+1.789	−6.63
100	−0.185	6.54	1.548	6.77
200	+0.103	6.32	1.294	6 85
300	0.389	6.05	1.029	6.87
400	+0.671	+5.72	+0.754	−6.83

* ☌ Mean Sun, Sept. 22.3.
* ☍ Mean Sun, Mar. 23.7.
* ☌ ☉, Sept. 24.4.

TABLE XXIV.—* β Chamæleontis.

R.A. 12^h 10.8^m Dec. — 78° 35′.

Upper transit at fictitious meridian.

Sidereal Day.	Mean Day.	$\Delta_\odot{}^a$			$\Delta_\odot{}^\delta$			Sidereal Day.	$\Delta_\Omega{}^a$	$\Delta_\Omega{}^\delta$	$\Delta_\Omega{}^a$	$\Delta_\Omega{}^\delta$
		1870.	Var. in 10 y.	Diff. for 10 d.	1870.	Var. in 10 y.	Diff. for 10 d.		1865.		1873.	
								0	+3.158	−3.79	−2.485	+5.74
								100	3.228	3.22	2.664	5.37
								200	3.269	2.64	2.820	4.96
		″			″			300	3.282	2.03	2.953	4.51
0, Jan. 0	− 0.27	+0.946	−13	+1209	+19.48	+ 1	−146	400	3.267	1.46	3.061	4.02
10	+ 9.70	2.130	− 6	1147	17.73	2	203					
20	19.67	3.230	0	1049	15.43	3	254		1866.		1874.	
30	29.65	4.218	+ 7	92	12.67	4	298	0	+3.275	−1.62	−3.027	+4.19
Feb. 9	8.62	5.070	13	778	9.51	4	333	100	3.241	0.98	3.119	3.67
19	18.59	5.770	19	619	6 04	5	359	200	3.178	−0.33	3.184	3.13
Mar. 1	0.57	6.306	24	45	+ 2.36	5	376	300	3.087	+0.32	3.223	2.57
11	10.54	6.673	29	283	− 1.44	5	384	400	2.970	0.96	3.235	1.98
21	20.51	6.870	33	+ 114	5.28	5	383					
31	30.48	6.901	36	− 51	9.07	5	374		1867.		1875.	
								0	+3.012	+0.74	−3.234	+2.18
100, Apr. 10	9.46	6.771	38	206	12.74	5	358	100	2.878	1.39	3.228	1.59
20	19.43	6.489	39	355	16.20	4	334	200	2.718	2.01	3.196	0.98
30	29.40	6.065	40	490	19.39	4	303	300	2.534	2.62	3.138	+0.36
May 10	9.38	5.514	39	611	22.95	3	267	400	2.328	3.21	3.054	−0.26
20	19.35	4.848	38	716	24.71	3	225					
									1868 B.		1876 B.	
30	29.32	4.084	35	806	26.73	2	178	0	+2.400	+3.02	−3.085	−0.05
June 9	8.29	3.242	32	875	28.25	+ 1	127	100	2.181	3.58	2.984	0.67
19	18.27	2.342	28	921	29.26	0	74	200	1.943	4.12	2.858	1.28
29	28.24	1.407	24	944	29.72	0	− 19	300	1.689	4.62	2.709	1.88
July 9	8.21	+0.463	19	946	29.63	− 1	+ 37	400	1.420	5.08	2.537	2.47
200, 19	18.18	−0.463	14	906	28.99	2	91		1869.		1877.	
29	28.16	1.343	8	846	27.82	3	143	0	+1.512	+4.93	−2.598	−2.27
Aug. 8	7.13	2.146	+ 3	755	26.15	4	190	100	1.235	5.36	2.412	2.85
18	17.10	2.843	− 3	635	24.04	4	231	200	0.948	5.74	2.205	3.40
28	27.08	3.407	8	485	21.56	5	264	300	0.654	6.07	1.981	3.92
Sept. 7	6.05	3.812	12	318	18.79	5	288	400	0.354	6.34	1.739	4.42
17	16.02	4.036	16	− 128	15.84	5	301		1870.		1878.	
27	25.99	4.063	19	+ 75	12.80	5	304	0	+0.456	+6.26	−1.822	−4.25
Oct. 7	5.96	3.884	21	284	9.81	5	293	100	+0.154	6.50	1.571	4.73
17	15.94	3.497	21	490	6.97	5	271	200	−0.148	6.68	1.305	5.16
300, 27	25.91	2.908	21	686	4.42	4	238	300	0.448	6.80	1.026	5.55
Nov. 6	4.88	2.132	20	862	2.24	4	194	400	0.743	6.87	0.742	5.89
16	14.86	1.192	17	1012	− 0.56	3	142					
26	24.83	−0.120	14	112	+ 0.58	2	84		1871.		1879.	
Dec. 6	4.80	+1.050	10	1205	1.10	− 1	+ 20	0	−0.644	+6.85	−0.840	−5.78
								100	0.935	6.88	0.548	6.09
16	14.77	2.277	− 4	1242	0.99	0	− 44	200	1.218	6.85	−0.252	6.36
26	24.75	3.520	+ 2	1237	+ 0.23	+ 1	108	300	1.489	6.76	+0.048	6.57
36	34.72	+4.739	+ 8	+1194	− 1.16	+ 2	−168	400	1.748	6.61	0.348	6.73
									1872 B.		1880 B.	
								0	−1.662	+6.07	+0.247	−6.68
								100	1.910	6.49	0.546	6.80
								200	2.142	6.25	0.841	6.86
								300	2.355	5.96	1.130	6.86
								400	−2.548	+5.62	+1.410	−6.81

✱ 𝛿 Mean Sun,   Mar. 24.9.
✱✱ ☌ ☉,   Sept. 25 6.
✱ ☌ Mean Sun,   Sept. 23.5.

TABLE XXIV.—η Virginis.

R.A. 12^h 13.3^m.   Dec. + 0$^°$ 3$^'$.

Upper transit at fictitious meridian.

Sidereal Day	Mean Day	$\Delta_\odot a$ 1870.	Var. in 10 y.	Diff. for 10 d.	$\Delta_\odot \delta$ 1870.	Var. in 10 y.	Diff. for 10 d.
0, Jan. 0	− 0.27	+0.157	− 3	+332	− 1.51	+ 2	−216
10	+ 9.70	0.483	3	320	3.63	2	207
20	19.67	0.793	3	297	5.62	1	190
30	29.65	1.075	2	267	7.41	1	169
Feb. 9	8.62	1.325	2	231	8.99	1	145
19	18.59	1.536	2	191	10.30	+ 1	118
Mar. 1	0.57	1.707	1	150	11.34	0	90
11	10.54	1.836	− 1	109	12.10	0	62
21	20.51	1.925	0	70	12.59	0	37
31	30.48	1.977	+ 1	34	12.84	0	− 14
100, Apr. 10	9.46	1.994	1	+ 3	12.87	0	+ 7
20	19.43	1.984	2	− 23	12.70	− 1	24
30	29.40	1.949	2	45	12.39	1	37
May 10	9.37	1.895	2	62	11.96	1	48
20	19.35	1.825	2	77	11.44	1	56
30	29.32	1.741	3	88	10.85	1	61
June 9	8.29	1.650	3	94	10.22	1	64
19	18.27	1.554	3	98	9.58	2	65
29	28.24	1.454	3	100	8.93	2	64
July 9	8.21	1.355	3	99	8.31	2	61
200, 19	18.18	1.258	3	94	7.72	1	56
29	28.16	1.168	3	86	7.20	1	50
Aug. 8	7.13	1.088	3	74	6.73	1	41
18	17.10	1.021	2	58	6.38	1	30
28	27.07	0.973	2	36	6.15	1	+ 15
Sept. 7	6.05	0.950	+ 1	− 11	6.08	− 1	− 3
17	16.02	0.953	0	+ 20	6.21	0	23
27	25.99	0.991	0	57	6.55	0	45
Oct. 7	5.96	1.067	0	95	7.12	0	71
17	15.94	1.182	0	137	7.97	+ 1	97
300, 27	25.91	1.341	− 1	180	9.07	1	124
Nov. 6	4.88	1.542	2	221	10.44	1	150
16	14.86	1.782	2	258	12.05	2	173
26	24.83	2.057	2	290	13.89	2	193
Dec. 6	4.80	2.360	2	314	15.90	3	208
16	14.77	2.683	3	329	18.03	3	216
26	24.75	3.016	3	335	20.20	3	217
33	34.72	+3.350	− 3	+328	−22.35	+ 3	−212

✳ ☌ ☉, Sept. 26.4.
✳ ☌ Mean Sun, Sept. 24.1.

Sidereal Day	$\Delta_\Omega a$	$\Delta_\Omega \delta$	$\Delta_\Omega a$	$\Delta_\Omega \delta$
	1865.		**1873.**	
0	+0.633	−3.69	−0.915	+5.69
100	0.551	3.13	0.864	5.31
200	0.464	2.54	0.806	4.89
300	0.373	1.93	0.740	4.43
400	0.278	1.30	0.669	3.94
	1866.		**1874.**	
0	+0.311	−1.52	−0.694	+4.11
100	0.214	0.88	0.619	3.59
200	0.116	−0.23	0.539	3.05
300	+0.017	+0.42	0.456	2.48
400	−0.083	1.06	0.368	1.89
	1867.		**1875.**	
0	−0.049	+0.85	−0.398	+2.09
100	0.148	1.49	0.308	1.49
200	0.246	2.11	0.216	0.88
300	0.342	2.72	0.123	+0.26
400	0.434	3.30	0.028	−0.36
	1868 B.		**1876 B.**	
0	−0.403	+3.11	−0.060	−0.15
100	0.493	3.67	+0.035	0.76
200	0.579	4.21	0.130	1.38
300	0.659	4.70	0.223	1.98
400	0.733	5.15	0.315	2.56
	1869.		**1877.**	
0	−0.709	+5.01	+0.284	−2.37
100	0.779	5.43	0.374	2.94
200	0.842	5.80	0.462	3.49
300	0.898	6.12	0.545	4.01
400	0.946	6.39	0.625	4.50
	1870.		**1878.**	
0	−0.930	+6.30	+0.598	−4.34
100	0.973	6.53	0.674	4.80
200	1.007	6.71	0.745	5.22
300	1.032	6.82	0.810	5.61
400	1.048	6.88	0.668	5.95
	1871.		**1879.**	
0	−1.043	+6.87	+0.849	−5.84
100	1.054	6.89	0.903	6.14
200	1.055	6.84	0.949	6.40
300	1.047	6.75	0.987	6.6)
400	1.031	6.59	1.017	6.75
	1872 B.		**1880 B.**	
0	−1.037	+6.65	+1.008	−6.70
100	1.015	6.46	1.032	6.61
200	0.984	6.21	1.048	6.57
300	0.945	5.91	1.055	6.86
400	−0.899	+5.57	+1.053	−6.80

TABLE XXIV.—α¹ Crucis.

R.A. 12^h 19^m.4.   Dec. − 62° 23′

Upper transit at fictitious meridian.

Sidereal Day	Mean Day	$\Delta_\odot a$ 1870.	Var. in 10y.	Diff. for 10d.	$\Delta_\odot \delta$ 1870.	Var. in 10y.	Diff. for 10d.
0, Jan. 0	− 0.27	+0.301	− 7	+588	+17.28	+ 2	−169
10	+ 9.71	0.877	5	561	15.34	2	219
20	19.68	1.417	4	518	12.93	3	263
30	29.65	1.908	3	462	10.11	4	297
Feb. 9	8.62	2.338	− 1	396	7.01	4	323
19	18.60	2.699	+ 1	325	3.67	4	343
Mar. 1	0.57	2.987	2	251	+ 0.18	4	353
11	10.54	3.200	4	175	− 3.37	4	354
21	20.52	3.338	6	101	6.88	4	349
31	30.49	3.404	7	+ 31	10.32	5	336
100, Apr. 10	9.46	3.402	8	− 34	13.58	4	315
20	19.43	3.337	9	95	16.61	3	290
30	29.41	3.214	10	150	19.36	3	259
May 10	9.38	3.039	10	199	21.78	2	224
20	19.35	2.819	11	241	23.82	2	184
30	29.32	2.559	11	277	25.44	2	139
June 9	8.30	2.268	11	305	26.60	+ 1	93
19	18.27	1.951	10	327	27.30	0	− 45
29	28.24	1.617	10	339	27.50	0	+ 5
July 9	8.21	1.276	9	342	27.21	− 1	53
200, 19	18.19	0.937	8	333	26.44	2	101
29	28.16	0.613	7	313	25.20	3	145
Aug. 8	7.13	0.314	6	282	23.55	3	186
18	17.11	+0.053	5	238	21.51	3	220
28	27.08	−0.158	3	182	19.18	4	246
Sept. 7	6.05	0.308	2	115	16.62	5	264
17	16.02	0.385	+ 1	− 38	13.93	5	271
27	26.00	0.381	0	+ 48	11.23	4	268
Oct. 7	5.97	0.288	− 1	137	8.60	4	255
17	15.94	−0.106	2	228	6.17	4	230
300, 27	25.91	+0.168	2	318	4.04	3	195
Nov. 6	4.89	0.528	3	400	2.30	2	151
16	14.86	0.965	2	471	1.04	2	99
26	24.83	1.466	2	529	0.31	− 1	+ 43
Dec. 6	4.81	2.017	2	570	0.18	0	− 17
16	14.78	2.601	2	593	0.65	0	76
26	24.75	3.197	− 1	596	1.70	+ 1	134
36	34.72	+3.786	0	+579	− 3.32	+ 3	−189

Sidereal Day	$\Delta_\Omega a$	$\Delta_\Omega \delta$	$\Delta_\Omega a$	$\Delta_\Omega \delta$
	1865.		**1873.**	
0	+1.626	−3.49	−1.548	+5.56
100	1.600	2.91	1.584	5.16
200	1.560	2.32	1.606	4.72
300	1.506	1.70	1.614	4.25
400	1.438	1.06	1.610	3.74
	1866.		**1874.**	
0	+1.463	−1.27	−1.613	+3.91
100	1.387	−0.63	1.599	3.39
200	1.299	+0.02	1.573	2.83
300	1.200	0.67	1.534	2.25
400	1.090	1.31	1.481	1.66
	1867.		**1875.**	
0	+1.128	+1.10	−1.500	+1.85
100	1.012	1.73	1.440	1.25
200	0.887	2.35	1.368	0.64
300	0.755	2.95	1.284	+0.02
400	0.616	3.52	1.191	−0.60
	1868 B.		**1876 B.**	
0	+0.664	+3.34	−1.223	−0.39
100	0.521	3.89	1.123	1.01
200	0.374	4.41	1.014	1.61
300	0.224	4.88	0.895	2.21
400	0.072	5.32	0.770	2.79
	1869.		**1877.**	
0	+0.124	+5.18	−0.814	−2.60
100	−0.028	5.59	0.684	3.17
200	0.180	5.94	0.548	3.70
300	0.329	6.24	0.407	4.21
400	0.475	6.49	0.263	4.68
	1870.		**1878.**	
0	−0.426	+6.41	−0.312	−4.53
100	0.570	6.62	0.166	4.98
200	0.708	6.77	−0.018	5.39
300	0.839	6.87	+0.130	5.75
400	0.964	6.90	0.278	6.07
	1871.		**1879.**	
0	−0.923	+6.89	+0.228	−5.97
100	1.041	6.89	0.374	6.26
200	1.151	6.83	0.518	6.49
300	1.250	6.71	0.658	6.67
400	1.339	6.53	0.792	6.80
	1872 B.		**1880 B.**	
0	−1.310	+6.59	+0.747	−6.76
100	1.391	6.38	0.878	6.85
200	1.460	6.12	1.001	6.88
300	1.517	5.80	1.117	6.85
400	1.561	+5.43	+1.223	−6.77

✱ ☌ ☉,   Sept. 28.1.
✱ ☌ Mean Sun,   Sept. 25.7.

TABLE XXIV.—β Corvi.

R.A. 12h 27m.6. Dec. −22° 41′.

Upper transit at fictitious meridian.

Sidereal Day	Mean Day	Δ⊙α 1870.	Var. in 10y.	Diff. for 10d.	Δ⊙δ 1870.	Var. in 10y.	Diff. for 10d.
0, Jan. 0	− 0.26	+0.091	− 3	+352	+ 6.50	+ 2	−214
10	+ 9.71	0.439	3	340	4.28	2	229
20	19.68	0.709	3	318	+ 1.95	3	238
30	29.66	1.073	2	289	− 0.45	3	240
Feb. 9	8.63	1.344	2	252	2.82	3	234
19	18.60	1.575	1	211	5.12	3	225
Mar. 1	0.58	1.766	− 1	170	7.31	3	211
11	10.55	1.916	0	128	9.32	2	192
21	20.52	2.024	+ 1	87	11.15	2	172
31	30.49	2.092	1	50	12.75	2	150
100, Apr. 10	9.47	2.126	2	+ 18	14.14	1	127
20	19.44	2.129	2	− 11	15.23	+ 1	103
30	29.41	2.106	3	36	16.20	0	81
May 10	9.38	2.058	3	58	16.89	0	56
20	19.36	1.991	4	76	17.33	0	32
30	29.33	1.907	4	90	17.54	0	− 9
June 9	8.30	1.811	4	102	17.52	− 1	+ 13
19	18.28	1.704	3	111	17.29	1	34
29	28.25	1.590	3	117	16.84	1	54
July 9	8.22	1.471	3	119	16.20	1	73
200, 19	18.19	1.354	3	118	15.37	2	90
29	28.17	1.238	3	112	14.40	2	104
Aug. 8	7.14	1.132	3	100	13.30	2	115
18	17.11	1.039	2	83	12.12	2	121
28	27.08	0.967	2	61	10.90	2	122
Sept. 7	6.06	0.919	2	− 33	9.60	2	117
17	16.03	0.902	1	+ 2	8.57	2	107
27	26.00	0.924	+ 1	42	7.57	2	90
Oct. 7	5.97	0.988	0	87	6.79	1	66
17	15.95	1.098	0	133	6.26	1	38
300, 27	25.92	1.255	− 1	180	6.04	− 1	+ 6
Nov. 6	4.89	1.460	1	226	6.15	0	− 30
16	14.87	1.709	1	269	6.64	0	68
26	24.84	1.907	1	304	7.51	+ 1	106
Dec. 6	4.81	2.315	2	331	8.75	1	141
16	14.78	2.656	2	348	10.32	2	172
26	24.76	3.008	2	355	12.17	2	199
36	34.73	+3.362	− 2	+350	−14.28	+ 3	−221

Sidereal Day — ΔΩα, ΔΩδ

Sidereal Day	ΔΩα	ΔΩδ	ΔΩα	ΔΩδ
	1865.		**1873.**	
0	+0.854	−3.21	−1.060	+5.38
100	0.784	2.62	1.027	4.96
200	0.706	2.01	0.985	4.50
300	0.623	1.38	0.936	4.00
400	0.533	0.73	0.879	3.47
	1866.		**1874.**	
0	+0.564	−0.95	−0.899	+3.66
100	0.472	−0.30	0.837	3.11
200	0.375	+0.35	0.768	2.54
300	0.275	1.00	0.693	1.95
400	0.173	1.64	0.613	1.34
	1867.		**1875.**	
0	+0.207	+1.42	−0.641	+1.55
100	0.104	2.06	0.557	0.94
200	0.000	2.67	0.469	+0.32
300	−0.104	3.26	0.377	−0.30
400	0.208	3.82	0.292	0.02
	1868 B.		**1876 B.**	
0	−0.173	+3.63	−0.314	−0.72
100	0.275	4.17	0.217	1.33
200	0.374	4.67	0.119	1.93
300	0.470	5.12	−0.019	2.52
400	0.562	5.54	+0.080	3.09
	1869.		**1877.**	
0	−0.532	+5.41	+0.047	−2.90
100	0.620	5.79	0.146	3.46
200	0.703	6.12	0.245	3.98
300	0.779	6.40	0.341	4.47
400	0.849	6.62	0.436	4.93
	1870.		**1878.**	
0	−0.826	+6.55	+0.403	−4.78
100	0.891	6.73	0.496	5.21
200	0.948	6.85	0.584	5.60
300	0.996	6.92	0.667	5.94
400	1.036	6.92	0.745	6.23
	1871.		**1879.**	
0	−1.024	+6.92	+0.719	−6.14
100	1.058	6.89	0.793	6.40
200	1.083	6.86	0.861	6.61
300	1.098	6.64	0.922	6.76
400	1.105	6.44	0.974	6.86
	1872 B.		**1880 B.**	
0	−1.103	+6.51	+0.958	−6.83
100	1.104	6.27	1.005	6.89
200	1.094	5.98	1.045	6.89
300	1.076	5.63	1.076	6.83
400	−1.049	+5.24	+1.097	−6.71

✳ ☌ ⊙, Sept. 30.3.
✳ ☌ Mean Sun, Sept. 27.8.

TABLE XXIV.—* κ Draconis,

R.A. 12 27.9 (h m)   Dec. + 70 30 (° ')

Upper transit at fictitious meridian.

Sidereal Day	Mean Day	Δ⊙a 1870.	Var. in 10 y.	Diff. for 10 d.	Δ⊙δ 1870.	Var. in 10 y.	Diff. for 10 d.
0, Jan. 0	− 0.26	+0.060	− 8	+773	−19.77	+ 1	−101
10	+ 9.72	0.831	10	764	20.46	0	− 36
20	19.69	1.580	11	730	20 49	− 1	+ 29
30	29 66	2.282	13	671	19.89	2	92
Feb. 9	8.63	2.914	14	589	18.67	2	150
19	18.60	3.455	14	490	16.91	3	201
Mar. 1	0.58	3.889	14	377	14.68	3	243
11	10.55	4.205	13	255	12.08	4	274
21	20.52	4.398	13	131	9.23	4	294
31	30.50	4.468	11	+ 9	6.25	4	301
100, Apr. 10	9.47	4.419	10	−106	3.26	4	296
20	19.44	4 260	8	210	− 0.38	4	280
30	29.41	4.003	6	302	+ 2.30	4	253
May 10	9.39	3 661	4	378	4 66	3	219
20	19.36	3.252	− 2	439	6.64	3	177
30	29.33	2.769	0	483	8.18	2	129
June 9	8.30	2.291	+ 2	512	9.22	2	79
19	18.28	1.771	3	525	9.75	− 1	+ 26
29	28.25	1.246	5	523	9 74	0	− 28
July 9	8.22	0.729	6	509	9.20	1	80
200, 19	18.19	+0.233	7	482	8.14	+ 1	131
29	28.17	−0.231	8	444	6.58	2	179
Aug. 8	7.14	0.650	9	394	4.56	2	224
18	17.11	1.015	9	334	+ 2.12	3	264
28	27.09	1.315	9	265	− 0.70	3	299
Sept. 7	6.06	1.542	8	186	3.84	4	328
17	16.03	1.685	7	99	7.25	4	352
27	26.00	1.737	6	− 4	10.85	4	368
Oct. 7	5.98	1.692	5	+ 96	14.58	4	377
17	15.95	1.543	3	201	18.37	5	376
300, 27	25.92	1.289	+ 1	308	22.12	4	371
Nov. 6	4.90	0.929	− 1	412	25.75	4	354
16	14.87	−0.466	3	511	29.17	4	328
26	24.84	+0.090	6	600	32.29	3	293
Dec. 6	4.81	0.729	8	675	35.01	3	249
16	14.79	1.433	10	730	37.25	2	198
26	24.76	2.182	12	764	38.95	2	140
36	34.73	+2.952	−14	+772	−40.03	+ 1	− 77

* δ Mean Sun, Mar. 29.3.
* δ ⊙, Sept. 30.4.
* δ Mean Sun, Sept. 27.9.

Sidereal Day	ΔΩa	ΔΩδ	ΔΩa	ΔΩδ
1865.			**1873.**	
0	−0.860	−3.19	+0.055	+5.37
100	1.020	2.61	0.232	4.95
200	1.17?	1.99	0.406	4 49
300	1.314	1.36	0.576	3.99
400	1.444	0.72	0.742	3.47
1866.			**1874.**	
0	−1.401	−0.94	+0.687	+3.65
100	1.524	−0.29	0.848	3.10
200	1.633	+0.36	1.001	2.53
300	1.727	1.01	1.147	1.94
400	1.807	1.65	1.282	1.33
1867.			**1875.**	
0	−1.782	+1.44	+1.237	+1.54
100	1.851	2.07	1.366	0 92
200	1.904	2.68	1.483	+0.30
300	1.941	3.27	1.588	−0.32
400	1.960	3.83	1.679	0.94
1868 B.			**1876 B.**	
0	−1.955	+3.65	+1.650	−0.73
100	1.963	4.18	1.732	1.34
200	1.954	4.68	1.800	1.94
300	1.928	5.14	1.854	2.53
400	1.885	5.55	1.892	3.10
1869.			**1877.**	
0	−1.902	+5.42	+1.881	−2 91
100	1.848	5.80	1.909	3.46
200	1.778	6.13	1.921	3.99
300	1.694	6.40	1.917	4.48
400	1.594	6.02	1.898	4.93
1870.			**1878.**	
0	−1.629	+6.55	+1.906	−4.78
100	1.521	6.73	1.876	5.21
200	1.400	6.85	1.836	5.60
300	1.267	6.92	1.769	5.94
400	1.124	6.92	1.694	6.24
1871.			**1879.**	
0	−1.173	+6.92	+1.723	−6.14
100	1.024	6.89	1.636	6.40
200	0.866	6.79	1.537	6.61
300	0.701	6.64	1.425	6.76
400	0.531	6.43	1.300	6.86
1872 B.			**1880 B.**	
0	−0.589	+6.51	+1.344	−6.83
100	0.416	6.27	1.212	6.89
200	0.240	5.97	1.070	6.89
300	0.063	5.62	0.917	6 83
400	+0.115	+5.23	+0.757	−6.71

TABLE XXIV.—* 32 Camelopardalis (II) (foll.)

R.A. 12ʰ 48ᵐ.2.   Dec. + 84° 7′.

Upper transit at fictitious meridian.

Sidereal Day	Mean Day	Δ☉α 1870.	Var. in 10 y.	Diff. for 10 d.	Δ☉δ 1870.	Var. in 10 y.	Diff. for 10 d.
0, Jan. 0	— 0.24	—1.051	+ 5	+2225	—20.45	0	— 96
10	+ 9.73	+1.193	—15	2250	21.07	0	— 29
20	19.70	3.423	34	2195	21.03	0	+ 37
30	29.67	5.556	53	2060	20.34	— 1	101
Feb. 9	8.65	7.517	69	1849	19.02	1	161
19	18.62	9.233	84	1572	17.14	1	213
Mar. 1	0.59	10.643	96	1241	14.79	1	256
11	10.56	11.701	104	869	12.06	1	288
21	20.54	12.374	109	475	9.07	1	307
31	30.51	12.648	111	+ 74	5.95	1	314
100, Apr. 10	9.48	12.529	108	— 319	— 2.83	1	309
20	19.46	12.019	103	688	+ 0.18	1	292
30	29.43	11.160	94	1023	2.97	1	264
May 10	9.40	9.986	82	1315	5.43	1	228
20	19.37	8.546	68	1557	7.50	1	184
30	29.35	6.890	52	1745	9.09	— 1	134
June 9	8.32	5.074	34	1876	10.16	0	81
19	18.29	3.152	—15	1957	10.69	0	+ 25
29	28.26	+1.177	+ 4	1981	10.67	0	— 31
July 9	8.24	—0.794	23	1955	10.08	0	86
200, 19	18.21	2.717	42	1883	8.95	0	139
29	28.18	4.545	59	1767	7.31	0	190
Aug. 8	7.16	6.238	76	1612	5.17	+ 1	235
18	17.13	7.757	90	1421	+ 2.62	1	276
28	27.10	9.068	103	1197	— 0.33	1	312
Sept. 7	6.07	10.141	113	945	3.60	1	342
17	16.05	10.948	120	666	7.14	1	364
27	26.02	11.466	125	365	10.87	1	380
Oct. 7	5.99	11.673	127	— 47	14.72	1	389
17	15.96	11.556	126	+232	18.60	1	388
300, 27	25.94	11.107	122	618	22.44	1	378
Nov. 6	4.91	10.322	114	950	26.14	1	360
16	14.88	9.212	104	1268	29.60	1	332
26	24.86	7.794	91	1562	32.74	1	295
Dec. 6	4.83	6.100	76	1818	35.47	1	249
16	14.80	4.174	59	2024	37.70	+ 1	195
26	24.77	—2.072	40	2166	39.36	0	136
36	34.75	+0.140	+20	+2241	—40.39	0	— 71

Sidereal Day	Δ☊α	Δ☊δ	Δ☊α	Δ☊δ
	1865.		**1873.**	
0	—4.681	—2.47	+2.707	+4.90
100	4.998	1.85	3.161	4.42
200	5.271	1.21	3.588	3.91
300	5.498	—0.56	3.984	3.36
400	5.677	+0.10	4.347	2.79
	1866.		**1874.**	
0	—5.622	—0.12	+4.228	+2.99
100	5.769	+0.53	4.566	2.40
200	5.865	1.19	4.866	1.80
300	5.910	1.85	5.124	1.18
400	5.904	2.46	5.340	0.56
	1867.		**1875.**	
0	—5.912	+2.25	+5.272	+0.77
100	5.871	2.86	5.459	+0.14
200	5.779	3.45	5.600	—0.49
300	5.637	4.01	5.695	1.11
400	5.447	4.53	5.743	1.73
	1868 B.		**1876 B.**	
0	—5.516	+4.36	+5.732	—1.52
100	5.294	4.86	5.749	2.13
200	5.026	5.31	5.719	2.72
300	4.715	5.72	5.641	3.28
400	4.363	6.07	5.517	3.82
	1869.		**1877.**	
0	—4.486	+5.96	+5.564	—3.65
100	4.110	6.28	5.410	4.16
200	3.699	6.54	5.211	4.65
300	3.257	6.75	4.969	5.10
400	2.789	6.90	4.686	5.51
	1870.		**1878.**	
0	—2.949	+6.85	+4.785	—5.37
100	2.466	6.96	4.476	5.75
200	1.962	7.01	4.129	6.08
300	1.443	7.00	3.747	6.37
400	0.913	6.95	3.333	6.60
	1871.		**1879.**	
0	—1.093	+6.96	+3.476	—6.52
100	0.559	6.85	3.042	6.72
200	—0.022	6.66	2.583	6.86
300	+0.514	6.45	2.101	6.94
400	1.044	6.17	1.600	6.96
	1872 B.		**1880 B.**	
0	+0.866	+6.27	+1.771	—6.96
100	1.390	5.96	1.260	6.95
200	1.909	5.60	0.738	6.87
300	2.392	5.19	+0.208	6.74
400	+2.803	+4.74	—0.325	—6.55

✳ ☌ Mean Sun, April 3.4.
✳ ☌ ☉, Oct. 6.1.
✳ ☌ Mean Sun, Oct. 3.0.

SPECIAL TABLES.

TABLE XXIV.—12 Canum Venaticorum.

R.A. 12^h 49.9^m.   Dec. + 39° 1′.

Upper transit at fictitious meridian.

Sidereal Day.	Mean Day.	Δ⊙α 1870.	Var. in 10 y.	Diff. for 10 d.	Δ⊙δ 1870.	Var. in 10 y.	Diff. for 10 d.
0, Jan. 0	− 0.25	−0.114	− 4	+392	−13.93	+ 2	−190
10	+ 9.73	+0.278	4	389	15.60	2	143
20	19.70	0.661	4	374	16.77	+ 1	91
30	29.67	1.023	4	348	17.41	0	− 37
Feb. 9	8.65	1.354	3	312	17.51	− 1	+ 15
19	18.62	1.644	3	268	17.11	1	65
Mar. 1	0 59	1.888	3	219	16.22	2	112
11	10.56	2.082	3	167	14.90	2	151
21	20.54	2.223	2	116	13 23	2	181
31	30.51	2.315	2	67	11.31	2	203
100, Apr. 10	9.48	2.359	1	+ 21	9.20	3	217
20	19.45	2.359	− 1	− 21	7.01	3	220
30	29.43	2.319	0	57	4.84	3	213
May 10	9.40	2.246	0	88	2.78	2	199
20	19.37	2.144	+ 1	113	− 0.88	2	179
30	29.35	2.021	1	133	+ 0.79	2	154
June 9	8.32	1.879	2	149	2.18	2	124
19	18.29	1.724	2	159	3.25	2	89
29	28.26	1.563	3	165	3.95	1	52
July 9	8.24	1.396	3	168	4.28	− 1	+ 15
200, 19	18.21	1.229	3	165	4.24	0	− 23
29	28.18	1.067	3	157	3.81	0	62
Aug. 8	7.15	0.916	2	144	2.99	0	100
18	17.13	0.781	2	127	1.81	+ 1	136
28	27.10	0.664	2	105	+ 0.28	1	170
Sept. 7	6.07	0.573	1	75	− 1.59	2	203
17	16.04	0.516	+ 1	− 39	3.77	3	234
27	26.02	0.497	0	+ 2	6.25	4	260
Oct. 7	5.99	0.521	0	49	8.95	4	280
17	15.96	0.596	− 1	99	11.84	4	298
300, 27	25.94	0.720	1	150	14.89	4	310
Nov. 6	4.91	0.897	2	203	18.02	4	315
16	14.88	1.126	2	255	21.17	4	312
26	24.85	1.405	3	301	24.23	4	300
Dec. 6	4.83	1.726	4	340	27.15	4	281
16	14.80	2.083	4	369	29.83	4	253
26	24.77	2.461	5	386	32.18	3	216
36	34.74	+2.851	− 5	+392	−34.13	+ 2	−173

✳ ♂ ⊙,   Oct. 6.5
✳ ♂ Mean Sun,   Oct. 3.5

Sidereal Day.	ΔΩα	ΔΩδ	ΔΩα	ΔΩδ
	1865.		**1873.**	
0	+0.191	−2.42	−0.610	+4.85
100	+0.090	1.79	0.525	4.36
200	−0.013	1.15	0.436	3.85
300	0.115	−0.50	0.343	3 30
400	0.217	+0.16	0.248	2.73
	1866.		**1874.**	
0	−0.182	−0.06	−0.281	+2.92
100	0.283	+0.60	0.184	2.34
200	0.381	1.25	−0.086	1.73
300	0.475	1.90	+0.012	1.11
400	0.566	2.52	0.110	0.48
	1867.		**1875.**	
0	−0.536	+2.32	+0.076	+0.69
100	0.623	2.93	0.175	−0.06
200	0.705	3.51	0.271	−0.57
300	0.781	4.07	0.364	1.19
400	0.849	4.59	0.455	1.80
	1868 B.		**1876 B.**	
0	−0.827	+4.42	+0.425	−1 60
100	0.891	4.91	0.513	2.20
200	0.947	5.36	0 597	2.79
300	0.994	5.76	0.676	3.35
400	1.033	6.11	0.750	3.89
	1869.		**1877.**	
0	−1.021	+6.00	+0.725	−3.72
100	1.054	6.32	0.795	4.24
200	1.077	6.58	0.858	4.72
300	1.091	6.78	0.914	5.16
400	1.096	6.92	0.963	5.57
	1870.		**1878.**	
0	−1.096	+6.88	+0.947	−5.43
100	1.094	6.98	0.991	5.81
200	1.085	7.02	1.020	6 13
300	1.063	7.01	1.053	6.41
400	1.034	6.93	1.072	6 63
	1871.		**1879.**	
0	−1.045	+6.96	+1 066	−6.56
100	1.009	6.84	1.079	6.75
200	0.936	6.67	1.082	6.88
300	0.914	6.44	1.077	6.95
400	0.854	6.14	1.063	6.97
	1872 B.		**1880 B.**	
0	−0.875	+6 25	+1.068	−6.97
100	0.811	5.93	1.048	6.95
200	0.740	5.56	1.019	6.87
300	0.664	5.15	0.980	6.73
400	−0.582	+4.69	+0.931	−6.53

TABLE XXIV.—θ Virginis.
R.A. 13^h 3.2^m. Dec. — 4° 51′.

Upper transit at fictitious meridian.

Sidereal Day.	Mean Day.	$\Delta_\odot\alpha$			$\Delta_\odot\delta$			Sidereal Day.	$\Delta_\Omega\alpha$	$\Delta_\Omega\delta$	$\Delta_\Omega\alpha$	$\Delta_\Omega\delta$
		1870.	Var. in 10 y.	Diff. for 10 d.	**1870.**	Var. in 10 y.	Diff. for 10 d.		**1865.**		**1873.**	
								0	+0.681	—1.94	—0.945	+4.51
								100	0.600	1.30	0.901	3.99
								200	0.515	—0.64	0.846	3.44
0, Jan. 0	— 0.24	—0.135	— 3	+333	+ 0.32	+ 2	—209	300	0.425	+0.03	0.783	2.87
10	+ 9.74	+0.197	3	331	— 1.77	3	208	400	0.330	0.69	0.715	2.27
20	19.71	0.523	3	317	3.83	3	199					
30	29.68	0.829	3	294	5.74	2	184		**1866.**		**1874.**	
Feb. 9	8.65	1.110	2	266	7.50	2	165	0	+0.362	+0.47	—0.732	+2.47
19	18.63	1.361	2	232	9.03	2	140	100	0.266	1.13	0.656	1.86
Mar. 1	0.60	1.573	1	195	10.30	2	115	200	0.168	1.76	0.585	1.24
11	10.57	1.750	— 1	158	11.33	1	91	300	+0.068	2.42	0.505	+0.61
21	20.55	1.889	0	122	12.11	1	65	400	—0.033	3.04	0.419	—0.03
31	30.52	1.994	0	87	12.62	+ 1	40		**1867.**		**1875.**	
100, Apr. 10	9.49	2.063	0	54	12.90	0	— 19	0	+0.001	+2.83	—0.445	+0.18
20	19.46	2.103	+ 1	+ 25	12.99	0	0	100	—0.099	3.43	0.359	—0.46
30	29.44	2.114	2	— 1	12.90	0	+ 16	200	0.199	4.00	0.268	1.09
May 10	9.41	2.101	3	24	12.67	0	29	300	0.297	4.53	0.174	1.71
20	19.38	2.067	3	44	12.32	0	40	400	0.392	5.03	0.078	2.32
30	29.35	2.013	3	61	11.87	— 1	48		**1868 B.**		**1876 B.**	
June 9	8.33	1.943	3	76	11.36	1	54	0	—0.360	+4.87	—0.111	—2.12
19	18.30	1.862	3	88	10.79	1	58	100	0.453	5.33	—0.015	2.71
29	28.27	1.770	3	97	10.20	1	61	200	0.541	5.75	+0.081	3.29
July 9	8.25	1.668	3	105	9.58	1	62	300	0.625	6.11	0.176	3.84
200, 19	18.22	1.561	3	109	8.96	1	62	400	0.703	6.42	0.270	4.35
29	28.19	1.451	3	109	8.35	1	59		**1869.**		**1877.**	
Aug. 8	7.16	1.343	3	104	7.79	1	53	0	—0.678	+6.33	+0.239	—4.19
18	17.14	1.244	3	93	7.30	1	45	100	0.752	6.60	0.331	4.64
28	27.11	1.158	2	77	6.89	— 1	35	200	0.819	6.82	0.421	5.14
Sept. 7	6.08	1.091	2	56	6.60	0	21	300	0.879	6.98	0.505	5.55
17	16.05	1.047	1	— 28	6.47	0	+ 4	400	0.932	7.07	0.591	5.92
27	26.03	1.036	+ 1	+ 7	6.52	0	— 15		**1870.**		**1878.**	
Oct. 7	6.00	1.062	0	46	6.76	0	37	0	—0.915	+7.05	+0.563	—5.80
17	15.97	1.129	0	88	7.26	0	63	100	0.962	7.10	0.643	6.14
300, 27	25.94	1.240	0	134	8.02	+ 1	89	200	1.001	7.10	0.717	6.43
Nov. 6	4.92	1.398	— 1	181	9.05	2	117	300	1.031	7.03	0.786	6.66
16	14.89	1.601	1	224	10.35	2	143	400	1.052	6.90	0.849	6.84
26	24.86	1.845	2	263	11.91	2	167		**1871.**		**1879.**	
Dec. 6	4.84	2.124	2	295	13.68	3	186	0	—1.045	+6.95	+0.828	—6.78
16	14.81	2.432	2	318	15.62	3	201	100	1.060	6.76	0.896	6.93
26	24.78	2.757	3	331	17.68	4	209	200	1.066	6.56	0.937	7.01
36	34.75	+3.091	— 3	+334	—19.78	+ 4	—210	300	1.063	6.28	0.986	7.04
								400	1.051	5.95	1.015	7.01
									1872 B.		**1880 B.**	
								0	—1.050	+6.07	+1.004	—7.03
								100	1.038	5.70	1.035	6.95
								200	1.012	5.29	1.054	6.82
								300	0.977	4.84	1.065	6.64
								400	—0.933	+4.35	+1.066	—6.59

✳ ♂ ⊙, Oct. 10.1.
✳ ♂ Mean Sun, Oct. 6.8.

TABLE XXIV.—ζ Virginis.

R. A. 13^{h} 28^{m}.1.   Dec. + 0° 4′.

Upper transit at fictitious meridian.

Sidereal Day	Mean Day	$\Delta_{\odot}a$ 1870.	Var. in 10 y.	Diff. for 10 d.	$\Delta_{\odot}\delta$ 1870.	Var. in 10 y.	Diff. for 10 d.
0, Jan. 0	− 0.22	−0.282	− 3	+329	− 1.35	+ 2	−213
10	+ 9.75	+0.048	3	329	3.45	2	205
20	19.73	0.374	3	321	5.43	2	190
30	29.70	0.687	3	304	7.24	3	171
Feb. 9	8.67	0.979	3	279	8.83	3	147
19	18.65	1.244	2	249	10.16	2	119
Mar. 1	0.62	1.476	2	215	11.21	2	90
11	10.59	1.673	1	180	11.97	1	61
21	20.56	1.835	1	144	12.44	1	33
31	30.54	1.962	− 1	109	12.64	+ 1	− 8
100, Apr. 10	9.51	2.054	0	77	12.61	0	+ 14
20	19.48	2.117	0	48	12.37	0	33
30	29.45	2.150	+ 1	+ 20	11.97	0	47
May 10	9.43	2.157	2	− 5	11.44	0	59
20	19.40	2.141	2	27	10.80	0	66
30	29.37	2.104	2	47	10.12	0	69
June 9	8.34	2.047	3	66	9.42	0	71
19	18.32	1.973	3	81	8.71	0	71
29	28.29	1.886	3	94	8.01	0	68
July 9	8.26	1.786	3	105	7.36	0	63
200, 19	18.24	1.677	3	113	6.76	0	57
29	28.21	1.562	3	116	6.23	− 1	49
Aug. 8	7.18	1.446	3	115	5.78	1	39
18	17.15	1.334	3	108	5.44	− 1	27
28	27.13	1.232	2	95	5.23	0	+ 14
Sept. 7	6.10	1.145	2	77	5.17	0	− 3
17	16.07	1.080	2	52	5.30	+ 1	22
27	26.04	1.044	1	− 18	5.61	1	42
Oct. 7	6.02	1.045	+ 1	+ 20	6.14	1	65
17	15.99	1.085	0	62	6.91	2	89
300, 27	25.96	1.170	0	108	7.93	2	115
Nov. 6	4.94	1.301	− 1	153	9.21	2	140
16	14.91	1.477	1	199	10.73	3	164
26	24.88	1.699	1	241	12.47	3	184
Dec. 6	4.85	1.958	2	277	14.39	3	199
16	14.83	2.251	2	305	16.43	3	208
26	24.80	2.566	3	323	18.54	3	213
36	34.77	+2.894	− 3	+330	−20.67	+ 4	−210

Sidereal Day	$\Delta_{\Omega}a$	$\Delta_{\Omega}\delta$	$\Delta_{\Omega}a$	$\Delta_{\Omega}\delta$
	1865.		**1873.**	
0	+0.633	−1.03	−0.915	+3.84
100	0.551	−0.35	0.864	3.26
200	0.464	+0.33	0.805	2.66
300	0.373	1.01	0.740	2.04
400	0.278	1.68	0.669	1.40
	1866.		**1874.**	
0	+0.310	+1.45	−0.694	+1.61
100	0.214	2.12	0.619	0.97
200	0.116	2.76	0.539	+0.31
300	+0.017	3.38	0.455	−0.34
400	−0.083	3.97	0.368	0.99
	1867.		**1875.**	
0	−0.049	+3.78	−0.398	−0.77
100	0.148	4.34	0.308	1.42
200	0.246	4.87	0.216	2.05
300	0.342	5.36	0.123	2.67
400	0.434	5.80	0.028	3.26
	1868 B.		**1876 B.**	
0	−0.403	+5.66	−0.060	−3.07
100	0.493	6.06	+0.035	3.64
200	0.579	6.42	0.130	4.19
300	0.659	6.71	0.223	4.70
400	0.734	6.95	0.315	5.17
	1869.		**1877.**	
0	−0.709	+6.88	+0.284	−5.02
100	0.779	7.08	0.374	5.47
200	0.842	7.21	0.462	5.87
300	0.898	7.28	0.545	6.23
400	0.945	7.29	0.625	6.53
	1870.		**1878.**	
0	−0.930	+7.29	+0.599	−6.43
100	0.973	7.26	0.675	6.70
200	1.006	7.16	0.745	6.91
300	1.031	7.00	0.810	7.07
400	1.048	6.79	0.868	7.17
	1871.		**1879.**	
0	−1.043	+6.87	+0.849	−7.14
100	1.053	6.61	0.903	7.20
200	1.055	6.30	0.949	7.20
300	1.047	5.94	0.987	7.14
400	1.031	5.52	1.017	7.01
	1872 B.		**1880 B.**	
0	−1.037	+5.67	+1.008	−7.06
100	1.015	5.23	1.032	6.90
200	0.984	4.74	1.048	6.68
300	0.945	4.22	1.055	6.40
400	−0.899	+3.66	+1.053	−6.07

✱ ♂ ☉,   Oct. 16.8.
✱ ♂ Mean Sun,   Oct. 13.1.

TABLE XXIV.—η Bootis.

R.A. 13h 48m.5.   Dec. + 19° 3′

Upper transit at fictitious meridian.

Sidereal Day	Mean Day	$\Delta_{\odot}a$ 1870.	Var. in 10y.	Diff. for 10 d.	$\Delta_{\odot}\delta$ 1870.	Var. in 10y.	Diff. for 10 d.
0, Jan. 0	− 0.20	−0.436	− 3	+331	− 7.54	+ 2	−234
10	+ 9.77	−0.101	3	338	9.75	2	207
20	19.74	+0.236	3	335	11.67	2	174
30	29.71	0.566	3	322	13.22	2	135
Feb. 9	8.69	0.877	3	299	14.36	2	93
19	18.66	1.162	3	271	15.08	+ 1	50
Mar. 1	0.63	1.417	2	239	15.37	0	− 8
11	10.60	1.638	2	203	15.23	0	+ 33
21	20.58	1.823	2	166	14.71	− 1	69
31	30.55	1.970	1	129	13.86	1	100
100, Apr. 10	9.52	2.081	− 1	93	12.73	1	124
20	19.50	2.157	0	60	11.40	1	141
30	29.47	2.201	0	+ 29	9.93	1	152
May 10	9.44	2.215	0	0	8.38	1	155
20	19.41	2.201	+ 1	− 27	6.84	1	153
30	29.39	2.162	2	50	5.33	1	145
June 9	8.36	2.102	2	72	3.95	1	131
19	18.33	2.019	3	90	2.71	1	116
29	28.30	1.922	3	105	1.64	1	96
July 9	8.28	1.809	3	119	0.80	1	73
200, 19	18.25	1.685	3	130	− 0.18	− 1	49
29	28.22	1.551	3	137	+ 0.18	0	+ 23
Aug. 8	7.19	1.414	3	136	0.28	0	− 3
18	17.17	1.281	3	130	+ 0.11	+ 1	31
28	27.14	1.155	3	120	− 0.34	1	60
Sept. 7	6.11	1.043	2	103	1.09	1	89
17	16.09	0.951	2	79	2.11	1	117
27	26.06	0.886	2	47	3.42	2	145
Oct. 7	6.03	0.858	1	− 9	5.00	2	172
17	16.00	0.869	+ 1	+ 33	6.66	3	198
300, 27	25.98	0.925	0	80	8.96	3	221
Nov. 6	4.95	1.029	0	129	11.26	3	241
16	14.92	1.183	− 1	178	13.76	3	257
26	24.89	1.384	1	223	16.37	4	265
Dec. 6	4.87	1.628	2	264	19.03	4	266
16	14.84	1.909	2	297	21.66	4	261
26	24.81	2.219	3	320	24.22	4	247
36	34.79	+2.547	− 3	+334	−26.58	+ 4	−224

✱ d ⊙,   Oct. 22.2.
✱ d Mean Sun, Oct. 18.3.

Sidereal Day	$\Delta_{\Omega}a$	$\Delta_{\Omega}\delta$	$\Delta_{\Omega}a$	$\Delta_{\Omega}\delta$
	1865.		1873.	
0	+0.437	−0.27	−0.762	+3.26
100	0.351	+0.43	0.699	2.64
200	0.261	1.12	0.631	1.99
300	0.169	1.80	0.558	1.33
400	0.075	2.47	0.480	0.67
	1866.		1874.	
0	+0.107	+2.25	−0.507	+0.89
100	+0.013	2.91	0.426	+0.22
200	−0.081	3.54	0.343	−0.45
300	0.175	4.14	0.257	1.12
400	0.267	4.70	0.168	1.77
	1867.		1875.	
0	−0.236	+4.52	−0.198	−1.56
100	0.327	5.06	0.109	2.20
200	0.415	5.55	−0.019	2.83
300	0.499	5.99	+0.071	3.43
400	0.578	6.39	0.160	4.01
	1868 B.		1876 B.	
0	−0.552	+6.26	+0.130	−3.82
100	0.624	6.62	0.219	4.37
200	0.699	6.91	0.306	4.89
300	0.763	7.15	0.390	5.37
400	0.821	7.32	0.471	5.80
	1869.		1877.	
0	−0.802	+7.27	+0.444	−5.67
100	0 855	7.40	0.523	6.07
200	0.901	7.47	0.598	6.42
300	0.938	7.47	0.667	6.72
400	0.967	7.40	0.732	6.97
	1870.		1878.	
0	−0.958	+7.43	+0.710	−6.89
100	0.982	7.32	0.771	7.10
200	0.997	7.15	0.825	7.25
300	1.004	6.92	0.873	7.34
400	1.002	6.64	0.913	7.37
	1871.		1879.	
0	−1.003	+6.74	+0.900	−7.37
100	0.996	6.41	0.936	7.36
200	0.979	6.03	0.964	7.28
300	0.955	5.60	0.984	7.15
400	0.922	5.13	0.995	6.96
	1872 B.		1880 B.	
0	−0.934	+5.29	+0.992	−7.03
100	0.897	4.79	0.998	6.80
200	0.852	4.24	0.996	6.51
300	0.800	3.67	0.985	6.16
400	−0.741	+3.06	+0.966	−5.76

TABLE XXIV.—β Centauri.

R.A. 13^h 54^m.7.   Dec. − 59° 45′.

Upper transit at fictitious meridian.

Sidereal Day	Mean Day	$\Delta_\odot a$ 1870.	Var. in 10 y.	Diff. for 10 d.	$\Delta_\odot \delta$ 1870.	Var. in 10 y.	Diff. for 10 d.
0, Jan. 0	− 0.20	−0.822	−10	+564	+16.01	− 1	− 50
10	+ 9.77	−0.252	8	572	15.25	0	100
20	19.75	+0.318	7	566	14.02	+1	146
30	29.72	0.875	6	544	12.34	3	188
Feb. 9	8.69	1.402	5	510	10.27	4	224
19	18.66	1.891	3	466	7.88	4	253
Mar. 1	0.64	2.332	− 2	415	5.23	5	276
11	10.61	2.719	0	358	+ 2.39	5	292
21	20.58	3.047	+ 1	299	− 0.58	6	301
31	30.55	3.316	3	239	3.61	6	304
100, Apr. 10	9.53	3.525	5	179	6.64	6	300
20	19.50	3.674	6	119	9.60	6	291
30	29.47	3.763	8	60	12.45	6	277
May 10	9.44	3.794	9	+ 2	15.13	5	259
20	19.42	3.768	10	− 54	17.61	5	234
30	29.39	3.686	11	108	19.79	5	204
June 9	8.36	3.553	12	158	21.68	4	172
19	18.34	3.372	13	203	23.21	3	134
29	28.31	3.148	13	243	24.35	2	94
July 9	8.28	2.887	13	275	25.08	1	51
200, 19	18.25	2.600	12	300	25.36	+ 1	− 6
29	28.23	2.291	12	315	25.19	0	+ 40
Aug. 8	7.20	1.974	11	317	24.57	0	84
18	17.17	1.662	10	305	23.52	− 1	125
28	27.14	1.369	9	280	22.09	2	162
Sept. 7	6.12	1.107	8	240	20.30	2	194
17	16.09	0.803	7	186	18.23	2	219
27	26.06	0.738	6	120	15.94	2	236
Oct. 7	6.04	0.656	5	− 42	13.54	3	243
17	16.01	0.656	4	+ 43	11.12	3	240
300, 27	25.98	0.744	2·	134	8.77	3	227
Nov. 6	4.95	0.924	+ 1	225	6.61	3	204
16	14.93	1.192	− 1	312	4.72	2	171
26	24.90	1.545	1	392	3.22	− 1	130
Dec. 6	4.87	1.972	1	459	2.14	0	85
16	14.84	2.459	1	512	1.54	+ 1	+ 34
26	24.82	2.991	1	549	1.46	2	− 17
33	34.79	+3.552	− 1	+569	− 1.88	+ 3	− 67

※ δ ☉,   Oct. 23.9.
※ δ Mean Sun,   Oct. 19.9.

Sidereal Day	$\Delta_\Omega a$	$\Delta_\Omega \delta$	$\Delta_\Omega a$	$\Delta_\Omega \delta$
	1865.		**1873.**	
0	+1.609	−0.04	−1.692	+3.08
100	1.547	+0.66	1.693	2.44
200	1.470	1.35	1.680	1.78
300	1.381	2.04	1.654	1.12
400	1.280	2.71	1.614	0.44
	1866.		**1874.**	
0	+1.315	+2.49	−1.628	+0.67
100	1.206	3.14	1.580	−0.01
200	1.086	3.77	1.518	0.69
300	0.957	4.36	1.444	1.35
400	0.820	4.91	−1.358	2.01
	1867.		**1875.**	
0	+0.867	+4.73	−1.388	−1.79
100	0.725	5.26	1.295	2.44
200	0.576	5.74	1.191	3.06
300	0.422	6.17	1.077	3.66
400	0.265	6.55	0.954	4.23
	1868 B.		**1876 B.**	
0	+0.318	+6.43	−0.996	−4.04
100	+0.160	6.77	0.869	4.59
200	0.000	7.05	0.734	5.10
300	−0.160	7.27	0.592	5.57
400	0.317	7.42	0.446	6.00
	1869.		**1877.**	
0	−0.265	+7.38	−0.496	−5.86
100	0.420	7.49	0.347	6.25
200	0.573	7.53	0.195	6.58
300	0.720	7.51	−0.041	6.87
400	0.858	7.43	+0.114	7.10
	1870.		**1878.**	
0	−0.813	+7.46	+0.061	−7.03
100	0.948	7.33	0.216	7.21
200	1.074	7.14	0.368	7.34
300	1.191	6.89	0.519	7.42
400	1.297	6.58	0.666	7.42
	1871.		**1879.**	
0	−1.263	+6.69	+0.616	−7.43
100	1.362	6.34	0.759	7.39
200	1.449	5.94	0.896	7.30
300	1.523	5.49	1.026	7.14
400	1.585	5.00	1.147	6.93
	1872 B.		**1880 B.**	
0	−1.566	+5.17	+1.107	−7.01
100	1.616	4.65	1.223	6.75
200	1.657	4.08	1.328	6.44
300	1.682	3.49	1.423	6.07
400	−1.693	+2.87	+1.506	−5.65

TABLE XXIV.—* a Draconis.

R.A. 14h 0m.9.   Dec. + 65° 0'.

Upper transit at fictitious meridian.

Sidereal Day	Mean Day	$\Delta_\odot\alpha$ 1870.	Var. in 10 y.	Diff. for 10 d.	$\Delta_\odot\delta$ 1870.	Var. in 10 y.	Diff. for 10 d.
0, Jan. 0	− 0.19	−1.217	− 2	+563	−17.69	+ 2	−227
. 10	+ 9.78	0.636	3	596	19.68	1	170
20	19.75	−0.031	4	609	21.07	+ 1	106
30	29.72	+0.576	5	601	21.79	0	− 39
Feb. 9	8.70	1.165	5	573	21.85	0	+ 27
19	18.67	1.716	6	527	21.25	− 1	92
Mar. 1	0.64	2.213	6	465	20.03	1	151
11	10.62	2.642	6	391	18.26	2	203
21	20.59	2.992	6	308	16.01	2	245
31	30.56	3.256	6	220	13.39	2	277
100, Apr. 10	9.53	3.430	6	129	10.51	2	297
20	19.51	3.515	5	+ 41	7.49	2	306
30	29.48	3.514	5	− 44	4.44	2	302
May 10	9.45	3.430	4	123	− 1.47	2	289
20	19.42	3.270	3	195	+ 1.31	2	266
30	29.40	3.043	2	258	3.81	2	234
June 9	8.37	2.757	1	312	5.96	1	195
19	18.34	2.422	0	357	7.70	1	151
29	28.31	2.047	+ 1	391	8.97	− 1	103
July 9	8.29	1.642	2	416	9.75	0	+ 52
200, 19	18.26	1.219	3	430	10.01	0	0
29	28.23	0.786	4	434	9.75	0	− 52
Aug. 8	7.20	+0.354	5	427	8.98	+ 1	103
18	17.18	−0.065	5	409	7.70	1	153
28	27.15	0.460	6	380	5.93	2	200
Sept. 7	6.12	0.821	6	340	3.72	2	243
17	16.10	1.136	7	287	+ 1.09	3	282
27	26.07	1.392	6	224	− 1.91	3	316
Oct. 7	6.04	1.580	6	151	5.22	3	345
17	16.01 ·	1.690	6	− 68	8.78	3	366
300, 27	25.99	1.714	5	+ 22	12.51	4	380
Nov. 6	4.96	1.645	5	116	16.34	4	385
16	14.93	1.481	4	212	20.17	4	380
26	24.90	1.222	3	306	23.91	4	366
Dec. 6	4.88	0.871	2	393	27.45	4	341
16	14.85	−0.439	+ 1	470	30.69	3	305
26	24.82	+0.064	0	532	33.52	3	260
36	34.80	+0.620	− 1	+577	−35.87	+ 3	−207

Sidereal Day	$\Delta_\Omega\alpha$	$\Delta_\Omega\delta$	$\Delta_\Omega\alpha$	$\Delta_\Omega\delta$
	1865.		**1873.**	
0	−0.588	+0.19	+0.064	+2.90
100	0.692	0.90	0.179	2.25
200	0.789	1.60	0.293	1.59
300	0.880	2.28	0.404	0.91
400	0.963	2.95	0.511	0.23
	1866.		**1874.**	
0	−0.936	+2.73	+0.475	+0.47
100	1.014	3.38	0.579	−0.23
200	1.083	4.00	0.678	0.01
300	1.142	4.58	0.772	1.58
400	1.193	5.13	0.859	2.24
	1867.		**1875.**	
0	−1.176	+4.95	+0.830	−2.01
100	1.219	5.47	0.912	2.66
200	1.251	5.94	0.987	3.28
300	1.272	6.35	1.053	3.88
400	1.282	6.72	1.111	4.44
	1868 B.		**1876 B.**	
0	−1.280	+6.60	+1.092	−4.26
100	1.282	6.92	1.144	4.79
200	1.274	7.18	1.187	5.29
300	1.254	7.38	1.219	5.75
400	1.223	7.52	1.241	6.16
	1869.		**1877.**	
0	−1.235	+7.48	+1.235	−6.03
100	1.197	7.57	1.250	6.40
200	1.149	7.59	1.256	6.73
300	1.092	7.55	1.251	6.99
400	1.025	7.44	1.236	7.21
	1870.		**1878.**	
0	−1.048	+7.49	+1.242	−7.14
100	0.976	7.34	1.220	7.31
200	0.894	7.12	1.188	7.42
300	0.806	6.85	1.146	7.48
400	0.711	6.52	1.094	7.47
	1871.		**1879.**	
0	−0.744	+6.64	+1.113	−7.49
100	0.644	6.27	1.055	7.42
200	0.540	5.85	0.988	7.31
300	0.432	5.38	0.913	7.13
400	0.320	4.86	0.830	6.90
	1872 B.		**1880 B.**	
0	−0.358	+5.04	+0.859	−6.98
100	0.244	4.50	0.771	6.71
200	0.129	3.93	0.676	6.37
300	−0.013	3.32	0.575	5.90
400	+0.103	+2.68	+0.470	−5.55

✳ ♉ Mean Sun, April 21.8.
✳ ♂ ☉, Oct. 25.5.
✳ ♂ Mean Sun, Oct. 21.4.

TABLE XXIV.—θ Bootis.

R.A. 14h 20m.8.   Dec. + 52° 27'.

Upper transit at fictitious meridian.

Sidereal Day	Mean Day	Δ☉a 1870.	Var.in 10y.	Diff. for 10d.	Δ☉δ 1870.	Var.in 10y.	Diff. for 10d.
0, Jan. 0	− 0.18	−1.005	− 2	+411	−15.18	+ 2	−261
10	+ 9.79	0.580	3	437	17.55	2	211
20	19.76	−0.135	3	440	19.37	2	153
30	29.74	+0.314	3	446	20.60	+ 1	91
Feb. 9	8.71	0.753	4	430	21.19	0	− 27
19	18.68	1.170	4	401	21.14	0	+ 36
Mar. 1	0.65	1.551	4	361	20.48	0	96
11	10.63	1.888	4	313	19.23	− 1	151
21	20.60	2.174	4	250	17.48	2	198
31	30.57	2.404	3	201	15.29	2	236
100, Apr. 10	9.54	2.576	3	142	12.79	2	264
20	19.52	2.689	2	84	10.05	3	281
30	29.49	2.744	2	+ 26	7.21	3	285
May 10	9.46	2.743	1	− 27	4.37	2	280
20	19.44	2.692	− 1	76	− 1.63	2	266
30	29.41	2.592	0	122	+ 0.93	2	244
June 9	8.38	2.450	0	162	3.22	1	213
19	18.35	2.269	+ 1	197	5.17	1	177
29	28.33	2.057	2	227	6.74	− 1	136
July 9	8.30	1.818	2	252	7.88	0	91
200, 19	18.27	1.556	3	269	8.56	0	+ 44
29	28.24	1.283	3	278	8.75	0	− 4
Aug. 8	7.22	1.002	3	282	8.47	+ 1	52
18	17.19	0.721	3	278	7.71	2	100
28	27.16	0.449	3	263	6.47	2	147
Sept. 7	6.14	+0.197	3	240	4.78	2	190
17	16.11	−0.028	3	208	2.67	2	232
27	26.08	0.216	3	167	+ 0.16	3	270
Oct. 7	6.05	0.360	3	117	− 2.71	3	302
17	16.03	0.447	2	− 58	5.88	4	330
300, 27	26.00	0.474	2	+ 7	9.30	4	352
Nov. 6	4.97	0.432	1	76	12.89	5	365
16	14.94	0.321	+ 1	147	16.57	5	368
26	24.92	−0.134	0	217	20.23	5	364
Dec. 6	4.89	+0.111	0	282	23.81	4	350
16	14.86	0.423	− 1	340	27.19	4	324
26	24.83	0.789	2	387	30.26	4	288
36	34.81	+1.194	− 3	+422	−32.92	+ 3	−243

✶ ♂ ☉,   Oct. 30.6
✶ ♂ Mean Sun,   Oct. 26.5

Sidereal Day	ΔΩa	ΔΩδ	ΔΩa	ΔΩδ
	1865.		1873.	
0	−0.103	+0.93	−0.302	+2.29
100	0.193	1.65	0.217	1.61
200	0.281	2.35	0.130	0.91
300	0.367	3.03	−0.042	+0.21
400	0.449	3.69	+0.045	−0.50
	1866.		1874.	
0	−0.422	+3.47	+0.016	−0.26
100	0.502	4.11	0.103	0.96
200	0.578	4.71	0.190	1.65
300	0.649	5.27	0.275	2.32
400	0.714	5.79	0.357	2.98
	1867.		1875.	
0	−0.693	+5.62	+0.328	−2.76
100	0.754	6.10	0.410	3.39
200	0.808	6.53	0.486	4.00
300	0.856	6.90	0.559	4.58
400	0.896	7.21	0.627	5.12
	1868 B.		1876 B.	
0	−0.883	+7.11	+0.605	−4.94
100	0.918	7.38	0.670	5.45
200	0.944	7.58	0.729	5.92
300	0.963	7.72	0.782	6.34
400	0.973	7.79	0.829	6.70
	1869.		1877.	
0	−0.970	+7.77	+0.813	−6.59
100	0.974	7 79	0.856	6.91
200	0.970	7.75	0.891	7.19
300	0.958	7.64	0.919	7.40
400	0.937	7.46	0.940	7.55
	1870.		1878.	
0	−0.945	+7.53	+0.934	−7.51
100	0.919	7.31	0.949	7.62
200	0.885	7.03	0.957	7.67
300	0.844	6.69	0.956	7.65
400	0.795	6.29	0.948	7.58
	1871.		1879.	
0	−0.812	+6.43	+0.952	−7.61
100	0.759	6.00	0.939	7.49
200	0.700	5.51	0.917	7.31
300	0.635	4.98	0.884	7.06
400	0.564	4.41	0.852	6.76
	1872 B.		1880 B.	
0	−0.588	+4.61	+0.865	−6.87
100	0.515	4.02	0.823	6.52
200	0.437	3 39	0.775	6.12
300	0.356	2.74	0.720	5.67
400	−0.273	+2.07	+0.658	−5.17

TABLE XXIV.—ᵃ 5 Ursæ Minoris.

R.A. 14ʰ 27ᵐ.8.   Dec. +76° 16′.

Upper transit at fictitious meridian.

Sidereal Day.	Mean Day.	$\Delta_\odot a$ 1870.	Var.in 10 y.	Diff. for 10 d.	$\Delta_\odot \delta$ 1870.	Var.in 10 y.	Diff. for 10 d.
0, Jan. 0	− 0.18	−2.803	+ 9	+847	−17.65	0	−239
10	+ 9.80	1.911	7	931	19.76	0	182
20	19.77	−0.951	4	982	21.26	0	118
30	29.74	+0.042	+ 2	993	22.11	0	− 51
Feb. 9	8.72	1.032	− 1	978	22.28	0	+ 17
19	18.69	1.985	4	923	21.77	0	83
Mar. 1	0.66	2.867	7	836	20.63	0	145
11	10 63	3.649	9	723	18.89	0	200
21	20.61	4.305	11	588	16.66	0	245
31	30.58	4.819	12	437	14.02	0	280
100, Apr. 10	9.55	5.176	13	277	11.09	0	304
20	19.52	5.372	14	+114	7.98	0	316
30	29.50	5.405	14	− 47	4.82	0	315
May 10	9.47	5.280	13	201	− 1.71	0	304
20	19.44	5.006	12	345	+ 1.23	0	283
30	29.42	4.595	11	474	3.91	0	252
June 9	8.39	4.063	9	588	6.25	0	214
19	18.36	3.425	7	683	8.18	0	171
29	28.33	2.702	4	761	9.65	0	122
July 9	8.31	1.911	− 1	818	10.61	0	70
200, 19	18.28	1.073	+ 2	855	11.05	0	+ 17
29	23.25	+0.207	5	873	10.95	0	− 36
Aug. 8	7.22	−0.667	8	870	10.33	0	89
18	17.20	1.527	11	847	9.17	0	141
28	27.17	2.355	14	805	7.52	0	190
Sept. 7	6.14	3.130	17	742	5.39	0	235
17	16.12	3.831	20	658	+ 2.83	0	276
27	26.09	4.440	22	556	− 0.11	0	312
Oct. 7	6.06	4.938	24	436	3.39	0	342
17	16.03	5.307	26	299	6.94	0	366
300, 27	26.01	5.532	27	−149	10.68	0	381
Nov. 6	4.98	5.601	27	+ 12	14.53	0	388
16	14.95	5.506	27	178	18.41	0	385
26	24.92	5.245	27	344	22.20	0	373
Dec. 6	4.90	4.820	26	505	25.82	0	349
16	14.87	4.241	25	653	29.16	0	315
26	24.84	3.523	23	780	32.10	0	271
36	34.82	−2.690	+21	+882	−34.55	0	−219

Sidereal Day.	$\Delta_\Omega a$	$\Delta_\Omega \delta$	$\Delta_\Omega a$	$\Delta_\Omega \delta$
	1865.		**1873.**	
0	−1.678	+1.20	+1.034	+2 08
100	1.778	1.92	1.186	1.38
200	1.862	2.62	1.327	+0,68
300	1.931	3.30	1.457	−0.03
400	1.982	3.95	1.574	0.74
	1866.		**1874.**	
0	−1.967	+3.73	+1.536	−0.50
100	2.007	4.36	1.645	1.21
200	2.029	4.96	1.740	1.90
300	2.034	5.51	1.820	2.57
400	2.021	6.01	1.886	3.22
	1867.		**1875.**	
0	−2.028	+5.85	+1.865	−3.01
100	2.003	6.31	1.920	3.64
200	1.961	6.72	1.960	4.24
300	1.902	7.08	1.983	4.81
400	1.827	7.37	1.989	5.34
	1868 B.		**1876 B.**	
0	−1.854	+7.28	+1.989	−5.17
100	1.768	7.53	1.985	5 67
200	1.667	7.71	1.964	6.12
300	1.551	7.82	1.928	6.52
400	1.422	7.87	1.875	6.87
	1869.		**1877.**	
0	−1.467	+7 86	+1.895	−6.76
100	1.330	7.86	1.832	7.07
200	1.182	7.79	1.754	7.33
300	1.024	7.66	1.661	7.52
400	0.858	7.46	1.553	7.66
	1870.		**1878.**	
0	−0.915	+7.53	+1.592	−7.62
100	0.743	7.29	1.477	7.71
200	0.566	6.98	1.349	7.74
300	0.385	6.62	1.210	7.70
400	0.200	6.20	1.060	7.60
	1871.		**1879.**	
0	−0.263	+6.34	+1.112	−7.64
100	−0.078	5.89	0.956	7.50
200	+0.108	5.38	0.792	7.29
300	0.292	4.84	0.621	7.03
400	0.473	4.25	0.444	6.70
	1872 B.		**1880 B.**	
0	+0.412	+4.45	+0 505	−6.81
100	0.590	3.84	0.325	6.45
200	0.763	3.20	+0.142	6.03
300	0.929	2.53	−0.042	5.56
400	+1.086	+1.84	−0.227	−5.04

✱ δ Mean Sun, April 28.7.
✱ ☌ ⊙, Nov. 1.5.
✱ ☌ Mean Sun, Oct. 28.3.

TABLE XXIV.—α² Centauri.

R.A. 14 30.8 (h m)   Dec. — 60 18 (° ')

Upper transit at fictitious meridian.

Sidereal Day	Mean Day	Δ☉α 1870.	Var.in 10y.	Diff. for 10 d.	Δ☉δ 1870.	Var.in 10y.	Diff. for 10 d.
0, Jan. 0	— 0.18	—1.231	— 9	+544	+15.04	— 2	+ 3
10	+ 9.80	0.675	8	566	14.83	— 1	— 46
20	19.77	—0.105	8	571	14.13	+ 1	93
30	29.74	+0.462	7	562	12.98	2	137
Feb. 9	8.72	1.015	6	540	11.41	2	175
19	18.69	1.538	4	505	9.50	3	207
Mar. 1	0.66	2.022	3	462	7.28	4	235
11	10.63	2.460	— 1	413	4.82	5	256
21	20.61	2.846	+ 1	360	+ 2.18	5	270
31	30.58	3.178	2	303	— 0.57	6	279
100, Apr. 10	9.55	3.451	3	244	3.39	6	283
20	19.52	3.666	5	186	6.21	7	281
30	29.50	3.820	6	125	8.99	7	273
May 10	9.47	3.913	8	62	11.66	6	261
20	19.44	3.944	9	+ 1	14.19	5	244
30	29.42	3.915	10	— 58	16.52	5	221
June 9	8.39	3.828	11	116	18.60	5	194
19	18.36	3.683	12	171	20.38	4	162
29	28.33	3.487	13	221	21.82	3	126
July 9	8.31	3.242	13	265	22.88	3	86
200, 19	18.28	2.958	13	301	23.53	3	— 44
29	28.25	2.642	13	329	23.75	2	0
Aug. 8	7.22	2.303	12	342	23.53	+ 1	+ 44
18	17.20	1.961	12	342	22.87	0	87
28	27.17	1.623	11	329	21.79	— 1	128
Sept. 7	6.14	1.307	9	299	20.32	1	165
17	16.11	1.030	8	253	18.51	2	196
27	26.09	0.805	6	193	16.42	2	220
Oct. 7	6.06	0.648	5	121	14.14	3	234
17	16.03	0.567	4	— 37	11.76	2	239
300, 27	26.01	0.577	3	+ 56	9.38	2	236
Nov. 6	4.98	0.679	+ 2	149	7.07	2	222
16	14.95	0.875	0	242	4.97	2	197
26	24.92	1.162	0	329	3.15	— 1	165
Dec. 6	4.90	1.530	0	406	1.68	0	125
16	14.87	1.970	— 1	471	0.67	+ 1	80
26	24.84	2.468	1	521	0.09	1	+ 33
36	34.81	+3.008	— 1	+555	— 0.02	+ 2	— 16

✳ ☌ ☉, Nov. 2.2.
✳ ☌ Mean Sun, Oct. 29.0.

Sidereal Day	Δ_Ωα	Δ_Ωδ	Δ_Ωα	Δ_Ωδ
1865.			**1873.**	
0	+1.620	+1.30	—1.756	+1.97
100	1.544	2.02	1.746	1.27
200	1.455	2.72	1.722	+0.56
300	1.354	3.40	1.683	—0.15
400	1.240	4.05	1.631	0.86
1866.			**1874.**	
0	+1.280	+3.84	—1.650	—0.62
100	1.158	4.46	1.589	1.33
200	1.027	5.05	1.515	2.02
300	0.887	5.60	1.428	2.69
400	0.738	6.09	1.330	3.34
1867.			**1875.**	
0	+0.789	+5.93	—1.365	—3.13
100	0.636	6.40	1.259	3.76
200	0.478	6.80	1.144	4 36
300	0.316	7.15	1.019	4.93
400	0.152	7.43	0.885	5.45
1868 B.			**1876 B.**	
0	+0.208	+7.34	—0.931	—5.29
100	0.042	7.58	0.793	5 77
200	—0.124	7.76	0.648	6.22
300	0.288	7.86	0.499	6.62
400	0.450	7.90	0.344	6.96
1869.			**1877.**	
0	—0.390	+7.90	—0.390	—6.85
100	0.555	7.89	0.239	7.16
200	0.709	7.81	—0.080	7.40
300	0.855	7.66	+0.080	7.59
400	0.995	7.45	0.239	7.71
1870.			**1878.**	
0	—0.949	+7.52	+0.185	—7.67
100	1.082	7.28	0.344	7.75
200	1.206	6.96	0.500	7.77
300	1.319	6.58	0.652	7.72
400	· 1.421	6.15	0.799	7.61
1871.			**1879.**	
0	—1.388	+6.31	+0.750	—7.65
100	1.481	5.84	0.893	7 50
200	1.562	5.33	1.030	7.28
300	1.629	4.77	1.157	7.00
400	1.682	4.17	1.276	6.66
1872 B.			**1880 B.**	
0	—1.665	+4.38	+1.237	—6.78
100	1.709	3.76	1.349	6.41
200	1.738	3.11	1.450	5.98
300	1.753	2.44	1.538	5.49
400	—1.753	+1.75	+1.614	—4.96

TABLE XXIV.—ε Bootis.

R.A. 14h 39m.3.   Dec. + 27° 37'

Upper transit at fictitious meridian.

Sidereal Day	Mean Day	$\Delta_\odot a$ 1870.	Var. in 10y.	Diff. for 10d.	$\Delta_\odot \delta$ 1870.	Var. in 10y.	Diff. for 10d.
0, Jan. 0	− 0.17	−0.779	− 2	+315	− 9.14	+ 2	−261
10	+ 9.80	0.454	3	334	11.60	2	230
20	19.78	−0.114	3	343	13.72	2	192
30	29.75	+0.229	3	340	15.42	2	146
Feb. 9	8.72	0.564	3	328	16.63	1	97
19	18.69	0.883	3	309	17.35	+ 1	− 46
Mar. 1	0.67	1.180	3	283	17.55	0	+ 5
11	10.64	1.448	3	252	17.25	0	54
21	20.61	1.683	2	217	16.48	0	99
31	30.58	1.882	2	182	15.30	− 1	137
100, Apr. 10	9.56	2.047	1	146	13.76	1	167
20	19.53	2.174	1	109	11.97	1	190
30	29 50	2.265	− 1	74	9.99	2	204
May 10	9.48	2.322	0	39	7.91	2	211
20	19.45	2.344	0	+ 6	5.80	1	209
30	29 42	2.335	+ 1	− 24	3.75	1	200
June 9	8.39	2.297	1	54	1.82	− 1	185
19	18.37	2.228	2	80	− 0.07	0	164
29	28.34	2.137	2	104	+ 1.45	0	140
July 9	8.31	2.020	2	127	2.72	0	111
200, 19	18.28	1.884	2	146	3.67	0	80
29	28.26	1.730	2	160	4 31	0	46
Aug. 8	7.23	1.566	2	169	4.59	0	+ 12
18	17.20	1.394	3	172	4.54	+ 1	− 23
28	27.18	1.225	3	167	4.12	1	59
Sept. 7	6.15	1.062	2	156	3.35	2	95
17	16.12	0.916	2	136	2.23	2	130
27	26.09	0.792	2	110	+ 0.74	3	164
Oct. 7	6.07	0.699	2	74	− 1.04	3	196
17	16.04	0.646	+ 1	− 30	3.16	4	227
300, 27	26.01	0.640	0	+ 18	5.56	4	253
Nov. 6	4.98	0.682	0	69	8.20	4	275
16	14.96	0.776	0	122	11.04	5	291
26	24.93	0.925	− 1	174	13.99	5	299
Dec. 6	4.90	1.123	2	222	16.99	5	301
16	14.87	1.368	2	265	19.98	5	294
26	24.85	1.651	2	298	22.83	5	276
36	34.82	+1.962	− 3	+323	−25.47	+ 5	−251

✳ ☌ ☉.   Nov. 4.3.
✳ ☌ Mean Sun,   Oct. 31.2.

Sidereal Day	$\Delta_\Omega a$	$\Delta_\Omega \delta$	$\Delta_\Omega a$	$\Delta_\Omega \delta$
	1865.		**1873.**	
0	+0.341	+1.62	−0.663	+1.71
100	0.256	2.34	0.600	1.00
200	0.172	3.04	0.532	+0.28
300	+0.085	3.71	0.460	−0.45
400	−0.003	4.35	0.384	1.16
	1866.		**1874.**	
0	+0.027	+4.14	−0.410	−0.92
100	−0.061	4.76	0.332	1.63
200	0.149	5.34	0.252	2.32
300	0.235	5.87	0.170	3.00
400	0.319	6.35	0.086	3.64
	1867.		**1875.**	
0	−0.291	+6.20	−0.114	−3.43
100	0.374	6.64	−0.030	4.06
200	0.453	7.03	+0.054	4.65
300	0.525	7.35	0.138	5.20
400	0.598	7.61	0.220	5.71
	1868 B.		**1876 B.**	
0	−0.575	+7.53	+0.192	−5.55
100	0.642	7.75	0.274	6.03
200	0.704	7.90	0.353	6.46
300	0.759	7.97	0.429	6.84
400	0.807	7.98	0.502	7.16
	1869.		**1877.**	
0	−0.791	+7.99	+0.478	−7.06
100	0.835	7.95	0.548	7.34
200	0.872	7.85	0.613	7.56
300	0.900	7.67	0.674	7.73
400	0.921	7.43	0.736	7.82
	1870.		**1878.**	
0	−0.915	+7.52	+0.712	−7.80
100	0.930	7.24	0.763	7.85
200	0.933	6.89	0.808	7.84
300	0.937	6.49	0.847	7.77
400	0.929	6.03	0.879	7.63
	1871.		**1879.**	
0	−0.932	+6.19	+0.869	−7.08
100	0.919	5.70	0.898	7.50
200	0.897	5.16	0.915	7.25
300	0.868	4.58	0.927	6.94
400	0.831	3 96	0.932	6.58
	1872 B.		**1880 B.**	
0	−0.844	+4.18	+0.931	−6.71
100	0.803	3.54	0.930	6.31
200	0.756	2.87	0.921	5 85
300	0.702	2.18	0.905	5.34
400	−0.642	+1.47	+0.890	−4.78

TABLE XXIV.—β Boötis.

R.A. 14h 57m.0.   Dec. +40° 54'.

Upper transit at fictitious meridian.

Sidereal Day	Mean Day	$\Delta_\odot a$ 1870.	Var. in 10 y.	Diff. for 10 d.	$\Delta_\odot \delta$ 1870.	Var. in 10 y.	Diff. for 10 d.
0, Jan. 0	− 0.16	−1.041	− 2	+330	−11.71	+ 2	−285
10	+ 9.82	0.697	2	357	14.37	2	246
20	19.79	−0.331	3	373	16.60	2	199
30	29 76	+0.046	3	378	18.32	1	146
Feb. 9	8.73	0.421	3	371	19.49	1	86
19	18.71	0.784	3	353	20.04	+ 1	− 25
Mar. 1	0.68	1.124	3	327	20.00	0	+ 34
11	10.65	1.436	3	296	19.38	0	90
21	20.62	1.715	3	259	18.22	− 1	140
31	30.60	1.953	3	217	16.59	1	183
100, Apr. 10	9.57	2.148	2	174	14.57	1	218
20	19.54	2.300	2	130	12.26	1	243
30	29.52	2.408	− 1	86	9.74	1	259
May 10	9.49	2.473	0	44	7.10	2	264
20	19.46	2.496	0	+ 3	4.48	1	260
30	29.43	2.479	0	− 36	1.92	1	249
June 9	8.41	2.424	+ 1	73	+ 0.48	1	229
19	18.38	2.333	1	108	2.64	1	202
29	28.35	2.208	2	140	4.50	− 1	170
July 9	8.32	2.055	2	167	6.02	0	134
200, 19	18.30	1.875	2	190	7.17	0	94
29	28.27	1.677	2	207	7.90	0	52
Aug. 8	7.24	1.462	2	220	8.20	+ 1	+ 9
18	17.21	1.238	3	225	8.07	1	− 35
28	27.19	1.014	3	222	7.51	2	79
Sept. 7	6.16	0.797	3	210	6.50	2	122
17	16.13	0.596	3	191	5.07	2	164
27	26.11	0.418	2	162	3.23	3	203
Oct. 7	6.08	0.274	2	123	+ 1.02	3	241
17	16.05	0.174	1	77	− 1.57	4	274
300, 27	26.02	0.122	1	− 25	4.44	4	301
Nov. 6	5.00	0.126	+ 1	+ 34	7.57	4	323
16	14.97	0.190	0	93	10.88	5	338
26	24.94	0.313	0	153	14.30	5	344
Dec. 6	4.91	0.496	− 1	211	17.73	5	342
16	14.89	0.734	1	263	21.10	5	329
26	24.86	1.019	1	307	24.27	5	304
36	34.83	+1.345	− 2	+341	−27.15	+ 5	−271

✱ ☌ ☉,   Nov. 8.8.
✱ ☌ Mean Sun,   Nov. 4.7.

Sidereal Day	$\Delta_\Omega a$	$\Delta_\Omega \delta$	$\Delta_\Omega a$	$\Delta_\Omega \delta$
	1865.		**1873.**	
0	+0.158	+2.26	−0.491	+1.14
100	+0.077	2.98	0.424	+0.41
200	−0.004	3.67	0.353	−0.33
300	0.085	4.34	0.279	1.07
400	0.166	4.97	0.204	1.79
	1866.		**1874.**	
0	−0.139	+4.76	−0.229	−1.55
100	0.219	5.36	0.153	2 26
200	0.297	5.91	−0.075	2.95
300	0.373	6.41	+0.003	3 62
400	0.445	6.87	0.082	4.26
	1867.		**1875.**	
0	−0.421	+6.72	+0.055	−4.05
100	0.491	7.11	0.133	4.66
200	0.556	7.47	0.209	5.23
300	0.617	7.74	0.284	5.77
400	0.672	7.96	0.356	6.25
	1868 B.		**1876 B.**	
0	−0.654	+7.89	+0.332	−6.09
100	0.705	8.06	0.403	6.54
200	0.750	8.15	0.470	6.93
300	0.788	8.17	0.533	7.27
400	0.820	8.12	0.592	7.55
	1869.		**1877.**	
0	−0.810	+8.15	+0.572	−7.47
100	0.836	8.05	0.628	7.70
200	0.856	7.89	0.679	7.88
300	0.868	7.65	0.724	7.99
400	0.872	7.35	0.763	8.03
	1870.		**1878.**	
0	−0.871	+7.46	+0.750	−8.02
100	0.871	7.12	0.786	8.02
200	0.863	6.72	0.815	7.96
300	0.847	6.26	0.837	7.82
400	0.824	5.75	0.852	7.63
	1871.		**1879.**	
0	−0.833	+5.93	+0.848	−7.70
100	0.805	5.39	0.858	7.46
200	0.771	4.80	0.861	7.16
300	0.730	4.17	0.858	6.79
400	0.684	3.51	0.847	6.37
	1872 B.		**1880 B.**	
0	−0.700	+3.74	+0.851	−6.52
100	0.650	3.06	0.835	6.06
200	0.594	2.35	0.813	5.55
300	0.533	1.63	0.783	4.99
400	−0.468	+0.90	0.747	−4.39

TABLE XXIV.—β Libræ.

R. A. 15h 10m.0.   Dec. — 8° 54′.

Upper transit at fictitious meridian.

Sidereal Day	Mean Day	$\Delta_\odot\alpha$ 1870.	Var.in 10y.	Diff. for 10d.	$\Delta_\odot\delta$ 1870.	Var.in 10y.	Diff. for 10d.
0, Jan. 0	− 0.15	−0.826	− 3	+298	+ 1.37	+ 1	−164
10	+ 9.82	0.519	3	316	− 0.29	1	168
20	19.80	−0.198	3	324	1.97	2	165
30	29.77	+0.126	3	323	3.58	2	157
Feb. 9	8.74	0.416	3	316	5.09	2	144
19	18.72	0.756	3	303	6.45	2	127
Mar. 1	0.69	1.050	3	283	7.62	2	107
11	10.66	1.321	2	259	8.58	2	85
21	20.63	1.568	2	235	9.31	2	62
31	30.61	1.790	1	208	9.81	2	40
100, Apr. 10	9.58	1.983	− 1	180	10.11	2	20
20	19.55	2.150	0	153	10.21	2	− 1
30	29.52	2.288	0	124	10.13	2	+ 15
May 10	9.50	2.398	+ 1	95	9.92	2	27
20	19.47	2.478	1	67	9.60	2	37
30	29.44	2.531	2	38	9.20	2	43
June 9	8.41	2.553	2	+ 8	8.75	2	47
19	18.39	2.547	2	− 21	8.26	1	49
29	28.36	2.511	3	49	7.76	1	50
July 9	8.33	2.450	3	75	7.26	1	51
200, 19	18.31	2.362	3	101	6.75	1	50
29	28.28	2.250	4	120	6.26	1	48
Aug. 8	7.25	2.123	4	135	5.80	1	45
18	17.22	1.981	4	145	5.37	1	40
28	27.20	1.834	4	147	5.00	0	36
Sept. 7	6.17	1.689	4	142	4.66	1	29
17	16.14	1.553	3	128	4.42	1	18
27	26.11	1.436	3	104	4.30	1	+ 7
Oct. 7	6.09	1.347	2	73	4.29	1	− 8
17	16.06	1.292	2	− 34	4.46	2	25
300, 27	26.03	1.281	2	+ 11	4.80	2	44
Nov. 6	5.01	1.315	+ 1	59	5.35	2	65
16	14.98	1.400	0	111	6.10	2	87
26	24.95	1.537	0	160	7.07	3	109
Dec. 6	4.92	1.720	0	206	8.27	4	129
16	14.90	1.948	− 1	247	9.64	4	145
26	24.87	2.212	1	284	11.16	4	158
36	34.84	+2.507	− 2	+305	−12.79	+ 5	−166

* ☌ ⊙, Nov. 12 0.
* ☌ Mean Sun, Nov. 8.0.

Sidereal Day	$\Delta_\Omega\alpha$	$\Delta_\Omega\delta$	$\Delta_\Omega\alpha$	$\Delta_\Omega\delta$
	1865.		**1873.**	
0	+0.718	+2.72	−0.993	+0.72
100	0.635	3.44	0.944	−0.03
200	0.547	4.13	0.887	0.78
300	0.454	4.78	0.823	1.53
400	0.357	5.39	0.753	2.25
	1866.		**1874.**	
0	+0.390	+5.19	−0.777	−2.00
100	0.290	5.78	0.703	2.72
200	0.188	6.31	0.622	3.41
300	+0.084	6.78	0.537	4.07
400	−0.021	7.20	0.447	4.69
	1867.		**1875.**	
0	+0.015	+7.07	−0.478	−4.49
100	−0.090	7.45	0.386	5.09
200	0.194	7.76	0.291	5.65
300	0.296	8.00	0.193	6.16
400	0.395	8.18	0.094	6.62
	1868 B.		**1876 B.**	
0	−0.362	+8.13	−0.128	−6.47
100	0.459	8.25	−0.029	6.89
200	0.552	8.31	+0.072	7.26
300	0.640	8.29	0.171	7.57
400	0.722	8.20	0.269	7.81
	1869.		**1877.**	
0	−0.695	+8.24	+0.236	−7.74
100	0.773	8.10	0.333	7.94
200	0.844	7.89	0.427	8.08
300	0.907	7.62	0.518	8.15
400	0.963	7.27	0.604	8.16
	1870.		**1878.**	
0	−0.945	+7.39	+0.576	−8.16
100	0.995	7.01	0.659	8.12
200	1.036	6.57	0.738	8.01
300	1.069	6.07	0.810	7.84
400	1.092	5.52	0.875	7.60
	1871.		**1879.**	
0	−1.085	+5.71	+0.851	−7.69
100	1.102	5.13	0.915	7.40
200	1.109	4.51	0.969	7.06
300	1.107	3.85	1.014	6.65
400	1.096	3.16	1.052	6.19
	1872 B.		**1880 B.**	
0	−1.100	+3.40	+1.040	−6.35
100	1.083	2.69	1.072	5.86
200	1.056	1.97	1.094	5.31
300	1.021	1.23	1.108	4.71
400	−0.978	+0.48	+1.112	−4.08

TABLE XXIV.—μ¹ Bootis.

R.A. 15h 19.6m   Dec. + 37° 50'

Upper transit at fictitious meridian.

Sidereal Day	Mean Day	$\Delta_\odot a$ 1870.	Var.in 10y.	Diff. for 10 d.	$\Delta_\odot \delta$ 1870.	Var.in 10y.	Diff. for 10 d.
0, Jan. 0	— 0.14	—1.125	— 1	+303	—10.26	+ 2	—292
10	+ 9.83	0.806	2	333	13.03	2	259
20	19.80	0.463	2	352	15.42	2	216
30	29.78	—0.106	3	361	17.33	1	165
Feb. 9	8.75	+0.255	3	359	18.70	1	109
19	18.72	0.609	3	348	19.50	1	— 51
Mar. 1	0.69	0.948	2	328	19.72	+ 1	+ 9
11	10.67	1.262	3	300	19.33	0	66
21	20.64	1.517	3	269	18.42	0	116
31	30.61	1.799	2	233	17.02	— 1	163
100, Apr 10	9.59	2.012	2	194	15.18	1	201
20	19.56	2.187	1	155	13.02	1	230
30	29.53	2.322	1	115	10.60	1	250
May 10	9.50	2.416	— 1	73	8.04	1	260
20	19.48	2.468	0	+ 33	5.43	2	261
30	29.45	2.482	0	— 6	2.85	2	253
June 9	8.42	2.456	0	45	— 0.40	1	237
19	18.39	2.393	+ 1	80	+ 1.87	1	214
29	28.37	2.297	2	112	3.87	1	186
July 9	8.34	2.169	2	144	5.58	1	154
200, 19	18.31	2.010	2	171	6.93	— 1	117
29	28.29	1.829	2	193	7.92	0	77
Aug. 8	7.26	1.626	3	210	8.48	0	+ 36
18	17.23	1.412	3	218	8.63	0	— 6
28	27.20	1.192	3	220	8.35	+ 1	50
Sept. 7	6.18	0.974	3	214	7.63	2	93
17	16.15	0.767	2	198	6.50	2	135
27	26.12	0.580	2	173	4.94	3	175
Oct. 7	6.09	0.423	2	139	3.00	3	213
17	16.07	0.304	2	97	+ 0.68	4	249
300, 27	26.04	0.231	1	— 47	— 1.96	4	279
Nov. 6	5.01	0.211	1	+ 9	4.88	4	304
16	14.98	0.249	+ 1	66	8.02	4	323
26	24.96	0.342	0	123	11.31	4	334
Dec. 6	4.93	0.495	0	181	14.68	5	336
16	14.90	0.704	0	234	18.00	5	328
26	24.88	0.961	— 1	279	21.21	5	310
36	34.85	+1.259	— 1	+315	—24.17	+ 4	—281

☿ ☌ ⊙,   Nov. 14.3.
☿ ☌ Mean Sun,   Nov. 10.4.

Sidereal Day | $\Delta_\Omega a$ | $\Delta_\Omega \delta$ | $\Delta_\Omega a$ | $\Delta_\Omega \delta$

1865.

Sidereal Day	$\Delta_\Omega a$	$\Delta_\Omega \delta$
0	+0.221	+3.06
100	0.144	3.77
200	+0.065	4.45
300	—0.014	5.10
400	0.093	5.70

1873.

Sidereal Day	$\Delta_\Omega a$	$\Delta_\Omega \delta$
0	—0.531	+0.42
100	0.469	—0.35
200	0.403	1.10
300	0.334	1.85
400	0.263	2.57

1866.

Sidereal Day	$\Delta_\Omega a$	$\Delta_\Omega \delta$
0	—0.066	+5.50
100	0.145	6.07
200	0.222	6.59
300	0.298	7.05
400	0.371	7.44

1874.

Sidereal Day	$\Delta_\Omega a$	$\Delta_\Omega \delta$
0	—0.287	—2.33
100	0.214	3.04
200	0.140	3.73
300	—0.065	4.38
400	+0.011	5.00

1867.

Sidereal Day	$\Delta_\Omega a$	$\Delta_\Omega \delta$
0	—0.347	+7.32
100	0.417	7.67
200	0.485	7.96
300	0.548	8.18
400	0.606	8.32

1875.

Sidereal Day	$\Delta_\Omega a$	$\Delta_\Omega \delta$
0	—0.014	—4.80
100	+0.062	5.39
200	0.137	5.93
300	0.211	6.43
400	0.283	6.87

1868 B.

Sidereal Day	$\Delta_\Omega a$	$\Delta_\Omega \delta$
0	—0.589	+8.25
100	0.641	8.38
200	0.690	8.40
300	0.733	8.35
400	0.768	8.25

1876 B.

Sidereal Day	$\Delta_\Omega a$	$\Delta_\Omega \delta$
0	+0.259	—6.73
100	0.330	7.13
200	0.398	7.48
300	0.463	7.76
400	0.524	7.99

1869.

Sidereal Day	$\Delta_\Omega a$	$\Delta_\Omega \delta$
0	—0.757	+8.25
100	0.789	8.11
200	0.814	7.87
300	0.832	7.57
400	0.842	7.19

1877.

Sidereal Day	$\Delta_\Omega a$	$\Delta_\Omega \delta$
0	+0.503	—7.92
100	0.562	8.10
200	0.615	8.21
300	0.664	8.25
400	0.707	8.23

1870.

Sidereal Day	$\Delta_\Omega a$	$\Delta_\Omega \delta$
0	—0.840	+7.35
100	0.846	6.91
200	0.844	6.44
300	0.835	5.92
400	0.819	5.34

1878.

Sidereal Day	$\Delta_\Omega a$	$\Delta_\Omega \delta$
0	+0.693	—8.24
100	0.733	8.17
200	0.767	8.04
300	0.794	7.83
400	0.812	7.56

1871.

Sidereal Day	$\Delta_\Omega a$	$\Delta_\Omega \delta$
0	—0.825	+5.54
100	0.805	4.94
200	0.777	4.29
300	0.744	3.61
400	0.703	2.90

1879.

Sidereal Day	$\Delta_\Omega a$	$\Delta_\Omega \delta$
0	+0.808	—7.66
100	0.825	7.35
200	0.836	6.97
300	0.837	6.54
400	0.833	6.05

1872 B.

Sidereal Day	$\Delta_\Omega a$	$\Delta_\Omega \delta$
0	—0.718	+3.15
100	0.674	2.42
200	0.624	1.68
300	0.569	0.92
400	—0.510	+0.16

1880 B.

Sidereal Day	$\Delta_\Omega a$	$\Delta_\Omega \delta$
0	+0.835	—6.22
100	0.826	5.70
200	0.810	5.12
300	0.797	4.50
400	+0.757	—3.84

TABLE XXIV.—* γ² Ursæ Minoris.

R.A. 15 21.0. (h m)   Dec. +72 18. (° ')

Upper transit at fictitious meridian.

Sidereal Day.	Mean Day.	Δ☉α 1870.	Var. in 10y.	Diff. for 10d.	Δ☉δ 1870.	Var. in 10y.	Diff. for 10d.
0, Jan. 0	− 0.13	−3.017	+ 6	+568	−14.75	0	−297
10	+ 9.84	2.402	5	659	17.48	0	249
20	19.81	1.706	4	727	19.69	0	192
30	29.78	0.956	3	770	21.29	0	128
Feb. 9	8.75	−0.176	+ 1	784	22.24	0	− 61
19	18.72	+0.604	0	772	22.51	0	+ 8
Mar. 1	0.70	1.359	− 1	733	22.09	0	74
11	10.67	2.063	2	671	21.03	0	137
21	20.64	2.695	3	589	19.37	0	193
31	30.62	3.235	4	490	17.20	0	240
100, Apr. 10	9.59	3 671	5	379	14.60	0	278
20	19.56	3.991	6	261	11.68	0	304
30	29.53	4.191	6	138	8.57	0	318
May 10	9.51	4.268	6	+ 16	5.36	0	321
20	19.48	4.223	6	−104	− 2.18	0	313
30	29.45	4.062	5	218	+ 0.87	0	295
June 9	8.42	3.791	5	323	3.70	0	269
19	18.40	3.420	4	418	6.22	0	234
29	28.37	2.959	3	502	8.36	0	194
July 9	8.34	2.421	− 2	572	10.08	0	149
200, 19	18.32	1.819	0	629	11.32	0	100
29	28.29	1.168	+ 1	670	12.06	0	+ 48
Aug. 8	7.26	+0.483	3	697	12.28	0	− 4
18	17.23	−0.220	4	706	11.98	0	57
28	27.21	0.923	6	698	11.14	0	109
Sept. 7	6.18	1.610	7	673	9.80	0	159
17	16.15	2.263	9	629	7.97	0	207
27	26.12	2.863	10	567	5.68	0	251
Oct. 7	6.10	3.391	12	488	+ 2.98	0	291
17	16 07	3.832	13	392	− 0.11	0	324
300, 27	26.04	4.170	14	280	3.50	0	352
Nov. 6	5.02	4.389	14	157	7.13	0	372
16	14.99	4.480	15	− 25	10.91	0	383
26	24.96	4.437	15	+113	14.76	0	384
Dec. 6	4.93	4.225	15	250	18.56	0	375
16	14.91	3.940	15	381	22.21	0	354
26	24.88	3.498	14	501	25.61	0	323
36	34.85	−2.944	+13	+604	−28.63	0	−280

Sidereal Day.	ΔΩα	ΔΩδ	ΔΩα	ΔΩδ
	1865.		**1873.**	
0	−1.029	+3.11	+0.637	+0.38
100	1.090	3.82	0.729	−0.38
200	1.141	4.50	0.816	1.14
300	1.183	5.15	0.895	1.88
400	1.214	5.75	0.967	2.61
	1866.		**1874.**	
0	−1.205	+5.55	+0.943	−2.37
100	1.229	6.12	1.010	3.08
200	1.243	6.63	1.068	3.77
300	1.245	7.09	1.117	4.42
400	1.237	7.46	1.157	5.04
	1867.		**1875.**	
0	−1.241	+7.35	+1.145	−4.83
100	1.226	7.70	1.178	5.42
200	1.200	7.99	1.202	5.97
300	1.164	8.20	1.216	6.46
400	1.117	8.34	1.219	6.90
	1868 B.		**1876 B.**	
0	−1.134	+8.30	+1.219	−6.76
100	1.081	8.40	1.216	7.16
200	1.019	8.42	1.204	7.50
300	0.948	8.36	1.181	7.79
400	0.869	8.24	1.145	8.01
	1869.		**1877.**	
0	−0.896	+8.29	+1.161	−7.94
100	0.812	8.11	1.122	8.11
200	0.721	7.87	1.074	8.22
300	0.624	7.56	1.017	8.26
400	0.522	7.18	0.951	8.24
	1870.		**1878.**	
0	−0.557	+7.32	+0.974	−8.25
100	0.452	6.90	0.903	8.18
200	0.343	6.43	0.825	8.04
300	0.232	5.90	0.739	7.83
400	0.119	5.32	0.647	7.56
	1871.		**1879.**	
0	−0 158	+5.52	+0.679	−7.66
100	−0.044	4.91	0.583	7.34
200	+0.070	4.26	0.483	6.96
300	0.182	3.58	0.378	6.53
400	0.293	2.87	0.269	6.04
	1872 B.		**1880 B.**	
0	+0.256	+3.11	+0.308	−6.21
100	0.365	2.38	0.196	5.68
200	0.471	1.64	+0.084	5.10
300	0.572	0.88	−0.029	4 48
400	+0.669	+0.12	−0.143	−3.82

✱ 8 Mean Sun, May 12.2.
✱ ☌ ☉, Nov. 14.7.
✱ ☌ Mean Sun, Nov. 10.8.

TABLE XXIV.—ε Serpentis.

R.A. 15 44.3 (h m).   Dec. + 4 52 (° ').

Upper transit at fictitious meridian.

Sidereal Day.	Mean Day.	$\Delta_\odot a$ 1870.	Var. in 10 y.	Diff. for 10 d.	$\Delta_\odot \delta$ 1870.	Var. in 10 y.	Diff. for 10 d.
0, Jan. 0	− 0.12	−0.975	− 2	+265	− 2.22	+ 1	−208
10	+ 9.85	0.698	3	289	4.27	1	201
20	19.82	0.399	3	305	6.21	1	185
30	29.79	−0.090	3	311	7.96	1	164
Feb. 9	8.77	+0.221	3	311	9.48	1	138
19	18.74	0.529	3	304	10.70	1	106
Mar. 1	0.71	0.826	2	290	11.59	1	72
11	10.68	1.107	2	273	12.14	2	37
21	20.66	1.370	2	251	12.33	2	− 2
31	30.63	1.608	2	227	12.19	1	+ 29
100, Apr. 10	9.60	1.824	1	202	11.76	1	57
20	19.58	2.013	1	·175	11.06	1	79
30	29.55	2.173	− 1	148	10.16	1	99
May 10	9.52	2.308	0	120	9.06	1	115
20	19.49	2.413	0	90	7.87	1	123
30	29.47	2.487	+ 1	59	6.62	1	126
June 9	8.44	2.531	1	+ 28	5.37	1	125
19	18.41	2.544	2	− 3	4.14	1	120
29	28.38	2.526	2	34	2.99	1	111
July 9	8.36	2.477	3	64	1.92	0	99
200, 19	18.33	2.399	3	91	1.00	0	86
29	28.30	2.296	3	115	− 0.21	1	71
Aug. 8	7.27	2.170	3	136	+ 0.42	1	55
18	17.25	2.025	3	150	0.89	1	38
28	27.22	1.872	3	157	1.17	2	+ 18
Sept. 7	6.19	1.713	3	158	1.25	2	− 2
17	16.17	1.559	2	148	1.13	2	23
27	26.14	1.419	2	130	0.79	2	45
Oct. 7	6.11	1.301	2	104	+ 0.22	3	68
17	16.08	1.213	2	70	− 0.58	3	91
300, 27	26.06	1.164	1	− 28	1.61	3	114
Nov. 6	5.03	1.159	+ 1	+ 17	2.87	3	138
16	15.00	1.200	0	67	4.37	3	161
26	24.97	1.294	0	118	6.08	4	181
Dec. 6	4.95	1.436	0	165	7.97	4	195
16	14.92	1.623	− 1	209	9.96	4	204
26	24.89	1.852	1	246	·12.04	5	209
36	34.87	+2.113	− 1	+274	−14.11	+ 5	−205

Sidereal Day.	$\Delta_\Omega a$	$\Delta_\Omega \delta$	$\Delta_\Omega a$	$\Delta_\Omega \delta$
1865.			**1873.**	
0	+0.591	+3.90	−0.874	−0.39
100	0.509	4.60	0.821	1.17
200	0.424	5.26	0.762	1.94
300	0.334	5.87	0.697	2.68
400	0.242	6.44	0.627	3.41
1866.			**1874.**	
0	+0.273	+6.25	−0.651	−3.17
100	0.179	6.78	0.577	3.87
200	+0.084	7.25	0.499	4.54
300	−0.013	7.66	0.416	5.18
400	0.109	8.00	0.330	5.77
1867.			**1875.**	
0	−0.077	+7.89	−0.359	−5.57
100	0.172	8.19	0.272	6.13
200	0.267	8.41	0.182	6.64
300	0.359	8.56	0.091	7.09
400	0.447	8.63	+0.001	7.48
1868 B.			**1876 B.**	
0	−0.418	+8.62	−0.030	−7.36
100	0.504	8.64	+0.062	7.71
200	0.585	8.59	0.154	8.00
300	0.661	8.46	0.244	8.22
400	0.731	8.26	0.333	8.38
1869.			**1877.**	
0	−0.709	+8.34	+0.303	−8.33
100	0.775	8.09	0.390	8.44
200	0.834	7.77	0.473	8.48
300	0.886	7.39	0.553	8.45
400	0.930	6.94	0.629	8.35
1870.			**1878.**	
0	−0.916	+7.10	+0.604	−8.40
100	0.954	6.61	0.676	8.25
200	0.985	6.07	0.743	8.04
300	1.006	5.47	0.803	7.75
400	1.020	4.83	0.858	7.41
1871.			**1879.**	
0	−1.016	+5.06	+0.840	−7.53
100	1.023	4.39	0.890	7.14
200	1.022	3.69	0.932	6.69
300	1.012	2.96	0.967	6.19
400	0.993	2.20	0.993	5.63
1872 B.			**1880 B.**	
0	−1.001	+2.46	+0.985	−5.82
100	0.976	1.70	1.006	5.23
200	0.944	0.92	1.019	4.59
300	0.904	+0.14	1.023	3.91
400	−0.857	−0.65	+1.019	−3.20

✶ ☌ ⊙,   Nov. 20.3.
✶ ☌ Mean Sun, Nov. 16.7.

TABLE XXIV.—ʼ ζ Ursæ Minoris.

R.A. 15 48.8. (h m)   Dec. + 78 12. (° ')

Upper transit at fictitious meridian.

Sidereal Day	Mean Day	$\Delta_\odot\alpha$ 1870.	Var. in 10y.	Diff. for 10d.	$\Delta_\odot\delta$ 1870.	Var. in 10y.	Diff. for 10d.
0, Jan. 0	− 0.12	−5.059	+20	+677	−13.26	− 2	−311
10	+ 9.85	4.301	20	834	16.16	2	267
20	19.83	3.401	19	961	18.58	2	215
30	29.80	2.391	17	1053	20.42	2	154
Feb. 9	8.77	1.308	15	1105	21.64	1	89
19	18.74	−0.191	13	1117	22.20	− 1	− 21
Mar. 1	0.72	+0.911	10	1088	22.07	0	+ 46
11	10.69	1.909	8	1021	21.28	0	111
21	20.66	2.942	4	920	19.88	+ 1	169
31	30.64	3.798	+ 1	789	17.93	1	220
100, Apr. 10	9.61	4.512	− 1	635	15.51	2	262
20	19.58	5.063	4	465	12.73	2	293
30	29.55	5.438	6	284	9.69	2	313
May 10	9.53	5.620	8	+ 97	6.51	2	321
20	19.50	5.633	9	− 88	3.30	2	319
30	29.47	5.456	11	266	− 0.17	2	307
June 9	8.44	5.104	11	436	+ 2.80	2	285
19	18.42	4.589	11	591	5.50	2	255
29	28.39	3.927	10	730	7.87	1	218
July 9	8.36	3.134	9	851	9.84	+ 1	176
200, 19	18.34	2.239	7	950	11.38	0	130
29	28.31	1.241	5	1028	12.43	0	80
Aug. 8	7.28	+0.184	− 2	1082	12.97	− 1	+ 29
18	17.25	−0.915	+ 1	1111	13.00	1	− 23
28	27.23	2.030	4	1115	12.51	2	75
Sept. 7	6.20	3.136	8	1093	11.50	3	126
17	16.17	4.207	12	1044	10.00	3	175
27	26.14	5.215	16	968	8.02	3	221
Oct. 7	6 12	6.135	20	866	5.60	4	263
17	16.09	6.939	23	739	+ 2.78	4	300
300, 27	26.06	7.604	27	588	− 0.38	5	331
Nov. 6	5.04	8.107	30	416	3.82	5	355
16	15.01	8.430	33	228	7.46	5	371
26	24.98	8.559	36	− 28	11.22	5	378
Dec. 6	4.95	8.486	38	+176	14.98	5	374
16	14.92	8.209	39	377	18.65	5	359
26	24.90	7.736	40	568	22.12	5	333
36	34.87	−7.080	+40	+740	−25.27	− 5	−296

Sidereal Day	$\Delta_\Omega\alpha$	$\Delta_\Omega\delta$	$\Delta_\Omega\alpha$	Δ_Ω
	1865.		**1873.**	
0	−1.767	+4.06	+1.452	−0.52
100	1.789	4.75	1.536	1.30
200	1.795	5.41	1 608	2.07
300	1.766	6.02	1.666	2.81
400	1.702	6.57	1.711	3.54
	1866.		**1874.**	
0	−1.772	+6.39	+1.697	−3.30
100	1.737	6.91	1.732	4.00
200	1.687	7.37	1.753	4.67
300	1.622	7.77	1.759	5.30
400	1.543	8.10	1.750	5.88
	1867.		**1875.**	
0	−1.571	+7.99	+1.755	−5.69
100	1.484	8.27	1.737	6.24
200	1.383	8.48	1.705	6.74
300	1.270	8.62	1.659	7.18
400	1.147	8.68	1.599	7.57
	1868 B.		**1876 B.**	
0	−1.190	+8.67	+1.621	−7.45
100	1.060	8.68	1.552	7.79
200	0.920	8.61	1.471	8.07
300	0.773	8.47	1.378	8.28
400	0.620	8.26	1.273	8.43
	1869.		**1877.**	
0	−0.673	+8.34	+1.309	−8.39
100	0.516	8.07	1.197	8.48
200	0.355	7.74	1.075	8.51
300	0.191	7.35	0.944	8.48
400	0 027	6.89	0.806	8.36
	1870.		**1878.**	
0	−0.082	+7.05	+0.853	−8.41
100	+0.082	6.55	0.710	8.25
200	0.246	5.99	0.560	8.03
300	0.407	5.39	0.405	7.73
400	0.565	4.74	0.246	7.38
	1871.		**1879.**	
0	+0.512	+4.96	+0.300	−7.51
100	0.666	4.29	+0.140	7.11
200	0.814	3.58	− 0.022	6.65
300	0.954	2.84	0.184	6.13
400	1.096	2.08	0.345	5.56
	1872 B.		**1880 B.**	
0	+1.043	+2.34	−0.291	−5.76
100	1.169	1.57	0.451	5.16
200	1.284	+0.79	0.607	4.51
300	1.389	0.00	0.758	3.83
400	+1.482	−0.78	−0.904	−3.11

✱ δ Mean Sun,   May 19.2.
✱ δ ☉,   Nov. 21.4.
✱ δ Mean Sun,   Nov. 17.8.

TABLE XXIV.—ε Coronæ Borealis.

R.A. 15h 52.2m   Dec. + 27° 15'.

Upper transit at fictitious meridian.

Sidereal Day	Mean Day	$\Delta_\odot\alpha$ 1870.	Var.in 10y.	Diff. for 10 d.	$\Delta_\odot\delta$ 1870.	Var.in 10y.	Diff. for 10 d.
0, Jan. 0	− 0.12	−1.143	− 1	+261	− 7.01	+ 2	−282
10	+ 9.85	0.866	2	292	9.73	2	259
20	19.83	0.563	3	313	12.17	2	227
30	29.80	−0.243	3	325	14.25	1	187
Feb. 9	8.77	+0.084	3	328	15.88	1	140
19	18.74	0.410	3	323	17.03	1	89
Mar. 1	0.72	0.727	3	311	17.65	1	− 35
11	10.69	1.031	3	293	17.74	+ 1	+ 18
21	20.66	1.312	3	260	17.30	0	68
31	30.64	1.569	2	244	16.40	0	114
100, Apr. 10	9.61	1.799	2	214	15.06	0	152
20	19.58	1.996	1	182	13.38	0	185
30	29.55	2.162	− 1	149	11.38	0	209
May 10	9.53	2.295	0	115	9.21	0	224
20	19.50	2.392	0	80	6.92	0	231
30	29 47	2.455	0	44	4.61	− 1	232
June 9	8.44	2.481	+ 1	+ 8	2.31	1	224
19	18.42	2.472	1	− 27	0.15	− 1	208
29	28.39	2.427	2	61	+ 1.83	0	188
July 9	8.36	2.350	2	93	3.59	0	163
200, 19	18.33	2.242	2	124	5.08	0	134
29	28.31	2.104	2	151	6.27	0	103
Aug. 8	7.28	1.943	2	172	7.14	+ 1	69
18	17.25	1.763	3	187	7 64	1	+ 32
28	27.23	1.572	3	195	7.78	1	− 4
Sept. 7	6.20	1.377	3	195	7.56	2	41
17	16.17	1.185	3	187	6.95	2	80
27	26.14	1.007	3	169	5.96	3	118
Oct. 7	6.12	0.851	2	141	4.60	3	153
17	16.09	0.728	2	106	2.90	4	188
300, 27	26.06	0.642	1	64	+ 0.85	4	221
Nov. 6	5.03	0.608	1	− 14	− 1.51	4	249
16	15.01	0.616	+ 1	+ 39	4.12	4	272
26	24.98	0.682	0	92	6.94	5	289
Dec. 6	4.95	0.800	0	144	9.88	5	299
16	14.93	0.970	0	194	12 88	5	301
26	24.90	1.186	− 1	237	15.85	5	293
36	34.87	+1.442	− 2	+273	−18.70	+ 6	−275

✳ ♂ ☉,   Nov. 22.1.
✳ ♂ Mean Sun,   Nov. 18.7.

Sidereal Day	$\Delta_\Omega\alpha$	$\Delta_\Omega\delta$	$\Delta_\Omega\alpha$	$\Delta_\Omega\delta$
	1865.		**1873.**	
0	+0.377	+4.16	−0.661	−0.64
100	0.302	4.85	0.606	1.43
200	0.224	5.50	0.547	2.19
300	0.144	6.11	0.483	2.94
400	0.063	6.66	0.415	3.66
	1866.		**1874.**	
0	+0.090	+6.48	−0.438	− 3.42
100	+0.008	7.00	0.368	4.12
200	−0.074	7.45	0.295	4.79
300	0.155	7.84	0.220	5.41
400	0.235	8.16	0.143	5.99
	1867.		**1875.**	
0	−0.208	+8.06	−0.170	−5.80
100	0.287	8.33	0.092	6.35
200	0.364	7.53	−0.014	6.84
300	0.437	8.66	+0.065	7.28
400	0.506	8.71	0.143	7.66
	1868 B.		**1876 B.**	
0	−0.483	+8.70	+0.117	−7.54
100	0.549	8.70	0.194	7.87
200	0.610	8.62	0.269	8.14
300	0.666	8.47	0.342	8.31
400	0.716	8.25	0.413	8.48
	1869.		**1877.**	
0	−0.700	+8.33	+0.389	−8.44
100	0.746	8.06	0.458	8.53
200	0.785	7.72	0.523	8.55
300	0.817	7.31	0.583	8.50
400	0.843	6.84	0.639	8.37
	1870.		**1878.**	
0	−0.835	+7.01	+0.621	−8 42
100	0.855	6.50	0.673	8.25
200	0.868	5.93	0.720	8.02
300	0.874	5.32	0.761	7 71
400	0.872	4.66	0.796	7.34
	1871.		**1879.**	
0	−0.873	+4.89	+0.785	−7.47
100	0.866	4.21	0.816	7.06
200	0.852	3.49	0.840	6.59
300	0.830	2.74	0.857	6.06
400	0.802	1.98	0 867	5.48
	1872 B.		**1880 B.**	
0	−0.812	+2.24	+0.864	−5.68
100	0.779	1.46	0.869	5.07
200	0.740	+0.67	0.867	4.42
300	0.694	−0.12	0.857	3.72
400	−0.643	−0.90	+0.840	−3.00

TABLE XXIV.—δ Scorpii.

R.A. 15^{h} 52^{m}.6.   Dec. — 22° 15$'$.

Upper transit at fictitious meridian.

Sidereal Day.	Mean Day.	$\Delta_\odot\alpha$			$\Delta_\odot\delta$			Sidereal Day.	$\Delta_\Omega\alpha$	$\Delta_\Omega\delta$	$\Delta_\Omega\alpha$	$\Delta_\Omega\delta$
		1870.	Var. in 10 y.	Diff. for 10 d.	1870.	Var. in 10 y.	Diff. for 10 d.		1865.		1873.	
								0	+0.837	+4.17	-1.119	-0.66
								100	0.750	4.86	1.069	1.44
								200	0.650	5.51	1.011	2.21
0, Jan. 0	— 0.12	-1.073	— 3	+289	+ 4.12	0	— 82	300	0.556	6.12	0.945	2.96
10	+ 9.85	0.771	3	315	3.22	0	97	400	0.451	6.67	0.871	3.68
20	19.83	0.445	3	332	2.19	+ 1	108					
30	29.80	-0.110	4	339	+ 1.08	1	114		1866.		1874.	
Feb. 9	8.77	+0.230	4	339	— 0.07	1	116	0	+0.487	+6.49	-0 897	-3.44
								100	0.379	7.01	0.819	4.14
19	18.74	0.566	3	332	·1.22	1	114	200	0.268	7.40	0.734	4.81
Mar. 1	0.72	0.892	3	319	2.34	2	109	300	0.154	7.85	0.643	5.43
11	10.69	1.202	3	302	3.39	2	100	400	0.039	8.17	0.547	6.01
21	20.66	1.495	2	281	4.34	3	90					
31	30.64	1.763	2	258	5.18	3	79		1867.		1875.	
100, Apr. 10	9.61	2.010	1	234	5.91	4	68	0	+0.078	+8.07	-0.580	-5.82
20	19.58	2.230	— 1	207	6.54	4	58	100	-0.037	8.34	0.451	6.36
30	29.55	2.423	0	179	7.08	3	49	200	0.152	8.54	0.377	6.86
May 10	9.53	2.588	0	149	7.52	3	40	300	0.265	8.66	0.272	7.29
20	19.50	2.720	+ 1	117	7.88	3	33	400	0.376	8.71	0.164	7.67
30	29.47	2.821	2	85	8.18	3	26		1868 B.		1876 B.	
June 9	8.44	2.890	· 2	51	8.40	3	20					
19	18.42	2.923	3	+ 16	8.57	3	14	0	-0.339	+8.71	-0.200	-7.55
29	28.39	2.922	3	— 20	8.67	3	8	100	0.448	8.76	-0.091	7.88
July 9	8.36	2.884	4	54	8.73	3	— 1	200	0.553	8.63	+0.019	8.15
								300	0.652	8.47	0.12	8.35
200, 19	18.34	2.814	4	86	8.70	3	+ 6	400	0.746	8.25	0.237	8.49
29	28.31	2.713	5	115	8.61	3	14		1869.		1877.	
Aug. 8	7.28	2.585	5	140	8.42	3	22					
18	17.25	2.436	4	157	8.16	2	30	0	-0.715	+8.33	+0.201	-8.45
28	27.23	2.274	4	167	7.82	2	37	100	0.865	8.06	0.308	8.54
								200	0.887	7.72	0.414	8.55
Sept. 7	6.20	2.106	4	168	7.42	2	44	300	0.931	7.31	0.516	8.50
17	16.17	1.942	4	159	6.95	2	49	400	1.027	6.83	0.614	8.37
27	26.14	1.792	4	140	6.45	1	51					
Oct. 7	6.12	1.665	3	111	5.95	1	49		1870.		1878.	
17	16.09	1.572	3	73	5.49	1	44	0	-1.006	+7.00	+0.581	-8.42
								100	1.066	6.49	0.676	8.25
300, 27	26.06	1.521	2	— 27	5.09	1	35	200	1.116	5.92	0.766	8.01
Nov. 6	5.03	1.519	2	+ 24	4.81	2	22	300	1.157	5 31	0.849	7.71
16	15.01	1.570	1	77	4.66	2	+ 6	400	1.188	4.65	0.920	7.34
26	24.98	1.674	+ 1	130	4.69	3	— 13					
Dec. 6	4.95	1.830	0	182	4.92	3	33		1871.		1879.	
16	14.93	2.037	— 1	229	5.35	4	53	0	-1.179	+4.88	+0.900	-7.47
26	24.90	2.287	— 1	269	5.98	4	72	100	1.203	4.19	0.972	7.05
36	34.87	+2.573	— 1	+300	— 6.78	+ 4	— 88	200	1.217	3.48	1.036	6.58
								300	1.220	2.75	1.091	6.05
								400	1.213	1.96	1.137	5.47
									1872 B.		1880 B.	
								0	-1.216	+2.21	+1.123	-5.67
								100	1.203	1.43	1.163	5.66
								200	1.179	+0.67	1.193	4.40
								300	1.145	-0.13	1.213	3.71
								400	-1.102	-0.92	+1.223	-2.98

✶ ♂ ⊙,   Nov. 22 2.
✶ ♂ Mean Sun,   Nov. 18.8.

TABLE XXIV.—β¹ Scorpii.

R.A. 15h 57.9m.   Dec. − 19° 27′.

Upper transit at fictitious meridian.

Sidereal Day	Mean Day	$\Delta_\odot a$ 1870.	Var. in 10 y.	Diff. for 10 d.	$\Delta_\odot \delta$ 1870.	Var. in 10 y.	Diff. for 10 d.
0, Jan. 0	− 0.11	−1.077	− 2	+281	+ 3.39	0	− 93
10	+ 9.86	0.781	3	307	2.39	0	106
20	19.83	0.465	3	324	1.29	0	114
30	29.80	−0.136	3	332	+ 0.13	+ 1	117
Feb. 9	8.78	+0.197	3	332	− 1.04	1	116
19	18.75	0.526	3	326	2.17	1	110
Mar. 1	0.72	0.848	3	315	3.23	1	101
11	10.69	1.154	3	298	4.19	2	91
21	20.67	1.443	2	279	5.04	2	79
31	30.64	1.711	2	257	5.76	3	66
100, Apr. 10	9.61	1.957	1	234	6.38	4	53
20	19.58	2.178	− 1	207	6.82	4	41
30	29.56	2.371	0	180	7.18	4	31
May 10	9.53	2.537	0	151	7.45	4	22
20	19.50	2.673	+ 1	121	7.62	4	14
30	29.48	2.779	1	89	7.74	4	8
June 9	8.45	2.850	2	55	7.79	3	− 4
19	18.42	2.888	2	+ 20	7.81	3	0
29	28.39	2.890	·	− 16	7.78	3	+ 5
July 9	8.37	2.857	3	49	7.70	2	10
200, 19	18.34	2.792	3	81	7.58	2	15
29	28.31	2.695	4	111	7.40	2	19
Aug. 8	7.28	2.572	4	135	7.20	2	24
18	17.26	2.427	4	153	6.91	2	30
28	27.23	2.268	4	164	6.59	2	34
Sept. 7	6.20	2.101	4	166	6.23	1	38
17	16.18	1.938	3	157	5.84	1	40
27	26.15	1.789	3	139	5.43	1	39
Oct. 7	6.12	1.662	3	113	5.06	1	36
17	16.09	1.566	3	76	4.72	1	30
300, 27	26 07	1.513	2	− 32	4.47	1	19
Nov. 6	5.04	1.504	2	+ 17	4.35	2	+ 5
16	15.01	1.547	1	70	4.36	2	− 11
26	24.98	1.644	+ 1	123	4.56	2	29
Dec. 6	4.96	1.793	0	175	4.94	3	47
16	14.93	1.992	0	221	5.51	3	66
26	24.90	2.232	− 1	259	6.27	4	83
36	34.87	+2.508	− 1	+291	− 7.18	+ 4	− 98

Sidereal Day	$\Delta_\Omega a$	$\Delta_\Omega \delta$	$\Delta_\Omega a$	$\Delta_\Omega \delta$
	1865.		**1873.**	
0	+0.807	+4.34	−1.090	−0.83
100	0 720	5.03	1.040	1.61
200	0.626	5.67	0.982	2.33
300	0.527	6.27	0.915	3.13
400	0.423	6 81	0.842	3.85
	1866.		**1874.**	
0	+0.459	+6.64	−0.867	−3.61
100	0.352	7.14	0.789	4.31
200	0.243	7.58	0.704	4.97
300	0.131	7.96	0.614	5.58
400	0.018	8.27	0.519	6.16
	1867.		**1875.**	
0	+0.056	+8.17	−0.552	−5.97
100	−0.057	8.43	0.454	6.51
200	0.169	8.62	0.352	6.99
300	0.280	8.73	0.248	7.41
400	0.389	8.76	0.141	7.78
	1868 B.		**1876 B.**	
0	−0.353	+8.76	−0.177	−7.66
100	0.459	8.74	−0.070	7.98
200	0.561	8.65	+0.038	8.24
300	0.658	8.48	0.146	8.43
400	0.749	8.23	0.252	8.55
	1869.		**1877.**	
0	−0.719	+8.32	+0.217	−8.52
100	0.805	8.03	0.322	8.50
200	0.885	7.68	0.425	8.50
300	0.956	7.25	0.524	8.52
400	1.020	6.76	0.620	8.38
	1870.		**1878.**	
0	−0.999	+6.94	+0.588	−8.44
100	1.057	6.41	0.680	8.25
200	1.104	5.83	0.767	7.99
300	1.143	5.21	0 848	7.67
400	1.171	4.53	0.922	7.29
	1871.		**1879.**	
0	−1.163	+4.76	+0.897	−7.42
100	1.185	4.07	0.966	6.99
200	1.196	3.34	1.027	6.51
300	1.198	2.59	1.080	5.96
400	1.190	1 81	1.124	5.37
	1872 B.		**1880 B.**	
0	−1.193	+2.07	+1.110	−5.58
100	1.178	1.29	1.147	4.95
200	1.153	+0.50	1.175	4.28
300	1.118	−0.30	1.194	3 57
400	−1.074	−1.09	+1.201	−2.83

✳ ♂ ⊙,   Nov. 23 5.
✳ ♂ Mean Sun,   Nov. 20.1.

TABLE XXIV.—* 87 Draconis (B): Groombridge 2320.

R.A. 16^h 6^m.0.   Dec. + 68$^°$ 9$^′$.

Upper transit at fictitious meridian.

Sidereal Day.	Mean Day.	$\Delta_\odot a$			$\Delta_\odot \delta$			Sidereal Day.	$\Delta_\Omega a$	$\Delta_\Omega \delta$	$\Delta_\Omega a$	$\Delta_\Omega \delta$
		1870.	Var. in 10 y.	Diff. for 10 d.	1870.	Var. in 10 y.	Diff. for 10 d.		1865.		1873.	
								0	−0.564	+4.60	+0.309	−1.08
								100	0.606	5.28	0.368	1.87
								200	0.643	5.92	0.424	2.63
0, Jan. 0	− 0.11	−2.937	+ 3	+389	−11.68	+ 1	−333	300	0.674	6.50	0.476	3.38
10	+ 9.87	2.502	3	477	14.83	0	294	400	0.700	7.03	0.524	4.09
20	19.84	1.987	2	549	17.54	0	245					
30	29.81	1.409	2	602	19.71	0	188		1866.		1874.	
Feb. 9	8.78	0.788	+ 1	635	21.27	0	124	0	−0.692	+6.86	+0.508	−3.86
								100	0.714	7.35	0.553	4.55
19	18.76	−0.145	0	646	22.18	0	− 57	200	0.729	7.77	0.594	5.20
Mar. 1	0.73	+0.497	0	635	22.40	0	+ 12	300	0.738	8.13	0.629	5.81
11	10.70	1.119	− 1	605	21.95	0	79	400	0.741	8.41	0.660	6.37
21	20.68	1.700	1	556	20.84	0	141					
31	30.65	2.225	2	492	19.15	0	197		1867.		1875.	
100, Apr. 10	9.62	2.680	2	415	16.94	0	244	0	−0.741	+8.33	+0.650	−6.19
20	19.59	3.052	2	329	14.31	0	281	100	0.739	8.56	0.677	6.71
30	29.56	3.335	2	236	11.36	0	307	200	0.731	8.73	0.698	7.18
May 10	9.54	3.502	3	139	8.21	0	322	300	0.717	8.81	0.713	7.59
20	19.51	3.612	3	+ 41	4.96	0	326	400	0.696	8.82	0.723	7.94
30	29.48	3.604	2	− 56	− 1.73	0	320		1868 B.		1876 B.	
June 9	8.46	3.500	2	150	+ 1.40	0	303	0	−0.704	+8.83	+0.720	−7.83
19	18.43	3.305	2	239	4.31	0	279	100	0.679	8.79	0.726	8.13
29	28.40	3.025	1	321	6.95	0	247	200	0.619	8.67	0.725	8.37
July 9	8.37	2.666	− 1	394	9.23	0	208	300	0.613	8.47	0.719	8.54
200, 19	18.35	2.239	0	458	11.09	0	165	400	0.571	8.21	0.706	8.63
29	28.32	1.754	+ 1	511	12.51	0	118		1869.		1877.	
Aug. 8	7.29	1.222	1	551	13.44	0	68	0	−0.586	+8.30	+0.711	−8.61
18	17.26	0.656	2	578	13.65	0	+ 16	100	0.541	7.99	0.695	8.66
28	27.24	+0.070	3	591	13.75	0	− 36	200	0.492	7.61	0.673	8.64
Sept. 7	6.21	−0.520	4	588	13.12	0	89	300	0.439	7.16	0.645	8.55
17	16.18	1.100	4	568	11.98	0	140	400	0.382	6.65	0.612	8.39
27	26.16	1.651	5	532	10.34	0	189		1870.		1878.	
Oct. 7	6.13	2.159	6	480	8.22	0	235	0	−0.401	+6.83	+0.624	−8.45
17	16.10	2.606	6	411	5.66	0	276	100	0.342	6.28	0.588	8.24
300, 27	26.07	2.976	7	328	+ 2.71	+ 1	313	200	0.290	5.68	0.546	7.96
Nov. 6	5.04	3.257	7	232	− 0.58	1	343	300	0.216	5 03	0.501	7.61
16	15.02	3.437	8	126	4.12	1	365	400	0.150	4.35	0.450	7.21
26	24.99	3.506	8	− 12	7.84	1	378		1871.		1879.	
Dec. 6	4.96	3.461	8	+104	11.64	1	380	0	−0.173	+1.58	+0.462	−7.35
16	14.94	3.300	8	218	15.41	1	372	100	0.106	3.87	0.415	6.90
26	24.91	3.027	7	326	19.04	1	352	200	−0.038	3.13	0.359	6.39
36	34.88	−2.651	+ 7	+424	−22.41	+ 1	−320	300	+0.02	2.36	0.299	5.83
								400	0.096	1.57	0.237	5.22
									1872 B.		1880 B.	
								0	+0.074	+1.84	+0.258	−5.43
								100	0.140	1.05	0.194	4.79
								200	0.205	+0.25	0.129	4.10
								300	0.269	−0.55	+0.062	3.38
								400	+0.329	−1.35	−0.005	−2.62

＊ ☌ Mean Sun,   May 23.6.
＊ ☌ ☉,   Nov. 25.4.
＊ ☌ Mean Sun,   Nov. 22.2.

TABLE XXIV.—δ Ophiuchi.

R.A. 16h 7.5m   Dec. − 3° 21′

Upper transit at fictitious meridian.

Sidereal Day	Mean Day	Δ⊙a 1870.	Var. in 10 y	Diff. for 10 d.	Δ⊙δ 1870.	Var. in 10 y	Diff. for 10 d.
0, Jan. 0	− 0.11	−1.059	2	+254	− 0.29	0	−167
10	+ 9.87	0.790	2	280	1.96	0	167
20	19.84	0.501	2	298	3.61	1	160
30	29.81	−0.196	3	309	5.15	1	147
Feb. 9	8.78	+0.114	3	311	6.54	1	130
19	18.76	0.423	3	306	7.73	1	107
Mar. 1	0.73	0.725	3	297	8.67	2	82
11	10.70	1.016	3	283	9.36	2	55
21	20.67	1.291	2	265	9.77	2	− 27
31	30.65	1.546	2	245	9.90	2	0
100, Apr 10	9.62	1.781	1	223	9.77	2	+ 24
20	19.59	1.992	1	199	9.43	2	44
30	29.56	2.180	− 1	173	8.90	2	61
May 10	9.54	2.339	0	145	8.23	2	74
20	19.51	2.470	0	116	7.44	2	83
30	29.48	2.572	+ 1	86	6.59	2	88
June 9	8.45	2.642	1	54	5.70	2	89
19	18.43	2.679	2	+ 21	4.83	2	86
29	28.40	2.685	2	− 12	3.99	2	81
July 9	8.37	2.656	2	45	3.21	2	75
200, 19	18.35	2.596	3	75	2.49	2	68
29	28.32	2.507	3	104	1.86	2	59
Aug. 8	7.20	2.390	3	129	1.31	2	50
18	17.26	2.252	3	146	0.87	2	39
28	27.24	2.101	3	157	0.54	2	27
Sept. 7	6.21	1.941	4	162	0.33	2	15
17	16.18	1.781	4	157	0.25	2	+ 1
27	26.15	1.631	3	141	0.32	2	− 14
Oct. 7	6.13	1.502	3	116	0.53	2	30
17	16.10	1.401	3	83	0.91	2	48
300, 27	26.07	1.338	2	− 44	1.49	2	67
Nov. 6	5.05	1.315	2	+ 1	2.26	3	86
16	15 02	1.341	+ 1	50	3.22	3	106
26	24.99	1.416	0	100	4.38	4	126
Dec. 6	4.96	1.541	0	149	5.73	4	143
16	14.94	1.713	0	194	7.22	4	156
26	24.91	1.928	− 1	233	8.84	4	164
36	34.88	+2.177	− 1	+264	−10.49	+ 5	−166

✳ δ ⊙,   Nov. 25.8.
✳ δ Mean Sun, Nov. 22.6.

Sidereal Day	ΔΩa	ΔΩδ	ΔΩa	ΔΩδ
	1865.		**1873.**	
0	+0.662	+4.64	−0.944	−1.14
100	0.579	5.32	0.893	1.93
200	0.491	5.96	0.835	2.69
300	0.398	6.54	0.769	3.44
400	0.302	7.07	0.698	4.15
	1866.		**1874.**	
0	+0.335	+6.90	−0.722	−3.91
100	0.236	7.38	0.647	4.60
200	0.136	7.80	0.566	5.25
300	+0.035	8.16	0.481	5.86
400	−0.067	8.44	0.392	6.42
	1867.		**1875.**	
0	−0.033	+8.35	−0.423	−6.24
100	0.134	8.59	0.332	6 76
200	0.234	8.74	0.238	7.22
300	0.332	8.83	0.142	7.63
400	0.427	8.83	0.046	7.97
	1868 B.		**1876 B.**	
0	−0.396	+8.84	−0.078	−7.86
100	0.488	8.79	+0.019	8.16
200	0.577	8.67	0.116	8.40
300	0.660	8.47	0.211	8.56
400	0.737	8.20	0.306	8.65
	1869.		**1877.**	
0	−0.712	+8.30	+0.274	−8.63
100	0.784	7.95	0 367	8.68
200	0.850	7.59	0.457	8.65
300	0.908	7.14	0.543	8.55
400	0.959	6.63	0.625	8.38
	1870.		**1878.**	
0	−0.943	+6.80	+0.598	−8.45
100	0.988	6.25	0.677	8.23
200	1.024	5.65	0.750	7.95
300	1.051	5.00	0.817	7.60
400	1.069	4.31	0.876	7.18
	1871.		**1879.**	
0	−1.064	+4.55	+0.858	−7.33
100	1.076	3.83	0.914	6.88
200	1.079	3.08	0.963	6.36
300	1 073	2.31	1.003	5.79
400	1.057	1.53	1.036	5.18
	1872 B.		**1880 B.**	
0	−1.064	+1.79	+1.026	−5.39
100	1.042	1.00	1.052	4.74
200	1.012	+0.20	1.070	4.05
300	0.974	−0.61	1.079	3.32
400	−0.928	−1.40	+1.079	−2.57

			TABLE XXIV.—τ Herculis.						
			R.A. 16ʰ 15ᵐ.8.		Dec. + 46° 37'.				
			Upper transit at fictitious meridian.						

Sidereal Day	Mean Day	$\Delta_{\odot}\alpha$			$\Delta_{\odot}\delta$			Sidereal Day	$\Delta_{\Omega}\alpha$	$\Delta_{\Omega}\delta$	$\Delta_{\Omega}\alpha$	$\Delta_{\Omega}\delta$
		1870.	Var. in 10 y.	Diff. for 10 d.	1870.	Var. in 10 y.	Diff. for 10 d.		1865.		1873.	
								0	+0.140	+4.90	−0.400	−1.40
								100	0.077	5.57	0.348	2.19
								200	+0.013	6.20	0.293	2.96
								300	−0.051	6.76	0.235	3.70
0, Jan. 0	− 0.10	−1.621	− 1	+261	− 9.10	+ 2	−330	400	0.115	7.27	0.176	4.40
10	+ 9.87	1.335	1	308	12.25	2	209					
20	19.84	1.008	2	344	15.05	3	258		1866.		1874.	
30	29.82	0.650	2	370	17.30	3	208	0	−0.093	+7.11	−0.196	−4.17
Feb. 9	8.79	−0.272	2	384	19.19	2	152	100	0.157	7.58	0.136	4.85
19	18.76	+0.115	2	388	20.41	2	91	200	0.219	7.98	0.076	5.49
Mar. 1	0.73	0.500	2	381	20.99	1	25	300	0.279	8.31	−0.014	6.09
11	10.71	0.874	3	365	20.91	1	+ 39	400	0.330	8.58	+0.048	6.63
21	20.68	1.227	3	340	20.23	+ 1	98					
31	30.65	1.552	2	309	18.97	0	154		1867.		1875.	
100, Apr. 10	9.62	1.843	2	272	17.17	0	203	0	−0.317	+8.50	+0.027	−6.46
20	19.60	2.095	2	231	14.94	− 1	241	100	0.373	8.71	0.089	6.96
30	29.57	2.304	2	186	12.38	1	271	200	0.425	8.84	0.149	7.41
May 10	9.54	2.467	1	139	9.56	− 1	290	300	0.474	8.90	0.209	7.80
20	19.52	2.582	− 1	91	6.61	0	299	400	0.518	8.88	0.266	8.13
30	29.49	2.648	0	+ 41	3.61	0	299		1868 B.		1876 B.	
June 9	8.46	2.663	0	− 9	− 0.66	0	290	0	−0.504	+8.90	+0.247	−8.02
19	18.43	2.631	0	57	+ 2.16	0	272	100	0.545	8.82	0.303	8.30
29	28.41	2.550	+ 1	103	4.76	0	246	200	0.582	8.68	0.356	8.52
July 9	8.38	2.425	2	147	7.06	0	214	300	0.613	8.45	0.407	8.66
200, 19	18.35	2.258	2	187	9.03	0	178	400	0.639	8.16	0.454	8.73
29	28.32	2.053	2	222	10.61	0	137		1869.		1877.	
Aug. 8	7.30	1.817	3	251	11.77	0	93	0	−0.631	+8.26	+0.441	−8.71
18	17.27	1.553	3	272	12.47	0	+ 47	100	0.654	7.92	0.483	8.74
28	27.24	1.275	3	285	12.70	+ 1	− 1	200	0.676	7.51	0.524	8.68
Sept. 7	6.21	0.986	3	289	12.45	1	49	300	0.681	7.03	0.561	8.56
17	16.19	0.700	3	281	11.72	1	97	400	0.686	6.50	0.593	8.37
27	26.16	0.427	3	263	10.51	2	143					
Oct. 7	6.13	+0.178	3	234	8.86	2	188		1870.		1878.	
17	16.11	−0.037	3	195	6.75	3	231	0	−0.685	+6.68	+0.583	−8.44
300, 27	26.08	0.209	2	147	4.25	3	260	100	0.686	6.11	0.612	8.21
Nov. 6	5.05	0.328	2	90	+ 1.39	3	302	200	0.681	5.49	0.636	7.90
16	15.02	0.387	2	− 28	− 1.77	3	329	300	0.670	4.82	0.655	7.52
26	25.00	0.322	1	+ 38	5.16	4	347	400	0.654	4.11	0.668	7.09
Dec. 6	4.97	0.311	+ 1	104	8.68	4	356					
16	14.94	−0.175	0	168	12.25	4	355		1871.		1879.	
26	24.91	+0.024	0	228	15.76	4	343	0	−0.666	+4.35	+0.664	−7.24
36	34.89	+0.279	0	+280	−19.08	+ 4	−319	100	0.640	3.62	0.674	6.76
								200	0.614	2.86	0.678	6.23
								300	0.584	2.08	0.677	5.64
								400	0.548	1.28	0.670	5.00

✶ ☌ ☉, Nov. 27.7.
✶ ☌ Mean Sun, Nov. 24.7.

	1872 B.		1880 B.	
0	−0.561	+1.55	+0.673	−5 23
100	0.522	+0.74	0.662	4.56
200	0.479	−0.06	0.646	3.85
300	0.433	0.87	0.623	3.11
400	−0.383	−1.67	+0.596	−2.34

TABLE XXIV.—η Draconis.

R.A. 16 22.2 (h m)   Dec. + 61 49 (° ')

Upper transit at fictitious meridian.

Sidereal Day	Mean Day	$\Delta_\odot\alpha$ 1870.	Var. in 10 y.	Diff. for 10 d.	$\Delta_\odot\delta$ 1870.	Var. in 10 y.	Diff. for 10 d.
0, Jan. 0	− 0.10	−2.421	0	+305	−10.17	+1	−343
10	+ 9.87	2.079	0	377	13.46	1	310
20	19.85	1.673	0	437	16.34	1	265
30	29.82	1.211	0	483	18.73	1	210
Feb. 9	8.79	0.714	− 1	511	20.52	0	148
19	18.77	−0.196	1	523	21.68	0	83
Mar. 1	0.74	+0.326	1	518	22.18	0	− 16
11	10.71	0.835	1	500	22.00	0	+ 51
21	20.68	1.317	2	468	21.16	0	116
31	30.66	1.766	2	422	19.70	− 1	175
100, Apr. 10	9.63	2.161	2	368	17.69	1	225
20	19.60	2.498	2	305	15.23	1	265
30	29.57	2.768	2	236	12.42	1	295
May 10	9.55	2.967	1	164	9.36	1	315
20	19.52	3.092	1	88	6.15	1	324
30	29.49	3.141	1	+ 12	2.90	1	323
June 9	8.46	3.115	− 1	− 62	+0.27	− 1	312
19	18.44	3.016	0	134	3.30	0	292
29	28.41	2.846	0	202	6.08	0	263
July 9	8.38	2.612	0	265	8.54	0	228
200, 19	18.36	2.318	+ 1	321	10.63	0	189
29	28.33	1.972	1	369	12.30	0	144
Aug. 8	7.30	1.582	1	408	13.50	0	96
18	17.27	1.158	2	437	14.21	0	+ 46
28	27.25	0.712	2	453	14.41	+ 1	− 6
Sept. 7	6.22	+0.256	3	456	14.09	1	58
17	16.19	−0.197	3	446	13.26	1	110
27	26.16	0.633	3	422	11.90	1	160
Oct. 7	6.14	1.038	4	384	10.07	1	207
17	16.11	1.399	4	333	7.77	1	251
300, 27	26.08	1.701	4	269	5.06	1	291
Nov. 6	5.06	1.934	4	193	+1.96	1	325
16	15.03	2.085	4	108	−1.42	2	351
26	25.00	2.149	4	− 18	5.03	2	370
Dec. 6	4.97	2.121	3	+ 75	8.78	2	377
16	14.95	2.001	3	167	12.51	2	373
26	24.92	1.790	2	254	16.21	2	359
36	34.89	−1.497	+ 2	+333	−19.68	+ 2	−332

✳ ☌ ⊙, Nov. 29.2.
✳ ☌ Mean Sun, Nov. 26.3.

Sidereal Day	$\Delta_\Omega\alpha$	$\Delta_\Omega\delta$	$\Delta_\Omega\alpha$	$\Delta_\Omega\delta$
	1865.		1873.	
0	−0.219	+5.10	−0.011	−1.60
100	0.265	5.76	+0.039	2.39
200	0.309	6.38	0.088	3.16
300	0.351	6.93	0.137	3.89
400	0.390	7.43	0.184	4.59
	1866.		1874.	
0	−0.377	+7.27	+0.169	−4.36
100	0.413	7.72	0.215	5.04
200	0.446	8.11	0.260	5.69
300	0.475	8.43	0.303	6.26
400	0.500	8.67	0.343	6.79
	1867.		1875.	
0	−0.492	+8.60	+0.329	−6.62
100	0.514	8.79	0.367	7.12
200	0.531	8.91	0.402	7.55
300	0.544	8.95	0.434	7.93
400	0.552	8.91	0.462	8.24
	1868 B.		1876 B.	
0	−0.550	+8.93	+0.453	−8.14
100	0.554	8.84	0.478	8.41
200	0.554	8.67	0.500	8.60
300	0.549	8.43	0.518	8.73
400	0.540	8.12	0.531	8.78
	1869.		1877.	
0	−0.544	+8.23	+0.526	−8.77
100	0.531	7.87	0.537	8.77
200	0.514	7.44	0.543	8.71
300	0.491	6.94	0.544	8.57
400	0.466	6.39	0.541	8.36
	1870.		1878.	
0	−0.475	+6.58	+0.543	−8.43
100	0.447	6.00	0.537	8.18
200	0.414	5.36	0.526	7.85
300	0.378	4.67	0.511	7.46
400	0.340	3.95	0.492	7.01
	1871.		1879.	
0	−0.353	+4.20	+0.499	−7.17
100	0.312	3.46	0.477	6.67
200	0.269	2.69	0.452	6.12
300	0.223	1.80	0.422	5.52
400	0.176	1.09	0.388	4.87
	1872 B.		1880 B.	
0	−0.192	+1.36	+0.400	−5.09
100	0.144	+0.56	0.364	4.41
200	0.094	−0.26	0.326	3.69
300	−0.044	1.07	0.284	2.94
400	+0.006	−1.87	+0.240	−2.16

TABLE XXIV.—' A Draconis.

R.A. 16 23.2 (h m)   Dec. + 69 3. (° ')

Upper transit at fictitious meridian.

Sidereal Day	Mean Day	Δ☉α 1870.	Var. in 10y.	Diff. for 10d.	Δ☉δ 1870.	Var. in 10y.	Diff. for 10d.
0, Jan. 0	− 0.09	−3.261	+ 3	+345	−10.18	0	−344
10	+ 9.88	2.866	3	444	13.47	0	311
20	19.85	2.378	3	528	16.36	0	266
30	29.83	1.815	2	594	18.75	0	212
Feb. 9	8.80	1.197	2	639	20.57	0	150
19	18.77	−0.545	1	661	21.74	0	84
Mar. 1	0.74	+0.119	+ 1	662	22.24	0	− 15
11	10.72	0.773	0	642	22.06	0	+ 52
21	20.69	1.396	0	601	21.21	0	116
31	30.66	1.970	− 1	544	19.74	0	176
100, Apr. 10	9.64	2.479	1	472	17.73	0	226
20	19.61	2.909	2	388	15.26	0	267
30	29.58	3.251	2	294	12.42	0	299
May 10	9.55	3.496	2	195	9.32	0	319
20	19.53	3.641	2	+ 94	6.08	0	328
30	29.50	3.683	2	− 9	−2.79	0	327
June 9	8.47	3.623	2	110	+0.43	0	316
19	18.44	3.465	2	206	3.49	0	296
29	28.42	3.212	2	297	6.31	0	267
July 9	8.39	2.873	1	380	8.82	0	232
200, 19	18.36	2.455	− 1	454	10.94	0	192
29	28.33	1.969	0	517	12.64	0	147
Aug. 8	7.31	1.426	0	567	13.87	0	98
18	17.28	0.839	+ 1	604	14.61	0	+ 48
28	27.25	+0.224	2	625	14.83	0	− 4
Sept. 7	6.22	−0.405	3	630	14.53	0	56
17	16.20	1.031	3	615	13 71	0	108
27	26.17	1.636	4	589	12.38	0	159
Oct. 7	6.14	2.204	5	542	10.55	0	207
17	16.12	2.715	6	478	8.25	0	251
300, 27	26.09	3.155	6	398	5.54	0	291
Nov. 6	5.06	3.506	7	303	+2.45	0	325
16	15.03	3.756	7	196	−0.95	0	352
26	25.01	3.896	7	− 81	4.56	0	370
Dec. 6	4.98	3.916	8	+ 40	8.31	0	378
16	14.95	3.816	8	160	12.08	0	375
26	24.92	3.597	7	276	15.76	0	360
36	34.90	−3.267	+ 7	+383	−19.24	0	−333

* ☍ Mean Sun, May 29.2.
* ☌ ☉, Nov. 30.6.
* ☌ Mean Sun, Nov. 27.8.

Sidereal Day	ΔΩα	ΔΩδ	ΔΩα	ΔΩδ
	1865.		**1873.**	
0	−0.536	+5.28	−0.343	−1.79
100	0.565	5.93	0.389	2.58
200	0.589	6.54	0.431	3.34
300	0.609	7.08	0.470	4.07
400	0.622	7.57	0.505	4.77
	1866.		**1874.**	
0	−0.618	+7.41	+0.494	−4.54
100	0.629	7.86	0.526	5.21
200	0.634	8.23	0.554	5.84
300	0.633	8.53	0.577	6.42
400	0.627	8.76	0.596	6 94
	1867.		**1875.**	
0	−0.629	+8.69	+0.590	−6.77
100	0.620	8.87	0.605	7.25
200	0.604	8.97	0.615	7.68
300	0.584	8.99	0.620	8.04
400	0.558	8.93	0.621	8.34
	1868 B.		**1876 B.**	
0	−0.568	+8.96	+0.621	−8.25
100	0.539	8.85	0.618	8.49
200	0.505	8.67	0.609	8.67
300	0.468	8.41	0.596	8.78
400	0.426	8.07	0.577	8.82
	1869.		**1877.**	
0	−0.440	+8.19	+0.584	−8.82
100	0.396	7.81	0.562	8.80
200	0.347	7.37	0.536	8.72
300	0.295	6.86	0.506	8.56
400	0.246	6.29	0.471	8.34
	1870.		**1878.**	
0	−0.264	+6.49	+0.483	−8.42
100	0.209	5.88	0.445	8.15
200	0.154	5.23	0.404	7.81
300	0.096	4.53	0.360	7.40
400	0.038	3.80	0.311	6.93
	1871.		**1879.**	
0	−0.058	+4.05	+0.328	−7.09
100	0.000	3.30	0.278	6.59
200	+0.057	2.52	0.226	6.02
300	0.115	1.72	0.172	5.40
400	0.170	0.91	0.116	4.74
	1872 B.		**1880 B.**	
0	+0.152	+1.18	+0.135	−4.97
100	0.207	+0.37	0.078	4.28
200	0.260	−0.45	+0.021	3.54
300	0.311	1.26	−0.037	2.78
400	+0.359	−2.06	−0.094	−1.99

TABLE XXIV.—ζ Ophiuchi.

R.A. 16^h 30^m.0.   Dec. — 10° 18ʹ.

Upper transit at fictitious meridian.

Sidereal Day	Mean Day	$\Delta_\odot a$ 1870.	Var. in 10 y.	Diff. for 10 d.	$\Delta_\odot \delta$ 1870.	Var. in 10 y.	Diff. for 10 d.
0, Jan. 0	− 0.09	−1.147	3	+243	+ 0.96	0	−124
10	+ 9.88	0.888	3	272	− 0.31	0	129
20	19.85	0.605	3	294	1.60	+1	128
30	29.83	−0.303	3	308	2.85	1	122
Feb. 9	8.80	+0.008	3	313	4.03	1	112
19	18.77	0.321	3	312	5.08	1	97
Mar. 1	0.74	0.630	3	306	5.94	1	78
11	10.72	0.932	3	297	6.63	1	58
21	20.69	1.222	2	282	7.11	2	38
31	30.66	1.495	2	264	7.39	2	− 17
100, Apr. 10	9.63	1.750	2	245	7.46	2	+ 2
20	19.61	1.985	2	224	7.35	2	18
30	29.58	2.197	1	199	7.10	3	32
May 10	9.55	2.382	− 1	172	6.72	3	42
20	19.52	2.541	0	143	6.26	3	49
30	29.50	2.668	0	112	5.74	3	54
June 9	8.47	2.764	+1	80	5.19	3	56
19	18.44	2.827	2	46	4.63	2	55
29	28.42	2.855	2	+ 10	4.10	2	53
July 9	8.39	2.846	2	− 27	3.58	2	50
200, 19	18.36	2.801	3	61	3.11	2	46
29	28.33	2.724	3	92	2.67	2	42
Aug. 8	7.31	2.617	3	120	2.28	2	37
18	17.28	2.485	3	143	1.92	2	32
28	27.25	2.332	3	158	1.63	2	27
Sept. 7	6.22	2.171	3	165	1.39	2	21
17	16.20	2.005	3	164	1.21	2	15
27	26.17	1.846	3	152	1.09	2	+ 7
Oct. 7	6.14	1.705	3	130	1.07	2	− 3
17	16.12	1.589	3	99	1.16	2	15
300, 27	26.09	1.509	2	60	1.37	2	28
Nov. 6	5.06	1.471	2	− 15	1.73	3	44
16	15.03	1.480	1	+ 34	2.25	3	60
26	25.01	1.539	+ 1	84	2.92	3	77
Dec. 6	4.98	1.647	0	133	3.77	3	93
16	14.95	1.804	0	180	4.77	4	107
26	24.92	2.006	0	221	5.90	4	119
36	34.90	+2.244	− 1	+254	− 7.14	+4	−127

Sidereal Day	$\Delta_\Omega a$	$\Delta_\Omega \delta$	$\Delta_\Omega a$	$\Delta_\Omega \delta$
	1865.		**1873.**	
0	+0.715	+5.32	−1.003	−1.86
100	0.629	5.99	0.951	2.64
200	0.538	6.58	0.891	3.40
300	0.441	7.12	0.824	4.14
400	0.341	7.60	0.751	4.83
	1866.		**1874.**	
0	+0.375	+7.45	−0.776	−4.60
100	0.273	7.89	0.699	5.27
200	0.168	8.26	0.615	5.89
300	+0.062	8.56	0.527	6.47
400	−0.045	8.78	0.435	6.99
	1867.		**1875.**	
0	−0.009	+8.71	−0.466	−6.82
100	0.116	8.89	0.372	7.30
200	0.221	8.98	0.274	7.72
300	0.325	9.00	0.174	8.08
400	0.425	8.94	0.073	8.37
	1868 B.		**1876 B.**	
0	−0.392	+8.97	−0.107	−8.28
100	0.490	8.85	−0.005	8.52
200	0.584	8.66	+0.097	8.70
300	0.672	8.40	0.197	8.80
400	0.755	8.06	0.297	8.83
	1869.		**1877.**	
0	−0.728	+8.18	+0.264	−8.83
100	0.806	7.80	0.362	8.62
200	0.877	7.34	0.457	8.72
300	0.940	6.83	0.549	8.56
400	0.905	6.26	0.636	8.33
	1870.		**1878.**	
0	−0.977	+6.46	+0.607	−8.41
100	1.026	5.85	0.691	8.13
200	1.066	5.19	0.770	7.79
300	1.097	4.49	0.842	7.37
400	1.118	3.76	0.908	6.90
	1871.		**1879.**	
0	−1.112	+4.01	+0.886	−7.06
100	1.127	3.25	0.947	6.55
200	1.133	2.47	1.000	5.98
300	1.128	1.67	1.044	5.36
400	1.115	0.85	1.081	4.69
	1872 B.		**1880 B.**	
0	−1.120	+1.13	+1.069	−4.92
100	1.100	+0.31	1.099	4.22
200	1.071	−0.51	1.120	3.48
300	1.033	1.32	1.132	2.72
400	−0.986	−2.12	+1.134	−1.93

✻ ♂ ☉,   Dec. 1.0.
✻ ♂ Mean Sun, Nov. 28.3.

TABLE XXIV.—• α Trianguli Australis.

R.A. 16h 34.9.   Dec. — 68° 47'

Upper transit at fictitous meridian.

Sidereal Day	Mean Day	Δ☉α 1870.	Var.in 10y.	Diff. for 10 d.	Δ☉δ 1870.	Var.in 10y.	Diff. for 10 d.
0, Jan. 0	— 0.09	-3.157	—12	+550	+ 9.53	— 7	+179
10	+ 9.80	2.565	14	632	11.15	6	143
20	19.86	1.809	15	696	12.38	5	103
30	29.88	1.178	16	742	13.21	3	61
Feb. 9	8.80	-0.422	16	768	13.61	— 1	+ 19
19	18.78	+0.353	15	778	13.58	0	— 23
Mar. 1	0.75	1.130	14	773	13.15	+ 2	63
11	10.72	1.894	13	753	12.34	4	100
21	20.70	2.632	11	722	11.16	5	135
31	30.67	3.334	9	679	9.65	7	166
100, Apr. 10	9.64	3.987	7	626	7.85	8	193
20	19.61	4.583	4	564	5.80	9	216
30	29.58	5.112	— 2	493	3.54	10	235
May 10	9.56	5.567	+ 1	415	+ 1.11	11	250
20	19.53	5.939	4	329	— 1.43	12	259
30	29.50	6.222	7	236	4.04	12	262
June 9	8.48	6.410	10	140	6.65	12	259
19	18.45	6.500	13	+ 40	9.21	12	251
29	28.42	6.490	15	— 60	11.65	12	236
July 9	8.39	6.380	17	158	13.90	11	214
200, 19	18.37	6.175	19	251	15.91	11	186
29	28.34	5.882	20	334	17.60	10	152
Aug. 8	7.31	5.512	22	405	18.92	9	113
18	17.28	5.078	22	460	19.83	7	69
28	27.26	4.598	22	496	20.29	6	— 22
Sept. 7	6.23	4.094	22	510	20.27	5	+ 26
17	16.20	3.586	21	501	19.77	4	74
27	26.18	3.100	20	467	18.80	2	120
Oct. 7	6.15	2.660	18	410	17.39	+ 1	162
17	16.12	2.289	16	330	15.58	0	198
300, 27	26.09	2.006	14	231	13.46	— 1	226
Nov. 6	5.07	1.831	11	—118	11.09	1	246
16	15.04	1.775	8	+ 6	8.58	1	255
26	25.01	1.845	6	134	6.02	1	256
Dec. 6	4.98	2.043	+ 3	261	3.51	— 1	245
16	14.96	2.365	0	391	— 1.14	0	227
26	24.93	2.801	— 2	489	+ 1.00	+1	200
36	34.90	+3.338	— 4	+583	+ 2.83	+ 2	+166

✱ ♂ Mean Sun, May 30.9.
✱ ♂ ☉, Dec. 2.2.
✱ ♂ Mean Sun, Nov. 29.5.

Sidereal Day	Δ☊α	Δ☊δ	Δ☊α	Δ☊δ
	1865.		1873.	
0	+1.761	+5.46	—2.148	—2.01
100	1.624	6.10	2.067	2.80
200	1.473	6.70	2.005	3.56
300	1.308	7.23	1.913	4.29
400	1.132	7.71	1.803	4.98
	1866.		1874.	
0	+1.193	+7.56	—1.842	—4.75
100	1.009	7.98	1.722	5.41
200	0.817	8.34	1.588	6.03
300	0.618	8.63	1.441	6.60
400	0.413	8.84	1.282	7.11
	1867.		1875.	
0	+0.482	+8.78	—1.337	—6.94
100	0.275	8.94	1.171	7.42
200	+0.065	9.02	0.996	7.83
300	—0.145	9.03	0.813	8.17
400	0.353	8.95	0.623	8.45
	1868 B.		1876 B.	
0	—0.283	+8.98	—0.688	—8.37
100	0.490	8.86	0.494	8.60
200	0.692	8.65	0.297	8.76
300	0.887	8.37	—0.097	8.85
400	1.075	8.02	+0.104	8.86
	1869.		1877.	
0	—1.013	+8.15	+0.037	—8.87
100	1.194	7.75	0.237	8.84
200	1.364	7.28	0.437	8.73
300	1.522	6.75	0.633	8.55
400	1.657	6.17	0.824	8.30
	1870.		1878.	
0	—1.619	+6.37	+0.761	—8.39
100	1.754	5.75	0.947	8.10
200	1.874	5.08	1.126	7.74
300	1.976	4.37	1.207	7.31
400	2.062	3.63	1.457	6.82
	1871.		1879.	
0	—2.035	+3.88	+1.404	—6.99
100	2.109	3.12	1.557	6.46
200	2.165	2.33	1.697	5.88
300	2.201	1.52	1.823	5.21
400	2.220	0.70	1.935	4.56
	1872 B.		1880 B.	
0	—2.216	+0.98	+1.899	—4.79
100	2.222	+0.15	2.000	4.09
200	2.209	—0.67	2.083	3.34
300	2.178	1.48	2.149	2.57
400	—2.129	—2.28	+2.199	—1.77

TABLE XXIV.—η Herculis.

R.A. 16^h 38^m.4.   Dec. + 39° 10′.

Upper transit at fictitious meridian.

Sidereal Day	Mean Day	Δ☉α 1870.	Var. in 10 y.	Diff. for 10 d.	Δ☉δ 1870.	Var. in 10 y.	Diff. for 10 d.
0, Jan. 0	− 0.09	−1.520	− 1	+224	− 6.99	+ 2	−322
10	+ 9.89	1.273	1	267	10.11	2	299
20	19.86	0.988	2	302	12.94	2	265
30	29.83	0.672	2	328	15.38	2	221
Feb. 9	8.80	−0.335	2	344	17.34	1	170
19	18.78	+0.013	3	351	18.77	1	114
Mar. 1	0.75	0.364	3	348	19.61	1	− 53
11	10.72	0.707	2	338	19.83	1	+ 7
21	20.69	1.038	2	323	19.47	+1	67
31	30.67	1.350	2	300	18.50	0	123
100, Apr 10	9.64	1.636	2	271	17.04	0	171
20	19.61	1.891	2	239	15.11	− 1	213
30	29.59	2.112	1	203	12.82	1	246
May 10	9.56	2.296	− 1	164	10.23	1	269
20	19.53	2.439	0	123	7.48	1	281
30	29.50	2.541	0	80	4.64	1	286
June 9	8.48	2.593	0	+ 35	− 1.79	1	282
19	18.45	2.611	0	− 9	+ 0.97	1	269
29	28.42	2.580	+ 1	54	3.57	− 1	249
July 9	8.39	2.504	1	96	5.93	0	222
200, 19	18.37	2.389	1	135	8.00	0	191
29	28.34	2.235	2	173	9.74	0	156
Aug. 8	7.31	2.046	2	203	11.11	0	116
18	17.29	1.832	3	226	12.06	+1	74
28	27.26	1.598	3	244	12.58	1	+ 30
Sept. 7	6.23	1.348	3	252	12.65	2	− 15
17	16.20	1.097	3	249	12.28	2	60
27	26.18	0.854	2	237	11.45	3	106
Oct. 7	6.15	0.627	2	215	10.17	3	150
17	16.12	0.427	2	183	8.46	4	192
300, 27	26.09	0.264	2	141	6.34	4	231
Nov. 6	5.07	0.148	2	91	3.85	4	266
16	15.04	0.083	1	− 37	+ 1.04	5	295
26	25.01	0.075	1	+ 22	− 2.03	5	317
Dec. 6	4.98	0.127	+ 1	81	5.28	5	332
16	14.96	0.237	0	139	8.64	5	338
26	24.93	0.405	0	193	12.00	6	331
36	34.90	+0.622	− 1	+240	−15.23	+ 6	−314

✶ ☌ ☉,   Dec. 2.9.
✶ ☌ Mean Sun, Nov. 30.4.

Sidereal Day	Δ☊α	Δ☊δ	Δ☊α	Δ☊δ
	1865.		**1873.**	
0	+0.282	+5.57	−0.528	−2.12
100	0.218	6.21	0.480	2.90
200	0.152	6.80	0.426	3.66
300	0.085	7.32	0.373	4.38
400	0.016	7.79	0.315	5.07
	1866.		**1874.**	
0	+0.040	+7.64	−0.335	−4.85
100	−0.029	8.06	0.275	5.50
200	0.097	8.41	0.213	6.12
300	0.165	8.69	0.150	6.65
400	0.231	8.89	0.085	7.18
	1867.		**1875.**	
0	−0.209	+8.83	−0.107	−7.02
100	0.274	8.98	−0.042	7.49
200	0.336	9.05	+0.024	7.89
300	0.395	9.04	0.089	8.23
400	0.451	8.96	0.154	8.50
	1868 B.		**1876 B.**	
0	−0.433	+8.99	+0.132	−8.42
100	0.486	8.86	0.196	8.64
200	0.535	8.64	0.258	8.79
300	0.579	8.35	0.318	8.87
400	0.618	7.99	0.375	8.88
	1869.		**1877.**	
0	−0.605	+8.12	+0.356	−8.89
100	0.640	7.71	0.411	8.85
200	0.670	7.23	0.463	8.73
300	0.694	6.70	0.512	8.54
400	0.712	6.10	0.556	8.29
	1870.		**1878.**	
0	−0.706	+6.31	+0.541	−8.38
100	0.721	5.68	0.583	8.08
200	0.728	5.01	0.619	7.71
300	0.729	4.29	0.651	7.27
400	0.724	3.54	0.677	6.77
	1871.		**1879.**	
0	−0.726	+3.80	+0.669	−6.95
100	0.717	3.03	0.691	6.41
200	0.702	2.23	0.708	5.82
300	0.681	1.42	0.719	5.18
400	0.654	0.60	0.724	4.49
	1872 B.		**1880 B.**	
0	−0.664	+0.88	+0.723	−4.73
100	0.633	+0.05	0.724	4.02
200	0.598	−0.77	0.719	3.27
300	0.557	1.58	0.708	2.49
400	−0.512	−2.38	+0.690	−1.69

TABLE XXIV.—κ Ophiuchi.

R.A. 16h 51.5m.   Dec. +9° 35′.

Upper transit at fictitious meridian.

Sidereal Day	Mean Day	$\Delta_\odot\alpha$ 1870.	Var. in 10 y.	Diff. for 10 d.	$\Delta_\odot\delta$ 1870.	Var. in 10 y.	Diff. for 10 d.
0, Jan. 0	− 0.08	−1.215	− 1	+208	− 2.42	0	−217
10	+ 9.89	0.990	1	242	4.56	0	210
20	19.87	0.734	2	267	6.60	+ 1	195
30	29.84	0.458	2	284	8.44	1	172
Feb. 9	8.81	−0.168	2	295	10.02	1	143
19	18.79	+0.130	2	301	11.29	1	110
Mar. 1	0.76	0.431	2	299	12.20	1	71
11	10.73	0.726	3	291	12.70	1	− 31
21	20.70	1.011	3	280	12.83	1	+ 8
31	30.68	1.285	2	265	12.55	1	46
100, Apr. 10	9.65	1.541	2	247	11.92	1	80
20	19.62	1.779	1	227	10.96	1	109
30	29.59	1.994	1	203	9.75	1	133
May 10	9.57	2.185	1	177	8.31	1	152
20	19.54	2.347	− 1	148	6.73	1	163
30	29.51	2.480	0	116	5.06	1	169
June 9	8.49	2.579	+ 1	82	3.36	1	169
19	18.46	2.644	1	47	1.69	1	164
29	28.43	2.673	1	+ 12	0.10	1	155
July 9	8.40	2.668	1	− 25	+ 1.39	2	142
200, 19	18.38	2.623	2	61	2.73	2	125
29	28.35	2.546	2	94	3.88	2	105
Aug. 8	7.32	2.437	2	123	4.83	2	85
18	17.29	2.302	3	147	5.57	2	62
28	27.27	2.144	3	165	6.07	2	38
Sept. 7	6.24	1.974	3	176	6.33	2	+ 14
17	16.21	1.795	3	177	6.35	2	− 11
27	26.18	1.623	3	168	6.11	3	37
Oct. 7	6.16	1.462	3	151	5.61	3	63
17	16.13	1.323	2	125	4.84	3	90
300, 27	26.10	1.215	2	89	3.81	4	116
Nov. 6	5.08	1.147	2	48	2.52	4	141
16	15.05	1.120	1	− 2	+ 0.99	4	165
26	25.02	1.143	+ 1	+ 46	− 0.77	4	186
Dec. 6	4.99	1.213	0	95	2.71	4	202
16	14.97	1.333	0	142	4.79	4	213
26	24.94	1.497	− 1	184	6.95	5	217
36	34.91	+1.700	− 1	+221	− 9.11	+ 6	−215

✳ ♂ ☉, Dec. 5.9.
✳ ♂ Mean Sun, Dec. 3.7.

Sidereal Day	$\Delta_\Omega\alpha$	$\Delta_\Omega\delta$	$\Delta_\Omega\alpha$	$\Delta_\Omega\delta$
	1865.		**1873.**	
0	+0.565	+5.93	−0.837	−2.52
100	0.487	6.55	0.787	3.30
200	0.404	7.11	0.730	4.05
300	0.318	7.61	0.667	4.76
400	0.230	8.05	0.599	5.44
	1866.		**1874.**	
0	+0.260	+7.91	−0.623	−5.22
100	0.170	8.30	0.552	5.86
200	+0.078	8.62	0.476	6.45
300	−0.015	8.86	0.397	6.99
400	0.107	9.03	0.314	7.47
	1867.		**1875.**	
0	−0.076	+8.98	−0.342	−7.32
100	0.168	9.10	0.258	7.76
200	0.258	9.13	0.172	8.13
300	0.346	9.08	−0.084	8.44
400	0.431	8.96	+0.004	8.68
	1868 B.		**1876 B.**	
0	−0.403	+9.01	−0.026	−8.60
100	0.485	8.83	+0.062	8.79
200	0.563	8.58	0.150	8.91
300	0.636	8.25	0.237	8.96
400	0.704	7.85	0.321	8.93
	1869.		**1877.**	
0	−0.662	+7.99	+0.293	−8.95
100	0.745	7.55	0.376	8.87
200	0.802	7.04	0.456	8.72
300	0.851	6.47	0.533	8.50
400	0.893	5.85	0.605	8.20
	1870.		**1878.**	
0	−0.880	+6.06	+0.581	−8.31
100	0.917	5.41	0.650	7.97
200	0.946	4.71	0.714	7.58
300	0.966	3.97	0.772	7.09
400	0.979	3.19	0.824	6.56
	1871.		**1879.**	
0	−0.975	+3.46	+0.807	−6.75
100	0.982	2.67	0.855	6.18
200	0.980	1.86	0.895	5.56
300	0.970	1.03	0.928	4.89
400	0.953	0.20	0.954	4.18
	1872 B.		**1880 B.**	
0	−0.960	+0.48	+0.946	−4.42
100	0.936	−0.35	0.966	3.69
200	0.905	1.17	0.976	2.91
300	0.866	1.99	0.982	2.12
400	−0.821	−2.78	+0.977	−1.30

TABLE XXIV.—d Herculis.

R.A. 16 56.8. (h m)   Dec. + 33 45. (° ')

Upper transit at fictitious meridian.

Sidereal Day	Mean Day	$\Delta_\odot a$ 1870.	Var. in 10 y.	Diff. for 10 d.	$\Delta_\odot \delta$ 1870.	Var. in 10 y.	Diff. for 10 d.
0, Jan. 0	− 0.07	−1.471	0	+201	− 5.48	+ 2	−310
10	+ 9.90	1.249	− 1	242	8.50	2	292
20	19.87	0.989	2	277	11.28	2	264
30	29.84	0.698	2	302	13.74	2	225
Feb. 9	8.82	0.387	2	320	15.76	2	178
19	18.79	−0.061	2	329	17.29	1	126
Mar. 1	0.76	+0.269	2	331	18.27	+ 1	69
11	10.73	0.598	2	325	18.67	0	− 11
21	20.71	0.917	2	312	18.49	0	+ 45
31	30.68	1.220	2	295	17.77	0	99
100, Apr. 10	9.65	1.506	2	273	16.53	0	149
20	19.63	1.765	2	246	14.81	0	191
30	29.60	1.996	1	215	12.73	− 1	224
May 10	9 57	2.195	1	181	10.35	1	249
20	19.54	2.357	− 1	144	7.77	1	266
30	29.52	2.482	0	105	5.06	− 1	274
June 9	8.49	2.567	0	63	− 2.32	0	272
19	18.46	2.609	0	+ 21	+ 0.36	0	263
29	28.43	2.609	+ 1	− 21	2.92	0	248
July 9	8.41	2.567	1	64	5.29	0	225
200, 19	18.38	2.482	1	105	7.40	0	197
29	28.35	2.359	1	141	9.21	0	165
Aug. 8	7 33	2.202	2	173	10.68	+ 1	129
18	17.30	2.015	2	200	11.78	1	91
28	27.27	1.805	2	220	12.50	1	50
Sept. 7	6.24	1.579	2	231	12.78	2	+ 8
17	16.22	1.347	3	232	12.65	2	− 35
27	26.19	1.119	3	224	12.09	3	78
Oct. 7	6.16	0.903	2	206	11.09	3	120
17	16.13	0.711	2	177	9.69	3	161
300, 27	26.11	0.552	2	140	7.87	4	201
Nov. 6	5.08	0.433	2	96	5.69	4	236
16	15.05	0 362	1	− 45	3.17	4	266
26	25.02	0.345	+ 1	+ 10	+ 0.38	5	291
Dec. 6	5.00	0.382	0	65	− 2.63	5	309
16	14.97	0.475	0	120	5.77	6	318
26	24.94	0.622	0	171	8.96	6	316
36	34.92	+0.816	− 1	+216	−12.06	+ 5	−303

Sidereal Day	$\Delta_\Omega a$	$\Delta_\Omega \delta$	$\Delta_\Omega a$	$\Delta_\Omega \delta$
	1865.		**1873.**	
0	+0.366	+6.07	−0.606	−2.68
100	0.301	6.68	0.560	3.46
200	0.233	7.23	0.510	4.20
300	0.16(8	7.73	0.456	4.91
400	0.092	8.15	0.398	5.58
	1866.		**1874.**	
0	+0.116	+8.01	−0.418	−5.36
100	+0.044	8.39	0.357	5.99
200	−0.029	8.70	0.295	6.58
300	0.101	8.93	0.229	7.11
400	0.172	9.08	0.162	7.58
	1867.		**1875.**	
0	−0.148	+9.04	−0.185	−7.43
100	0.218	9.14	0.117	7.86
200	0.287	9.15	−0.048	8.22
300	0.353	9.09	+0.021	8.51
400	0.416	8.95	0.090	8 74
	1868 B.		**1876 B.**	
0	−0.393	+9.01	+0.067	−8.67
100	0.455	8.82	0.135	8.85
200	0.512	8.55	0.203	8.95
300	0.563	8.20	0.269	8 93
400	0.610	7.79	0.332	8.94
	1869.		**1877.**	
0	−0 595	+7.94	+0.311	−8.96
100	0.638	7.48	0.373	8.87
200	0.676	6.96	0.432	8.71
300	0.707	6.38	0.487	8.47
400	0.733	5.74	0.539	8.16
	1870.		**1878.**	
0	−0.725	+5.96	+0.522	−8.27
100	0.746	5.29	0.571	7.92
200	0.761	4.58	0.615	7.49
300	0.769	3.83	0.654	7.01
400	0.770	3.05	0.688	6.47
	1871.		**1879.**	
0	−0.771	+3.32	+0.677	−6.66
100	0.767	2.52	0.707	6.08
200	0.758	1.70	0.731	5.45
300	0.743	0.84	0.749	4.77
400	0.721	+0.04	0.762	4.05
	1872 B.		**1880 B.**	
0	−0.729	+0.32	+0.758	−4.30
100	0.703	−0.51	0.766	3.55
200	0.671	1.34	0.767	2.77
300	0.633	2.15	0.762	1.97
400	−0.591	−2.94	+0.751	−1.15

✶ d ☉,   Dec. 7.2.
✶ d Mean Sun,   Dec. 5.1.

TABLE XXIV.—* ε Ursæ Minoris.

R.A. 16 59.4 (h m)   Dec. + 82 15 (° ')

Upper transit at fictitious meridian.

Sidereal Day	Mean Day	$\Delta_\odot a$ 1870	Var.in 10y	Diff. for 10d	$\Delta_\odot \delta$ 1870	Var.in 10y	Diff. for 10d
0, Jan. 0	− 0.07	9.311	+35	+ 498	− 8.03	− 9	−342
10	+ 9.90	8.664	41	792	11.33	8	315
20	19.88	7.737	46	1056	14.30	7	277
30	29.85	6.565	50	1280	16.84	6	230
Feb. 9	8.82	5.193	52	1455	18.86	5	174
19	18.79	3.678	52	1572	20.29	4	112
Mar. 1	0.77	2.068	51	1629	21.08	3	− 46
11	10.74	− 0.436	48	1625	21.21	− 1	+ 21
21	20.71	+ 1.162	44	1561	20.68	0	85
31	30.68	2.668	39	1442	19.54	+ 2	145
100, Apr. 10	9.66	4.029	33	1273	17.82	3	198
20	19.63	5.260	26	1063	15.61	4	243
30	29.60	6.145	18	822	13.00	5	278
May 10	9.58	6.837	11	558	10.09	5	305
20	19.55	7.257	+ 4	+ 279	6.97	6	318
30	29.52	7.394	− 3	− 5	3.76	6	323
June 9	8.49	7.248	10	287	− 0.55	6	317
19	18.47	6.824	16	558	+ 2.56	5	303
29	28.44	6.137	21	814	5.48	4	281
July 9	8.41	5.203	25	1049	8.14	3	251
200, 19	18.38	4.046	28	1259	10.47	2	215
29	28.36	2.695	29	1430	12.42	+ 1	174
Aug. 8	7.33	+ 1.179	29	1587	13.94	− 1	130
18	17.30	− 0.467	28	1700	15.01	2	83
28	27.28	2.208	26	1775	15.59	4	+ 33
Sept. 7	6.25	4.008	22	1812	15.67	6	− 17
17	16.22	5.818	18	1808	15.25	8	68
27	26.19	7.606	12	1761	14.32	9	118
Oct. 7	6 16	9.326	− 5	1672	12.90	11	166
17	16.14	10.936	+ 2	1540	11.02	12	211
300, 27	26.11	12.392	11	1366	8 69	14	253
Nov. 6	5.08	13.655	19	1153	5.96	15	290
16	15.06	14.686	28	904	+ 2.90	16	321
26	25.03	15.453	37	625	− 0.43	17	344
Dec. 6	5.00	15.929	46	324	3.94	17	357
16	14.97	16.097	54	− 11	7.54	18	361
26	24.95	15.949	62	+ 306	11.12	18	353
36	34.92	−15.489	+68	+ 612	−14.56	−17	−333

* δ Mean Sun, June 6.1.
* δ ⊙, Dec. 7.8.
* δ Mean Sun, Dec. 5.7.

Sidereal Day	$\Delta_\Omega a$	$\Delta_\Omega \delta$	$\Delta_\Omega a$	$\Delta_\Omega \delta$
1863.	s	"	**1873.** s	"
0	−2.263	+6.15	+2.464	−2.74
100	2.154	6.76	2.447	3.52
200	2.025	7.31	2.410	4.26
300	1.879	7.79	2.353	4.97
400	1.716	8.21	2.277	5.63
1866.			**1874.**	
0	−1.773	+8.07	+2.305	−5.41
100	1.600	8.45	2.217	6.04
200	1.413	8.74	2.110	6.62
300	1.213	8.96	1.986	7.15
400	1.003	9.10	1.846	7.62
1867.			**1875.**	
0	−1.075	+9.06	+1.895	−7.46
100	0.859	9.16	1.746	7.89
200	0.636	9.17	1.582	8.25
300	0.407	9.10	1.405	8.54
400	0.175	8.95	1.216	8.76
1868 B.			**1876 B.**	
0	−0.254	+9.01	+1.281	−8.69
100	−0.021	8.81	1.026	8.86
200	+0.212	8.53	0.882	8.96
300	0.443	8.18	0.671	8.99
400	0.669	7.76	0.454	8.94
1869.			**1877.**	
0	+0.593	+7.91	+0.527	−8.97
100	0.815	7.44	0.308	8.87
200	1.029	6.91	+0.086	8.70
300	1.234	6.33	−0.138	8.46
400	1.428	5.69	0.361	8.15
1870.			**1878.**	
0	+1.364	+5.91	−0.286	−8.26
100	1.549	5.24	0.507	7.90
200	1.721	4.52	0.725	7.48
300	1.877	3.77	0.957	6.99
400	2.017	2.98	1.143	6.45
1871.			**1879.**	
0	+1.971	+3.25	−1.074	−6.64
100	2.100	2.45	1.27?	6.06
200	2.210	1.63	1.462	5.42
300	2.301	+0.81	1.640	4.74
400	2.373	−0.03	1.804	4.02
1872 B.			**1880 B.**	
0	+2.351	+0.25	−1.750	−4.27
100	2.409	−0.58	1.904	3.52
200	2.447	1.41	2.043	2.74
300	2.464	2.22	2.165	1.94
400	+2.461	−3.01	−2.269	−1.12

TABLE XXIV.—44 Ophiuchi.

R.A. 17 18.4. (h m)   Dec. − 24 3. (° ')

Upper transit at fictitious meridian.

Sidereal Day	Mean Day	$\Delta_\odot a$ 1870.	Var. in 10 y.	Diff. for 10 d.	$\Delta_\odot \delta$ 1870.	Var. in 10 y.	Diff. for 10 d.
0, Jan. 0	− 0.06	−1.370	− 1	+221	+ 1.99	− 2	− 23
10	+ 9.91	1.130	2	256	1.70	2	33
20	19.89	0.860	2	285	1.33	1	41
30	29.86	0.582	3	307	0.89	0	46
Feb. 9	8.83	−0.248	3	321	+ 0.42	0	48
19	18.80	+0.078	3	330	− 0 06	+ 1	47
Mar. 1	0.78	0.410	4	331	0.50	1	44
11	10.75	0.738	4	328	0.92	1	39
21	20.72	1.064	4	322	1.28	2	33
31	30.69	1.380	4	311	1.58	2	27
100, Apr. 10	9.67	1.684	4	297	1.82	3	20
20	19.64	1.972	3	280	1.99	3	15
30	29.61	2.242	2	259	2.13	3	12
May 10	9.59	2.489	1	234	2.24	4	11
20	19.56	2.708	− 1	205	2.35	5	10
30	29.53	2.898	0	173	2.44	5	10
June 9	8.50	3.053	0	137	2.54	4	12
19	18.48	3.172	+ 1	99	2.68	4	14
29	28.45	3.251	2	57	2.82	4	15
July 9	8.42	3.286	2	+ 14	2.99	4	16
200, 19	18.39	3.280	3	− 28	3.14	4	16
29	28.37	3.231	3	69	3.31	4	15
Aug. 8	7.34	3.144	3	105	3.44	4	11
18	17.31	3.023	4	137	3.53	4	− 6
28	27.29	2.872	4	162	3.56	4	0
Sept. 7	6.26	2.701	4	177	3.53	3	+ 7
17	16.23	2.520	4	183	3.42	3	14
27	26.20	2.338	4	179	3.24	3	22
Oct. 7	6.18	2.165	4	164	2.99	3	27
17	16.15	2.013	3	138	2.71	3	29
300, 27	26.12	1.893	3	102	2.41	3	30
Nov. 6	5.09	1.812	3	58	2.11	3	29
16	15.07	1.778	2	− 9	1.83	3	24
26	25.04	1.795	2	+ 43	1.63	3	16
Dec. 6	5.01	1.865	+ 1	97	1.51	3	+ 7
16	14.99	1.988	0	148	1.50	3	− 4
26	24.96	2.159	0	194	1.60	3	15
36	34.93	+2.374	− 1	+235	− 1.80	+ 3	− 27

＊ ☌ ☉,   Dec. 12.1.
＊ ☌ Mean Sun,   Dec. 10.6.

Sidereal Day	$\Delta_\Omega a$	$\Delta_\Omega \delta$	$\Delta_\Omega a$	$\Delta_\Omega \delta$
	1865.		1873.	
0	+0.795	+6.61	−1.114	−3.33
100	0.700	7.18	1.056	4.09
200	0.599	7.69	0.990	4.81
300	0.492	8.13	0.916	5.50
400	0.381	8.51	0.835	6.13
	1866.		1874.	
0	+0.418	+8.40	−0.863	−5.92
100	0.305	8.72	0.777	6.52
200	0.189	8.97	0.684	7.07
300	+0.071	9 14	0.587	7.56
400	−0.048	9.23	0.484	7.98
	1867.		1875.	
0	−0.008	+9.21	−0.519	−7.85
100	0.126	9.24	0.414	8.23
200	0.243	9.20	0.306	8.54
300	0.358	9.08	0.195	8.78
400	0.470	8.85	0.082	8.95
	1868 B.		1876 B.	
0	−0.433	+8.95	−0.120	−8.90
100	0.542	8.70	−0.008	9.02
200	0.646	8.37	+0.106	9.07
300	0.744	7.97	0.218	9.04
400	0.836	7.50	0.329	8.94
	1869.		1877.	
0	−0.806	+7.66	+0.202	−8.98
100	0.893	7.15	0.400	8.83
200	0.972	6.57	0.506	8.60
300	1.042	5.94	0.608	8.30
400	1.103	5.26	0.705	7.94
	1870.		1878.	
0	−1.083	+5.50	+0.673	−8 07
100	1.138	4.79	0.766	7.66
200	1.182	4.04	0.853	7.18
300	1.217	3.26	0.935	6.65
400	1.241	2.45	1.006	6.06
	1871.		1879.	
0	−1.234	+2.73	+0.982	−6.26
100	1.251	1.96	1.050	5.64
200	1.257	1.07	1.109	4 96
300	1.252	+0.23	1.158	4.24
400	1.257	−0.62	1.198	3.48
	1872 B.		1880 B.	
0	−1.243	−0.33	+1.186	−3.74
100	1.221	1.17	1.220	2.97
200	1.189	1.99	1.243	2 16
300	1.147	2.80	1.256	1.33
400	−1.096	−3.55	+1.258	−0.50

TABLE XXIV.—β Draconis.

R.A. 17^h 27^m.5.   Dec. + 52° 24′.

Upper transit at fictitious meridian.

Sidereal Day	Mean Day	Δ☉α 1870.	Var. in 10y.	Diff. for 10 d.	Δ☉δ 1870.	Var. in 10y.	Diff. for 10 d.
0, Jan. 0	− 0.05	−2.123	0	+170	− 5.15	+ 2	−353
10	+ 9.92	1.922	− 1	232	8.61	2	336
20	19.89	1.663	1	287	11.84	2	307
30	29.87	1.351	1	334	14.71	1	266
Feb. 9	8.84	0.998	1	370	17.13	1	216
19	18.81	0.614	2	396	19.00	1	157
Mar. 1	0.78	−0.210	2	410	20.25	1	94
11	10.76	+0.202	2	413	20.88	+ 1	− 29
21	20.73	0.613	2	407	20.83	0	+ 38
31	30.70	1.013	2	390	20.13	0	100
100, Apr. 10	9.67	1.390	2	363	18.84	0	158
20	19.65	1.727	2	329	16.99	0	209
30	29.62	2.046	2	289	14.68	0	252
May 10	9.59	2.313	1	242	11.98	− 1	286
20	19.56	2.529	1	189	8.99	1	309
30	29.54	2.690	− 1	134	5.83	1	322
June 9	8.51	2.796	0	75	− 2.58	1	326
19	18.48	2.839	0	+ 15	+ 0.65	1	320
29	28.46	2.825	+ 1	− 44	3.79	− 1	305
July 9	8.43	2.751	1	104	6.73	0	283
200, 19	18.40	2.618	1	160	9.42	0	254
29	28.37	2.433	1	211	11.78	0	219
Aug. 8	7.35	2.198	2	258	13.78	0	179
18	17.32	1.920	2	295	15.35	0	135
28	27.29	1.610	2	324	16.48	+ 1	88
Sept. 7	6.26	1.275	2	345	17.11	1	+ 39
17	16.24	0.924	2	354	17.25	2	− 11
27	26.21	0.572	2	349	16.88	2	61
Oct. 7	6.18	+0.230	2	333	16.03	2	112
17	16.16	−0.090	2	305	14.63	2	162
300, 27	26.13	0.376	2	265	12.78	3	209
Nov. 6	5.10	0.616	2	213	10.45	3	252
16	15.07	0.800	2	153	7.74	3	289
26	25.05	0.921	1	87	4.68	4	321
Dec. 6	5.02	0.973	1	− 17	+ 1.34	4	344
16	14.99	0.955	+ 1	+ 55	− 2.17	4	357
26	24.96	0.864	0	126	5.76	4	359
36	34.94	−0.704	0	+192	− 9.31	+ 4	−349

✱ ☌ ☉,   Dec. 14.1.
✱ ☌ Mean Sun,   Dec. 12.9.

Sidereal Day	Δ_Ω α	Δ_Ω δ	Δ_Ω α	Δ_Ω δ
	1865.		**1873.**	
	s.	″	s.	″
0	+0.189	+6.82	−0.351	−3.58
100	0.146	7.37	0.319	4.34
200	0.103	7.87	0.285	5.05
300	0.058	8.29	0.249	5.72
400	0.013	8.64	0.211	6.34
	1866.		**1874.**	
0	+0.028	+8.53	−0.224	−6.14
100	−0.017	8.83	0.184	6.72
200	0.062	9.06	0.143	7.25
300	0.107	9.20	0.101	7.72
400	0.150	9.27	0.059	8.13
	1867.		**1875.**	
0	−0.135	+9.25	−0.073	−8.00
100	0.178	9.27	0.030	8.36
200	0.220	9.20	+0.013	8.65
300	0.259	9.05	0.056	8.67
400	0.296	8.82	0.099	9.01
	1868 B.		**1876 B.**	
0	−0.284	+8.91	+0.085	−8.97
100	0.319	8.63	0.127	9.07
200	0.351	8.27	0.168	9.09
300	0.381	7.85	0.207	9.04
400	0.407	7.35	0.245	8.91
	1869.		**1877.**	
0	−0.398	+7.53	+0.233	−8.96
100	0.422	6.99	0.269	8.79
200	0.442	6.40	0.304	8.54
300	0.458	5.75	0.336	8.22
400	0.470	5.05	0.366	7.83
	1870.		**1878.**	
0	−0.466	+5.29	+0.356	−7.97
100	0.475	4.57	0.383	7.54
200	0.481	3.80	0.409	7.04
300	0.482	3.01	0.429	6.49
400	0.479	2.19	0.446	5.87
	1871.		**1879.**	
0	−0.480	+2.47	+0.441	−6.09
100	0.474	1.64	0.456	5.44
200	0.464	+0.80	0.467	4.75
300	0.451	−0.04	0.475	4.02
400	0.433	0.99	0.478	3.25
	1872 B.		**1880 B.**	
0	−0.440	−0.60	+0.478	−3.51
100	0.420	1.44	0.479	2.72
200	0.396	2.26	0.475	1.91
300	0.370	3.07	0.468	1.08
400	−0.340	−3.84	+0.457	−0.23

TABLE XXIV.—* ω Draconis.

R.A. 17h 37m.7.   Dec. + 68° 49'.

Upper transit at fictitious meridian.

Sidereal Day	Mean Day	Δ⊙a 1870.	Var. in 10 y.	Diff. for 10 d.	Δ⊙δ 1870.	Var. in 10 y.	Diff. for 10 d.
0, Jan. 0	− 0.04	−3.652	+ 1	+162	− 4.83	− 1	−363
10	+ 9.93	3.433	1	275	8.39	− 1	346
* 20	19.90	3.106	1	378	11.71	0	317
30	29.88	2.682	1	468	14.69	0	277
Feb. 9	8.85	2.176	1	542	17.21	0	226
19	18.82	1.605	1	597	19.18	0	167
Mar. 1	0.79	0.988	1	632	20.54	0	103
11	10.77	−0.347	1	647	21.23	0	− 35
21	20.74	+0.293	1	641	21.25	0	+ 32
31	30.71	0.929	1	616	20.59	0	98
100, Apr. 10	9.68	1.524	1	572	19.31	0	158
20	19.66	2.068	1	513	17.45	0	212
30	29.63	2.546	+ 1	440	15.10	0	257
May 10	9.60	2.945	0	356	12.35	0	293
20	19.58	3.235	0	263	9.28	0	319
30	29.55	3.469	0	164	6.01	0	334
June 9	8.52	3.582	0	+ 62	− 2.64	0	339
19	18.49	3.592	0	− 41	+ 0.74	0	334
29	28.46	3.499	0	143	4.02	0	321
July 9	8.44	3.307	− 1	241	7.13	0	299
200, 19	18.41	3.019	1	333	9.98	0	270
29	28.38	2.644	1	417	12.52	0	236
Aug. 8	7.36	2.189	1	490	14.68	0	195
18	17.33	1.667	1	551	16.41	0	151
28	27.30	1.091	− 1	599	17.68	0	103
Sept. 7	6.27	+0.474	0	631	18.45	0	+ 52
17	16.25	−0.166	0	646	18.71	0	0
27	26.22	0.812	0	644	18.45	0	− 53
Oct. 7	6.19	1.448	0	623	17.66	− 1	106
17	16.16	2.052	+ 1	584	16.34	1	157
300, 27	26.14	2.609	1	526	14.52	1	206
Nov. 6	5.11	3.100	1	452	12.22	1	252
16	15.08	3.508	1	363	9.50	1	292
26	25.06	3.820	2	260	6.41	1	325
Dec. 6	5.03	4.025	2	148	+ 3.04	1	349
16	15.00	4.115	2	− 31	− 0.54	1	364
26	24.97	4.086	2	+ 89	4.20	1	367
36	34.95	−3.938	+ 2	+209	− 7.84	− 1	−358

* 8 Mean Sun, June 15.8.
* ♂ ⊙, Dec. 16.5.
* ♂ Mean Sun, Dec. 15.4.

Sidereal Day	ΔΩa	ΔΩδ	ΔΩa	ΔΩδ
	1865.		**1873.**	
0	−0.197	+7.04	+0.179	−3.87
100	0.196	7.58	0.185	4.61
200	0.193	8.05	0.190	5.31
300	0.188	8.44	0.193	5.95
400	0.182	8.77	0.194	6.57
	1866.		**1874.**	
0	−0.184	+8.67	+0.194	−6.37
100	0.177	8.94	0.194	6.94
200	0.168	9.14	0.192	7.45
300	0.157	9.26	0.189	7.89
400	0.146	9.29	0.185	8.28
	1867.		**1875.**	
0	−0.150	+9.29	+0.187	−8.15
100	0.137	9.27	0.181	8.49
200	0.123	9.18	0.174	8.76
300	0.108	9.00	0.166	8.95
400	0.092	8.74	0.156	9.07
	1868 B.		**1876 B.**	
0	−0.098	+8.84	+0.159	−9.04
100	0.081	8.53	0.149	9.11
200	0.064	8.15	0.137	9.10
300	0.047	7.70	0.124	9.02
400	0.029	7.18	0.110	8.87
	1869.		**1877.**	
0	−0.035	+7.36	+0.115	−8.95
100	−0.017	6.80	0.100	8.73
200	+0.002	6.19	0.085	8.45
300	0.020	5.52	0.068	8.11
400	0.038	4.80	0.051	7.69
	1870.		**1878.**	
0	+0.032	+5.05	+0.057	−7.84
100	0.049	4.31	0.040	7.38
200	0.067	3.53	0.023	6.86
300	0.083	2.73	+0.005	6.29
400	0.099	1.90	−0.013	5.66
	1871.		**1879.**	
0	+0.094	+2.18	−0.007	−5.88
100	0.109	1.34	0.025	5.21
200	0.123	+0.50	0.043	4.51
300	0.137	−0.35	0.060	3.76
400	0.149	1.19	0.077	2.98
	1872 B.		**1880 B.**	
0	+0.145	−0.91	−0.071	−3.24
100	0.156	1.74	0.088	2.44
200	0.166	2.56	0.103	1.62
300	0.175	3.36	0.118	−0.78
400	+0.182	−4.12	−0.132	+0.07

TABLE XXIV.—μ Herculis.

R.A. 17h 41.4m.   Dec. + 27° 48′.

Upper transit at fictitious meridian.

Sidereal Day	Mean Day	$\Delta_{\odot}a$ 1870.	Var.in 10y.	Diff. for 10 d.	$\Delta_{\odot}\delta$ 1870.	Var.in 10y.	Diff for 10 d.
0, Jan. 0	− 0.04	−1.475	0	+153	− 3.00	+ 1	−250
10	+ 9 93	1.300	− 1	196	5.85	2	280
20	19.90	1.086	1	231	8.57	2	262
30	29.87	0.840	2	260	11.05	2	232
Feb. 9	8.85	0.569	2	282	13.18	2	193
19	18.82	−0.278	2	299	14.89	1	148
Mar. 1	0.79	+0 027	2	309	16.12	1	96
11	10.77	0.337	3	310	16.82	1	− 43
21	20.74	0.646	3	308	16.98	1	+ 11
31	30.71	0.952	2	301	16.61	+ 1	64
100, Apr 10	9.68	1.246	2	287	15.72	0	113
20	19.66	1.525	2	269	14.36	0	156
30	29.63	1.783	2	246	12.62	0	193
May 10	9.60	2.016	1	219	10.53	− 1	223
20	19.57	2.221	1	188	8.18	1	244
30	29.55	2.392	− 1	153	5.67	− 1	257
June 9	8.52	2.527	0	116	3.07	0	262
19	18.49	2.623	0	74	− 0.46	0	258
29	28.47	2.675	0	+ 32	+ 2.07	0	248
July 9	8.44	2.636	+ 1	− 11	4.49	0	232
200, 19	18.41	2.653	2	54	6.70	0	210
29	28.38	2.579	2	94	8.68	+ 1	184
Aug. 8	7 36	2.466	2	131	10.37	1	154
18	17.33	2.318	2	163	11.74	1	120
28	27.30	2.141	3	190	12.76	1	84
Sept. 7	6.27	1.940	3	209	13.42	2	47
17	16.25	1.727	3	218	13.69	2	+ 8
27	26.22	1.508	3	218	13.57	2	− 32
Oct. 7	6.19	1.295	3	207	13.05	3	73
17	16.16	1.098	3	186	12.12	3	112
300, 27	26.14	0.926	2	157	10.81	3	150
Nov. 6	5.11	0.786	2	119	9.12	4	187
16	15.08	0.689	1	75	7.08	4	220
26	25.06	0.637	1	− 27	4.75	4	249
Dec. 6	5.03	0.636	+ 1	+ 24	+ 2.14	5	271
16	15.00	0.685	0	74	− 0.64	6	285
26	24.97	0.784	0	123	3.53	6	292
36	34.95	+0.931	− 1	+169	− 6.44	+ 6	−288

Sidereal Day	$\Delta_{\Omega}a$	$\Delta_{\Omega}\delta$	$\Delta_{\Omega}a$	$\Delta_{\Omega}\delta$
	1865.		**1873.**	
0	+0.468	+7.12	−0.694	−3.97
100	0.403	7.64	0.653	4.71
200	0.335	8 10	0.605	5.41
300	0.263	8.49	0.554	6.06
400	0.190	8.81	0.497	6.65
	1866.		**1874.**	
0	+0.215	+8.71	−0.517	−6.46
100	0.140	8.98	0.457	7.02
200	+0.063	9.16	0.395	7.52
300	−0.013	9.27	0.329	7.96
400	0.090	9.30	0.260	8.33
	1867.		**1875.**	
0	−0.064	+9.30	−0.284	−8.21
100	0.140	9.27	0.214	8.54
200	0.215	9.16	0.142	8.80
300	0.288	8.97	−0.069	8.96
400	0.359	8.71	+0.004	9.09
	1868 B.		**1876 B.**	
0	−0.336	+8.81	−0.021	−9.06
100	0.404	8.49	+0.053	9.12
200	0.469	8.10	0.125	9.10
300	0.529	7.64	0.197	9.01
400	0.585	7.11	0.269	8.85
	1869.		**1877.**	
0	−0.567	+7.30	+0.244	−8.91
100	0.619	6.73	0.313	8.70
200	0 666	6.11	0.379	8.41
300	0.707	5.45	0.443	8.06
400	0.742	4.71	0.503	7.63
	1870.		**1878.**	
0	−0.731	+4.96	+0.483	−7.78
100	0.761	4.21	0.540	7.32
200	0.783	3.43	0.593	6.79
300	0.802	2.62	0.641	6.20
400	0.812	1.79	0.685	5.57
	1871.		**1879.**	
0	−0.810	+2.07	+0.670	−5.79
100	0.815	1.23	0.710	5.12
200	0.814	+0.39	0.743	4.40
300	0.806	−0.46	0.771	3.65
400	0.791	1.30	0.792	2.86
	1872 B.		**1880 B.**	
0	−0.796	−1.02	+0.785	−3.13
100	0.777	1.86	0.802	2.33
200	0.751	2.67	0.812	1.50
300	0.719	3 46	0.815	−0.66
400	−0.681	−4.22	+0.811	+0.19

✳ ☌ ☉,   Dec. 17.3.
✳ ☌ Mean Sun,   Dec. 16.4.

TABLE XXIV.—* ψ¹ Draconis.

R.A. 17^h 44^m.3.　　　　Dec. +72° 13'.

Upper transit at fictitious meridian.

Sidereal Day	Mean Day	$\Delta_\odot\alpha$ 1870.	Var. in 10y.	Diff. for 10 d.	$\Delta_\odot\delta$ 1870.	Var. in 10y.	Diff. for 10 d.
0, Jan. 0	− 0.04	4.353	+ 2	+147	− 4.31	− 1	−363
10	+ 9.93	4.137	2	283	7.88	1	348
20	19.91	3.791	3	408	11.23	1	321
30	29.88	3.326	3	519	14.25	1	282
Feb. 9	8.85	2.760	3	611	16.83	1	233
19	18.82	2.112	3	682	18.86	1	175
Mar. 1	0.80	1.405	4	728	20.32	1	111
11	10.77	−0.663	4	751	21.10	− 1	− 45
21	20.74	+0.088	4	748	21.20	0	+ 23
31	30.72	0.824	3	721	20.64	0	88
100, Apr. 10	9.69	1.523	3	673	19.45	0	149
20	19.66	2.163	3	604	17.68	0	204
30	29.63	2.726	2	519	15.40	+ 1	250
May 10	9.61	3.196	2	419	12.71	1	287
20	19.58	3.561	1	309	9.70	1	314
30	29.55	3.811	+ 1	191	6.47	1	330
June 9	8.52	3.942	0	+ 70	− 3.13	1	337
19	18.50	3.951	− 1	− 53	+ 0.24	1	334
29	28.47	3.837	1	174	3.52	1	322
July 9	8.44	3.604	1	290	6.64	1	301
200, 19	18.42	3.259	2	399	9.53	1	274
29	28.39	2.809	2	499	12.10	+ 1	240
Aug. 8	7.36	2.266	2	586	14.31	0	201
18	17.33	1.642	2	660	16.10	0	157
28	27.31	0.952	2	717	17.44	0	110
Sept. 7	6.28	+0.214	2	757	18.29	− 1	60
17	16.25	−0.555	2	777	18.63	1	+ 8
27	26.22	1.333	2	777	18.44	1	− 45
Oct. 7	6.20	2.102	2	756	17.73	2	98
17	16.17	2.838	− 1	714	16.49	2	150
300, 27	26.14	3.522	0	650	14.75	2	199
Nov. 6	5.12	4.132	0	566	12.53	2	245
16	15.09	4.648	+ 1	465	9.88	3	285
26	25.06	5.056	1	348	6.85	3	320
Dec. 6	5.03	5.340	2	218	+ 3.51	3	346
16	15.00	5.490	2	− 81	− 0.03	3	361
26	24.98	5.500	3	+ 60	3.68	3	366
36	34.95	−5.370	+ 3	+199	− 7.31	− 3	−359

Sidereal Day	$\Delta_\Omega\alpha$	$\Delta_\Omega\delta$	$\Delta_\Omega\alpha$	$\Delta_\Omega\delta$
	1865.		**1873.**	
0	−0.328	+7.18	+0.384	−4.05
100	0.306	7.70	0.376	4.78
200	0.281	8.15	0.365	5.47
300	0.254	8.53	0.351	6.11
400	0.225	8.84	0.334	6.71
	1866.		**1874.**	
0	−0.234	+8.75	+0.340	−6.51
100	0.205	9.00	0.322	7.07
200	0.172	9.18	0.301	7.57
300	0.138	9.28	0.277	8.00
400	0.103	9.30	0.251	8.36
	1867.		**1875.**	
0	−0.115	+9.30	+0.260	−8.25
100	0.080	9.27	0.233	8.57
200	0.043	9.15	0.204	8.82
300	−0.006	8.95	0.173	8.99
400	+0.030	8.68	0.141	9.10
	1868 R.		**1876 B.**	
0	−0.018	+8.78	+0.152	−9.07
100	0.055	8.46	0.119	9.12
200	0.091	8 06	0.085	9.10
300	0.126	7.59	0.051	9.00
400	0.160	7.06	0.015	8.83
	1869.		**1877.**	
0	+0.148	+7.25	+0.027	−8.90
100	0.182	6.67	−0.008	8.68
200	0.213	6.04	0.043	8.39
300	0.243	5.36	0.078	8.02
400	0.270	4.64	0.112	7.60
	1870.		**1878.**	
0	+0.261	+4.89	−0.101	−7.75
100	0.287	4.14	0.135	7.28
200	0.310	3.35	0.167	6.74
300	0.331	2.54	0.199	6.15
400	0.348	1.71	0.229	5.51
	1871.		**1879.**	
0	+0.343	+1.99	−0.215	−5.73
100	0.358	1.15	0.248	5.06
200	0.371	+0.30	0.274	4.34
300	0.380	−0.55	0.299	3 58
400	0.386	1.39	0.321	2.80
	1872 B.		**1880 B.**	
0	+0.385	−1.10	−0.314	−3.07
100	0.389	1.94	0.334	2.26
200	0.390	2.75	0.352	1.43
300	0.387	3.54	0.366	−0.59
400	+0.381	−4.30	−0.378	+0.26

```
*  δ Mean Sun,  June 17.5.
*  δ ☉,         Dec. 17.9.
*  δ Mean Sun,  Dec. 17.1.
```

TABLE XXIV.—γ² Sagittarii.

R.A. 17h 57m.5.   Dec. — 30° 25′.

Upper transit at fictitious meridian.

Sidereal Day.	Mean Day.	$\Delta_\odot a$ 1870.	Var. in 10y.	Diff. for 10 d.	$\Delta_\odot \delta$ 1870.	Var. in 10y.	Diff. for 10 d.
0, Jan. 0	− 0.03	−1.521	0	+191	+ 1.07	− 3	+ 34
10	+ 9.94	1.308	− 1	233	1.37	3	26
20	19.91	1.058	2	268	1.59	2	18
30	29.89	0.775	3	295	1.74	2	11
Feb. 9	8.86	0.470	3	316	1.82	1	6
19	18.83	−0.144	4	332	1.87	− 1	+ 2
Mar. 1	0.80	+0.192	4	340	1.87	0	− 1
11	10.78	0.535	4	345	1.86	0	2
21	20.75	0.881	4	345	1.83	+ 1	3
31	30.72	1.224	4	340	1.79	2	4
100, Apr. 10	9.69	1.560	4	331	1.75	2	6
20	19.67	1.885	3	319	1.68	3	8
30	29.64	2.196	3	302	1.59	4	11
May 10	9.61	2.487	2	280	1.45	4	16
20	19.59	2.754	2	253	1.27	4	22
30	29.56	3.992	1	222	1.02	5	28
June 9	8.53	3.196	− 1	186	0.70	5	35
19	18.50	3.362	0	145	+ 0.32	5	41
29	28.48	3.485	+ 1	99	− 0.12	5	47
July 9	8.45	3.560	1	52	0.60	6	50
200, 19	18.42	3.589	2	+ 5	1.11	6	51
29	28.39	3.571	2	− 41	1.62	6	50
Aug. 8	7.37	3.507	3	85	2.11	5	47
18	17.34	3.402	3	124	2.55	5	41
28	27.31	3.260	4	157	2.92	4	32
Sept. 7	6.29	3.090	4	180	3.18	4	21
17	16 26	2.902	4	194	3.33	4	− 8
27	26 23	2.705	4	197	3.33	4	+ 6
Oct. 7	6.20	2.511	4	188	3.21	4	19
17	16.18	2.332	4	168	2.96	3	31
300, 27	26.15	2.179	4	136	2.59	3	42
Nov. 6	5.12	2.063	3	95	2.13	3	49
16	15.09	1.991	3	− 48	1.62	2	53
26	25.07	1.968	2	+ 4	1.07	2	55
Dec. 6	5.04	1.999	+ 1	59	0.53	2	52
16	15.01	2.085	0	111	− 0.04	2	47
26	24.98	2.221	0	161	+ 0.40	2	40
36	34.96	+2.407	0	+207	+ 0.76	+ 2	+ 32

Sidereal Day.	$\Delta_\Omega a$	$\Delta_\Omega \delta$	$\Delta_\Omega a$	$\Delta_\Omega \delta$
	1865.		**1873.**	
0	+0.799	+7.43	−1.151	−4.41
100	0.696	7.92	1.086	5.12
200	0.587	8.34	1.013	5.80
300	0.473	8.69	0.932	6.42
400	0.354	8.97	0.843	6.98
	1866.		**1874.**	
0	+0.395	+8.86	−0.874	−6.80
100	0.274	9.10	0.780	7.33
200	0.151	9.25	0.680	7.79
300	+0.026	9.31	0.575	8.19
400	−0.099	9.20	0.465	8.53
	1867.		**1875.**	
0	−0.057	+9.31	−0.503	−8.42
100	0.181	9.23	0.391	8.71
200	0.304	9.08	0.275	8.92
300	0.424	8.85	0.158	9.06
400	0.540	8.54	0.039	9.13
	1868 B.		**1876 B.**	
0	−0.501	+8.65	−0.079	−9.11
100	0.614	8.29	+0.040	9.13
200	0.722	7.86	0.159	9.07
300	0.823	7.36	0.276	8.94
400	0.916	6.80	0.392	8.73
	1869.		**1877.**	
0	−0.836	+7.00	+0.353	−8.81
100	0.974	6.39	0.467	8.55
200	1.054	5.74	0.577	8.22
300	1.123	5.04	0.682	7.83
400	1.184	4.29	0.781	7.37
	1870.		**1878.**	
0	−1.165	+4.55	+0.748	−7.53
100	1.219	3.78	0.844	7.03
200	1.262	2.98	0.933	6.47
300	1.293	2.16	1.014	5.85
400	1.314	1.32	1.087	5.18
	1871.		**1879.**	
0	−1.309	+1.60	+1.064	−5.41
100	1.322	+0.75	1.131	4.71
200	1.324	−0.10	1.189	3.98
300	1.315	0.94	1.237	3.20
400	1.294	1.76	1.275	2.40
	1872 B.		**1880 B.**	
0	−1.302	−1.50	+1.264	−2 67
100	1.275	2.33	1.295	1.85
200	1.237	3.13	1.315	1.03
300	1.188	3.91	1.324	−0 17
400	−1.130	−4.65	+1.322	+0.68

✳ ♂ ⊙,   Dec. 20.9.
✳ ♂ Mean Sun,   Dec. 20.4.

TABLE XXIV.—μ¹ Sagittarii.

R.A. 18h 6.0m　　　　　　Dec. — 21° 5′

Upper transit at fictitious meridian.

Sidereal Day	Mean Day	$\Delta_\odot a$ 1870.	Var. in 10 y.	Diff. for 10 d.	$\Delta_\odot \delta$ 1870.	Var. in 10 y.	Diff. for 10 d.
0, Jan. 0	− 0.03	−1.413	− 1	+169	+ 0.19	− 2	− 18
10	+ 9.95	1.224	1	207	− 0.01	2	23
20	19.92	1.000	2	240	0.27	1	27
30	29.89	0.746	2	267	0.55	− 1	27
Feb. 9	8.86	0.468	3	287	0.80	0	24
19	18.84	−0.173	3	303	1.02	0	20
Mar. 1	0.81	+0.136	3	313	1.19	0	13
11	10.78	0.452	4	317	1.28	+ 1	− 5
21	20.76	0.769	4	319	1.29	1	+ 5
31	30.73	1.088	4	317	1.19	2	14
100, Apr. 10	9.70	1.401	3	310	1.01	2	21
20	19.67	1.707	3	300	0.77	2	27
30	29.65	1.999	3	284	0.48	3	31
May 10	9.62	2.274	2	265	− 0.16	3	32
20	19.59	2.528	2	242	+ 0.16	3	32
30	29.56	2.756	1	214	0.48	4	28
June 9	8.54	2.954	− 1	181	0.73	4	23
19	18.51	3.116	0	143	0.94	4	17
29	28.48	3.238	0	101	1.08	4	11
July 9	8.45	3.318	+ 1	57	1.16	5	+ 5
200, 19	18.43	3.353	1	+ 13	1.18	5	− 1
29	28.40	3.345	2	− 31	1.13	5	6
Aug. 8	7.37	3.292	2	73	1.06	5	9
18	17.35	3.201	3	110	0.96	5	11
28	27.32	3.075	4	141	0.85	5	10
Sept. 7	6.29	2.922	4	164	0.76	4	8
17	16.26	2.750	4	178	0.70	4	5
27	26.24	2.568	3	182	0.67	4	− 1
Oct. 7	6.21	2.389	3	175	0.68	4	+ 3
17	16.18	2.221	3	158	0.73	4	6
300, 27	26.15	2.076	3	129	0.80	3	8
Nov. 6	5.13	1.965	2	92	0.89	3	8
16	15.10	1.893	2	51	0.96	3	6
26	25.07	1.864	2	− 4	1.00	3	+ 3
Dec. 6	5.05	1.885	+ 1	+ 46	1.01	3	− 2
16	15.02	1.956	0	96	0.96	3	9
26	24.99	2.076	0	142	0.84	3	16
36	34.96	+2.238	0	+182	+ 0.65	+ 3	− 21

Sidereal Day	$\Delta_\Omega a$	$\Delta_\Omega \delta$	$\Delta_\Omega a$	$\Delta_\Omega \delta$
	1865.		**1873.**	
0	+0.735	+7.58	−1.066	−4.63
100	0.639	8.05	1.005	5.33
200	0.537	8.45	0.936	5.99
300	0.431	8.78	0.860	6.59
400	0.320	9.06	0.777	7.14
	1866.		**1874.**	
0	+0.358	+8.95	−0.805	−6.96
100	0.245	9.15	0.718	7.47
200	0.130	9.27	0.624	7.92
300	+0.014	9.31	0.526	8.30
400	−0.102	9.27	0.424	8.61
	1867.		**1875.**	
0	−0.063	+9.29	−0.459	−8.52
100	0.178	9.20	0.354	8.78
200	0.292	9.02	0.247	8.97
300	0.404	8.76	0.137	9.09
400	0.512	8.43	0.027	9.13
	1868 B.		**1876 B.**	
0	−0.476	+8.55	−0.064	−9.13
100	0.580	8.17	+0.047	9.12
200	0.680	7.72	0.157	9.04
300	0.773	7.20	0.267	8.88
400	0.860	6.62	0.373	8.65
	1869.		**1877.**	
0	−0.832	+6.82	+0.338	−8.74
100	0.913	6.20	0.443	8.46
200	0.986	5.53	0.545	8.11
300	1.051	4.82	0.642	7.69
400	1.106	4.06	0.734	7.21
	1870.		**1878.**	
0	−1.089	+4.32	+0.704	−7.38
100	1.138	3.54	0.792	6.86
200	1.177	2.73	0.874	6.28
300	1.205	1.91	0.949	5.65
400	1.224	1.06	1.017	4.97
	1871.		**1879.**	
0	−1.219	+1.35	+0.995	−5.21
100	1.230	+0.50	1.057	4.50
200	1.231	−0.35	1.110	3.75
300	1.222	1.20	1.154	2.96
400	1.202	2.03	1.189	2.15
	1872 B.		**1880 B.**	
0	−1.210	−1.75	+1.178	−2.43
100	1.183	2.57	1.206	1.61
200	1.147	3.37	1.224	−0.77
300	1.101	4.14	1.332	+0.08
400	−1.046	−4.87	+1.229	+0.93

✱ ♂ ☉,　　· Dec. 22.8.
✱ ♂ Mean Sun,　Dec. 22.6.

TABLE XXIV.—*σ Octantis.†

R.A. 18h 6.4m   Dec. −89° 17′

Upper transit at fictitious meridian.

Sidereal Day	Mean Day	$\Delta_\odot\alpha$ 1870	Var. in 10y	Diff. for 10d	$\Delta_\odot\delta$ 1870	Var. in 10y	Diff. for 10d
0, Jan. 0	− 0.02	−106.05	−108	+693	+ 3 16	−160	+323
10	+ 9.95	97.54	243	1004	6.30	14?	304
20	19.92	86.08	368	1283	9.20	131	276
30	29.90	72.01	481	1524	11.79	110	241
Feb. 9	8.87	55.75	578	1721	14.00	85	200
19	18.84	37.73	657	1873	15.78	58	155
Mar. 1	0.81	− 18.43	718	1979	17.09	− 29	108
11	10.79	+ 1.71	758	2040	17.92	+ 1	59
21	20.76	22.22	777	2056	18.26	32	+ 9
31	30.73	42.68	781	2028	18.10	64	− 40
100, Apr. 10	9.70	62.66	755	1962	17.47	94	87
20	19.68	81.78	714	1854	16.37	122	132
30	29.65	99.62	655	1709	14.84	149	174
May 10	9.62	115.84	578	1530	12.90	174	212
20	19.60	130.10	486	1317	10.62	195	244
30	29.57	142.09	381	1076	8.04	213	271
June 9	8.54	151.55	265	811	5.22	226	291
19	18.51	158.24	142	525	+ 2.23	236	305
29	28.48	162.01	− 13	+226	− 0.85	242	310
July 9	8.46	162.75	+118	− 79	3.94	242	306
200, 19	18.43	160.45	245	381	6.95	239	294
29	28.40	155.17	367	673	9.79	230	272
Aug. 8	7.38	147.08	478	943	12.37	218	242
18	17.35	136 41	576	1183	14.61	202	204
28	27.32	123.56	657	1382	16.42	183	157
Sept. 7	6.29	108.95	717	1532	17.74	161	105
17	16.27	93.12	753	1620	18.52	137	48
27	26.24	76.66	763	1656	18.70	112	+ 11
Oct. 7	6.21	60.24	755	1619	18.29	87	72
17	16.18	44.50	716	1518	17.28	64	131
300, 27	26.16	30.10	654	1352	15.70	42	185
Nov. 6	5.13	17.65	568	1129	13.61	23	233
16	15.10	7.68	464	857	11.07	+ 8	274
26	25.08	+ 0.63	342	548	8.18	− 3	304
Dec. 6	5.05	− 3.19	210	−214	5.03	9	324
16	15.02	3.61	+ 70	+131	− 1.74	10	333
26	24.99	− 0.58	− 72	473	+ 1.59	− 5	331
36	34.97	+ 5.80	−211	+799	+ 4.84	+ 4	+318

Sidereal Day	1865 $\Delta_\Omega\alpha$	$\Delta_\Omega\delta$	1873 $\Delta_\Omega\alpha$	$\Delta_\Omega\delta$
1865.			**1873.**	
0	+22.88	+7.43	−31.21	−4.77
100	19.92	7.93	29.14	5.48
200	16.77	8.35	26.80	6.13
300	13.46	8.70	24.24	6.73
400	10.02	8.98	21.47	7.28
1866.			**1874.**	
0	+11.19	+8.89	−22.43	−7.10
100	7.68	9.12	19.53	7.60
200	4.11	9.25	16.47	8.04
300	+ 0.49	9.31	13.27	8.40
400	− 3.14	9.28	9.95	8.70
1867.			**1875.**	
0	− 1.92	+9.30	−11.08	−8.61
100	5.52	9.21	7.70	8.85
200	9.08	9.05	4.27	9.02
300	12.54	8.80	− 0.79	9.11
400	15.89	8.47	+ 2.69	9.12
1868 B.			**1876 B.**	
0	−14.78	+8.59	+ 1.51	−9.13
100	18.03	8 21	4.98	9.09
200	21.11	7.76	8.40	8.97
300	23.99	2.23	11.75	8.78
400	26.65	6.65	15.00	8.51
1869.			**1877.**	
0	−25.78	+6.85	+13.91	−8.61
100	28.27	6.23	17.08	8.29
200	30.50	5.55	20.09	7.90
300	32.45	4.82	22.95	7.45
400	34.09	4.05	25.59	6.93
1870.			**1878.**	
0	−33.57	+4.31	+24.72	−7.11
100	35.00	3.52	27.22	6.55
200	36.11	2.70	29.49	5.93
300	36.89	1.85	31.50	5.26
400	37.33	0.99	33.23	4.54
1871.			**1879.**	
0	−37.22	+1.29	+32.68	−4.79
100	37.43	0.42	34.22	4.04
200	37.31	−0.44	35.46	3.26
300	36.86	1.30	36.39	2.44
400	36.07	2.15	37.00	1.61
1872 B.			**1880 B.**	
0	−36.37	−1.86	+36.83	−1.89
100	35.37	2.70	37.22	1.05
200	34.06	3.50	37.27	−0.19
300	32.45	4.28	36.99	+0.68
400	−30.57	−5.01	+36.38	+1.53

✳ ☊ Mean Sun, June 23.1.
✳ ♂ ⊙, Dec. 22.9.
✳ ☌ Mean Sun, Dec. 22.7.

† See pages 248. 250 for additional corrections.

TABLE XXIV.—* δ Ursæ Minoris.†

R.A. 18ʰ 14ᵐ.3.　　　　　Dec. + 86° 36'.

Upper transit at fictitious meridian.

Sidereal Day	MeanDay.	Δ☉α 1870.	Var.in 10y.	Diff.for 10 d.	Δ☉δ 1870.	Var.in 10y.	Diff.for 10 d.
0, Jan. 0	− 0.02	−22 98	0	− 23	− 1.54	−29	−341
10	+ 9.95	22.84	+ 5	+ 51	4.93	29	335
20	19.93	21.97	10	122	8.20	23	317
30	29.90	20.42	15	187	11.23	26	288
Feb. 9	8.87	18.25	20	245	13.92	23	247
19	18.85	15.54	24	294	16.15	20	197
Mar. 1	0.82	12.41	26	329	17.85	16	141
' 11	10.79	8.99	28	351	18.96	12	80
21	20.76	5.42	29	359	19.44	8	− 17
31	30.74	− 1.84	30	354	19.29	− 3	+ 47
100, Apr. 10	9.71	+ 1.63	29	336	18.51	+ 1	108
20	19.68	4.85	28	306	17.15	5	162
30	29.65	7.71	25	265	15.28	9	210
May 10	9.63	10.11	21	215	12.96	12	252
' 20	19.60	11.98	17	159	10.27	14	284
30	29.57	13.27	13	99	7.31	15	306
June 9	8.55	13.94	8	+ 35	4.18	16	318
19	18.52	13.96	+ 3	− 30	− 0.96	16	322
29	28.49	13.35	− 2	93	+ 2.25	15	318
July 9	8.46	12.11	7	154	5.38	13	305
200, 19	18.44	10.28	12	211	8.34	11	285
29	28.41	7.91	17	263	11.06	8	258
Aug. 8	7.38	5.04	21	310	13.48	+ 4	226
18	17.35	+ 1.73	24	350	15.56	0	189
28	27.33	− 1.94	27	382	17.24	− 5	148
Sept. 7	6.30	5.90	30	406	18.50	10	103
17	16.27	10.05	31	423	19.29	15	55
27	26.24	14.33	32	431	19.00	20	+ 7
Oct. 7	6.22	18.63	32	428	19.42	26	− 43
17	16.19	22.85	31	415	18.73	32	94
300, 27	26.16	26.89	30	392	17.53	37	144
Nov. 6	5.14	30.66	28	360	15.86	41	191
16	15.11	34.06	25	318	13.73	46	234
26	25.08	36.98	21	265	11.20	50	272
Dec. 6	5.05	39.34	17	205	8.31	53	· 303
16	15.03	41.07	13	139	5.15	55	325
26	25.00	42.10	8	− 67	+ 1.82	56	333
36	34.97	−42.40	− 2	+ 8	− 1.57	−56	−338

Sidereal Day	ΔΩα	ΔΩδ	ΔΩα	ΔΩδ
	1865. ʼ ʺ		**1873.** ʼ ʺ	
0	− 3.40	+7.75	+ 5.48	−4.81
100	2.85	8.20	5.11	5.49
200	2.27	8.57	4.70	6.14
300	1.68	8.87	4.25	6.73
400	1.07	9.09	3.77	7.26
	1866.		**1874.**	
0	− 1.28	+9.02	+ 3 94	−7.09
100	0.66	9.19	3.44	7.58
200	− 0.04	9.29	2.91	8.01
300	+ 0.59	9.30	2.36	8.37
400	1.21	9.23	1.79	8.67
	1867.		**1875.**	
0	+ 1.00	+9.26	+ 1.99	−8.58
100	1.61	9.13	1.41	8.82
200	2.21	8.93	0.82	9.00
300	2.79	8.65	+ 0.22	9.11
400	3.35	8.36	− 0.37	9.13
	1868 B.		**1876 B.**	
0	+ 3.17	+8.43	− 0.17	−9.12
100	3.70	8.03	0.77	9.10
200	4.21	7.56	1.36	9.00
300	4.67	7.03	1.93	8.83
400	5.10	6.43	2.50	8.59
	1869.		**1877.**	
0	+ 4.96	+6.64	− 2.31	−8.68
100	5.35	6.01	2.86	8.39
200	5.70	5.32	3.39	8.03
300	6.00	4.60	3.89	7.61
400	6.25	3.83	4.38	7.12
	1870.		**1878.**	
0	+ 6.18	+4.69	− 4.20	−7.28
100	6.39	3.30	4.65	6.75
200	6.54	2.49	5.06	6.17
300	6.65	1.66	5.43	5.53
400	6.69	0.82	5.75	4.84
	1871.		**1879.**	
0	+ 6.68	+1.11	− 5.65	−5.08
100	6.69	+0.26	5.94	4.36
200	6.64	−0.59	6.19	3.61
300	6.53	1.43	6.39	2 81
400	6.38	2.25	6.53	2.02
	1872 B.		**1880 B.**	
0	+ 6.43	−1.98	− 6 49	−2.29
100	6.24	2.79	6.60	1.47
200	5.99	3.58	6.65	−0.63
300	5.70	4.33	6.65	+0.22
400	+ 5.36	−5.05	− 6 60	+1.06

✳ δ Mean Sun, ·June 25.2.
✳ δ ☉, Dec. 24 7.
✳ δ Mean Sun, Dec. 24 8.

† See pages 251–253 for additional corrections.

TABLE XXIV.—η Serpentis.

R.A. 18 14.6.   Dec. — 2 56.

Upper transit at fictitious meridian.

Sidereal Day	Mean Day	$\Delta_\odot a$ 1870.	Var. in 10 y.	Diff. for 10 d.	$\Delta_\odot \delta$ 1870.	Var. in 10 y.	Diff. for 10 d.
0, Jan. 0	− 0.02	−1.329	0	+141	− 0.76	0	−129
10	+ 9.95	1.168	− 1	178	2.06	0	130
20	19.92	0.975	1	209	3.34	0	124
30	29.90	0.752	2	236	4.53	0	113
Feb. 9	8.87	0.505	2	257	5.58	0	97
19	18.84	−0.240	2	272	6.45	0	77
Mar. 1	0 82	+0.037	3	284	7.10	+ 1	52
11	10.79	0.326	3	291	7.47	1	25
21	20.76	0.618	3	292	7.59	1	+ 2
31	30.73	0.910	2	291	7.42	1	30
100, Apr. 10	9.71	1.199	2	287	6.99	1	56
20	19.68	1.482	2	278	6.31	1	79
30	29.65	1.754	2	264	5.42	1	97
May 10	9.62	2.009	2	246	4.38	2	112
20	19.60	2.245	2	225	3.19	2	121
30	29.57	2.458	1	198	1.96	2	126
June 9	8.54	2.641	1	166	− 0.60	2	127
19	18.52	2.790	− 1	132	+ 0.56	3	122
29	28.49	2.904	0	94	1.77	3	117
July 9	8.46	2.978	0	53	2.89	3	106
200, 19	18.43	3.010	+ 1	+ 12	3 90	3	95
29	28.41	3.002	1	− 29	4.78	3	81
Aug. 8	7.38	2.952	2	69	5.52	3	67
18	17.35	2.865	2	104	6.12	4	52
28	27.32	2.746	2	133	6.56	4	38
Sept. 7	6.30	2.601	2	156	6.87	4	24
17	16.27	2.437	3	171	7 04	4	+ 9
27	26.24	2.263	3	176	7.06	4	− 6
Oct. 7	6.22	2.080	3	171	6.92	4	20
17	16.19	1.925	3	156	6.65	4	35
300, 27	26.16	1.781	2	133	6.22	4	50
Nov. 6	5.13	1.663	2	100	5.64	4	65
16	15.11	1.584	2	60	4.91	4	80
26	25.08	1.544	1	− 18	4.03	4	95
Dec. 6	5.05	1.548	+ 1	+ 27	3.01	4	108
16	15.02	1.598	0	72	1.87	4	119
26	25.00	1.691	0	115	+ 0.64	4	127
36	34.97	+1.827	− 1	+155	− 0.65	+ 4	−130

✱ ♂ ☉, Dec. 24 7.
✱ ♂ Mean Sun, Dec. 24.8.

Sidereal Day	$\Delta_\Omega a$	$\Delta_\Omega \delta$	$\Delta_\Omega a$	$\Delta_\Omega \delta$
	1865.		**1873.**	
0	+0.646	+7.72	−0.935	−4.84
100	0.562	8.17	0.882	5.53
200	0.473	8.55	0.822	6.17
300	0.380	8.86	0.756	6.76
400	0.283	9.06	0.683	7.29
	1866.		**1874.**	
0	+0.316	+9.02	−0.708	−7.12
100	0.218	9.19	0.632	7.01
200	0.117	9.29	0.550	8.04
300	+0.016	9.30	0.461	8.40
400	−0.086	9.23	0.375	8.69
	1867.		**1875.**	
0	−0.052	+9.27	−0.405	−8.60
100	0.153	9.14	0.314	8.84
200	0.253	8.94	0.220	9.01
300	0.350	8.67	0.124	9.10
400	0.445	8.31	0.027	9.12
	1868 B.		**1876 B.**	
0	−0.413	+8.44	−0.060	−9.13
100	0.505	8.04	+0.037	9.09
200	0.592	7.57	0.131	8.99
300	0.674	7.03	0.230	8.81
400	0.750	6.43	0.324	8.56
	1869.		**1877.**	
0	−0.726	+6.64	+0.292	−8.65
100	0.797	6.00	0.384	8.35
200	0.862	5.32	0.474	7.98
300	0.918	4.59	0.559	7.55
400	0.967	3.82	0.640	7.05
	1870.		**1878.**	
0	−0.952	+4.09	+0.613	−7.23
100	0.995	3.30	0.691	6.69
200	1.029	2.45	0.763	6.09
300	1.055	1.65	0.829	5.44
400	1.071	0.81	0.888	4.75
	1871.		**1879.**	
0	−1.067	+1.09	+0.869	−4 99
100	1.077	+0.24	0.924	4.27
200	1.078	−0.61	0.971	3.51
300	1.070	1.45	1.009	2.72
400	1.053	2.25	1.040	1.90
	1872 B.		**1880 B.**	
0	−1.060	−2.00	+1.031	−2.18
100	1.037	2.82	1.056	1.35
200	1.006	3.60	1.072	−0.51
300	0.966	4.36	1.079	+0 34
400	−0.918	−5.08	+1.076	+1.19

TABLE XXIV.—1 Aquilæ.

R.A. 18ʰ 23ᵐ.1.　　　Dec. − 8° 20′.

Upper transit at fictitious meridian.

Sidereal Day	Mean Day	$\Delta_\odot \alpha$ 1870.	Var. in 10y.	Diff. for 10d.	$\Delta_\odot \delta$ 1870.	Var. in 10y.	Diff. for 10d.
0, Jan. 0	− 0.01	−1.346	0	+133	− 0.74	− 1	− 90
10	+ 9.96	1.194	0	171	1.65	0	91
20	19.93	1.005	− 1	204	2 56	0	+8
30	29.91	0.787	2	231	3.41	0	81
Feb. 9	8.88	0.545	2	253	4.17	0	68
19	18.85	0.282	3	271	4.77	0	51
Mar. 1	0.83	−0.004	3	284	5.19	0	33
11	10.80	+0.284	3	292	5.42	0	− 12
21	20.77	0.579	3	297	5.43	+ 1	+ 11
31	30.74	0.878	3	299	5.21	1	33
100, Apr. 10	9.72	·1.175	3	295	4.76	1	53
20	19.69	1.467	3	288	4.14	1	71
30	29.66	1.750	2	277	3.35	1	85
May 10	9.63	2.019	2	261	2.44	2	96
20	19.61	2.271	2	241	1.44	2	103
30	29 58	2.500	1	215	− 0.40	3	105
June 9	8.55	2 700	1	185	+ 0.65	3	103
19	18.52	2.868	− 1	150	1.66	3	98
29	28.50	2.999	0	111	2.61	3	91
July 9	8.47	3.090	0	70	3.47	3	81
200, 19	18.44	3.139	0	+ 28	4.22	3	70
29	28.42	3.146	+ 1	− 14	4.87	3	58
Aug. 8	7.39	3.112	2	56	5.38	3	46
18	17.36	3.036	3	94	5.79	4	35
28	27.33	2.927	3	125	6.08	4	24
Sept. 7	6.31	2.789	3	150	6.27	4	14
17	16.28	2.629	3	166	6.36	4	+ 4
27	26.25	2.459	·3	173	6.35	4	− 6
Oct. 7	6.22	2.286	3	171	6.25	4	15
17	16.20	2.121	3	159	6.06	4	24
330, 27	26.17	1.972	2	136	5.78	4	34
Nov. 6	5.14	1.852	2	105	5.39	4	44
16	15.12	1.705	2	67	4.89	4	54
26	25.09	1.719	2	− 25	4.30	4	64
Dec. 6	5.06	1.715	1	+ 19	3.62	4	74
16	15.03	1.757	+ 1	64	2.83	4·	83
26	25.01	1.843	0	108	1.97	4	89
36	34.98	+1.971	0	+148	+ 1.06	+ 4	− 92

Sidereal Day	$\Delta_\Omega \alpha$	$\Delta_\Omega \delta$	$\Delta_\Omega \alpha$	$\Delta_\Omega \delta$
	1865.		**1873.**	
0	+0.665	+7.92	−0.968	−5.17
100	0.577	8.34	0.912	5.83
200	0.484	8.68	0.849	6.45
300	0.387	8.95	0.779	7.01
400	0.286	9.14	0.703	7.51
	1866.		**1874.**	
0	+0.320	+9.09	−0.730	−7.35
100	0.218	9.22	0.650	7.81
200	0.113	9.26	0.564	8.20
300	+0.007	9.26	0.475	8.53
400	−0.098	9.15	0.381	8.78
	1867.		**1875.**	
0	−0.063	+9.20	−0.413	−8.70
100	0.168	9.04	0.318	8.91
200	0.272	8.80	0.220	9.04
300	0.373	8.49	0.120	9.10
400	0.471	8.10	0.019	9.08
	1868 B.		**1876 B.**	
0	−0.438	+8.24	−0.053	−9.10
100	0.533	7.80	+0.048	9.03
200	0.624	7.30	0.148	8.89
300	0.709	6.74	0.248	8.68
400	0.787	6.11	0.345	8.39
	1869.		**1877.**	
0	−0.761	+6.33	+0.313	−8.49
100	0.835	5.67	0.408	8.16
200	0.902	4.97	0.501	7.76
300	0.960	4.22	0.589	7.29
400	1.010	3.44	0.673	6.77
	1870.		**1878.**	
0	−0.994	+3 71	+0.645	−6.95
100	1.038	2.91	0.725	6.39
200	1.073	2.08	0.800	5.77
300	1.098	1.24	0.868	5.11
400	1.115	+0.40	0.929	4.39
	1871.		**1879.**	
0	−1.111	+0.68	+0.909	−4.63
100	1.121	−0.17	0.965	3.90
200	1.121	1.01	1.013	3.12
300	1.112	1.85	1.053	2.32
400	1.094	2.66	1.084	1.50
	1872 B.		**1880 B.**	
0	−1.101	−2.39	+1.075	−1.78
100	1.076	3.19	1.099	0.95
200	1.043	3.96	1.115	−0.10
300	1.000	4.70	1.122	+0.74
400	−0.950	−5.39	+1.119	+1.59

✱ ♂ ☉, Dec. 27.8.
✱ ♂ Mean Sun, Dec. 28.2.

TABLE XXIV.—β Lyræ.

R.A. 18h 45.3m.   Dec. +33° 13'.

Upper transit at fictitious meridian.

Sidereal Day	Mean Day	Δ⊙a 1870.	Var. in 10 y.	Diff. for 10 d.	Δ⊙δ 1870.	Var. in 10 y.	Diff. for 10 d.
0, Jan. 0	0.00	−1.600	0	+ 77	− 0.21	+ 2	−294
10	9.98	1.499	− 1	124	3.16	2	294
20	19.95	1.353	1	168	6.05	2	282
30	29.92	1.165	1	206	8.76	2	259
Feb. 9	8.89	0.942	1	240	11.20	2	227
19	18.87	0.687	2	268	13.28	2	186
Mar. 1	0.84	0.408	2	291	14.90	2	138
11	10.81	−0.107	2	308	16.02	1	85
21	20.79	+0.206	2	318	16.58	+ 1	− 28
31	30.76	0.527	3	322	16.58	0	+ 29
100, Apr. 10	9.73	0.848	3	320	16.00	0	84
20	19.70	1.165	2	311	14.90	0	135
30	29.68	1.469	2	297	13.31	0	182
May 10	9.65	1.757	2	276	11.29	0	220
20	19.62	2.020	2	249	8.94	0	251
30	29.59	2.254	1	217	6.30	− 1	274
June 9	8.57	2.453	1	180	3.48	− 1	298
19	18.54	2.613	− 1	138	0.56	0	293
29	28.51	2.729	0	92	+2.36	0	291
July 9	8.48	2.797	0	+ 44	5.24	0	282
200, 19	18.46	2.817	+ 1	− 4	7.99	0	266
29	28.43	2.790	1	51	10.55	0	244
Aug. 8	7.40	2.716	1	96	12.86	+ 1	217
18	17.38	2.599	1	138	14.88	1	186
28	27.35	2.442	2	174	16.57	1	151
Sept. 7	6.32	2.253	2	203	17.89	1	112
17	16.29	2.039	3	223	18.81	2	72
27	26.27	1.810	3	234	19.32	2	+ 30
Oct. 7	6.24	1.574	2	235	19.41	2	− 14
17	16.21	1.343	2	225	19.03	2	58
300, 27	26.18	1.128	2	205	18.24	3	102
Nov. 6	5.16	0.936	2	177	17.00	3	145
16	15.13	0.776	1	142	15.38	4	184
26	25.10	0.654	1	99	13.35	4	220
Dec. 6	5.08	0.579	1	51	10.99	4	250
16	15.05	0.552	+ 1	− 2	8.37	4	274
26	25.02	0.575	0	+ 46	5.53	5	259
36	34.99	+0.647	− 1	+ 95	+ 2.61	+ 5	−294

✻ ☌ ⊙,   Dec. 31.7.
✻ ☌ Mean Sun,   Jan. 1.3.

Sidereal Day	ΔΩa	ΔΩδ	ΔΩa	ΔΩδ
	1865.		**1873.**	
0	+0.521	+8.14	−0.699	−5.55
100	0.466	8.51	0.668	6.19
200	0.407	8.81	0.631	6.76
300	0.344	9.03	0.590	7.29
400	0.278	9.17	0.543	7.75
	1866.		**1874.**	
0	+0.301	+9.13	−0.560	−7.60
100	0.233	9.22	0.510	8.01
200	0.163	9.23	0.457	8.37
300	0.092	9.15	0.400	8.65
400	0.020	9.00	0.339	8.85
	1867.		**1875.**	
0	+0.045	+9.06	−0.360	−8.79
100	−0.029	8.86	0.296	8.95
200	0.100	8.57	0.233	9.04
300	0.171	8.22	0.167	9.05
400	0.240	7.79	0.099	8.99
	1868 B.		**1876 B.**	
0	−0.217	+7.94	−0.122	−9.02
100	0.285	7.47	0.054	8.91
200	0.350	6.93	+0.015	8.72
300	0.412	6.33	0.084	8.46
400	0.471	5.68	0.152	8.14
	1869.		**1877.**	
0	−0.451	+5.90	+0.129	−8.25
100	0.507	5.22	0.196	7.88
200	0.559	4.49	0.264	7.44
300	0.605	3.73	0.326	6.94
400	0.646	2.93	0.387	6.38
	1870.		**1878.**	
0	−0.633	+3.21	+0.367	−6.58
100	0.670	2.39	0.426	5.98
200	0.701	1.56	0.482	5.34
300	0.726	+0.72	0.534	4.65
400	0.745	−0.12	0.582	3.91
	1871.		**1879.**	
0	−0.740	+0.16	+0.566	−4.17
100	0.754	−0.68	0.611	3.41
200	0.762	1.52	0.651	2.62
300	0.764	2.34	0.685	1.81
400	0.760	3.14	0.714	0.93
	1872 B.		**1880 B.**	
0	−0.762	−2.87	+0.705	−1.27
100	0.753	3.65	0.729	−0.43
200	0.739	4.40	0.748	+0.41
300	0.716	5.11	0.760	1.25
400	−0.689	−5.77	+0.766	+2.08

TABLE XXIV.—σ Sagittarii.

R.A. 18ʰ 47ᵐ.2.   Dec. − 26° 27′

Upper transit at fictitious meridian.

Sidereal Day	Mean Day	Δ☉α 1870.	Var. in 10y.	Diff. for 10 d.	Δ☉δ 1870.	Var. in 10y.	Diff for 10 d.
0, Jan. 0	0.01	−1.489	0	+132	− 1.13	− 3	+ 30
10	9.98	1.335	0	174	0.84	2	28
20	19.95	1.143	− 1	210	0.57	2	26
30	29.92	0.917	2	242	0.32	2	26
Feb. 9	8.90	0.661	2	269	− 0.05	2	28
19	18.87	0.381	2	290	+ 0.24	1	30
Mar. 1	0.84	−0.082	3	307	0.55	− 1	32
11	10.81	+0.232	3	319	0.88	0	36
21	20.79	0.555	4	327	1 26	+ 1	40
31	30.76	0.835	4	331	1.67	1	43
100, Apr 10	9.73	·1.216	4	331	2.11	1	45
20	19.70	1.546	4	327	2.57	2	44
30	29 68	1.869	3	318	3.00	3	42
May 10	9.65	2.181	3	303	3.41	3	39
20	19.62	2.474	3	283	3.77	3	32
30	29.60	2.746	3	258	4.04	4	23
June 9	8 57	2.988	2	225	4.22	4	13
19	18.54	3.195	1	189	4.30	4	+ 2
29	28.51	3.364	− 1	147	4.26	5	− 9
July 9	8.49	3.488	+ 1	101	4.12	5	19
200, 19	18.46	3 566	1	54	3.88	5	28
29	28.43	3.595	1	+ 5	3.57	5	35
Aug. 8	7.40	3.577	2	− 41	3.19	5	39
18	17.38	3.514	2	85	2.79	5	41
28	27.35	3.408	3	124	2.38	5	40
Sept. 7	6.32	3.269	3	153	2.00	5	36
17	16.30	3.104	4	176	1.66	5	30
27	26.27	2 920	4	188	1.41	5	21
Oct. 7	6.24	2.732	4	188	1.25	4	11
17	16.21	2.548	3	178	1.19	4	− 1
300, 27	26.19	2.380	3	156	1.22	4	+ 8
Nov. 6	5.16	2.239	3	124	1.35	3	17
16	15.13	2.134	3	86	1.56	3	24
26	25.10	2.069	2	− 42	1.82	3	28
Dec. 6	5.08	2.051	1	+ 7	2.11	3	30
16	15.05	2.083	+ 1	56	2.42	3	31
26	25.02	2.163	0	103	2.73	3	31
36	34.99	+2.299	0	+147	+ 3.03	+ 3	+ 29

✳ ☌ ☉,   Jan. 1.1.
✳ ☌ Mean Sun,   Jan. 1.8.

Sidereal Day	ΔΩα	ΔΩδ	ΔΩα	ΔΩδ
	1865.		**1873.**	
0	+0.717	+8.16	−1.079	−5.60
100	0.615	8.53	1.011	6.23
200	0.507	8.82	0.936	6.80
300	0.394	9.03	0.853	7.32
400	0.278	9.17	0.763	7.77
	1866.		**1874.**	
0	+0.317	+9.13	−0.794	−7.63
100	0.199	9.22	0.700	8.04
200	+0.079	9.22	0.600	8.38
300	−0.042	9.14	0.496	8.66
400	0.162	8.9e	0.388	8.86
	1867.		**1875.**	
0	−0.122	+9.04	−0.425	−8.80
100	0.241	8.83	0.314	8.95
200	0.359	8.55	0.201	9.04
300	0.473	8.19	−0 087	9.04
400	0.583	7.75	+0.028	8.97
	1868 B.		**1876 B.**	
0	−0.546	+7.91	−0.011	−9.01
100	0.652	7.43	0.104	8.89
200	0.753	6.89	0.219	8.70
300	0.847	6.29	0.331	8.44
400	0.933	5.63	0.441	8.10
	1869.		**1877.**	
0	−0.905	+5.85	+0.404	−8.22
100	0.986	5.17	0.512	7.84
200	1.058	4.44	0.615	7.40
300	1.121	3.67	0.714	6.89
400	1.174	2.88	0.807	6.33
	1870.		**1878.**	
0	−1.157	+3.15	+0.776	−6.53
100	1.203	2.34	0.865	5.93
200	1.239	1.51	0.946	5.28
300	1.264	+0.66	1.021	4.59
400	1.278	−0.18	1.086	3.85
	1871.		**1879.**	
0	−1.274	+0.11	+1.065	−4.11
100	1.281	−0.74	1.125	3.35
200	1.277	1.57	1.176	2.56
300	1.262	2.39	1.217	1.75
400	1.236	3.19	1.248	0.92
	1872 B.		**1880 B.**	
0	−1.246	−2.93	+1.239	−1.20
100	1.213	3.70	1.262	−0.37
200	1.171	4.44	1.276	+0.47
300	1.118	5.15	1.279	1.31
400	−1.057	−5.81	+1.271	+2.14

TABLE XXIV.—* 50 Draconis.

R.A. 18^h 50.6^m. Dec. +75° 17'.

Upper transit at fictitious meridian.

Sidereal Day	Mean Day	$\Delta_\odot a$ 1870.	Var.in 10 y.	Diff. for 10 d.	$\Delta_\odot \delta$ 1870.	Var.in 10 y.	Diff. for 10 d.
0, Jan. 0	0.01	-5.329	-5	-99	+1.38	-2	-319
10	9.98	5.345	4	+68	-2.14	2	353
20	19.95	5.195	3	233	5.63	2	343
30	29.92	4.882	-2	329	8.96	2	321
Feb. 9	8.90	4.420	0	531	12.01	2	287
19	18.87	3.826	+1	654	14.67	2	242
Mar. 1	0.84	3.120	3	754	16.83	2	188
11	10.82	2.328	4	826	18.41	1	128
21	20.79	1.477	5	870	19.37	1	-63
31	30.76	-0.598	5	884	19.67	-1	+3
100, Apr. 10	9.73	+0.252	6	870	19.30	0	68
20	19.71	1.132	7	826	18.31	0	130
30	29.68	1.926	7	758	16.73	+1	186
May 10	9.65	2.641	6	667	14.62	1	235
20	19.02	3.254	6	557	12.05	2	276
30	29.60	3.750	6	432	9.14	2	307
June 9	8.57	4.113	5	294	5.95	2	329
19	18.54	4.336	4	150	-2.58	2	342
29	28.52	4.412	2	+2	+0.86	2	346
July 9	8.49	4.339	+1	-146	4.30	1	340
200, 19	18.46	4.120	0	290	7.64	1	327
29	28.43	3.761	-2	427	10.81	1	306
Aug. 8	7.41	3.269	4	544	13.73	+1	278
18	17.38	2.657	5	667	16.35	0	244
28	27.35	1.940	6	765	18.60	0	205
Sept. 7	6.32	1.134	8	844	20.44	-1	162
17	16.30	+0.259	9	902	21.82	1	112
27	26.27	-0.663	10	938	22.71	2	64
Oct. 7	6.24	1.610	11	951	23.09	2	+11
17	16.22	2.556	12	938	22.94	3	-43
300, 27	26.19	3.477	12	900	22.24	3	97
Nov. 6	5.16	4.348	13	837	21.00	4	150
16	15.13	5.143	13	749	19.24	4	201
26	25.11	5.838	12	639	17.00	5	247
Dec. 6	5.08	6.413	12	508	14.33	5	287
16	15.05	6.849	12	362	11.29	5	319
26	25.02	7.132	11	203	7.98	5	341
36	35.00	-7.252	-10	-37	+4.51	-5	-352

* ♂ ☉, Jan. 1.7.
* ♂ Mean Sun, Jan. 2.7.
* ☍ Mean Sun, July 4.3.

Sidereal Day	$\Delta_\Omega a$	$\Delta_\Omega \delta$	$\Delta_\Omega a$	$\Delta_\Omega \delta$
	1865.		**1873.**	
0	+0.029	+8.20	+0.313	-5.66
100	0.106	8.56	0.242	6.28
200	0.182	8.84	0.169	6.85
300	0.257	9.04	0.095	7.36
400	0.330	9.17	0.021	7.81
	1866.		**1874.**	
0	+0.305	+9.13	+0.046	-7.66
100	0.376	9.21	-0.029	8.07
200	0.444	9.20	0.103	8.40
300	0.507	9.11	0.176	8.67
400	0.567	8.94	0.246	8.87
	1867.		**1875.**	
0	+0.547	+9.01	-0.224	-8.81
100	0.603	8.79	0.294	8.93
200	0.654	8.49	0.362	9.02
300	0.699	8.12	0.427	9.03
400	0.738	7.68	0.488	8.95
	1868 B.		**1876 B.**	
0	+0.725	+7.84	-0.468	-8.99
100	0.760	7.35	0.526	8.86
200	0.788	6.80	0.581	8.66
300	0.809	6.19	0.630	8.39
400	0.823	5.54	0.675	8.06
	1869.		**1877.**	
0	+0.819	+5.77	-0.660	-8.18
100	0.825	5.08	0.701	7.80
200	0.830	4.34	0.736	7.35
300	0.824	3.57	0.765	6.84
400	0.813	2.78	0.788	6.27
	1870.		**1878.**	
0	+0.818	+3.05	-0.781	-6.47
100	0.801	2.23	0.800	5.87
200	0.777	1.40	0.811	5.21
300	0.746	+0.56	0.817	4.52
400	0.710	-0.28	0.816	3.78
	1871.		**1879.**	
0	+0.723	+0.01	-0.817	-4.03
100	0.682	-0.84	0.811	3.28
200	0.636	1.67	0.798	2.49
300	0.584	2.48	0.779	1.69
400	0.528	3.27	0.753	0.85
	1872 B.		**1880 B.**	
0	+0.548	-3.01	-0.762	-1.13
100	0.488	3.78	0.732	-0.29
200	0.425	4.52	0.696	+0.55
300	0.358	5.22	0.653	1.38
400	+0.299	-5.87	-0.605	+2.21

TABLE XXIV.—ζ Aquilæ.

R.A. 18 59.4 (h m)   Dec. +13 40 (° ')

Upper transit at fictitious meridian.

Sidereal Day	Mean Day	$\Delta_\odot\alpha$ 1870.	Var. in 10 y.	Diff. for 10 d.	$\Delta_\odot\delta$ 1870.	Var. in 10 y.	Diff. for 10 d.
0, Jan. 0	0.01	−1.367	0	+ 84	− 0.34	+ 1	−205
10	9.99	1.263	0	123	2.40	1	205
20	19.96	1.122	− 1	159	4.42	1	198
30	29.93	0.947	1	191	6.33	1	182
Feb. 9	8.90	0.742	1	218	8.04	1	159
19	18.88	0.513	2	241	9.48	1	128
Mar. 1	0.85	−0.261	2	261	10.58	0	92
11	10.82	+0.008	2	276	11.31	0	52
21	20.79	0.289	3	286	11.62	0	− 10
31	30.77	0.578	3	292	11.50	0	+ 33
100, Apr. 10	9.74	0.872	3	294	10.96	0	75
20	19.71	1.165	2	291	10.02	0	112
30	29.69	1.452	2	282	8.74	0	145
May 10	9.66	1.728	2	269	7.14	0	173
20	19.63	1.988	2	250	5.30	0	196
30	29.60	2.227	1	226	3.25	0	211
June 9	8.58	2.438	1	196	− 1.10	1	218
19	18.55	2.617	− 1	161	+ 1.10	1	221
29	28.52	2.759	0	122	3.30	1	217
July 9	8.49	2.861	+ 1	81	5.42	1	207
200, 19	18.47	2.921	1	+ 38	7.43	1	193
29	28.44	2.937	1	− 6	9.27	1	175
Aug. 8	7.41	2.909	1	49	10.92	2	154
18	17.39	2.840	2	87	12.35	2	130
28	27.36	2.736	2	121	13.52	2	104
Sept. 7	6.33	2.599	2	151	14.44	2	77
17	16.30	2.437	2	172	15.07	2	49
27	26.28	2.258	2	183	15.42	3	+ 20
Oct. 7	6.25	2.074	2	186	15.48	4	− 10
17	16.22	1.890	2	179	15.22	4	39
300, 27	26.19	1.720	2	162	14.69	4	68
Nov. 6	5.17	1.569	2	137	13.85	4	97
16	15.14	1.448	2	104	12.75	4	124
26	25.11	1.362	2	68	11.37	4	151
Dec. 6	5.09	1.314	1	− 28	9.75	5	172
16	15.06	1.307	1	+ 15	7 95	5	188
26	25.03	1.344	+ 1	58	6.00	5	201
36	35.00	+1.423	0	+ 90	+ 3.94	+ 5	−206

✳ ♂ ☉,   Jan. 3.6.
✳ ♂ Mean Sun, Jan. 4.9.

Sidereal Day	$\Delta_\Omega\alpha$	$\Delta_\Omega\delta$	$\Delta_\Omega\alpha$	$\Delta_\Omega\delta$
	1865.		**1873.**	
0	+0.600	+8.29	−0.841	−5.85
100	0.529	8.02	0.798	6.45
200	0.452	8.87	0.748	7.00
300	0.372	9.05	0.693	7.49
400	0.288	9.14	0.631	7.91
	1866.		**1874.**	
0	+0.316	+9.13	−0.652	−7.77
100	0.231	9.18	0.587	8.15
200	0.143	9.14	0.517	8.47
300	+0.054	9.05	0.444	8.71
400	−0.035	8.84	0.366	8.88
	1867.		**1875.**	
0	−0.005	+8.91	−0.393	−8.83
100	0.094	8.67	0.314	8.95
200	0.183	8.35	0.233	9.00
300	0.270	7.96	0.148	8.97
400	0.354	7.50	0.064	8.87
	1868 B.		**1876 B.**	
0	−0.326	+7.66	−0.092	−8.91
100	0.408	7.10	−0.007	8.76
200	0.487	6.55	+0.078	8.54
300	0.561	5.97	0.163	8.25
400	0.630	5.36	0.246	7.89
	1869.		**1877.**	
0	−0.607	+5.55	+0.218	−8.02
100	0.673	4.83	0.300	7.61
200	0.732	4.08	0.380	7.14
300	0.785	3.31	0.457	6.62
400	0.831	2.50	0.530	6.04
	1870.		**1878.**	
0	−0.817	+2.78	+0.506	−6.24
100	0.858	1.90	0.576	5 62
200	0.892	1.13	0.642	4.95
300	0.918	+0.29	0.703	4.25
400	0.936	−0.55	0.758	3.50
	1871.		**1879.**	
0	−0.930	−0.27	+0.740	−3.76
100	0.943	1.10	0.791	2.99
200	0.948	1.93	0.835	2.20
300	0.945	2.73	0.873	1.38
400	0.933	3.5	0.903	−0.56
	1872 B.		**1880 B.**	
0	−0.938	−3.25	+0.894	−0.84
100	0.922	4.01	0.919	0.00
200	0.897	4.74	0.937	+0.83
300	0.866	5.42	0.947	1.66
400	−0.827	−6.06	+0.949	+2.48

TABLE XXIV.—d Sagittarii.

R.A. 19ʰ 10ᵐ.0. Dec. — 19° 11′.

Upper transit at fictitious meridian.

Sidereal Day	Mean Day	$\Delta_\odot \alpha$ 1870	Var.in 10y	Diff.for 10d	$\Delta_\odot \delta$ 1870	Var.in 10y	Diff.for 10d
0, Jan. 0	0.02	−1.397	0	+100	− 1.76	− 1	− 10
10	9.99	1.277	0	139	1.85	1	9
20	19.97	1.119	− 1	176	1.93	1	6
30	29.94	0.9t6	1	209	1.97	1	− 1
Feb. 9	8.91	0.703	2	236	1.95	1	+ 5
19	18.88	0.456	2	258	1.87	− 1	13
Mar. 1	0.86	−0.188	3	277	1.69	0	23
11	10.83	+0.097	3	293	1.39	0	35
21	20.80	0.396	3	304	0.97	0	47
31	30.78	0.703	3	312	− 0.44	+ 1	57
100, Apr. 10	9.75	1.018	4	316	+ 0.17	1	66
20	19.72	1.334	4	315	0.88	1	74
30	29.69	1.646	3	309	1.65	2	78
May 10	9.67	1.951	3	300	2.44	2	79
20	19.64	2.244	2	284	3.23	2	77
30	29.61	2.517	2	261	3.98	3	72
June 9	8.58	2.764	2	232	4.66	3	64
19	18.56	2.980	1	199	5.25	4	54
29	28.53	3.161	− 1	160	5.74	4	43
July 9	8.50	3.299	0	117	6.12	5	31
200, 19	18.47	3.394	0	72	6.37	5	18
29	28.45	3.443	0	+ 25	6.48	5	+ 6
Aug. 8	7.42	3.445	+ 1	− 20	6.49	5	− 3
18	17.39	3.404	2	63	6.42	5	12
28	27.37	3.320	2	103	6.26	5	18
Sept. 7	6.34	3.200	2	135	6.06	5	21
17	16.31	3.052	2	158	5.83	5	22
27	26.28	2.886	3	173	5.61	4	22
Oct. 7	6.26	2.710	3	178	5.38	4	21
17	16.23	2.534	3	171	5.19	4	18
300, 27	26.20	2.371	3	156	5.02	4	15
Nov. 6	5.17	2.226	3	130	4.89	4	13
16	15.15	2.114	3	95	4.77	3	11
26	25.12	2.037	2	57	4.67	3	10
Dec. 6	5.09	2.001	2	− 14	4.58	3	10
16	15.07	2.009	1	+ 30	4.48	3	10
26	25.04	2.062	+ 1	74	4.30	3	10
36	35.01	+2.156	0	+115	+ 4.28	+ 3	− 10

Sidereal Day	$\Delta_\Omega \alpha$	$\Delta_\Omega \delta$	$\Delta_\Omega \alpha$	$\Delta_\Omega \delta$
	1865.		**1873.**	
0	+0.673	+8.37	−1.016	−6.06
100	0.576	8.67	0.952	6.64
200	0.474	8.90	0.880	7.16
300	0.367	9.05	0.802	7.62
400	0.257	9.12	0.716	8.01
	1866.		**1874.**	
0	+0.294	+9.10	−0.746	−7.89
100	0.182	9.12	0 657	8 24
200	0.069	9.06	0.563	8.52
300	−0.045	8.92	0.464	8.73
400	0.159	8.70	0.361	8.87
	1867.		**1875.**	
0	−0.120	+8.78	−0.396	−8.84
100	0.233	8.51	0.292	8.93
200	0.344	8.17	0.185	8 95
300	0.451	7.75	0.077	8.89
400	0.555	7.27	+0.031	8.76
	1868 B.		**1876 B.**	
0	−0.521	+7.44	−0.005	−8.81
100	0.621	6.91	+0.103	8.64
200	0.716	6.33	0.211	8 39
300	0.804	5.69	0.317	8.07
400	0.885	5.00	0.421	7.69
	1869.		**1877.**	
0	−0.859	+5.24	+0.387	−7.82
100	0.935	4.52	0.488	7.39
200	1.003	3.77	0.585	6.90
300	1.061	2 98	0.678	6.36
400	1.111	2.18	0.766	5.76
	1870.		**1878.**	
0	−1.095	+2.45	+0.737	−5.96
100	1.134	1.63	0.824	5.33
200	1.172	+0.80	0.897	4.65
300	1.194	−0.04	0.967	3.93
400	1.207	0.87	1.029	3.18
	1871.		**1879.**	
0	−1.204	−0.59	+1.009	−3.44
100	1.210	1.42	1.065	2.67
200	1.206	2.23	1.112	1.87
300	1.191	3.02	1.151	1.05
400	1.166	3.79	1.180	0.23
	1872 B.		**1880 B.**	
0	−1.176	−3.53	+1.171	−0.51
100	1.145	4.28	1.193	+0.32
200	1.104	4.98	1.206	1.15
300	1.054	5.64	1.208	1.97
400	−0.996	−6.26	+1.200	+2.78

✳ d ☉, Jan. 6.0.
✳ d Mean Sun, Jan. 7.6.

14

TABLE XXIV.—* δ Draconis.

R.A. 19h 12.5m.　　　　　Dec. + 67° 26'.

Upper transit at fictitious meridian.

Sidereal Day	Mean Day	Δ☉α 1870.	Var.in 10 y.	Diff. for 10 d.	Δ☉δ 1870.	Var.in 10 y.	Diff. for 10 d.
0, Jan. 0	+ 0.02	−3.474	− 3	− 75	+ 2.94	0	−344
10	10.00	3.495	3	+ 32	− 0.55	0	352
20	19.97	3.409	3	139	4.07	0	348
30	29.94	3.218	3	242	7.47	0	331
Feb. 9	8.91	2.928	3	357	10.63	0	301
19	18.89	2.548	2	421	13.44	0	260
Mar. 1	0.86	2.090	2	492	15.79	0	208
11	10.83	1.569	2	547	17.59	0	150
21	20.80	1.001	1	585	18.77	0	86
31	30.78	−0.405	1	605	19.30	0	− 20
100, Apr. 10	9.75	+0.203	− 1	607	19.17	0	+ 46
20	19.72	0.804	0	591	18.39	0	109
30	29.70	1.380	0	558	17.00	0	168
May 10	9.67	1.915	+ 1	509	15.05	0	220
20	19.64	2.393	1	446	12.62	0	265
30	29.61	2.802	1	371	9.78	0	301
June 9	8.59	3.132	2	286	6.64	0	327
19	18.56	3.372	2	193	− 3.27	0	345
29	28.53	3.517	2	+ 97	0.23	0	352
July 9	8.50	3.565	1	− 2	3.75	0	351
200, 19	18.48	3.513	1	102	7.22	0	342
29	28.45	3.362	+ 1	198	10.55	0	324
Aug. 8	7.42	3.119	0	289	13.68	0	300
18	17.40	2.788	0	372	16.52	0	269
28	27.37	2.379	0	444	19.03	0	232
Sept. 7	6.34	1.903	0	506	21.14	0	190
17	16.31	1.372	− 1	553	22.81	0	144
27	26.29	0.803	1	584	24.00	0	94
Oct. 7	6.26	+0.209	1	600	24.68	0	+ 41
17	16.23	−0.391	2	603	24.82	0	− 14
300, 27	26.20	0.980	2	578	24.41	0	69
Nov. 6	5.18	1.541	3	541	23.45	0	124
16	15.15	2.057	3	487	21.95	0	177
26	25.12	2.511	4	418	19.93	0	226
Dec. 6	5.10	2.889	4	336	17.44	0	270
16	15.07	3.180	4	243	14.56	0	306
26	25.04	3.372	5	141	11.36	0	333
36	35.01	−3.461	− 5	− 35	+ 7.95	0	−348

✳ δ ☉, Jan. 6.7.
✳ δ Mean Sun, Jan. 8.2
✳ δ Mean Sun, July 9.8.

Sidereal Day	ΔΩα	ΔΩδ	ΔΩα	ΔΩδ
	1865.		**1873.**	
0	+0.378	+8.39	−0.230	−6.10
100	0.402	8.69	0.265	6.67
200	0.422	8.90	0.298	7.19
300	0.438	9.05	0.328	7.64
400	0.451	9.11	0.356	8.03
	1866.		**1874.**	
0	+0.447	+9.09	−0.347	−7.01
100	0.457	9.10	0.373	8.25
200	0.463	9.03	0.395	8.53
300	0.465	8.88	0.414	8.74
400	0.463	8.66	0.430	8.87
	1867.		**1875.**	
0	+0.464	+8.74	−0.425	−8.83
100	0.459	8.47	0.438	8.92
200	0.450	8.12	0.448	8.93
300	0.438	7.69	0.454	8.87
400	0.421	7.21	0.456	8.73
	1868 B.		**1876 B.**	
0	+0.427	+7.38	−0.456	−8.79
100	0.408	6.85	0.456	8.61
200	0.386	6.26	0.452	8.35
300	0.360	5.62	0.444	8.03
400	0.331	4.93	0.433	7.64
	1869.		**1877.**	
0	+0.341	+5.17	−0.437	−7.78
100	0.310	4.45	0.423	7.35
200	0.277	3.69	0.406	6.85
300	0.242	2.91	0.386	6.31
400	0.204	2.10	0.362	5.70
	1870.		**1878.**	
0	+0.217	+2.37	−0.370	−5.91
100	0.178	1.56	0.344	5.28
200	0.137	+0.72	0.316	4.59
300	0.096	−0.11	0.284	3.87
400	0.054	0.94	0.256	3.12
	1871.		**1879.**	
0	+0.068	−0.66	−0.202	−3.38
100	+0.026	1.49	0.227	2.60
200	−0.017	2.30	0.189	1.81
300	0.059	3.09	0.150	0.99
400	0.100	3.85	0.110	0.17
	1872 B.		**1880 B.**	
0	−0.086	−3.60	−0.124	−0.45
100	0.127	4.34	0.084	+0.38
200	0.167	5.04	−0.041	1.21
300	0.206	5.69	+0.002	2.03
400	−0.242	−6.30	+0.044	+2.83

TABLE XXIV.—* τ Draconis.

R.A. 19 18.0. (h m)   Dec. + 73 7. (° ')

Upper transit at fictitious meridian.

Sidereal Day	Mean Day	Δ⊙a 1870	Var. in 10y	Diff. for 10 d	Δ⊙δ 1870	Var. in 10y	Diff. for 10 d
0, Jan. 0	0.03	-4.576	-6	-160	+3.64	-1	-339
10	10.00	4.665	5	-16	+0.19	1	350
20	19.97	4.609	5	+123	-3.31	1	348
30	29.94	4.410	4	267	6.72	1	343
Feb. 9	8.92	4.077	4	398	9.92	1	305
19	18.89	3.619	3	517	12.78	1	266
Mar. 1	0.86	3.053	2	613	15.20	1	216
11	10.83	2.400	-1	691	17.08	1	159
21	20.81	1.679	0	745	18.36	1	97
31	30.78	0.917	+1	775	19.00	-1	31
100, Apr. 10	9.75	-0.138	2	779	18.98	0	+34
20	19.73	+0.633	3	759	18.32	0	98
30	29.70	1.371	4	715	17.04	0	157
May 10	9.67	2.055	4	650	15.19	0	210
20	19.64	2.665	4	566	12.85	+1	256
30	29.62	3.182	4	466	10.09	1	294
June 9	8.59	3.593	4	354	7.01	1	322
19	18.56	3.887	4	232	3.69	1	341
29	28.53	4.055	3	+104	-0.23	1	350
July 9	8.51	4.095	2	-26	+3.29	1	351
200, 19	18.48	4.004	+1	155	6.77	1	344
29	28.45	3.787	0	280	10.13	+1	328
Aug. 8	7.42	3.447	-1	398	13.30	0	305
18	17.40	2.994	2	506	16.21	0	276
28	27.37	2.440	3	601	18.80	0	241
Sept. 7	6.34	1.797	4	681	21.01	0	200
17	16.32	1.083	5	745	22.79	-1	155
27	26.29	+0.314	6	789	24.10	1	105
Oct. 7	6.26	-0.488	7	813	24.90	2	54
17	16.23	1.303	8	815	25.18	2	+1
300, 27	26.21	2.110	9	795	24.91	2	-55
Nov. 6	5.18	2.884	10	752	24.08	2	111
16	15.15	3.605	10	687	22.70	2	164
26	25.13	4.251	11	602	20.80	2	214
Dec. 6	5.10	4.803	11	498	18.43	3	260
16	15.07	5.242	12	379	15.63	3	298
26	25.04	5.556	12	247	12.51	3	326
36	35.02	-5.733	-11	-106	+9.15	-3	-344

Sidereal Day	ΔΩa	ΔΩδ	ΔΩa	ΔΩδ
	1865.		**1873.**	
0	+0.329	+8.43	-0.009	-6.20
100	0.393	8.71	0.079	6.76
200	0.454	8.91	0.148	7.26
300	0.511	9.03	0.216	7.70
400	0.563	9.08	0.282	8.08
	1866.		**1874.**	
0	+0.546	+9.07	-0.260	-7.96
100	0.595	9.06	0.324	8.29
200	0.639	8.98	0.386	8.55
300	0.677	8.81	0.444	8.74
400	0.710	8.57	0.499	8.86
	1867.		**1875.**	
0	+0.700	+8.66	-0.481	-8.83
100	0.728	8.37	0.532	8.90
200	0.750	8.01	0.580	8.89
300	0.766	7.57	0.622	8.82
400	0.774	7.08	0.659	8.67
	1868 B.		**1876 B.**	
0	+0.772	+7.25	-0.648	-8.73
100	0.777	6.71	0.681	8.53
200	0.774	6.11	0.709	8.26
300	0.765	5.46	0.732	7.93
400	0.749	4.77	0.748	7.53
	1869.		**1877.**	
0	+0.755	+5.01	-0.743	-7.67
100	0.735	4.28	0.756	7.23
200	0.709	3.52	0.762	6.73
300	0.676	2.74	0.762	6.17
400	0.638	1.93	0.755	5.56
	1870.		**1878.**	
0	+0.652	+2.20	-0.758	-5.77
100	0.610	1.39	0.747	5.13
200	0.563	+0.55	0.731	4.44
300	0.511	-0.28	0.708	3.71
400	0.455	1.11	0.679	2.96
	1871.		**1879.**	
0	+0.474	-0.83	-0.689	-3.22
100	0.416	1.65	0.657	2.44
200	0.354	2.45	0.619	1.64
300	0.289	3.23	0.575	0.83
400	0.222	3.99	0.527	0.00
	1872 B.		**1880 B.**	
0	+0.245	-3.74	-0.544	-0.28
100	0.177	4.47	0.492	+0.54
200	0.108	5.16	0.436	1.37
300	+0.037	5.80	0.377	2.18
400	-0.033	-6.40	-0.314	+2.98

* ♂ ⊙.   Jan. 7.9.
* ♂ Mean Sun,   Jan. 9.6.
* ☍ Mean Sun,   July 11.2.

TABLE XXIV.—δ Aquilæ.

R.A. 19^h 18.9^m. Dec. +2° 51′.

Upper transit at fictitious meridian.

Sidereal Day	Mean Day	$\Delta_\odot\alpha$ 1870.	Var. in 10 y.	Diff. for 10 d.	$\Delta_\odot\delta$ 1870.	Var. in 10 y.	Diff. for 10 d.
0, Jan. 0	0 03	−1.311	0	+ 75	− 0.67	0	−140
10	10.00	1.217	0	112	2.07	0	140
20	19.97	1.087	0	146	3.46	0	135
30	29.94	0.925	− 1	179	4.75	0	122
Feb. 9	8.92	0.731	1	207	5.89	0	106
19	18.89	0.513	2	229	6.85	0	83
Mar. 1	0.86	0.274	2	249	7.53	0	55
11	10.84	−0.016	2	267	7.93	0	− 24
21	20.81	+0 258	2	280	8.00	+ 1	+ 8
31	30.78	0.542	3	288	7.77	1	41
100, Apr. 10	9.75	0.833	3	293	7.18	1	73
20	19 73	1.126	3	294	6.31	1	102
30	29 70	1.419	2	290	5.15	1	127
May 10	9.67	1.705	2	280	3.78	1	147
20	19.64	1.977	2	265	2.22	1	162
30	29.62	2.233	2	244	0.55	1	172
June 9	8.59	2.464	1	217	+ 1.20	1	176
19	18.56	2.665	1	185	2.95	2	175
29	28.54	2.833	− 1	148	4.68	2	170
July 9	8.51	2.961	0	108	6.33	2	159
200, 19	18 48	3 049	0	66	7.84	3	145
29	28.45	3.093	0	+ 22	9.22	3	120
Aug. 8	7.43	3.093	+ 1	− 22	10.42	3	112
18	17.40	3.050	1	02	11.45	3	93
28	27.37	2.970	1	98	12.27	3	72
Sept. 7	6.34	2.856	2	129	12 89	3	52
17	16.32	2.714	2	152	13.31	3	32
27	26.29	2.555	2	167	13.52	3	+ 12
Oct. 7	6.26	2.384	2	172	13.53	4	− 8
17	16.24	2.214	3	167	13.35	4	28
200, 27	26.21	2.052	3	154	12.98	4	48
Nov. 6	5.18	1.908	2	133	12.40	4	67
16	15.15	1.789	2	104	11 61	5	84
26	25.13	1.703	2	68	10.72	4	102
Dec. 6	5.10	1.654	1	− 30	9.61	4	117
16	15.07	1.644	1	+ 10	8.39	4	128
26	25.04	1.674	+ 1	51	7.06	4	137
36	35.02	+1.745	0	+ 89	+ 5.66	+ 4	−141

✻ δ ☉, Jan. 8.1.
✻ δ Mean Sun, Jan. 9.9.

Sidereal Day	$\Delta_\Omega\alpha$	$\Delta_\Omega\delta$	$\Delta_\Omega\alpha$	$\Delta_\Omega\delta$
	1865.		**1873.**	
0	+0.629	+8.43	−0.902	−6.22
100	0.550	8.71	0 852	6 78
200	0 485	8.91	0.790	7 28
300	0.376	9.03	0.733	7.71
400	0.284	9.07	0.664	8.09
	1866.		**1874.**	
0	+0.315	+9 07	−0 688	−7.96
100	0.221	9.06	0 615	8 30
200	0.125	8 97	0 538	8.55
300	+0.028	8.80	0.456	8.74
400	−0.070	8.56	0 370	8 86
	1867.		**1875.**	
0	−0.037	+8 65	−0.400	−8 83
100	0.134	8 36	0 312	8 89
200	0.230	7.99	0.222	8.89
300	0 324	7 56	0.131	8 81
400	0.416	7.06	0.038	8.65
	1868 B.		**1876 B.**	
0	−0.385	+7 23	−0 069	−8.71
100	0 473	6.69	0.024	8 51
200	0.558	6.09	0 116	8.24
300	0.637	5.44	0.208	7.91
400	0 710	4.74	0.298	7.50
	1869.		**1877.**	
0	−0 686	+4 98	+0.268	−7.64
100	0.756	4.26	0.357	7.20
200	0.818	3 50	0.443	6 69
300	0.874	2.71	0 525	6.13
400	0.921	1.90	0.604	5.52
	1870.		**1878.**	
0	−0 906	+2.17	+0.578	−5.73
100	0 948	1.35	0.653	5 08
200	0.983	+0.52	0.723	4.40
300	1.008	−0 31	0.787	3 67
400	1.025	1.14	0.844	2.91
	1871.		**1879.**	
0	−1.020	−0.86	+0 825	−3.17
100	1.031	1.68	0.879	2 39
200	1.034	2.48	0.925	1.59
300	1.027	3.26	0.963	−0.78
400	1.012	4.01	0.993	+0.04
	1872 B.		**1880 B.**	
0	−1.018	−3.76	+0.984	−0.24
100	0.997	4.49	1.009	+0.59
200	0 968	5.18	1.026	1.41
300	0.931	5.82	1 033	2.23
400	−0.886	−6.41	+1.033	+3.02

TABLE XXIV.—κ Aquilæ.

R.A. 19 29.9. (h m)   Dec. — 7 19. (°)

Upper transit at fictitious meridian.

Sidereal Day	Mean Day	Δ⊙α 1870.	Var. in 10y.	Diff. for 10d.	Δ⊙δ 1870.	Var. in 10y.	Diff. for 10d.
0, Jan. 0	0.03	−1.308	+ 1	+ 73	− 1.44	0	— 78
10	10.01	1.216	0	110	2.22	0	77
20	19.98	1.088	0	144	2.97	0	71
30	29.95	0.928	— 1	175	3.64	0	62
Feb. 9	8.93	0.739	1	202	4.21	0	50
19	18.90	0.524	1	227	4.63	0	33
Mar. 1	0.87	0.285	2	249	4.87	0	— 13
11	10.84	−0.027	2	266	4.88	0	+ 10
21	20.82	+0.247	3	280	4.67	0	33
31	30.79	0.533	3	291	4.22	0	56
100, Apr 10	9.76	0.827	3	298	3.55	0	77
20	19.73	1.128	3	301	2.68	+ 1	96
30	29.71	1.427	3	298	1.63	1	112
May 10	9.68	1.723	3	291	— 0.44	1	124
20	19.65	2.007	3	278	+ 0.84	1	131
30	29.63	2.277	2	259	2.17	2	134
June 9	8.60	2.523	2	233	3.51	2	132
19	18.57	2.741	2	203	4.81	2	126
29	28.54	2.927	1	166	6.02	3	117
July 9	8.52	3.072	1	125	7.14	3	105
200, 19	18.49	3.176	— 1	83	8.12	3	91
29	28.46	3.237	0	+ 39	8.96	3	77
Aug. 8	7.43	3.253	+ 1	— 6	9.65	3	62
18	17.41	3.225	1	48	10.19	4	46
28	27.38	3.153	2	86	10.57	4	31
Sept. 7	6.35	3.054	2	120	10.80	4	17
17	16.32	2.920	2	144	10.92	4	+ 5
27	26.30	2.768	2	161	10.92	4	— 6
Oct. 7	6.27	2.601	3	169	10.80	4	17
17	16.24	2.433	3	165	10.58	4	27
300, 27	26.22	2.273	3	153	10.27	4	36
Nov. 6	5.19	2.129	3	133	9.87	4	45
16	15.16	2.009	2	104	9.38	4	53
26	25.13	1.922	2	70	8.82	4	60
Dec. 6	5.11	1.870	2	— 32	8.18	4	67
16	15.08	1.858	1	+ 8	7.47	4	73
26	25.05	1.886	+ 1	48	6.72	4	76
36	35.02	+1.953	0	+ 86	+ 5.95	+ 4	— 77

✳ δ ⊙,   Jan. 10.6.
✳ δ Mean Sun, Jan. 12.7.

Sidereal Day	Δ_Ω α	Δ_☊ δ	Δ_Ω α	Δ_☊ δ
	1865.		**1873.**	
0	+0.642	+8.49	−0.948	—6.41
100	0.554	8.73	0.892	6.94
200	0.461	8.90	0.828	7.41
300	0.364	8.99	0.757	7.82
400	0.264	9.00	0.681	8.16
	1866.		**1874.**	
0	+0.298	+9.01	−0.707	—8.05
100	0.196	8.97	0.627	8.35
200	+0.092	8.85	0.542	8.58
300	−0.012	8.65	0.432	8.73
400	0.117	8.38	0.359	8.82
	1867.		**1875.**	
0	−0.081	+8.49	−0.391	—8.79
100	0.185	8.16	0.296	8.83
200	0.288	7.77	0.199	8.79
300	0.387	7.31	0.100	8.69
400	0.484	6.79	0.000	8.50
	1868 B.		**1876 B.**	
0	−0.452	+6.97	−0.034	—8.57
100	0.545	6.41	+0.066	8.35
200	0.633	5.79	0.166	8 05
300	0.716	5.12	0.264	7.69
400	0.793	4.41	0.359	7.26
	1869.		**1877.**	
0	−0.768	+4.65	+0.327	—7.41
100	0.839	3.92	0.421	6.94
200	0.904	3.15	0.512	6.41
300	0.960	2.36	0.599	5.84
400	1.008	1.55	0.681	5.21
	1870.		**1878.**	
0	−0.992	+1.83	+0.654	—5.42
100	1.035	1.01	0.732	4.77
200	1.068	+0.18	0.804	4.07
300	1.091	−0.64	0.870	3.33
400	1.106	1.46	0.929	2.57
	1871.		**1879.**	
0	−1.102	−1.19	+0.910	—2.83
100	1.110	1.99	0.964	2.05
200	1.109	2.78	1.010	1.25
300	1.098	3 55	1.048	−0.44
400	1.078	4.28	1.077	+0.38
	1872 B.		**1880 B.**	
0	−1.086	−4.03	+1.068	+0.10
100	1.060	4.74	1.091	0.92
200	1.025	5.41	1.105	1.73
300	0.981	6.03	1.110	2.53
400	−0.930	−6.59	+1.105	+3.32

TABLE XXIV.—ε Draconis.

R.A. 19 48.6 (h m)   Dec. + 69 56 (° ')

Upper transit at fictitious meridian.

Sidereal Day.	Mean Day.	Δ☉α 1870.	Var.in 10y.	Diff.for 10d.	Δ☉δ 1870.	Var.in 10y.	Diff.for 10d.
0, Jan. 0	0.05	−3 729	− 4	−193	+ 5.96	0	−323
10	10.02	3.804	5	− 77	+ 2.64	0	341
20	19.99	3.882	5	+ 43	− 0.81	0	346
30	29.97	3.780	5	161	4.25	0	339
Feb. 9	8.94	3.562	5	275	7.55	0	319
19	18.91	3.234	5	380	10.59	0	287
Mar. 1	0.88	2.807	4	473	13.24	0	243
11	10.86	2.293	4	550	15.43	0	190
21	20.83	1.712	3	610	17.03	0	131
31	30.80	1.079	2	651	18.02	0	67
100, Apr. 10	9.78	−0.416	− 1	671	18.36	0	− 2
20	19.75	+0.256	0	670	18.05	0	+ 63
30	29.72	0.918	0	649	17.11	0	125
May 10	9.69	1.549	+ 1	610	15.57	0	182
20	19.67	2.131	2	552	13.50	0	232
30	29.64	2.647	2	479	10.93	0	274
June 9	8.61	3.084	2	392	8.04	0	309
19	18.58	3.429	3	296	4.82	0	334
29	28.56	3.673	3	192	− 1.39	0	350
July 9	8.53	3.810	3	+ 83	+ 2.16	0	357
200, 19	18.50	3.837	2	− 28	5.73	0	356
29	28.48	3.754	2	138	9.25	0	246
Aug. 8	7.45	3.564	2	243	12.63	0	329
18	17.42	3.271	+ 1	342	15.81	0	305
28	27.39	2.893	0	431	18.71	0	274
Sept. 7	6.36	2.412	0	509	21.28	0	238
17	16.34	1.870	− 1	573	23.45	0	196
27	26.31	1.271	2	622	25.18	0	149
Oct. 7	6.28	+0.632	3	653	26.42	0	99
17	16.26	−0.030	4	667	27.15	0	+ 45
300, 27	26.23	0.696	5	662	27.32	0	− 11
Nov. 6	16.21	1.347	5	638	26.93	0	67
16	15.17	1.965	6	595	25.98	0	123
26	25.15	2.532	7	538	24.48	0	177
Dec. 6	5.12	3.029	8	458	22.45	0	227
16	15.09	3.442	8	366	19.96	0	270
26	25.06	3.758	9	263	17 07	0	306
36	35.04	−3.965	− 9	−150	+13.88	0	−331

✳ ☌ ☉, Jan. 14 9.
✳ ☌ Mean Sun, Jan. 17.4.
✳ ☍ Mean Sun, July 19.0.

Sidereal Day.	ΔΩα	ΔΩδ	ΔΩα	ΔΩδ
	1865.		**1873.**	
0	+0.587	+8.54	−0.320	−6.69
100	0.632	8.73	0.382	7.17
200	0.671	8.84	0.441	7.59
300	0.705	8.87	0.496	7.95
400	0.733	8.83	0.547	8.24
	1866.		**1874.**	
0	+0 724	+8.85	−0.530	−8.15
100	0.747	8.75	0.578	8 39
200	0.764	8.58	0.621	8.57
300	0.775	8.34	0.659	8.67
400	0.778	8.02	0.691	8 70
	1867.		**1875.**	
0	+0.778	+8.13	−0.681	−8.70
100	0.776	7.77	0.710	8.68
200	0.769	7.33	0.732	8.59
300	0.754	6.84	0.749	8.44
400	0.733	6.28	0.760	8.21
	1868.B.		**1876 B.**	
0	+0.741	+6.47	−0.757	−8.29
100	0.716	5.88	0.763	8.02
200	0.684	5.24	0.763	7.68
300	0.647	4.55	0.757	7.28
400	0.604	3.81	0.744	6.82
	1869.		**1877.**	
0	+0.619	+4.07	−0.749	−6 98
100	0.572	3.33	0.733	6.48
200	0.521	2.55	0.710	5.92
300	0.464	1.76	0.682	5.32
400	0.406	0.95	0.648	4.67
	1870.		**1878.**	
0	+0.427	+1.22	−0.663	−4.89
100	0.365	+0.41	0.622	4.22
200	0.300	−0.40	0.579	3.50
300	0.233	1.21	0.531	2.76
400	0.164	2.01	0.479	1.99
	1871.		**1879.**	
0	+0.187	−1.74	−0.497	−2.25
100	0.117	2 52	0 442	1.47
200	+0.046	3.29	0 383	−0.68
300	−0.025	4.02	0.320	+0.13
400	0.095	4.71	0.255	0.93
	1872 B.		**1880 B.**	
0	−0.072	−4.48	−0.277	+0.66
100	0.142	5.15	0.216	1.47
200	0.210	5.77	0.142	2.26
300	0.277	6.34	−0.071	3.03
400	−0.341	−6.86	0.000	+3.78

TABLE XXIV.—ˀ λ Ursæ Minoris.†

R.A. 19ʰ 54.3ᵐ   Dec. + 88° 55′

Upper transit at fictitious meridian.

Sidereal Day	Mean Day	$\Delta_\odot\alpha$ 1870	Var. in 10y.	Diff. for 10 d.	$\Delta_\odot\delta$ 1870	Var. in 10y.	Diff. for 10 d.
0, Jan. 0	0.06	− 67.68	−277	−578	+ 7.25	− 82	−293
10	10.03	72.38	243	360	4.21	88	315
20	20.00	74.84	201	−130	+ 0.99	91	326
30	29.98	74.97	152	+102	− 2.27	92	324
Feb. 9	8.95	72.81	98	327	5.45	89	310
19	18.92	68.48	− 44	536	8.43	84	284
Mar. 1	0.89	62.17	+ 11	720	11.10	76	247
11	10.87	54.18	65	872	13.34	67	200
21	20.84	44.85	115	988	15.08	55	147
31	30.81	34.56	158	1063	16.26	43	88
100, Apr. 10	9.78	23.73	194	1096	16.84	30	− 27
20	19.76	12.77	221	1088	16.80	1t	+ 34
30	29.73	− 2.10	238	1041	16.17	− 3	93
May 10	9.70	+ 7.93	244	958	14.96	+ 9	148
20	19.68	16.96	240	843	13.23	20	198
30	29.65	24.71	226	703	11.03	29	241
June 9	8.62	30.95	202	542	8.44	36	276
19	18.59	35.56	169	366	5.53	42	304
29	28.56	38 24	127	+190	− 2.39	45	323
July 9	8.54	39.06	79	− 11	+ 0.91	46	335
200, 19	18.51	38.02	+ 25	209	4.27	44	338
29	28.48	35.06	− 34	388	7.63	40	333
Aug. 8	7.46	30.28	95	567	10.91	34	321
18	17.43	23.76	159	734	14.04	26	302
28	27.40	15.64	223	887	16.95	16	278
Sept. 7	6.37	+ 6.08	287	1022	19.57	+ 4	247
17	16.35	− 4.73	348	1138	21.87	− 9	210
27	26.32	16.59	407	1230	23.77	24	169
Oct. 7	6.29	29.25	459	1297	25.23	39	123
17	16.26	42.44	507	1337	26.21	55	73
300, 27	26.24	55.88	547	1346	26.69	72	+ 21
Nov. 6	5.21	69.24	581	1322	26.63	88	− 33
16	15.18	82.21	602	1265	26.03	104	88
26	25.16	94.43	615	1173	24.88	119	141
Dec. 6	5.13	105.56	618	1048	23.21	132	192
16	15.10	115.28	609	890	21.07	144	236
26	25.07	123.27	591	704	18.51	154	274
36	35.05	−129.25	−502	−495	+15.62	−162	−303

Sidereal Day	$\Delta_\Omega\alpha$	$\Delta_\Omega\delta$	$\Delta_\Omega\alpha$	$\Delta_\Omega\delta$
	1865.		**1873.**	
0	+ 1.11	+ 8.54	+10.41	−6.73
100	3.45	8.70	8.26	7.20
200	5.76	8.78	6.05	7.61
300	8.03	8.79	3.80	7.96
400	10.24	8.72	1.52	8.24
	1866.		**1874.**	
0	+ 9.50	+ 8.75	+ 2 29	−9.15
100	11.66	8.63	0.00	8.39
200	13.71	8.44	−2.28	8.56
300	15.66	8.17	4.55	8.66
400	17.47	7.84	6.77	8.60
	1867.		**1875.**	
0	+16.87	+7.96	− 6.02	−8 69
100	18.59	7.58	8.21	8.68
200	20.15	7.13	10.33	8.59
300	21.53	6.63	12.37	8.44
400	22.74	6.07	14.31	8.21
	1868 B.		**1876 B.**	
0	+22.35	+6.26	−13.67	−8.30
100	23.43	5.67	15.54	8.03
200	24.30	5.02	17.28	7.70
300	24.97	4.34	18.89	7.31
400	25.43	3.61	20.35	6.85
	1869.		**1877.**	
0	+25.30	+3.86	−19.87	−7.01
100	25.62	3.12	21.23	6.52
200	25.71	2.35	22.41	5.98
300	25.59	1.57	23.42	5.38
400	25.26	0.77	24.25	4.75
	1870.		**1878.**	
0	+25.40	+1.04	−23.99	−4.97
100	24.92	0.24	24.69	4.30
200	24.24	−0.57	25.20	3.60
300	23.36	1.36	25.50	2.87
400	22.28	2.14	25.60	2.11
	1871.		**1879.**	
0	+22.67	−1.88	−25.59	−2.37
100	21.47	2.65	25.55	1.59
200	20.10	3.39	25.31	0.80
300	18.56	4.11	24.86	−0.01
400	16.88	4.79	24.21	+0.80
	1872 B.		**1880 B.**	
0	+17.47	−4.56	−24.45	+0.53
100	15.69	5.22	23.66	1.32
200	13.79	5.83	22.68	2.12
300	11.79	6.39	21.51	2.89
400	+ 9.69	−6.90	−20.16	+3.64

✱ ☍ ☉,   Jan. 16.3.
✱ ☌ Mean Sun, Jan. 18.9.
✱ ☌ Mean Sun, July 20.5.

† See pages 248, 250, 251–253 for additional corrections.

TABLE XXIV.—τ Aquilæ.

R.A. 19 57.8 (h m).   Dec. + 6 55 (° ').

Upper transit at fictitious meridian.

Sidereal Day	Mean Day	$\Delta_\odot a$ 1870.	Var. in 10 y.	Diff. for 10 d.	$\Delta_\odot \delta$ 1870.	Var. in 10 y.	Diff. for 10 d.
0, Jan. 0	0.05	-1.257	+1	+36	-0.01	+1	-149
10	10.03	1.203	0	71	1.52	1	152
20	20.00	1.115	0	106	3.03	1	148
30	29.97	0.992	-1	138	4.46	1	136
Feb. 9	8.94	0.839	1	168	5.74	1	119
19	18.92	0.656	2	197	6.82	1	96
Mar. 1	0.89	0.446	2	221	7.64	1	68
11	10.86	-0.214	2	243	8.17	1	36
21	20.84	+0.039	2	263	8.35	1	-1
31	30.81	0.310	2	278	8.19	0	+35
100, Apr. 10	9.78	0.593	3	289	7.65	0	71
20	19.75	0.886	3	296	6.78	0	103
30	29.73	1.184	3	298	5.59	1	134
May 10	9.70	1.480	2	293	4.12	1	159
20	19.67	1.763	2	282	2.43	1	178
30	29.64	2.042	2	266	-0.57	1	192
June 9	8.62	2.298	2	244	+1.39	1	199
19	18.59	2.528	2	214	3.40	1	202
29	28.56	2.725	1	180	5.41	1	199
July 9	8.54	2.886	-1	141	7.36	1	190
200, 19	18.51	3.005	0	98	9.20	2	178
29	28.48	3.082	0	54	10.92	2	162
Aug. 8	7.45	3.112	+1	+10	12.44	2	143
18	17.43	3.101	1	-33	13.78	2	122
28	27.40	3.046	1	73	14.89	2	100
Sept. 7	6.37	2.956	1	108	15.77	2	77
17	16.34	2.833	1	136	16.43	3	54
27	26.32	2.687	2	155	16.85	3	31
Oct. 7	6.29	2.525	2	167	17.04	3	+8
17	16.26	2.356	2	168	17.00	4	-16
300, 27	26.23	2.191	2	161	16.73	4	39
Nov. 6	5.21	2.036	3	146	16.22	4	62
16	15.18	1.901	3	124	15.50	5	82
26	25.15	1.791	2	95	14.58	5	102
Dec. 6	5.13	1.713	2	61	13.47	5	120
16	15.10	1.669	2	-25	12.18	5	135
26	25.07	1.663	1	+12	10.76	5	144
36	35.04	+1.693	+1	+48	+9.30	+5	-150

Sidereal Day	$\Delta_\Omega a$	$\Delta_\Omega \delta$	$\Delta_\Omega a$	$\Delta_\Omega \delta$
	1865.		**1873.**	
0	+0.635	+8.54	-0.891	-6.82
100	0.558	8.70	0.845	7.28
200	0.477	8.78	0.792	7.67
300	0.391	8 79	0.732	8.00
400	0.302	8.72	0.667	8.26
	1866.		**1874.**	
0	+0.332	+8.75	-0.690	-8.18
100	0.241	8.63	0.620	8.39
200	0.148	8.44	0.546	8.54
300	+0.054	8.17	0.468	8.62
400	-0.041	7.83	0.385	8.62
	1867.		**1875.**	
0	-0.009	+7.95	-0.414	-8.63
100	0.104	7.56	0.329	8.58
200	0.198	7.11	0.242	8.47
300	0.290	6.60	0.154	8.29
400	0.380	6.02	0.063	8.04
	1868 B.		**1876 B.**	
0	-0.350	+6.22	-0.094	-8.13
100	0.437	5.62	-0.003	7.83
200	0.520	4.96	+0.087	7.48
300	0.599	4.27	0.177	7.05
400	0.672	3.53	0.265	6.57
	1869.		**1877.**	
0	-0.648	+3.78	+0.236	-6.74
100	0.718	3.03	0.323	6.22
200	0.781	2.26	0.408	5.65
300	0.837	1.46	0.489	5.03
400	0.885	0.66	0.567	4.37
	1870.		**1878.**	
0	-0.870	+0.93	+0.541	-4.60
100	0.913	+0.12	0.615	3.91
200	0.949	-0.69	0.685	3.20
300	0.976	1.49	0.749	2.45
400	0 995	2.27	0.808	1.68
	1871.		**1879.**	
0	-0.989	-2.01	+0.789	-1.94
100	1.003	2.78	0.842	1.16
200	1.007	3.53	0.889	-0.37
300	1.005	4.24	0.929	+0.43
400	0.991	4.91	0.961	1.23
	1872 B.		**1880 B.**	
0	-0.996	-4.69	+0.951	+0.96
100	0.978	5.34	0.978	1.75
200	0.952	5.94	0.996	2.53
300	0.918	6.49	1.006	3.29
400	-0.877	-6.98	+1.008	+4.02

✻ ♂ ☉,   Jan. 17.1.
✻ ♂ Mean Sun,   Jan. 19.7.

· TABLE XXIV.—' κ Cephei.

R.A. 20 13.2. (h m)   Dec. + 77 19. (° ')

Upper transit at fictitious meridian.

Sidereal Day.	Mean Day.	$\Delta_\odot a$ 1870.	Var. in 10y.	Diff. for 10 d.	$\Delta_\odot \delta$ 1870.	Var. in 10y.	Diff. for 10 d.
0, Jan. 0	0.06	−5.587	−17	−465	+ 8.34	− 2	−298
10	10.04	5.965	17	2e9	5.22	2	324
20	20.01	6.161	16	−102	+ 1.90	2	338
30	29.98	6.167	15	+ 89	− 1.49	3	339
Feb. 9	8.96	5.984	14	276	4.84	3	327
19	18.93	5.618	12	454	8.00	2	303
Mar. 1	0.90	5 082	10	616	10.85	2	266
11	10.87	4.394	7	754	13.29	2	220
21	20.85	3.581	4	866	15.22	2	165
31	30.82	2.672	− 2	948	16.58	1	105
100, Apr. 10	9.79	1.697	+ 1	996	17.31	1	− 42
20	19.76	−0.690	3	1011	17.41	− 1	+ 23
30	29.74	+0.315	5	993	16.86	0	85
May 10	9.71	1.286	7	943	15.71	0	144
20	19.68	2.191	9	864	13.99	+ 1	198
30	29.66	3.005	10	760	11.77	1	245
June 9	8.63	3.704	10	634	9.12	1	285
19	18.60	4.268	10	491	6 11	1	316
29	28.57	4.681	9	335	− 2.83	1	339
July 9	8.55	4.935	8	170	+ 0.64	1	353
200, 19	18.52	5.021	7	+ 3	4.20	1	358
29	28.49	4.940	5	−164	7.77	1	355
Aug. 8	7.46	4.693	+ 2	327	11.28	1	345
18	17.44	4.287	0	482	14 64	+ 1	327
28	27.41	3.733	− 3	625	17.80	0	302
Sept. 7	6 38	3.043	6	752	20.67	0	271
17	16.36	2.235	9	861	23.19	0	234
27	26.33	1.327	12	950	25.33	− 1	191
Oct. 7	6.30	+0.343	16	1016	27.01	1	144
17	16.27	−0.696	19	1056	28.19	2	93
300, 27	26.25	1.760	22	1069	28.85	2	+ 38
Nov. 6	5.22	2.825	24	1055	28.94	3	− 19
16	15.19	3.861	27	1012	28 47	3	76
26	25.16	4.840	29	941	27.42	3	133
Dec. 6	5.14	5.733	31	841	25.82	4	186
16	15.11	6.513	32	716	23.71	4	235
26	25.08	7.157	33	568	21.15	4	277
36	35.06	−7.643	−33	−401	+18.21	− 5	−309

✳ ♂ ☉,   Jan. 20 7.
✳ ♂ Mean Sun,   Jan. 23 6.
✳ ☍ Mean Sun,   July 25 2.

Sidereal Day.	$\Delta_\Omega a$	$\Delta_\Omega \delta$	$\Delta_\Omega a$	$\Delta_\Omega \delta$
	1865.		**1873.**	
0	+0.831	+8.52	−0.166	−7.01
100	0.959	8.63	0.313	7.42
200	1.080	8.66	0.457	7.76
300	1.191	8.62	0.597	8.05
400	1.292	8.51	0.732	8.26
	1866.		**1874.**	
0	+1.260	+8.55	−0.686	−8.20
100	1.353	8.39	0.818	8.37
200	1.435	8.15	0.942	8.47
300	1.504	7.84	1.058	8.50
400	1.560	7.46	1.165	8.46
	1867.		**1875.**	
0	+1.543	+7.60	−1.130	−8.48
100	1.590	7.18	1.231	8.40
200	1.624	6.69	1.321	8.24
300	1.643	6.15	1.401	8.02
400	1.648	5.56	1.469	7.74
	1868 B.		**1876 B.**	
0	+1.648	+5.76	−1.447	−7.84
100	1.644	5.14	1.507	7.51
200	1.625	4.47	1.554	7.12
300	1.592	3.76	1.589	6.67
400	1.545	3.02	1.611	6.16
	1869.		**1877.**	
0	+1.565	+3 27	−1.605	−6.34
100	1.507	2.51	1.618	5.80
200	1.439	1.74	1.618	5.21
300	1.358	0.95	1.605	4.57
400	1.265	0.15	1.578	3.90
	1870.		**1878.**	
0	+1.298	+0.42	−1.588	−4.13
100	1.198	−0.38	1.553	3.44
200	1.089	1.17	1.504	2.71
300	0.970	1.95	1.443	1.96
400	0.843	2.71	1.370	1.20
	1871.		**1879.**	
0	+0.827	−2.45	−1.396	−1.46
100	0.755	3.20	1.315	−0.68
200	0.618	3 91	1.223	+0.10
300	0.476	4.59	1.121	0.89
400	0.330	5.23	1.009	1.67
	1872 B.		**1880 B.**	
0	+0.380	−5.02	−1.048	+1.41
100	0 232	5.63	0.929	2.18
200	+0 083	6.19	0.803	2.93
300	−0 067	6.70	0.670	3.67
400	−0 216	−7.15	−0.530	+4.37

TABLE XXIV.—a Pavonis.

R.A. 20 15.4. Dec. —57 9.

Upper transit at fictitious meridian.

Sidereal Day	Mean Day	$\Delta_\odot a$ 1870.	Var. in 10 y.	Diff. for 10 d.	$\Delta_\odot \delta$ 1870.	Var. in 10 y.	Diff. for 10 d.
0, Jan. 0	0.07	−2.266	+ 6	+ 18	− 7.37	− 5	+216
10	10.04	2.213	4	88	5.13	5	231
20	20.01	2.091	+ 2	155	2.77	5	240
30	29.99	1.905	0	217	− 0.35	5	243
Feb. 9	8.96	1.658	− 1	276	+ 2.07	5	240
19	18.93	1.354	3	328	4.43	5	232
Mar. 1	0.90	1.003	4	375	6.70	4	220
11	10.87	0.605	5	417	8.82	3	204
21	20.85	−0.170	7	452	10.77	2	184
31	30.82	+0.297	8	480	12.50	2	161
100, Apr. 10	9.79	0.788	9	502	13.99	− 1	135
20	19.77	1.298	10	516	15.20	+ 1	105
30	29.74	1.817	11	522	16.09	2	74
May 10	9.71	2.338	11	517	16.67	3	41
20	19.69	2.848	11	503	16.91	4	+ 6
30	29.66	3.340	10	478	16.79	5	− 29
June 9	8.63	3.800	10	442	16.33	6	63
19	18.60	4.220	9	396	15.52	6	96
29	28.57	4.588	8	338	14.41	7	127
July 9	8.55	4.894	7	272	12.98	8	154
200, 19	18.52	5.130	7	200	11.33	9	175
29	28.49	5.292	6	123	9.49	9	191
Aug. 8	7.47	5.375	5	+ 43	7.52	10	200
18	17.44	5.379	3	− 36	5.51	9	202
28	27.41	5.304	− 2	111	3.51	9	196
Sept. 7	6.38	5.159	0	179	+ 1.61	9	182
17	16.36	4.950	+ 1	237	− 0.10	8	160
27	26.33	4.689	2	281	1.56	8	131
Oct. 7	6.30	4.393	3	310	2.70	7	96
17	16.27	4.074	4	324	3.47	6	57
300, 27	26.25	3.749	4	320	3.83	5	− 15
Nov. 6	5.22	3.438	4	300	3.77	4	+ 28
16	15.19	3.153	4	266	3.28	3	70
26	25.17	2.910	3	218	2.37	2	110
Dec. 6	5.14	2.721	2	160	− 1.09	2	147
16	15.11	2.592	2	95	+ 0.55	1	178
26	25.08	2.532	+ 1	− 25	2.46	+ 1	203
36	35.06	+2.542	− 1	+ 44	+ 4.59	0	+222

✳ ☌ ☉, Jan. 21.2.
✳ ☌ Mean Sun, Jan. 24.2.

Sidereal Day	$\Delta_\Omega a$	$\Delta_\Omega \delta$	$\Delta_\Omega a$	$\Delta_\Omega \delta$
	1865.		**1873.**	
0	+0.559	+8.51	−1.168	−7.03
100	0.403	8.62	1.047	7.44
200	0.244	8.65	0.918	7.73
300	+0.082	8.60	0.781	8.05
400	−0.081	8.48	0.638	8.26
	1866.		**1874.**	
0	−0.026	+8.53	−0.687	−8.20
100	0.188	8.36	0.540	8.36
200	0.349	8.12	0.390	8.45
300	0.507	7.80	0.236	8.48
400	0.661	7.42	0.081	8.43
	1867.		**1875.**	
0	−0.611	+7.56	−0.133	−8.45
100	0.761	7.13	+0.022	8.36
200	0.904	6.64	0.177	8.20
300	1.039	6.10	0.331	7.97
400	1.165	5.50	0.482	7.68
	1868 B.		**1876 B.**	
0	−1.123	+5.71	+0.432	−7.78
100	1.242	5.06	0.580	7.45
200	1.350	4.40	0.723	7.05
300	1.446	3.69	0.861	6.59
400	1.530	2.95	0.992	6.08
	1869.		**1877.**	
0	−1.503	+3.20	+0.949	−6.25
100	1.577	2.44	1.075	5.71
200	1.638	1.67	1.191	5.11
300	1.684	0.88	1.298	4.48
400	1.716	0.08	1.395	3.80
	1870.		**1878.**	
0	−1.707	+0.35	+1.364	−4.03
100	1.728	−0.45	1.453	3.34
200	1.735	1.24	1.530	2.61
300	1.727	2.01	1.595	1.86
400	1.703	2.77	1.647	1.09
	1871.		**1879.**	
0	−1.713	−2.52	+1.631	−1.36
100	1.681	3.26	1.674	−0.58
200	1.634	3.97	1.703	+0.20
300	1.573	4.64	1.718	0.99
400	1.439	5.28	1.718	1.76
	1872 B.		**1880 B.**	
0	−1.526	−5.07	+1.719	+1.50
100	1.444	5.67	1.710	2.27
200	1.350	6.23	1.667	3.02
300	1.245	6.73	1.649	3.75
400	−1.130	−7.17	+1.597	+4.45

TABLE XXIV.—π Capricorni.

R.A. 20h 19m.9.   Dec. − 18° 38′.

Upper transit at fictitious meridian.

Sidereal Day	Mean Day	Δ☉α 1870.	Var. in 10 y.	Diff. for 10 d.	Δ☉δ 1870.	Var. in 10 y.	Diff. for 10 d.
0, Jan. 0	0.07	−1.269	+2	+30	−3.64	−1	−1
10	10.04	1.220	1	67	3.62	1	+6
20	20.01	1.135	+1	103	3.52	1	14
30	29.99	1 015	0	136	3.34	1	23
Feb. 9	8.96	0.863	−1	168	3.06	2	34
19	18 93	0.680	1	197	2.67	2	46
Mar. 1	0.91	0.469	2	223	2.14	1	59
11	10.88	−0.235	2	247	1.48	0	73
21	20.85	+0.023	3	270	0.68	0	87
31	30.82	0.303	3	289	+0.26	0	100
100, Apr. 10	9.80	0.599	4	303	1.31	0	110
20	19.77	0.907	4	314	2.45	0	118
30	29.74	1.225	4	320	3.65	0	123
May 10	9.71	1.545	4	321	4.89	0	124
20	19.69	1.864	4	315	6.11	+1	121
30	29.66	2.172	4	301	7.30	1	115
June 9	8.63	2.464	3	281	8.40	2	105
19	18.61	2 732	3	254	9.38	2	91
29	28.58	2.970	2	221	10.21	3	74
July 9	8.55	3.172	2	182	10.85	4	57
200, 19	18.52	3.333	1	138	11.34	4	40
29	28.50	3.448	1	91	11.64	4	22
Aug. 8	7 47	3.516	−1	+44	11.78	5	+5
18	17.44	3.536	0	−3	11.74	5	−11
28	27.41	3.510	+1	47	11.57	5	23
Sept. 7	6.39	3.443	1	86	11.29	5	32
17	16.36	3.339	1	120	10.92	5	40
27	26.33	3.205	2	145	10.49	4	43
Oct. 7	6.30	3.051	2	160	10.06	4	43
17	16.28	2.888	3	166	9.63	4	43
300, 27	26.25	2.722	3	164	9.21	4	39
Nov. 6	5.22	2.563	3	150	8.86	4	34
16	15.20	2.424	2	128	8.53	4	29
26	25.17	2.309	2	100	8.27	3	23
Dec. 6	5.14	2.225	2	68	8.07	3	17
16	15.11	2.175	1	−32	7.93	3	11
26	25.09	2.102	+1	+6	7.84	3	−5
36	35.06	+2.157	0	+44	+7.83	+3	+2

✶ ☌ ☉, Jan. 22.3.
✶ ☌ Mean Sun, Jan. 25.3.

Sidereal Day	ΔΩα	ΔΩδ	ΔΩα	ΔΩδ
	1865.		**1873.**	
0	+0.614	+8.49	−0.965	−7.08
100	0.516	8.59	0.901	7.47
200	0.413	8.60	0.827	7.80
300	0.306	8.54	0.746	8.06
400	0.197	8.41	0.659	8.25
	1866.		**1874.**	
0	+0.234	+8.46	−0.689	−8.20
100	0.123	8.28	0.599	8.34
200	+0.011	8.03	0.503	8.42
300	−0.100	7.70	0.404	8 44
400	0.212	7.31	0.302	8.38
	1867.		**1875.**	
0	−0.174	+7.45	−0.337	−8.40
100	0.284	7.01	0.233	8.30
200	0.392	6.51	0.127	8.13
300	0.496	5.96	−0.021	7.89
400	0.595	5.36	+0.086	7.58
	1868 B.		**1876 B.**	
0	−0.562	+5.57	+0.050	−7.69
100	0.658	4.93	0.157	7.35
200	0.748	4.25	0.262	6.94
300	0.831	3.54	0.365	6.47
400	0.908	2.80	0.465	5.96
	1869.		**1877.**	
0	−0.883	+3.05	+0.431	−6.13
100	0.954	2.29	0.529	5.58
200	1.016	1.51	0.623	4.98
300	1.069	+0.73	0.711	4.34
400	1.113	−0.07	0.794	3.66
	1870.		**1878.**	
0	−1.099	+0.20	+0.767	−3.89
100	1.137	−0.59	0.845	3.20
200	1.164	1.37	0.917	2.47
300	1.182	2.14	0.981	1.72
400	1.189	2.89	1.038	0.95
	1871.		**1879.**	
0	−1.188	−2.64	+1.020	−1.21
100	1.189	3.37	1.071	−0.44
200	1.179	4.08	1.113	+0.34
300	1.160	4.74	1.145	1.12
400	1.131	5.37	1.169	1.89
	1872 B.		**1880 B.**	
0	−1.141	−5.16	+1.162	+1.63
100	1.106	5.75	1.179	2.39
200	1.061	6.30	1.196	3.14
300	1.008	6.79	1.183	3.86
400	−0.946	−7.22	+1.170	+4.54

TABLE XXIV.—ε Delphini.

R.A. 20h 27m.0.   Dec. + 10° 52'.

Upper transit at fictitious meridian.

Sidereal Day	Mean Day	ΔΘα 1870.	Var.in 10y.	Diff. for 10d.	ΔΘδ 1870.	Var.in 10y.	Diff. for 10d.
0, Jan. 0	0.07	−1.198	+1	+6	+0.90	+1	−158
10	10.05	1.175	+1	40	−0.71	1	162
20	20.02	1.118	0	74	2.33	1	161
30	29.99	1.028	0	107	3.91	1	152
Feb. 9	8.96	0.905	0	139	5.35	1	136
19	18.94	0.750	−1	169	6.61	1	114
Mar. 1	0.91	0.567	2	197	7.61	1	85
11	10.88	0.356	2	223	8.30	1	52
21	20.86	−0.121	2	246	8.64	0	−15
31	30.83	+0.136	2	267	8.60	0	+23
100, Apr 10	9.80	0.412	3	283	8.19	0	61
20	19.77	0.701	3	295	7.39	0	98
30	29.75	1.000	3	301	6.24	0	132
May 10	9.72	1.301	2	302	4.76	0	162
20	19.69	1.601	2	295	3.02	0	185
30	29.66	1.889	2	281	−1.08	0	203
June 9	8.64	2.161	2	261	+1.02	0	217
19	18.61	2.409	2	235	3.23	0	223
29	28.58	2.629	1	203	5.45	0	221
July 9	8.56	2.813	−1	164	7.63	1	215
200, 19	18.53	2.956	0	122	9.74	1	205
29	28.50	3.057	0	79	11.72	1	190
Aug. 8	7.47	3.113	+1	+33	13.53	1	172
18	17.45	3.124	1	−10	15.15	2	151
28	27.42	3.093	1	52	16.55	2	128
Sept. 7	6.39	3.021	1	90	17.71	2	104
17	16.36	2.915	1	120	18.63	2	78
27	26.34	2.783	2	143	19.27	2	52
Oct. 7	6.31	2.631	2	159	19.66	3	+26
17	16.28	2.467	3	166	19.78	3	−1
300, 27	26.25	2.301	3	164	19.64	4	27
Nov. 6	5.23	2.141	3	153	19.25	4	52
16	15.20	1.996	2	135	18.61	4	76
26	25.17	1.872	2	112	17.73	4	100
Dec. 6	5.15	1.773	2	84	16.62	4	122
16	15.12	1.706	2	51	15.31	4	139
26	25.09	1.672	2	−17	13.85	4	152
36	35.06	+1.672	+1	+17	+12.29	+4	−160

✶ ☌ ☉,   Jan. 24.0.
✶ ☌ Mean Sun,   Jan. 27.1.

Sidereal Day	ΔΩα	ΔΩδ	ΔΩα	ΔΩδ
	1865.		**1873.**	
0	+0.649	+8.46	−0.890	−7.15
100	0.576	8.55	0.846	7.52
200	0.498	8.53	0.797	7.82
300	0.415	8.45	0.741	8.06
400	0.329	8.29	0.679	8.23
	1866.		**1874.**	
0	+0.358	+8.35	−0.700	−8.18
100	0.270	8.15	0.635	8.31
200	0.179	7.87	0.564	8.37
300	+0.087	7.55	0.488	8.36
400	−0.006	7.12	0.409	8.28
	1867.		**1875.**	
0	+0.026	+7.27	−0.436	−8.32
100	−0.067	6.82	0.355	8.19
200	0.160	6.31	0.271	8.00
300	0.251	5.75	0.184	7.74
400	0.340	5.13	0.096	7.42
	1868 B.		**1876 B.**	
0	−0.310	+5.34	−0.126	−7.54
100	0.397	4.70	−0.038	7.17
200	0.480	4.02	+0.051	6.75
300	0.559	3.30	0.140	6.28
400	0.632	2.55	0.227	5.75
	1869.		**1877.**	
0	−0.608	+2.81	+0.197	−5.93
100	0.678	2 05	0.284	5.36
200	0.742	1.27	0.36?	4.76
300	0.799	+0.49	0.449	4.11
400	0.850	−0.30	0.526	3.43
	1870.		**1878.**	
0	−0.834	−0.03	+0.501	−3.66
100	0.879	0.8?	0.576	2.96
200	0.917	1.5?	0.646	2.23
300	0.947	2.35	0.711	1.48
400	0.968	3.0?	0.770	0.72
	1871.		**1879.**	
0	−0.962	−2.84	+0.751	−0.98
100	0.978	3.5?	0.806	−0.21
200	0.986	4.?5	0.855	+0.56
300	0.985	4.89	0.897	1.33
400	0.976	5.5?	0.931	2.10
	1872 B.		**1880 B.**	
0	−0.980	−5.3?	+0.918	+1.84
100	0.966	5.8?	0.949	2.59
200	0.943	6.4?	0.971	3.32
300	0.913	6.87	0.984	4.03
400	−0.875	−7.2?	+0.989	+4.70

TABLE XXIV.—Groombridge 3241.

R.A. 20^h 30.5^m.　　　　Dec. + 72° 5′.

Upper transit at fictitious meridian.

Sidereal Day	Mean Day	$\Delta_\odot a$ 1870.	Var. in 10 y.	Diff. for 10 d.	$\Delta_\odot \delta$ 1870.	Var. in 10 y.	Diff. for 10 d.
0, Jan. 0	0.07	−3.826	→ 7	−341	+ 9.32	0	−289
10	10.05	4.108	8	222	6.28	0	317
20	20.02	4.266	8	− 93	+ 3.01	0	335
30	29.99	4.293	9	+ 39	− 0.38	0	339
Feb. 9	8.96	4.187	8	171	3.74	0	331
19	18.94	3.952	8	297	6.95	0	310
Mar. 1	0.91	3.595	8	417	9.89	0	276
11	10.89	3.126	7	521	12.44	0	232
21	20.86	2.561	6	606	14.50	0	179
31	30.83	1.919	4	674	15.99	0	120
100, Apr. 10	9.80	1.220	3	720	16.88	0	− 57
20	19.77	−0.488	2	742	17.13	0	+ 7
30	29.75	+0.257	− 1	741	16.74	0	71
May 10	9.72	0.988	+ 1	718	15.73	0	131
20	19.69	1.686	2	673	14.13	0	187
30	29.66	2.328	3	608	12.01	0	236
June 9	8.64	2.897	3	527	9.43	0	278
19	18.61	3.377	4	431	6.47	0	312
29	28.58	3.754	4	323	− 3.22	0	338
July 9	8.56	4.022	4	208	+ 0.25	0	355
200, 19	18.53	4.170	4	+ 88	3.84	0	363
29	28.50	4.198	4	− 33	7.48	0	363
Aug. 8	7.47	4.105	3	153	11.07	0	355
18	17.45	3.894	3	268	14.55	0	339
28	27.42	3.572	2	375	17.83	0	316
Sept. 7	6.39	3.147	+ 1	472	20.85	0	287
17	16.36	2.633	− 0	557	23.54	0	251
27	26.34	2.040	2	626	25.85	0	210
Oct. 7	6.31	1.396	3	679	27.72	0	163
17	16.28	+0.688	4	714	29.10	0	112
300, 27	26.25	−0.036	6	730	29.96	0	58
Nov. 6	5.23	0.766	7	726	30.25	0	+ 1
16	15.20	1.481	8	701	29.97	0	− 58
26	25.17	2.161	10	656	29.10	0	115
Dec. 6	5.15	2.786	11	592	27.67	0	170
16	15.12	3.338	12	509	25.71	0	221
26	25.09	3.799	13	410	23.27	0	265
36	35.06	−4.154	−14	−298	+20.43	0	−301

Sidereal Day	$\Delta_\Omega a$	$\Delta_\Omega \delta$	$\Delta_{\dot\Omega} a$	$\Delta_{\dot\Omega} \delta$
	1865.		**1873.**	
0	+0.902	+8.44	−0.505	−7.18
100	0.968	8.50	0.598	7.54
200	1.026	8.48	0.685	7.83
300	1.075	8.39	0.767	8.06
400	1.114	8.23	0.843	8.22
	1866.		**1874.**	
0	+1.102	+8.29	−0.818	−8.18
100	1.135	8.08	0.889	8.29
200	1.158	7.79	0.952	8.34
300	1.171	7.44	1.007	8.32
400	1.174	7.03	1.054	8.23
	1867.		**1875.**	
0	+1.174	+7.17	−1.039	−8.27
100	1.171	6.72	1.081	8.14
200	1.157	6.20	1.115	7.94
300	1.132	5.63	1.136	7.67
400	1.098	5.01	1.150	7.34
	1868 B.		**1876 B.**	
0	+1.111	+5.23	−1.146	−7.46
100	1.071	4.58	1.154	7.09
200	1.021	3.89	1.152	6.66
300	0.963	3.17	1.140	6.18
400	0.896	2.43	1.119	5.65
	1869.		**1877.**	
0	+0.919	+2.68	−1.127	−5.83
100	0.848	1.92	1.100	5.27
200	0.769	1.15	1.064	4.66
300	0.683	+0.37	1.019	4.01
400	0.592	−0.41	0.965	3.32
	1870.		**1878.**	
0	+0.624	−0.15	−0.985	−3.56
100	0.529	0.93	0.926	2.85
200	0.430	1.70	0.859	2.13
300	0.328	2.45	0.785	1.34
400	0.223	3.18	0.704	0.62
	1871.		**1879.**	
0	+0.259	−2.94	−0.732	−0.87
100	0.153	3.65	0.647	−0.11
200	+0.046	4.33	0.557	+0.66
300	−0.062	4.97	0.462	1.43
400	0.168	5.57	0.362	2.19
	1872 B.		**1880 B.**	
0	−0.133	−5.37	−0.396	+1.93
100	0.238	5.93	0.295	2.68
200	0.341	6.45	0.190	3.41
300	0.441	6.91	0.082	4.10
400	−0.537	−7.31	+0.024	+4.77

✻ ♂ ☉, Jan. 24 9.
✻ ♂ Mean Sun, Jan. 28 0.
✻ ☍ Mean Sun, July 29.6.

TABLE XXIV.—μ Aquarii.

R. A. 20h 45m.6.   Dec. − 9° 28′.

Upper transit at fictitious meridian.

Sidereal Day	Mean Day	$\Delta_\odot a$ 1870.	Var. in 10 y.	Diff. for 10 d.	$\Delta_\odot \delta$ 1870.	Var. in 10 y.	Diff. for 10 d.
0, Jan. 0	0.09	−1.143	+2	+4	−2 67	0	−50
10	10.06	1.121	1	38	3.15	0	45
20	20.03	1.067	+1	70	3.57	0	38
30	30.01	0.981	0	102	3.90	0	27
Feb. 9	8.98	0.863	0	133	4.10	0	−13
19	18.95	0.716	−1	162	4.16	0	+3
Mar. 1	0.92	0.540	1	190	4.04	0	22
11	10.90	0.336	2	217	3.71	0	43
21	20.87	−0.107	3	241	3.18	0	64
31	30.84	+0.145	3	263	2.43	0	85
100, Apr. 10	9.81	0.417	3	282	1.47	0	106
20	19.79	0.707	3	297	0.31	0	124
30	29.76	1.009	3	306	+0.99	0	138
May 10	9.73	1.318	3	310	2.43	0	149
20	19.70	1.628	3	309	3.95	0	154
30	29 68	1.933	3	300	5.50	+1	155
June 9	8.65	2.225	3	283	7.04	1	152
19	18.62	2.497	3	259	8.53	1	144
29	28.60	2.742	2	230	9.90	1	132
July 9	8.57	2.955	2	195	11.16	2	118
200, 19	18.54	3.130	2	154	12.26	2	100
29	28.51	3.262	1	110	13.16	2	81
Aug. 8	7.49	3.349	−1	64	13.88	3	62
18	17.46	3.390	0	+18	14.41	3	43
28	27.43	3.386	0	−26	14.75	3	26
Sept. 7	6.40	3.340	+1	64	14.93	4	+10
17	16.38	3.259	2	.8	14.95	4	−5
27	26.35	3.146	2	125	14.83	4	17
Oct. 7	6.32	3.011	2	143	14.62	4	27
17	16.30	2.862	2	154	14.30	4	36
300, 27	26.27	2.706	2	155	13.91	4	42
Nov. 6	5.24	2.555	2	145	13.47	4	46
16	15 21	2.418	2	129	13.00	4	49
26	25.19	2.298	2	108	12.49	4	53
Dec. 6	5.16	2.203	2	80	11.94	4	54
16	15.13	2.138	2	50	11.42	3	52
26	25.10	2.103	1	−18	10.90	3	52
36	35.08	+2.102	+1	+16	+10.38	+3	−50

✶ ☌ ☉,   Jan. 28.5.
✶ ☌ Mean Sun,   Jan. 31.9.

Sidereal Day	$\Delta_\Omega a$	$\Delta_\Omega \delta$	$\Delta_\Omega a$	$\Delta_\Omega \delta$
	1865.		**1873.**	
0	+0.613	+8.34	−0.932	−7.29
100	0.523	8.35	0.873	7.61
200	0.428	8.29	0.806	7.85
300	0.330	8.15	0.733	8.03
400	0.228	7.95	0.654	8.15
	1866.		**1874.**	
0	+0.263	+8.02	−0.681	−8.12
100	0.159	7.77	0.599	8.19
200	+0.055	7.45	0.511	8.19
300	−0.050	7.06	0.420	8.12
400	0.155	6.62	0.325	7.99
	1867.		**1875.**	
0	−0.120	+6.77	−0.358	−8.04
100	0.223	6.29	0.261	7.87
200	0.325	5.74	0.103	7.63
300	0.424	5.15	−0.063	7.33
400	0.520	4.52	+0.037	6.96
	1868 B.		**1876 B.**	
0	−0.488	+4.74	+0 004	−7.09
100	0.580	4.07	0.104	6.69
200	0.667	3.38	0.203	6.23
300	0.748	2.65	0.301	5.73
400	0.822	1.91	0.396	5.17
	1869.		**1877.**	
0	−0.798	+2.16	+0.364	−5.36
100	0.867	1.40	0.457	4.77
200	0.929	+0.64	0.547	4.14
300	0.983	−0.14	0.632	3.48
400	1.028	0.90	0.712	2.79
	1870.		**1878.**	
0	−1.013	−0.64	+0.686	−3.03
100	1.053	1.41	0.762	2.32
200	1.082	2.15	0.832	1.59
300	1.103	2.88	0.896	0.85
400	1.114	3.58	0.952	0.10
	1871.		**1879.**	
0	−1.111	−3.35	+0.934	−0.35
100	1.116	4.03	0.986	+0.40
200	1.111	4.67	1.029	1.16
300	1.097	5.27	1.063	1.90
400	1.073	5.83	1.089	2.63
	1872 B.		**1880 B.**	
0	−1.082	−5.65	+1.081	+2.39
100	1.053	6.17	1.101	3.11
200	1.014	6.64	1.112	3.80
300	0.968	7.05	1.113	4.47
400	−0.913	−7.41	+1.105	+5.10

TABLE XXIV.—ν Cygni.

R.A. 20ʰ 52ᵐ.3.   Dec. + 40° 40′.

Upper transit at fictitious meridian.

Sidereal Day	Mean Day	$\Delta_\odot\alpha$ 1870	Var. in 10 y.	Diff. for 10 d.	$\Delta_\odot\delta$ 1870	Var. in 10 y.	Diff. for 10 d.
0, Jan. 0	0.09	−1.449	+1	−77	+6.83	+3	−248
10	10.06	1.504	0	−34	4.23	3	269
20	20.04	1.516	0	+10	+1.48	3	280
30	30.01	1.483	0	57	−1.34	3	281
Feb. 9	8.98	1.402	−1	103	4.10	3	271
19	18.96	1.277	1	148	6.72	3	250
Mar. 1	0.93	1.106	2	193	9.06	3	218
11	10.90	0.891	2	233	11.04	2	177
21	20.87	0.641	3	270	12.57	2	129
31	30.85	0.353	3	304	13.60	1	76
100, Apr. 10	9.82	−0.036	3	328	14.07	1	−19
20	19.79	+0.300	3	345	13.97	+1	+37
30	29.76	0.652	2	356	13.32	0	92
May 10	9.74	1.009	2	357	12.13	0	145
20	19.71	1.364	2	350	10.43	−1	192
30	29.68	1.706	1	333	8.30	1	233
June 9	8.65	2.028	1	308	5.79	1	268
19	18.63	2.320	−1	275	−2.97	1	294
29	28.60	2.576	0	234	+0.06	1	312
July 9	8.57	2.787	0	188	3.24	1	323
200, 19	18.55	2.950	0	138	6.49	1	325
29	28.52	3.061	+1	84	9.72	1	320
Aug. 8	7.49	3.117	1	+30	12.86	1	309
18	17.46	3.121	2	−23	15.87	1	291
28	27.44	3.072	2	75	18.06	−1	267
Sept. 7	6.41	2.973	2	121	21.20	0	238
17	16.38	2.832	2	161	23.41	0	204
27	26.35	2.653	3	193	25.26	+1	166
Oct. 7	6.33	2.448	3	216	26.72	1	126
17	16.30	2.224	3	232	27.77	2	82
300, 27	26.27	1.987	3	238	28.35	3	+34
Nov. 6	5.25	1.750	3	233	28.45	3	−14
16	15.22	1.523	3	221	28.07	3	62
26	25.19	1.311	3	202	27.21	3	109
Dec. 6	5.16	1.122	3	175	25.90	4	154
16	15.14	0.964	2	141	24.15	4	195
26	25.11	0.842	2	104	22.03	5	230
36	35.08	+0.758	+1	−62	+19.58	+5	−257

✻ ☌ ☉,   Jan. 30 1.
✻ ☌ Mean Sun,   Feb. 2.6.

Sidereal Day	1865 $\Delta_\Omega\alpha$	$\Delta_\Omega\delta$	1873 $\Delta_\Omega\alpha$	$\Delta_\Omega\delta$
0	+0.754	+8.28	−0.841	−7.33
100	0.713	8.27	0.832	7.62
200	0.666	8.19	0.815	7.85
300	0.613	8.03	0.792	8.01
400	0.554	7.81	0.762	8.11
	1866.		**1874.**	
0	+0.575	+7.89	−0.773	−8.09
100	0.513	7.62	0.739	8.13
200	0.447	7.28	0.699	8.11
300	0.377	6.88	0.654	8.03
400	0.303	6.42	0.603	7.88
	1867.		**1875.**	
0	+0.328	+6.58	−0.621	−7.94
100	0.253	6.06	0.567	7.74
200	0.176	5.53	0.508	7.49
300	0.097	4.93	0.445	7.17
400	0.017	4.29	0.378	6.79
	1868 B.		**1876 B.**	
0	+0.044	+4.51	−0.401	−6.92
100	−0.036	3.84	0.333	6.51
200	0.115	3.14	0.261	6.05
300	0.193	2.42	0.187	5.52
400	0.260	1.67	0.112	4.96
	1869.		**1877.**	
0	−0.244	+1.92	−0.138	−5.15
100	0.318	1.17	−0.062	4.56
200	0.390	+0.41	+0.014	3.92
300	0.458	−0.36	0.031	3.26
400	0.523	1.12	0.167	2.57
	1870.		**1878.**	
0	−0.501	−0.86	+0.141	−2.80
100	0.563	1.62	0.217	2.10
200	0.619	2.35	0.290	1.37
300	0.669	3.07	0.362	−0.63
400	0.714	3.75	0.430	+0.12
	1871.		**1879.**	
0	−0.699	−3.52	+0.407	−0.13
100	0.740	4.19	0.474	+0.62
200	0.774	4.82	0.536	1 36
300	0.802	5.40	0.595	2.10
400	0.823	5.94	0.646	2.82
	1872 B.		**1880 B.**	
0	−0.816	−5.76	+0.631	+2.58
100	0.833	6.27	0.681	3 29
200	0.842	6.71	0.725	3.97
300	0.844	7.11	0.764	4.62
400	−0.839	−7.44	+0.795	+5.23

TABLE XXIV.—* 81 Cephei (B): 12 Year Cat. 1879.

R.A. 20^h 53^m.4.   Dec. + 80° 4$'$.

Upper transit at fictitious meridian.

Sidereal Day	Mean Day	Δ☉a 1870.	Var.in 10y.	Diff. for 10d.	Δ☉δ 1870.	Var.in 10y.	Diff. for 10d.	Sidereal Day	ΔΩa	ΔΩδ	ΔΩa	ΔΩδ
									1865.		**1873.**	
								0	+1.448	+8.27	−0.432	−7.34
								100	1.639	8.25	0.059	7.63
								200	1.817	8.17	0.880	7.85
0, Jan. 0	0.09	−6.411	−32	−799	+11.52	− 3	−257	300	1.979	8.01	1.094	8.01
10	10.07	7.109	34	595	8.76	3	294	400	2.124	7.76	1.298	8.10
20	20.04	7.593	34	370	5.69	3	319					
30	30.01	7.844	33	−132	+ 2.42	3	332		**1866.**		**1874.**	
Feb. 9	8.98	7.855	32	+112	− 0.91	3	332	0	+2.077	+7.86	−1 230	−8.08
19	18.96	7.622	29	351	4.18	3	319	100	2.210	7.59	1.427	8.12
Mar. 1	0.93	7.157	25	577	7.25	3	294	200	2.323	7.25	1.612	8.10
11	10.90	6.477	21	780	10.02	3	257	300	2.417	6.85	1.783	8.02
21	20.88	5.606	16	955	12.36	3	210	400	2.490	6.35	1.939	7.86
31	30.85	4.578	11	1094	14.19	2	156					
									1867.		**1875.**	
100, Apr. 10	9.82	3.431	6	1194	15.46	2	96	0	+2.468	+6.54	−1.890	−7.92
20	19.79	2.204	− 1	1252	16.11	1	− 34	100	2.526	6.04	2.034	7.73
30	29.77	−0.941	+ 4	1267	16.14	− 1	+ 29	200	2.562	5.49	2.163	7.47
May 10	2.74	+0.316	8	1240	15.54	0	90	300	2.576	4.89	2.273	7.15
20	19.71	1.526	12	1174	14.34	0	148	400	2.567	4.25	2.365	6.77
30	29.68	2.653	15	1073	12.60	+ 1	201					
June 9	8.66	3.662	17	940	10.35	1	247		**1868 B.**		**1876 B.**	
19	18.63	4.524	18	781	7.68	1	286	0	+2.573	+4.47	−2.336	−6.91
29	28.60	5.217	18	602	4.66	2	318	100	2.550	3.80	2.416	6.49
July 9	8.57	5.723	17	407	− 1.36	2	341	200	2.504	3.10	2.475	6.02
								300	2.437	2.37	2.514	5.50
200, 19	18.55	6.029	16	+204	+ 2.14	2	356	400	2.348	1.63	2.533	4.94
29	28.52	6.129	13	− 4	5.74	2	363					
Aug. 8	7.49	6.021	10	211	9.37	2	362		**1869.**		**1877.**	
18	17.46	5.709	6	412	12.95	1	353	0	+2.380	+1.88	−2.529	−5.13
28	27.44	5.201	+ 1	603	16.40	1	337	100	2.279	1.13	2.534	4.54
								200	2.157	+0.37	2.518	3.91
Sept. 7	6.41	4.508	− 4	779	19.66	+ 1	314	300	2.018	−0.39	2.481	3.24
17	16.38	3.649	10	937	22.65	0	284	400	1.861	1.13	2.423	2.55
27	26.36	2.642	16	1074	25.32	0	247					
Oct. 7	6.33	1.510	22	1186	27.57	− 1	205		**1870.**		**1878.**	
17	16.30	+0.280	28	1270	29.40	1	158	0	+1.916	−0.90	−2.445	−2.79
								100	1.748	1.65	2.374	2.08
300, 27	23.27	−1.019	34	1323	30.72	2	105	200	1.566	2.36	2.284	1.35
Nov. 6	5.25	2.355	40	1344	31.49	3	+ 49	300	1.371	3.09	2.174	−0.61
16	15.22	3.695	45	1330	31.70	4	− 8	400	1.165	3.78	2.046	+0.13
26	25.19	5.003	50	1280	31.32	4	68					
Dec. 6	5.16	6.243	55	1193	30.35	4	126		**1871.**		**1879.**	
								0	+1.235	−3.55	−2.091	−0.11
16	15.14	7.376	59	1070	28.82	5	180	100	1.023	4.21	1.952	+0.63
26	25.11	8.370	62	912	26.76	5	230	200	0.802	4.84	1.795	1.37
36	35.08	−9.191	−64	−725	+24.24	− 5	−272	300	0.575	5.42	1.624	2.11
								400	0.343	5.95	1.438	2.83
									1872 B.		**1880 B.**	
		✳ ♂ ☉,		Jan. 30.4.				0	+0.422	−5.78	−1.502	+2.59
		✳ ♂ Mean Sun,		Feb. 2.9.				100	+0.189	6.28	1.308	3.29
		✳ ☊ Mean Sun,		Aug. 4.5.				200	−0.046	6.72	1.102	3.97
								300	0.279	7.11	0.886	4.62
								400	−0.509	−7.44	−0.662	+5.23

TABLE XXIV.—61 Cygni (pr.)

R.A. 21h 1m.1.   Dec. +38° 7'.

Upper transit at fictitious meridian.

Sidereal Day	Mean Day	$\Delta_\odot a$ 1870.	Var. in 10y.	Diff. for 10d.	$\Delta_\odot \delta$ 1870.	Var. in 10y.	Diff. for 10d.
0, Jan. 0	0.10	-1.357	+1	-69	+6.77	+3	-226
10	10.07	1.406	0	-28	1.40	3	247
20	20.04	1.411	0	+15	+1.85	3	260
30	30.02	1.375	-1	58	-0.77	3	262
Feb. 9	8.99	1.294	1	103	3.35	3	252
19	18.96	1.169	2	147	5.78	3	231
Mar. 1	0.93	1.001	3	189	7.95	3	201
11	10.91	0.791	3	229	9.78	2	163
21	20.88	0.543	3	266	11.18	2	117
31	30.85	-0.261	3	298	12.09	2	65
100, Apr. 10	9.82	+0.052	3	323	12.47	+1	-10
20	19.80	0.385	3	343	12.29	0	+45
30	29.77	0.737	3	356	11.57	0	98
May 10	9.74	1.096	3	360	10.34	0	149
20	19.72	1.454	2	354	8.61	0	197
30	29.69	1.802	2	340	6.43	-1	237
June 9	8.66	2.132	2	318	3.90	1	269
19	18.63	2.435	1	287	-1.07	2	295
29	28.61	2.705	-1	250	+1.98	2	313
July 9	8.58	2.935	0	206	5.17	1	323
200, 19	18.55	3.117	0	157	8.42	1	327
29	28.52	3.250	+1	106	11.69	-1	323
Aug. 8	7.50	3.329	2	53	14.86	0	311
18	17.47	3.357	2	+1	17.90	0	294
28	27.44	3.333	3	-49	20.73	0	272
Sept. 7	6.42	3.262	3	94	23.32	+1	213
17	16.39	3.148	3	133	25.58	1	210
27	26.36	2.998	3	166	27.51	1	174
Oct. 7	6.33	2.820	4	191	29.06	2	135
17	16.31	2.620	4	206	30.20	2	92
300, 27	26.28	2.410	4	213	30.89	3	47
Nov. 6	5.25	2.198	4	211	31.14	3	+1
16	15.22	1.992	4	200	30.92	4	-45
26	25.20	1.801	3	182	30.24	4	92
Dec. 6	5.17	1.631	3	157	29.09	5	135
16	15.14	1.488	3	127	27.55	5	174
26	25.11	1.379	2	91	25.62	5	209
36	35.09	+1.307	+2	-52	+23.40	+6	-235

Sidereal Day	$\Delta_\Omega a$	$\Delta_\Omega \delta$	$\Delta_\Omega a$	$\Delta_\Omega \delta$
	1865.		1873.	
0	+0.759	+8.20	-0.863	-7.38
100	0.715	8.16	0.850	7.64
200	0.664	8.05	0.837	7.84
300	0.608	7.87	0.804	7.97
400	0.546	7.62	0.771	8.04
	1866.		1874.	
0	+0.567	+7.71	-0.782	-8.02
100	0.502	7.42	0.745	8.04
200	0.432	7.06	0.702	8.00
300	0.359	6.64	0.653	7.89
400	0.282	6.16	0.598	7.72
	1867.		1875.	
0	+0.308	+6.33	-0.617	-7.78
100	0.230	5.81	0.560	7.57
200	0.150	5.25	0.497	7.29
300	+0.068	4.64	0.431	6.95
400	-0.014	3.99	0.361	6.55
	1868 B.		1876 B.	
0	+0.014	+4.21	-0.385	-6.69
100	-0.068	3.54	0.314	6.26
200	0.149	2.83	0.239	5.78
300	0.229	2.11	0.163	5.24
400	0.307	1.36	0.085	4.68
	1869.		1877.	
0	-0.281	+1.61	-0.112	-4.86
100	0.356	0.86	-0.033	4.26
200	0.429	+0.10	+0.046	3.62
300	0.495	-0.65	0.124	2.95
400	0.562	1.40	0.202	2.26
	1870.		1878.	
0	-0.541	-1.15	+0.176	-2.50
100	0.602	1.89	0.252	1.79
200	0.657	2.61	0.327	1.06
300	0.707	3.30	0.400	-0.33
400	0.751	3.98	0.469	+0.41
	1871.		1879.	
0	-0.737	-3.75	+0.446	+0.16
100	0.776	4.39	0.513	0.90
200	0.808	5.00	0.575	1.64
300	0.834	5.56	0.633	2.36
400	0.853	6.07	0.686	3.06
	1872 B.		1880 B.	
0	-0.847	-5.90	+0.669	+2.83
100	0.861	6.38	0.718	3.52
200	0.868	6.80	0.761	4.18
300	0.867	7.17	0.798	4.81
400	-0.859	-7.47	+0.829	+5.40

✳ ☌ ⊙, Feb. 1.2.
✳ ☌ Mean Sun, Feb. 4.8.

15

TABLE XXIV.—ζ Cygni.

R.A. 21^h 7.4^m.   Dec. +20° 42′.

Upper transit at fictitious meridian.

Sidereal Day	Mean Day	$\Delta_\odot a$ 1870.	Var. in 10 y.	Diff. for 10 d.	$\Delta_\odot \delta$ 1870.	Var. in 10 y.	Diff. for 10 d.
0, Jan. 0	0.10	−1.203	+2	−59	+5.42	+2	−209
10	10.07	1.244	+1	−24	3.23	2	227
20	20.05	1.250	0	+13	+0.91	2	236
30	30.02	1.218	0	51	−1.46	2	236
Feb. 9	8.99	1.148	−1	90	3.78	2	226
19	18.97	1.039	1	128	5 95	2	206
Mar. 1	0.94	0.892	2	165	7.87	2	177
11	10.91	0.709	2	201	9.46	2	141
21	20.88	0.490	2	235	10.66	1	98
31	30.86	−0.239	3	265	11.40	1	51
100, Apr. 10	9.83	+0.038	3	290	11.66	+1	−1
20	19.80	0.339	3	310	11.41	0	+50
30	29.77	0.656	2	323	10.67	0	98
May 10	9.75	0.982	2	328	9.46	0	143
20	19.72	1.310	2	326	7.81	0	185
30	29.69	1.632	2	316	5.77	−1	221
June 9	8.67	1.940	2	298	3.41	1	249
19	18.64	2 225	1	271	−0.81	1	270
29	28.61	2.480	1	238	+1.96	1	284
July 9	8.58	2.699	−1	199	4.84	1	291
200, 19	18.56	2 877	0	155	7.75	1	291
29	28.53	3.009	0	108	10.64	1	284
Aug. 8	7.50	3.093	0	60	13.42	1	272
18	17.47	3.129	+1	+12	16.07	1	254
28	27.45	3.117	2	−35	18.50	0	231
Sept. 7	6.42	3.059	2	78	20.68	0	204
17	16.39	2.962	3	115	22.57	+1	174
27	26.36	2.831	3	146	24.15	1	141
Oct. 7	6 34	2.672	3	169	25.38	1	104
17	16.31	2.495	3	183	26.23	2	66
300, 27	26.28	2.308	3	189	26.70	3	+26
Nov. 6	5.26	2.119	3	188	26.75	3	−14
16	15.23	1.935	3	179	26.42	3	54
26	25.20	1.764	3	161	25.68	4	94
Dec. 6	5.17	1.614	3	138	24.55	4	133
16	15.15	1.489	3	112	23.04	5	166
26	25.12	1.391	2	81	21.25	5	194
36	35.09	+1.328	+2	−46	+19.18	+5	−217

✻ ☌ ☉, Feb. 2.8.
✻ ☌ Mean Sun, Feb. 6.4.

Sidereal Day	$\Delta_\Omega a$	$\Delta_\Omega \delta$	$\Delta_\Omega a$	$\Delta_\Omega \delta$
	1865.		**1873.**	
0	+0.734	+8 13	−0.895	−7.40
100	0.679	8.07	0.862	7.64
200	0.615	7.94	0.832	7.82
300	0.552	7.74	0.795	7.94
400	0.481	7.48	0.751	7.98
	1866.		**1874.**	
0	+0.505	+7.57	−0.767	−7.97
100	0.431	7.26	0.719	7.98
200	0.353	6.89	0.666	7 91
300	0.272	6.46	0.607	7.78
400	0.189	5.96	0.543	7.59
	1867.		**1875.**	
0	+0.218	+6.14	−0.566	−7.66
100	0.133	5.61	0.499	7 43
200	+0.047	5.04	0.428	7.13
300	−0.039	4.42	0.354	6.78
400	0.124	3.76	0.277	6.37
	1868 B.		**1876 B.**	
0	−0.095	+3.99	−0.303	−6.52
100	0.180	3.31	0.225	6.07
200	0.263	2.60	0.145	5 58
300	0.344	1.88	−0.063	5.04
400	0.421	1.14	+0 019	4.46
	1869.		**1877.**	
0	−0.396	+1.39	−0.009	−4.65
100	0.471	+0.64	+0.074	4.04
200	0.542	−0.11	0.156	3.40
300	0.608	0.86	0.236	2.73
400	0.668	1.60	0.315	2.04
	1870.		**1878.**	
0	−0.648	−1.35	+0.289	−2.27
100	0.705	2 08	0.366	1.56
200	0.755	2 79	0.440	0 84
300	0.799	3.48	0.511	−0.11
400	0.836	4.13	0.578	+0.62
	1871.		**1879.**	
0	−0.824	−3.9:	+0.556	+0.38
100	0 856	4.54	0.020	1.11
200	0.881	5 13	0.679	1.83
300	0.89⁻	5 67	0.732	2.55
400	0.908	6.16	0.780	3.24
	1872 B.		**1880 B.**	
0	−0.905	−6.00	+0.765	+3.01
100	0.910	6.46	0.808	3.68
200	0 907	6.86	0.841	4.33
300	0.895	7.21	0.874	4.94
400	−0.878	−7.49	+0.896	+5.51

TABLE XXIV.—1 Pegasi.

R.A. 21 16.1. (h m)   Dec. + 19 15. (° ')

Upper transit at fictitious meridian.

Sidereal Day	Mean Day	$\Delta_\odot\alpha$ 1870.	Var. in 10 y.	Diff. for 10 d.	$\Delta_\odot\delta$ 1870.	Var. in 10 y.	Diff. for 10 d.
0, Jan. 0	0.11	−1.073	+1	− 46	+ 3.43	+2	−170
10	10.08	1.104	1	− 15	+ 1.67	2	181
20	20.05	1.102	+1	+ 19	− 0.18	2	187
30	30.03	1.066	0	52	2.05	2	185
Feb. 9	9.00	0.998	−1	86	3.85	2	173
19	18.97	0.895	1	121	5.49	2	154
Mar. 1	0.94	0.757	1	154	6.91	1	128
11	10.92	0.587	2	186	8.03	1	95
21	20.89	0.386	2	217	8.79	1	56
31	30.86	−0.154	2	246	9.15	1	− 15
100, Apr 10	9.84	+0.105	3	271	9.09	+1	+ 27
20	19.81	0.386	3	291	8.61	0	70
30	29.78	0.684	3	305	7.68	0	112
May 10	9.75	0.993	3	313	6.38	0	149
20	19.73	1.307	2	314	4.72	0	182
30	29.70	1.618	2	307	2.76	0	209
June 9	8.67	1.918	2	292	− 0.56	0	232
19	18.64	2.199	2	270	+ 1.85	0	246
29	28.62	2.456	1	242	4.34	−1	253
July 9	8.59	2.679	−1	206	6.90	1	256
200, 19	18.56	2.865	0	165	9.44	1	251
29	28.53	3.008	0	121	11.91	−1	242
Aug. 8	7.51	3.107	0	76	14.26	0	227
18	17.48	3.161	0	+ 31	16.44	0	209
28	27.45	3.170	+1	− 13	18.42	0	186
Sept. 7	6.43	3.135	1	54	20.15	+1	161
17	16.40	3.063	2	90	21.63	1	134
27	26.37	2.957	2	120	22.82	2	105
Oct. 7	6.34	2.825	3	142	23.72	2	74
17	16.32	2.676	3	156	24.30	3	42
300, 27	26.29	2.516	3	163	24.56	3	+ 10
Nov. 6	5.26	2.352	3	162	24.50	3	− 22
16	15.23	2.194	3	153	24.13	3	53
26	25.21	2.048	3	138	23.44	4	84
Dec. 6	5.18	1.920	2	118	22.45	4	113
16	15.15	1.814	2	93	21.19	4	128
26	25.13	1.736	2	64	19.70	4	159
36	35.10	+1.686	+1	− 34	+18.03	+4	−175

✳ ☌ ☉, Feb. 5.0.
✳ ☌ Mean Sun, Feb. 8.6.

Right-hand tables ($\Delta_\Omega\alpha$, $\Delta_\Omega\delta$):

Sidereal Day	1865. $\Delta_\Omega\alpha$	$\Delta_\Omega\delta$	1873. $\Delta_\Omega\alpha$	$\Delta_\Omega\delta$
0	+0.702	+8.02	−0.903	−7.43
100	0.637	7.94	0.869	7.64
200	0.566	7.78	0.828	7.79
300	0.490	7.56	0.781	7.87
400	0.410	7.27	0.727	7.89

Sidereal Day	1866.		1874.	
0	+0.437	+7.37	−0.746	−7.89
100	0.354	7.04	0.688	7.87
200	0.266	6.66	0.624	7.78
300	0.179	6.20	0.555	7.63
400	0.089	5.69	0.482	7.41

Sidereal Day	1867.		1875.	
0	+0.120	+5.87	−0.507	−7.49
100	0.029	5.33	0.432	7.23
200	−0.062	4.74	0.355	6.92
300	0.152	4.11	0.271	6.55
400	0.241	3.45	0.186	6.12

Sidereal Day	1868 B.		1876 B.	
0	−0.211	+3.68	−0.215	−6.27
100	0.299	3.00	0.130	5.91
200	0.383	2.29	−0.043	5.30
300	0.464	1.56	+0.044	4.75
400	0.541	0.85	0.130	4.16

Sidereal Day	1869.		1877.	
0	−0.516	+1.07	+0.101	−4.36
100	0.590	+0.37	0.187	3.74
200	0.658	−0.41	0.271	3.09
300	0.721	1.15	0.354	2.42
400	0.777	1.88	0.433	1.73

Sidereal Day	1870.		1878.	
0	−0.759	−1.63	+0.407	−1.96
100	0.811	2.35	0.484	1.26
200	0.855	3.04	0.558	−0.54
300	0.892	3.70	0.627	+0.19
400	0.922	4.34	0.691	0.91

Sidereal Day	1871.		1879.	
0	−0.913	−4.13	+0.670	+0.67
100	0.937	4.73	0.731	1.39
200	0.953	5.30	0.785	2.10
300	0.961	5.81	0.833	2.80
400	0.961	6.28	0.875	3.47

Sidereal Day	1872 B.		1880 B.	
0	−0.962	−6.13	+0.862	+3.25
100	0.956	6.56	0.894	3.90
200	0.943	6.94	0.927	4.53
300	0.922	7.25	0.946	5.12
400	−0.893	−7.51	+0.964	+5.67

TABLE XXIV.—β Aquarii.

R.A. 21h 24.7m.   Dec. — 6° 9′.

Upper transit at fictitious meridian.

Sidereal Day	Mean Day	Δ☉a 1870	Var.in 10y	Diff. for 10d	Δ☉δ 1870	Var.in 10y	Diff. for 10d
0, Jan. 0	0.11	−0.992	+ 2	− 29	2.40	0	− 62
10	10.09	1.006	2	0	3.00	0	57
20	20.06	0.992	2	+ 30	3.53	0	49
30	30.03	0.946	+ 1	60	3.97	0	39
Feb. 9	9.00	0.871	0	90	4.30	0	25
19	18.98	0.765	0	121	4.46	0	− 8
Mar. 1	0.95	0.629	− 1	151	4.44	0	+ 13
11	10.92	0.463	1	181	4.19	0	37
21	20.90	0.268	2	209	3.70	− 1	61
31	30.87	−0.045	2	236	2.98	1	84
100, Apr. 10	9.84	+0.204	2	261	2.03	1	107
20	19.81	0.475	3	281	− 0.84	− 1	129
30	29.79	0.764	3	297	+ 0.54	0	148
May 10	9.76	1.067	3	307	2.10	0	162
20	19.73	1.376	3	312	3.76	0	171
30	29.70	1.688	3	309	5.50	0	176
June 9	8.68	1.991	3	297	7.26	0	176
19	18.65	2.280	3	279	9.00	0	170
29	28.62	2.547	2	255	10.65	+ 1	161
July 9	8.60	2.787	2	223	12.20	1	147
200, 19	18.57	2.991	2	185	13.58	1	130
29	28.54	3.156	1	143	14.79	2	111
Aug. 8	7.51	3.276	− 1	99	15.80	2	91
18	17.49	3.354	0	54	16.61	2	70
28	27.46	3.385	0	+ 10	17.20	2	49
Sept. 7	6.43	3.375	+ 1	− 31	17.59	3	29
17	16.40	3.325	1	67	17.79	3	+ 11
27	26.38	3.242	2	98	17.82	3	− 6
Oct. 7	6.35	3.131	2	121	17.68	3	20
17	16.32	3.002	2	136	17.42	3	32
300, 27	26.29	2.861	2	143	17.05	4	41
Nov. 6	5.27	2.718	2	142	16.60	4	49
16	15.24	2.579	2	133	16.08	4	55
26	25.21	2.454	2	118	15.50	4	60
Dec. 6	5.19	2.344	2	98	14.89	4	62
16	15.16	2.258	2	74	14.26	4	63
26	25.13	2.197	1	48	13.63	4	63
36	35.10	+2.163	+ 1	− 19	+13.00	+ 4	− 61

✶ ☾ ☌ ☉,   Feb. 7.1.
✶ ☾ ☌ Mean Sun,   Feb. 10 8.

Sidereal Day	Δ☊a	Δ☊δ	Δ☊a	Δ☊δ
	1865.		**1873.**	
0	+0.611	+7.92	−0.917	−7.44
100	0.523	7.79	0.860	7.63
200	0.432	7.61	0.796	7.75
300	0.336	7.37	0.726	7.80
400	0.237	7.04	0.650	7.79
	1866.		**1874.**	
0	+0.271	+7.17	−0.676	−7.80
100	0.170	6.81	0.596	7.75
200	0.068	6.40	0.512	7.64
300	−0.034	5 93	0.423	7.46
400	0.136	5.41	0.331	7.22
	1867.		**1875.**	
0	−0.102	+5.59	−0.363	−7.31
100	0.204	5 04	0.269	7.03
200	0.303	4.44	0 173	6.69
300	0.400	3 81	−0.076	6.30
400	0.494	3.14	+0.022	5.83
	1868 B.		**1876 B.**	
0	−0.463	+3.37	−0.011	−6.02
100	0.553	2.68	+0.087	5.54
200	0.638	1.97	0.184	5.02
300	0.718	1.25	0.279	4.46
400	0.792	0.52	0.372	3.83
	1869.		**1877.**	
0	−0.768	+0.76	+0.341	−4 04
100	0.837	+0.03	0.433	3.42
200	0.898	−0.71	0.521	2.77
300	0.951	1.44	0.604	2.10
400	0.997	2.15	0.683	1.40
	1870.		**1878.**	
0	−0.982	−1.91	+0.657	−1.64
100	1.022	2.61	0.735	0.94
200	1.052	3.24	0.802	−0.22
300	1.073	3.93	0.866	+0.49
400	1.085	4.54	0.922	1.21
	1871.		**1879.**	
0	−1.082	−4.33	+0.903	+0.97
100	1.088	4.92	0.955	1.67
200	1.085	5.46	0 908	2.37
300	1.072	5.95	1.033	3.05
400	1.051	−6.39	1.060	3.70
	1872 B.		**1880 B.**	
0	−1.059	−6.25	+1.052	+3.49
100	1.031	6.65	1.072	4.12
200	0.995	7.00	1.084	4.72
300	0.951	7.29	1.086	5.29
400	−0.899	−7.51	+1.060	+5.81

TABLE XXIV.—ς Aquarii.

R.A. 21^h 30^m.8.   Dec. — 8° 26′.

Upper transit at fictitious meridian.

Sidereal Day	Mean Day	$\Delta_\odot\alpha$ 1870.	Var. in 10y.	Diff. for 10d.	$\Delta_\odot\delta$ 1870.	Var. in 10y.	Diff. for 10d.
0, Jan. 0	0.12	−0.973	+2	−33	−3.00	+1	−51
10	10.09	0.992	2	−5	3.48	+1	44
20	20.06	0.982	1	+25	3.87	0	35
30	30.04	0.941	+1	55	4.17	−1	24
Feb. 9	9.01	0.871	0	86	4.34	1	−9
19	18.98	0.770	0	117	4.35	1	+8
Mar. 1	0.95	0.638	−1	147	4.18	1	28
11	10.93	0.476	1	177	3.78	1	50
21	20.90	0.284	2	206	3.18	1	73
31	30.87	−0.065	2	233	2.32	1	95
100, Apr. 10	9.85	+0.181	3	259	1.27	1	116
20	19.82	0.451	3	280	−0.00	1	135
30	29.79	0.740	3	297	+1.43	1	151
May 10	9.76	1.043	3	309	3.01	−1	163
20	19.74	1.355	3	314	4.68	0	171
30	29.71	1.668	3	312	6.41	0	174
June 9	8.68	1.976	3	302	8.14	0	172
19	18.65	2.270	3	285	9.84	0	165
29	28.63	2.543	2	260	11.42	0	153
July 9	8.60	2.788	2	228	12.88	+1	138
200, 19	18.57	2.998	2	192	14.17	1	120
29	28.54	3.171	1	151	15.27	2	100
Aug. 8	7.52	3.300	1	105	16.16	2	78
18	17.49	3.382	−1	60	16.83	2	56
28	27.46	3.421	0	+17	17.29	3	36
Sept. 7	6.44	3.417	0	−25	17.56	3	+17
17	16.41	3.373	+1	62	17.64	3	−1
27	26.38	3.295	1	93	17.55	3	16
Oct. 7	6.35	3.189	1	118	17.32	3	29
17	16.33	3.062	1	134	16.98	4	39
300, 27	26.30	2.924	2	142	16.55	4	46
Nov. 6	5.27	2.781	2	142	16.06	4	52
16	15.24	2.643	2	134	15.52	4	56
26	25.22	2.515	2	120	14.95	4	57
Dec. 6	5.19	2.405	2	100	14.38	4	57
16	15.16	2.316	2	77	13.81	4	56
26	25.14	2.251	2	51	13.26	4	54
36	35.11	+2.214	+2	−22	+12.74	+4	−49

Sidereal Day	$\Delta_\Omega\alpha$	$\Delta_\Omega\delta$	$\Delta_\Omega\alpha$	$\Delta_\Omega\delta$
	1865.		**1873.**	
0	+0.600	+7.82	−0.916	−7.45
100	0.511	7.69	0.857	7.61
200	0.417	7.49	0.791	7.71
300	0.320	7.22	0.719	7.75
400	0.219	6.90	0.640	7.71
	1866.		**1874.**	
0	+0.253	+7.01	−0.667	−7.74
100	0.151	6.64	0.586	7.67
200	+0.048	6.22	0.499	7.53
300	−0.055	5.74	0.469	7.31
400	0.158	5.21	0.315	7.08
	1867.		**1875.**	
0	−0.124	+5.39	−0.347	−7.17
100	0.226	4.83	0.252	6.83
200	0.326	4.22	0.155	6.53
300	0.424	3.56	−0.057	6.13
400	0.517	2.91	+0.042	5.67
	1868 B.		**1876 B.**	
0	−0.496	+3.14	+0.009	−5.83
100	0.577	2.45	0.108	5.34
200	0.662	1.75	0.206	4.81
300	0.741	1.03	0.302	4.24
400	0.814	0.30	0.395	3.64
	1869.		**1877.**	
0	−0.791	+0.54	+0.364	−3.84
100	0.859	−0.19	0.456	3.21
200	0.919	0.92	0.544	2.56
300	0.972	1.64	0.627	1.88
400	1.015	2.34	0.706	1.19
	1870.		**1878.**	
0	−1.001	−2.10	+0.680	−1.43
100	1.040	2.79	0.755	0.73
200	1.068	3.45	0.824	−0.02
300	1.088	4.08	0.887	+0.69
400	1.098	4.68	0.942	1.40
	1871.		**1879.**	
0	−1.096	−4.48	+0.924	+1.16
100	1.100	5.04	0.974	1.86
200	1.095	5.57	1.017	2.55
300	1.080	6.04	1.050	3.22
400	1.056	6.46	1.075	3.86
	1872 B.		**1880 B.**	
0	−1.065	−6.32	+1.067	+3.65
100	1.036	6.71	1.066	4.27
200	0.998	7.04	1.086	4.86
300	0.951	7.30	1.097	5.40
400	−0.897	−7.51	+1.088	+5.91

✱ ♂ ⊙,   Feb. 8.6.
✱ ♂ Mean Sun, Feb. 12.3.

TABLE XXIV.—ε Pegasi.

R.A. 21h 37m.8.   Dec. + 9° 17'.

Upper transit at fictitious meridian.

Sidereal Day	Mean Day	$\Delta_\odot\alpha$ 1870.	Var.in 10 y.	Diff. for 10 d.	$\Delta_\odot\delta$ 1870.	Var.in 10 y.	Diff. for 10 d.
0, Jan. 0	0.12	−0.939	+2	−49	+1.37	+2	−124
10	10.10	0.976	1	−21	+0.10	2	130
20	20.07	0.981	1	+8	−1.21	2	·131
30	30.04	0.960	+1	37	2.50	2	126
Feb. 9	9.01	0.907	0	69	3.71	2	115
19	18.99	0.821	−1	102	4.77	1	97
Mar. 1	0.96	0.703	1	133	5.63	1	74
11	10.93	0.555	2	164	6.24	+1	45
21	20.90	0.376	2	195	6.53	0	−13
31	30.88	−0.165	2	225	6.50	0	+20
100, Apr. 10	9.85	+0.074	2	252	6.12	0	56
20	19.82	0.337	3	275	5.38	0	91
30	29.80	0.622	3	292	4.31	0	122
May 10	9.77	0.920	3	305	2.94	−1	151
20	19.74	1.229	3	310	1.29	1	177
30	29.71	1.538	3	307	+0.59	1	198
June 9	8.69	1.840	2	297	2.65	1	211
19	18.66	2.130	2	281	4.79	−1	217
29	28.63	2.399	2	255	6.98	0	221
July 9	8.60	2.638	1	223	9.19	0	219
200, 19	18.58	2.844	1	188	11.34	0	210
29	28.55	3.013	−1	148	13.37	0	197
Aug. 8	7.52	3.139	0	103	15.26	0	180
18	17.50	3.219	0	59	16.96	+1	160
28	27.47	3.257	+1	+16	18.47	1	139
Sept. 7	6.44	3.252	1	−25	19.74	1	116
17	16.41	3.208	2	62	20.78	1	91
27	26.39	3.129	2	92	21.56	2	67
Oct. 7	6.36	3.025	3	116	22.12	2	43
17	16.33	2.899	3	134	22.43	2	+19
300, 27	26.30	2.760	3	143	22.50	3	−5
Nov. 6	5.28	2.616	3	144	22.33	3	28
16	15.25	2.474	2	139	21.94	3	50
26	25.22	2.340	2	127	21.34	4	70
Dec. 6	5.19	2.222	2	110	20.55	4	88
16	15.17	2.122	2	89	19.58	4	105
26	25.14	2.045	2	65	18.46	4	118
36	35.11	+1.992	+2	−40	+17.23	+4	−127

✳ ☌ ☉,   Feb. 10.4.
✳ ☌ Mean Sun,   Feb. 14.1.

Sidereal Day	$\Delta_\Omega\alpha$	$\Delta_\Omega\delta$	$\Delta_\Omega\alpha$	$\Delta_\Omega\delta$
	1865.		**1873.**	
0	+0.674	+7.71	−0.918	−7.45
100	0.599	7.56	0.875	7.58
200	0.520	7.34	0.824	7.66
300	0.435	7.05	0.767	7.68
400	0.347	6.71	0.704	7.62
	1866.		**1874.**	
0	+0.377	+6.83	−0.726	−7.65
100	0.287	6.45	0.659	7.56
200	0.194	6.01	0.587	7.40
300	0.099	5.51	0.510	7.19
400	0.003	4.97	0.429	6.92
	1867.		**1875.**	
0	+0.036	+5.16	−0.457	−7.01
100	−0.060	4.58	0.373	6.70
200	0.155	3.97	0.287	6.34
300	0.249	3.32	0.199	5.92
400	0.341	2.65	0.109	5.45
	1868 B.		**1876 B.**	
0	−0.310	+2.88	−0.139	−5.61
100	0.399	2.19	−0.048	5.12
200	0.485	1.49	+0.043	4.58
300	0.567	0.77	0.134	4.00
400	0.643	0.05	0.224	3.39
	1869.		**1877.**	
0	−0.618	+0.29	+0.194	−3.59
100	0.690	−0.44	0.283	2.96
200	0.757	1.16	0.369	2.31
300	0.816	1.86	0.453	1.63
400	0.869	2.55	0.534	0.94
	1870.		**1878.**	
0	−0.852	−2.32	+0.507	−1.17
100	0.900	3.00	0.584	−0.48
200	0.939	3.64	0.657	+0.23
300	0.970	4.25	0.725	0.93
400	0.994	4.83	0.786	1.63
	1871.		**1879.**	
0	−0.987	−4.64	+0.766	+1.39
100	1.004	5.19	0.824	2.08
200	1.013	5.69	0.874	2.76
300	1.013	6.14	0.918	3.41
400	1.005	6.54	0.954	4.03
	1872 B.		**1880 B.**	
0	−1.009	−6.41	+0.943	+3.83
100	0.995	6.77	0.974	4.43
200	0.972	7.07	0.996	5.00
300	0.942	7.32	1.011	5.53
400	−0.904	−7.50	+1.016	+6.01

TABLE XXIV.—° 11 Cephei.

R.A. 21h 40m 0.0.   Dec. + 70° 43'.

Upper transit at fictitious meridian.

Sidereal Day	Mean Day	$\Delta_\odot a$ 1870.	Var. in 10 y.	Diff. for 10 d.	$\Delta_\odot \delta$ 1870.	Var. in 10 y.	Diff. for 10 d.
0, Jan. 0	0.12	−2.784	− 4	−441	+13.76	+ 2	−218
10	10.10	3.188	6	359	11.36	2	261
20	20.07	3.498	7	259	8.57	2	295
30	30.04	3.703	8	148	5.50	2	317
Feb. 9	9.02	3.792	9	− 30	+ 2.27	2	327
19	18.99	3.762	10	+ 91	− 0.99	2	323
Mar. 1	0.96	3.610	10	212	4.15	2	307
11	10.93	3.340	10	327	7.09	2	279
21	20.91	2.960	10	432	9.69	1	239
31	30.88	2.480	9	525	11.85	1	191
100, Apr. 10	9.85	1.916	8	601	13.49	1	136
20	19.82	1.286	7	657	14.55	+ 1	76
30	29.80	−0.608	6	694	15.00	0	− 14
May 10	9.77	+0.695	4	709	14.83	0	+ 48
20	19.74	0.802	2	702	14.04	0	108
30	29.72	1.492	− 1	675	12.67	0	165
June 9	8.69	2.145	+ 1	629	10.76	− 1	216
19	18.66	2.743	2	565	8.37	1	261
29	28.63	3.270	3	486	5.56	1	299
July 9	8.61	3.711	4	395	− 2.41	1	330
200, 19	18.58	4.057	5	295	+ 1.00	1	352
29	28.55	4.299	6	189	4.60	1	366
Aug. 8	7.52	4.434	6	+ 80	8.30	1	372
18	17.50	4.458	7	− 30	12.01	1	370
28	27.47	4.374	7	137	15.68	1	361
Sept. 7	6.44	4.186	6	238	19.21	1	344
17	16.42	3.900	6	332	22.53	− 1	319
27	26.39	3.525	6	416	25.57	0	288
Oct. 7	6.36	3.072	5	488	28.27	0	250
17	16.33	2.553	4	547	30.56	0	207
300, 27	26.31	1.984	3	590	32.38	0	157
Nov. 6	5.28	1.378	+ 2	618	33.69	0	103
16	15.25	0.754	0	628	34.44	+ 1	+ 46
26	25.22	+0.127	− 1	622	34.60	1	− 14
Dec. 6	5.20	−0.483	3	596	34.16	1	74
16	15.17	1.060	5	553	33.13	2	132
26	25.14	1.584	7	493	31.53	2	187
36	35.12	−2.039	− 8	−415	+29.41	+ 2	−235

Sidereal Day	$\Delta_\Omega a$	$\Delta_\Omega \delta$	$\Delta_\Omega a$	$\Delta_\Omega \delta$
	1865.		**1873.**	
0	+1.349	+7.67	−0.962	−7.44
100	1.401	7.51	1.058	7.58
200	1.440	7.29	1.146	7.65
300	1.467	6.99	1.224	7.65
400	1.482	6.64	1.291	7.60
	1866.		**1874.**	
0	+1.478	+6.77	−1.269	−7.62
100	1.481	6.38	1.330	7.52
200	1.477	5.93	1.379	7.36
300	1.457	5.43	1.417	7.14
400	1.424	4.89	1.442	6.86
	1867.		**1875.**	
0	+1.437	+5.08	−1.435	−6.96
100	1.397	4.50	1.453	6.65
200	1.342	3.89	1.459	6.28
300	1.277	3.24	1.454	5.85
400	1.201	2.57	1.436	5.38
	1868 B.		**1876 B.**	
0	+1.229	+2.80	−1.443	−5.55
100	1.145	2.11	1.417	5.05
200	1.053	1.40	1.380	4.51
300	0.951	+0.68	1.331	3.92
400	0.841	−0.04	1.272	3.31
	1869.		**1877.**	
0	+0.679	+0.21	−1.293	−3.52
100	0.764	−0.52	1.226	2.89
200	0.643	1.23	1.149	2.24
300	0.517	1.93	1.063	1.56
400	0.346	2.62	0.967	0.87
	1870.		**1878.**	
0	+0.431	−2.40	−1.000	−1.10
100	0.298	3.06	0.899	−0.41
200	0.163	3.70	0.790	+0.29
300	+0.027	4.31	0.675	0.99
400	−0.109	4.88	0.555	1.69
	1871.		**1879.**	
0	−0.063	−4.69	−0.595	+1.45
100	0.196	5.23	0.470	2.14
200	0.331	5.72	0.341	2.81
300	0.461	6.17	0.208	3.46
400	0.587	6.56	0.074	4.08
	1872 B.		**1880 B.**	
0	−0.545	−6.43	−0.119	+3.88
100	0.668	6.79	+0.016	4.48
200	0.784	7.08	0.151	5.04
300	0.894	7.32	0.286	5.56
400	−0.996	−7.50	+0.417	+6.04

✳ ♂ ⊙, Feb. 11.0.
✳ ♂ Mean Sun, Feb. 14.7.
✳ ☍ Mean Sun, Aug. 16.3.

TABLE XXIV.—μ Capricorni.

R.A. 21^h 46^m.2.　　　　Dec. — 14° 10′.

Upper transit at fictitious meridian.

Sidereal Day	Mean Day	$\Delta_\odot a$ 1870.	Var. in 10 y.	Diff. for 10 d.	$\Delta_\odot \delta$ 1870.	Var. in 10 y.	Diff. for 10 d.
0, Jan. 0	0.13	−0.929	+ 3	− 44	− 4.60	+ 1	− 23
10	10.10	0.959	2	− 16	4.78	0	13
20	20.07	0.961	1	+ 13	4.86	0	− 1
30	30.05	0.933	+ 1	42	4.79	0	+ 14
Feb. 9	9.02	0.876	0	73	4.57	0	30
19	18.99	0.787	0	105	4.19	0	47
Mar. 1	0.97	0.667	− 1	136	3.63	− 1	66
11	10.94	0.516	1	167	2.86	1	85
21	20.91	0.333	2	198	1.92	1	104
31	30.88	−0.121	2	226	− 0.78	1	123
100, Apr. 10	9.86	+0.119	3	253	+ 0.54	2	140
20	19.83	0.385	3	278	2.01	2	155
30	29.80	0.674	3	298	3.62	1	165
May 10	9.77	0.978	4	312	5.30	1	171
20	19.75	1.295	3	320	7.02	− 1	174
30	29.72	1.616	3	321	8.76	0	171
June 9	8.69	1.934	3	314	10.43	0	163
19	18.66	2.241	3	299	12.02	0	151
29	28.64	2.529	3	276	13.46	+ 1	135
July 9	8.61	2.790	2	247	14.72	1	116
200, 19	18.58	3.020	2	212	15.78	2	95
29	28.56	3.210	2	170	16.62	2	72
Aug. 8	7.53	3.357	2	125	17.22	2	48
18	17.50	3.459	1	80	17.58	3	25
28	27.47	3.516	− 1	+ 34	17.73	3	+ 4
Sept. 7	6.45	3.527	0	− 9	17.66	3	− 15
17	16.42	3.498	0	48	17.43	3	30
27	26.39	3.432	0	82	17.06	4	43
Oct. 7	6.36	3.335	+ 1	109	16.57	4	54
17	16.34	3.216	1	128	15.99	4	60
300, 27	26.31	3.082	2	139	15.38	4	62
Nov. 6	5.28	2.941	3	141	14.76	4	61
16	15.26	2.802	3	136	14.17	4	58
26	25.23	2.671	3	124	13.61	3	54
Dec. 6	5.20	2.555	3	108	13.10	3	47
16	15.17	2.457	2	86	12.67	3	39
26	25.15	2.384	2	60	12.32	3	30
36	35.12	+2.336	+ 1	− 34	+12.07	+ 3	− 20

☆ ♂☉,　Feb. 12.6.
☆ ♂ Mean Sun,　Feb. 16.2.

Sidereal Day	$\Delta_\Omega a$	$\Delta_\Omega \delta$	$\Delta_\Omega a$	$\Delta_\Omega \delta$
	1865.		**1873.**	
0	+0.567	+7.57	−0.908	−7.43
100	0.473	7.39	0.843	7.55
200	0.375	7.15	0.772	7.59
300	0.274	6.84	0.694	7.58
400	0.170	6.48	0.611	7.50
	1866.		**1874.**	
0	+0.205	+6.60	−0.640	−7.54
100	+0.100	6.20	0.553	7.42
200	−0.006	5.74	0.463	7.24
300	0.112	5.23	0.368	7.00
400	0.218	4.68	0.270	6.71
	1867.		**1875.**	
0	−0.182	+4.87	−0.304	−6.81
100	0.286	4.29	0.205	6.48
200	0.388	3.67	0.104	6.09
300	0.486	3.02	−0.003	5.66
400	0.579	2.34	+0.09	5.18
	1868 B.		**1876 B.**	
0	−0.544	+2.57	+0.064	−5.34
100	0.638	1.88	0.165	4.83
200	0.723	1.17	0.264	4.29
300	0.801	+0.46	0.361	3.70
400	0.872	−0.26	0.456	3.08
	1869.		**1877.**	
0	−0.849	−0.02	+0.424	−3.29
100	0.914	0.73	0.516	2.65
200	0.972	1.44	0.604	1.99
300	1.021	2.13	0.687	1.32
400	1.063	2.81	0.765	0.63
	1870.		**1878.**	
0	−1.049	−2.58	+0.739	−0.87
100	1.083	3.24	0.813	−0.17
200	1.108	3.86	0.880	+0.52
300	1.123	4.46	0.940	1.22
400	1.128	5.01	0.992	1.90
	1871.		**1879.**	
0	−1.128	−4.83	+0.975	+1.67
100	1.127	5.35	1.022	2.35
200	1.116	5.82	1.060	3.00
300	1.096	6.25	1.080	3.64
400	1.067	6.62	1.111	4.24
	1872 B.		**1880 B.**	
0	−1.078	−6.50	+1.105	+4.04
100	1.043	6.83	1.119	4.63
200	0.999	7.11	1.125	5.17
300	0.947	7.32	1.120	5.68
400	−0.897	−7.48	+1.106	+6.13

TABLE XXIV.—° 79 Draconis.

R.A. 21h 51m.2.   Dec. + 73° 5'.

Upper transit at fictitious meridian.

Sidereal Day	Mean Day	Δ⊙α 1870.	Var. in 10 y.	Diff. for 10 d.	Δ⊙δ 1870.	Var. in 10 y.	Diff. for 10 d.
0, Jan. 0	0.13	−2.991	− 6	−544	+14.64	+ 1	−202
10	10.11	3.490	8	450	12.38	2	248
20	20.08	3.886	10	340	9.70	2	285
30	30.05	4.165	11	216	6.71	2	311
Feb. 9	9.02	4.315	12	− 82	3.52	2	325
19	19.00	4.328	13	+ 56	+ 0.26	2	325
Mar. 1	0.97	4.202	13	195	− 2.94	2	313
11	10.94	3.940	13	329	5.95	1	290
21	20.92	3.548	13	452	8 66	1	252
31	30.89	3.040	12	562	10.95	1	206
100, Apr. 10	9.86	2.431	10	653	12.75	1	153
20	19.83	1.741	9	723	13.99	+ 1	94
30	29.80	0.993	7	769	14.63	0	− 33
May 10	9.78	−0.210	5	792	14.65	0	+ 29
20	19.75	+0.583	3	790	14.06	0	90
30	29.72	1.362	− 1	764	12.87	0	147
June 9	8 70	2.104	+ 1	717	11.12	0	200
19	18.67	2.789	3	649	8.88	− 1	247
29	28.64	3.397	4	564	6.20	1	288
July 9	8.61	3.913	6	466	− 3.16	1	321
200, 19	18.59	4.325	7	356	+ 0.18	1	346
29	28.56	4.622	8	239	3.73	1	363
Aug. 8	7 53	4.800	9	+117	7.41	1	372
18	17.50	4.856	9	− 5	11.15	1	374
28	27.48	4.790	9	126	14.86	1	367
Sept. 7	6.45	4.607	8	241	18.46	1	353
17	16.42	4.311	8	349	21.90	1	331
27	26.40	3.912	7	447	25.07	1	302
Oct. 7	6.37	3.422	6	532	27.92	− 1	267
17	16.34	2.853	5	603	30.39	0	225
300, 27	26.31	2.220	3	659	32.41	0	177
Nov. 6	5.29	1.540	+ 1	697	33.91	0	124
16	15.26	0 832	− 1	717	34.87	+ 1	67
26	25.23	+0.112	3	717	35.25	1	+ 7
Dec. 6	5.20	−0.596	5	696	35.01	1	− 54
16	15.18	1.274	7	655	34.18	1	113
26	25.15	1 899	9	593	32.77	2	169
36	35.12	−2.452	−11	−511	+30.81	+ 2	−220

Sidereal Day	ΔΩα	ΔΩδ	ΔΩα	ΔΩδ
	1865.		**1873.**	
0	+1.538	+7.48	−1.049	−7.42
100	1.606	7.28	1.169	7.52
200	1.664	7.02	1.279	7.55
300	1.706	6.70	1.378	7.52
400	1.733	6.33	1.465	7.43
	1866.		**1874.**	
0	+1.725	+6.46	−1.437	−7.47
100	1.742	6.04	1.517	7.33
200	1.744	5.57	1.584	7.14
300	1.730	5.06	1.637	6.80
400	1.701	4.49	1.677	6.58
	1867.		**1875.**	
0	+1.713	+4.69	−1.665	−6.69
100	1.674	4.10	1.696	6.35
200	1.621	3.48	1.713	5.95
300	1.554	2.82	1.716	5.51
400	1.473	2.14	1.705	5.02
	1868 B.		**1876 B.**	
0	+1.502	+2.37	−1.710	−5.19
100	1.413	1.68	1.689	4.67
200	1.311	0.96	1.655	4.11
300	1.199	+0.27	1.606	3.52
400	1.075	−0.44	1.545	2.90
	1869.		**1877.**	
0	+1.118	−0.19	−1.567	−3.11
100	0.989	0.91	1.497	2.48
200	0.852	1.61	1.415	1.82
300	0.707	2 29	1.320	1.15
400	0.557	2.96	1.215	0.46
	1870.		**1878.**	
0	+0.608	−2.74	−1.252	−0.69
100	0.455	3.38	1.139	0.00
200	0.298	3.99	1.017	+0.69
300	+0.139	4.57	0.887	1.37
400	−0.021	5.11	0.748	2.05
	1871.		**1879.**	
0	+0.033	−4.93	−0.796	+1.82
100	−0.127	5.44	0.653	2.49
200	0.295	5.90	0.504	3.14
300	0.440	6.31	0.350	3.76
400	0.591	6.67	0.194	4.36
	1872 B.		**1880 B.**	
0	−0.541	−6.55	−0.247	+4.16
100	0.689	6.87	−0.089	4.73
200	0.830	7.13	+0.071	5.26
300	0.965	7.33	0.230	5.75
400	−1.091	−7.46	+0.388	+6.20

✳ ☌ ⊙, Feb. 13.9.
✳ ☌ Mean Sun, Feb. 17 5.
✳ ☌ ☊ Mean Sun, Aug. 19.1.

TABLE XXIV.—α Gruis.

R.A. 22h 0.0m   Dec. — 47° 35′.

Upper transit at fictitious meridian.

Sidereal Day.	Mean Day.	Δ☉a 1870.	Var.in 10y.	Diff. for 10d.	Δ☉δ 1870.	Var.in 10y.	Diff. for 10d.
0, Jan. 0	0.14	−1.275	+5	−106	−12.19	−2	+125
10	10.11	1.361	5	64	10.77	3	157
20	20.08	1.404	4	−21	9.06	3	186
30	30.06	1.402	3	+24	7.07	4	210
Feb. 9	9.03	1.356	2	69	4.88	4	229
19	19.00	1.264	+1	115	2.51	4	244
Mar. 1	0.97	1.126	0	161	−0.02	4	253
11	10.95	0.943	−1	205	+2.54	4	257
21	20.92	0.716	2	249	5.11	4	257
31	30.89	0.446	3	291	7.67	3	253
100, Apr. 10	9.87	−0.136	4	329	10.15	3	242
20	19.84	+0.210	5	362	12.49	3	227
30	29.81	0.585	6	390	14.67	2	207
May 10	9.78	0.987	6	412	16.61	1	182
20	19.76	1.406	7	426	18.29	−1	154
30	29.73	1.835	7	430	19.67	0	121
June 9	8.70	2.262	8	423	20.70	+1	84
19	18.67	2.677	8	406	21.35	2	46
29	28.65	3.070	7	379	21.61	3	+7
July 9	8.62	3.431	7	343	21.49	3	−31
200, 19	18.59	3.752	7	296	20.99	4	69
29	28.57	4.021	6	242	20.12	5	104
Aug. 8	7.54	4.234	6	183	18.91	5	135
18	17.51	4.386	5	120	17.43	5	160
28	27.48	4.473	4	+55	15.73	6	179
Sept. 7	6.46	4.496	4	−8	13.88	6	190
17	16.43	4.458	3	68	11.96	6	193
27	26.40	4.363	2	120	10.04	6	188
Oct. 7	6.37	4.221	−1	164	8.22	7	175
17	16.35	4.039	0	197	6.57	6	154
300, 27	26.32	3.830	0	219	5.16	5	126
Nov. 6	15.29	3.605	+1	230	4.06	4	93
16	15.26	3.374	1	229	3.31	4	56
26	25.24	3.151	1	217	2.95	3	−16
Dec. 6	5.21	2.944	1	195	2.99	2	+25
16	15.18	2.763	2	166	3.44	2	65
26	25.16	2.614	2	131	4.28	+1	103
36	35.13	+2.503	+1	−91	+5.48	0	+137

※ ☌ ☉,   Feb. 16.1.
※ ☌ Mean Sun, Feb. 19.7.

Sidereal Day.	Δ☊a	Δ☊δ	Δ☊a	Δ☊δ
	1865.		1873.	
0	+0.312	+7.32	−0.850	−7.39
100	0.180	7.10	0.741	7.46
200	+0.046	6.81	0.627	7.46
300	−0.088	6.47	0.507	7.40
400	0.222	6.07	0.384	7.28
	1866.		1874.	
0	−0.178	+6.21	−0.426	−7.33
100	0.311	5.78	0.300	7.17
200	0.441	5.29	0.173	6.95
300	·0.567	4.76	−0.044	6.67
400	0.689	4.19	+0.085	6.34
	1867.		1875.	
0	−0.648	+4.36	+0.042	−6.46
100	0.766	3.76	0.170	6.09
200	0.877	3.13	0.297	5.68
300	0.980	2.47	0.421	5.22
400	1.074	1.80	0.543	4.71
	1868 B.		1876 B.	
0	−1.043	+2.04	+0.502	−4.89
100	1.131	1.3?	0.620	4.36
200	1.209	+0.6?	0.733	3.79
300	1.277	−0.0?	0.840	3.19
400	1.333	0.7?	0.940	2.57
	1869.		1877.	
0	−1.315	−0.52	+0.907	−2.77
100	1.364	1.22	1.002	2.13
200	1.400	1.91	1.089	1.48
300	1.425	2.5?	1.167	0.80
400	1.437	3.22	1.235	0.12
	1870.		1878.	
0	−1.434	−3.00	+1.213	−0.35
100	1.438	3.63	1.275	+0.33
200	1.429	4.24	1.327	1.01
300	1.408	4.78	1.368	1.68
400	1.375	5.29	1.397	2.34
	1871.		1879.	
0	−1.387	−5.12	+1.388	+2.12
100	1.347	5.60	1.410	2.77
200	1.294	6.03	1.420	3.40
300	1.232	6.41	1.419	4.00
400	1.158	6.74	1.405	4.57
	1872 B.		1880 B.	
0	−1.184	−6.63	+1.411	+4.39
100	1.104	6.92	1.390	4.93
200	1.016	7.15	1.356	5.44
300	0.919	7.32	1.311	5.90
400	−0.815	−7.4?	+1.255	+6.31

TABLE XXIV.—θ Aquarii.

R.A. 22h 10m.0.   Dec. — 8° 26'

Upper transit at fictitious meridian.

Sidereal Day	Mean Day	$\Delta_{\odot}\alpha$ 1870.	Var. in 10 y.	Diff. for 10 d.	$\Delta_{\odot}\delta$ 1870.	Var. in 10 y.	Diff. for 10 d.
0, Jan. 0	0.15	−0.799	+3	−62	3.45	+1	−48
10	10.12	0.849	2	36	3.85	+1	40
20	20.09	0.871	2	−10	4.21	0	30
30	30.06	0.869	2	+16	4.45	0	18
Feb. 9	9.04	0.838	+1	45	4.56	0	−2
19	19.01	0.778	0	76	4.49	0	+16
Mar. 1	0.98	0.686	0	107	4.23	0	36
11	10.95	0.563	−1	139	3.77	0	57
21	20.93	0 408	1	171	3.09	0	81
31	30.90	0.221	2	203	2.16	0	104
100, Apr. 10	9.87	−0.002	2	234	1.01	0	125
20	19.85	+0.245	2	260	+0.34	−1	145
30	29.82	0.516	3	283	1.88	1	162
May 10	9.79	0.809	3	301	3.56	1	175
20	19.76	1.116	3	312	5.36	1	183
30	29.74	1.431	4	316	7.20	1	186
June 9	8.71	1.746	4	313	9.06	1	184
19	18.68	2.054	3	302	10.87	−1	177
29	28.65	2.347	3	283	12.59	0	166
July 9	8.63	2.617	3	256	14.17	+1	150
200, 19	18.60	2.856	2	223	15 58	1	132
29	28.57	3.061	2	185	16.80	1	111
Aug. 8	7.54	3.225	1	142	17.79	2	87
18	17.52	3.345	−1	99	18.54	2	64
28	27.49	3.422	0	55	19.07	2	41
Sept. 7	6.46	3.455	0	+12	19 36	2	+18
17	16.44	3.447	0	−27	19.44	2	−1
27	26.41	3.403	+1	61	19.35	3	18
Oct. 7	6.38	3.327	1	90	19.09	3	33
17	16.35	3.226	2	111	18.70	3	44
300, 27	26.33	3.108	2	125	18.23	3	53
Nov. 6	5.30	2.978	2	132	17.66	3	58
16	15.27	2.847	2	131	17.08	3	60
26	25.24	2.719	3	124	16.47	2	62
Dec. 6	5.22	2.601	3	111	15.85	3	61
16	15.19	2.499	3	94	15.25	3	58
26	25.16	2.414	2	74	14.69	3	53
36	35.14	+2.351	+2	−52	+14.20	+3	−46

✱ ☌ ☉,   Feb. 18.7.
✱ ☌ Mean Sun,   Feb. 22.3.

Sidereal Day	$\Delta_{\Omega}\alpha$	$\Delta_{\Omega}\delta$	$\Delta_{\Omega}\alpha$	$\Delta_{\Omega}\delta$
	1865.		**1873.**	
0	+0 587	+7.12	−0.904	−7.35
100	0.496	6.87	0.844	7.38
200	0.405	6.56	0.778	7.35
300	0.308	6.19	0.706	7.26
400	0.208	5.77	0.628	7.11
	1866.		**1874.**	
0	+0.242	+5.92	−0.655	−7.16
100	0.141	5.46	0.573	6.97
200	+0 039	4.96	0.487	6.73
300	−0.664	4.41	0.397	6.42
400	0.166	3.82	0.304	6.07
	1867.		**1875.**	
0	−0.131	+4.02	−0.336	−6.19
100	0.233	3.41	0.241	5.80
200	0.332	2.77	0.145	5.37
300	0.428	2.11	−0.047	4.89
400	0.521	1.43	+0.051	4.37
	1868 B.		**1876 B.**	
0	−0.490	+1.66	+0.018	−4.55
100	0.579	0.97	0.115	4.01
200	0.664	+0.28	0.212	3 43
300	0.742	−0.42	0.308	2.83
400	0.814	1.11	0.400	2.20
	1869.		**1877.**	
0	−0.790	−0.88	+0.369	−2.40
100	0.857	1.57	0.460	1.76
200	0.916	2.24	0.547	1.10
300	0.968	2.89	0.629	−0.44
400	1.010	3.51	0.707	+0.24
	1870.		**1878.**	
0	−0.997	−3.30	+0.681	+0.01
100	1.034	3.90	0.755	0.68
200	1.062	4.47	0.823	1.35
300	1.080	4.99	0.884	2.01
400	1.090	5.48	0.935	2.66
	1871.		**1879.**	
0	−1.088	−5.32	+0.921	+2.44
100	1.091	5.77	0.970	3.07
200	1.085	6.17	1.011	3.68
300	1.069	6.52	1.043	4.26
400	1.045	6.81	1.067	4.80
	1872 B.		**1880 B.**	
0	−1.054	−6.72	+1.060	+4.62
100	1.024	6 97	1.078	5.14
200	0.986	7.16	1.087	5.62
300	0.939	7.30	1.087	6.05
400	−0.884	−7.37	+1.078	+6.43

TABLE XXIV.—π Aquarii.

R.A. 22h 18.6m.   Dec. + 0° 43'.

Upper transit at fictitious meridian.

Sidereal Day	Mean Day	Δ☉α 1870.	Var. in 10 y.	Diff. for 10 d.	Δ☉δ 1870.	Var. in 10 y.	Diff. for 10 d.
0, Jan. 0	0.15	−0.745	+ 2	− 68	− 0.83	+ 1	− 83
10	10.12	0.802	2	46	1.66	1	81
20	20.10	0.836	2	− 22	2.45	1	77
30	30.07	0.845	1	+ 5	3.18	1	68
Feb. 9	9.04	0.826	+ 1	33	3.80	1	56
19	19.01	0.779	0	62	4.28	+ 1	40
Mar. 1	0.99	0.701	− 1	94	4.58	0	19
11	10.96	0.590	1	127	4.64	0	+ 6
21	20.93	0.446	1	161	4.46	0	31
31	30.91	0.263	2	193	4.01	0	59
100, Apr. 10	9.88	−0.060	2	223	3.27	− 1	88
20	19.85	+0.178	2	252	2.26	1	114
30	29.82	0.443	3	275	− 0.99	1	140
May 10	9.80	0.727	3	294	+ 0.53	1	162
20	19.77	1.030	3	308	2.24	1	179
30	29.74	1.341	3	312	4.09	2	192
June 9	8.71	1.652	3	310	6.07	1	199
19	18.69	1.959	3	300	8.07	1	200
29	28.66	2.250	3	281	10.06	1	197
July 9	8.63	2.518	2	254	11.99	0	189
200, 19	18.61	2.756	2	222	13 83	0	176
29	28.58	2.961	1	186	15.50	0	159
Aug. 8	7.55	3.127	1	146	17.01	0	141
18	17.52	3.252	− 1	103	18.31	+ 1	119
28	27.49	3.333	0	59	19.38	1	96
Sept. 7	6.47	3.371	0	+ 19	20.23	2	74
17	16.44	3.371	+ 1	− 20	20.86	2	51
27	26.41	3.333	1	55	21.26	2	30
Oct. 7	6.39	3.263	1	82	21.46	2	+ 10
17	16.36	3.170	2	103	21.47	3	− 7
300, 27	26.33	3.058	2	119	21.32	3	23
Nov. 6	5.30	2.934	3	126	21.01	3	38
16	15.28	2.807	3	126	20.56	3	52
26	25.25	2.683	3	123	19.98	3	62
Dec. 6	5.22	2.563	3	113	19.32	4	70
16	15.20	2.456	2	98	18.59	4	76
26	25.17	2.367	2	81	17.81	4	80
36	35.14	+2.297	+ 2	− 60	+16.99	+ 3	− 82

✱ ♂ ☉,   Feb. 20.3.
✱ ♂ Mean Sun,   Feb. 24.5.

Sidereal Day	ΔΩα	ΔΩδ	ΔΩα	ΔΩδ
	1865.		1873.	
0	+0.638	+6.93	−0.917	−7.30
100	0.556	6.66	0.866	7.30
200	0.470	6.33	0.808	7.24
300	0.379	5.94	0.744	7.12
400	0.285	5.50	0.673	6.94
	1866.		1874.	
0	+0.317	+5.65	−0.698	−7.01
100	0.221	5.17	0.624	6.79
200	0.123	4.65	0.545	6.52
300	+0.024	4.09	0.461	6.19
400	−0.075	3.50	0.374	5.82
	1867.		1875.	
0	−0.041	+3.70	−0.404	−5.95
100	0.140	3.08	0.315	5.54
200	0.238	2.44	0.223	5.09
300	0.333	1.78	0.130	4.60
400	0.426	1.10	0.035	4.06
	1868 B.		1876 B.	
0	−0.395	+1.32	−0.067	−4.25
100	0.485	+0.64	+0.027	3.69
200	0.571	−0.05	0.122	3.11
300	0.651	0.74	0.215	2.50
400	0.726	1.42	0.307	1.87
	1869.		1877.	
0	−0.701	−1.20	+0.276	−2.08
100	0.772	1.87	0.366	1.43
200	0.835	2.53	0.454	0.78
300	0.892	3.15	0.538	−0.11
400	0.940	3.75	0.617	+0.55
	1870.		1878.	
0	−0.924	−3.55	+0.591	+0.33
100	0.967	4.13	0.667	0.99
200	1.002	4.68	0.738	1.65
300	1.027	5.18	0.803	2.29
400	1.044	5.63	0.862	2.92
	1871.		1879.	
0	−1.040	−5.49	+0.843	+2.71
100	1.051	5.91	0.897	3.33
200	1.053	6.28	0.943	3.91
300	1.046	6.60	0.982	4.47
400	1.030	6.86	1.013	4.99
	1872 B.		1880 B.	
0	−1.036	−6.78	+1.003	+4.82
100	1.015	7.00	1.028	5.31
200	0.985	7.16	1.045	5.76
300	0.946	7.26	1.053	6.16
400	−0.901	−7.30	+1.051	+6.52

TABLE XXIV.—η Aquarii.

R.A. 22h 28.7.   Dec. — 0° 47'.

Upper transit at fictitious meridian.

Sidereal Day	Mean Day	$\Delta_\odot a$ 1870.	Var. in 10y.	Diff. for 10d.	$\Delta_\odot \delta$ 1870.	Var. in 10y.	Diff. for 10d.
0, Jan. 0	0.16	—0.695	+ 3	— 73	— 1.30	+ 1	— 75
10	10.13	0.758	2	52	2.04	1	73
20	20.10	0.799	2	29	2.75	1	68
30	30.08	0.816	2	— 4	3.39	1	59
Feb. 9	9.05	0.806	+ 1	+ 24	3.91	1	46
19	19.02	0.768	0	53	4.29	1	29
Mar. 1	0.99	0.699	0	84	4.48	+ 1	— 8
11	10.97	0.599	— 1	117	4.44	0	+ 15
21	20.94	0.464	1	152	4.17	0	40
31	30.91	0.295	2	185	3.63	— 1	67
100, Apr. 10	9.88	—0.094	2	216	2.83	1	94
20	19.86	+0.137	2	245	1.75	1	121
30	29.83	0.395	2	272	— 0.41	1	144
May 10	9.80	0.679	2	293	+ 1.13	1	164
20	19.78	0.978	2	306	2.86	1	181
30	29.75	1.288	3	313	4.74	1	192
June 9	8.72	1.602	3	312	6.68	1	198
19	18.69	1.910	2	303	8.68	1	200
29	28.67	2.206	2	287	10.65	1	194
July 9	8.64	2.481	2	262	12.55	— 1	185
200, 19	18.61	2.728	2	231	14.35	0	172
29	28.59	2.941	1	195	15.97	0	153
Aug. 8	7.56	3.117	— 1	155	17.40	0	133
18	17.53	3.251	0	113	18.63	0	112
28	27.50	3.343	0	70	19.64	+ 1	89
Sept. 7	6.48	3.392	0	+ 29	20.41	1	66
17	16.45	3.401	+ 1	— 10	20.96	2	44
27	26.42	3.373	1	45	21.29	2	22
Oct. 7	6.39	3.313	2	75	21.40	3	+ 2
17	16.37	3.226	2	97	21.34	3	— 13
300, 27	26.34	3.121	2	112	21.14	3	29
Nov. 6	5.31	3.004	2	122	20.76	3	43
16	15.28	2.879	2	125	20.29	3	52
26	25.26	2.755	3	121	19.72	3	62
Dec. 6	5.23	2.638	3	113	19.06	3	69
16	15.20	2.530	3	100	18.35	3	72
26	25.18	2.438	3	84	17.62	3	75
36	35.15	+2.362	+ 3	— 66	+16.85	+ 3	— 75

Sidereal Day	$\Delta_\Omega a$	$\Delta_\Omega \delta$	$\Delta_\Omega a$	$\Delta_\Omega \delta$
	1865.		**1873.**	
0	+0.629	+6.71	—0.914	—7.22
100	0.546	6.40	0.862	7.19
200	0.459	6.05	0.803	7.10
300	0.367	5.63	0.737	6.94
400	0.272	5.17	0.665	6.74
	1866.		**1874.**	
0	+0.304	+5.33	—0.690	—6.81
100	0.207	4.84	0.615	6.57
200	0.109	4.30	0.534	6.27
300	+0.010	3.72	0.450	5.92
400	—0.090	3.12	0.362	5.52
	1867.		**1875.**	
0	—0.057	+3.32	—0.392	—5.66
100	0.156	2.70	0.302	5.23
200	0.254	2.05	0.210	4.76
300	0.349	1.38	0.116	4.25
400	0.442	0.71	0.021	3.70
	1868 B.		**1876 B.**	
0	—0.411	+0.93	—0.053	—3.89
100	0.501	+0.25	+0.042	3.33
200	0.586	—0.43	0.137	2.73
300	0.663	1.11	0.231	2.12
400	0.740	1.77	0.323	1.48
	1869.		**1877.**	
0	—0.716	—1.56	+0.292	—1.70
100	0.786	2.21	0.382	1.05
200	0.848	2.85	0.469	—0.39
300	0.904	3.46	0.553	+0.26
400	0.951	4.03	0.632	0.92
	1870.		**1878.**	
0	—0.936	—3.84	+0.600	+0.69
100	0.978	4.40	0.681	1.35
200	1.011	4.91	0.752	1.99
300	1.036	5.38	0.816	2.62
400	1.051	5.80	0.874	3.23
	1871.		**1879.**	
0	—1.047	—5.67	+0.855	+3.03
100	1.057	6.06	0.908	3.62
200	1.057	6.40	0.954	4.18
300	1.049	6.68	0.992	4.71
400	1.032	6.90	1.021	5.20
	1872 B.		**1880 B.**	
0	—1.038	—6.83	+1.012	+5.04
100	1.015	7.02	1.036	5.50
200	0.984	7.15	1.051	5.92
300	0.944	7.21	1.058	6.29
400	—0.897	—7.22	+1.053	+6.61

✶ ♂ ⊙,   Feb. 23.6.
✶ ♂ Mean Sun,   Feb. 27.0.

TABLE XXIV.—* 226 Cephei (B).

R.A. 22^h 30^m.0.   Dec. + 75° 33'.

Upper transit at fictitious meridian.

Sidereal Day	Mean Day	$\Delta_{\odot}\alpha$ 1870.	Var. in 10 y.	Diff. for 10 d.	$\Delta_{\odot}\delta$ 1870.	Var. in 10 y.	Diff. for 10 d.
0, Jan. 0	0.16	−2.739	− 6	−721	+16.80	+ 1	−150
10	10.13	3.419	9	635	15.03	2	203
20	20.10	4.001	12	525	12.77	2	248
30	30.08	4.463	14	396	10.09	2	284
Feb. 9	9.05	4.786	16	249	7.12	2	309
19	19.02	4.957	18	− 91	3.96	2	321
Mar. 1	1.00	4.967	19	+ 72	+ 0.75	2	320
11	10.97	4.813	19	235	− 2.38	2	305
21	20.94	4.499	19	391	5.32	2	279
31	30.91	4.035	18	535	7.93	2	242
100, Apr. 10	9.89	3.434	17	661	10.13	2	196
20	19.86	2.719	15	765	11.84	1	144
30	29.83	1.913	13	843	12.99	1	86
May 10	9.80	1.042	10	894	13.55	+ 1	− 26
20	19.78	−0.134	7	917	13.50	0	+ 35
30	29.75	+0.783	4	912	12.85	0	94
June 9	8.72	1.681	− 1	881	11.63	0	151
19	18.70	2.536	+ 2	824	9.86	− 1	203
29	28.67	3.322	5	746	7.59	1	249
July 9	8.64	4.022	7	649	4.90	1	289
200, 19	18.61	4.616	10	537	− 1.84	1	322
29	28.59	5.091	12	413	+ 1.51	2	347
Aug. 8	7.56	5.439	13	281	5.08	2	365
18	17.53	5.652	14	144	8.79	2	375
28	27.50	5.728	15	+ 7	12.56	2	378
Sept. 7	6.48	5.667	15	−128	16.32	2	372
17	16.45	5.473	15	260	19.98	1	359
27	26.42	5.153	14	381	23.47	1	338
Oct. 7	6.40	4.715	13	493	26.71	1	309
17	16.37	4.170	12	593	29.63	1	274
300, 27	26.34	3.534	10	678	32.17	− 1	231
Nov. 6	5.31	2.821	8	745	34.24	0	183
16	15.29	2.050	6	794	35.80	0	128
26	25.26	1.240	+ 3	822	36.79	+ 1	70
Dec. 6	5.23	+0.413	0	827	37.19	1	+ 9
16	15.20	−0.406	− 4	807	36.97	2	− 53
26	25.18	1.192	7	762	36.14	2	114
36	35.15	−1.921	−10	−692	+34.72	+ 2	−170

✳ ☌ ☉, Feb. 23.9.
✳ ☌ Mean Sun, Feb. 27.4.
✳ ☍ Mean Sun, Aug. 29.0.

Sidereal Day	$\Delta_{\Omega}\alpha$	$\Delta_{\Omega}\delta$	$\Delta_{\Omega}\alpha$	$\Delta_{\Omega}\delta$
	1865.		**1873.**	
0	+2.011	+6.68	−1.395	−7.21
100	2.097	6.37	1.547	7.18
200	2.165	6.06	1.686	7.08
300	2.215	5.58	1.811	6.92
400	2.245	5.12	1.920	6.71
	1866.		**1874.**	
0	+2.237	+5.25	−1.885	−6.79
100	2.254	4.78	1.984	6.54
200	2.252	4.25	2.066	6.24
300	2.230	3.67	2.132	5.58
400	2.188	3.06	2.179	5.48
	1867.		**1875.**	
0	+2.207	+3.27	−2.165	−5.62
100	2.151	2.64	2.201	5.19
200	2.078	1.99	2.218	4.72
300	1.986	1.35	2.218	4.21
400	1.878	0.65	2.199	3.66
	1868 B.		**1876 B.**	
0	+1.917	+0.88	−2.207	−3.85
100	1.798	+0.20	2.177	3.28
200	1.662	−0.48	2.127	2.69
300	1.514	1.16	2.061	2.07
400	1.352	1.82	1.977	1.44
	1869.		**1877.**	
0	+1.408	−1.60	−2.007	−1.65
100	1.239	2.26	1.913	1.01
200	1.059	2.89	1.802	−0.36
300	0.870	3.49	1.677	+0.30
400	0.674	4.07	1.537	0.96
	1870.		**1878.**	
0	+0.741	−3.88	−1.586	+0.73
100	0.541	4.43	1.43-	1.39
200	0.338	4.94	1.277	2.03
300	+0.132	5.41	1.105	2.65
400	−0.075	5.83	0.924	3.26
	1871.		**1879.**	
0	−0.006	−5.60	−0.986	+3.06
100	0.212	6.08	0.799	3.65
200	0.416	6.41	0.605	4.21
300	0.616	6.69	0.406	4.73
400	0.810	6.91	0.202	5.22
	1872 B.		**1880 B.**	
0	−0.745	−6.84	−0.271	+5.06
100	0.934	7.02	−0.066	5.52
200	1.116	7.16	+0.141	5.94
300	1.287	7.21	0.347	6.30
400	−1.448	+7.21	+0.550	+6.62

TABLE XXIV.—ζ Pegasi.

R.A. 22 35.0.   Dec. + 10 9.

Upper transit at fictitious meridian.

Sidereal Day	Mean Day	Δ⊙α 1870.	Var. in 10 y.	Diff. for 10 d.	Δ⊙δ 1870.	Var. in 10 y.	Diff. for 10 d.
0, Jan. 0	0.16	−0.669	+2	−83	+2.04	+2	−105
10	10.14	0.743	2	64	+0.95	2	113
20	20.11	0.797	2	41	−0.21	2	117
30	30.08	0.825	1	−16	1.38	2	115
Feb. 9	9.05	0.828	+1	+12	2.49	2	106
19	19.03	0.801	0	43	3.49	1	93
Mar. 1	1.00	0.742	−1	75	4.34	1	74
11	10.97	0.650	1	109	4.96	+1	50
21	20.94	0.523	2	145	5.32	0	−21
31	30.92	0.360	2	180	5.37	0	+11
100, Apr. 10	9.89	−0.164	2	213	5.10	0	44
20	19.86	+0.066	2	245	4.49	0	78
30	29.84	0.325	2	271	3.55	−1	111
May 10	9.81	0.607	3	292	2.20	1	141
20	19.78	0.907	3	308	−0.75	1	167
30	29.75	1.220	3	315	+1.03	1	189
June 9	8.73	1.534	3	313	3.01	1	206
19	18.70	1.843	2	305	5.13	2	217
29	28.67	2.141	2	289	7.33	2	222
July 9	8.64	2.418	2	264	9.56	2	222
200, 19	18.62	2.667	2	234	11.75	1	216
29	28.59	2.884	1	198	13.86	1	206
Aug. 8	7.56	3.061	−1	157	15.86	1	191
18	17.53	3.197	0	115	17.68	0	173
28	27.51	3.291	0	73	19.32	0	153
Sept. 7	6.48	3.343	+1	+31	20.74	0	131
17	16.45	3.354	1	−8	21.93	0	107
27	26.43	3.329	2	41	22.89	+1	83
Oct. 7	6.40	3.273	2	72	23.60	2	59
17	16.37	3.187	2	96	24.07	2	35
300, 27	26.34	3.083	3	112	24.31	2	+12
Nov. 6	5.32	2.965	3	122	24.32	2	−10
16	15.29	2.841	3	127	24.11	2	31
26	25.26	2.713	3	126	23.70	3	51
Dec. 6	5.23	2.591	3	119	23.10	3	69
16	15.21	2.477	3	109	22.32	3	86
26	25.18	2.374	3	95	21.39	4	99
36	35.15	+2.2~9	+3	−76	+20.34	+4	−108

Sidereal Day	ΔΩα 1865.	ΔΩδ 1865.	ΔΩα 1873.	ΔΩδ 1873.
0	+0.699	+6.56	−0.940	−7.17
100	0.625	6.24	0.898	7.12
200	0.545	5.86	0.848	7.00
300	0.460	5.43	0.792	6.83
400	0.371	4.96	0.729	6.60

Sidereal Day	ΔΩα 1866.	ΔΩδ 1866.	ΔΩα 1874.	ΔΩδ 1874.
0	+0.401	+5.12	−0.751	−6.68
100	0.310	4.62	0.684	6.42
200	0.216	4.07	0.612	6.10
300	0.120	3.49	0.535	5.74
400	0.023	2.88	0.454	5.33

Sidereal Day	ΔΩα 1867.	ΔΩδ 1867.	ΔΩα 1875.	ΔΩδ 1875.
0	+0.056	+3.08	−0.481	−5.47
100	−0.041	2.45	0.397	5.03
200	0.138	1.80	0.316	4.55
300	0.234	1.14	0.221	4.03
400	0.327	0.46	0.129	3.47

Sidereal Day	ΔΩα 1868 B.	ΔΩδ 1868 B.	ΔΩα 1876 B.	ΔΩδ 1876 B.
0	−0.295	+0.69	−0.160	−3.66
100	0.387	+0.01	0.068	3.09
200	0.475	−0.67	+0.024	2.49
300	0.558	1.34	0.117	1.87
400	0.637	2.00	0.209	1.24

Sidereal Day	ΔΩα 1869.	ΔΩδ 1869.	ΔΩα 1877.	ΔΩδ 1877.
0	−0.611	−1.78	+0.178	−1.45
100	0.686	2.43	0.268	0.81
200	0.755	3.05	0.357	−0.16
300	0.817	3.64	0.443	+0.50
400	0.872	4.20	0.525	1.15

Sidereal Day	ΔΩα 1870.	ΔΩδ 1870.	ΔΩα 1878.	ΔΩδ 1878.
0	−0.854	−4.02	+0.498	+0.93
100	0.904	4.56	0.577	1.57
200	0.946	5.05	0.652	2.21
300	0.979	5.50	0.722	2.82
400	1.004	5.91	0.786	3.42

Sidereal Day	ΔΩα 1871.	ΔΩδ 1871.	ΔΩα 1879.	ΔΩδ 1879.
0	−0.997	−5.78	+0.765	+3.22
100	1.016	6.15	0.825	3.80
200	1.027	6.46	0.878	4.34
300	1.029	6.72	0.924	4.86
400	1.022	6.92	0.962	5.33

Sidereal Day	ΔΩα 1872 B.	ΔΩδ 1872 B.	ΔΩα 1880 B.	ΔΩδ 1880 B.
0	−1.026	−6.86	+0.950	+5.17
100	1.013	7.03	0.983	5.62
200	0.992	7.13	1.008	6.02
300	0.963	7.18	1.024	6.36
400	−0.926	−7.16	+1.032	+6.66

✳ ☌ ⊙, Feb. 25.2.
✳ ☌ Mean Sun, Feb. 28.6.

TABLE XXIV.—' ι Cephel.

R.A. 22h 45.1m.   Dec. + 65° 31'.

Upper transit at fictitious meridian.

Sidereal Day	Mean Day	$\Delta_\odot a$ 1870.	Var.in 10y.	Diff. for 10 d.	$\Delta_\odot \delta$ 1870.	Var.in 10y.	Diff. for 10 d.
0, Jun. 0	0.17	−1.451	+2	−399	+16.13	+2	−144
10	10.14	1.829	0	355	14.43	3	194
20	20.12	2.156	−1	297	12.26	3	238
30	30.09	2.419	2	227	9.70	4	273
Feb. 9	9.06	2.606	4	146	6.84	4	296
19	19.03	2.709	5	− 57	3.82	4	307
Mar. 1	1.01	2.719	6	+ 37	+ 0.74	4	306
11	10.98	2.634	7	133	− 2.27	3	293
21	20.95	2.453	7	228	5.08	3	267
31	30.92	2.179	7	318	7.58	3	231
100, Apr. 10	9.90	1.820	7	399	9.67	2	187
20	19.87	1.384	7	469	11.28	2	135
30	29.84	0.886	7	525	12.36	1	79
May 10	9.82	−0.339	6	565	12.85	+1	− 20
20	19.79	+0.239	5	589	12.76	0	+ 39
30	29.76	0.834	3	595	12.08	0	97
June 9	8.73	1.424	3	584	10.83	− 1	152
19	18.71	1.997	− 2	558	9.06	1	202
29	28.68	2.535	0	517	6.81	2	247
July 9	8.65	3.025	+ 1	462	4.14	2	286
200, 19	18.62	3.455	2	396	− 1.12	2	317
29	28.60	3.814	4	322	+ 2.18	2	341
Aug. 8	7.57	4.096	5	242	5.68	3	358
18	17.54	4.296	6	158	9.31	3	366
28	27.52	4.411	7	+ 72	12.99	3	368
Sept. 7	6.49	4.441	8	− 11	16.64	3	362
17	16.46	4.389	8	92	20.20	2	348
27	26.43	4.258	9	168	23.58	2	327
Oct. 7	6.40	4.055	9	238	26.71	2	299
17	16.38	3.786	9	299	29.53	1	264
300, 27	26.35	3.460	9	351	31.97	− 1	223
Nov. 6	5.32	3.088	9	393	33.96	0	175
16	15.30	2.679	9	423	35.46	0	123
26	25.27	2.245	8	442	36.41	+ 1	67
Dec. 6	5.24	1.799	7	448	36.79	2	+ 9
16	15.21	1.354	6	441	36.57	2	− 51
26	25.19	0.923	5	419	35.77	2	109
36	35.16	+0.520	+ 4	−384	+34.41	+ 3	−163

Sidereal Day	$\Delta_\Omega a$	$\Delta_\Omega \delta$	$\Delta_\Omega a$	$\Delta_\Omega \delta$
	1865.		**1873.**	
0	+1.475	+6.31	−1.256	−7.08
100	1.485	5.96	1.319	6.99
200	1.483	5.56	1.371	6.84
300	1.467	5.11	1.411	6.64
400	1.438	4.61	1.440	6.38
	1866.		**1874.**	
0	+1.449	+4.78	−1.431	−6.47
100	1.412	4.26	1.452	6.18
200	1.363	3.70	1.461	5.84
300	1.302	3.10	1.458	5.44
400	1.229	2.46	1.443	5.01
	1867.		**1875.**	
0	+1.255	+2.69	−1.449	−5.16
100	1.175	2.05	1.426	4.70
200	1.086	1.40	1.391	4.19
300	0.986	0.73	1.345	3.66
400	0.878	0.06	1.288	3.10
	1868 B.		**1876 B.**	
0	+0.915	+0.29	−1.308	−3.29
100	0.802	−0.35	1.244	2.71
200	0.682	1.05	1.169	2.10
300	0.557	1.71	1.085	1.48
400	0.427	2.35	0.992	0.85
	1869.		**1877.**	
0	+0.471	−2.13	−1.024	−1.06
100	0.338	2.76	0.925	−0.42
200	0.203	3.36	0.818	+0.22
300	+0.067	3.93	0.708	0.87
400	−0.071	4.47	0.585	1.51
	1870.		**1878.**	
0	−0.024	−4.29	−0.626	+1.29
100	0.161	4.80	0.503	1.92
200	0.295	5.27	0.375	2.54
300	0.427	5.60	0.244	3.14
400	0.555	6.06	0.111	3.71
	1871.		**1879.**	
0	−0.512	−5.94	−0.156	+3.52
100	0.637	6.28	−0.021	4.07
200	0.756	6.56	+0.114	4.60
300	0.868	6.78	0.248	5.08
400	0.973	6.95	0.381	5.52
	1872 B.		**1880 B.**	
0	−0.938	−6.90	+0.336	+5.38
100	1.037	7.03	0.467	5.79
200	1.127	7.10	0.595	6.16
300	1.208	7.10	0.717	6.47
400	−1.278	−7.05	+0.835	+6.73

* ☌ ☉,   Feb. 27.9.
* ☌ Mean Sun,   Mar. 3.2.
* ☍ Mean Sun,   Sept. 1.9.

TABLE XXIV.—λ Aquarii.

R.A. 22^h 45.8^m.   Dec. — 8° 16'.

Upper transit at fictitious meridian.

Sidereal Day	Mean Day	Δ☉α 1870	Var.in 10y	Diff.for 10d	Δ☉δ 1870	Var.in 10y	Diff.for 10d
0, Jan. 0	0.17	-0.618	+ 3	- 81	- 3.66	+ 1	- 50
10	10.14	0.690	2	63	4.12	1	41
20	20.12	0.743	2	41	4.47	1	29
30	30.09	0.772	2	- 16	4.70	1	- 15
Feb. 9	9.06	0.775	1	+ 9	4.77	+ 1	+ 1
19	19.03	0.753	+ 1	37	4.68	0	20
Mar. 1	1.01	0.700	0	69	4.37	0	41
11	10.98	0.615	0	102	3.86	0	63
21	20.95	0.495	- 1	136	3.12	- 1	85
31	30.92	0.342	1	171	2.15	1	108
100, Apr. 10	9.90	-0.154	2	206	- 0.95	1	131
20	19.87	+0.068	2	237	+ 0.46	1	151
30	29.84	0.318	2	264	2.06	2	168
May 10	9.82	0.594	2	289	3.81	2	182
20	19.79	0.893	3	306	5.68	1	191
30	29.76	1.203	3	314	7.62	1	196
June 9	8.73	1.519	3	318	9.58	1	194
19	18.71	1.836	3	313	11.49	- 1	189
29	28.68	2.142	3	297	13.34	0	179
July 9	8.65	2.428	3	275	15.05	0	162
200, 19	18.62	2.600	3	248	16.57	0	142
29	28.60	2.922	2	213	17.89	0	121
Aug. 8	7.57	3.115	2	174	18.98	0	97
18	17.54	3.269	2	132	19.83	+ 1	71
28	27.51	3.379	1	89	20.41	1	46
Sept. 7	6.49	3.447	- 1	47	20.76	1	23
17	16.46	3.474	0	+ 7	20.88	2	+ 1
27	26.43	3.463	0	- 29	20.78	2	- 20
Oct. 7	6.41	3.417	+ 1	60	20.50	3	36
17	16.38	3.344	1	86	20.08	4	48
300, 27	26.35	3.248	2	105	19.56	4	58
Nov. 6	5.32	3.137	2	116	18.94	3	65
16	15.30	3.018	2	122	18.28	3	67
26	25.27	2.895	3	121	17.61	3	67
Dec. 6	5.24	2.777	3	114	16.94	3	65
16	15.21	2.667	3	105	16.31	3	61
26	25.19	2.567	3	92	15.73	2	55
36	35.16	+2.484	+ 3	- 74	+15.22	+ 2	- 47

✳ ☌ ☉,   Feb. 28.1.
✳ ☌ Mean Sun,   Mar. 3.4.

Sidereal Day	ΔΩα	ΔΩδ	ΔΩα	ΔΩδ
1865.			**1873.**	
0	+0.578	+6.30	-0.893	-7.07
100	0.490	5.94	0.834	6.98
200	0.397	5.54	0.768	6.83
300	0.301	5.09	0.696	6.62
400	0.202	4.59	0.618	6.36
1866.			**1874.**	
0	+0.235	+4.76	-0.645	-6.45
100	0.135	4.23	0.564	6.16
200	-0.031	3.67	0.479	5.81
300	-0.068	3.08	0.390	5.42
400	0.169	2.45	0.297	4.98
1867.			**1875.**	
0	-0.135	+2.66	-0.329	-5.14
100	0.236	2.03	0.245	4.67
200	0.334	1.37	0.139	4.17
300	0.429	0.71	-0.042	3.63
400	0.520	0.04	+0.055	3.07
1868 B.			**1876 B.**	
0	-0.490	+0.26	+0.022	-3.26
100	0.578	-0.41	0.119	2.69
200	0.661	1.09	0.215	2.08
300	0.739	1.73	0.309	1.45
400	0.809	2.37	0.401	0.82
1869.			**1877.**	
0	-0.786	-2.16	+0.370	-1.03
100	0.852	2.79	0.460	-0.39
200	0.911	3.39	0.546	+0.26
300	0.961	3.96	0.627	0.90
400	1.003	4.49	0.704	1.54
1870.			**1878.**	
0	-0.990	-4.32	+0.679	+1.33
100	1.026	4.82	0.752	1.96
200	1.053	5.29	0.819	2.57
300	1.071	5.70	0.879	3.17
400	1.080	6.07	0.932	3.74
1871.			**1879.**	
0	-1.078	-5.95	+0.915	+3.55
100	1.081	6.29	0.963	4.10
200	1.074	6.56	1.003	4.62
300	1.059	6.79	1.035	5.10
400	1.035	6.95	1.059	5.54
1872 B.			**1880 B.**	
0	-1.044	-6.90	+1.052	+5.40
100	1.013	7.03	1.069	5.81
200	0.975	7.09	1.078	6.17
300	0.928	7.10	1.077	6.48
400	-0.874	-7.05	+1.067	+6.74

TABLE XXIV.—* σ Cephei.

R.A. 23h 13m.3.　　　　Dec. + 67° 24'.

Upper transit at fictitious meridian.

Sidereal Day	Mean Day	$\Delta_{\odot}\alpha$			$\Delta_{\odot}\delta$		
		1870.	Var. in 10 y.	Diff. for 10 d.	1870.	Var. in 10 y.	Diff. for 10 d.
0, Jan. 0	0.19	−1.164	+ 4	−457	+17.31	+ 2	−104
10	10.16	1.605	+ 2	422	15.99	3	159
20	20.14	2.002	0	371	14.16	3	208
30	30.11	2.340	− 1	304	11.97	4	248
Feb. 9	9.08	2.606	3	224	9.22	4	279
19	19.05	2.785	4	133	6.33	4	298
Mar. 1	1.03	2.868	6	− 33	3.31	4	305
11	11.00	2.849	7	+ 72	+ 0.28	4	299
21	20.97	2.725	8	177	− 2.63	4	281
31	30.94	2.497	8	279	5.31	3	252
100, Apr. 10	9.92	2.169	8	374	7.64	3	213
20	19.89	1.753	8	458	9.55	3	167
30	29.86	1.258	8	528	10.95	2	114
May 10	9.84	0.701	7	583	11.82	1	− 58
20	19.81	−0.098	6	620	12.11	+ 1	0
30	29.78	+0.532	5	638	11.81	0	+ 58
June 9	8.75	1.172	4	639	10.95	− 1	114
19	18.73	1.804	2	622	9.54	1	167
29	28.70	2.410	− 1	587	7.62	2	215
July 9	8.67	2.974	+ 1	539	5.25	2	258
200, 19	18.64	3.483	2	477	− 2.48	3	294
29	28.62	3.924	4	405	+ 0.62	3	324
Aug. 8	7.59	4.290	5	326	3.98	3	346
18	17.56	4.574	7	240	7.52	3	361
28	27.54	4.770	8	152	11.17	3	368
Sept. 7	6.51	4.878	9	+ 64	14.86	3	369
17	16.48	4.897	10	− 23	18.51	3	361
27	26.45	4.831	11	108	22.05	3	345
Oct. 7	6.42	4.684	12	186	25.39	3	323
17	16.40	4.461	12	258	28.48	2	293
300, 27	26.37	4.170	12	322	31.23	2	256
Nov. 6	5.34	3.820	12	377	33.57	1	213
16	15.32	3.420	12	421	35.46	− 1	163
26	25.29	2.981	12	454	36.83	0	109
Dec. 6	5.26	2.517	11	474	37.63	+ 1	+ 52
16	15.23	2.039	10	480	37.85	2	− 8
26	25.21	1.562	9	471	37.47	2	68
36	35.18	+1.103	+ 7	−446	+36.51	+ 3	−125

✱ ☌ ☉, Mar. 7.5.
✱ ☌ Mean Sun, Mar. 10.3.
✱ ☍ Mean Sun, Sept. 9.0.

Sidereal Day	$\Delta_{\Omega}\alpha$	$\Delta_{\Omega}\delta$	$\Delta_{\Omega}\alpha$	$\Delta_{\Omega}\delta$
	1865.		1873.	
0	+1.671	+5.56	−1.424	−6.74
100	1.682	5.13	1.495	6.55
200	1.679	4.66	1.554	6.31
300	1.661	4.15	1.600	6.02
400	1.628	3.60	1.632	5.68
	1866.		1874.	
0	+1.641	+3.79	−1.622	−5.80
100	1.598	3.22	1.646	5.43
200	1.542	2.62	1.655	5.02
300	1.473	2.00	1.651	4.56
400	1.390	1.36	1.634	4.07
	1867.		1875.	
0	+1.419	+1.58	−1.641	−4.24
100	1.329	0.93	1.615	3.72
200	1.227	+0.27	1.575	3.18
300	1.114	−0.38	1.522	2.61
400	0.991	1.04	1.457	2.02
	1868 B.		1876 B.	
0	+1.034	−0.82	−1.480	−2.22
100	0.906	1.47	1.407	1.62
200	0.770	2.10	1.322	1.00
300	0.627	2 72	1.226	−0.37
400	0.480	3.30	1.120	+0.26
	1869.		1877.	
0	+0.530	−3.11	−1.157	+0.04
100	0.380	3.64	1.045	0.67
200	0.229	4.22	0.924	1.29
300	+0.072	4.71	0.795	1.91
400	−0.084	5.17	0.659	2.51
	1870.		1878.	
0	−0.031	−5.02	−0.706	+2.31
100	0.186	5.45	0.566	2.90
200	0.338	5.83	0.421	3.46
300	0.488	6.15	0.272	4.00
400	0.632	6.43	0.121	4.50
	1871.		1879.	
0	−0.584	−6.34	−0.173	+4.34
100	0.725	6.58	0.020	4.82
200	0.860	6.76	+0.133	5.26
300	0.987	6.88	0.285	5.66
400	1.105	6.94	0.435	6.01
	1872 B.		1880 B.	
0	−1.066	−6.93	+0.385	+5.90
100	1.178	6.96	0.533	6.22
200	1.280	6.92	0.678	6.49
300	1.370	6.83	0.817	6.71
400	−1.450	−6.68	+0.949	+6.86

TABLE XXIV.—θ Piscium.

R.A. 23h 21m.4.   Dec. + 5° 40'.

Upper transit at fictitious meridian.

Sidereal Day	Mean Day	$\Delta_{\odot}a$ 1870	Var. in 10y.	Diff. for 10d.	$\Delta_{\odot}\delta$ 1870	Var. in 10y.	Diff. for 10d.
0, Jan. 0	0.19	−0.413	+3	−100	+0.74	+2	−83
10	10.17	0.507	3	88	−0.10	2	85
20	20.14	0.587	2	71	0.95	2	86
30	30.11	0.648	2	52	1.80	2	82
Feb. 9	9.09	0.690	1	29	2.58	2	73
19	19 06	0.706	+1	−1	3.24	2	60
Mar. 1	1.03	0.692	0	+29	3.75	1	43
11	11.00	0.648	0	62	4.07	+1	−21
21	20.98	0.567	0	99	4.15	0	+5
31	30.95	0.449	−1	137	3.97	0	32
100, Apr. 10	9.92	0.293	1	174	3.51	0	61
20	19.89	−0.102	2	210	2.75	0	90
30	29.87	+0.125	2	243	1.71	0	118
May 10	9.84	0.382	2	270	−0.39	−1	144
20	19.81	0.664	2	293	+1.17	1	167
30	29.79	0.966	3	308	2.94	1	185
June 9	8.76	1.277	3	315	4.85	1	199
19	18.73	1.593	3	314	6.92	1	208
29	28.70	1.903	2	305	9.02	2	211
July 9	8.68	2.200	2	288	11.12	2	208
200, 19	18.65	2.477	2	264	13.17	2	201
29	28.62	2.726	1	233	15.12	1	187
Aug. 8	7.59	2.941	1	198	16.90	1	171
18	17.57	3.121	1	160	18.53	−1	153
28	27.54	3.261	−1	120	19.96	0	132
Sept. 7	6.51	3.360	0	80	21.17	0	109
17	16.48	3.421	+1	41	22.13	0	85
27	26.46	3.443	1	+4	22.87	+1	62
Oct. 7	6.43	3.430	2	−29	23.38	1	39
17	16.40	3.387	2	55	23.67	1	+19
300, 27	26.38	3.322	2	77	23.76	2	−1
Nov. 6	5.35	3.235	3	95	23.66	2	19
16	15.32	3.134	3	105	23.39	2	35
26	25.29	3.026	3	111	22.97	2	49
Dec. 6	5.27	2.913	4	113	22.41	2	61
16	15.24	2.801	3	111	21.75	3	71
26	25.21	2.692	3	106	21.00	3	79
36	35.18	+2.591	+3	−96	+20.17	+3	−85

✳ ☌ ☉,   Mar. 9 7.
✳ ☌ Mean Sun, Mar. 12.4.

Sidereal Day	$\Delta_{\Omega}a$	$\Delta_{\Omega}\delta$	$\Delta_{\Omega}a$	$\Delta_{\Omega}\delta$
	1865.		**1873.**	
0	+0.678	+5.33	−0.932	−6.62
100	0.599	4.86	0.892	6.41
200	0.516	4.40	0.839	6.14
300	0.428	3.87	0.777	5.83
400	0.335	3.31	0.711	5.47
	1866.		**1874.**	
0	+0.367	+3.50	−0.734	−5.59
100	0.273	2.92	0 663	5.20
200	0.176	2.31	0.587	4.77
300	+0.076	1.68	0.506	4.30
400	−0.021	1.04	0.422	3.79
	1867.		**1875.**	
0	+0.012	+1.25	−0.451	−3.96
100	−0.087	+0.60	0.364	3.44
200	0.185	−0.05	0.274	2.88
300	0.281	0.70	0.191	2.30
400	0.375	1.35	0.098	1.70
	1868 B.		**1876 B.**	
0	−0.344	−1.13	−0.126	−1.91
100	0.435	1.77	−0.025	1.30
200	0.523	2.39	+0.069	0.68
300	0.606	2.99	0.163	−0.04
400	0.683	3.57	0.255	+0.57
	1869.		**1877.**	
0	−0.658	−3.38	+0.224	+0.37
100	0.731	3.93	0.315	0.99
200	0.799	4.45	0.404	1.60
300	0.858	4.93	0.490	2.21
400	0.911	5.35	0.572	2.79
	1870.		**1878.**	
0	−0.894	−5.22	+0.545	+2.60
100	0.941	5.62	0.624	3.17
200	0.980	5.97	0.697	3.72
300	1.010	6.27	0.766	4.24
400	1.032	6.52	0.828	4.72
	1871.		**1879.**	
0	−1.026	−6.44	+0.808	+4.56
100	1.042	6.65	0.865	5.02
200	1.048	6.80	0.916	5 44
300	1.046	6.89	0.959	5 81
400	1.036	6.92	0.994	6.14
	1872 B.		**1880 B.**	
0	−1.040	−6.92	+0.983	+6.03
100	1.023	6.92	1.013	6 33
200	0.999	6.85	1.034	6.57
300	0.965	6.73	1.047	6.75
400	−0.923	−6.56	+1.051	+6.88

244

TABLE XXIV.—ι Piscium.

R.A. 23h 33m.3   Dec. + 4° 55'

Upper transit at fictitious meridian.

Sidereal Day	Mean Day	Δ☉a 1870.	Var.in 10y.	Diff.for 10d.	Δ☉δ 1870.	Var.in 10y.	Diff.for 10d.
0, Jan. 0	0.20	−0.345	+3	−102	+0.49	+2	−80
10	10.18	0.442	3	92	−0.32	2	82
20	20.12	0.527	2	78	1.14	2	82
30	30.12	0.596	2	60	1.94	2	77
Feb. 9	9.09	0.646	2	38	2.66	2	68
19	19.07	0.671	1	−13	3.28	1	55
Mar. 1	1.04	0.670	+1	+18	3.75	1	38
11	11.01	0.634	0	52	4.03	1	−17
21	20.98	0.565	−1	87	4 08	+1	+8
31	30.96	0.459	1	126	3.86	0	35
100, Apr. 10	9.93	0.313	1	164	3.37	0	62
20	19.90	−0.131	2	201	2.61	−1	91
30	29.88	+0.069	2	236	1.55	1	119
May 10	9.85	0.339	3	265	−0 24	1	144
20	19.82	0.617	3	289	+1.33	1	166
30	29.79	0.915	3	305	3.09	1	184
June 9	8.77	1.225	3	315	5.00	1	197
19	18.74	1.542	3	317	7.02	1	205
29	28.71	1.856	2	309	9.09	2	208
July 9	8.68	2.158	2	294	11.17	2	205
200, 19	18.66	2.441	2	271	13.18	1	197
29	28.63	2.698	2	242	15.09	1	185
Aug. 8	7.60	2.924	2	209	16.86	1	169
18	17.58	3.116	1	172	18.45	−1	149
28	27.55	3.267	1	132	19.83	0	127
Sept. 7	6.52	3.379	−1	93	20.98	0	103
17	16.49	3.453	0	54	21.89	0	80
27	26.47	3.487	+1	+17	22.59	0	57
Oct. 7	6.44	3.488	1	−16	23.04	+1	34
17	16.41	3.457	1	44	23.28	1	+13
300, 27	26.38	3.402	2	66	23.31	1	−5
Nov. 6	5.36	3.326	2	85	23.18	1	22
16	15.33	3.233	3	98	22.88	1	37
26	25.30	3 131	3	106	22.44	2	50
Dec. 6	5.27	3.023	4	110	21.88	2	62
16	15.25	2.913	4	110	21.20	2	71
26	25.22	2.804	4	106	20 46	2	77
36	35.19	+2.702	+3	−98	+19.67	+2	−81

Sidereal Day	ΔΩa	ΔΩδ	ΔΩa	ΔΩδ
	1865.		**1873.**	
0	+0.674	+4.97	−0.937	−6.43
100	0.595	4.50	0.890	6.18
200	0.510	3.99	0.836	5.88
300	0.422	3.44	0.774	5.53
400	0.329	2.86	0.707	5.14
	1866.		**1874.**	
0	+0.360	+3.05	−0.730	−5.28
100	0.266	2.46	0.659	4.85
200	0.169	1.84	0.582	4.39
300	+0.070	1.20	0.501	3.89
400	−0.029	0.56	0.416	3.37
	1867.		**1875.**	
0	+0.005	+0.77	−0.445	−3.55
100	−0.095	+0.12	0.357	3.00
200	0.193	−0.53	0.267	2.43
300	0.283	1.17	0.174	1.84
400	0.383	1.81	0.081	1.24
	1868 B.		**1876 B.**	
0	−0.351	−1.66	−0.112	−1.44
100	0.443	2.22	−0.018	0.83
200	0.531	2.82	+0.077	−0.21
300	0.614	3.40	0.171	+0.41
400	0.691	3.95	0.263	1.03
	1869.		**1877.**	
0	−0.666	−3.77	+0.232	+0.83
100	0.739	4.36	0.324	1.44
200	0.806	4.78	0.412	2.05
300	0.865	5.22	0.498	2.63
400	0.917	5.63	0.580	3.20
	1870.		**1878.**	
0	−0 900	−5.49	+0.553	+3.01
100	0.947	5.86	0.631	3 56
200	0.985	6.17	0.705	4.08
300	1.015	6.42	0.773	4.57
400	1.036	6.6.	0.835	5.02
	1871.		**1879.**	
0	−1.030	−6.57	+0.814	+4.88
100	1.045	6.73	0.872	5.30
200	1.051	6.84	0.922	5.68
300	1.049	6.89	0 964	6.02
400	1.037	6.88	0.999	6.31
	1872 B.		**1880 B.**	
0	−1.042	−6.89	+0.985	+6.22
100	1.024	6.84	1.017	6.47
200	0.998	6.74	1.038	6.67
300	0.964	6.58	1.050	6.87
400	−0.922	−6.36	+1.053	+6.89

✳ ☌ ☉,   Mar. 12.9.
✳ ☌ Mean Sun,   Mar. 15.4.

TABLE XXIV.—° γ Cephei.

R.A. 23h 34.0m.   Dec. + 76° 54'.

Upper transit at fictitious meridian.

Sidereal Day	Mean Day	Δ⊙a 1870.	Var. in 10 y.	Diff. for 10 d.	Δ⊙δ 1870.	Var. in 10 y.	Diff. for 10 d.
0, Jan. 0	+ 0.20	−1.467	+ 4	−869	+19.03	+ 2	− 59
10	10.18	2.316	0	823	18.14	2	119
20	20.15	3.104	− 4	748	16.66	3	175
30	30.12	3.801	9	642	14.66	3	224
Feb. 9	9.10	4.379	13	511	12.21	4	263
19	19.07	4.815	16	357	9.43	4	292
Mar. 1	1.04	5.088	20	187	6.42	4	306
11	11.01	5.186	22	− 7	3.30	4	312
21	20.99	5.102	23	+175	+ 0.22	4	303
31	30.96	4.837	24	353	− 2.72	4	282
100, Apr. 10	9.93	4.400	24	519	5.39	3	250
20	19.90	3.805	23	668	7.63	3	209
30	29.88	3.071	21	794	9.55	3	161
May 10	9.85	2.224	19	895	10.89	2	107
20	19.82	1.291	16	967	11.68	1	− 50
30	29.79	−0.301	12	1008	11.89	+ 1	+ 9
June 9	8.77	+0.716	8	1020	11.51	0	67
19	18.74	1.730	− 4	1003	10.56	− 1	122
29	28.71	2.714	0	960	9.07	1	175
July 9	8.68	3.641	+ 5	892	7.07	2	223
200, 19	18.66	4.491	9	803	4.62	2	266
29	28.63	5.241	13	698	− 1.77	3	303
Aug. 8	7.60	5.878	17	575	+ 1.41	3	333
18	17.58	6.338	20	443	4.86	3	356
28	27.55	6.763	23	305	8.49	4	371
Sept. 7	6.52	6.996	26	162	12.25	4	379
17	16.49	7.086	28	+ 18	16.04	4	379
27	26.47	7.033	29	−124	19.80	4	371
Oct. 7	6.44	6.839	30	262	23.44	3	356
17	16.41	6.511	30	393	26.88	3	332
300, 27	26.38	6.056	30	515	30.05	3	300
Nov. 6	5.36	5.486	29	624	32.86	2	261
16	15.33	4.814	27	718	35.25	2	215
26	25.30	4.056	25	795	37.15	− 1	162
Dec. 6	5.28	3.232	22	849	38.49	0	105
16	15.25	2.365	18	879	39.23	+ 1	+ 43
26	25.22	1.482	14	883	39.35	2	− 19
36	35.19	+0.610	+10	−856	+38.84	+ 2	− 81

Sidereal Day	Δ☊a	Δ☊δ	Δ☊a	Δ☊δ
	1865.		**1873.**	
0	+2.626	+4.95	−1.997	−6.42
100	2.698	4.47	2.160	6.17
200	2.748	3.96	2.304	5.87
300	2.773	3.41	2.429	5.51
400	2.775	2.82	2.533	5.12
	1866.		**1874.**	
0	+2.777	+3.02	−2.501	−5.26
100	2.763	2.43	2.591	4.83
200	2.724	1.80	2.630	4.37
300	2.662	1.17	2.707	3.87
400	2.576	0.52	2.732	3.34
	1867.		**1875.**	
0	+2.608	+0.74	−2.731	−3.52
100	2.507	+0.09	2.741	2.97
200	2.384	−0.56	2.729	2.40
300	2.241	1.20	2.693	1.81
400	2.078	1.84	2.636	1.20
	1868 B.		**1876 B.**	
0	+2.135	−1.63	−2.658	−1.41
100	1.961	2.25	2.586	0.80
200	1.769	2.85	2.493	−0.18
300	1.562	3.43	2.379	+0.44
400	1.342	3.98	2.246	1.06
	1869.		**1877.**	
0	+1.418	−3.80	−2.293	+0.95
100	1.190	4.32	2.147	1.47
200	0.953	4.80	1.983	2.07
300	0.708	5.24	1.802	2.66
400	0.457	5.64	1.606	3.22
	1870.		**1878.**	
0	+0.542	−5.51	−1.674	+3.03
100	0.299	5.87	1.469	3.58
200	+0.034	6.18	1.251	4.10
300	−0.221	6.44	1.022	4.59
400	0.474	6.64	0.784	5.04
	1871.		**1879.**	
0	−0.389	−6.57	−0.865	+4.90
100	0.638	6.74	0.622	5.32
200	0.882	6.84	0.374	5.70
300	1.117	6.89	−0.121	6.03
400	1.343	6.97	+0.134	6.32
	1872 B.		**1880 B.**	
0	−1.268	−6.85	+0.049	+6.23
100	1.486	6.83	0.303	6.48
200	1.690	6.73	0.555	6.67
300	1.880	6.56	0.803	6.81
400	−2.054	−6.34	+1.045	+6.89

✳ ♂ ⊙,   Mar. 13.1.
✳ ♂ Mean Sun,   Mar. 15.6.
✳ ☍ Mean Sun,   Sept. 14.3.

TABLE XXIV₅.—° Groombridge 4163.

R.A. 23 48.5. (h m)   Dec. + 73 41. (° ')

Upper transit at fictitious meridian.

Sidereal Day	Mean Day	$\Delta_\odot a$ 1870.	Var. in 10 y.	Diff. for 10 d.	$\Delta_\odot \delta$ 1870.	Var. in 10 y.	Diff. for 10 d.
0, Jan. 0	0.21	−0.880	+ 7	−681	+18.94	+ 2	− 45
10	10.19	1.550	5	655	18.19	2	105
20	20.16	2.181	+ 1	604	16 85	3	161
30	30 13	2.750	− 2	529	14.98	4	211
Feb. 9	9.10	3.233	5	432	12.66	4	252
19	19.08	3.608	8	315	9.98	5	282
Mar. 1	1.05	3.858	10	183	7.65	5	301
11	11.02	3.970	12	− 41	4.01	5	307
21	21.00	3.938	14	+106	+ 0.96	5	300
31	30.97	3.760	15	251	− 1.96	4	282
100, Apr. 10	9.94	3.438	16	390	4.64	4	253
20	19.91	2.984	16	516	6.98	3	214
30	29.89	2.411	15	627	8.89	3	168
May 10	9.86	1.737	14	717	10.31	2	116
20	19.83	0.985	12	784	11.19	2	60
30	29.80	−0.177	10	828	11.51	+ 1	− 3
June 9	8.78	+0.663	8	848	11.24	0	+ 55
19	18.75	1.510	5	843	10.42	− 1	110
29	28.72	2.341	− 2	816	9.05	1	163
July 9	8.70	3.135	+ 1	768	7.17	2	212
200, 19	18.67	3.872	4	702	4.83	3	255
29	28.64	4.535	7	621	− 2.09	3	292
Aug. 8	7.61	5.111	10	528	+ 0.99	4	323
18	17.59	5.587	13	424	4.34	4	347
28	27.56	5.957	16	314	7.90	4	363
Sept. 7	6.53	6.214	18	200	11.59	4	373
17	16.50	6.356	20	+ 84	15.33	4	374
27	26.48	6.382	22	− 31	19.05	4	368
Oct. 7	6.45	6.295	23	143	22.67	4	354
17	16.42	6.097	24	251	26.11	4	333
300, 27	26.40	5.796	25	351	29.30	3	303
Nov. 6	5.37	5.398	25	443	32.15	3	266
16	15.34	4.914	24	523	34.59	2	222
26	25.31	4.356	24	590	36.56	1	171
Dec. 6	5.29	3.738	22	642	38.00	− 1	115
16	15.26	3.078	20	674	38.86	0	+ 56
26	25.23	2.397	18	686	39.10	+ 1	− 6
36	35.20	+1.715	+15	−674	+38.73	+ 2	− 68

✳ δ ☉,   Mar. 17.1.
✳ δ Mean Sun,   Mar. 19.3.
✳ 8 Mean Sun,   Sept. 18.0.

Sidereal Day	$\Delta_\Omega a$	$\Delta_\Omega \delta$	$\Delta_\Omega a$	$\Delta_\Omega \delta$
	1865.		**1875.**	
0	+2.285	+4.50	−1.866	−6.17
100	2.319	3.99	1.981	5.87
200	2.333	3.45	2.079	5.52
300	2.326	2.87	2.159	5.13
400	2.300	2.27	2.221	4.69
	1866.		**1874.**	
0	+2.311	+2.47	−2.202	−4.85
100	2.271	1.86	2.252	4.39
200	2.211	1.23	2.284	3.89
300	2.132	+0.58	2.296	3.36
400	2.034	−0.07	2.290	2.81
	1867.		**1875.**	
0	+2.069	+0.15	−2.294	−3.00
100	1.959	−0.50	2.275	2.43
200	1.832	1.14	2.238	1.84
300	1.690	1.77	2.182	1.24
400	1.532	2.40	2.108	0.63
	1868 B.		**1876 B.**	
0	+1.587	−2.18	−2.135	−0.83
100	1.421	2.79	2.049	−0.22
200	1.243	3 36	1.947	+0.40
300	1.054	3.91	1.828	1.02
400	0.856	4.43	1.695	1.63
	1869.		**1877.**	
0	+0.924	−4.26	−1.741	+1.42
100	0.721	4.74	1.598	2.02
200	0.512	5.19	1.441	2.61
300	0.301	5.59	1.273	3.17
400	0.086	5.94	1.093	3.71
	1870.		**1878.**	
0	+0.158	−5.82	−1.155	+3.53
100	−0.057	6.14	0.968	4.05
200	0.271	6.40	0.774	4.53
300	0.482	6.60	0.572	4.99
400	0.688	6.75	0.365	5.40
	1871.		**1879.**	
0	−0.619	−6.71	−0.436	+5.26
100	0.822	6.82	0.226	5.64
200	1.016	6.87	−0.014	5.98
300	1.202	6.86	+0.198	6.26
400	1.377	6.79	0.410	6.50
	1872 B.		**1880 B.**	
0	−1.319	−6.82	+0.339	+6.43
100	1.487	6.72	0.549	6.62
200	1.641	6.56	0.756	6.77
300	1.782	6.34	0.955	6.86
400	−1.907	−6.08	+1.147	+6.88

TABLE XXIV.—ω Piscium.

R.A. 23^h 52^m.6.　　　　Dec. + 6° 9'.

Upper transit at fictitious meridian.

Sidereal Day	Mean Day	$\Delta_\odot a$ 1870.	Var.in 10y.	Diff.for 10d.	$\Delta_\odot \delta$ 1870.	Var.in 10y.	Diff.for 10d.
0, Jan. 0	0.22	-0.232	+3	-108	+0.91	+2	-77
10	10.19	0.337	3	101	+0.12	2	81
20	20.16	0.433	3	90	-0.69	2	81
30	30.13	0.516	3	76	1.48	2	77
Feb. 9	9.11	0.583	2	56	2.21	1	70
19	19.08	0.626	2	31	2.86	1	58
Mar. 1	1.05	0.643	+1	-2	3.36	1	42
11	11.03	0.629	0	+31	3.67	1	-22
21	21.00	0.580	0	68	3.78	+1	+1
31	30.97	0.492	-1	107	3.64	0	27
100, Apr. 10	9.94	0.365	1	147	3.24	0	55
20	19.92	-0.199	2	186	2.54	0	83
30	29.89	+0.005	2	222	1.57	-1	111
May 10	9.86	0.243	2	254	-0.32	1	138
20	19.83	0.511	3	280	+1.17	1	161
30	29.81	0.801	3	300	2.88	1	180
June 9	8.78	1.108	3	313	4.75	2	194
19	18.75	1.425	3	318	6.75	2	204
29	28.73	1.741	2	313	8.82	2	209
July 9	8.70	2.048	2	301	10.91	2	207
200, 19	18.67	2.340	2	281	12.95	2	200
29	28.64	2.608	2	255	14.91	2	190
Aug. 8	7.62	2.848	1	224	16.73	2	174
18	17.59	3.054	1	187	18.38	1	156
28	27.56	3.222	-1	149	19.84	1	135
Sept. 7	6.53	3.353	0	111	21.08	-1	112
17	16.51	3.445	0	73	22.07	0	88
27	26.48	3.500	+1	36	22.85	0	65
Oct. 7	6.45	3.519	2	+3	23.39	+1	43
17	16.42	3.507	2	-26	23.72	1	22
300, 27	26.40	3.468	3	51	23.83	2	+2
Nov. 6	5.37	3.407	3	72	23.77	2	-15
16	15.34	3.326	3	88	23.54	2	31
26	25.32	3.233	3	98	23.16	2	45
Dec. 6	5.29	3.131	4	106	22.65	2	56
16	15.26	3.022	4	110	22.04	2	67
26	25.23	2.912	4	110	21.32	2	74
36	35.21	+2.804	+4	-105	+20.56	+2	-78

$\Delta_\Omega a$ and $\Delta_\Omega \delta$ by Sidereal Day:

Sidereal Day	$\Delta_\Omega a$	$\Delta_\Omega \delta$	$\Delta_\Omega a$	$\Delta_\Omega \delta$
	1865.		**1873.**	
0	+0.686	+4.37	-0.947	-6.10
100	0.608	3.85	0.900	5.78
200	0.524	3.30	0.847	5.42
300	0.435	2.72	0.786	5.02
400	0.343	2.11	0.719	4.57
	1866.		**1874.**	
0	+0.374	+2.32	-0.742	-4.73
100	0.280	1.70	0.672	4.26
200	0.183	1.06	0.595	3.75
300	+0.084	+0.42	0.515	3.22
400	-0.016	-0.23	0.429	2.66
	1867.		**1875.**	
0	+0.018	-0.01	-0.459	-2.85
100	-0.081	0.66	0.371	2.28
200	0.180	1.30	0.281	1.69
300	0.277	1.93	0.188	1.08
400	0.372	2.54	0.094	0.47
	1868 B.		**1876 D.**	
0	-0.349	-2.34	-0.126	-0.68
100	0.433	2.94	-0.031	-0.06
200	0.521	3.51	+0.064	+0.56
300	0.605	4.05	0.158	+1.17
400	0.683	4.55	0.251	1.78
	1869.		**1877.**	
0	-0.657	-4.39	+0.220	+1.58
100	0.732	4.86	0.312	2.18
200	0.800	5.29	0.402	2.76
300	0.860	5.68	0.488	3.31
400	0.913	6.01	0.571	3.84
	1870.		**1878.**	
0	-0.896	-5.91	+0.543	+3.67
100	0.944	6.21	0.623	4.18
200	0.984	6.45	0.698	4.65
300	1.015	6.64	0.767	5.09
400	1.037	6.78	0.830	5.49
	1871.		**1879.**	
0	-1.031	-6.74	+0.809	+5.36
100	1.047	6.83	0.868	5.73
200	1.055	6.87	0.919	6.05
300	1.053	6.85	0.963	6.33
400	1.043	6.76	0.999	6.55
	1872 B.		**1880 B.**	
0	-1.047	-6.80	+0.988	+6.48
100	1.031	6.68	1.018	6.66
200	1.006	6.51	1.040	6.79
300	0.973	6.29	1.053	6.86
400	-0.932	-6.00	+1.057	+6.87

✳ ☌ ☉,　　　　Mar. 18.2.
✳ ☌ Mean Sun,　　Mar. 20.3.

	TABLE XXV.						TABLE XXVI.		

Terms to be multiplied by $\left(\dfrac{t-1870}{10}\right)^2$

Motion of $\odot + \Omega$ and $\odot - \Omega$ for sidereal days;

(In thousandths of the circumference.)

Sidereal Day.	51 Cephei.		σ Octantis.		λ Ursæ Minoris.		Sidereal Day.	$\odot + \Omega$	$\odot - \Omega$
	R.A.	Dec.	R.A.	Dec.	R.A.	Dec.			
Jan. 0	−0.01	−0.01	+0.69	−0.01	+0.04	−0.03	Jan. 0	0	0
10	0.00	0.01	0.64	0.02	0.06	0.03	10	26	29
20	0.00	0.01	0.56	0.03	0.09	0.03	20	52	58
30	+0.01	0.01	0.48	0.04	0.11	0.02	30	78	86
Feb. 9	0.01	−0.01	0.37	0 05	0.14	0.02	Feb. 9	103	115
19	0.01	0.00	0.26	0.05	0.15	0.01	19	129	144
Mar. 1	+0.01	0.00	0.14	0.06	0.17	0.01	Mar. 1	155	173
11	0.00	0.00	+0 01	0.06	0.17	−0.01	11	181	201
21	0.00	+0.01	−0.13	0.06	0.17	0.00	21	207	230
31	−0.01	+0.01	0.26	0.06	0.17	0.00	31	233	259
Apr. 10	0.02	0.00	0.39	0.06	0.16	+0.01	Apr. 10	258	288
20	0.02	0.00	0.51	0.05	0.14	0.01	20	284	316
30	0.03	0.00	0.63	0.05	0.13	0.01	30	310	345
May 10	0.02	0.00	0.73	0.04	0.10	0.02	May 10	336	374
20	0.02	0.00	0.82	0.03	0.08	0.02	20	362	403
30	0.02	−0.01	0.90	0.02	0.05	0.02	30	388	432
June 9	−0.01	0 01	0.97	0.02	+0.02	0 02	June 9	413	460
19	0.00	0.01	1.01	−0.01	−0.01	0.02	19	439	489
29	+0.01	0.01	1.03	0.00	0.03	0.02	29	465	518
July 9	0.02	−0.01	1.04	+0.01	0.06	0.01	July 9	491	547
19	0.02	0.00	1.02	0.03	0.08	+0.01	19	517	575
29	0.03	0.00	0.99	0.03	0.10	0.00	29	543	604
Aug. 8	0.03	0.00	0.94	0.04	0.12	0.00	Aug. 8	568	633
18	0.03	+0.01	0 87	0.05	0.13	−0.01	18	594	662
28	0.02	0.01	0.79	0.06	0.15	0.01	28	620	690
Sept. 7	0 02	0.01	0.70	0.06	0.15	0.02	Sept. 7	646	719
17	+0.01	0.01	0.60	0 06	0.16	0 02	17	672	748
27	0.00	0.02	0.48	0.06	0.15	0.03	27	698	777
Oct. 7	−0.01	0.02	0.38	0.06	0.15	0.03	Oct. 7	723	806
17	0.02	0.01	0.28	0.06	0.14	0.04	17	749	834
27	0 03	+0.01	0.19	0.05	0.13	0.04	27	775	863
Nov. 6	0.04	0.00	0.11	0.04	0.11	0.05	Nov. 6	801	892
16	0.04	0.00	−0.04	0.04	0.09	0.05	16	827	921
26	0 05	0.00	+0.01	0.03	0.06	0.05	26	853	949
Dec. 6	0.04	−0.01	0.03	0.02	0.04	0.05	Dec. 6	879	978
16	0 04	0.01	0 04	+0.01	−0 01	0.06	16	904	7
26	0.03	0.01	+0.03	0 00	+0.02	0.06	26	930	36
36	−0.02	−0.01	−0 01	−0.02	+0.05	−0.06	36	956	65

TABLE XXVII.

Terms for Circumpolar Stars depending on $\odot + \Omega$ and $\odot - \Omega$.

Arguments—*

For α Ursæ Minoris and 51 Cephei.

Year.	$\odot + \Omega$	$\odot - \Omega$
1835	377	177
1866	323	230
1867	269	284
1868	215	338
1869	161	392
1870	107	446
1871	53	500
1872	0	553
1873	946	607
1874	892	631
1875	839	715
1876	785	768
1877	731	822
1878	677	876
1879	623	929
1880	570	983

For λ Ursæ Minoris and σ Octantis.

Year.	$\odot + \Omega$	$\odot - \Omega$
1865	379	179
1866	325	232
1867	271	286
1868	217	340
1869	163	394
1870	109	448
1871	55	502
1872	2	555
1873	948	609
1874	894	663
1875	841	717
1876	787	770
1877	733	824
1878	679	878
1879	625	931
1880	572	985

* Add to the argument for the beginning of the year Its motion for the Sidereal Day, on p. 248.

Argument	α Ursæ Minoris Arg.=$\odot+\Omega$ R.A.	Dec.	Arg.=$\odot-\Omega$ R.A.	Dec.	51 Cephei Arg.=$\odot+\Omega$ R.A.	Argument
0	−0.05+	−0.01+	0.00	−0.02+	+0.01−	500
10	0.05	0.01	0.00	0.02	0.01	510
20	0.04	0.01	0.00	0.02	0.01	520
30	0.04	0.02	0.00	0.02	0.01	530
40	0.03	0.02	0.00	0.02	+0.01−	540
50	0.03	0.02	0.00	0.02	0.00	550
60	0.02	0.02	0.00	0.02	0.00	560
70	0.02	0.02	0.00	0.02	0.00	570
80	−0.01+	0.02	0.00	0.02	0.00	580
90	0.00	0.02	0.00	0.02	0.00	590
100	0.00	0.02	0.00	0.01	0.00	600
110	+0.01−	0.02	+0.01−	0.01	0.00	610
120	0.01	0.02	0.01	0.01	−0.01+	620
130	0.01	0.02	0.01	0.01	0.01	630
140	0.02	0.02	0.01	0.01	0.01	640
150	0.03	0.02	0.01	0.01	0.01	650
160	0.03	0.02	0.01	0.01	0.01	660
170	0.04	0.02	0.01	0.01	0.01	670
180	0.04	0.01	0.01	0.01	0.01	680
190	0.05	0.01	0.01	0.01	0.01	690
200	0.05	0.01	0.01	0.01	0.02	700
210	0 06	0.01	0.01	−0.01+	0.02	710
220	0.06	0.01	0.01	0.00	0.02	720
230	0.07	0.01	0.01	0.00	0.02	730
240	0.07	0.01	0.01	0.00	0.02	740
250	0.07	0.01	0.01	0.00	0.02	750
260	0.08	0.01	0.01	0.00	0.02	760
270	0.08	0.01	0.01	0.00	0.02	770
280	0.08	0.01	0.01	0.00	0.02	780
290	0.08	−0.01+	0.01	0.00	0.02	790
300	0.08	0.00	0.01	0.00	0.02	800
310	0.09	0.00	0.01	0.00	0.02	810
320	0.09	0.00	0.01	0.00	0.02	820
330	0.09	0.00	0.01	+0.01−	0.02	830
340	0.09	0.00	0.01	0.01	0.02	840
350	0.09	0.00	0.01	0.01	0.02	850
360	0.09	0.00	0.01	0.01	0.02	860
370	0.10	0.00	0.01	0 01	0.02	870
380	0.09	+0.01−	0.01	0.01	0.02	880
390	0.08	0.01	0.01	0.01	0.02	890
400	0.08	0.01	0.01	0.01	0.02	900
410	0.08	0.01	0.01	0.01	0.02	910
420	0.08	0.01	0.01	0.01	0.02	920
430	0.08	0.01	0.01	0.01	0.02	930
440	0.07	0.01	0.01	0.02	0.02	940
450	0.07	0.01	0.01	0.02	0.02	950
460	0.07	0.01	0.01	0.02	0.02	960
470	0.06	0.01	0.01	0.02	0.01	970
480	0.06	0.01	0.01	0.02	0.01	980
490	0.06	0.01	+0.01−	0.02	0.01	990
500	+0.05−	+0.01−	0.00	+0.02−	−0.01+	1000

TABLE XXVII.

Terms for Circumpolar Stars depending on ☉ + ☊ and ☉ − ☊.

Argument	σ Octantis.				λ Ursæ Minoris.				Argument
	Arg. = ☉ + ☊		Arg. = ☉ − ☊		Arg. = ☉ + ☊		Arg. = ☉ − ☊		
	R.A.	Dec.	R.A.	Dec.	R.A.	Dec.	R.A.	Dec.	
0	−0.02+	+0.03−	0.00	−0.03+	+0.12−	+0.01−	+0.01−	−0.02+	500
10	0.00	0.03	0.00	0.03	0.11	0.01	0.01	0.02	510
20	+0.02−	0.03	+0.01−	0.03	0.11	0.01	0.01	0.02	520
30	0.04	0.03	0.01	0.03	0.10	0.01	0.01	0.02	530
40	0.06	0.03	0.01	0.03	0.10	0.01	0.01	0.02	540
50	0.08	0.03	0.02	0.02	0.09	0.01	0.01	0.02	550
60	0.10	0.03	0.02	0.02	0.08	0.01	0.01	0.02	560
70	0.12	0.03	0.02	0.02	0.08	0.02	0.01	0.02	570
80	0.14	0.02	0.03	0.02	0.07	0.02	0.01	0.02	580
90	0.16	0.02	0.03	0.02	0.06	0.02	+0.01−	0.01	590
100	0.18	0.02	0.03	0.02	0.05	0.02	0.00	0.01	600
110	0.19	0.02	0.04	0.02	0.04	0.02	0.00	0.01	610
120	0.21	0 02	0.04	0.02	0.03	0.02	0.00	0.01	620
130	0.22	0.02	0.04	0.02	0.03	0.02	0.00	0.01	630
140	0.24	0.02	0.05	0.02	0.02	0.02	0.00	0.01	640
150	0.25	0.02	0.05	0.01	+0.01−	0.02	0.00	0.01	650
160	0.26	0.02	0.05	0.01	0.00	0.02	0.00	0.01	660
170	0.27	0.01	0.05	0.01	−0.01+	0.02	0.00	−0.01+	670
180	0.28	0.01	0.05	0.01	0.02	0.02	0.00	0.00	680
190	0.29	0.01	0.06	0.01	0.03	0.02	−0.01+	0.00	690
200	0.30	0.01	0.06	0.01	0.04	0.02	0.01	0.00	700
210	0.31	0.01	0.06	−0.01+	0.05	0.02	0.01	0.00	710
220	0.31	0.01	0.06	0.00	0.05	0.02	0.01	0.00	720
230	0.32	0.01	0.06	0.00	0.06	0.02	0.01	0.00	730
240	0.32	+0.01−	0.06	0.00	0.07	0.02	0.01	0.00	740
250	0.32	0.00	0.06	0.00	0.08	0.02	0.01	0.00	750
260	0.32	0.00	0.06	0.00	0.08	0.02	0.01	+0.01−	760
270	0.32	0.00	0.06	0.00	0.09	0.02	0.01	0.01	770
280	0.32	0.00	0.06	+0.01−	0.10	0.02	0 01	0.01	780
290	0.32	−0.01+	0.06	0.01	0.11	0.01	0.02	0.01	790
300	0.31	0.01	0.06	0.01	0.11	0.01	0.02	0.01	800
310	0.31	0.01	0.06	0.01	0.12	0.01	0.02	0.01	810
320	0.30	0.01	0.06	0.01	0.12	0.01	0.02	0.01	820
330	0.29	0.01	0.05	0.01	0.13	0.01	0.02	0.01	830
340	0.28	0.01	0.05	0.01	0.13	0.01	0.02	0 01	840
350	0.27	0.01	0.05	0.02	0.13	0.01	0.02	0.01	850
360	0.26	0.02	0.05	0.02	0.14	0.01	0.02	0.01	860
370	0.25	0.02	0.05	0.02	0.14	0.01	0.02	0.02	870
380	0.23	0.02	0.04	0.02	0.14	+0.01−	0.02	0.02	880
390	0.22	0.02	0.04	0.02	0.14	0.00	0.02	0.02	890
400	0.20	0.02	0 04	0.02	0.14	0.00	0.02	0.02	900
410	0.19	0.02	0.03	0.02	0.14	0.00	0.02	0.02	910
420	0.17	0.02	0.03	0.02	0.14	0.00	0.02	0.02	920
430	0.15	0.02	0.03	0.03	0.14	0.00	0.02	0.02	930
440	0.13	0.02	0.02	0.03	0.14	0.00	0 02	0.02	940
450	0.12	0 03	0.02	0.03	0.14	0.00	0.02	0.02	950
460	0.10	0.03	0.02	0.03	0.14	0.00	0.02	0.02	960
470	0.08	0.03	0.01	0.03	0.13	−0.01+	0.02	0.02	970
480	0.06	0.03	0.01	0.03	0.13	0.01	0.02	0 02	980
490	0.04	0.03	+0.01−	0.03	0.12	0.01	0.02	0.02	990
500	+0.02−	−0.03+	0.00	+0.03−	−0.12+	−0.01+	−0.01+	+0 02−	1000

TABLE XXVIII.

Terms for Circumpolar Stars depending on 2 ☽.

Argument = Arg. 2 ☽ (p. 253) + Sidereal Day (Tab. xxiv.) —

Argument.	α Ursæ Minoris.		51 Cephei.		δ Ursæ Minoris.		λ Ursæ Minoris.	
	R.A.	Dec.	R.A.	Dec.	R.A.	Dec.	R.A.	Dec.
d	s	''	s	''	s	''	s	''
0.0	−0.20	+0.05	+0.05	+0.08	−0.01	−0.09	−0.14	−0.08
1.0	0.24	+0.02	−0.01	0.09	+0.03	0.08	−0.02	0.09
2.0	0.24	−0.03	0.06	0.08	0.06	0.06	+0.09	0.06
3.0	0.19	0.05	0.10	0.05	0.08	−0.02	0.21	0.05
4.0	−0.09	0.08	0.12	+0.01	0.08	+0.02	0.27	−0.01
5.0	+0.02	0.08	0.12	−0.03	0.06	0.05	0.28	+0.02
6.0	0.12	0.07	0.09	0.06	+0.04	0.08	0.23	0.06
7.0	0.20	0.05	−0.04	0.08	0.00	0.09	+0.13	0.08
8.0	0.24	−0.01	+0.02	0.09	−0.03	0.08	0.00	0.09
9.0	0.23	+0.03	0.07	0.07	0.06	0.05	−0.12	0.08
10.0	0.17	0.06	0.11	−0.05	0.08	+0.01	0.22	0.05
11.0	+0.08	0.08	0.13	0.00	0.08	−0.02	0.23	+0.01
12.0	−0.03	0.08	0.12	+0.04	0.06	0.06	0.27	−0.03
13.0	0.14	0.07	0.08	0.07	−0.03	0.08	0.21	0.06
0.3	0.21	+0.04	+0.03	0.09	+0.01	0.09	−0.11	0.08
1.3	0.25	0.00	−0.03	0.09	0.04	0.08	+0.02	0.09
2.3	0.23	−0.03	0.08	0.07	0.07	0.05	0.14	0.07
3.3	0.16	0.06	0.11	+0.04	0.08	−0.01	0.24	−0.04
4.3	−0.06	0.08	0.13	0.00	0.07	+0.03	0.28	0.00
5.3	+0.05	0.08	0.11	−0.04	0.06	0.06	0.27	+0.03
6.3	0.15	0.06	0.08	0.07	+0.03	0.09	0.20	0.07
7.3	0.22	−0.04	−0.02	0.09	−0.01	0.09	+0.09	0.09
8.3	0.25	0.00	+0.03	0.09	0.04	0.07	−0.04	0.08
9.3	0.22	+0.04	0.08	0.07	0.07	+0.04	0.16	0.07
10.3	0.15	0.07	0.12	−0.03	0.08	0.00	0.25	+0.04
11.3	+0.05	0.08	0.13	+0.01	0.07	−0.03	0.28	−0.01
12.3	−0.07	0.08	0.11	0.05	0.05	0.07	0.26	0.04
13.3	0.16	0.06	0.07	0.07	−0.02	0.09	0.19	0.07
0.6	0.23	+0.03	+0.01	0.09	+0.02	0.09	−0.07	0.09
1.6	0.25	−0.01	−0.04	0.08	0.05	0.07	+0.06	0.08
2.6	0.21	0.04	0.09	0.06	0.07	−0.04	0.17	0.07
3.6	0.13	0.07	0.12	+0.03	0.08	0.00	0.25	−0.03
4.6	−0.03	0.08	0.12	−0.01	0.07	+0.04	0.28	+0.01
5.6	+0.08	0.08	0.10	0.05	0.05	0.07	0.25	0.04
6.6	0.18	0.06	0.06	0.08	+0.02	0.09	0.17	0.08
7.6	0.23	−0.03	−0.01	0.09	−0.02	0.08	+0.05	0.09
8.6	0.24	+0.01	+0.05	0.08	0.05	0.07	−0.07	0.08
9.6	0.20	0.04	0.10	0.06	0.07	+0.03	0.19	0.06
10.6	0.12	0.07	0.12	−0.02	0.08	−0.01	0.26	+0.02
11.6	+0.01	0.08	0.12	+0.02	0.07	0.04	0.28	−0.02
12.6	−0.10	0.08	0.10	0.06	0.04	0.08	0.24	0.05
13.6	0.19	0.05	+0.05	0.08	−0.01	0.09	0.15	0.08
0.9	0.24	+0.02	0.00	0.09	+0.03	0.08	−0.03	0.09
1.9	0.24	−0.02	−0.06	0.08	0.06	0.06	+0.09	0.08
2.9	0.20	0.05	0.10	0.05	0.08	−0.03	0.20	0.06
3.9	−0.10	0.07	0.12	+0.02	0.08	+0.02	0.27	−0.02
4.9	0.00	0.08	0.12	−0.03	0.07	0.05	0.28	+0.02
5.9	+0.11	0.07	0.09	0.06	+0.04	0.08	0.23	0.05
6.9	0.20	0.05	−0.05	0.08	0.00	0.09	0.14	0.08
7.9	0.24	−0.02	+0.01	0.08	−0.03	0.08	+0.02	0.09
8.9	0.24	+0.02	0.06	0.08	0.06	0.06	−0.11	0.08
9.9	0.18	0.05	0.11	0.05	0.08	+0.02	0.22	0.05
10.9	+0.09	0.08	0.12	−0.01	0.08	−0.02	0.28	+0.01
11.9	−0.02	0.06	0.12	+0.03	0.06	0.05	0.23	−0.03
12.9	−0.13	+0.07	+0.09	+0.07	−0.03	−0.08	−0.22	−0.06

TABLE XXVIII.

Terms for Circumpolar Stars depending on 2 ☽.

Argument = Arg. 2 ☽ (p. 253) + Sidereal Day (Tab. xxiv.) —

Argument.	α Ursæ Minoris.		51 Cephei.		δ Ursæ Minoris.		λ Ursæ Minoris.	
	R.A.	Dec.	R.A.	Dec.	R.A.	Dec.	R.A.	Dec.
	s	"	s	"	s	"	s	"
0.2	—0.21	+0.04	+0.04	+0.08	0.00	—0.09	—0.12	—0.08
1.2	0.25	+0.01	—0.02	0.09	+0.04	0.08	0.00	0.09
2.2	0.23	—0.03	0 07	0.07	0.06	0.05	+0.13	0.07
3.2	0.17	0.06	0.11	+0.04	0.08	—0.01	0.23	0.05
4.2	—0.07	0.08	0.13	0.00	0.08	+0.03	0.28	—0.01
5 2	+0.04	0.08	0.11	—0.04	0.06	0.06	0.27	+0.03
6.2	0.14	0.07	0.08	0.07	+0.03	0.08	0.21	0.06
7.2	0.22	—0.04	—0.03	0.09	—0.01	0.09	+0.10	0.08
8 2	0.25	0.00	+0.03	0.09	0.04	0.07	—0.02	0.09
9.2	0.22	+0.03	0.08	0.07	0.07	0.05	0.15	0.07
10.2	0.16	0.06	0.11	—0.03	0.08	+0.01	0.24	+0.04
11.2	+0.06	0.08	0.13	0.00	0.07	—0.03	0.28	0.00
12.2	—0.05	0.08	0.11	+0.04	0.05	0.06	0.27	—0.04
13.2	0.16	0.06	0.07	0.07	—0.02	0.09	0.20	0.07
0.5	0.22	+0.03	+0.02	0.09	+0.01	0.00	—0.09	0.09
1 5	0.25	0.00	—0.04	0.08	0.05	0.07	+0.04	0.08
2 5	0.22	—0.04	0.08	0.07	0.07	—0.04	0.16	0.07
3.5	0.14	0.07	0.12	+0.03	0.08	0.00	0.25	—0.04
4.5	—0.04	0.08	0.12	—0.01	0.07	+0.04	0.28	+0.01
5.5	+0.07	0.08	0.11	0.05	0.05	0.07	0.26	0.04
6.5	0.17	0.06	0.07	0.07	+0.02	0.09	0.18	0.07
7.5	0.23	—0.03	—0.01	0.09	—0.02	0.09	+0.07	0.09
8.5	0.25	+0.01	+0.04	0.08	0.05	0.07	—0.06	0.08
9 5	0.21	0.04	0.09	0.06	0.07	+0.04	0.18	0.06
10 5	0.13	0.07	0.12	—0.02	0.08	0.00	0.26	+0.03
11.5	+0.02	0.08	0.12	+0.01	0.07	—0.04	0.28	—0.01
12.5	—0.09	0.08	0.10	0.05	0.05	0.07	0.25	0.05
13 5	0.18	0.06	+0.06	0.08	—0.01	0.09	0.17	0.08
0.8	0.24	+0.02	0.00	0.09	+0.02	0.08	—0.05	0.09
1.8	0.24	—0.01	—0.05	0.08	0.05	0.06	+0 08	0.08
2.8	0.21	0.04	0.10	0.06	0.07	—0.03	0.19	0.06
3.8	0.11	0.07	0.12	+0.02	0.08	+0.01	0.26	—0.02
4.8	—0.01	0.08	0.12	—0.02	0 07	0.05	0.28	+0.02
5.8	+0.10	0.07	0.10	0.06	0.04	0.08	0.24	0.05
6.8	0.19	0.05	—0.05	0 08	+0.01	0.09	0.15	0.08
7 8	0.24	—0.02	+0.01	0.09	—0.03	0.08	+0.03	0.09
8.8	0.24	+0.02	0.06	0.08	0.06	0.06	—0.10	0.08
9.8	0.19	0.05	0.10	0.05	0.08	+0.03	0-21	0 05
10.8	+0.10	0.07	0.12	—0.01	0.08	—0.02	0.27	+0.02
11 8	—0.01	0.08	0.12	+0.03	0.06	0.05	0.28	—0.02
12.8	0.12	0.07	0.09	0.06	—0.04	0.08	0.23	0.05
0.1	0.20	0.05	+0.04	0.08	0.00	0.09	0.13	0.08
1.1	0.24	+0.01	—0.01	0.09	+0.03	0.08	—0.01	0.09
2.1	0.24	—0.02	0.07	0 08	0.06	0.05	+0.12	0.08
3.1	0.18	0.06	0.11	+0.05	0.08	—0.02	0.22	0.05
4.1	—0.09	0.08	0.12	0.00	0.08	+0.02	0.28	—0.01
5.1	+0.03	0.08	0.12	—0.03	0.06	0.06	0.28	+0.03
6.1	0.13	0.07	0.08	0.07	+0.03	0.08	0.22	0.06
7.1	0.21	—0.04	—0.03	0.08	0.00	0.09	+0.12	0.08
8.1	0.25	0.00	+0.02	0.09	—0.04	0.08	—0.01	0.09
9.1	0.23	+0.03	0.07	0.07	0.06	0.05	0.13	0.07
10.1	0.17	0.06	0.11	—0.04	0.08	+0.01	0 23	0.04
11.1	+0 07	0.08	0.13	0.00	0.08	—0.03	0.28	+0.01
12.1	—0.04	0 08	0.11	+0.04	0.06	0.06	0.27	—0.03
13.1	—0.15	+0.07	+0.08	+0.07	—0.03	—0.08	—0.20	—0.06

TABLE XXVIII.

Terms for Circumpolar Stars depending on 2 ☽.

Argument = Arg. 2 ☽ (p. 253) + Sidereal Day   (Tab. xxiv.)

Argument.	α Ursæ Minoris.		51 Cephei.		δ Ursæ Minoris.		λ Ursæ Minoris.	
	R.A.	Dec.	R.A.	Dec.	R.A.	Dec.	R.A.	Dec.
	s	"	s	"	s	"	s	"
0.4	−0.22	+0.04	+0 03	+0.09	+0 01	−0.09	−0.10	−0.08
1.4	0.25	0.00	−0.03	0.09	0.04	0.07	+0.03	0.09
2.4	0.22	−0 03	0.08	0.07	0.07	0.04	0.15	0.07
3 4	0.15	0.07	0.12	+0.03	0.08	−0.01	0.24	−0.04
4.4	−0.05	0.08	0.13	−0.01	0.07	+0.03	0.28	0.00
5 4	+0.06	0.08	0.11	0.04	0.05	0.07	0.26	+0.04
6.4	0.16	0.06	0.07	0.07	+0.02	0.09	0.19	0.07
7.4	0.23	−0.03	−0.02	0.09	−0.01	0.09	+0.08	0.09
8.4	0.25	+0.01	+0.04	0.08	0.05	0.07	−0.05	0.08
9.4	0.21	0.04	0.09	0.07	0.07	+0.04	0.16	0.07
10.4	0.14	0 07	0.12	−0.03	0.08	0.00	0.25	+0.03
11.4	+0.03	0.08	0.12	+0.01	0.07	−0.04	0.28	−0.01
12.4	−0.08	0.08	0.11	0.05	0.05	0.07	0.26	0.04
13.4	0.17	0.06	0.06	0.08	−0.02	0.09	0.18	0.07
0.7	0.23	+0.03	+0.01	0.09	+0.02	0.08	−0.06	0.09
1.7	0.24	−0.01	−0.05	0.08	0.05	0.07	+0.07	0.08
2 7	0 21.	0.04	0.09	0.06	0.07	−0.03	0.18	0.06
3.7	0.12	0.07	0.12	+0.02	0.08	0.00	0.26	−0.02
4.7	−0.02	0.08	0.12	−0.02	0.07	+0.04	0.28	+0.01
5.7	+0.09	0.08	0.10	0.05	0.05	0.08	0.25	0.03
6.7	0.18	0.06	−0.06	0.08	+0.01	0.09	0.16	0.08
7.7	0.24	−0.02	0.00	0.09	−0.02	0.08	+0.04	0.09
8.7	0.24	+0.02	+0.06	0.08	0.05	0.06	−0.09	0 08
9.7	0.20	0.05	0 10	0.06	0.07	+0.03	0.20	0.06
10.7	+0.11	0.07	0.12	−0.02	0.08	−0.01	0.27	+0.02
11.7	0.00	0.08	0.12	+0.03	0.07	0.05	0.28	−0.02
12.7	−0.11	+0.07	+0.09	+0.06	−0.04	−0.08	−0.24	−0.05

The argument 2 ☽.		Multiples of the Period of the Argument 2 ☽.			
	d		d		d
1860	0.88	1	13.70	16	219.17
1861	10.97	2	27.40	17	232.87
1862	7.36	3	41.09	18	246.57
1863	3.75	4	54.79	19	260.27
1864	0.14	5	68.49	20	273.96
1865	10.23	6	82.19	21	287.66
1866	6.62	7	95 89	22	301.36
1867	3.01	8	109.59	23	315.06
1868	13.10	9	123.28	24	328.76
1869	9.49	10	136.98	25	342.45
1870	5.88	11	150.68	26	356.15
1871	2.27	12	164.38	27	369.85
1872	12.36	13	178.08		
1873	8.76	14	191.77		
1874	5.15	15	205.47		
1875	1.54				
1876	11.63				
1877	8.02				
1878	4.41				
1879	0.80				
1880	10.89				

TABLE XXIX.—Reductions of the mean places of the Stars in the American Ephemeris, 1865-69, to those adopted in these Tables.

[*t* is reckoned from 1865.0.]

IN RIGHT ASCENSION.

	R.A.	s	s		R.A.	s	s
β Hydri	0h	−0.221	−0.0188t	α² Centauri . . .	14h	−0.025	−0.0020t
ε Piscium . . .	0	−0.050	−0 0010t	β¹ Scorpii	15	+0.042	+0.0002t
α Ursæ Minoris . .	1	+1.113	+0.0512t	η Draconis . . .	16	−0.519	−0.0196t
η Piscium	1	+0.005	−0.0005t	ζ Ophiuchi . . .	16	−0.023	−0.0003t
α Persei	3	−0.022	−0.0002t	β Draconis . . .	17	+0.024	+0.0003t
α Columbæ	5	−0.033	−0.0013t	δ Ursæ Minoris . .	18	−0.084	−0.0022t
51 Cephei	6	+0.483	+0.0332t	d Sagittarii . . .	19	−0.050	−0.0010t
μ Leonis	9	+0.027	+0.0007t	τ Aquilæ	19	−0.073	−0.0013t
ι Leonis	10	+0.040	0.0000t	λ Ursæ Minoris . .	19	+0.537	−0.0048t
o Virginis	11	−0.049	−0.0009t	Groombridge 3241 .	20	+0.210	+0.0050t
β Chamæleontis . .	12	−0.007	−0 0002t	61¹Cygni	21	+0.287	+0.0138t
α¹ Crucis.	12	−0.005	−0.0004t	1 Pegasi	21	−0.010	−0.0010t
β Corvi	12	+0.079	+0.0029t	μ Capricorni . . .	21	−0.035	−0.0015t
θ Centauri	13	−0.003	0.0000t	λ Aquarii	22	+0.025	+0.0005t

IN DECLINATION.

	R.A.	''	''		R.A.	''	''
α Andromedæ . . .	0h	−0.23	−.005t	γ Geminorum . . .	6h	+0.76	+.013t
γ Pegasi	0	+0.38	+.012t	51 Cephei	6	−0.40	−.048t
β Hydri	0	−0.03	.000t	ε Canis Majoris . .	6	+1.80	+.024t
α Cassiopeæ . . .	0	−0.48	−.006t	δ Canis Majoris . .	6	+0.94	+.027t
β Ceti	0	+1.11	+.019t	δ Geminorum . . .	7	+1.02	+.029t
ε Piscium	0	+0.61	+.025t	β Geminorum . . .	7	+0.63	+.017t
α Ursæ Minoris . .	1	−0.15	−.005t	φ Geminorum . . .	7	+1.28	+.036t
θ¹ Ceti	1	+1.42	+ 027t	15 Argus	8	−0.89	+.013t
μ Piscium	1	+1.05	+.018t	ε Hydræ	8	+0.62	+.018t
o Piscium	1	+0 41	+.028t	ι Ursæ Majoris . .	8	−0.13	+.014t
β Arietis	1	+0.74	+.016t	κ Cancri	9	+1.16	+.031t
α Arietis	1	+0.11	+.003t	α Hydræ	9	+0.15	+.006t
ξ¹ Ceti	2	−0.20	+.029t	θ Ursæ Majoris . .	9	+0.17	+.015t
γ Ceti	2	+1.73	+.037t	ε Leonis	9	+0.83	+.014t
α Ceti	2	+0.40	+.014t	μ Leonis	9	+0.34	+.014t
ζ Arietis	3	+0.47	+.013t	α Leonis	10	+0.62	+.011t
α Persei	3	−0.04	+.001t	γ¹ Leonis	10	+1.50	+.031t
δ Persei	3	−0.35	.000t	ρ Leonis	10	+1.07	+.031t
η Tauri	3	+0 29	+.012t	ι Leonis	10	+1.34	+.019t
ζ Persei	3	+0.17	+.026t	α Ursæ Majoris . .	10	+0.19	+.006t
γ¹ Eridani	3	+1 44	+.031t	δ Leonis	11	+1.06	+.015t
γ Tauri	4	+0.86	+.028t	δ Crateris	11	+1.57	+.016t
ε Tauri	4	+1.27	+.022t	τ Leonis	11	+0 58	+.011t
α Tauri	4	−0.08	−.001t	ν Leonis	11	+0.74	+.023t
ι Aurigæ	4	+0.73	+.008t	β Leonis	11	+0.37	+.010t
11 Orionis	4	+0.29	+.019t	γ Ursæ Majoris . .	11	+0.10	+.005t
α Aurigæ	5	−0.38	−.004t	o Virginis	11	+1.35	+.030t
β Orionis	5	+0.60	+.016t	η Virginis	12	+0.65	+.018t
β Tauri	5	+0.61	+.020t	β Corvi	12	+2.32	+.033t
δ Orionis	5	+0.88	+.030t	12 Can. Venat. . . .	12	+0.26	+.005t
α Leporis	5	+0.74	+.026t	θ Virginis	13	+0.83	+.020t
ε Orionis	5	+0.73	+.014t	α Virginis	13	+0.56	+.016t
α Columbæ	5	−0.76	−.022t	ζ Virginis	13	+0.70	+.008t
α Orionis	5	+0.79	+.017t	η Ursæ Majoris . .	13	−0.22	−.002t
μ Geminorum . . .	6	+1.35	+.033t	η Bootis	13	+1.21	+.027t

TABLE XXIX.—Reductions of the mean places of the Stars in the American Ephemeris, 1865-69, to those adopted in these Tables.

[t is reckoned from 1865.0.]

IN DECLINATION.

	R.A.	"	"		R.A.	"	"
α Bootis	14h	+0.09	+.005t	σ Sagittarii	18h	+0.73	+.018t
θ Bootis	14	+0.85	+.015t	ζ Aquilæ	18	+0.24	+.015t
α² Centauri	14	−0.10	−.012t	d Sagittarii	19	+3.84	+.030t
ε Bootis	14	+0.97	+.020t	δ Aquilæ	19	+0.67	−.007t
α² Libræ	14	+0.95	.000t	κ Aquilæ	19	+1.61	+.022t
β Bootis	14	+1.06	+.021t	γ Aquilæ	19	+0.04	.000t
β Libræ	15	+1.20	+.006t	α Aquilæ	19	+0.01	−.003t
μ¹ Bootis	15	+0.48	+.009t	β Aquilæ	19	+0.53	+.014t
α Coronæ Borealis	15	−0.39	−.012t	τ Aquilæ	19	+0.97	+.009t
α Serpentis	15	+0.11	.000t	λ Ursæ Minoris	19	−0.52	−.014t
ε Serpentis	15	+0.63	+.010t	α² Capricorni	20	+0.26	+.006t
ε Coronæ Borealis	15	+1.16	+.016t	π Capricorni	20	+0.53	−.050t
δ Scorpii	15	+1.60	+.012t	ε Delphini	20	+0.94	−.020t
β¹ Scorpii	15	+0.29	+.001t	α Cygni	20	−0 24	−.005t
δ Ophiuchi	16	+1.45	+.002t	μ Aquarii	20	+0.95	+.020t
τ Herculis	16	+0.32	−.004t	ν Cygni	20	+0.97	+.003t
α Scorpii	16	−0.21	−.004t	61¹Cygni	21	+0.88	+.025t
η Draconis	16	−0.70	−.012t	ζ Cygni	21	+0.77	+.014t
ζ Ophiuchi	16	+1.11	+.017t	1 Pegasi	21	+0.03	−.003t
η Herculis	16	+0.75	+.006t	β Aquarii	21	+1.10	+.008t
κ Ophiuchi	16	+1.25	+.003t	ξ Aquarii	21	+0.82	+.023t
d Herculis	16	+0.70	+.001t	ε Pegasi	21	+0.70	+.00?t
α¹ Herculis	17	−0.05	−.002t	μ Capricorni	21	+1.73	+.011t
44 Ophiuchi	17	+2.09	+.033t	α Aquarii	21	+0.18	−.002t
β Draconis	17	−0.06	−.004t	θ Aquarii	22	+0.43	+.019t
α Ophiuchi	17	−0.22	−.011t	π Aquarii	22	+1.04	+.012t
μ Herculis	17	+1.46	+.017t	η Aquarii	22	+0.53	+.01?t
γ³ Sagittarii	17	+0.92	+.010t	ζ Pegasi	22	+0.65	+.007t
μ¹ Sagittarii	18	+1.08	+.013t	λ Aquarii	22	+1.08	+.023t
δ Ursæ Minoris	18	+1.01	+.024t	α Piscis Australis	22	+0.66	+.010t
η Serpentis	18	+1.60	+.010t	α Pegasi	22	−0.30	−.011t
1 Aquilæ	18	+1.85	+.020t	θ Piscium	23	+1.86	+.034t
α Lyræ	18	−0.33	−.002t	ι Piscium	23	+0.89	+ 014t
β Lyræ	18	+0.92	+.017t	ω Piscium	23	+0.94	+.028t

TABLE XXX.—Correction of the place of α Canis Majoris (*Sirius*) due to orbital motion, for the beginning of each year.*

Years.	R. A. q	Dec. r	Years.	R. A. q	Dec. r	Years.	R. A. q	Dec. r
1750	+0.183	+0.85	1800	+0.134	+0.81	1850	+0.086	+0.76
1751	161	0.81	1801	113	0.75	1851	066	0.69
1752	140	0.75	1802	093	0.68	1852	047	0.61
1753	121	0.67	1803	075	0.59	1853	029	0.51
1754	103	0.58	1804	058	0.50	1854	+0.013	0.41
1755	087	0.47	1805	042	0.39	1855	−0.001	0.31
1756	072	0.37	1806	028	0.28	1856	015	0.19
1757	058	0.25	1807	015	0.16	1857	027	+0.07
1758	045	0.14	1808	+0.003	+0.05	1858	038	−0.04
1759	034	+0.02	1809	−0.007	−0.07	1859	048	0.16
1760	024	−0.10	1810	017	0.19	1860	057	0.28
1761	015	0.22	1811	025	0.31	1861	065	0.41
1762	+0.007	0.34	1812	033	0.43	1862	072	0.53
1763	0.000	0.46	1813	039	0.55	1863	078	0 64
1764	−0.006	0.58	1814	044	0.67	1864	083	0.76
1765	011	0.70	1815	049	0.79	1865	086	0.88
1766	015	0.82	1816	052	0.90	1866	089	0.99
1767	018	0.93	1817	055	1.02	1867	091	1.10
1768	020	1.04	1818	056	1.13	1868	092	1.21
1769	021	1.15	1819	057	1.23	1869	092	1.31
1770	021	1.25	1820	056	1.33	1870	091	1.41
1771	020	1.35	1821	055	1.43	1871	089	1.51
1772	018	1.45	1822	052	1.53	1872	086	1.60
1773	016	1.54	1823	049	1.61	1873	082	1.68
1774	012	1.63	1824	045	1.70	1874	077	1.76
1775	007	1.71	1825	041	1.77	1875	072	1.84
1776	−0.002	1.78	1826	033	1.84	1876	065	1.90
1777	+0.005	1.84	1827	026	1.90	1877	057	1.96
1778	013	1.90	1828	018	1.96	1878	048	2.00
1779	022	1.95	1829	−0.008	2.00	1879	038	2.04
1780	032	1.99	1830	+0.002	2.03	1880	026	2.07
1781	043	2.02	1831	014	2.05	1881	−0 014	2.08
1782	055	2.04	1832	027	2.06	1882	0.000	2.08
1783	068	2.04	1833	041	2.05	1883	+0.015	2.07
1784	083	2.03	1834	057	2.03	1884	031	2 03
1785	099	1.99	1835	074	1.99	1885	049	1.97
1786	117	1.94	1836	092	1.91	1886	068	1.88
1787	136	1.85	1837	112	1.82	1887	088	1.77
1788	156	1.74	1838	133	1.68	1888	110	1.60
1789	178	1.59	1839	155	1.51	1889	133	1.40
1790	200	1.39	1840	178	1.27	1890	156	1.12
1791	223	1.13	1841	200	0.96	1891	176	0 77
1792	244	0.79	1842	219	0.59	1892	190	−0.37
1793	259	−0.39	1843	228	−0.16	1893	191	+0.06
1794	263	+0.04	1844	222	+0.24	1894	178	0.41
1795	252	0.40	1845	205	0.53	1895	156	0.63
1796	231	0.64	1846	182	0.71	1896	131	0.75
1797	206	0.78	1847	156	0.79	1897	106	0.80
1798	181	0.83	1848	132	0.82	1898	082	0.79
1799	157	0.84	1849	108	0.80	1899	060	0.76
1800	+0.134	+0.81	1850	+0.083	+0.76	1900	+0.039	+0.70

* Prepared from the formulæ of AUWERS.—Astronomische Nachrichten, vol. 63, No. 1506.

SUPPLEMENTARY TABLES,

FOR SMALL TERMS OF NUTATION.

17

TABLE XXXI.—Terms in the reduction of Mean to App't R. Ascensions depending on 2 ☾ .

$\triangle'_C a = -0^s.0125 \sin 2 ☾ .$ $\triangle''_C a = -[0^s.00542 \sin 2 ☾ \sin a + 0^s.00590 \cos 2 ☾ \cos a] \tan \delta.$

Side Arg. = Arg. IV (p. 34) + d' + day of year. Hor. Arg. = Star's R. Ascension.

Arg. IV.	$\triangle'_C a.$	$\triangle''$ a + tan δ. To be multiplied by tan δ													Arg. IV.
		0ʰ	1ʰ	2ʰ	3ʰ	4ʰ	5ʰ	6ʰ	7ʰ	8ʰ	9ʰ	10ʰ	11ʰ	12ʰ	
d	s	s													d
0.0	−0.000	−0.0059	−57	−51	−42	−29	−15	−00	+15	+29	+42	+51	+57	+59	0.0
0.5	03	57	59	56	50	39	26	12	+03	18	32	44	52	57	0.5
1.0	05	53	58	58	54	47	37	24	−10	+05	20	34	45	53	1.0
1.5	08	45	53	57	57	53	45	35	22	−07	+07	22	35	45	1.5
2.0	10	36	46	52	55	55	51	43	32	19	−06	+09	23	36	2.0
2.5	11	24	36	45	52	54	54	49	42	31	18	−04	+11	24	2.5
3.0	12	11	25	36	45	51	54	53	49	40	30	17	−03	+11	3.0
3.5	12	− 02	−12	25	37	46	51	54	52	48	39	29	16	−02	3.5
4.0	12	+ 15	+02	−13	26	37	46	52	54	53	48	39	29	15	4.0
4.5	11	28	15	00	14	27	39	48	53	55	53	48	40	28	4.5
5.0	09	39	27	+14	−01	15	29	40	49	55	56	54	48	39	5.0
5.5	07	48	39	26	+12	−02	18	31	42	51	56	57	55	48	5.5
6.0	05	54	48	37	24	+10	−05	21	33	45	53	57	59	54	6.0
6.5	−0.002	58	54	47	36	22	+07	−08	23	36	47	55	59	58	6.5
7.0	+0.001	59	58	53	45	33	19	+04	−11	25	39	49	56	59	7.0
7.5	04	56	59	57	52	42	30	16	+01	14	28	41	50	56	7.5
8.0	06	51	58	58	55	49	39	28	14	−01	16	30	42	51	8.0
8.5	09	42	51	55	57	54	47	37	25	+11	−03	18	31	42	8.5
9.0	10	32	43	50	55	55	52	45	36	23	+09	−05	20	32	9.0
9.5	12	20	33	43	50	54	54	51	44	34	22	+08	−07	20	9.5
10.0	12	+ 07	21	32	43	50	53	53	50	43	33	21	+07	−07	10.0
10.5	12	− 07	+07	21	33	43	50	53	53	50	43	32	21	+07	10.5
11.0	12	20	−07	+08	22	34	44	51	54	54	50	43	33	20	11.0
11.5	10	32	20	−05	+09	23	36	45	52	55	55	50	43	32	11.5
12.0	09	42	31	18	−03	+11	25	37	47	54	57	55	51	42	12.0
12.5	06	51	43	30	16	−01	14	27	39	49	55	58	58	51	12.5
13.0	04	56	50	41	28	14	+01	16	31	42	52	57	59	56	13.0
13.5	+0.001	59	56	49	39	26	−11	+04	19	32	45	53	58	59	13.5
14.0	−0.002	−0.0058	−59	−55	−47	−36	−23	−08	+07	+22	+36	+46	+54	+58	14.0
		12ʰ	13ʰ	14ʰ	15ʰ	16ʰ	17ʰ	18ʰ	19ʰ	20ʰ	21ʰ	22ʰ	23ʰ	24ʰ	

TABLE XXXII.—Terms in the reduction of Mean to App't R. Ascensions depending on ☾ − Γ'.

$\triangle'''_C a = +0^s.0041 \sin (☾ − Γ').$ $\triangle^{iv}_C a = +0^s.00180 \sin (☾ − Γ') \sin a \times \tan \delta.$

Side Arg. = Arg. V (p 34) + d' + day of year. Hor. Arg. = Star's Right Ascension.

Arg. V.	$\triangle'''_C a.$	$\triangle^{iv}_C$ a + tan δ. To be multiplied by tan δ.							Arg. V.	$\triangle'''_C a.$	$\triangle^{iv}_C$ a + tan δ. To be multiplied by tan δ.						
		$a=\begin{cases}0ʰ\\12ʰ\end{cases}$	$\begin{cases}1ʰ\\11ʰ\end{cases}$	$\begin{cases}2ʰ\\10ʰ\end{cases}$	$\begin{cases}3ʰ\\9ʰ\end{cases}$	$\begin{cases}4ʰ\\8ʰ\end{cases}$	$\begin{cases}5ʰ\\7ʰ\end{cases}$	$\begin{cases}6ʰ\\6ʰ\end{cases}$			$a=\begin{cases}0ʰ\\12ʰ\end{cases}$	$\begin{cases}1ʰ\\11ʰ\end{cases}$	$\begin{cases}2ʰ\\10ʰ\end{cases}$	$\begin{cases}3ʰ\\9ʰ\end{cases}$	$\begin{cases}4ʰ\\8ʰ\end{cases}$	$\begin{cases}5ʰ\\7ʰ\end{cases}$	$\begin{cases}6ʰ\\6ʰ\end{cases}$
d	s	s							d	s	s						
0	+0.000	0.0000	+0	+0	+0	+0	+0	+0	14	−0.000	0.0000	−0	−0	−1	−1	−1	−1
1	1	0	1	2	3	4	4	4	15	1	0	1	2	3	3	4	4
2	2	0	2	4	6	7	8	8	16	2	0	2	4	6	8	9	9
3	3	0	3	6	8	10	11	11	17	3	0	3	6	9	10	12	12
4	3	0	4	7	10	12	14	14	18	3	0	4	7	10	13	14	15
5	4	0	4	8	11	14	16	16	19	4	0	4	8	12	14	16	17
6	4	0	5	9	13	15	17	18	20	4	0	5	9	13	15	17	18
7	4	0	5	9	13	16	18	18	21	4	0	5	9	13	15	17	18
8	4	0	4	9	12	15	17	17	22	4	0	4	9	12	15	17	17
9	4	0	4	8	11	14	15	16	23	4	0	4	8	11	13	15	15
10	3	0	3	7	10	12	13	14	24	3	0	3	7	9	11	13	13
11	2	0	3	5	8	9	10	11	25	2	0	3	5	7	9	10	10
12	2	0	2	4	5	6	7	7	26	1	0	2	3	4	5	6	6
13	1	0	+1	2	+3	+3	+3	+3	27	1	0	−1	−1	−2	−2	−2	−2
14	+0.000	0.0000	0	0	−1	−1	−1	−1	28	−0.000	0.0000	0	+1	+1	+2	+2	+2
		$a=\begin{cases}12ʰ\\24ʰ\end{cases}$	$\begin{cases}13ʰ\\23ʰ\end{cases}$	$\begin{cases}14ʰ\\22ʰ\end{cases}$	$\begin{cases}15ʰ\\21ʰ\end{cases}$	$\begin{cases}16ʰ\\20ʰ\end{cases}$	$\begin{cases}17ʰ\\19ʰ\end{cases}$	$\begin{cases}18ʰ\\18ʰ\end{cases}$			$a=\begin{cases}12ʰ\\24ʰ\end{cases}$	$\begin{cases}13ʰ\\23ʰ\end{cases}$	$\begin{cases}14ʰ\\22ʰ\end{cases}$	$\begin{cases}15ʰ\\21ʰ\end{cases}$	$\begin{cases}16ʰ\\20ʰ\end{cases}$	$\begin{cases}17ʰ\\19ʰ\end{cases}$	$\begin{cases}18ʰ\\18ʰ\end{cases}$

Change the signs of $\triangle''_C$ a and $\triangle^{iv}_C$ a when a > 12ʰ.

TABLE XXXIII.—Terms in the reduction of Mean to App't Declinations depending on 2 ☾ .

$$\Delta'_d \delta = -0\overset{''}{.}0813 \sin 2 \,\text{☾} \cos a + 0\overset{''}{.}0886 \cos 2 \,\text{☾} \sin a.$$

Side Arg. = Arg. IV (p. 34) + d' + day of year. Hor. Arg. = Star's R. Ascension.

Arg. IV	0ʰ	1ʰ	2ʰ	3ʰ	4ʰ	5ʰ	6ʰ	7ʰ	8ʰ	9ʰ	10ʰ	11ʰ	12ʰ	Arg. IV
d	″	″	″	″	″	″	″	″	″	″	″	″	″	d
0.0	−0.00	+0.02	+0.04	+0.06	+0.08	+0.08	+0.09	+0.08	+0.08	+0.06	+0.04	+0.02	+0.00	0.0
0.5	.02	.00	.02	.05	.07	.08	.09	.09	.08	.07	.06	.04	.02	0.5
1.0	.04	− .01	+ .01	.03	.05	.07	.08	.09	.09	.08	.07	.06	.04	1.0
1.5	.05	.03	− .01	+ .01	.03	.05	.07	.08	.09	.09	.08	.06	.05	1.5
2.0	.06	.05	.03	− .01	+ .01	.03	.05	.07	.08	.08	.08	.08	.06	2.0
2.5	.07	.06	.05	.03	− .01	+ .02	.04	.05	.07	.08	.08	.08	.07	2.5
3.0	.08	.07	.06	.04	.03	.00	+ .02	.04	.05	.07	.08	.08	.08	3.0
3.5	.08	.08	.07	.05	.04	− .02	− .01	+ .02	.04	.05	.07	.08	.08	3.5
4.0	.08	.08	.08	.07	.06	.04	.02	.00	+ .02	.04	.06	.07	.08	4.0
4.5	.07	.08	.08	.08	.08	.06	.05	− .02	.00	+ .02	.04	.06	.07	4.5
5.0	.06	.07	.08	.08	.08	.07	.06	.04	− .02	.00	+ .02	.04	.06	5.0
5.5	.05	.06	.08	.08	.09	.08	.07	.06	.04	− .02	.00	.03	.05	5.5
6.0	.03	.05	.07	.08	.09	.09	.08	.07	.06	.04	− .02	+ .01	.03	6.0
6.5	− .01	.03	.05	.07	.08	.09	.09	.08	.07	.05	.03	− .01	+ .01	6.5
7.0	+ .01	− .02	.04	.06	.07	.08	.09	.09	.08	.07	.05	.03	− .01	7.0
7.5	.02	.00	− .02	.04	.06	.07	.08	.09	.08	.08	.06	.04	.02	7.5
8.0	.04	+ .02	.00	− .02	.04	.06	.08	.08	.09	.08	.07	.06	.04	8.0
8.5	.06	.04	+ .01	.00	− .03	.05	.06	.08	.08	.08	.08	.07	.06	8.5
9.0	.07	.05	.03	+ .01	.01	.03	.05	.06	.08	.08	.08	.07	.07	9.0
9.5	.08	.07	.05	.03	+ .01	− .01	.03	.05	.06	.07	.08	.08	.08	9.5
10.0	.08	.08	.06	.05	.03	+ .01	− .01	.03	.05	.06	.07	.08	.08	10.0
10.5	.08	.08	.07	.06	.05	.03	+ .01	− .01	.03	.05	.06	.07	.08	10.5
11.0	.08	.08	.08	.07	.06	.05	.03	+ .01	− .01	.03	.05	.07	.08	11.0
11.5	.07	.08	.08	.08	.07	.06	.05	.03	+ .01	− .01	.04	.05	.07	11.5
12.0	.06	.07	.08	.08	.08	.08	.06	.05	.03	+ .01	− .02	.04	.06	12.0
12.5	.04	.06	.07	.08	.09	.08	.08	.06	.05	.02	.00	− .02	.04	12.5
13.0	+ .02	.05	.06	.08	.09	.09	.08	.08	.06	.04	+ .02	.00	− .02	13.0
13.5	.00	.03	.05	.07	.09	.09	.09	.08	.06	.04	+ .02	.00	.03	13.5
14.0	−0.01	+0.01	+0.03	+0.05	+0.07	+0.08	+0.09	+0.09	+0.08	+0.07	+0.05	+0.03	+0.01	14.0

| | 12ʰ | 13ʰ | 14ʰ | 15ʰ | 16ʰ | 17ʰ | 18ʰ | 19ʰ | 20ʰ | 21ʰ | 22ʰ | 23ʰ | 24ʰ | |

TABLE XXXIV.—Terms in the reduction of Mean to App't Declinations depending on ☾ − Γ'.

$$\Delta''_d \delta = +0\overset{''}{.}0270 \sin (\text{☾} - \Gamma') \cos a.$$

Side Arg. = Arg. V (p. 34) + d' + day of year. Hor. Arg. = Star's R. Ascension.

Arg. V	$a = \begin{cases} 0^h \\ 24^h \end{cases}$	1ʰ 23ʰ	2ʰ 22ʰ	3ʰ 21ʰ	4ʰ 20ʰ	5ʰ 19ʰ	6ʰ 18ʰ	Arg. V	$a = \begin{cases} 0^h \\ 24^h \end{cases}$	1ʰ 23ʰ	2ʰ 22ʰ	3ʰ 21ʰ	4ʰ 20ʰ	5ʰ 19ʰ	6ʰ 18ʰ
d	″	″	″	″	″	″	″	d	″	″	″	″	″	″	″
0	+0.00	+0.00	+0.00	+0.00	+0.00	+0.00	0.00	14	−0.00	−0.00	−0.00	−0.00	−0.00	−0.00	0.00
1	.01	.01	.01	.00	.00	.00	.00	15	.01	.01	.01	.00	.00	.00	.00
2	.01	.01	.01	.01	.01	.00	.00	16	.01	.01	.01	.01	.01	.00	.00
3	.02	.02	.01	.01	.01	.00	.00	17	.02	.02	.02	.01	.01	.00	.00
4	.02	.02	.02	.01	.01	.00	.00	18	.02	.02	.02	.02	.01	.01	.00
5	.02	.02	.02	.02	.01	.01	.00	19	.02	.02	.02	.02	.01	.01	.00
6	.03	.03	.02	.02	.01	.01	.00	20	.03	.03	.02	.02	.01	.01	.00
7	.03	.03	.02	.02	.01	.01	.00	21	.03	.03	.02	.02	.01	.01	.00
8	.03	.02	.02	.02	.01	.01	.00	22	.03	.02	.02	.02	.01	.01	.00
9	.02	.02	.02	.02	.01	.01	.00	23	.02	.02	.02	.02	.01	.01	.00
10	.02	.02	.02	.01	.01	.00	.00	24	.02	.02	.02	.01	.01	.00	.00
11	.02	.02	.01	.01	.01	.00	.00	25	.01	.01	.01	.01	.01	.00	.00
12	.01	.01	.01	.01	.00	.00	.00	26	.01	.01	.01	.01	.00	.00	.00
13	.01	.00	.00	.00	.00	.00	.00	27	.00	.00	.00	.00	.00	.00	.00
14	+0.00	+0.00	+0.00	+0.00	+0.00	0.00	+0.00	28	−0.00	−0.00	−0.00	−0.00	−0.00	−0.00	0.00

| $a = \begin{cases} 12^h \\ 12^h \end{cases}$ | 11ʰ 13ʰ | 10ʰ 14ʰ | 9ʰ 15ʰ | 8ʰ 16ʰ | 7ʰ 17ʰ | 6ʰ 18ʰ | | $a = \begin{cases} 12^h \\ 12^h \end{cases}$ | 11ʰ 13ʰ | 10ʰ 14ʰ | 9ʰ 15ʰ | 8ʰ 16ʰ | 7ʰ 17ʰ | 6ʰ 18ʰ |

Change the signs in these two tables when a is taken at the bottom.

TABLE XXXV.—Arguments of small terms in A and B.

Arg. VI for terms in $2 \odot - \Omega$.   **Arg. IX** for terms in $2 \Gamma' - \Omega$.
Arg. VII for terms in $2 \odot - 2 \Omega$.   **Arg. X** for terms in Γ'.
Arg. VIII for terms in $2 \odot - 2 \Gamma'$.

For Washington Mean Noon of Jan. 0 in common years, Jan. 1 in bissextile years.

Years.	VI.	VII.	VIII.	IX.	X.	Years.	VI.	VII.	VIII.	IX.	X.
	d	d	d	d	d		d	d	d	d	d
1750	138.4	0	125	223	3150	1800	82.5	64	63	209	2023
1751	147.7	18	78	588	284	1801	91.8	83	16	574	2388
1752 B	158.0	38	32	954	650	1802	101.1	101	175	939	2753
1753	167.3	56	192	14	1015	1803	110.4	119	128	1304	3118
1754	176.6	74	145	379	1380	1804 B	120.7	139	82	364	253
1755	8.1	93	98	744	1745	1805	130.1	157	36	729	618
1756 B	18.4	112	52	1110	2111	1806	139.4	2	195	1094	983
1757	27.7	131	5	169	2476	1807	148.7	21	148	154	1348
1758	37.1	149	165	534	2841	1808 B	159.0	40	102	520	1714
1759	46.4	167	118	899	3206	1809	168.3	58	55	885	2079
1760 B	56.7	13	72	1265	340	1810	177.6	77	8	1250	2444
1761	66.0	32	25	325	705	1811	9.1	95	168	309	2809
1762	75.3	50	184	690	1070	1812 B	19.4	115	122	675	3175
1763	84.6	69	137	1055	1435	1813	28.7	133	75	1040	309
1764 B	94.9	88	92	115	1801	1814	38.0	151	28	100	674
1765	104.2	106	45	460	2166	1815	47.3	170	187	465	1039
1766	113.6	125	204	845	2531	1816 B	57.6	16	142	831	1405
1767	122.9	143	157	1210	2896	1817	67.0	34	95	1196	1770
1768 B	133.2	162	111	271	31	1818	76.3	53	48	255	2135
1769	142.5	8	65	636	396	1819	85.6	71	1	620	2500
1770	151.8	26	18	1001	761	1820 B	95.9	90	161	986	2866
1771	161.1	44	177	61	1126	1821	105.2	109	115	46	3231
1772 B	171.4	64	131	427	1492	1822	114.5	127	68	411	364
1773	2.9	82	84	792	1857	1823	123.8	145	21	776	729
1774	12.2	100	38	1157	2222	1824 B	134.1	165	181	1142	1095
1775	21.5	119	197	216	2587	1825	143.5	10	134	202	1460
1776 B	31.8	138	151	582	2953	1826	152.8	28	88	567	1825
1777	41.1	157	104	947	86	1827	162.1	47	41	932	2190
1778	50.5	2	57	7	451	1828 B	172.4	66	201	1298	2556
1779	59.8	20	11	372	816	1829	3.9	84	154	357	2921
1780 B	70.1	39	171	738	1182	1830	13.2	103	107	722	55
1781	79.4	58	124	1103	1547	1831	22.5	121	60	1087	420
1782	88.7	76	77	162	1912	1832 B	32.8	141	15	148	786
1783	98.0	95	30	527	2277	1833	42.1	159	174	513	1151
1784 B	108.3	114	190	893	2643	1834	51.4	4	127	878	1516
1785	117.6	132	144	1258	3008	1835	60.7	22	80	1243	1881
1786	127.0	151	97	318	142	1836 B	71.0	42	34	303	2247
1787	136.3	169	50	683	507	1837	80.4	60	194	668	2612
1788 B	146.6	15	4	1049	873	1838	89.7	79	147	1033	2977
1789	155.9	33	163	108	1238	1839	99.0	97	100	93	110
1790	165.2	52	117	473	1603	1840 B	109.3	116	54	459	476
1791	174.5	70	70	838	1968	1841	118.6	135	7	824	841
1792 B	7.0	90	24	1204	2334	1842	127.9	153	167	1189	1206
1793	16.3	108	183	264	2699	1843	137.2	171	120	248	1571
1794	25.6	126	136	629	3064	1844 B	147.5	18	74	614	1937
1795	34.9	145	90	994	197	1845	156.9	36	27	979	2302
1796 B	45.2	164	44	54	563	1846	166.2	54	186	39	2667
1797	54.6	9	203	419	928	1847	175.5	73	139	404	3032
1798	63.9	28	156	784	1293	1848 B	8.0	92	94	770	167
1799	73.2	46	109	1149	1658	1849	17.3	110	47	1135	532
1800	82.5	64	63	209	2023	1850	26.6	129	0	194	897

TABLE XXXV.—Arguments of small terms in A and B.

For Washington Mean Noon of Jan. 0 in common years, Jan. 1 in bissextile years.

Arg. for the Inequalities = Arg. I + Ineq's + d' + day of year.

Years.	VI.	VII.	VIII.	IX.	X.
	d	d	d	d	d
1850	26.6	129	0	194	897
1851	35.9	147	159	559	1262
1852 B	46.2	167	113	925	1628
1853	55.5	12	67	1290	1993
1854	64.8	30	20	350	2358
1855	74.1	48	179	715	2723
1856 B	84.5	66	133	1081	3089
1857	93.8	86	86	140	222
1858	103.1	105	40	505	587
1859	112.4	123	199	870	952
1860 B	122.7	142	153	1236	1318
1861	132.0	161	106	296	1683
1862	141.3	6	59	661	2048
1863	150.6	24	13	1026	2413
1864 B	161.0	43	173	86	2779
1865	170.3	62	126	451	3144
1866	1.7	80	79	816	278
1867	11.0	99	32	1181	643
1868 B	21.4	118	192	242	1009
1869	30.7	136	146	607	1374
1870	40.0	155	99	972	1739
1871	49.3	0	52	31	2104
1872 B	59.6	19	6	397	2470
1873	68.9	38	165	762	2835
1874	78.2	56	119	1127	3200
1875	87.5	74	72	187	333
1876 B	97.9	94	26	553	699
1877	107.2	112	185	918	1064
1878	116.5	131	138	1283	1429
1879	125.8	149	92	343	1794
1880 B	136.1	168	46	709	2160
1881	145.4	13	205	1074	2525
1882	154.7	32	158	133	2890
1883	164.0	50	111	498	24
1884 B	174.4	69	66	864	390
1885	5.8	88	19	1229	755
1886	15.1	106	178	239	1120
1887	24.4	125	131	654	1485
1888 B	34.8	144	85	1020	1851
1889	44.1	162	39	79	2216
1890	53.4	7	198	444	2581
1891	62.7	26	151	809	2946
1892 B	73.0	45	105	1175	80
1893	82.3	64	58	235	445
1894	91.6	82	11	600	810
1895	100.9	100	171	965	1175
1896 B	111.3	120	125	25	1541
1897	120.6	138	78	390	1906
1898	129.9	156	31	755	2271
1899	139.2	2	190	1120	2636
1900	148.5	20	144	180	3001

Arg. I + d' + day.	Inequalities of Arguments.		
	VI.	VII.	VIII.
d	d	d	d
0	0.0	0	0
10	+0.3	0	0
20	0.6	+1	+1
30	0.9	1	1
40	1.2	1	1
50	1.4	1	2
60	1.6	2	2
70	1.8	2	2
80	1.9	2	2
90	1.9	2	2
100	1.9	2	2
110	1.8	2	2
120	1.7	2	2
130	1.5	2	2
140	1.3	1	2
150	1.1	1	1
160	0.8	+1	1
170	0.5	0	+1
180	+0.2	0	0
190	−0.1	0	0
200	0.5	0	−1
210	0.8	−1	1
220	1.0	1	1
230	1.3	1	1
240	1.5	1	2
250	1.7	2	2
260	1.8	2	2
270	1.9	2	2
280	1.9	2	2
290	1.8	2	2
300	1.7	2	2
310	1.6	2	2
320	1.4	1	2
330	1.1	1	1
340	0.8	1	1
350	0.5	−1	−1
360	−0.2	0	0
370	+0.1	0	0

Periods and Multiples.

Of Arg. VI.
	d
1	177.8
2	355.7
3	533.5

Of Arg. VII.
	d
1	173
2	347
3	520

Of Arg. VIII.
	d
1	206
2	412

Of Arg. IX.
	d
1	1305

Of Arg. X.
	d
1	3231

TABLE XXXVI.—Small terms in A and B.

In units of the *fifth* decimal place for *A*, and of the *fourth* for *B*.

Arguments = Arg's of Tables VI and XXXV + inequalities + d' + day of year.

Arg.	I. A	I. B	VI. A	VI. B	VII. A	VIII. A	Arg.	I. A	I. B	Arg.	IX. A	IX. B	Arg.	X. A	X. B
d 0	+3	+26	0	+67	0	0	d 215	−10	+8	d 0	0	+24	d 0	+5	8
5	6	23	+4	66	−1	+2	220	9	15	50	+2	23	100	6	+3
10	8	19	9	63	2	3	225	7	20	100	4	21	200	7	−3
15	10	13	13	58	3	4	230	5	24	150	6	18	300	8	10
20	11	+6	16	51	3	6	235	−3	26	200	7	14	400	8•	16
25	11	0	19	43	4	7	240	0	27	250	8	9	500	7	22
30	11	−8	22	33	4	8	245	+3	26	300	9	+3	600	5	27
35	9	14	24	22	5	9	250	5	24	350	9	−3	700	+2	30
40	7	20	25	+10	5	9	255	8	19	400	8	8	800	0	31
45	5	24	25	−1	5	10	260	9	14	450	7	13	900	−2	30
50	+2	26	25	13	5	10	265	10	8	500	6	18	1000	4	28
55	0	27	23	24	5	10	270	11	+1	550	4	21	1100	−6	23
60	−3	26	21	35	4	10	275	11	−6	600'	+2	23	1200	7	17
65	6	23	19	44	4	9	280	10	12	650	0	24	1300	8	11
70	8	18	16	53	3	8	285	8	18	700	−2	23	1400	7	−4
75	10	12	12	59	2	8	290	6	•23	750	4	21	1500	6	+2
80	11	−6	8	64	−1	6	295	3	26	800	6	18	1600	5	7
85	11	+1	+3	66	0	5	300	+1	27	850	7	13	1700	4	12
90	10	8	−1	67	+1	4	305	−2	26	900	8	8	1800	2	14
95	9	14	5	65	1	2	310	5	24	950	9	−3	1900	−1	16
100	7	20	10	62	2	+1	315	7	20	1000	9	+3	2000	0	16
105	5	24	13	56	3	−1	320	9	15	1050	8	9	2100	+1	16
110	−3	26	17	49	4	2	325	10	8	1100	7	14	2200	+1	16
115	0	27	20	40	4	4	330	11	−1	1150	6	18	2300	0	15
120	+3	26	22	30	5	5	335	11	+6	1200	4	21	2400	0	15
125	5	23	24	20	5	6	340	10	13	1250	−2	23	2500	0	15
130	8	19	25	−8	5	7	345	8	18	1300	0	24	2600	−1	16
135	9	14	25	+4	5	8	350	6	.23	1350	+2	+23	2700	−1	16
140	10	8	24	15	5	9	355	−3	26				2800	−1	1ó
145	11	+1	23	27	4	10	360	0	27				2900	0	16
150	11	−6	21	37	4	10	365	+3	26				3000	+1	15
155	10	12	18	46	3	10	370	5	23				3100	3	13
160	8	18	15	54	2	10	375	8	19				3200	5	10
165	6	22	11	60	1	9	380	+10	+13				3300	+6	+5
170	4	25	7	64	+1	9									
175	+1	27	−3	67	0	8									
180	−1	27	+2	67	−1	7									
185	4	25	6	65	2	6									
190	6	22	11	61	3	5									
195	8	17	14	55	4	3									
200	10	11	17	47	4	−2									
205	11	−5	20	39	5	0									
210	−11	+2	+23	+28	−5	+1									

www.ingramcontent.com/pod-product-compliance
Lightning Source LLC
Chambersburg PA
CBHW020500270326
41926CB00008B/681